D1218429

Cape Sunium, the southern point of Attica, which grain ships, plying between the Piraeus and the Hellespont, had to round in the teeth of northeast and southwest winds. The temple of Poseidon crowns the promontory.

THE GEOGRAPHY
OF THE
MEDITERRANEAN REGION
ITS RELATION TO ANCIENT HISTORY

BY

ELLEN CHURCHILL SEMPLE

M.A., LL.D.

Professor of Anthropogeography at Clark University
and author of
"Influences of Geographical Environment"

D
973
.S45
1971

One generation passeth away
and another generation cometh,
but the Earth abideth forever.
ECCLESIASTES.

AMS PRESS
NEW YORK

INDIANA
PURDUE
LIBRARY
OCT 22 1979

FORT WAYNE

Reprinted from the edition of 1931, New York

First AMS EDITION published 1971

Manufactured in the United States of America

International Standard Book Number: 0-404-05751-9

Library of Congress Catalog Number: 70-137267

AMS PRESS INC.
NEW YORK, N.Y.   10003

TO

WALLACE W. ATWOOD,

A MAN ENDOWED WITH VISION
AND THE POWER OF EXECUTION
THIS BOOK IS DEDICATED
IN APPRECIATION OF HIS NOTABLE
SERVICES TO THE SCIENCE OF
GEOGRAPHY

PREFACE

The preparation of this book has involved twenty years of research and numerous journeys to the Mediterranean for field work, in the course of which I visited nearly all parts of the coasts and their immediate hinterland.

My thanks are due to Dr. Wallace W. Atwood for his unfailing encouragement and help in securing me leisure for research in the midst of my professorial activities at Clark University; to my good friend Dick Mack of San Francisco, who took me on long motor trips through Greece, Corfu, Dalmatia, Bosnia and Herzegovina, and with generous interest planned the tours with reference to my purposes rather than his own preferences; to my brother-in-law Francis B. Keene of Rome and my nieces Emerin and Carolyn Keene, who enabled me to explore by motor little-known parts of Italy, thus contributing to that intimate knowledge of the country invaluable to a geographer; to Professor Clarence F. Jones of Clark University, for his careful supervision of the maps while they were being prepared for this volume.

Finally I wish to express my lasting gratitude to Dr. Ruth E. Baugh, Assistant Professor of geography at the University of California in Los Angeles, for her intelligent, efficient and devoted service in helping me put this book through press, at a time when illness compelled me to delegate a large part of the task to another. This service, for which her knowledge of Mediterranean geography equipped her in a peculiar degree, can never be sufficiently repaid.

Ellen Churchill Semple.

Clark University,
Worcester, Massachusetts,
September 30, 1931.

CONTENTS

PART I

GENERAL GEOGRAPHIC CONDITIONS

PART II

THE BARRIER BOUNDARIES OF THE MEDITERRANEAN REGION

PART III

VEGETATION AND AGRICULTURE

vii

1*

PART IV

MARITIME ACTIVITIES

LIST OF MAPS

PART I

GENERAL GEOGRAPHIC CONDITIONS

CHAPTER I

THE MEDITERRANEAN IN UNIVERSAL HISTORY

All the world is heir of the Mediterranean. All the world is her debtor. Much that is finest in modern civilization traces back to seeds of culture matured in the circle of the Mediterranean lands and transplanted thence to other countries, whence they have been disseminated over the world. In this wide distribution they have developed new local varieties, which however reveal their kinship with the original Mediterranean species. The fine colonial dwellings of rural Virginia, the mission architecture of California trace back alike to Mediterranean forms. Modern science in many lands resorts to the storehouse of ancient Greek to equip itself with a terminology. Roman government and law stamp the political organization of the youngest states. Transplanted Mediterranean languages have given the name of Latin America to half the Western Hemisphere. Poets, dramatists, sculptors, musicians, and dancers have found their earliest and best models in the fine arts of ancient Mediterranean lands. Even the crassly modern dollar mark claims a like old and honorable origin, derived from the "pillar dollar" of Emperor Charles V; this was stamped with the Pillars of Hercules connected with an ornamental scroll, a design used on an early coin of Phœnician Gades.[1]

Mediterranean civilization has given the world standards. These are embodied in classical culture and Christianity, and they still represent ideals of achievement and of conduct. The new faith, born of a narrow tribal belief in the hill country of Judea and Galilee, emerged as a principle of universal brotherhood from the gradual breakdown of local religions incident to the active intercourse between all parts of the Mediterranean basin under the *pax Romana*. Transplanted from its small tribal habitat to the cosmopolitan field of the Roman Mediterranean, Christian dogma underwent modification; and in its

Roman and Greek forms it entered its career of conquest. Its teachings and scriptures were disseminated along Roman routes of trade and dominion. Its organization into a church was modelled after the Roman imperial system, while rituals and festivals were borrowed from the discarded religions of Saturn, Zeus, Jupiter and Vesta.

COMPOSITE ELEMENTS IN MEDITERRANEAN CIVILIZATION— This Mediterranean Sea with its bordering lands has been a melting-pot for the peoples and civilizations which have seeped into it from its continental hinterlands. It has been a catchment basin, and it has been also a distributing center for its composite cultural achievements. This double rôle in history is an outgrowth of its geographical location and its relation to the neighboring continents.

The Mediterranean is a great gulf of the Atlantic cutting back into the land mass of the Eastern Hemisphere. It carries the waters of the ocean 2,330 miles inland to the foot of the Lebanon Mountains, and yet farther through the Black Sea to the rugged coast of the Caucasus. It gives Asia an Atlantic seaboard, and hence rendered it possible for Asiatic navigators from Phœnicia to make the first recorded discovery of Britain. This is the *mare internum*, enclosed by three contrasted continents which it helps to divide, but whose differences in climate, flora, fauna, peoples and civilizations it helps to reconcile. Its coastlands, peninsulas and islands form a broad transition belt. It defines the shoreline of southern Europe and northern Africa, yet it has never served to hold apart the history of these two regions, so far as records show. The Levantine Sea has linked Egypt with Asia Minor more effectively than has the Suez and Syrian bridge between. The line of the Ægean, Marmara, Black Sea and Azof divides Asia and Europe in a physical sense, but unites them in an historical sense. The Greek names for these two continents trace back to Assyrian words meaning sunrise and sunset, used to designate the lands lying east and west of the Ægean Sea. Beyond the Euxine the ancient civilized peoples penetrated little into the interior. Hence from the geography of the Mediterranean they adopted the three-fold division of the continents, which popular usage has retained. The continent of Eurasia is a modern scientific concept, based upon much later Asiatic explorations.[2]

For the ancients, therefore, the Mediterranean had an Asiatic, a European, and an African front, each the long portico of a separate continent. Each continent, in turn, possessed distinctive features of coastline, relief, hinterland connections, and differentiated types of the prevailing Mediterranean climate. Each had its own native race or native peoples, speaking different tongues, having different manners, customs and religions, showing different degrees of proficiency in the arts, and representing different stages of economic and social development. But all made their contributions to the Mediterranean civilization; all helped to give it the cosmopolitan character which was the expression of its rich content and the reason for its survival through the ages.

The Mediterranean frontage of these continents differs both in length and character. Europe has a long coastline of about 8,000 miles (13,000 kilometers) measured from the Strait of Gibraltar to the mouth of the Don River (Tanais), the ancient boundary of eastern Europe.[3] It comprises a fringe of peninsulas and islands; a great variety and rapid alternation of reliefs, from the snowy Sierras of Spain to the lowlands of the Ebro; a decided range of climates between sub-tropical Crete and the frozen winters of the Scythian plains, between the rain-drenched slopes of Dalmatia and the arid steppes of the Don. Back of this European front moreover lay a varied and productive hinterland, contrasted in climate and in natural products, and in ancient times lingering in a backward civilization as compared with the Mediterranean coastland. Here were both motive and opportunity for maritime trade and for trade with the back country. Europe therefore made notable contributions to Mediterranean civilization, by reason of its ready contact with the sea and the diversified character of its coastlands harboring a maritime population; it stimulated the aptitude of its people for exploiting their own geographic advantages and especially for appropriating the best methods of their overseas neighbors. Europe appeared first as a borrower from Asia and Egypt, but soon developed into a dispenser of gifts.

Africa's front promised and gave far less. Its coastline measures only 3,100 miles (5,000 km.) and comprises few marine inlets either great or small, few peninsulas and almost no islands. It is sharply divided into a long stretch of mountain coast to the west, and a longer stretch of plateau coast to the east, each characterized by monotony till they combine in the Tunisian Peninsula, and each backed by the same desert hinterland. This whole African front has suffered also from monotonous heat and drought, except where the coastal mountains in the wintèr half of the year achieve a more or less ample rainfall. From the Strait of Gibraltar to the Nile valley, Africa has made meager contribution to Mediterranean life and civilization. It has been a poor mediator, limited in its power either to give or to receive. Stim'uli which have reached its shores have been blunted against its vast inertia. Phœnician, Greek, Roman, Vandal and Arab colonists have exploited its local resources here and there but in time succumbed to local conditions, without forcing from African soil any outstanding native achievement, except the elephant corps of Hannibal's army, the dauntless Numidian cavalry, and perhaps a winning horse for the races of the Greek games.

On the eastern edge of the African front lay Egypt, a striking contrast to the rest. So different was it that the ancients counted the Nile valley as part of Asia until the maritime ventures of the Ptolemies on the Red Sea made the deep cleft between Arabia and Libya a part of common knowledge; [4] but even so, the assignment of Egypt to continental Asia returned again in the early middle ages, as if its grouping with Africa did violence to fundamental geographic principles. The reasons are obvious. The long river oasis which was Egypt, the multiform adjustments of individual and national life to its peculiar geographic conditions, the whole elaborate fluvial civilization was more affiliated to Asia than to Africa. Moreover, the Nile valley, both in its military campaigns and its trade, was more closely connected with Asia across the Isthmus of Suez and along the Red Sea route than with Africa across the economic void of the Libyan Desert, or along the sandy reaches of the upper Nile. The ancients therefore displayed geographical insight in regarding Egypt as part of Asia; for its contributions to Mediterranean civilization were similar to those of Asia and in large measure duplicated those of the Tigris-Euphrates valley.

The Asiatic front, from the Don River to the Isthmus of Suez, measures 3,700 miles (6,000 km.) and therefore exceeds that of Africa. It owes its length largely to the Asia Minor Peninsula, which also supplies its only well indented coast and gives it immediate access to Thrace and the Balkan Peninsula. Despite a varied but none too productive hinterland, despite poor hinterland connections except at a few favored points, this Asiatic front made invaluable contributions to Mediterranean civilization, because it was a great irregular isthmus between the western sea and the Indian Ocean. As such it formed a natural passway through all time between Orient and Occident. It was the Mediterranean base for the multiform cultural influences which emanated primarily from the fluvial civilization of the Tigris and Euphrates valley, or which filtered in from Persia and India. A series of middlemen states grew up on this Asiatic front, in Philistia, Phœnicia, northern Syria, Lydia, Phrygia and the Hellenic colonial coast of Asia Minor. Moreover, the hinterland nations—Hittites, Assyrians, Babylonians and Persians—reached out westward to seize Mediterranean termini of the Isthmian trade routes. The result was a constant outpouring of Asiatic gifts, whether crafts, commodities or religions, into the all-receiving lap of Mediterranean culture. They were carried by armies, migrant tribes, traders, colonists and slaves, who infused a strain of Asiatic blood into the Mediterranean stock of Europe and Africa.

COMPOSITE RACE ELEMENTS—The three continents contributed also diverse elements of race and language. The predominant ethnic stocks along the Mediterranean coastlands belonged presumably to the Mediterranean race of narrow head and short stature, as early grave findings seem to indicate. But alien strains trickled or flowed in from the hinterlands. Sometimes they freshened the native ethnic spring; sometimes they muddied it, occasionally they engulfed it. Broadheaded Celts from middle Europe drifted southward into Spain where they blended with the native Iberians. Others occupied the

Po valley, while a different type of tall broad-heads from
Illyria formed a constituent or dominant element in the ancient
Hellenes.[5]   The Black Sea steppes of Europe contributed
Iranian elements in the Cimmerians and Sarmatians, with a
probable Mongolian admixture in the ruling Scythian tribes,
who came from northwest Asia; [6] but the immediate hinterland
was occupied by Slav and Finnish stocks.[7] Representatives of
all these peoples undoubtedly found their way in to more
southern Mediterranean lands, both by incursions like that of
the Cimmerians into Asia Minor and of the Scythians into
Thrace, reported by Herodotus, and also by the slave trade
with the Greeks, which was always exceedingly active along
the Euxine coasts.   Scythian slaves were the police of Athens.

Asia's ethnic contributions were varied.   They comprised
the large Semitic stocks of Palestine, Syria and Arabia which
were scattered eventually over the whole Mediterranean area
through Phœnician colonization, through the widespread sale
of Syrian and Hebrew slaves after the Roman conquest, and
finally through the Saracen conquests; and they included also
the congeries of diverse, unclassified peoples found in Asia
Minor—Lydians, Carians, Lycians, Pisidians, Hittites—all
variants of one original racial group, neither Semitic nor Indo-
European in language, but all later modified, displaced or
diluted by later migrations from Europe.[8] From the Asiatic
hinterland Assyrians of Semitic speech and Aryan Persians
reached out westward and dominated stretches of the Mediterranean seaboard for long periods, leaving there elements of
their race and culture.

Africa brought to the Mediterranean coastland its dark
Hamitic race, representing many stages of civilization in the
Egyptians, the nomads of the northern plateau, and the secluded mountaineers of the Atlas ranges; but this continent
also contributed strains of Negro blood, drawn from its remote
southern hinterland.   The infiltration was slight through the
broad Sahara barrier; but where the upper Nile opened a path
across the desert to Ethiopia and Nubia, the northward movement of Negro elements into Egypt seems to have been considerable.

The various ethnic strains from three continents multiplied

and complicated the reactions between race and environment in the Mediterranean lands; but they undoubtedly enriched the ancient Mediterranean culture.

Detached centers of civilization developed also outside this cosmopolitan Mediterranean region of diverse contacts, but they remained provincial, monotonous, uni-type. The culture which grew up in China and India was in each case confined to an Asiatic area. Even when it encompassed a maritime region, it failed to achieve a cosmopolitan character. Chinese civilization spread around the enclosed basin formed by Pechili Gulf and the Yellow Sea, and embraced Manchuria, Korea and Japan. In this expansion it evolved some interesting minor variants. But the Yellow Sea indented the coast of one continent.[9] Its shores and hinterland were confined to one monotonous race area of Mongolians. Hence its variations of language, art, architecture, religion and social customs never deviated far from the parent Chinese type.

MEDITERRANEAN ELEMENTS OF THIS CULTURE—The intercontinental location of the Mediterranean Sea afforded the fundamental geographic conditions for a cosmopolitan culture; but further refinements and differentiations ensued as a response to conditions within the circle of the Mediterranean lands. These lands, owing to a great diversity of coastal articulation and relief, comprise a succession of small naturally defined regions, separated from each other by barriers of mountain, sea, or desert, but in general fronting some marine inlet, which gave their ancient inhabitants accessibility to the sea and its stimulating contacts. These detached districts became the sites of strongly individualized states and federations, like Athens or Bœotia, Achaia or Sybaris, the Etruscan or the Latin League, Egypt or Carthage; but all together formed one big Mediterranean neighborhood. Whatever flower of culture each small region developed in its own garden plot was disseminated over the whole basin by the multitudinous paths of the sea. So varied were the local conditions of temperature, rainfall, soil, relief, area, coastline and vicinal grouping, that each district commanded some peculiar combination of natural advantages in the production of its distinctive contribution to the civilization of the whole. These cultural achievements in turn, transplanted to distant shores, took on new aspects in response to a changed environment or were remodeled by the genius or needs of new masters. The lyrics of Athens became war songs in Sparta. The swift Liburnian cutters of the Dalmatian pirates were conscripted into the fleet of the Roman navy. Irrigation methods of the keen Sidonian cosmopolite were adopted by the dull Bœotian peasant in his fertile lacustrine plain. The fine horticulture of Syria lived again in the gardens of Sallust and Mæcenas on the Pincian Hill of Rome.

The Mediterranean basin thus stimulated the development of a cosmopolitan civilization such as was unknown to the historical countries of Asia. These were all essentially continental; they had their nuclei in isolated river valleys,—the Tigris and Euphrates, the stream oases of highland Persia, the Oxus and Jaxartes, the Indus, the Ganges, and the rivers of China. The dominant geographic factors were the same in all; a river fed by rains or snows on distant mountains, watering a land of chronic or seasonal aridity; a fertile alluvial soil generally of large extent; barrier boundaries of mountains or deserts; and about the river mouths widespread deltaic flats, saline marshes, shifting channels, hidden sandbars, and silted coasts, discouraging contact with the sea. The inhabitants made the most of the fecund soil by early developing a more or less elaborate system of tillage dependent upon irrigation. Thus they secured an abundant and reliable food supply which led to great concentration of population with all its derivative effects; but they lacked stimuli from without. The isolation which protected their nascent civilization from overwhelming attack overshot the mark and induced stagnation. It not only shut out but it shut in. The people were corralled in their fertile valley plains; they were tethered in their lush meadows. Little motive or chance for them to get out and away. This was the blight upon the great civilizations of Asia and early Egypt. Intermittent and few were the caravans of land-borne commerce which reached or crossed these valley kingdoms. Only Egypt and Mesopotamia lay near enough to the Mediterranean to profit by its contacts, and then chiefly through the agency of Phœnician, Arab, and Hellenic traders. What they gave had to be fetched; what they received had to be delivered.

The Mediterranean Sea with its close-hugging shores promoted many-sided relations, as opposed to the one-sided relations of the land. Rhodes was equally linked with the Bosporus and the Nile, with Tyre and Sicily. Athens drew its wheat supply from Scythia and Egypt, from Syria and Sicily, as prices or sailing conditions might dictate. To its universities came students from the whole circle of the Mediterranean lands. And no matter what their native tongue, they spoke Greek, the cosmopolitan language of education, and they recognized a cosmopolitan standard of breeding and culture. Easy communications conduced to good manners: the Rhodians, in an hour of national disaster, resolved to cherish their "reputation of being the best-mannered people" of the Mediterranean. Ceaseless intercourse back and forth along "the wet ways" bound together the Mediterranean peoples into one great community life, transmuted their diverse civilizations into one great culture, reconciled their differences into harmony, their antagonisms into tolerance; and mingled their race strains and languages in innumerable over-seas colonies.

This process of cultural unification began early and continued long. It permeated the economic, colonial and finally the political history of the basin as a whole. The ancient Mediterranean reveals a succession of maritime commercial states,—Phœnician, Cretan, Hellenic, Carthaginian, Etruscan, —each maintaining a large sphere of influence which overlapped that of its neighbors at one or more points. Through these interlocking spheres, each participated to some extent in the world events of its day. Minoan interests extended from Egypt to Sicily, north to Athens and probably to Troy. Greeks and Phœnicians became rival traders and colonists in the western Mediterranean as they had earlier been in the Levantine Sea, the Ægean and the Euxine. The Hebrew prophet Ezekiel, writing about 590 B.C., looked down from the Judean hills upon the blue Mediterranean and enumerated the products of its shores and hinterlands which were to be seen in the markets of Tyre.[10] There were horses and mules from Armenia, rams and lambs from the Syrian grassland, spices from Arabia, wheat and oil from Judea, Egyptian linen, African ivories, purple dye from the Greek islands, slaves from

Ionia, silver, iron and tin from Spain, wealth from everywhere; because "thy borders are in the midst of the sea." Ezekiel's list gives a geographical index of the known world of his time and epitomizes its economic development. Later these Tyrian wares were duplicated or multiplied in the markets of Miletos, Rhodes, Athens, Corinth, Alexandria, Carthage or Roman Ostia. The commercial center shifted, but always to some focal point of the sea routes.

Such was the uniting power of the Mediterranean. It consolidated the ancient world in a cultural sense, even before the political unification under the Roman Empire put a finishing touch to the work. The ancient world was small. It comprised little beyond the Mediterranean coasts and their immediate hinterlands. This was the *orbis terrarum*, "the seabound circle of the whole dry land" [11] according to an anonymous Greek poet. "Like frogs around a pond we have settled down upon the shores of this sea from the Phasis River to the Pillars of Heracles," said Plato.[12] Every city state, every dwarf principality, every far-flung colony, every pirate league faced seaward towards the Mediterranean. Inland countries were left out in the cold, condemned to poverty and provincialism. Highland Judea tried again and again to secure a foothold upon its shore. Its shining waters formed the real center of ancient life. Back and forth along its dissolving paths moved commerce, colonies, and the multiform elements of classical culture,—alphabets and scripts, literatures and languages, arts and industries, laws and infant sciences, gods and rituals, a vast give and take.

Finally Rome, the heir of long Mediterranean ages, combined the whole into one political dominion and made Latin a second cosmopolitan tongue. "Rome the capital of the world, Italy the land which is at once the foster-child and parent of all lands; chosen by the providence of the gods to render heaven itself more glorious, to unite the scattered empires of the earth, to bestow a polish on men's manners, to unite the discordant and uncouth dialects of many different nations by the powerful ties of a common language, to confer the enjoyments of discourse and of civilization upon mankind, and to

become in short the mother-country of all nations of the earth."
Thus Pliny depicted Rome as the embodiment of Mediterranean culture, heart of the ancient world, focus of the earliest
universal history.[13]

THE ORIENTAL TRADE ROUTE—The Mediterranean Sea
belongs to the series of marine subsidences which extend eastward from Suez through the marginal basins of the Indian
Ocean to the Pacific, and reappear in the Caribbean Sea and
Gulf of Mexico, thus belting the earth. In ancient times the
effect of this thalassic grouping reached eventually to the
Malay Peninsula or "The Golden Chersonnesus" and China; it
gave the Mediterranean traders access to the Orient, a region
of contrasted tropical climates and of contrasted civilizations,
facilitated intercourse between East and West, and stimulated
commercial exchanges. Phœnician and later Greek merchantmen reached the ports of India and Ceylon, while Indian and
later Chinese vessels steered westward to the seaboard markets
of the Persian Gulf and Strait of Bab-el-Mandeb. Thus the
geographical horizon of the Mediterranean peoples was greatly
extended eastward and also southward along the African coast
by the time of Claudius Ptolemy (160 A.D.), and their circle of
commercial exchanges was yet more enlarged by the time of
Justinian (552 A.D.). Their participation in the history of
the Far East, however, except for Alexander's conquests in
Persia and India, was restricted to the peaceful activities of
trade and early Christian missions.

As part of this great maritime track between Europe and
the Orient, the Mediterranean had the compass of its historical
associations constantly widened through the ancient and medieval periods. The Saracen conquests in the seventh century
brought its southern and western shores into political and cultural union with Arabia, Persia and western India, and introduced from the East new field crops like rice and cotton, new
fruits like oranges and lemons, improved technique in ceramics
and textiles, and oriental standards of beauty in color and
design. All these spread from their distributing centers in
Alexandria, Sicily, North Africa and Spain, and went to enrich the culture of medieval Italy and France.

After the Caliphate was disrupted, the commercial states of Genoa, Pisa, Venice, Amalfi and Barcelona maintained the oriental trade through the ports of the Levant, and the Crusaders established their short-lived Frankish principalities in Syria and Palestine, whence they carried away valuable suggestions from the finished industries of the East. Genoese trading stations on Lesbos, Samos and the Crimean coast, Venetian holdings in the Ægean islands, Crete and Cyprus outlived the Byzantine Empire. So active was Venetian trade through Alexandria and the Red Sea with the Orient, that after the Portuguese discovery of the outside route to the Indies, the Doge in 1504 hastily negotiated with the Mameluke government of Egypt for the restoration of the old canal communication between the Nile delta and the Gulf of Suez, as a means of expediting and cheapening transportation. But the Turkish conquest of Egypt in 1517 blocked the enterprise. The Mediterranean was paralyzed by the ensuing dislocation of the world trade routes. Instead of the chief thoroughfare to the Orient, it became an untravelled *cul-de-sac*, idle except for local traffic.

So it remained for centuries. Meantime, Europe established colonial empires in southern Asia and drew the whole Orient into the circle of its trade. Need for rapid communication between East and West began to revive the old Mediterranean thoroughfare. Its seaboard began to take on new significance in the eighteenth century, and the opening of the Suez Canal in 1869 restored it to its old position as a dominant factor in world history.

AUTHORITIES—CHAPTER I

1. F. Cajori, "Evolution of the Dollar Mark," *Pop. Sci. Mo.*, Vol. 81, pp. 521-530.
2. A. Philippson, *Das Mittelmeergebiet*, p. 6, note 1. Leipzig, 1907. H. Kiepert, *Ancient Geography*, p. 17. London, 1881.
3. Strabo, XI, Chap. II, 1-2. Strabo was the most famous geographer of ancient times; born at Amasia in Pontus in 66 B.C., died in 24 A.D.
4. Kiepert, *op. cit.*, p. 18.
5. W. Z. Ripley, *Races of Europe*, passim.
6. E. H. Mimms, *Scythians and Greeks*, pp. 35-47. Cambridge, 1913.
7. *Ibid.*, 102-106.
8. Eduard Meyer, *Geschichte des Altertums*, pp. 613, 615-619, 624. Stuttgart, 1909.
9. T. Fischer, *Mittelmeerbilder*, pp. 2, 31. Leipzig, 1908.
10. *Ezekiel*, Chap. XXVII.
11. W. R. Paton, *Greek Anthology*, Vol. III, p. 375. Loeb Classical Library, London, 1907.
12. Plato, *Phædo*.
13. Pliny, *Historia Naturalis*, Lib. III, Chap. VI.

CHAPTER II

THE PHYSIOGRAPHIC HISTORY OF THE MEDITER-
RANEAN AND ITS EFFECTS

The geological history of the Mediterranean Sea and its bordering lands has given this region a complex physiographic character, and thereby afforded the natural conditions for an extraordinary human development. The Mediterranean is a young sea, formed in the Tertiary and early Quaternary Periods, when man was already living on the earth. It occupies the areas of depression interposed between the areas of upheaval constituting the belt of young folded mountains which stretches across northwest Africa, southern Europe, and nearby Asia as far as the Caucasus and the Taurus ranges of Armenia. The West Basin lies wholly within this mountain zone. The East Basin stretches across it, penetrating through the Black Sea to the low plains of present-day Russia on the north, to the plateau rim of Africa on the south, where no folding has taken place, and to the young block mountains of Syria and Palestine on the east.

This geological history has involved extensive elevations and subsidences. These have converted islands into peninsulas and peninsulas into islands; they have altered the contact of continent with continent and sea with sea, and ultimately resulted in an endless variety of land and sea forms, grouped in close proximity.[1] The region includes every degree of coast articulation from the compact Iberian Peninsula with its 230,000 square miles (584,000 sq. km.) of area to the finger promontories of the Peloponnesos and Chalcidice, and the Gibraltar headland with its two square miles (5 sq. km.) of area. It embraces every form of relief from the level plain of the Guadalquivir valley to the plateau of the Spanish Meseta and the steep slopes of the Sierra Nevada; from the deltaic flats of the Sperchius River, which merge into the silted shallows of the Malic Gulf, to the old lake basin of Thessaly overlooked by the snowy massif of Mount Olympos. Land forms alternate with every gradation of sea, from the great rectangular area of the Levantine Sea to the crater harbor of half-sunk Santorin Island, from the long lane of the Adriatic to the slender runnel of the Hellespont and Bosporus, which make the Black Sea a vast alcove of the Mediterranean.

Changes of outline during a momentous geological history have extended the reach of the Mediterranean and thereby the range of climates in its bordering lands. Subsidences north and south expanded the Mediterranean domain till it included coastlands distinguished by marked variations of the Mediterranean type of climate, from the Po basin and rain-drenched slope of the Carso Plateau with its brief summer drought, to the Libyan grassland with its short shrift of winter rains. Subsidence also stretched the Mediterranean northward till it penetrated into the alien climatic province of the Scythian or Russian plains, and southward till it impinged on another alien climatic province in the Libyan Desert of Africa with its long-drawn fluvial oasis of the Nile valley. These two contrasted climatic provinces, accessible to the waterways of the Mediterranean Sea, have exercised a strong influence to diversify the economic, commercial and political history of the other Mediterranean lands.

OLD RESIDUAL PLATEAUS—Additional forms of relief in the Mediterranean region were provided by old residual plateaus of archæan and crystalline rocks, which were embraced by the young folded mountains in their process of uplifting.[2] These present the appearance of tablelands crossed by worn-down ranges, or of dissected plateaus with steep escarpments, or of high peaks of granite or marble which have resisted erosion and therefore offer rugged fronts like unto the younger mountains. Five of these old highland areas remain. I. The plateau or Meseta of Spain, filling the space between the young Pyrenees on the north and the Sierra Nevada on the south, cemented to the former by the Ebro valley and to the latter by the Guadalquivir plain. II. The Central Plateau of France, linking the Pyrenees with the Maritime Alps by the bold Cevenne escarpment, cemented to the Pyrenees by the Garonne-Aude furrow and to the Alps by the Rhone valley. III. Frag-

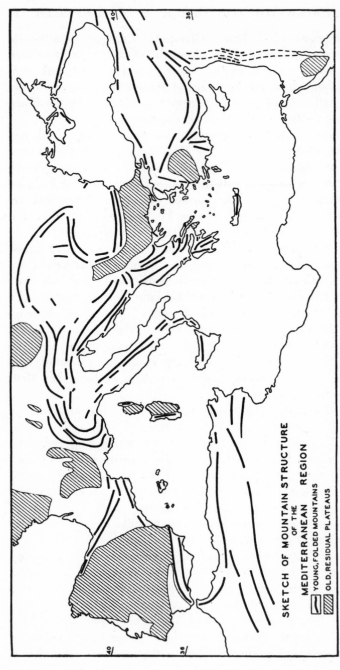

MAP 1—Heavy lines show the trend of the young folded mountains. Shaded areas indicate the old crystalline plateaus. Dotted lines on the east bound the Lebanon Trough and the Jordan-Dead Sea Depression.

SKETCH OF MOUNTAIN STRUCTURE
OF THE
MEDITERRANEAN   REGION

YOUNG, FOLDED MOUNTAINS

OLD, RESIDUAL PLATEAUS

ments of the old Tyrrhenian massif surviving in Corsica, Sardinia, Elba and the hill country of Tuscany, around which curves the long crescent of the Apennine folds. IV. The Rhodope or Thracian massif, welded to the young folded Balkan Mountains on the north by the upper Maritza River valley (ancient Hebrus), and merging into the Macedonian fold mountains on the west. V. The Lydian massif, occupying the middle section of western Asia Minor and embracing the valleys of the Gediz (Hermus) and Menderes (Meander) rivers, which are graben or rift valleys.

The structural valleys which lie between these old plateaus and their flanking fold systems appear as ancient scars on the face of the earth, marking old wounds which healed imperfectly. Practically they open highways of gentle gradient into the hinterland and only near their head do they meet steep ascents where plateau and fold system join.

These old crystalline highlands were the chief repositories of valuable metals in the ancient Mediterranean region. Spain attracted the early Phœnician metallurgists who were searching for tin, gold, and silver; it provided also copper, lead, mica which took the place of glass, and cinnabar from which the much prized vermilion was obtained. Tin, so important in the Bronze Age, was said by Ezekiel and Posidonius to have come from Tarshish,[3] probably from mines in the mountain district of Orenso. Tin was found in the old crystalline area of Etruria (Tuscany) about Mount Amiata and Monte Catini, and may have contributed to the ancient Etruscan bronze work. Etruria furnished also iron and mercury, while the iron mines of Elba were worked from early times. Sardinia also, which yielded iron, copper and silver, attracted Phœnician traders to its coasts.

Phœnicians were the first people to colonize Thasos island, which is a fragment of the Rhodope massif, and from this protected base they exploited the gold mines in the Rhodope Mountains. Centuries later Athens founded the colony of Amphipolis at the southern foot of the Rhodope, and there drew upon the gold mines of Mount Pangæus to replenish her treasury, much as Carthage, after the first Punic War, exploited the gold and silver of Spain in order to prepare for the next great struggle with Rome. Gold found in Lydia in the sands of the Pactolus River doubtless contributed to the wealth of Crœsus and stimulated the early coinage of money in the Lydian Kingdom; it also encouraged the long continued trade of the Phœnicians on this part of the Asia Minor coast. We find these inveterate gold-seekers at an early date founding a colony on the island of Siphnos near gold deposits where the crystalline core of the half-submerged Cyclades folds had been uncovered.

YOUNG FOLD SYSTEMS—Two systems of folded mountains may be distinguished within the Mediterranean region: I. A Western system, which quite encircles the West Basin, except where erratic fractures and subsidences cut across the grain of mountains and form straits or gulfs. II. An Eastern system, which radiates in three arms from the eastern Alps, encircles the Ægean Sea and much of the Black Sea, and finally converges again in the great mountain node of the Caucasus and the corrugated highland of Armenia.[4]

The Alps, as the conspicuous relief feature of the Mediterranean, may be taken as the focus of these fold systems. The Western system begins with the Maritime Alps and merges eastward into the narrow Ligurian Apennines which, spreading out into the multiple folds of the Italian Apennines, continue southeastward through the length of the peninsula. Turning westward across Sicily, they are cleft by the narrow Strait of Messina, dip below the sea in the Sicilian Straits, marked by a shallow submarine isthmus, and emerge again in the Atlas Mountain system, whose parallel ranges first appear as Cape Bon and Cape Blanco of the Tunisian Peninsula. The massive Atlas folds traverse North Africa for 1,200 miles (3,000 km.) to the Atlantic, throwing off a branch range as the Rif Atlas, which curves northward to the Tangier peninsula, breaks asunder in the narrow Strait of Gibraltar, and reappears on the Spanish side as the Granada Mountains and the Sierra Nevada. These describe a gentle curve northeastward along the Spanish coast, protrude in the bold headlands of Cape Palos and Cape Nao before they dive beneath the sea, and emerge again in fragments as the Pityus and Balearic Islands, whose parallel ranges and submarine plateaus reveal the former connection with the Iberian Peninsula.

The eastern escarpment of the Spanish Meseta and a single narrow range forming the seaward rim of the Ebro River plain link the southern mountains with the Pyrenean folds. These spring from the old Cantabrian mountains bordering the Spanish Meseta on the north, and continue eastward with scarcely a dip in their high skyline till they run out to the Mediterranean in bold headlands. There they sink beneath the subsidence area of the Gulf of Lyons, emerge again beyond the Rhone as the low parallel hill ranges of Provence, and join the Maritime Alps. These inconspicuous hills have exercised local geographic influences out of all proportion to their relief. Between the Pyrenees and the Alps, at the head of the Gulf of Lyons, the high escarpment of the Central Plateau of France presents the rugged relief characteristic of mountain backgrounds in Mediterranean lands.

The link between the Western and Eastern fold systems is formed by the Alps, which from the Gulf of Lyons bend northward and eastward till they run out near the Danube in the wooded hills of Vienna. Beyond the Vienna basin the Eastern folds resume their way as the Carpathian Mountains, then swing around to the east and southeast in a vast inverted S as they join the Balkans, sink beneath the Black Sea, emerge again as the Jaila Mountains along the Crimean littoral, and are cleft by the narrow channel of the Kertch or Crimean Bosporus before they continue eastward as the Caucasus Mountains. This northern arm of the Eastern fold system at no point touches the Mediterranean Sea proper, but it serves to endow the northeast coast of the Black Sea with a Mediterranean type of relief and climate.

The southern arm of the Eastern fold system branches off southeastward from the Carnic Alps, traverses the Adriatic side of the Balkan Peninsula as the Dinaric Alps, breaks at the sharp cross fracture of the Corinthian Gulf, recovers again in the mountainous Peloponnesos, and runs out southward in four bold finger peninsulas into the Mediterranean. Here subsidence has had its way. The half-submerged ranges, their parallelism still evident, can be traced in the long island crescent formed by Cythera, Crete, Carpathos and Rhodes which represent the mountains of the Peloponnesos; while the Cyclades islands maintain their alignment with Attica and Eubœa, which together form the half drowned ranges of an older massif. On the southwest coast of Asia Minor these Eastern folds rise again in rocky promontories and merge into the high Taurus system, which runs eastward along the Levantine littoral of the Anatolian Peninsula, bends northward in the corrugated highland of Armenia, and merges into the Anti-Caucasus.

The mountains of Macedonia send off an intermediate arm which runs out seaward as the three-pronged peninsula of Chalcidice, sinks beneath the north Ægean, emerges as the east-west ranges of the Trojan Peninsula on the Asiatic side, and continues eastward along the Black Sea front of Asia Minor as the Pontic Ranges. These folds mingle almost inextricably with the block mountains marking the escarpment of the Anatolian Plateau. Along the whole western front of Asia Minor, mountain ranges, irrespective of their geologic origin, run out endwise into the Ægean and the Sea of Marmara. They therefore give this slope of the peninsula the appearance of a vast fluted surface, alternate valleys and ridges, alternate bays and promontories, the latter sinking seaward beneath the waves and rising again as rugged offshore islands, like Lesbos, Chios and Samos, which show a strict alignment with the ranges of the mainland. The general type of relief is that of young folded mountains with steep slopes, because the recent subsidence which formed the Ægean Sea submerged the old shelving piedmont, and brought the wash of the waves or the alluvial valley floor right up to the foot of the sudden acclivity. Hence the Mediterranean type of landscape prevails even along the littoral of the old Lydian massif.

The same is true in pronounced form along the eastern front of the Mediterranean. Where the Taurus system bends northward away from the sea, it sends off a short fold southward in Mount Amanus, which rounding the Bay of Issus (Alexandretta) on the east shows a perfect alignment with the Olympos range of Cyprus. The Amanus links the Eastern folds with the young block mountains of Syria and Palestine.

These block mountains, formed by the great monocline of the Arabian plateau where it sinks abruptly to the Mediterranean, present on the seaward front the characteristic bold relief of young ranges. Moreover, the sinking of the arched crest in the Quaternary Period formed a long rift valley comprising the Lebanon Trough, Jordan-Dead Sea depression, and Gulf of Akabah, which divided the monocline lengthwise into two parallel heights, with a vast canyon-like groove between. This process emphasized the already rugged relief, and lent these highlands in some degree the outward appearance of young folded mountains flanking a longitudinal furrow, though the details of the relief reveal the true geological origin. However, the result is that the bold outline of the typical Mediterranean highlands prevails also on the eastern front, though only the Bay of Issus breaks the even line of the shore.

At the Isthmus of Suez the relief changes. The characteristic Mediterranean type gives place to the low monotonous relief of northeast Africa, to level plain and even coastline, backed by the canyon-carved buttresses of the plateau interior. Only where the rounded bight of the Great Syrtis balances and perhaps explains the Tertiary elevation of the rounded Barca plateau does northeast Africa reveal the typical Mediterranean topography. This isolated highland rises from the coast in a bold escarpment to the height of 2,000 feet or more (600 meters), attaining its greatest elevation within a few miles of the sea, and gradually sinking inland to the prevailing level of the interior. Its whole history is one of elevation, so that no inlet nicks the smooth contour of its coast. With the exception of the Barca plateau therefore, the African platform is alien to the dominant Mediterranean physiographic region, though it forms part of the Mediterranean maritime region. It is a distinct region in point of relief, and because of its low elevation and southern location has only an attenuated form of the Mediterranean climate; because of excessive dryness its steppes are more closely related to the African deserts than to the winter crop-lands of other Mediterranean coasts.

This African type of relief appears again on the northwest coast of the Black Sea. Where the great alcove of the Mediterranean penetrates beyond the northern belt of folded mountains and reaches the low plains of southeast Europe about the Gulf of Odessa and the Sea of Azof, it includes an alien type of relief and an alien climate within the Mediterranean maritime region. Elsewhere young folded mountains of bold relief nearly encircle the Euxine shores and preserve a modified type of the Mediterranean climate, except on the east Pontic ranges and the Caucasus.

TERTIARY DEPOSITS—Repeated elevations, alternating with shorter periods of subsidence, have characterized the geologic history of the Mediterranean lands. These changes of level have resulted in a wide distribution of late Tertiary deposits, consisting of loose clay, marl and sandstone with harder limestone between. These deposits mantle the feet and even the shoulders of many mountain ranges, cloaking the sharp forms of relief and spreading a border of plain along the coastal hem. Their anthropo-geographic significance has been twofold. As natural terraces built up in the course of ages against the steep rock core of the folded mountains, they have eased the gradient from lowland to highland and thus facilitated human intercourse between the two. At the same time they have improved the conditions for agriculture, both in point of relief and of soils. Though less fertile than the deltaic lands and alluvial valleys, their mixed soils have proved far more productive under tillage than the old mountain slopes of weathered limestone or crystalline rock.[5]

The narrow coastal plains found along the Mediterranean consist for the most part of these Tertiary deposits, overlaid in places by alluvium. Such were the Plain of Sharon, symbol of fertility to the ancient Hebrews; and the maritime plain of Elis in the Peloponnesos, "goodly Elis," as Homer called it, land of grainfield and meadow, land of the blossoming flax, whose acres of unbroken blue seemed a bit of the Mediterranean sky dropped down to earth. Such too was the southern coast belt of the Corinthian Gulf, which from the earliest times had its flourishing farms and vineyards, and supported populous cities like ancient Sicyon, Ægyra, Helice and Patræ. But the opposite coast, rising steeply from the Gulf, offered no level land for tillage except a rare erosion valley, like that of the little Crissian plain at the foot of Mount Parnassos, which was a bone of contention between the hungry Phocians and the priests of Delphi.

The same contrast of geographic conditions and resulting development was apparent on the opposite coasts of the Adriatic Sea. The steep Illyrian front of barren limestone, with no veneer of Tertiary deposits and no vestige of alluvial soil in its drowned valleys, afforded abundant harbors but scant footing for field or settlement. Adjustment to these conditions produced the ancient Illyrian pirates, driven to robbery on the sea by their step-mother land. On the opposite Italian coast, a narrow belt of Tertiary deposits, guiltless of harbors but productive as to soil, nurtured the hard-working peasants of Picenum who cultivated their orchards, vineyards and wheat fields,[6] and sent out their little fishing boats on the Adriatic as their descendants do today.

These coastal plains rise by gentle gradient and merge into the piedmont terraces of Tertiary deposits, which combine various other geographic advantages. In the warm Mediterranean climate they unite in a narrow zone of cultivation both sub-tropical and temperate products. They command facilities for irrigation during the summer drought, and are to some extent protected by effective drainage against malaria, which has long infested the lowlands. Tertiary deposits cover also the floors of longitudinal valleys within the mountains, as in the Apennines of Italy [7] and in western Asia Minor, where they have extended the level land and improved the quality of the soil. The barren history of Corsica and Sardinia can in large measure be ascribed to the fact that their granitic massifs, part of the old Tyrrhenian continent, towered above the Mediterranean throughout the Tertiary Period; hence they acquired no sedimentary coastland to serve as intermediary between sea and highland, and to maintain an industrious peasant population. Only the Cagliari valley of southwest Sardinia, cementing a Tertiary limestone ridge to the crystalline core of the island, is also endowed with a fertile volcanic soil. Its wheat fields drew thither Phœnician traders from early times, and later filled the Roman granaries.

LIMESTONES AND CAVES—Old sea caves registered every halt in the emergence of fold and block mountains out of the early

sea of the Mesozoic Epoch, and recorded their vertical oscilla-
tions later mid the waters of the Mediterranean. Widespread
limestones, which form part of nearly every mountain foreland
and run out seaward in bold white promontories, bear witness
to the marine birth of many parts of the Mediterranean lands.
Along the old beaches of the receding sea these limestones and
other sedimentary rocks have been hollowed out by the surf
into numerous caves. These abound along the coast, but are
also found far inland where the sea once penetrated, or where
underground waters dissolved out the porous limestone. Caves
and grottoes are therefore so common a feature of the Mediterranean landscape that they figured conspicuously in Mediterranean life and literature, especially in ancient times.
Homer could find no better term to describe the domain of
Menelaus than "caverned Lacedæmon." The Messenian hero
Aristomenes escaped from a deep pit cave, into which he had
been cast by his Spartan captors, by seizing the tail of a fox
which had come to feed on the dead bodies, and clinging to it as
it ran along an underground passage to an outside opening.[8]
Aristomenes enlarged the outlet with his hands, and so got
away, returning to Messenia to resume the leadership of his
people in the war with Sparta. Stories like this recur in all
classical literature.

Primitive troglodytes were apparently common in most ancient Mediterranean times.[9] They were represented by the barbarous Cyclops,[10] who dwelt with their sheep in the caves of
the Sicilian coast; and by the savage shepherd Cacus who inhabited a cave on the Aventine Mount by the Tiber, raided the
country about, and stole from Hercules the cattle of Geryon.[11]
Even in historical times the Sardinian mountaineers were barbarian cave-dwellers who tilled a little land, but lived chiefly by
plundering the valley farms.[12] Robber tribes of the Lebanon
Mountains and Mount Hermon made their homes in caves, while
they ravaged the lowlands and beset the caravan routes.[13] As
late as 1878 troglodytes were still found on the little island
of Linosa off the Tunisian coast.[14]

Caves served as sheepcotes in the limestone plateau of Judea,
and as shelters both for the sheep and swine of Ulysses in the
mountains of Ithaca.[15] A wide cavern in the acropolis hill of

Pylos in Messenia passed in Pausanias' time as the cattle-shed of Nestor and of his father Neleus.[16]   Vergil advises that the brood mares of Italy should graze in meadows "where caves may shelter them and rock ledges give them shade." [17]   According to a tradition, perpetuated by the artists of Italy and Spain, the stable where Christ was born was a grotto, and around it the Church of the Nativity in Bethlehem was built.

In all the Mediterranean lands caves were places of refuge during times of war or persecution—for the prophets of Jehovah like Elijah, fleeing from the vengeance of Ahab and Jezebel; for David fleeing from the wrath of Saul; [18] and for the Phrygians near Laodicea during the Gallic invasion of the third century A.D., when the women and children were secreted in a cave later consecrated to the cavern-gods, Apollo, Heracles and Hermes.[19]   Rhea gave birth to Zeus in a cavern high up on Mount Dikte in Crete, whither she had fled to save her child from the devouring Cronos.   A similar grotto on Mount Lycæus in Arcadia was also a reputed birthplace of Zeus, and was held sacred to Rhea.[20]   The Corycian Cave on Mount Parnassos served as a hiding place for the Delphians and their property during the Persian attack on Delphi in 490 B.C.[21]   In the Balearic Isles caves were both the homes and refuges of the natives. In Sardinia they afforded safe asylums for the people when the Carthaginians tried to conquer the island, because the invaders dared not venture into the winding underground passages.

Sea caves were without number, as Pausanias says, and therefore they figured conspicuously in epic and history, in exploration and navigation. They served as lairs for the pirates who often infested the Mediterranean coasts, and as places of refuge for ship-wrecked mariners.   When Ulysses finally landed in his native Ithaca, he concealed his treasure in a grotto near the harbor of Phorkys.[22]   The sea-monster Scylla lurked in a cave on the Strait of Messina where she swallowed up unlucky sailors with their craft.[23]

Caves abound in Greek mythology, and have been embodied thence in Roman mythology.   Grottoes with stalactites and dripping roofs, their entrances masked by overhanging trees and swaying vines, were the haunts of Pan and the nymphs,

creatures of mountain and forest.   Such was the Corycian
Cave far up on the slope of Mount Parnassos.[24]   Others, sacred
to various gods as Apollo, Poseidon, Aphrodite and Æscu-
lapius, suggest the modern grottoes dedicated to the Virgin and
the saints throughout the Catholic Mediterranean lands.   This
manner, of religious thinking bears a Mediterranean stamp.
Æolus, King of the Winds, ruled in a cave of the Lipari Isles
north of Sicily, where he confined his boisterous subjects.
Caves regarded as gateways to the infernal regions were found
all the way from Asia Minor to the Vesuvian district and
Sicily.[25]   Pluto seized Proserpine in a Sicilian meadow and carried her through a nearby cave down to Hades.   Æneas descended to the nether world through a cave near Lake Avernus.
A grotto or limestone sink-hole near Hermione on the southeast
coast of Argolis was reputed to be the spot where Heracles
brought up Cerberus from the lower regions; and a cave on
the Tænarum promontory of Laconia claimed the same distinction.[26]   Hence Heracles was one of the Cavern-gods.   In Palestine and Syria, where this association was wanting, caves of
burial were common, like that which finally received Abraham,
Sarah, Isaac, Rebeccah and Jacob.[27]   It was doubtless such a
grotto as this, enlarged and finished on the inside, which received
the body of the dead Christ, now the holiest shrine of all
Christendom.

LOST RIVERS—The widespread limestone formations and
especially the karst regions of underground drainage gave
rise to the phenomenon of lost rivers which permeate classical
mythology and literature.[28]   The abundance and volume of
many limestone springs, important as water supply in the dry
summers, could be explained only on the theory that they were
the issue of subterranean streams or drainage channels of
katavothra lakes, a connection which the ancients early surmised.   Pausanias states that the Stymphalus Lake of highland
Arcadia had its outlet in an underground rift, through which
the water flowed to reappear as a spring 22 miles away in
Argolis; there it was called the Erasinus River.[29]   Today the
traveller may see this copious Erasinus spring, three miles
from the city of Argos, driving a dozen mills with a hydraulic
force gained in its descent of nearly 2,000 feet.

The lost rivers mentioned by Herodotus, Plato, Sophocles, Pindar, Theophrastus, Strabo, Vergil, Seneca, Ovid and Pliny are distributed through the Mediterranean lands from Syria and Cilicia [30] in the east to the Anas River (Guadiana) of Spain in the west,[31] and from the Carso Plateau in the north to African Cyrenaica in the south. The phenomenon was so common that it probably provided the natural models for the tunnel aqueducts which were constructed by the ancients for their domestic water supply in extraordinarily early times,—by the builders of Mycenæ before the Trojan War, by Hezekiah of Jerusalem in the eighth century B.C., by the rulers of Samos and Athens in the seventh and sixth centuries B.C. The Greeks used to clean out or enlarge the underground discharge channels of the katavothra lakes in Epirus, Bœotia and Arcadia in order to drain them and reclaim arable land from the margins, and thus acquired experience in such enterprises. Hence the subterranean outlets of Pheneus Lake in Arcadia were said to be artificial, the work of the engineer hero Heracles.[32] Cyprus had its ancient underground conduits for irrigation, according to Cesnola. The Romans at a very early date constructed a tunnel emissarium through the hard lava wall of Lake Albanus, to drain the lake and secure water for irrigation.

A phenomenon so striking as that of disappearing and reappearing rivers was inevitably embodied in classical mythology in the effort to explain the strange occurrence. The River Helicon, which maintained an underground course for three miles on its way from Mount Olympos to the sea, gave rise to the story that the women who murdered Orpheus, because he had lured away their husbands, sought to wash the tell-tale blood from their hands in the waters of the Helicon, but that the river dived underground in order to escape pollution.[33] The Eridanus River, the modern Po, since it runs underground for two miles near its source in the Alps, was said to spring from the lower world; there Æneas accordingly saw it flowing through the Elysian Fields.[34] The River Styx rises on Mount Aroania of northern Arcadia, flows over a cliff and loses itself in a mass of broken rock before it emerges some distance below as a tributary of the "ever-flowing Cratis." [35] This hidden part of its course was assigned to Tartarus, into whose geography therefore the River Styx was incorporated. The same thing was true of the Acheron and Cocytus Rivers of Thesprotia,[36] an old katavothra district of Epirus inhabited by early Pelasgian Greeks. Pausanias surmises that Homer, having seen these streams, introduced them under their own names into his description of the nether world.[37] The story of the Lethe may have originated in Cyrenaica, a typical karst country of sink-holes, caverns and underground rivers.[38] Here the famous Cave of Lethe is traversed by a stream which has only a subterranean course and emerges thence as a spring.

Familiarity with the hidden rivers gave rise among the ancients to erratic geographical conclusions about the reappearance of these underground streams in distant lands.[39] Sophocles, misled by identical names, concluded that the Inachus River of southern Epirus crossed to the Peloponnesos and joined the Inachus of Argolis, which had an underground course below its springs on Mount Artemisium.[40] The Fons Timavus at the head of the Adriatic, flowing out from the base of the Carso Plateau as a spring of nine mouths, had such volume that it was correctly interpreted as the issue of a considerable river; hence it was regarded as a subterranean offshoot of the Danube,[41] whose tributary the Save River rose in a limestone cave above Nauportus (Upper Laibach) only 35 miles to the east. (See map Carso Plateau, Chap. X.) For this karst region, honey-combed with underground channels, and having no visible surface watershed, the conjecture was not far-fetched. Pausanias surmised that the little salt stream Rheti, which defined the ancient boundary between Attica and Eleusis, had its source in the Eubœan Sound near Chalcis, whence it followed an underground course to the salt lakes by the Bay of Eleusis.[42]

The River Alpheus of Elis, whose headstreams were known to pursue an elusive hide-and-seek course through the karst plateau of Arcadia,[43] drawing surreptitiously from the waters of the katavothra lakes, was accredited by the ancients with a submarine course from its mouth "across the wide and stormy Ionia Sea" to Sicily, where it reappeared in the Fountain of Arethusa at Syracuse.[44] The story was believed and repeated by Pindar, Vergil, Erastosthenes, and others, from the analogy of the underground drainage; but it was rejected by Strabo.[45] The acceptance of these daring physiographic theories by men of extraordinary intelligence warns against an off-hand estimate of the ancient mind as unscientific, and suggests a search for other facts which might seem to support the theory.

Such a group of facts is found in the fresh-water springs in the sea which are common off the Mediterranean coast, and which were well known to the ancients, according to the testimony of their literature. Submarine springs were found moreover in much frequented bays, whence their fame spread abroad; and they welled up in such volume and with such force that they domed up above the surface of the surrounding sea. Hence they were properly interpreted as the issue of considerable subterranean rivers which had found their way out under the sea. Moreover as their water was in some cases potable and was distinguished by its color from marine water, they seemed to maintain a distinct flow which conceivably might be extended from coast to coast beneath the sea.

Perhaps the earliest known of these submarine springs was that off the coast of Phœnicia between the island of Aradus and the mainland. The citizens of Aradus utilized it to supplement their scant cistern water. They rowed out in boats and inverted over the spring a lead funnel, from which the fresh water mounted through a leathern hose to the surface and was poured thence into earthen jars.[46] Another such spring was found near the Chelidonian Isles off the coast of Lycia in Asia Minor,[47] about 30 miles south of the busy port of Phaselis; others were known near various islands of the Cyclades group. The submarine spring of Deine, described by Pausanias, can be seen today where it wells up in the Argolic Gulf, about a quarter of a mile from the shore. It is so copious that it forms a convex surface fifty feet in diameter, and is evidently fed by a subterranean river draining the high Mantinean Lake plain of Arcadia, whence it gets its hydraulic pressure.[48] "The water is sweet though it comes up from the sea," says Pausanias. This spring must have been familiar to every seaman or voyager of ancient Argos or Tiryns who sailed the Argolic Gulf from the port of Nauplia; and to every wayfarer who travelled the coast road from Argos to Lerna it must have been visible as it was to the author on a recent journey through Greece. Another fresh water spring is found in the Messenian Gulf at the foot of the high Taygetos Mountain, five miles south of the ancient port of Cardamyle.[49] On the west coast of Thesprotia in Epirus was Sweet Water Harbor or *Dulcis Portus*, the Harbor of Chimæra mentioned by Thucydides,[50] in which a powerful fresh water spring wells up in a dome, probably fed by a katavothra stream or subterranean river from the mountain interior.

Such springs were known in the West Mediterranean. Pliny describes a warm fresh spring in the sea off the Bay of Naples, between Baiæ and the island of Ænaria (Ischia);[51] and another is mentioned by Pausanias off Dicæarchia or Puteoli in this same region, where an artificial island was constructed in order that the hot water might be utilized for baths.[52] A fresh water spring bubbled up in the Atlantic Ocean near Gades,[53] where limestone ridges run out west from the Andalusian ranges. The limestone region of the Provençal coast, once dotted with Greek colonies, has several subterranean rivers which debouch as fresh water springs beneath the surface of the Mediterranean. The most powerful of these, which gushes forth in the sea only ten miles southeast of ancient Massilia,[54] was probably known to the early Greek and Roman navigators sailing along this coast to the busy port near the Rhone mouth.

When sailors' reports yielded the chief information about distant lands, their accounts of these submarine springs were doubtless widely circulated, and furnished the basis for the hypothesis of submarine rivers, as set forth in the story of the Alpheus. Curiously enough the adventurous career of the Alpheus was still invoked in the middle of the nineteenth century by the monks of the Strophades Islands, to explain a surprisingly strong spring near the monastery. They surmised that the water came either from Sicily or from the Peloponnesos, since the Strophades lay on the direct line of the supposed submarine course of the Alpheus.[55]

AUTHORITIES—CHAPTER II

1. Philippson, *Das Mittelmeergebiet*, p. 30. Leipzig, 1907.
2. *Ibid.*, pp. 10-11.
3. *Ezekiel*, XXVII, 12.
4. Philippson, *op. cit.*, pp. 11-14.
5. *Ibid.*, pp. 19-20.
6. Strabo, V, Chap. IV, 2.
7. W. Deecke, *Italy*, p. 45. New York, 1904.
8. Pausanias, IV, Chap. 18.
9. Strabo, VIII, Chap. VI, 2.
10. *Odyssey*, IX, 105-115, 216-465.
11. Livy, Bk. I, Chap. VII, 4-9. Vergil, *Æneid*, VIII, 190-270.
12. Strabo, V, Chap. II, 7.
13. *Ibid.*, XVI, Chap. II, 18, 20.
14. Deecke, *op. cit.*, p. 447.
15. I *Samuel*, XXIV, 3. *Odyssey*, XIV, 532-533.
16. Pausanias, IV, Chap. 36.
17. Vergil, *Georgic* III, 144-145.
18. I *Samuel*, XIII, 6; XXII, 1; XXIV, 3; I *Kings*, XVIII, 4; XIX, 9.
19. Pausanias, X, Chap. XXXII, 2-7.
20. *Ibid.*, VIII, Chap. XXXVI, 3.
21. Herodotus, VIII, 36.
22. *Odyssey*, XIX, 188; XIII, 348-375.
23. Vergil, *Æneid*, III, 423. *Odyssey*, XII, 80-84.
24. Strabo, IX, Chap. III, 2.
25. *Ibid.*, V, Chap. IV, 5; XIII, Chap. IV, 14; XIV, I, 11. Diodorus Siculus, V, Chap. 3, 2-3.
26. Pausanias, II, Chap. 35. Pindar, *Pythian Ode*, IV, 77. Lucan, IX, 36.
27. *Genesis*, XXIII, 9; XLIX, 29-32.
28. Seneca, *Quæstiones Naturales*, III, 26.
29. Pausanias, VIII, Chap. 22, 3.
30. Strabo, XIV, Chap. V, 5.
31. Pliny, *Historia Naturalis*, III, 2.
32. Pausanias, VIII, Chap. 14, 1.
33. *Ibid.*, IX, Chap. 30, 8.
34. Vergil, *Æneid*, VI, 658.
35. Herodotus, VI, 74. Pausanias, VIII, Chaps. 17 and 18.
36. Cicero, *De Natura Deorum*, III, 17. Vergil, *Æneid*, VI, 295-8, 705.
37. Pausanias, I, Chap. 17.
38. Hildebrand, *Cyrenaika*, p. 167. Bonn, 1904. Strabo, XV, Chap. I, 39.
39. Neumann and Partsch, *Physikalische Geographie von Griechenland*, pp. 255-256. Breslau, 1885.
40. Strabo, VI, Chap. II, 4. Pausanias, II, Chap. 25.
41. Vergil, *Æneid*, I, 243-246. Pliny, *op. cit.*, II, 103, 106. Strabo, V, Chap. I, 8.
42. Pausanias, I, Chap. 38, 1-2.
43. *Ibid.*, VIII, Chap. 14, 1; Chap. 23, 2-7; Chap. 44, 1-3; Chap. 54, 1-4.
44. Vergil, *Eclogue*, X, 1-4. Polybius, XII, Chap. IV.
45. Strabo, VI, Chap. II, 4.

46. *Ibid.,* XVI, Chap. II, 13.
47. Pliny, *op. cit.,* II, 106.
48. Leake, *Morea,* Vol. II, pp. 480-481.
49. Neumann and Partsch, *op. cit.,* p. 253.
50. Thucydides, I, 46.
51. Pliny, *op. cit.,* II, 106.
52. Pausanias, VIII, Chap. 7, 3.
53. Pliny, *op. cit.,* II, 106.
54. E. Reclus, *Europe,* Vol. III, p. 108.   New York.
55. Tozer, *Highlands of Turkey,* Vol. I, p. 106.

CHAPTER III

EARTHQUAKES AND VOLCANOES

Many physiographic features of the Mediterranean region are so clearly the result of subsidence that they were correctly interpreted as such by the ancients. They were ascribed, however, to convulsive movements and not to the slow action of cosmic forces. These physiographic features were so striking, moreover, that they challenged attention. They stimulated observation, the correlation of facts; and finally they stirred the scientific imagination of the ancients to formulate theories of their origin. This intellectual response of a people to their environment was conspicuous and persistent in Egypt and that widespread Hellenic world from Cyprus to Sicily; it appeared with abated keenness and originality in the Roman and Carthaginian lands.

ANCIENT THEORIES OF ELEVATION AND SUBSIDENCE—Geographers and philosophers, noting the distribution of sea shells and salt deposits far inland, reached the conclusion that various Mediterranean districts had undergone extensive subsidence followed by elevation. From such evidence Xanthus of Lydia (496 B.C.) surmised the former connection between the Mediterranean and the Red Sea,—the old Strait of Suez whose existence has been established by modern geology.[1] Strabo from a review of his data arrived at the general conclusion "that formerly at various periods a large portion of the mainland has been covered and again uncovered by the sea." [2] Aristotle stated the same principle three centuries earlier: "Inroads and withdrawals of the sea have often converted dry land into sea and sea into dry land." [3]

Living in a region of recurrent seismic disturbances, reasoning from actual experience, the ancients attributed these earth changes to natural convulsions.[4] Their thinking reflected their geographic environment. They observed the effects of earthquakes and volcanic activity registered in the alteration of

35

shorelines, widening or narrowing of sea-beaches, changes in offshore soundings, and the submergence of coast cities or buildings by the encroaching waves; and they had seen volcanic islands rise from the sea and vanish again. From such local occurrences the ancients deduced cataclysmic changes on a vast scale. Strabo made the step from the particular to the general when he wrote: "Extensive sinkings of the land no less than small ones have been known." [5] He himself experienced in Egypt a sudden encroachment of the sea upon the Isthmus of Suez; he saw the Pelusium district flooded and Mount Cassius converted into an island. Wherefore he considered it probable that "at some future time the isthmus which separates the Egyptian Sea from the Erythræan should part asunder or subside, and becoming a strait, should connect the outer and inner seas, similarly to what has taken place at the Strait of the Pillars." [6]

Reasoning thus, the ancients attributed the straits and sounds of the Mediterranean and the formation of many islands to convulsions of nature. They found evidences of previous land connection in the similarity of relief and rock structure on both sides of the intervening channels, as do modern geographers, but they erred as to the time element in the problem. They attributed the Bosporus and Hellespont to a cataclysm which opened a passage from the Euxine to the Ægean Sea.[7] Æschylus repeats an ancient tradition that Sicily was torn asunder from Italy and thus the Strait of Messina was formed.[8] Vergil and Diodorus Siculus adopt the same explanation.[9] Seneca in a scientific treatise states that earthquakes severed Sicily from Italy and Spain from Africa. According to a folk-lore tale explaining the Strait of Gibraltar, *Mons Abila* on the African side and *Mons Calpe* on the Iberian shore once formed a continuous mountain; but they were wrenched apart by Hercules and called his Pillars.[10] In like manner Euboea was rent away from Bœotia, and the Eubœan Sound formed between.[11] Other islands were supposed to have had a similar origin. Ceos was torn away from the southern end of Eubœa, according to Pliny,[12] Atalanta from Opuntian Locris, Leucas from Acarnania, the islet of Besbycus in the Propontis from the Bithynian headland of Mount Arganthonius, with which it is in alignment, and Lesbos from the Mount Ida range. Italy told the same tale of geologic tragedy. Not only had Sicily been severed from Bruttium, but Leucosia Isle from the Promontory of the Sirens in western Lucania,[13] Capri from the Sorrento peninsula, Procida and Ischia from Cape Mesino.[14] The obvious relation of the mountains of Cyprus to the Taurus ranges of Asia Minor suggested the former connection of this island with the mainland. In all these regions of subsidence, frequent earthquakes testified to one persistent agency in changing the land forms.

Where earthquake had torn a passage, the sea rushed in and encroached upon the land, according to ancient theory. Thus the Mediterranean penetrated through the new-made Bosporus and Hellespont to form the Propontis and the Euxine, and yet farther through the fresh rift of the Crimean Bosporus to cover the shallow reaches of the *Palus Mæotis*. The rupture of the Strait of Rhium admitted the Ionian Sea into the deep-running Gulf of Corinth, and a similar breach farther north enabled the Gulf of Ambracia to encroach upon the territory of Acarnania; for in both these inlets the ancients observed fluctuations of the shoreline marking the advance or recession of the sea.[15] Moreover, the width of the Strait of Rhium varied. It is given as seven stadia (4,249 feet) by Thucydides, as five stadia (3,035 feet) by Strabo, as less than a mile by Pliny, and as ten stadia (6,070 feet) by Scylax,[16] which approximates the present width. These variations could hardly have been overlooked, because the Strait was the busy ferry point of the Gulf of Corinth and its control was contested by Athens and Corinth, by Achaia and Ætolia. Moreover, it lay in an active earthquake zone.

Cataclysms were invoked to explain certain changes in the surface of the land. The Vale of Tempe was ascribed to an earthquake which rent apart Mount Ossa from Olympos, cleft a passage through the old barrier for the River Peneus, and thus drained the mountain-locked lake of Thessaly.[17] According to popular belief, an earthquake also made a channel for the River Ladon from a mountain basin of Arcadia to the Alpheus, whereby it reached the sea.[18] This explanation was probably deduced from the commonly known fact that the

Ladon rose in the katavothra lake Pheneus, whose underground drainage fissures were often obstructed and reopened by local tremors.[19]

Plato's lost island of Atlantis, which by tradition sank with its palaces and gardens and temples beneath the waves of the outer ocean, did not tax the credulity of the ancients. They were familiar with volcanic islands which rose from the sea and sank again among the Cyclades, the Lipari, and in other groups of the Ægean and Tyrrhenian seas; and they regularly associated inundations of the sea with earthquakes.[20] They thought scientifically in terms of cataclysms, and even formulated an hypothesis of terrestrial catastrophes which was current in Plato's time. This doctrine ascribed changes on the earth's surface, either local or widespread, to floods and earthquakes which recurred periodically and which marked off the ages of man, just as Noah's flood closed a period in Judaic legend.[21] Plato applied this theory in his Atlantis story, according to which a very ancient, glorified Athens had been destroyed by flood and earthquake in a single day and night.[22] Significantly enough, Plato considered Egypt immune from the secular disasters.

This doctrine persisted in more rational form in the physiographic principles of Eratosthenes (c. 200 B.C.) who explained changes in the aspect of the earth by the action of water, fire, earthquakes and volcanic eruptions;[23] and in those of Posidonius (c. 120 B.C.), who attributed "to earthquakes and other similar causes . . . the risings, slips and changes which at various times come over the earth."[24] Strato the philosopher (288 B.C.), on the other hand, conceived a slow secular process in the formation of the Bosporus, Hellespont and Strait of Gibraltar. He supposed that the Euxine, raised by the influx of many rivers, overflowed into the Propontis and Ægean; and that a like rise in the Mediterranean enabled this sea to force a passage for itself at the Pillars of Hercules into the lower level of the Atlantic.[25] Strabo shows that this explanation did not accord with observed facts so well as the theory of elevation and subsidence.

This theory was deduced from observation and experience. Earthquakes and tidal waves were widespread phenomena in the Mediterranean physiographic region, in consequence of its geological history. Egypt, as part of the great desert platform of north Africa with its horizontal strata, belonged to a different physiographic province, and was therefore practically exempt from both forms of physical catastrophe—a fact recognized by Plato, Seneca and Pliny. It possessed the same character as the Russian platform,[26] the land of the ancient Scythians, who were so unfamiliar with earthquakes that they regarded them as contrary to the laws of nature.[27]

Modern evidence supports ancient testimony as to constant earthquakes in the Mediterranean region. A natural concomitant of mountain-building, they occurred with greatest frequency and violence along lines of fracture and subsidence marked by rift valleys, straits, sounds, mountain-locked gulfs, and volcanic fissures. Seneca observed that they were practically universal, and especially active along the coasts. "Tyre is as regularly shaken by earthquakes as it is washed by the waves," he says.[28] Thucydides, Aristotle, Eratosthenes, Strabo, Pliny and Pausanias attest their frequent occurrence and discuss their causes, various movements or directions, attendant phenomena, and their effects. They were so usual in the Ægean region, where the vast subsidences of the Quaternary Period left countless active faults, that they were considered natural phenomena like thunder and lightning. The younger Pliny, describing the great eruption of Vesuvius in 79 A.D., states that the premonitory earthquakes which occurred for several days before "were less alarming as they are frequent in Campania." [29] Livy in his industrious enumeration of prodigies in the Second Punic War includes no earthquakes. In two instances he mentions the formation of a local cave-in or sink-hole, but in terms which exclude seismic phenomena: "*terra consedit in sinum immensum*" and "*consedit in cavernis.*" [30] He alludes to the tremor during the Battle of Lake Trasimenus which passed unnoticed by the combatants, only to indicate the intensity of the fighting.

Few parts of the Mediterranean region, aside from Egypt and the Libyan plateau, escaped seismic disturbances. This is a fair conclusion, despite gaps in the ancient evidence caused by the destruction of the two great libraries of the ancient

world, that of Carthage in 146 B.C. and of Alexandria in 640
A.D. Evidence is lacking in regard to Spain and the Atlas
Mountain section, where, however, seismic disturbances in ancient times may be assumed from their repeated occurrence in
recent times. Ancient testimony, which is supported by modern experience,[31] points to a middle zone of intense earthquake
activity, characterized by faulting and subsidence on a vast
scale. It stretched across Sicily, southern Italy, Greece, the
Ægean isles, western Asia Minor and Cyprus to the north Syrian coast, where it joined at right angles a second meridional
belt, marked by the faulted scarps of the Lebanon block mountains and the long-drawn rift valley of the Lebanon Trough
and Jordan-Dead Sea depression. This was the great fracture
zone of seismic unrest. It was crossed by lines of active or
extinct volcanoes; it was overlaid here and there by old lava
fields or veneered by volcanic ash; and it was sprinkled then as
now with countless thermal springs. Its coasts were swept by
tidal waves, which added horror to the desolation caused by
the earthquakes; for the destructive agencies wrought their
worst along the littoral of the Mediterranean Sea. There
faults slipped oftenest and subsidence was most marked. There
market towns and active ports fronted the busy trade routes
which traversed straits and sounds and sheltered shores. There
population clustered thickest on alluvial coasts and deltaic
flats, which provided fertile soil for tillage, but offered no resistance to the deep-seated crustal movements and no protection against tidal waves sweeping in from the shaken sea.

GEOGRAPHIC DISTRIBUTION OF EARTHQUAKES—A survey of
the earthquakes recorded by ancient authorities, in regard both
to distribution and character, will present the basis of these
generalizations.

In ancient Palestine seismic disturbances were common. References to them abound in biblical literature. Every associated
phenomenon is mentioned: earth tremors, land-slides, yawning
chasms in the ground, the thunderous subterranean roar, tidal
waves or the recession of the sea, and reversal of river currents.
All are described in poetical language and attributed to the
devastating power of a wrathful Jehovah. "He removeth the
mountains by the roots," and "overturneth them in his

anger." [32]   "He calleth for the waters of the sea and poureth
them out on the face of the earth." [33]   His punishment descends
upon Jerusalem "with thunder and with earthquake and with
great noise." [34]   The Mount of Olives is cleft in twain.   "Thou
hast made the earth to tremble: thou hast broken it: heal the
breaches thereof, for it shaketh." [35]   In the presence of the
Lord, "The sea saw it and fled: the Jordan was driven back.
The mountains skipped like rams and the little hills like
lambs." [36]   These lines would accurately describe many an
earthquake along the mountain coast of California.

Earth tremors in Palestine were frequent but rarely destructive, because the Hebrew towns and villages lay for the most
part in the highlands and rested on bed-rock foundations.   The
site of Sodom, Gomorrah and the other cities of the Jordan
valley [37] invited destruction by earthquake.   They lay in the
Jordan rift on the soft alluvium which yielded to every crustal
wave, near enough to the Dead Sea to be submerged, when a
local subsidence followed a slip in the flanking faults.   All authorities from Strabo down assign the initial cause of this
catastrophe to an earthquake, and attribute the fire described
in *Genesis* to the presence of oil and asphalt springs.[38]   Jericho
was situated 450 feet above the Jordan River on a natural terrace, formed by one of the numerous longitudinal graben faults,
and marked for a stretch of twelve miles by a typical series of
fault springs.[39]   The collapse of Jericho's walls at the time of
the Israelite invasion points to an earthquake, not to a miracle
wrought by the shouts and trumpetings of Joshua's army.
Slips along the step-faults of the Jordan rift also caused severe
quakes in the abutting highland of Judea.   Such a one occurred about 763 B.C. in the reign of Uzziah.[40]   It rent the wall
and roof of the temple of Jerusalem, destroyed roads and gardens, and started a vast landslide on the Mount of Olives.[41]

The block and fault mountains of the Lebanon system and
Lebanon Trough had a long history of seismic disturbances.
Tyre and Sidon suffered frequently, exposed alike to shock and
to tidal waves.[42]   According to Posidonius, an earthquake destroyed two-thirds of Sidon, swallowed up another town located
up on the Lebanon slope, and extended in lighter form through
all Syria.[43]   The island city of Tyre was especially vulnerable,

because its many-storied houses, seventy feet high or more, were easily shaken down.[44] A tidal wave inundated the coast near Ptolemais (Akko) at the end of a battle and overwhelmed the defeated Syrians, sweeping the fugitives out to sea.[45] The rift valley of the Lebanon constitutes an earthquake belt and registered its destructive powers from Baalbec, where it damaged the great Temple of the Sun,[46] along the Orontes valley to Antioch. This city, located in the alluvial plain of the lower Orontes, was scourged by earthquakes through the ages. It was demolished in 184 B.C. and was damaged ten times during the first six centuries of the Christian era; but each time it revived, owing to its commanding position at the Mediterranean terminus of the caravan route across northern Mesopotamia.

The Quaternary subsidences which ruptured Greece from Asia Minor and formed the Ægean Sea left the scars of fault line and fracture, graben and flooded rift valley upon the surrounding lands.[47] They condemned the whole Ægean region to recurrent seismic disturbances, and marked as exceptional any spot which in ancient times boasted exemption from the prevailing evil. Delos was reputed to be the only Ægean isle immune from earthquakes; Zeus himself had anchored it to the sea floor. Hence Pindar called Delos "the wide earth's immovable wonder";[48] but Pindar spoke too soon. An earthquake struck the island in 490 B.C. during the Persian invasion of Greece;[49] and again in 431 B.C. immediately before the outbreak of the Peloponnesian War. In both instances the phenomenon was regarded as ominous because it happened on the sacred island of the prophet god Apollo.[50]

The islands of Cos, Nisyros and Rhodes, lying at the sea door of Halicarnassos and facing the deep subsidence bays of the nearby coast, shared the seismic disturbances of western Asia Minor. Nisyros, a volcanic island, lost its original population by a violent earthquake.[51] Cos, which also showed traces of old volcanic activity, experienced a cataclysmic earthquake in 412 B.C.[52] Rhodes in 224 B.C. saw the walls of its capital city, its dockyards and famous Colossus overthrown by a shock, which elicited for the stricken island sympathy and help from practically the whole Mediterranean world. The Rhodians "turned necessity to glorious gain," though not in the Words-

worthian sense. They played upon public sympathy, solicited
lavish gifts from numerous states, and secured exemption from
import and export duties in their trade with Syracuse and
other cities,[53] so that the island gained both in prestige and
privilege.

The Ægean slope of Asia Minor, crossed from east to west
by belts of subsidence opening into the great Ægean sink, was
a natural seismic region from Lycia in the south to the Troad
in the north, as it is today.[54] The fertile valley floors of these
graben, covered with alluvium by their drainage streams, became the attractive but perilous sites of numerous cities, which
again and again paid for a choice location with their existence.
The young graben of the Meander valley was devastated by
earthquakes in ancient as in recent times; the cities which lined
this main thoroughfare of Lydia suffered accordingly. The
ancient town of Tralles, like its modern successor Aidin,[55] was
frequently demolished. A catastrophe in the reign of Augustus
was mitigated by the Emperor's generosity. A similar disaster
at Carura swallowed up the local inn, which disappeared bodily
with all its guests. In Laodicea and Apamea Cibotus at the
head of the valley in Phrygia earthquakes were common occurrences.[56] One had just destroyed Apamea when the city surrendered to Alexander the Great; and again two centuries later
when its empty shell was taken by Mithradates.[57]

TIDAL WAVES AND EARTHQUAKES—Along the coasts of the
Ægean earthquakes displayed their most destructive powers.
Here tidal waves added their horrors to the scene, flooding the
soft alluvium detached by fault slips from the rock structure
of the land, causing it to slide off into the watery abyss, or
sweeping away its settlements and population. The violent
agitation of the sea during earthquakes, its vast reflux from
the shore, its overwhelming return over shelving beaches, its
swift advance up river mouths, were known also to the
Romans; [58] but to the Greeks these associated phenomena were
a common attendant of seismic disturbances, owing to the close
succession of subsidence areas along the deeply embayed Ægean
coasts and also to the concentrated population located on these
vantage grounds of protected harbor and fertile littoral. Pic-
turing the earth as a disk floating on the surface of the cir-

cumambient ocean, the Greeks called Poseidon "the Earth-shaker" or "the earth-shaking son of Cronos" [59] because orig-inally they attributed earthquakes to tidal waves. By the time of Thucydides, however, they recognized the true relation be-tween the two.[60] To Pindar tidal waves were "the emptying of the sea upon the land," [61] mark of the wrath of Zeus. Their frequent occurrence in the Ægean region explains the Greek traditions of repeated floods like those of Deucalion and Dar-danus, which have been connected with Noah's flood by ardent supporters of the biblical myths. The two have scant geo-graphical bases in common, though later Greek versions of the Deucalion cataclysm borrowed details from the old Chaldean account.[62]

The coastal belts of the Balkan Peninsula furnish examples of ancient earthquakes attended by tidal waves, wherever old fracture lines met the sea. Ancient Samothrace, a half sub-merged fragment of the crystalline Rhodope massif, had a tradi-tion of the Dardanian flood, antedating all others, caused by the irruption of the Euxine through the new-made Bosporus and Hellespont into the Ægean. The people of Samothrace fled to the mountains from the rising waters which permanently inundated the coast of the island. Centuries later, so they said, fishermen caught their nets on the marble columns of the drowned cities.[63] The scientific facts are obvious: a local slip on an old fault line, detachment of the alluvial hem from the granite mass of the island and its subsidence beneath the sea. Farther west Chalcidice, with its three finger promontories separated by sunken troughs, experienced a tidal wave of seis-mic origin in 479 B.C. The Persians were besieging Potidæa from the land side at the neck of the Pallene promontory, when they observed a reflux of the sea, "which lasted for a long time," says Herodotus. Endeavoring to cross the broadened beach of the isthmus and thus reach the Pallene side of the city, they were caught by the returning tidal wave and destroyed. The Potidæans attributed this disaster to the desecration of the nearby temple of Poseidon by the Persians; [64] because their rescue by an irresistible natural force demanded a *deus ex machina*. The episode suggests the destruction of the Pharaoh of the Exodus in the Red Sea. A similar divine delivery occurred on this Macedonian littoral in 62 A.D., when an earthquake shattered the jail at Philippi and released the apostles Paul and Barnabas from prison.[65]

Earthquakes and tidal wave multiplied their tragedies in Greece itself, where lines of fracture scarred the face of the peninsula. They recurred through the centuries along the transverse subsidence which formed the Malic Gulf and the Strait of Oreus, and rent asunder the ranges of northern Euboea from the Othrys Mountains of Hellas; along the Euboean Sound which divides Euboea from middle Hellas; and along the yet larger trough forming the Corinthian and the Saronic Gulfs. Minor earthquake faults in the Peloponnesos, visible in the rift valleys and embayed coasts of that peninsula, added their list to the seismic tragedies which left so profound an impress on the scientific thinking of the Hellenic people.

The sounds and gulfs which indented the coast of Hellas and the Peloponnesos by their very shape exaggerated the destructive force of every tidal wave by penning it up and driving it toward the land. The loose Tertiary deposits or looser alluvium which fringed the sounds, and the deltaic flats which headed every funnel-shaped bay offered themselves and their settlements as unresisting victims to the Earth-shaker. Therefore the seismic history of these Hellenic coastlands has repeated itself with tragic uniformity through the ages.

The Deucalion flood myth, which eventually became the common property of all the Mediterranean lands visited or colonized by the Greeks, was originally localized in the north Euboean Sound and the Strait of Oreus, where earthquakes and tidal waves have an ancient record. The earliest legends make Deucalion land his ark or chest after the deluge on Mount Othrys, which overlooks the Strait of Oreus. His immediate descendants ruled Thessaly, according to Hesiod, while his name and that of his wife lingered in the Gulf of Pagasæ in the Pyrrha Promontory and the two islets, Pyrrha and Deucalion.[66] The mountain resting place of the ark, which recurs in the deluge myths, may possibly be linked with the flight to the mountains from the coast which recurs in all historical account of tidal waves and earthquakes along the Mediterranean littoral.

Bœotia, which lay between the two great fracture zones of

Greece, had a seismic history which reached back into the legendary period.[67] Earthquakes affected the drainage of the katavothra lake Copais, now obstructing the underground outlets, now opening new fissures, now stopping all, with a resulting inundation of the whole lake basin, like that embodied in the mythical flood of Bœotian Ogyges. This state suffered severely in the earthquake winter of 427 and 426 B.C. reported by Thucydides, when Orchomenos was the chief victim; [68] and again in 551 A.D. when Coronea and Chæronea were destroyed.

The great cross rift formed by the Corinthian and Saronic Gulfs has been the breeding place of earthquakes through the centuries. Slips along its countless fracture lines have shaken the bordering coasts, and been propagated along fault lines into Bœotia and with diminished effect as far as Attica. Earthquakes in 420 B.C. broke up assemblies at Athens and at Corinth, important interstate conferences; in 426 B.C. they were violent enough to turn back a Peloponnesian army *en route* to invade Attica.[69] Corinth suffered repeatedly and severely. The succession of small alluvial plains which constituted the coastland of Achaia and Sicyon saw their fertile fields and populous cities desolated again and again.[70] Sicyon, the home of artists and skilled artisans, lost much of its splendor by an earthquake in 227 B.C. and nearly all its population.[71] Severe shocks, accompanied by an overwhelming tidal wave, struck the Achaian coast in 373 B.C. It engulfed the thriving city of Helice and the ground on which it stood, detaching the low coast alluvium from the mountain base and precipitating it into the Gulf, where the submerged ruins of the city were visible long afterwards. At the same time, the town of Bura, located on a natural terrace of fault origin 2,577 feet (785 m.) up the mountain above Helice, was swallowed up by a yawning chasm.[72] Ægium, located ten miles west of Helice, suffered severely from an earthquake in 23 A.D.; [73] and in 1861 it duplicated the tragic experience of ancient Helice in every detail.

The northern coast belt of the Corinthian Gulf, especially the faulted front of Mount Parnassos, shared the seismic history of the rift. The Temple of Delphi was destroyed by an earthquake, probably in 373 B.C. When the Persians attempted to plunder the temple in 480 B.C. Apollo frightened them away with earthquakes and the detonations of falling crags sundered from the cliffs of Parnassos.[74] He used the same efficacious method again in the Sacred War (353 B.C.) against a party of Phocians who were digging for treasures under the sanctuary;[75] and in 279 B.C. against the invading Gauls who were attracted by the riches of Delphi.[76]

The subsidence trough of the Saronic Gulf continues the record of seismic disturbance in the great cross rift. A volcanic fissure traces its western edge, beginning with the solfataras and young igneous rocks near Crommyon on the Isthmus of Corinth. Thence it extends through Ægina, an old seismic spot,[77] through Methana, an active volcano in ancient and present times,[78] and through Calauria off the coast of Argolis. It swings thence across the Ægean Sea through the volcanic islands of Melos and Thera (Santorin) to Cos and Nisyros. Thus it traces the southern margin of the submarine plateau supporting the Cyclades,[79] and explains in part the ancient seismic movement on those islands. The inner Saronic Gulf, nearly enclosed by islands, made a dangerous setting for tidal waves attending the local earthquakes. Euripides in his Hippolytus gives an impressive description of one sweeping across the Saronic Gulf upon the coast of Corinth and Argolis. It came on with "an angry sound, slow-swelling like God's thunder underground." Then:

> A wave unearthly crested in the sky;
> Till Sciron's Cape first vanished from my eye,
> Then sank the Isthmus hidden, then the rock
> Of Epidauros. Then it broke, one shock
> And roar of gasping sea and spray flung far,
> And shoreward swept.[80]

It is interesting to note that a similar wave swept the Saronic Gulf in an earthquake in 365 A.D. and threatened disaster to Epidauros, averted only by a miracle, according to the ancient chronicler Procopius.

A subsidence zone flanks Argolis also on the west. Beginning as a submarine trench far out in the Ægean, it extends northward forming the Gulf of Nauplia and the Inachus River plain; crossing the low watershed to the north, as the basin of

Cleonæ and the Longopotamos valley, it descends to the Isthmian corner of the Corinthian Gulf.[81] Dislocations along its fault lines explain the frequent earthquakes which figure in Argolic history and the mythological allusions to inundations from the sea. Argos had a shrine to Poseidon the flood-maker (Prosklystios) as one to be propitiated, because he overwhelmed the flat Argive plain, when his claim to the land had been ignored by Inachus and the counter-claim of Hera recognized.[82] Euripides, who treated life objectively, seized upon a common experience of the Argives when he let Iphigenia, child of Mycenæ but an exile in Tauris, have a prophetic dream of an earthquake working the downfall of Agamemnon's dynasty.

> Meseemed in sleep, far over distant seas,
> I lay in Argos, and about me slept
> My maids: and lo the level earth was swept
> With quaking like the sea. Out, out I fled,
> And turning, saw the cornice overhead
> Reel, and the beams and mighty door-trees down
> In blocks of ruin round me overthrown.
> One single oaken pillar, so I dreamed,
> Stood of my father's house.[83]

The earthquakes of Argolis discouraged invasions by its hereditary enemies, the Lacedæmonians. In the spring of 414 B.C. they checked a Spartan campaign which had advanced into Argolic territory as far as Cleonæ, and by the terror inspired forced the enemy to retire. Again in 388 B.C., the Spartan king Agesipolis invaded the country from the northwest through the faulted basins of Phlius and Nemea, where he was met by repeated tremors and underground rumblings.[84] Despite the reluctance of his soldiers, he advanced to Argos; but when the disturbances continued during the siege and demoralized his men, he withdrew, for the Lacedæmonians were the most superstitious of all the Greeks.[85]

If earthquakes could break the nerve and nullify the life-long training of Spartan troops, there must have been abundant reason. The Lacedæmonians, owing to their geographical seclusion, restricted commerce and limited intellectual life, were characterized by strong religious reverence and regard for

portents. They looked upon earthquakes as the most significant omens, for they were warnings from Poseidon, who constantly displayed his power as the Earth-shaker in the valley
of the Eurotas.

The recent geological structure of Laconia favors earthquakes. The middle subsidence zone of the Peloponnesos begins in the Megalopolis basin of highland Arcadia, continues
south down the Eurotas furrow and runs out into the Laconian
Gulf. To the west, a companion subsidence belt comprises the
Messenian lowland and Messenian Gulf, long under the dominion
of Sparta, and divided from Laconia by the fold ranges of the
Taygetos Mountains, whose base is defined by an earthquake
fault marking the edge of the Eurotas furrow.[86] Other longitudinal and transverse fractures multiplied the sources of seismic shocks. Moreover, out in the Ionian Sea a submarine fracture line, running from Zacynthos past the Peloponnesian coast
to the western end of Crete,[87] was doubtless responsible for
earth tremors and tidal waves which in ancient times threatened
that island, and also for the earthquake in Elis in 402 B.C.
which sent the Lacedæmonian invaders under Agis scurrying
out of the country.[88]

Laconia therefore lay in a seismic region, which gave it a
sinister reputation in ancient times. Earthquake chasms
Cæti were common in the country. One of them formed the
deep pit-cave or limestone rift which served as the Spartan
prison, called the *Cæietas*.[89] The first recorded seismic tragedy,
which was predicted by the physicist Anaximander (died 547
B.C.), demolished Sparta, while a huge projection from Mount
Taygetos broke off and added to the previous destruction in
the valley.[90] The same disastrous combination of shock and
landslide recurred in 464 B.C. It destroyed many lives and
nearly all the houses, opened chasms far and wide through the
country, by reason of the resulting confusion impelled the
Helots to revolt in concert with the Messenians, and thus
brought on the protracted third Messenian War.[91] An earthquake in Sparta in 411 B.C. was sufficiently severe to disor-
ganize the naval program for the prosecution of the Peloponnesian War off the Ionian coast.[92]

Many of these earthquakes which desolated Greece and the

neighboring coastlands were attributed by the ancients to the wrath of Poseidon, aroused by some desecration of his temples or violations of the right of sanctuary there. Hence as a kind of earthquake insurance, the devout or cautious built shrines to him where the danger seemed imminent: that is, along the fracture lines of recurrent seismic disturbances, like the Euboean Sound or the Corinthian and Saronic Gulfs. Here headlands consecrated to Poseidon with sacred groves or imposing temples dotted the shores and marked the entrance to every busy port. But these waters were also well-travelled marine highways, where the venturesome seaman looked to the god of the waves and the storm, not of the heaving land, for protection on his wide-ranging voyages. Hence in these sea-lane shrines of Poseidon the obvious connection is that between religion and navigation, rather than between religion and earthquakes. On the other hand, the earthquake theory of the Poseidon cult gains support from the ascription of the Helice catastrophe, with the destruction of the Poseidon grove and temple, to the wrath of the Earth-shaker; and from the primitive worship of Poseidon at Delphi, far up on the unsteady slope of Mount Parnassos. Moreover since Strabo states that the Poseidon cult at Apamea in Phrygia, an inland town, was probably due to the frequent earthquakes in that district,[93] the same construction may be placed upon his worship in inland Bœotia and Laconia.

Italy like the Balkan Peninsula suffered in ancient times as today from frequent and violent earthquakes. These were in part tectonic, due to folding and faulting in the Alps and Apennines, where they were common, according to Pliny. The shock at Lake Trasimenus in 217 B.C. was evidently propagated along longitudinal fracture lines to various parts of Italy for months, as fifty-seven earthquakes were reported to Rome during that year.[94]

VOLCANIC RIFTS—Italy had a second source of earthquakes in the series of volcanic rifts, which run from the border of the Alps to the coast of Africa. They begin near Padua in the old cones of Monti Birici and to the Euganean Hills, whose thermal springs have been used since Roman days, and reappear in the extinct volcanoes—Monte Catini, Monte Amiata

(1,734 meters) and Monte Ciminio (1,050 meters)—and the crater lakes of Tuscany. The Etrurian district was not recognized as volcanic by the ancients, though its hot springs, owing to their proximity to Rome, were as popular as those of Baiæ. The Alban Mountains near Rome continue this volcanic series, which farther south expands to include the Ponza Islands (*Pontiæ Insulæ*), Pandateria and the extinct cone of Monte Croce (*Saltus Vescinus*) on the border of Latium and Campania. Then follow the volcanoes of the Neapolitan district, some of which were active from the earliest times; all were associated with traditions or historical accounts of earthquakes. The same holds true of the Lipari or Æolian Islands, the large volcanic region of eastern Sicily, Pantelleria and that elusive cone which through the ages has alternately emerged and vanished in the Sicilian Strait. Apart from this long rift series are Mount Ferru in Sardinia and Mount Vultur, which formed the ancient boundary stone between Samnium, Lucania and Apulia. Extinct during historical times, they have nevertheless been centers of seismic disturbances.

In these Italian regions of active vulcanism, earthquake and tidal wave heralded or accompanied the eruptions, and often increased the horrors of the catastrophe. This was especially true of the Neapolitan district. According to Strabo, the island of Ænaria (Ischia) had been rent apart from the island of Procida by some prehistoric cataclysm. Greek colonists who first occupied it were driven out by earthquakes, tidal waves and eruptions from Mount Epomeus. Later colonists sent from Syracuse by Hiero to hold the island (474 B.C.) were forced to abandon it for the same reasons. Ischia again about 300 B.C. repeated the experience of eruption, earthquake and tidal wave, the withdrawal of the sea for three stadia (600 yards), its recoil and inundation of the island. All the coastland of the Bay of Naples or *Crater* was recognized as volcanic by the ancients, who read the signs in the character of Vesuvius itself, the solfataras, and the hot springs which gave rise to numerous popular resorts, like Baiæ with its sumptuous villas.[95] The natural charm of the district, however, was abated by the frequent earthquakes, like the one in Nero's reign which nearly destroyed Pompeii. We get a picture of the crowded theater of Naples quivering under a shock when Nero makes his debut on the primitive concert stage; we see the pale faces of the audience, afraid to stay and afraid to leave while the imperial artist sings on; we see them finally rush out to escape the bad music and impending death, as the vast structure collapses behind them.[96] For a decade or more before the great eruption of Vesuvius in 79 A.D. the pent up forces within the earth repeatedly shook Herculaneum, Pompeii and all Campania in their struggle for an outlet; and finally became almost incessant.[97] Tidal waves accompanied the eruption of Vesuvius in 79 A.D. and increased the widespread destruction.[98]

The ancients recognized evidences of convulsions of nature in southern Italy and Sicily. They surmised, however, that the earthquakes there had declined in violence after volcanic vents were opened in Ætna and the Æolian Islands and the rift at the Sicilian Strait was formed.[99] Seismic phenomena figure in all the mythology of this district. According to one version of the Proserpine story, Pluto carried the goddess down to Hades through a chasm which opened in the earth near Syracuse.[100] The Sicani, according to tradition, abandoned their fertile territory in eastern Sicily owing to a devastating eruption of Ætna, and migrated to the western part. Centuries later the Siculi crossed from Italy and occupied the vacant land.[101] At every eruption the earth groaned and shook, owing to the movements of a wounded giant imprisoned beneath the mountain. In one of the Æolian Isles, where earthquakes and eruptions were frequent, the god of the winds confined his boisterous subjects in a cave where "they roared around the enclosure." [102] Their struggles to get out caused the earthquakes, according to the general theory of seismic disturbances current in the time of Aristotle, Strabo and Pliny. An earthquake in this group in 183 B.C. and again in 125 B.C. was attended by a submarine eruption and the emergence of a small island from the sea.[103] Incidents like these gave support to the ancient theory of cataclysmic modification of the earth's surface. So did the marked changes wrought on the summits and slopes of Ætna by successive eruptions, and the alteration in Sicily's shoreline as lava streams flowed down into the sea,[104] the transformation of Vesuvius by the eruption of 79 A.D., the changes in the soundings and coastline of the Bay of Naples.

Volcanic activity in the Ægean world, on the other hand, made little havoc during historical times. It assumed mild forms like gaseous exhalations or minor eruptions, and was confined to the headland of Methana and small islands. The formation of the Methana volcano about 250 B.C., the plutonic birth of ash-cone isles in the flooded crater of Thera in 197 B.C. and again in 46 A.D., and the emergence of an island from a submarine rift near Crete [105] were only local disturbances, spectacular enough with their boiling sea, hovering flames, sulphurous steam, and perhaps a tidal wave rolling out to distant shores.[106] Quite different was that prehistoric eruption on Thera, tentatively dated as 2000 B.C., which mantled the island with ash and pumice, buried farmhouses, barley fields, olive orchards with their oil presses, and the artifacts of an advanced neolithic civilization. Thus it preserved a "prehistoric Pompeii." [107] Obsidian knives excavated there indicate trade with Melos, the only source of this volcanic glass, while a few gold and copper articles point to probable connections with Cnossos. Hence this catastrophe could not have passed unknown. Reports of it probably impressed the imagination of Cretans and those shadowy Leleges who inhabited the Cyclades of that youthful world. Memory of it passed, but left perhaps some dim tradition, which haunted the Hellenic mind and was embodied in Plato's theory of secular cataclysms.

Volcanoes, in the nature myths of the ancient Mediterranean lands, were the work shops of Hephæstus, whose furnaces belched forth flames, smoke and ashes. The fire god therefore had his forges on Lemnos, reputed in ancient times to have "a fire mountain" like the Chimæra of Lycia; [108] in Mount Ætna, where he forged the thunderbolts of Zeus; and in the island of Hiera (Volcano) in the Lipari group.[109] The earthquakes and subterranean roar of volcanoes, preceding or during eruption, were embodied in the story of the rebellious giants imprisoned beneath. Enceladus, pierced by a thunderbolt of Zeus, groaned and struggled under the mass of Ætna,[110] as did the fire-breathing monster Typhœus beneath the trembling cone of Ænaria (Ischia). None of these myths were attached to Vesuvius, which first became active in 79 A.D.

Volcanoes wrought temporary destruction, but they also conferred lasting benefits. The good which they did lived after them, the evil was oft interred in oblivion. Centuries after their fiery outbreaks subsided, ages after their throbbing hearts were stilled, wide fields of basalt, leucitic lava, trachyte, and tufa were disintegrated into fertile soil and remained as a permanent gift to generations of farmers toiling under the Mediterranean sun. These rocks contain potash, soda, silica and phosphoric acid, all valuable elements of plant food, which are slowly fed to the vegetation as the rocks disintegrate, and thus maintain the productivity of the land. Such soil had special value because it was peculiarly retentive of moisture, and therefore resisted the long summer droughts of the Mediterranean climate.

Sicily, Campania, Etruria and much of Latium owed their great fertility to the outpourings of volcanic materials in the Tertiary period, and to the renewal of the supply from active centers like Ætna, Ischia, Phlegræan Fields and Vesuvius in historical times.[111]   Strabo understood the law of compensation operative in Mount Ætna: "After the burning ashes have caused temporary damage, they fertilize the country for future years, and render the soil good for the vine and very strong for other produce." [112]   Wind-borne volcanic ash provided a top dressing to the fields on the slopes of the Apennines and Nebrodes Mountains; or washed thence by the rains, it accumulated in thick layers on the valley floors. Thus it increased the sources of subsistence for the highland tribes. Mount Amiata, Mount Vultur and Mount Croce (Vescinus) have dispensed these blessings to the valleys of their lower slopes. More meager were the volcanic ejecta in the Ægean world. Yet Thera and Melos, both mere breached rims of half-submerged craters, were famous in antiquity for their fertile vineyard soil and for their export of alum and sulphur, typical products of volcanic districts.[113] Lemnos, Cos and Nisyros in the Sporades Islands had limited but productive land; so that Homer could speak of "well-peopled Cos" and "well-peopled Lemnos." The fertility of the Troad, of Mysia and Lydia was due in large part to the veneer of tufa, andesite or trachyte which covered the older limestones and mica schists in the middle or late Tertiary.[114] Lesbos drew from these volcanic sources the rich soil which made this island a garden, fit home for Sappho. The ancient granary of Syria was Bashan, a district on the western slope of the volcanic Hauran Mountains. It had a dark red-brown soil composed of disintegrated lava. In good years, when the rainfall was adequate and the irrigation streams flowed full from Mount Hauran, it raised wheat enough for local consumption and for export.[115]

The varied character of the Mediterranean lands and seas challenged early effort to explain the environment. It not only stimulated thought, but influenced the mode of thought, whether in the groping science of early mythology or in the oft brilliant deductions of the later physiography and cosmography. To the observed effects of subsidence, elevation and volcanic upheaval the ancients applied a wide cataclysmic theory of earth mutations which became embodied in classical literature— Greek, Roman and Semitic. Thence it was transmitted through medieval learning to northern literature, by means of the Bible, Latin authors like Pliny and Seneca, or Latin translations of Plato and Aristotle, till it finally became saddled on the western mind. It dominated modern scientific thought till near a century ago, when the hard, slow process of intellectual emancipation began. Still it lingers in popular books and common parlance; and it still permeates the mental fiber of reactionaries like the fundamentalists. This cataclysmic point of view, in Philippson's opinion, could never has arisen in northern Europe, but represents an inheritance from the ancient Mediterranean mind.[116]

AUTHORITIES—CHAPTER III

1. Suess, *Face of the Earth*, Vol. I, pp. 323-324, 379-384. Oxford, 1904.
2. Strabo, I, Chap. III, 4, 5, 10.
3. Aristotle, *De Mundo*, VI, 25-30. Compare Pomponius Mela, I, 32.
4. Neumann and Partsch, *Physikalische Geographie von Griechenland*, p. 340. Breslau, 1885.
5. Strabo, I, Chap. III, 10.
6. Strabo, I, Chap. III, 17.
7. Aristotle, *Meteorology*, I, 14, 24; Diodorus Siculus, V, 47.
8. Lost book quoted in Strabo, VI, Chap. I, 6.
9. Vergil, *Æneid*, III, 414. Diod. Sic., *op. cit.*, IV, 85.
10. Diod. Sic., *op. cit.*, IV, 20.
11. Strabo, I, Chap. III, 19. Pliny, *Hist. Nat.*, IV, 21.
12. Pliny, IV, 20.
13. Pliny, II, 90, 92.
14. Strabo, I, Chap. III, 19.
15. Pliny, II, 92; IV, 5.
16. Thucydides, II, 86. Strabo, VIII, Chap. II, 3. Pliny, IV, 3. Scylax, *Periplus*, 35.
17. Herodotus, VII, 129.
18. Seneca, *Quæstiones Naturales*, VI, 25. English translation, London, 1910.
19. Strabo, VIII, Chap. VIII, 4.
20. Pliny, II, 86-89.
21. Seneca, *op. cit.*, III, 27-29. J. A. Stewart, *Myths of Plato*, pp. 196, 466. London, 1905.
22. Plato, *Timæus*, 20 A-25 D.
23. Quoted in Strabo, I, Chap. III, 3.
24. Quoted in Strabo, I, Chap. III, 6.
25. Quoted in Strabo, II, Chap. III, 6.
26. Suess, *op. cit.*, Vol. I, 356, 370-376.
27. Herodotus, IV, 28.
28. Seneca, *op. cit.*, VI, Chaps. 1, 26.
29. Pliny the Younger, Letter to Tacitus, VI, 20.
30. Livy, Bk. XXX, 2 and 38. Compare Livy, Bk. I, 13; VII, 6.
31. Philippson, *Das Mittelmeergebiet*, p. 28. Leipzig, 1907.
32. *Job*, IX, 5-6; XXVIII, 9.
33. *Amos*, V, 8; IX, 6.
34. *Isaiah*, XXIX, 6.
35. *Psalms*, LX, 2.
36. *Psalms*, CXIV, 3-4.
37. *Genesis*, XIV, 2-10; XIII, 3-10.
38. Strabo, XVI, Chap. II, 44. G. Adam Smith, *Historical Geography of the Holy Land*. London, 1895.
39. Suess, *op. cit.*, Vol. I, p. 373.
40. *Amos*, I, 1; *Zachariah*, XIV, 4-5.
41. Josephus, *Antiquities of the Jews*, Bk. IX, Chap. 10; Bk. XV, Chap. 5.
42. Seneca, *op. cit.*, Bk. VI, Chap. 24, 5; 26, 4.
43. Strabo, I, Chap. III, 16.
44. Strabo, XVI, Chap. II, 23. Compare *Ibid.*, V, Chap. III, 7.
45. Strabo, XVI, Chap. II, 26.

46. E. Banse, *Die Turkei*, p. 327, 336, 351. Braunschweig, 1919.
47. Philippson, *op. cit.*, p. 18.
48. Pindar, *Fragment in Honor of Delos*.
49. Herodotus, VI, 98.
50. Thucydides, II, 8. Pliny, IV, 22.
51. Diod. Sic., V, Chap. 54, 3.
52. Thucydides, VIII, 41.
53. Polybius, V, 88-90. Diod. Sic., XXVI, 8.
54. Strabo, I, Chap. III, 16-19. Banse, *op. cit.*, p. 124.
55. Banse, *op. cit.*, 144-45.
56. Tacitus, *Annales*, XIV, 27; XII, 50. Pliny, II, 93.
57. Strabo, XII, Chap. VII, 16-18.
58. Livy, *Historia*, XXII, 5. Pliny the Younger, *Epistulæ*, VI, 16, 20.
59. *Iliad*, XX, 11. *Odyssey*, I, 74. Pindar, *Isth. Ode*, I, 53, III, 37.
60. Thucydides, III, 89.
61. Pindar, *Frag. Song on Eclipse of 463* B.C.
62. Suess, *op. cit.*, Vol. I, pp. 67-69.
63. Diod. Sic., V, Chap. 47, 3-4.
64. Herodotus, VIII, 129.
65. *Acts of the Apostles*, XVI, 26.
66. Hesiod, *Catalogue of Women*, V. Strabo, IX, Chap. V, 6, 14.
67. Pausanias, II, Chap. 23, 2; IX, Chap. 36, 2.
68. Thucydides, III, 87.
69. *Ibid.*, V, 45, 50; III, 89.
70. Philippson, *Der Peloponnes*, pp. 116-119, 146-149, 437-438.
71. Pausanias, II, Chap. 7, 1.
72. Diod. Sic., XV, 49. Strabo, I, Chap. III, 18; VIII, Chap. VII, 2. Paus., VII, 24-25. Seneca, VI, 23.
73. Tacitus, *Annales*, IV, 13.
74. Herodotus, VIII, 38.
75. Strabo, IX, Chap. III, 8.
76. Pausanias, X, Chap. 23, 1-3.
77. Herodotus, V, 85.
78. Strabo, I, Chap. III, 18. Pausanias, II, Chap. 34, 1.
79. Philippson, *Der Peloponnes*, pp. 427-428. Berlin, 1892.
80. Euripides, *Hippolytus*, Gilbert Murray translation, pp. 62-63. Oxford, 1904.
81. Philippson, *Der Peloponnes*, p. 31, pp. 419-420, 428-429. Berlin, 1892.
82. Pausanias, II, Chap. XXII, 4-5.
83. Euripides, *Iphigenia in Tauris*, Gilbert Murray translation, p. 5. Oxford, 1915.
84. Philippson, *Der Peloponnes*, pp. 78-79, 116.
85. Xenophon, *Hellenes*, IV, Chap. 7, 4-7. Pausanius, III, Chap. V, 8.
86. Philippson, *Der Peloponnes*, p. 238-239. Berlin, 1892.
87. *Ibid.*, p. 156, 425-430.
88. Pausanias, III, Chap. 8, 2.
89. Strabo, VIII, Chap. V, 7.
90. Cicero, *De Divinatione*, I, 112.
91. Thucydides, I, 101. Plutarch, *Cimon*, XVI. Diod. Sic., XV, 66.
92. Thucydides, VIII, 6.
93. Strabo, XII, Chap. VIII, 18. Discussed in Neumann and Partsch, *op. cit.*, pp. 332-336.

94. Pliny, II, 82, 86.
95. Strabo, V, Chap. IV, 5-9.
96. Tacitus, *Annales*, XV, 33-34. Suetonius, *Nero*, XX.
97. Seneca, *op. cit.*, VI, 1 and 27. Tacitus, *Annales*, XV, 22.
98. Pliny Younger, *Epistulæ*, VI, 16 and 20.
99. Strabo, VI, Chap. I, 6.
100. Diod. Sic., V, 1. Compare E. A. Freeman, *History of Sicily*.
101. *Ibid.*, V, Chap. 6, 3.
102. *Odyssey*, X, I. Vergil, *Æneid*, I, 52-78.
103. Strabo, VI, Chap. II, 11. Pliny, II, 89.
104. Strabo, VI, Chap. II, 8. Diod. Sic., XIV, Chap. 59, 3.
105. Pliny, II, 89.
106. Seneca, *op. cit.*, II, 26. Strabo, I, Chap. III, 16-18.
107. Neumann and Partsch, *op. cit.*, 277-279.
108. Strabo, XIV, Chap. III, 5. Pliny, II, 110; V, 28.
109. Thucydides, III, 88. Vergil, *Æneid*, VIII, 415.
110. Pindar, *Pythian Ode*, I, 15.
111. Strabo, V, Chap. IV, 3-4, 8, 9. Deecke, *Italy*, pp. 55-65, 438. London, 1904.
112. Strabo, VI, Chap. II, 3.
113. Pliny, XXXV, 15 and 95.
114. Banse, *op. cit.*, pp. 41-42, 68, 124-125, 132.
115. *Ibid*, p. 353, 357-358.
116. Philippson, *Das Mittelmeergebiet*, p. 30. 1907.

CHAPTER IV

THE MEDITERRANEAN AS AN ENCLOSED SEA

The successive geological elevations and subsidences in the middle mountain zone of the Old World resulted in the formation of the Mediterranean, with its vestibule in the Gulf of Cadiz, and its innermost chamber in the Black Sea 2,600 miles from the Atlantic. Today this sea links the grain of Odessa and the oranges of Joppa with the markets of Liverpool, as once it linked the tin mines of Cornwall with the bronze factories of ancient Phœnicia. It imposes a Mediterranean policy upon all European nations with colonial holdings or commercial enterprises in the Asiatic Orient, as it once motivated a Mediterranean policy for the Mesopotamian empires which had commercial or territorial ambitions in "the Western Sea."

In ancient times when the Mediterranean and its encircling lands embraced most of the known world, the whole outlook of ancient life was directed toward its blue waters. This was the view of Plato and Strabo. The latter says: "As Ephorus follows the coast in his measurements, and begins thence, considering the sea as the most important guide, so ought I, observing the natural character of regions, to keep in view the sea as the mark by which I should direct the course of my description." [1]

In his opinion geography should deal with the physical features, the flora and fauna of each country: "To these should be added its maritime history, for we are in a certain sense amphibious, not exclusively connected with the land, but with the sea as well. . . . The sea and the land in which we dwell furnish theaters for action, limited for limited actions and vast for grander deeds." [2] All ancient books of travel were the Periplus type or coasting voyage, as the Periplus of Hanno, Scylax, Nearchus, Erythæan Sea, and evidently that of Pytheas. They reflected the contact between human life and the marine field of intercourse.

This was the geographical standpoint of the ancients. The

sea yielded them salt and the famous purple dye. The pastures
of the land were poor and uncertain owing to variable rainfall,
but the pastures of the deep furnished abundant fish, especially
the tunny seeking the brackish coast waters to spawn. Land
transportation was hard and costly owing to the prevailing
mountain relief, so goods were carried chiefly by sea. Oversea
markets promised generally big profits. Military campaigns
of wide scope required a fleet and transports. Hence the Mediterranean was the plaza of ancient life. Lands remote from its
sunny expanse were back lots. They missed the pageants and
the throngs, the traffic and the commercial profits of the open
square. Here each nation staged its historical drama, sacrificed to its gods, cried its wares, flaunted its fine apparel and
contracted its international marriages, while the mixed crowd
had its common language in Greek or Latin which served the
purpose of a *lingua franca.*

COMPONENT SEAS OF THE MEDITERRANEAN—The numerous
sub-basins comprised in the Mediterranean Sea resulted from
the varied tectonic processes, both elevation and subsidence,
which this region had undergone, and in turn their long indented coastlines go far to explain the seaward outlook of the
ancients. The Mediterranean as a whole is a vast composite
of minor seas, whose varieties in point of size, form and degree
of enclosure are great. It is cleft almost in twain by the stricture at the Sicilian Strait, and thus falls naturally into two
major basins, the West and the East. The West Basin (area
328,225 square miles, 841,600 square kilometers), triangular in
shape and comparatively simple in outline, was nevertheless
divided by the ancients. The long corridor of the Iberian Sea
lay between Spain and Africa, leading to the Gibraltar Gate.
The Balearic Sea lay between eastern Spain and the Balearic
Islands, and beyond this group towards Corsica was the Sardinian Sea. Yet farther east lay the well defined Tyrrhenian
Sea, surrounded by Corsica, Sardinia, Italy, and Sicily, while
Sinus Gallicus and *Sinus Ligusticus* specified the Gulf of Lyons
and the Gulf of Genoa. Between Sicily and nearby Africa was
the Sicilian Strait and African Sea. In these almost minute
sub-divisions speaks the ancients' sense of the home waters to

be exploited and monopolized, just as the Roman Empire appropriated the whole Mediterranean as the *Mare Nostrum*.

The larger and more complex East Basin (area 643,890 square miles, 1,651,000 square kilometers) was sub-divided naturally and also artificially by the ancients. The Sicilian Strait opened into the ancient *Mare Africum*, which merged into the Sicilian Sea. This merged into the Ionian Sea on the east. This in turn was linked by the Strait of Otranto with the long *cul-de-sac* of the Adriatic to the north, and opened on the east into the island-strewn Ægean, which included the Cretan Sea in the south, the *Mare Myrtoum* in the west towards Laconia and Argolis, and the Thracian Sea in the north off the Thracian coast. Beyond the Ægean [3] lay the Propontis, like a lacustrine expansion in the salty stream of the Hellespont and Bosporus, and beyond this in turn the Euxine or Black Sea which the ancients generally considered part of the Mediterranean.[4] They pushed their fishing and trading ships to the mouth of the Tanais River (Don) in the Lake Mæotis (Azof) and to the Phasis River at the foot of the Caucasus, and based their classification on this practical test.

The East Basin included also the Levantine Sea, a great quadrangle lying between Asia Minor, Syria, and North Africa, and defined on the west by Crete and a submarine ridge extending from this island to the Barca Peninsula on the Libyan coast. The Levantine Sea included in turn the Phœnician Sea between Cyprus and the Lebanon coast, and the Egyptian Sea at the Nilotic corner of the Mediterranean. The East Basin, owing to its ready connection with the Red Sea and the Persian Gulf, drew the chief elements of its culture from Asia and the Orient. These it passed on in Europeanized form to the West Basin, where they were distributed to all the surrounding shores.

In those ancient times when the Mediterranean was the plaza of the known world, it was also the western terminus of the trade track to the Orient. Hence the eastern sub-basins developed entrepôts for the profitable eastern trade, and enjoyed intercourse with the old civilized states of Mesopotamia and the Nile, which in turn received stimuli from other states in the remoter East. From one to another incentives to progress were

passed on with the exchange of new agricultural and industrial
products. These embodied new standards of civilization, which
were forthwith appropriated on the Mediterranean coasts.
Oriental crops, so far as climatic conditions permitted, were
domiciled in Mediterranean fields and orchards, Oriental industrial methods were mastered and their patterns imitated, till
local genius improved upon the Eastern model, and developed
higher artistic merit. Thus, the seed of Mediterranean civilization germinated in the eastern end of the East Basin and spread
thence westward to the surrounding shores, modified in every
locality to which it was transplanted, developing in each new
habitat a fresh and improved variety. All these together contributed to the richness of Mediterranean civilization, through
the constant interchanges of trade and the intercourse of merchants passing from shore to shore.

This is the history of most enclosed seas. The majority
have had on their coasts some favored strip, where civilization
first developed and from which it spread. This early center of
distribution is favored in climate, or location near older centers
of civilization, or situation on natural highways heading to
such older centers, or in local conditions forcing the intelligent
development of local resources, and necessitating an outreach
overseas for foreign supplies.

BOTTLE FORM OF TYPICAL SUB-BASINS—The various basins
and sub-basins of this Midland Sea reveal certain type forms,
with a common stamp, due partly to the common history of
subsidence in a region of young folded mountains. The Mediterranean Sea as a whole is reproduced in miniature in the
Gulf of Corinth. Here we have the same east-and-west inlet
with mountainous coasts, the same single gateway in a strait
affording entrance from a westward facing bay, which in turn
opens into a larger western sea. At its eastern end is the same
low and narrow isthmus, which in both cases has been pierced
by a canal in the past few decades—Suez in 1869 and the Isthmus of Corinth in 1893—in order to give access to a smaller
enclosed sea and avoid a long detour around a stormy peninsula, the Cape of Good Hope and Cape Malea.

The resemblance here indicated is more than a superficial
likeness; it embodies a homologous geographical form. The

whole Mediterranean Sea has the shape of a bottle of which the nine-mile Strait of Gibraltar is the neck. This feature makes it unlike other enclosed seas of similar size, such as the Gulf of Mexico or the Caribbean, and lends this single entrance peculiar strategic importance, a fact appreciated by its ancient Phœnician warders. This bottle form and bottle neck occur elsewhere in the Mediterranean, making the neck always the scene of active historical events. The West Basin has its bottle neck in the Sicilian Strait, the Adriatic in the Strait of Otranto, the Propontis or Marmara in the Hellespont, the Black Sea in the Bosporus, and the Sea of Azof or Mæotis Lake in the Crimean Bosporus or Kertch. This homologous form appears on a smaller scale in the Strait of Lepanto (Rhium) giving access to the Gulf of Corinth, in the thread-like passage heading into the Gulf of Ambracia (Arta), and the tortuous channel leading into the Gulf of Volo.

All these straits have afforded strategic locations for the control of their respective basins. These were, therefore, early selected as sites for trading stations or colonies by progressive peoples reaching out for commercial or political control. These choice sites as bases for control, reinforced by the small area of the sub-basin, early gave rise to the political idea of the *mare clausum* or monopolized sea, over which exclusive trading rights were exercised by a single state.[5] This idea was finally extended to the whole Mediterranean as the *Mare Nostrum* under the Roman Empire, and its application to the open ocean was attempted by medieval Spain and Portugal.

The marine vestibule is a recurrent feature of the Mediterranean sub-basins. The Gulf of Cadiz, structurally a part of the Mediterranean, flanked by the same folded mountains and depressed by the same subsidences that gave rise to the larger basin, plays the part of vestibule to the sea as a whole. The Ionian Sea holds a like relation to the Adriatic, the Gulf of Patras on a smaller scale to the Gulf of Corinth, the African Sea to the West Basin, the Cretan Sea to the Ægean, and the Propontis to the Euxine.

These vestibules have staged dramatic scenes in history. They have shared the significance of the marine gateways or straits. Here great historical movements have lingered preparatory to the next outward step to the larger unknown. Euripides called the Propontis "the many bayed water-key of the boundless deep," for in the latter terms he described the unbroken expanse of the *Pontus Euxine.* Ancient Hellenic colonial enterprise paused in this vestibule and the Bosporus gateway before pressing on into the big inner chamber of the Black Sea. The compactness of their settlements here, founded alike by Dorians, Æolians and Ionians and crowded in wherever favorable sites offered themselves along these sheltered and familiar shores, indicates the enduring attraction of the smaller sea for colonization even after the big commercial possibilities of the Euxine had become apparent. Greek colonial expansion seized upon the island of Corcyra guarding the Strait of Otranto in 734 B.C., and in a few decades lined the nearby shores of the Ionian Seas with thriving cities. But it was a century or more before Corcyra planted her daughter colonies within the Adriatic, beyond the outpost settlements of Aulon (modern Avlona) and Apollonia which commanded the northern entrance of the Strait of Otranto.

The Phœnicians pushed westward along the whole Mediterranean through the Strait of the Pillars into the *Sinus Emporicus* or Bay of the Merchants; there they planted their colonies or factories and gathered in the wealth of Tarshish, for decades before rumors of the tin of Britain induced them to leave the familiar vestibule and face the untried dangers of the Atlantic.

The value of these various marine basins, straits, vestibules or island-rimmed gulfs lay in their early encouragement to nautical venture. The ancient Mediterranean sailor, once familiar with the little inlet which made his home port, then with the sub-basin which formed his home sea, gradually pushed his enquiring prow out into the unknown waters of the next basin, and so on until by successive steps he explored the whole Mediterranean.[6] The first timorous navigator crept coastwise around the shores of his sub-basin, until he had circled the whole; only then would he strike out boldly across the body of water whose farther shore was no longer unknown. This is the step from coastwise to crosswise navigation which enclosed seas early make possible.

VARIOUS EFFECTS OF SUBSIDENCE—Complementary to the fringe of peninsulas and island groups which break the surface of the Mediterranean are the numerous sub-basins, bays, inlets and straits which make this body of water a composite or mosaic sea. Subsidence has separated districts of like origin and relief and joined together unlike ones. It has cut across the grain of mountain systems and given a bottle form to the Adriatic and the Gulf of Corinth. At the Gibraltar breach it nipped in two a massive range, leaving a high submarine door-sill at the Gibraltar gates. This door-sill, rising within 1,200 feet of the surface, excludes the cold deep waters of the Atlantic, admits only the warm surface waters to the Mediterranean, whose level is constantly lowered by evaporation. Hence it helps to maintain the high temperature of the interior sea, and thereby moderates the winter temperature of the surrounding lands, maintaining their mild Mediterranean climate.

As late as the Quaternary Period, when man was already on the earth, subsidence radically modified the character of the East Basin, sundered Asia Minor from the Balkan Peninsula, and created the Ægean Sea. It depressed the old river valleys of the Hellespont and Bosporus into marine channels, drowned the mountain ranges of the old Ægean land till their half-submerged summits appeared as island groups or finger peninsulas, and converted the Euxine into a vast alcove of the Mediterranean, thus opening the productive Scythian plains to Mediterranean enterprise.

The river parentage of the Bosporus and Hellespont is revealed in their tortuous course and parallel banks, while the narrow harbor of the Golden Horn is the flooded mouth of a tributary stream, deepened by subsidence and made hospitable to large vessels. The Bosporus, 18 miles long, has a minimum breadth of 800 yards, but widens to nearly three miles at its northern entrance. A rapid current flows through it from the Black Sea at an average rate of three miles an hour. At certain narrows in the channel the current nearly doubles this rate, and shoots with such force around the bends of the shore that boats have to be towed up-stream.[7] The ancient mariners found it difficult to beat up against this current and the strong north wind of the summer sailing season which swept down the

Bosporus. This same difficulty was repeated in the Hellespont farther south. The Bosporus cuts across a spur of the ancient Thracian crystalline plateau, which here rises in a line of hills 700 feet high on either bank, and forms a canyon through which the air currents pour.

The Hellespont or Dardanelles also reveals its prefluvial character, but on a larger scale, as it is three-fourths to three and three-fourths miles wide. Its surface current flows from the Marmara Sea into the Ægean at about three miles an hour; but this increases in the narrows to over five miles an hour. This point is only 1,475 yards wide, and lies just north of Dardanos, where were located the Dardanelles Castles, built by Mohammed II in 1470 to control this passage. At the next narrows (1,585 yards) once lay the important Greek city of Abydos on the east shore, and Sestos on the west, located on a rocky promontory. Here Leander swam the Strait to Hero, here Lord Byron swam it in 1810, and here Xerxes, on his invasion of Thrace in 480 B.C., threw a pontoon across the channel [8] as his father had done in the case of the Bosporus. Here a *Zeugma* or swinging ferry was maintained in Strabo's time.[9] Here Alexander crossed in 334 B.C., and the Turks bound westward in 1357 here set foot on European soil.

The forty-mile length of the Hellespont made this narrows a strategic point. The Greeks called it the Strait of the Seven Stadia or the Hepta Stadia. Hence the shrewd Milesians selected it as the site of Abydos about 680 B.C., to offset the commanding position of the Megaran settlement at Calchedon at the entrance to the Bosporus. The whole stretch of the Marmara district, including the two Straits and the Propontis between, measures 150 miles; by reason of its various geographic features and its strategic location it has profoundly influenced both European and Asiatic history in their mutual relations. Moreover, it has stretched the span of the East Basin of the Mediterranean Sea from the mouth of the Nile to the mouth of the Dnieper and the Don, thus uniting to the Mediterranean region, with its sub-tropical climate, the cold-temperate lands of the Scythian plains.

The typical Mediterranean landscape of ancient times was the small mountain-rimmed valley opening out between sheltering promontories to enclose a harbor or small bay. Here the ancient immigrants or colonists established themselves, and exploited the slopes and valley floor by differentiated crops, till the plain was covered with grain, the piedmont with orchards and vineyards. Then with a view to safeguarding their ownership, they appropriated neighboring inlets by throwing out settlements, as the Greek colonists did about the Thermic Gulf or the Massiliots did about the *Sinus Gallicus,* or the various Greek tribes did in the Ægean Sea. They seized upon all points of advantage, both to secure their own privileges and to exclude intruders. Thus they put their own stamp on a basin or sub-basin, so far as their needs or aptitudes enabled them to cope with the geographic conditions amid which they worked. These conditions reacted in turn upon the people. Hence each basin developed a certain industrial, commercial and cultural character, result of the interaction of race and environment, and played a certain rôle in the history of the Mediterranean as a whole.

These geographic conditions depended in large part upon the nature of the local subsidences, their degree and direction, because these determined the coast of the basin as embayed or not, and therefore its accessibility from the sea. Coasts of scant subsidence show few breaks in the straight or sinuous shore-line to serve as harbors, as along the coast of Numidia, where a few inlets assumed only local importance in the history of Africa. Such were Hippo Diarrhytus (Bizerta), Hippo Regius (Bône) and Saldæ (Bougie); but they were barred by the Atlas Mountains from hinterland intercourse.

This type of coast, poor in harbors and in hinterland connections, recurs along the Mediterranean front of the Iberian peninsula. There a few favored ports like Carteia (Gibraltar), Malaca (Malaga), Carthaga Nova (Carthagena) have persisted through historical times; though only Gades with its river valley highway into the interior has conspicuously influenced the economic and cultural history of Spain. This type of shoreline recurs on the whole east coast of Italy, where only the river mouths afford poor harbors of refuge, except where Brundisium appropriated the one small indentation; on the coast of Phœnicia and Syria with their inferior harbors, found only

where the Lebanon, Bargylus and Amanus Mountains have
thrust out a buttress here and there towards an inshore reef,
and enabled human enterprise to convert it into a breakwater
to fend off the westerly or northerly winds. The Phœnicians
developed their maritime activities despite paucity of natural
harbors and poor hinterland connection because of their location at the threshold of the Orient, the big profits of their trade
with Mesopotamia and Egypt, and the field for maritime carriers offered by the East Basin. Incidentally, they became distributors of culture, and made the Levantine Sea the starting
point for the spread of the finer arts and sciences over the
Mediterranean shores.

Elsewhere on the Mediterranean coasts longitudinal subsidence was more pronounced. It depressed the southern base
of the Taurus Mountains in Lycia and Rugged Cilicia just
enough to flood the outlets of the erosion valleys and convert
these into harbors commodious enough for ancient vessels; but
the steep, forbidding slopes barred the hinterland and condemned this seaboard to a minor historical rôle, despite the
maritime activity of its population. On the eastern coast of
the Adriatic, also, subsidence took a longitudinal direction, submerged the long-stretched flank of the Dinaric Alps, admitted
the Adriatic among the drowned valleys, converted these into
a maze of straits and sounds among a swarm of slender rocky
islands, which marked the old half-submerged ridges. Barred
from the hinterland by successive mountain ranges, this deeply
embayed coast bred a race of seamen who found easy profit only
as pirates preying upon the commerce of the long Adriatic
lane; they contributed nothing to civilization.

TRANSVERSE SUBSIDENCE AND MARITIME ACTIVITY—Transverse subsidence has endowed other sections of the Mediterranean littoral with deep inlets protected by mountains running out endwise into the sea and backed by longitudinal valleys opening up natural highways into the hinterland. Such
favored seaboards are found preëminently on the Ægean shores
of Asia Minor, Greece and Crete, and the coasts of the Propontis; on the eastern end of the Atlas and Pyrenees Mountains
where they dip into the sea, as along the submerged ends of the
hills of Provence on the Mediterranean coast of Gaul. It is a

significant fact that all these coasts bore in ancient times a record of great nautical efficiency and maritime activity which exploited all their natural advantages.   The Massiliot sailors in the Second Punic War were sent "in their fast-sailing Massilian vessels to reconnoitre" the east coast of Spain by their Roman allies. "They were first in every service of difficulty and danger." [10]   Corinth built the first triremes and taught this art to the Samians in 704 B.C.   Samos had a powerful fleet in 526 B.C., and so had Chios, Lesbos and the Ionian ports of Asia Minor about the same time.[11]   Long before this the Minoan kings of Crete had established commercial relations north as far as Troy, Athens, Megara and Mycenæ, east to Cyprus, Philistia and the Nile, and west to Sicily,[12] while evidences of their civilization are found in Sardinia, Spain and at Massilia. The latter places are significant because Crete led the Ægean civilization in the Bronze Age 2000 to 1000 B.C., and probably drew upon the western sources of tin.[13]

The physical character of the Ægean and its location in the center of the East Basin made it a natural field for constant coastwise and crosswise communication, the amalgamation of races and of culture, the exchange of commodities and ideas. Never has it been a race boundary, and from legendary times its maritime relations have penetrated to the Syrian coast of the Levantine Sea and to the Caucasus shores of the Euxine, so that it has been a well travelled transit region between the north and south limits of the East Basin.   Conditions in the Ægean "occasioned active maritime intercourse and thereby a steady development of material and intellectual achievement, wherein the islands took a central position.   On them culture progressed steadily and spread thence to the mainland coast. When this culture reached its zenith the continental stocks, armed with the products of this culture acquired from the islands, and relying on the great advantage of their larger hinterland and population, attained increased importance and overthrew the island world." [14]

Streams of races have poured back and forth across this sea. A thousand years before the northern invaders of Aryan speech emerged upon its shores, the local Ægean race had settled upon the fringes and fragments of the lands, and resorted to maritime intercourse for their trade and colonization. These early people of Greece and the Ægean isles were ethnic kindred to those inhabiting the Asia Minor coast. Judged from place names on both peninsulas and islands, their languages were closely related.[15] Homer, Hesiod and Herodotus, who give the earliest records of the heroic age, show that Leleges and Pelasgi, who were probably survivors of the Ægean race, were found on both sides of the Ægean and occasionally in the islands. Eventually all these aborigines of the Ægean lands were submerged by the floods of Greek migration which swept this region in the thirteenth to tenth centuries before Christ and made the basin an Hellenic Sea.

The turmoil of successive migrations and resettlement, as described by Thucydides,[16] led to the decline of organized sea power in the Ægean as expressed in maritime commerce and the suppression of piratical activities. The irruption of the northern mountaineers brought disorder on the sea as well as on the land; and it undoubtedly checked the industries which had made the life of previous Ægean commerce. Therefore, during this period, though we see the glint of while sails and the flash of wet oars over the whole Ægean, the new Hellenic occupants of its shores had to learn the business of sea-trade. They served a long apprenticeship, and while their fingers were fumbling at the unaccustomed task, their sea power was retarded from lack of motive force, and failed to resist the Phœnicians who entered the field. Seawise, offering for sale the rich products of Oriental industries, at once manufacturers and sailors, they captured the profitable part of Ægean commerce, till the Hellenes advanced in nautical and industrial efficiency and finally produced a succession of Greek sea powers, like Samos, Chios, Miletos, Rhodes, Corinth, and Ægina, who seized the leadership in Ægean trade.

They finally monopolized this basin as an Hellenic field of enterprise. Then they made it the base of expansion into the Levantine Sea by the establishment of colonies along its northern shores and the coast of Cyprus to tap the Oriental trade; then into the Euxine where they wove a border of Hellenic colonies around the coasts but never altered the backwoods character of the basin, with its inhospitable coasts, its adverse conditions for navigation, and harsh climate. At length the commercial cities along the Eubœan Sound, like Chalcis and Eretria, and those grouped about the Saronic Gulf and the Isthmus of Corinth, profiting by their accessibility to the Isthmian route to the west, made their first wide commercial and colonial ventures into the Ionian and Sicilian Seas, establishing belts of Ionian and Dorian settlements on their congenial shores amid perfect Mediterranean conditions of climate, soil, and coastline.

The transverse subsidence of the Gulf of Corinth and the Saronic Gulf opened a marine passage across the middle of Greece, broken only by the narrow isthmus, over which the small ships of ancient times were conveyed on rollers. This seaway enabled ships to avoid the long and stormy detour around the Peloponnesos, and thus it became a focus of sea routes from east to west. Along the east coast of Hellas a combination of longitudinal and transverse subsidences had separated the long mountainous island of Eubœa from the mainland, converting it into a breakwater, sundered the island ranges from the Othrys Mountains to the north, and opened a passage from the Sound to the Ægean. Thus was formed a busy marine Broadway along the coast of Hellas, protected from the Hellespontine winds sweeping down from the Black Sea.

MEDITERRANEAN STRAITS—Owing to such active subsidences, the Mediterranean more than any other enclosed sea is distinguished by its number of straits. In all times these have offered strategic positions. Powers holding one side have constantly tried to acquire a foothold on the opposite shore and thus control the passage. Since a strait is a gateway in a sea route and a break in a land route, this strategic location enabled a power holding it to bottle up the sub-basin of which the strait was the outlet by means of blockades or tolls; or to profit by the trade converging upon the narrow passage from the flanking seas and the traffic crossing by ferry from shore to shore. This has been the commercial and political history of all the Mediterranean straits. It is fair to say that no power which has held one side of any one of these straits has ever refrained from designs upon the opposite shore. Most often these designs have succeeded for longer or shorter periods. Sometimes they have endured for centuries, and sometimes control has been divided, or it has shifted from one side of the passage to the other. But this effort to dominate the straits must always be taken into account in Mediterranean history, both ancient and modern.

The Mediterranean has many of these strategic passways—Gibraltar, the Elba passage (30 miles wide) forming the northern entrance into the Tyrrhenian Sea, Strait of Messina, Sicilian Strait, Strait of Otranto, Lepanto, the Cretan Strait between Crete and Cape Malea which forms a 60-mile wide passage into the Ægean Sea, the Carpathian Strait between Crete and Rhodes which provides a 90-mile wide entrance into the Ægean from the east, the Hellespont, the Bosporus, and the Crimean Bosporus or Kertch which links the Black Sea with the Sea of Azof. Besides these major straits could be enumerated many inshore channels or sounds which provided protected "inside passages" for ancient coastwise traffic and offered choice sites along their coasts for commercial settlements. Such was the location of the capital or leading cities on the islands of Rhodes, Samos, Chios, and Lesbos.

The ancients early discovered the principle of getting "astride the straits." The initial discovery was probably incident to the drift of peoples along a peninsula bridge and across the intervening strip of sea to the dimly seen opposite shore. Having occupied the location, they gradually came to realize its strategic and commercial possibilities for the acquisition of wealth and power. Such was the drift of the Mysians and Phrygians from Macedonia and Thrace across the Hellespont into the Troad and nearby districts of Asia Minor.[17] Hence during the Trojan War kindred people held both sides of the strait, and enlisted as allies of Priam [18] to defend their control of the Euxine trade [19] against Greek attack. Later the commercial cities of the Ægean, vitally interested in the raw products of the Euxine lands, such as Megara, Athens, Mytilene, and Miletos, established colonies on the straits and the Propontis primarily as way-stations on the long voyage to the northern sea. Control of the passage was therefore divided. But eventually one or the other colony, like Chrysopolis,[20] Calchedon,[21] or Byzantium [22] took advantage of their geographic opportunity to levy tolls on passing vessels. Athens finally secured

her right of way to the Pontic grainfields. In time of war she
levied ship tolls at Chrysopolis and Byzantium on the Bosporus [23] or at Sestos on the Hellespont to fill her depleted
treasury, and regulated the export of Pontic grain from the
Euxine as a contraband of war.[24] She maintained her power
over the Straits by judicious alliances except for short intervals, till the establishment of the Macedonian Empire.

The Cimmerian Bosporus, exit of the *Palus Mæotis* (Sea of
Azof) into the Euxine, was dominated by the two Greek colonies of Panticapæum on the European side and Phanagoria on
the Asiatic. Founded by Miletos with the help of Teos, they
became the basis for the Greek Kingdom of the Bosporus which
attained wealth and power as early as 480 B.C. by reason of
its favorable commercial location and natural resources, and
continued as a kingdom under the protection of the Roman
Emperors.

Bosporus and Hellespont constituted only a break in a land
route, a stream across the path, to the invaaing Persians in
512 B.C.,[25] in 490 and 480 B.C., and again to Alexander of
Macedon when launched upon the conquest of Asia. Hence the
Straits, which were merely submerged river valleys, were crossed
by pontoon bridges,[26] as they frequently were in later centuries
by land powers bent upon territorial expansion. But to the
commercial sea powers of the Ægean the Straits were a sea-way
to the north. Therefore, at the dissolution of Alexander's empire, the territory of the Straits was assigned to the little Kingdom of Lysimachus in the character of trustee, because it was
too weak to exploit its strategic position and, as it proved, even
to hold it.

For this whole Marmara district was inevitably a goal of expansion, destined by its geographic conditions to be held only
by some strong land power seated either in Asia Minor or the
Balkan Peninsula.[27] Hence in 192 B.C. the kingdom of the
Seleucids began edging forward to occupy both shores of the
Hellespont at the cost of Lysimachia, while control of the Bosporus was divided between Bithynia and the independent state
of Byzantium. History repeated itself in a striking manner
when the Latin Powers of the Crusades imitated Alexander's
successors, and in 1204 set up the slender kingdom of Romania

comprising a narrow zone either side of this historic water-way,[28] but with no more permanent result. Its Asiatic neighbor, the inland Greek Empire of Nikaia, began to spread westward in 1240 and by 1260 was fully astride the Hellespont and the Marmara, leaving only the little Byzantine peninsula as a remnant of the former kingdom of the Straits. Finally Constantinople fell in 1261 and the Byzantine Empire was reestablished astride the Straits from the former Greek Empire of Nikaia.[29] Once more the shadow of Asia crept westward across the Bosporus and Hellespont under the form of the advancing Turks, by 1340 enveloping all their Asiatic shores except the east coast of the Bosporus, sweeping across the Hellespont and Marmara by 1391 and the Bosporus in 1453. In the light of these events, the futile attempt of the European powers in 1919 to establish a small dominion of the Straits is significant.

The southern end of the Ægean Sea resembles the mouth of a bag rather than the neck of a bottle. Across the opening Crete stretches its length of 160 miles and divides the entrance into two straits, on which the island holds a commanding position. It was doubtless this strategic location which enabled the early Minoan navy to exclude Phœnician ships from the lucrative maritime field of the Ægean until the Cretan power was overwhelmed by Dorian invasions in the twelfth century B.C.[30] and the sea trade passed to Phœnicians and Greeks. Later the demoralized Cretans turned pirates and utilized their location to prey upon the traffic which converged on the flanking routes into the Ægean.[31] The island of Cythera, which shared with Crete the frontage on the western channel, also became a base for piratical activities, while Illyrian pirates came down from the Adriatic to maintain their sinister patrol of this strait.[32] Centuries later, Venice, at the height of her power between 1206 and 1669, animated with truly Minoan ambitions for commercial supremacy in the Ægean, occupied Crete and Cythera for several centuries, besides various bases in the Peloponnesos or Morea. Thus she secured control of the western channel. With the cooperation of the Knights of St. John in Rhodes she (1340 to 1500) insured her command of the eastern channel and the sea route from the Ægean to Cyprus and Alexandria. The position of Venice astride the straits had an ethnic parallel centuries earlier in the Dorian occupation of Cythera, Crete, Rhodes and the intervening islands; but only in Rhodes did the Dorians fully exploit the advantage of their location on the eastern strait as the Venetians did later.

An even more critical channel was the narrow Strait of Rhium linking the Ionian Sea with the Gulf of Corinth and the trans-isthmian route to the Ægean. Only a mile wide, it became the chief ferry point between Hellas and Peloponnesos.[33] Here in legendary times the returning Heraclidæ or Dorians crossed the Strait to invade the southern peninsula. They built their fleet in the harbor of Naupactos, which lay in the wind-shadow of the Antirrhium Promontory, and crossed thence to Rhium. Control of the Strait was desired by Corinth and Athens during their long commercial rivalry in the fifth century B.C. as later by the competing Achaian and Ætolian Leagues. Corinth secured her western trade connections by acquiring Molycria on the north shore of the Strait of Rhium, and Chalcis twenty miles outside the passage on the Ætolian coast, while she made an alliance with Œniadæ commanding the sea approach to the Gulf of Patras.[34] Rising Athens, to impair these Corinthian connections, in 460 B.C. seized the excellent harbor of Naupactos within the Strait and made it her chief naval station, captured Chalcis from Corinth and made a futile attack upon Œniadæ.[35] She also forced Cephallenia into her alliance in 456 B.C. During the Peloponnesian War several naval engagements were staged in or near the Strait. Naupactos, as the key to the Gulf of Corinth, was taken from Athens at the end of this war.

Later Achaia [36] got astride the Strait [37] in the struggle between the Achaian and Ætolian Leagues; Achaia generally managed to hold Naupactos and through their great ally Philip V of Macedon it controlled Cephallenia, which was recognized as the island warder of the Strait, holding the same relation as Tenedos to the Hellespont, or as Corcyra to the Strait of Otranto. Significantly enough in the late middle ages both Naupactos and Cephallenia were occupied by the Venetians, who with their Spanish allies won the naval battle of Lepanto against the Turks in these waters in 1571.

The Strait of Otranto reveals a similar record. Between its

two shores the shuttle of history has passed back and forth
weaving into a common fabric the big events on the Calabrian
peninsula of Italy and the opposite Illyrian-Epirote coast.
At a very early date, Messapians and Calabrians of Illyrian
stock pushed westward across the fifty-mile passage and established themselves on the heel of Italy,[38] where in time they came
to exploit the port of Brundisium, the one good harbor on the
west side of the marine ferry from Corcyra. Hence they were
already astride the Strait when Greek Dorians colonized Corcyra in 724 B.C., gradually occupied points on the seaboard
of Epiros and Illyria, and secured a base at Hydruntum and
Tarentum in order to control the transit route to Italy and the
trade of the Adriatic. The next domination emanated from the
western side. Dionysius I of Syracuse (c. 380 B.C.), having
extended his sway over Greek Sicily and much of Greek Italy,
proposed to make the Adriatic a Syracusan lake. He planted
colonies on the Apulian coast, secured dependencies among the
native communities in the Calabrian peninsula and on the
Illyrian coast opposite, made an alliance with the King of
Molossia in Epiros, and thus acquired a dominant position
at the gates of the Adriatic.[39]

Two similar purposes emanated from Epiros on the east,
that of Alexander of Molossia in 334 B.C. who apparently
aimed at an Epirote dominion astride the Strait of Otranto;[40]
and later that of Pyrrhus (281-275 B.C.) who for a time extended his dominion across the Strait over all southern Italy
into Sicily[41] in a manner to alarm Rome. Hence a Roman
colony was established at Brundisium in 224 B.C., probably
as an outpost against aggression from the Epirote or Macedonian side of the Strait. The need of policing the Adriatic
against Illyrian pirates led Rome (229-228 B.C.) to establish
a protectorate over the whole east coast of this sea; but she
appropriated as her own territory only Corcyra, Apollonia
and Epidamnos or Dyrrhachium. After the war with Antiochus
the Great she saw the wisdom of occupying Cephallenia and
Zacynthos as the other island warders of the Strait. Her position was duplicated centuries later by the Norman power in
Sicily and Italy, which at times held all these strategic locations. In 1480, the Turks under Mahmet the Conqueror held

the Illyrian coast and Otranto passage.   The latest episode in this recurrent history took place in August, 1914, when Italy seized the port of Avlona, opposite Brundisium to safeguard herself against the Austrian fleet; and again in 1919, when the Italian fleet bombarded Corfu in protest against Grecian hostility—an act which Greece interpreted as the ghost of an ancient aggression once more stalking abroad.

The Strait of Messina presents a close resemblance to the Hellespont, because its narrow two-mile width facilitated crosswise expansion and control, making Sicily both a physical and political appendage of Italy.   Like Hellespont and Otranto, this channel linked a backward northern coast region of raw products around the lower Tyrrhenian Sea with a southern region of advanced civilization and industrial development facing the Sicilian Sea.   At the dawn of history the native Sicils occupied both the lower peninsula of Italy and eastern Sicily, whither they had migrated, probably attracted by the fertile soil.   These were dislodged from the coasts of the Strait and driven into the immediate hinterland by the intruding Greeks,[42] who with an eye to commercial opportunity colonized Rhegium on the toe of Italy and Zancle or Messana on the opposite corner of Sicily, and thus dominated the Strait.[43]   In order to exploit its strategic possibilities, Anaxilaus of Rhegium in 482 B.C. seized Zancle and by means of a fortress and fleet closed the Strait against the Etruscan pirates who were infesting the passage.[44]   Next Dionysius of Syracuse, a century later, having consolidated the Greek power in eastern Sicily, got astride of the Strait of Messina, and brought all the lower peninsula of Italy under his sway as far as the Crathis River.[45]   At the stricture between Scylletium and the Terinæan Gulf, he planned to delimit his nearer Italian territory by a wall and ditch across the 20-mile isthmus [46] in order to emphasize its union with Sicily.[47]   His domain to some extent anticipated the Norman Kingdom of the Two Sicilies, which developed fifteen centuries later.

Expanding Rome, with an eye to strategic possibilities, having acquired Rhegium in Italy, accepted the offer of Messana as a gift from the rebellious Mamertines in 265 B.C.   She thus gained a much-needed bridge-head on the Sicilian side and command of one of the two straits linking the East and West Mediterranean.   Her rival Carthage held the other and revealed designs upon the Messina passage by attacks on Messana and Rhegium; but these two vital points remained in the grip of Rome through all the vicissitudes of the Second Punic War.[48] Victory gave Rome Sicily and sole control of the sea-way, while the Third Punic War carried her across the Sicilian Straits into Carthaginian Africa.

The history of the Messinian passage is closely linked with that of the Sicilian Strait. Expanding powers, either from the Italian or Tunisian side, have repeatedly swept across Sicily and the two straits to the opposite mainland.   Carthage early (550 B.C.) converted the Phœnician cities of the nearby Sicilian shore into dependencies, and thus commanded the lucrative trade passing between the East and West Basins—two maritime regions differing somewhat in climate, conspicuously in their civilizations, and furnishing therefore contrasted products and contrasted markets.   Soon after the expulsion of the able Tarquins from Rome, Carthage, confident of her power to control the 85-mile channel of the Sicilian Strait, imposed on the young Roman Republic a commercial treaty designed to limit its maritime field, which had expanded under its sea-wise Etruscan kings.   This treaty (508 B.C.) inhibited the Romans and their allied coast towns of Latium from trading in any African port north or east of the Hermæan Promontory, the modern Cape Bon; thus it excluded them from the busy market towns on the Lesser Syrtis and prevented their opening up direct trade with Egypt.[49]   Carthage wished to be sole middleman for the industrial products of the East Basin and the luxury articles of the Orient, while she restricted Roman commerce to the backward economic regions of the West Basin.

The Phœnician settlements in Sicily yielded their early sites on the east coast to Hellenic colonization, but stood their ground in the northwest corner of the island, in Panormus, Drepanum, Lilybæum and Motye, facing the shortest passage to Africa.[50]   These served Carthage as land bases for the extension of her control along the southwest coast of Sicily (400 B.C.); but they became in turn the object of repeated attacks by Dionysius of Syracuse, who tried to dislodge the Carthaginian power from its bridgehead in Sicily [51] and break the Punic control of the Strait.

The dream of Dionysius was realized momentarily by Agathocles of Syracuse, who extended his territory in southern Sicily, and then in a four years' war (310-307 B.C.) conquered the opposite African coasts, from Hippo Diarrhytus in the north to Hadrumetum in the south, but failed to take Carthage.[52] Thus he stood astride the Strait for a time, but was unable to maintain his position. It remained for Rome to expel the Carthaginians from Sicily and to dominate Africa and the Strait. During the Punic Wars, the Strait became the scene of great naval battles, like that of Ecnomus,[53] Drepanum and the Ægatian Islands. The storms which visit this channel even in summer occasioned great loss of men, ships and military stores as these were being conveyed to one side or the other, while fleets were driven from their course onto perilous coasts.[54] The land abutting on the narrows of the Strait, the Hermæan Promontory (Cape Bon) in Africa and the western angle of Sicily, were the scene of departing and landing fleets. Lilybæum, the chief fortress of the Carthaginians in Sicily, was the object of a long and futile siege from 249 to 241 B.C. by the Romans during the First Punic War; during the Second Punic War it was the Roman base for practically all naval operations against the African coast, and the home port for the return of victorious or booty-laden ships.[55] Hence Carthage made the recovery of Lilybæum, its old bridgehead on the Sicilian coast, the constant aim of the Punic navy.[56] Lilybæum was the first landing place of the Saracens in 827 and the base of their military operations until they conquered Sicily in 895. So important was it that they called it the "Port of Allah." [57]

History continued to repeat itself on the Sicilian Strait. A Norman King of the Two Sicilies (1127-1140) held Mahdia and other points on the opposite African coast during his life. Charles V of Spain, as king of the Two Sicilies, seized Tunis in 1531. Similarly the modern kingdom of Italy hoped to acquire Tunisia till her ambition was dashed by the French occupation of that territory in 1875. But the ethnic drift across the Strait continues, for Tunisia today contains only 35,000 French and over 100,000 Italians. Most of these are Sicilians who came over to supply the demand for rough labor for which Tunisians are unfit. They form more or less compact groups, tenacious of their language and customs, ominously prolific, and constitute a sort of *imperium in imperio*. The import of their birth-rate and great industry as means for political domination is not lost upon the French government.[58]

The Strait of Gibraltar, a nine-mile breach in the mountain wall enclosing the Mediterranean on the west, was gateway to the Atlantic and the early tin route; it was immemorial ferry site for intercourse between the Iberian peninsula and Africa. Phœnician traders, possibly as early as the fifteenth century before Christ, secured their tenure of this strategic passage by colonies on the Pillars of Hercules at Calpe and Abila, the modern Gibraltar and Ceuta; at Carteia near the present Algiceras, at Tartessus probably in the vicinity though its site is unlocated, and at Tingis, the modern Tangier. Gades (Cadiz) near the mouth of the Bætis or Guadalquivir and Lixus yet older served as Atlantic outposts of the Strait, which was called the Strait of the Pillars of Heracles by the Greeks and later *Fretum Gaditanum* by the Romans.

Control of the Strait was jealously guarded. Greek traders from Phocæa who tried to found a colony at Mænaca, later Malaca, were warned off and the site later occupied by Phœnicians. Carthaginian power consolidated these colonies and dominated the Strait. At this point Hamilcar Barca and his son Hannibal crossed into Spain,[59] when the Carthaginians set out in 238 B.C. to recover the Iberian possessions of Carthage after the revolt of the mercenary troops. The Roman power conquered Spain in the Second Punic War but not till the time of Augustus did it acquire the opposite coast of Mauretania Tingitania, though an active export trade went on from the Iberian side to the African.[60] Only in the later days of the Empire was this district incorporated in the Prefecture of Gaul and thus administered from Spain.[61] Migrant Germanic tribes like the Franks and Goths in 260 A.D. and Vandals two centuries later crossed the Strait but as inland people found no temptation to hold it. But the Saracens or Moors got astride the Strait in 711 A.D. and maintained their position till 1492, when Spain drove them from the peninsula, reversed the situation by acquiring Ceuta, the old Mount Abila, and four other presidios or forts along the Rif coast, to check further invasion from the African mainland and police Spanish shipping against the Rif pirates.

AUTHORITIES—CHAPTER IV

1. Strabo, VIII, Chap. I, 3; IX, Chap. II, 21.
2. *Ibid.,* I, Chap. I, 16.
3. Pliny, *Historia Naturalis,* III, 10, 15, 29. Strabo, II, Chap. V, 18-25.
4. Procopius, *Vandal War,* I, 4. Pliny, IV, 18-19, 24-26. Strabo, I, Chap. III, 2. Pliny, Bk. III, Introduction and Chap. I.
5. Ellen C. Semple, *Influences of Geographic Environment,* pp. 314-315. New York, 1911.
6. Ellen C. Semple, *op. cit.,* pp. 300-302.
7. A. Philippson, *Das Mittelmeergebiet,* p. 52. Leipzig, 1907.
8. Herodotus, IV, 83, 85, 87, 88.
9. Strabo, XIII, Chap. I, 22.
10. Polybius, III, 95. Strabo, IV, Chap. I, 6.
11. Thucydides, I, 13; II, 9, 56; III, 10; VIII, 76.
12. Herodotus, VII, 170. Hogarth, *Ionia and the East,* pp. 25-30; 47, 87-89; 108-110. Oxford, 1909.
13. J. B. Bury, *History of Greece,* pp. 31-39. London, 1909.
14. Eduard Meyer, *Geschichte des Altertums,* pp. 677-678. Stuttgart, 1909.
15. J. B. Bury, *op. cit.,* p. 34.
16. Thucydides, I, 12.
17. Herodotus, VI, 45; VII, 73-74. E. Meyer, *op. cit.,* pp. 614-616. Strabo, XII, Chap. IV, 4; Chap. VIII, 3-4; XIII, Chap. I, 21.
18. *Iliad,* II, 825-877.
19. Walter Leaf, *Troy,* pp. 201, 255-279. London, 1912.
20. Xenophon, *Hellenes,* I, Chap. I, 21-22.
21. Aristotle, *Economics,* II, 11.
22. Polybius, IV, 46, 47, 52. Xenophon, *Hellenes,* IV, Chap. VIII, 27.
23. Xenophon, *Hellenes,* I, Chap. I, 14, 22; IV, Chap. 8, 27, 31. Polybius, IV, 44.
24. Boeckh, *Public Economy of the Athenians,* p. 78. English translation. London and Boston, 1857.
25. Herodotus, IV, 33-36, 83-88.
26. T. A. Dodge, *Alexander,* Vol. I, p. 231. Boston, 1890. Arrian, *Anabasis of Alexander,* Bk. I, Chap. XI.
27. John L. Myres, "The Marmara Region," *Scottish Geographical Magazine,* Vol. 40, pp. 129-150. 1924.
28. E. A. Freeman, *Historical Geography of Europe,* p. 396.
29. *Ibid.,* pp. 399-400.
30. Hogarth, *Ionia and the East,* pp. 40, 99. Oxford, 1909.
31. Polybius, XIII, 8.
32. *Ibid.,* V, 101.
33. Polybius, IV, 11.
34. E. Curtius, *History of Greece,* Vol. I, p. 290. New York.
35. Thucydides, I, 111.

36. Xenophon, *Hellenes,* IV, Chap. VI, 14.
37. Polybius, V, 3.
38. Pliny, Bk. III, 111. J. B. Bury, *op. cit.,* p. 102.
39. Diodorus Siculus, XV, Chap. 2. Bury, *op. cit.,* 661-662.
40. Bury, *op. cit.,* p. 680.
41. Mommsen, *History of Rome,* Vol. II, pp. 3, 7, 9, 12, 15, 21, 22, 28. New York, 1906.
42. Thucydides, VI, 2-4. Freeman, *History of Sicily,* Vol. I, pp. 20, 100-102, 124-137. London, 1891.
43. J. B. Bury, *op. cit.,* pp. 96, 99.
44. *Ibid.,* 297-8.
45. Freeman, *History of Sicily,* Vol. IV, pp. 177-179, 189-192, 202-203. Oxford, 1894.
46. Strabo, VI, Chap. I, 10.
47. Pliny, III, 15.
48. Mommsen, *op. cit.,* Vol. II, pp. 165-169.
49. Polybius, III, 22, 23. Niebuhr, *History of Rome,* Vol. I, pp. 534-535. London, 1855.
50. Thucydides, VI, 2.
51. Diodorus Siculus, XIV, 47. Freeman, *History of Sicily,* Vol. IV, pp. 65-68, 206-209. Oxford, 1894.
52. Diodorus Siculus, XX, 3.
53. Polybius, I, 25-28.
54. Livy, XXI, 49; XXIII, 34. Compare Vergil, *Æneid,* I, 84-89.
55. *Ibid.,* XXV, 31; XXVII, 5; XXVIII, 4; XXIX, 24.
56. *Ibid.,* XXI, 49; XXII, 46.
57. Augustus Hare, *Cities of Southern Italy and Sicily,* p. 519. New York.
58. R. Devereux, *Aspects of Algeria,* pp. 267-268. London and New York, 1912.
59. Polybius, II, 1.
60. Strabo, III, Chap. IV, 2, 8.
61. Shepherd, *Historical Atlas,* p. 42.

CHAPTER V

THE MEDITERRANEAN CLIMATE

The Mediterranean Sea and its bordering lands constitute a climatic region characterized by winter rains and summer droughts.[1] Despite the sharp contrasts in rainfall and temperature to be found on the north and south coasts, in highlands and lowlands, the region is in the main a climatic unit. It has an outstanding type of climate, in which the essential feature is the seasonal distribution of the rainfall. This type is not confined to the Mediterranean region of Europe. It recurs, attended by a distinctive type of vegetation armed with drought-resisting qualities, on the west side of the continents in about the same latitudes both in the northern and southern hemispheres,—in California, middle Chile, the west side of Cape Colony and southwest Australia. All these districts have their Mediterranean climate restricted to a narrow coastal strip too limited in area to attain historical significance.

The Mediterranean Climatic Region under consideration, when compared with the others, has a vastly greater extent. This is due to the presence of the Midland Sea and the Euxine, extending east and west along the main axis of the 36th parallel as from Monterey, California, to the coast of North Carolina, and along a north-south axis as from Lake Nipissing to New Orleans. This expanse has therefore a definite relation to the Mediterranean Maritime Region. Compared with other Mediterranean climatic regions, it combines the advantage of large area with a whole complex of other geographic advantages,—with varied relief, location on an enclosed sea, command of a long indented coastline, access to three contrasted continents, proximity to land routes and marine routes, all contributing to the stimulating environment which left its mark upon ancient Mediterranean civilization; for advancing civilization was chiefly progressive adjustment to this environment, made by the peoples living within reach of the Mediterranean coasts.

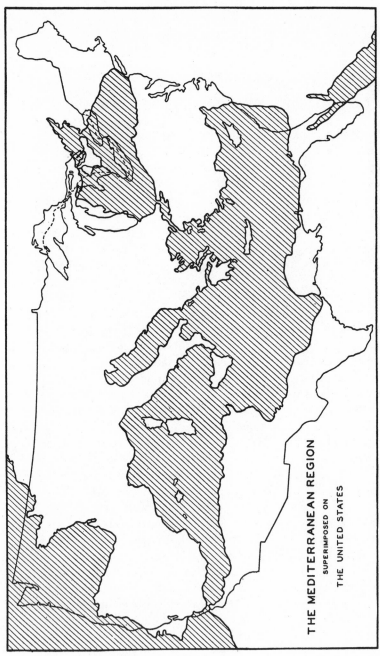

MAP 2—The extent of the Mediterranean Maritime Region as compared with the United States. The Mediterranean Sea is the chief source of moisture for the bordering lands.

THE MEDITERRANEAN REGION

SUPERIMPOSED ON

THE UNITED STATES

WINTER RAINS AND SUMMER DROUGHTS—The significant characteristic of the Mediterranean climate is not the amount of the rainfall, but the fact that the rain is nearly confined to the colder months of the year, while the summers are relatively dry. The Mediterranean lands form a region of winter rains and summer droughts.

The dearth of rainfall in summer and the relative abundance in winter is due to the location of the Mediterranean Basin between two regions of sharply contrasted precipitation. It lies on the northern margin of the trade wind or desert tract of Africa; and on the southern margin of the prevailing westerly winds, which all year round bring rain from the Atlantic to northern and middle Europe. The Mediterranean Basin occupies a transition zone between the two, and partakes in turn of the climatic character of each according to the season of the year. In summer it approximates the arid conditions of the Sahara; in winter it reproduces the stormy skies and frequent rains of France and Germany.

At the time of the equinoxes when the sun's rays are vertical at the equator, the southern lands of the Mediterranean Basin come under the influence of the dry northeast trade winds. These winds, blowing from a cooler to a warmer region, get an increase of temperature which raises the point of saturation and enables the air to suck up more moisture from the thirsting earth. The trades are therefore hot, drying winds, which drop no rain except upon the chilly slopes of high mountains. At this same time, the northern parts of the Basin, like the Pyrenean district of Spain, the Po Basin and northern Apennines, lie within the belt of the prevailing westerlies and approximate the climate of France and Germany, with their ample spring and autumn showers.

With the advance of summer, the heat belt moves northward from the equator, and makes the rain-bearing westerlies retire to Middle Europe, where they merely brush the northern rim of the Basin. In their place come the heat and drought of Saharan Africa, which spread like a hot blanket over most of the Mediterranean Basin. Only the northernmost rim protrudes beyond this dry covering. The whole region, overheated, makes an area of low barometric pressure, over which the air rises

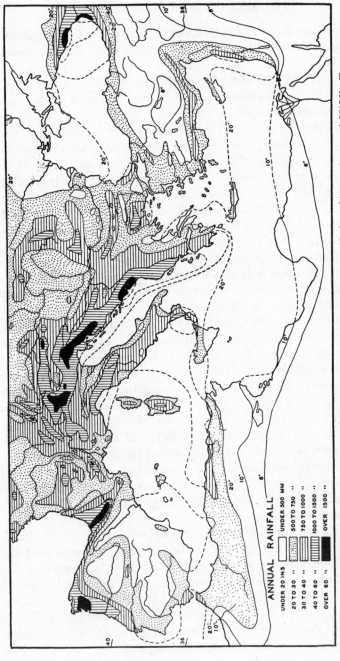

ANNUAL RAINFALL

UNDER 20 INS   UNDER 500 MM
20 TO 30   ″   500 TO 750   ″
30 TO 40   ″   750 TO 1000   ″
40 TO 60   ″   1000 TO 1500 ″
OVER 60   ″   OVER 1500   ″

Map 3—Distribution of annual rainfall in the Mediterranean Region and the adjacent parts of Middle Europe.

and sucks in winds from the high-pressure belt extending over Middle Europe. These winds, blowing from the north and growing warmer as they reach the Mediterranean, absorb moisture but part with none. Hence the steady north winds and long drought of the Mediterranean summer.

After the autumnal equinox, the sun moves southward from the equator and shifts the heat belt into southern Africa; the northeast trades forsake the Mediterranean and withdraw into the desert belt of the Sahara; the wind system of the prevailing westerlies follow, and in their turn spread like a wet blanket over the whole Mediterranean Basin and bring occasional rains even to the desert rim of Africa. The Basin then shares the winter weather conditions of western Europe. It is surrounded by high-pressure areas over the encircling continents, and by the high-pressure area in the Atlantic west of Spain and Morocco. The warm air above the Sea forms a low-pressure area, which draws in the winds from all sides. These grow warm and moisture-laden, as they sweep across the Sea; but as they impinge upon the lands which are colder, they release their moisture as rain. There are local, low-pressure areas over the several sub-basins of the Mediterranean, and corresponding high-pressure areas over the several peninsulas, islands and coastal plains. The boundaries of these areas frequently shift, with the result that the winds shift also and bring constantly changing weather during the winter season. These variable cyclonic winds, always of a more or less stormy nature, were dreaded by the ancient Mediterranean seamen, who therefore deferred their maritime enterprises till the steady winds of summer made navigation safe and easy.

The chief source of moisture in the Mediterranean Climatic Region is the Midland Sea itself, supplemented by the Black Sea and the Caspian. This sea as a whole constitutes a low pressure area during the colder part of the year; but in this area specific "lows" of the cyclonic storms originate in the extreme northwest of the Western Basin and advance thence eastward to the Egyptian coast, bringing the rare showers to the Nile Delta. This eastward course of the "lows" gives the western side of coastlands, islands, peninsulas and mountain ranges a heavier precipitation than the eastern flanks receive.

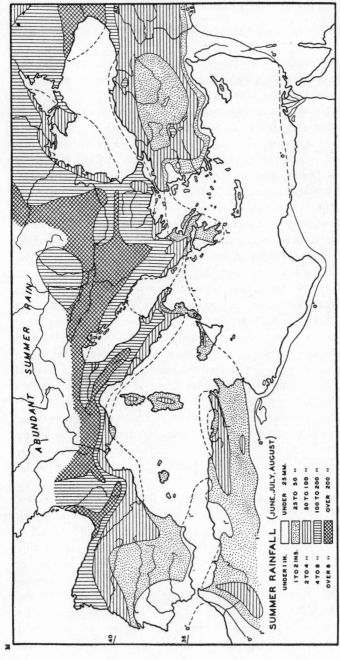

SUMMER RAINFALL (JUNE, JULY, AUGUST)

UNDER 1 IN.	UNDER 25 MM.
1 TO 2 INS.	25 TO 50 "
2 TO 4 "	50 TO 100 "
4 TO 8 "	100 TO 200 "
OVER 8 "	OVER 200 "

MAP 4—Map showing the scant rainfall of the Mediterranean Region during the three summer months. Rainfall of 4 to 8 inches confined to high mountains and to Middle Europe.

West, southwest or northwest winds bring Athens 16 inches of rain distributed over 93 days, or half the time between October and April; but they arrive bereft of most of their moisture by the mountains behind them, except the few winds that happen to strike a straight passage through the Gulf of Corinth and thus meet no obstruction.[2]   Blowing on eastward across the Ægean, these winds renew their store of moisture, bring Smyrna 26 inches (655 mm.) and a higher quota of about 30 inches (750 mm.) to the mountain ranges near the coast; but fifty miles inland they dispense only 20 inches (500 mm.), and when they reach the mountain-walled interior of Asia Minor, they drop only 8 to 12 inches (200 to 300 mm.) annually.

Syria, Lebanon and Palestine present a bold front to these rain-bearing winds from the west and thus intercept most of their moisture.   The Lebanon Mountains, rising to an altitude of 8,000 feet or more, get an annual precipitation of 40 inches on the summit.   Beirut at their base gets only 32 inches; the Palestine coast farther south gets 16 to 23 inches.   Jerusalem located on the Judean Plateau at an altitude of 2,600 feet, gets a rainfall of 25.6 inches (650 mm.).   Behind this rain screen aridity increases rapidly to the Syrian Desert.   East of Jordan, however, Gilead and the Hauran Plateau face the broad wind-gap formed by the low Samarian hills and Galilean hills, and lie high enough (2,000 feet to 6,133 feet on Hauran Massif) to condense the moisture left in the west winds.   Hence these districts receive enough rain for pastures, grain fields and even oak groves, like that in which David's son Absalom was caught by his long hair when riding through on horseback. Farther north, Mount Hermon (9,380 ft.) and the high peaks of Anti-Lebanon (8,330 ft.) get abundant snow and rain, with which they feed the rushing "rivers of Damascus," despite an inland location.

This same contrast between the precipitation on western and eastern slopes reappears in the Balkan, Apennine and Iberian peninsulas.   The table for Greece and Italy on p. 90 gives the data for the first two in similar latitudes.[3]

In the Iberian Peninsula the contrast between east and west in point of rainfall is even more marked.   Owing to the high relief and location of the northwest coast within the belt of the prevailing westerly winds, the Atlantic front gets a generous rainfall, ranging from 25 to 48 inches. The rest of the peninsula is very arid. The east coast south of Barcelona and the plateau interior average from 15 to 19 inches a year, while cloudiness and humidity are scant.[4] Hence evaporation is intense.

GREECE				ITALY			
West	*Inches*	*East*	*Inches*	*West*	*Inches*	*East*	*Inches*
Valona	42.1	Constantinople	28.0	ˉGenoa	51.7	Venice	29.5
Corfu	47.9	Volos	21.6	Florence	34.9	Bologna	28.3ˉ
Arta	42.6	Lamia	23.7	Leghorn	34.8	Ancona	26.5
Patras	26.5	Athens	16.0	Rome	31.5	North Apulia	22.0
Pyrgos	33.8	Nauplia	20.0	Naples	32.7	Foggia	18.3
Kalamata	33.0	Leonidin	25.8	Palermo	34.2	Catania	20.9
Zante	43.4	Andros	26.2				

The rainfall in the Mediterranean and the duration of the rainy season decrease not only from west to east but from north to south; and the summer drought increases in the same direction both in length and intensity. This is another way of saying that the half of the Basin north of the fortieth parallel is assimilated to the climate of Middle Europe, but has a marked minimum of rainfall in summer; and that the southern half is assimilated to that of desert Africa, with a long rainless or nearly rainless summer. Deviations from this rule of decreased precipitation from north to south occur only where high mountains like the Sierra Nevada of Spain and the Lebanon rob the clouds of their moisture and make local climatic islands of relatively heavy rainfall. Occasionally they break the summer drought by thunderstorms on their higher slopes, while after midday their chilly summits are usually enveloped in clouds, which seem to give a delusive promise of rain to the thirsty and semi-baked plains below. "Boastful people without gifts are as clouds without rain," or "The light of the king's countenance is life, and his favor is as a cloud of the latter rain,"— welcome but unreliable, for the summer drought is imminent.[5]

The summer drought on the southern margin of the East Basin is very pronounced. In Alexandria it lasts seven months, from April till November; in Palestine six months, from May till late November, and in Greece, four months, from the middle of May till the middle of September. Farther north, about the Sea of Marmara, it is limited to July and August. In Tripoli,

as in the Nile Delta, the drought lasts seven months, in Malta
from four to five months, in Sicily the four months from May
till September, but in Naples and Rome it is shorter and is
broken by occasional heavy showers. On the Mediterranean'
coast of France and the Italian Riviera only July is rainless.
All the northernmost belt of the Basin resembles Middle Europe
and gets heavy spring and autumn rains which curtail the summer drought.

The drought is hard upon vegetation because it occurs in
summer when evaporation is increased by heat, low atmospheric
humidity, and strong drying winds which prevail for two to six
months. Plant life loses its moisture at an excessive rate, unless it is specially equipped to resist desiccation or has its needs
supplied by artificial irrigation. An annual rainfall of 23
inches, which maintains the fresh vegetation of southern England with its mild moist summers, is inadequate at Jerusalem
or Palermo for garden or vineyard, which then require irrigation to maintain growth.

On the highlands of the Mediterranean Basin, however, the
sharp drop of temperature at night precipitates the moisture
held in solution by the warm air of the day, and causes heavy
dews which revive the vegetation. On the Plateau of Barca,
the Judean Plateau, and the highlands of Gilead and Hauran,
the dew is so abundant that it partly atones for the lack of rain.[6]
The ancient Greek and Roman colonists in Cyrenaica and the
Libyan coast regularly counted upon its aid. The Jewish peasants of Palestine recognized the dew as a power to mitigate the
effects of the heat and drought, and therefore considered it a
divine gift.[7] "God give thee the dew of Heaven and the fatness
of the earth, and plenty of corn and wine," was Isaac's blessing
on his son. The threat to withhold dew and rain was Elijah's
curse. Refreshing dews were enumerated in the Odyssey among
the natural advantages of ancient Ithaca,[8] and rightly; for
though the island lies on the rainy western side of Greece, it has
practically rainless summers, since it receives less than an inch
of rain (25 mm.) during the period of June, July and August.
Apollo, as god of agriculture, had the title of Hersos, "dispenser of fertilizing dews," in ancient mythology. The value
of dew is less emphasized by the ancient Romans, probably be-

cause of the ampler rains and cooler summers in Italy and the lands of the Western Basin.

VARIABILITY OF RAINFALL—A minor source of moisture like dew assumes increased importance in view of the great variability of rainfall from year to year. This feature distinguishes precipitation in all Mediterranean climatic regions of the world. In Los Angeles, representing Southern California, the rainfall attained a maximum of 34 inches in 1889 and a minimum of 5.6 inches in 1898. In Athens the rainfall varied from 34 inches in 1883 to 4.5 inches in 1898; in the decade 1894 to 1903 it was subnormal seven years with a marked deficiency, and supernormal three years with very slight excess, so that this whole period was a dry one. This also is characteristic of the Mediterranean climate, resulting in failing springs, exhaustion of water reserves, and ultimate famine. Jerusalem, with a mean annual rainfall of 26 inches, saw its precipitation fluctuate from 43 inches in 1877 to 12.5 inches in 1869. In a period of 60 years it fell twelve times below 20 inches so critical for grain crops, and as often exceeded 32 inches.[9] Years of heavy rains do not bring commensurate benefit to field and pasture, because they are attended by violent downpours and rapid run-off, so that the soil soaks up relatively little of the moisture.

Variations in rainfall increase from north to south and from west to east; hence they are most pronounced and most disastrous on the semi-arid eastern and southern margins of the Basin. In the Tripolis district of North Africa, which lies on the mere fringe of the Mediterranean Climatic Region, the rainfall ranged in five years from 26 inches in 1894 to 8.8 inches in 1895: hence the mean could have little significance for agriculture.

Variable too is the advent of the autumn and spring showers which respectively open and close the rainy period, and hence fix the length of the growing season. These are "the former and the latter rains" of the Bible. The "former rains" begin in Palestine any time between October fourth and November twenty-eighth. An early beginning means a long growing season and easy germination in a soil still warm. The "latter rains" may end from April first to May twenty-seventh. A premature arrival of the summer drought shortens the growing season and catches the crops before the grains have filled out and accumulated moisture for the long dry season before harvest, which is due in May and June. "I have withholden the rain from you when there were yet three months to the harvest," or in February. This was Jehovah's threat of punishment uttered through the mouth of Amos.

In Greece the initial showers appear with more regularity in October and the final ones linger through April into May, while occasional storms terminate the summer drought with short downpours. Italy, farther west, has the drought broken with some regularity in September and can usually depend upon the rains till the end of May. In 1922 the rains ceased in early May and caused a partial failure of the wheat crops, with the result that the Italian government removed the import duty on wheat flour, and the native population had to eat dark bread most of the ensuing winter. The Cyclades Islands—Naxos, Syros and Santorin—lying in the rain-shadow of the Cretan highlands, have a low rainfall (less than 20 inches) of short duration; Santorin is often forced to import water from the mainland. An agreement between the amount and duration of the rainfall may generally be observed, if the records are taken at several stations with different wind exposures.

IMPORTANCE OF THE WINDS—The winds are arbiters of human fate in the Mediterranean world. This fact was recognized by the ancients. To them the direction of the wind meant scorching heat or refreshing coolness, rain or drought, abundant or meager crops, food or famine, conditions favorable or adverse to navigation. Weather was a despot to the ancient Mediterranean folk, and the weather was governed by the winds. Hence there was an adage, old even in the time of Theophrastus: "*Annus fructum fert, non tellus.*" "The season produces the crop, not the soil." The Greeks and Romans distinguished eight to twelve different winds, and named them not from the direction whence they blew, but gave them proper names and distinguished them according to their force, temperature, humidity, source and the season of their blowing. Hence the abundant vocabulary of the winds which confuses the young reader of Vergil or Homer. Aristotle in his Meteorology enumerates twelve winds and the quarters whence they blow; [10]

but only eight were popularly known, as indicated by the names inscribed on the so-called Tower of the Winds at Athens. This same discrimination survives among the modern seamen and peasants of Mediterranean lands, and reveals a fine observation of the air currents rare among peoples of Middle Europe. They know the winds and their effects. *Vorias*, the ancient *Boreas*, the Italian Bora or *Transmontana* is a stormy wind from the north, northwest or northeast, which dries up the vegetation in summer; but in winter it brings cold rain and snow. Theophrastus made the generalization that sea winds were better for plant life than land breezes, and west winds better than east winds, cool winds better than warm ones as a rule, unless the trees and shrubs had just germinated.[11] In Palestine and Egypt the east wind had a bad reputation because it blew from the desert and devastated the crops.[12] "Behold seven thin ears and blasted with the east wind sprung up," representing the seven years of famine in Pharaoh's dream.

Most important are the dry northeast trade winds of summer, to which the Greeks gave the name of Etesian, and which blow over the entire Eastern Basin. They appear in late May, alternate with south winds or with calms till July 25th, the heliotic rising of the Dog Star; then they become established and dominate the East Basin till about September 15th, when they begin to give way. As they are coupled with the summer drought, they share its variability in duration and intensity. In the West Basin north of the 40th parallel they give place to north, northwest and southwest winds. The last two, which prevail on the west coast of Italy, are due to the permanent low pressure area in the Adriatic and sometimes bring rain.

The ancients knew how to utilize the winds not only in naval warfare but also on the land. Hannibal at the Battle of Cannæ disposed his forces to escape the violence of the Bora, which blew clouds of dust into the face of the Roman army to their confusion. Centuries later Theodoric the Great, invading Italy by way of the Carso Plateau, disposed his army in the same way upon the Venetian plain with their backs to the stormy Bora while the Roman defenders were exposed to its full violence.

TEMPERATURES—The Mediterranean seasons have little to
characterize them in point of temperature. The summers are
hot but not debilitating, because the heat is tempered by the
dry. north winds and the diurnal breezes which penetrate from
ten to twenty miles inland. The July heat in the West Basin
varies from 75° F. in northern Italy and the coast of France to
79° F. along the African littoral; but in the East Basin it averages somewhat higher, owing to the hot continental winds of
Asia and Africa. The western sides of the fringe of peninsulas
and islands are cooler in summer and warmer in winter owing
to the westerly winds, while the autumns in general are warmer
than the springs.

The winter temperatures are cold enough to be bracing, but
nevertheless are mild, considering the northern latitudes in
which the encircling lands are located. This is due to the
ameliorating influence of a large central body of water whose
winter temperature along the coasts is four to nine degrees F.
higher than that of the land, and in mid-sea from 1.6 to 3.4
degrees higher; to the submarine barrier in the Gibraltar Strait
which excludes the cold water of the Atlantic; and to the mountain screen on the north which fends off the cold blasts or
compels them to abate their chill in process of descent over the
barrier.

Extremes of winter temperature are less marked in the West
Basin than in the East Basin, because the former feels the
ameliorating influences of the Atlantic. The latter is swept by
cold northeast continental winds which chill the bordering lands
and force the January isotherm of 50° F. (10° C.) down to
the extremity of Italy, Greece and Cyprus, while this line in the
West Basin follows the coast of the Riviera and Spanish Catalonia. They give to Rhodes, Athens and Tarentum about the
same winter temperature as to Genoa, Nice and Barcelona,
though the latter lie 350 miles farther north.

Frost and snow occur at times almost everywhere in the encircling lands, but they are evanescent except in the mountains
and the Po valley, where snow may linger for a week. Athens
has a snowfall five or six days in the year; its temperature occasionally drops below freezing point. The southern limit of
frosts at sea level for the whole Basin runs along the southern

coast of the Iberian Peninsula, crosses to Sicily and the Ionian Isles, and crosses the extremity of the Peloponnesos to the Syrian coast.

However, the winter climate is mild. This fact, combined with the winter rains, makes the cooler half of the year the season of plant growth, both for natural vegetation and field crops, while the dry summer is the period of rest. The growing season in general is a long one, lasting from the warm humid autumn favorable for germination through the cool spring to the warm summer, which even at Rome begins before the end of May. Plant life is quiescent at the height of winter in January through half of February. There are numerous bright clear days in winter which make the sun effective in stimulating vegetation. Athens has 200 days annually with skies entirely clear or merely flecked with clouds, and only 93 days on which rain falls heavily for a few hours as a rule, and then gives way to brilliant sunshine. The mild rainy winters therefore form the climatic basis of Mediterranean agriculture, and assure to this favored region an adequate and varied food supply not obtainable by a system of summer tillage by irrigation.

SPECIAL PROVINCES—The Mediterranean region is only approximately a climatic unit. Owing to its great extent, its penetration through the Black Sea to the Caucasus Mountains and the Russian steppes at Odessa (46° N. Lat.) on the north, and nearly to the 30th parallel on the south; owing to the northward reach of the Adriatic and the Po River Basin to the foot of the Alps (46° N. Lat.), owing also to the large size and massive form of its big peninsulas, it includes within its geographic boundaries several minor climatic provinces which are only partly akin or even alien to the Mediterranean climate. They exercised a potent influence especially in ancient Mediterranean economic history because of their considerable area, and because they brought into close juxtaposition to the Mediterranean Climatic Region districts of contrasted climate and contrasted economic or social condition. The result was stimulation of commercial exchanges, the barter of finished Mediterranean manufactured articles like wine and textiles for the raw products of the retarded districts, or for the abundant supplies of food-stuffs furnished by a favored district of contrasted climate, soil and relief. The result was a mutual financial advantage, and a sounder, broader basis for economic security.

These special provinces were: I. The Scythian plains of southeast Europe forming the hinterland of the Black Sea. This is a district of low relief, continental climate with extremes of heat and cold, a meager rainfall of 12 to 20 inches, most of which comes between May and early July at an opportune season for the big wheat crops yielded by the fertile black-earth or chestnut soils. The rains are too scant for tree growth but suffice for the wide spread pastures of the steppes till late summer. This region supplied the ancient Greeks with wool, hides, cattle and grain. It included the lowland of the Crimea, but not the mountain coast belt of this peninsula, which had a genuine Riviera of typical Mediterranean climate, and furnished the Greek colonists settled on this coast with a congenial environment of mild winters and familiar vegetation.

II. The Caucasus and Armenian highlands enclosing the eastern end of the Black Sea, east of the 38th meridian, a densely forested region with a rainfall ranging from 30 to 60 inches, distributed throughout the year. In contrast to the rather scant woodlands of the Mediterranean Region, these lofty and rain-soaked highlands yielded a virtually inexhaustible supply of lumber, ship-timber, honey, wax and other forest products, which formed part of the return cargo on all the Grecian and Phœnician vessels visiting the Euxine coasts.

III. The Anatolian Plateau, rimmed around by the high and massive coastal ranges of Asia Minor, is a region of scant rainfall and interior drainage, with all the typical features of a steppe country. The rains come chiefly in spring and autumn. Draining the interior slopes of the mountains, they form occasional irrigation streams. These provide the water for the few settlements which dot the piedmont of both the northern and southern margin, and occupy the same sites marked in ancient times by the road towns of the main Anatolian highways leading to Persia and Mesopotamia. The vast salt pastures of this climatic province provided the wool of fine quality and exquisite color which found its way down to the Ægean coast of Asia Minor. There it furnished the raw material for the highly developed textile industry of Miletos and other Greek cities of

Ionia and Ætolia. This arid core of Asia Minor was also a breeding ground for nomadic hordes, which from time to time harried the frontier of the civilized seaboard, and later, in the Middle Ages, swarmed across the Hellespont into the Balkan Peninsula.

IV. Egypt, which is a climatic desert crossed by a fluvial oasis, is an alien province when compared with the Mediterranean Climatic Region. A rainfall of 8 inches at Alexandria, 3.2 inches at Port Said, 1.3 inches at Helwan, and virtually none up the Nile above this point would impose genuine desert conditions upon all life, were it not for the mountain-born Nile. On the other hand, the concept of "Mediterranean climate," from the standpoint of human geography as opposed to the science of climatology, includes the idea of sufficient rainfall for winter tillage without irrigation in average years, though not in exceptional years of deficient precipitation.

Tested by these standards Egypt is an alien in the Mediterranean climatic group of countries. As such it assumed enormous importance in ancient times, because its 10,000 square miles of fertile soil, yielding large and dependable harvests under irrigation tillage, made it the granary for the populous Mediterranean countries which were rather scantily provided by nature with good wheat land. One result was that the imperial politicians of Rome, in the second and third centuries of the Empire, based their hopes of power and office upon control of Egyptian wheat fields.

V. The Meseta Plateau of Spain, with the Ebro Valley, resembles the Anatolian Plateau in its extreme continental climate. It has cold winters with frequent frost and snow, hot dry summers, and scant rains which fall chiefly in spring and autumn. Hence it has extremely meager vegetation, and the country is in part only treeless steppes. Owing to the border barriers of mountains, it is not easily accessible from the coast, and bears all the marks of extreme isolation. In ancient times it supported a retarded race of warlike mountaineers, poor and intolerant of drudgery, who contributed nothing to Mediterranean trade except animals or hides to purchase wine from the Mediterranean coast settlements.

VI. The intermontane valley of the Po constitutes a transi-

tion province from the Mediterranean Climatic Region to the
rainy lands of Middle Europe. Owing to its location between
two mountain systems near the northern margin of the Mediterranean Basin, it gets its maximum rainfall in spring and
autumn with frequent thunderstorms in summer, with the result
that it receives the larger share of its precipitation in the warm
half of the year. Hence the rich alluvial soil gets abundant
moisture during the entire year, and tillage is uninterrupted
though the winters are cold. From ancient times it was famous
for its ample agricultural products, and its live-stock pastured
in meadows whose grass crops were doubled or tripled by irrigation. The tall forests on its mountains or plains'exported lumber, casks or barrels to the urban centers of Italy, so that its
contributions to Mediterranean exchanges were generous and
valuable.

CHANGES OF CLIMATE IN HISTORICAL TIMES—The question has been repeatedly raised as to whether there have been
changes of climate in historical times, especially rainfall fluctuations, sufficient to explain the decline and fall of the Roman
Empire and the decadence of civilization, by reason of which
large sections of the Mediterranean lands, once thriving and
populous, have become depopulated or impoverished. Arguments supporting this position have been advanced chiefly by
historians, archæologists, and other incompetent authorities not
concerned with climatology. The large majority of competent
authorities have reached a contrary conclusion. These are
Hann, Sir Napier Shaw, Alfred Philippson, Robert DeC. Ward,
L. Berg, De Martonne and D. G. Hogarth, though Philippson
thinks increased desiccation on the fringe of the Syrian steppe
possible. Arrayed on the side of these authorities are Egnitis,
Mariolopoulos, Bursian, Neumann and Partsch for Greece;
Hildebrand, J. W. Gregory and Hermann Leiter for Cyrenaica
and Egypt; Eduard Meyer, P. Rohrbach and Ewald Banse for
Palestine, Syria, and Mesopotamia; and Dr. von Geisan for
Samos. Theobald Fischer cited Cyrenaica in evidence of a
change of climate, but his arguments were refuted by Gregory
and Hildebrand. Ellsworth Huntington attributed the decline
of Palestine, Syria, Asia Minor, Greece and Italy to the same

cause, but his arguments have been questioned both by historians and climatologists.

More than this, many facts of ancient and modern Mediterranean life point to marked stability of climatic conditions in historical times. This is proved by the practical identity of crops, leaving out of account certain fruits and grains introduced by the Saracens in the seventh and eighth centuries; by the persistence of old tillage methods, of the dates of ploughing, sowing and harvesting, and the time taken by the crops for maturing. In Hesiod's time (750 b.c.) wheat fields were sown between October 20th and November 25th, and the harvest began May 15th. These were the dates for Bœotia.[13] Today the sowing of wheat takes place in all Greece in general from the middle of October to the middle of November; but in Bœotia, according to the Minister of Agriculture for Greece, it begins precisely on the 20th of October. After a detailed study of ancient Mediterranean tillage, the author has been struck by the amazing agreement between ancient and modern dates and methods. The climate of Bœotia today is just as Hesiod described it—cold and raw in winter, hot and humid in summer, the continental climate of a mountain-rimmed lake basin.

The causes of decline are to be sought not in a changed climate, but in denudation of the hillside soil, deforestation with the failure of springs, destruction of irrigation works by barbarian or nomad attack, collapse of orderly government under repeated barbarian inroads, and possibly to the exhaustion of the soil, causing agricultural decline.

AUTHORITIES—CHAPTER V

1. Bibliography for the Mediterranean climate, providing the data used in this chapter.
   Sir Napier Shaw, *Manual of Meteorology*, 2 Vols. Cambridge, 1926.
   J. Hann, *Handbuch der Klimatologie*, 3 Vols. Stuttgart, 1908-1911.
   Theobald Fischer, *Studien über das Klima der Mittelmeerländer, Pet. Mitt. Ergänz.* No. 58, 1879. *Mittelmeerbilder.* Leipzig, 1908. *Die Sudeuropäischen Halbinseln*, in *Kirchhofs Länderkunde von Europa.* Leipzig, 1893.
   A. Philippson, *Das Mittelmeergebiet.* Leipzig, 1907.
   F. Trzebitsky, *Studien über die Niederschlagsverhältnisse auf den Sudosteuropäischen Halbinseln.* 1911.
   R. Fitzner, *Niederschlag und Bewölkung in Kleinasien, Pet. Mitt. Ergänz*, No. 140. 1902.

Neumann und Partsch, *Physikalische Geographie von Griechenland.* Breslau, 1885.

E. G. Mariolopoulos, *Etude sur le climat de la Grèce.* Paris, 1925.

G. Hildebrand, *Cyrenaika.* Bonn, 1904.

Alexander Knox, *Climate of Africa.* Cambridge, 1911.

E. Banse, *Die Turkei.* Braunschweig, 1916 and 1919.

A. E. Mitard, *Pluviosité de la Bordure sud-oriental du Massif Central, Revue de Géographie Alpine,* Vol. XV, pp. 8-45. 1927.

H. Leiter, *Die Frage der Klimaänderung während historischer Zeit in Nordafrika.* Vienna, 1909.

E. Huntington, *Palestine and Its Transformation.* Boston, 1911.

J. L. Myres, "The Burial of Olympia," *Geog. Jour.,* Vol. 36, pp. 657-687.

L. Berg, *Das Problem der Klimaänderung in geschichtlicher Zeit.* Leipzig, 1914.

C. E. P. Brooks, *Evolution of Climate.* London, 1922.

J. W. Gregory, "Is the Earth Drying up?" *Geog. Jour.,* Vol. 48, pp. 148-172, 293-318. 1914. "Cyrenaica," *Geog. Jour.,* pp. 321-345. 1916.

E. Huntington and Visher, *Climatic Changes: Their Nature and Causes.* Yale University Press, 1922.

H. A. Matthews, "The Mediterranean Climates of Eurasia and the Americas," *Scott. Geog. Mag.,* Vol. 40, pp. 150-159. 1924.

Th. Findiklis, "La Température de l'air a Athènes," *Annales de l'Observatoire National d'Athènes,* Vol. X. 1928. Athens.

2. Mariolopoulos, *op. cit.,* pp. 24-25.

3. Figures from Mariolopoulos and Hann.

4. A. Woeikoff, *Klimate der Erde,* Vol. II, pp. 106-107. Jena, 1887.

5. *Proverbs,* XIII, 15; XVI, 15.

6. Theophrastus, *De Historia Plantarum,* IV, Chap. III, 7; VIII, Chap. VI, 6.

7. *Deuteronomy,* XXXIII, 13, 28; *Genesis,* XXVII, 28; I. *Kings,* XVII, 1.

8. *Odyssey,* XIII, 243-244.

9. E. Huntington, *Palestine and Its Transformation,* p. 425. Boston, 1911.

10. Aristotle, *Meteorology,* II, 6.

11. Theophrastus, *De Causis Plantarum,* II, Chap. III, 1-2.

12. *Isaiah,* XXVII, 8; *Hosea,* XII, 1; XIII, 15.

13. Hesiod, *Works and Days,* 385, 614.

CHAPTER VI

THE RIVERS OF THE MEDITERRANEAN LANDS

ALIEN RIVERS—Large river systems with stable volume do not properly belong to the Mediterranean region. Various natural conditions militate against their development: climate, relief, close-hugging barriers of mountains and deserts, deeply indented coasts breaking up the adjacent lands into peninsulas and islands with small drainage areas. A few big rivers of this kind debouch into the Mediterranean, but they have their sources far outside the region: they are foreign-born. One such immigrant, the Nile, comes from Africa, progeny of the great Equatorial Lakes and the monsoon rains on the highlands of Abyssinia. Asia's fluvial contributions are insignificant. But Europe sends the Rhone, the Danube draining a series of mountain-rimmed basins, and the group of long Russian rivers flowing with gentle currents down the southeastern plains and maintaining an even volume by the summer rains of a continental climate.

These intruding streams, few in number, attained great historical importance in ancient and medieval times because they opened up to Mediterranean trade and colonization regions of contrasted climate and civilization. In addition, each had a distinctive rôle. The Nile was a busy highway connecting the Mediterranean Sea with the Orient; it supported the chief granary of the basin; and its punctual, mysterious floods were a century-long riddle which stirred scientific speculation among ancient geographers. The Rhone stimulated Mediterranean industry and trade from that unknown date when the river traffic began to deliver tin to Massiliot merchants, introduced competitive prices, and broke the Phœnician tin monopoly of Gades. The northern Euxine rivers delivered the bulky products of pasture land and grain fields at their debouchure ports, which were colonized by Greeks; but their hinterland was too cold and too alien in culture to invite Hellenic settlement. The Scythian

102

rivers, moreover, afforded admirable port sites, ten to twenty
miles from the sea on their high right banks, which rose in
bluffs above the broad *liman* or estuary mouth.   Such was the
site of Tyras, a Milesian colony on the Dneister *liman*, of Olbia
on the Bug and Tanais on the Don, protected from floods, accessible to cargo boats from the Ægean and to hinterland products arriving by barge or skiff from the upper river or by
Scythian wagon lumbering over the level steppe.[1]

The Danube delta, on the other hand, afforded its first feasible sites far up its southern distributary, where the Dobrudja
Highland extended to the river and overlooked its flood plain.
This arm of the Danube was navigated by the fleet of Darius in
512 B.C. and later by that of Alexander the Great, but its backward hinterland repelled Greek traders.   However, an Argo-
naut tradition indicates the exploration of the Danube to the
upper Save, and the pseudo-Aristotle reports a trading post
somewhere on the middle Danube,[2] where merchants from the
Adriatic brought Corcyrean jars to exchange for wares from
Lesbos, Thasos, and Chios, thus indicating some commercial
traffic on this river.

The tributaries of the Danube which had their sources near
the Adriatic in the Carnic Alps and Illyria were known to the
Romans as navigable and utilized by Augustus to forward supplies downstream to the frontier province of Dacia.   Native
tribes of the Drave, Save, and Kulpa navigated these streams
in dug-outs and rafts, and were employed by the Roman forces
in 35 B.C. for the river attack on the Pannonian stronghold of
Siscia (Segesta) which was needed as a base for operations
against the Dacians.[3]   The most straight west-east course of
the Save-Danube subtended the base of the Balkan Peninsula,
and offered a waterway of gentle current from the Adriatic
divide to the Euxine.   It therefore became a highway for the
expanding Romans, who in time constructed a canal around the
rapids of the Iron Gate.

CLIMATIC FACTORS—To these large continental rivers, the
native-born Mediterranean streams present a marked contrast.
They all bear the stamp of the Mediterranean climate.   The
vast majority are periodic, flowing full during the winter rains,
swollen to flood proportions by storms or spring thaws in the

mountain snows, shrinking in the summer droughts to mere
trickles, or drying up into drifts of sand and gravel, broken
here and there by stagnant pools. The variability of their
volume is intensified by their small catchment basins and rapid
run-off, due to the prevailing mountain relief. Hence many
torrents plunging down their canyons become intermittent even
in winter. They are wet-weather streams, born of the mountain storm and dying in the sunshine—the old familiar myth
of the children of Niobe slain by the darts of Apollo. Such are
the *wadis* of Syria and north Africa, the *fiumares* of Italy and
the *ramblas* of Spain. In summer their broad sandy or pebbly
beds afford natural highways of easy gradient, which are used
today in various Mediterranean countries. They served this
purpose even more in antiquity. Along such wadis Ptolemy
Philadelphus (274 B.C.) opened the roads from Coptos on the
Nile southeast to Berenice on the Red Sea, and east to *Leucos
Limen* (Kosseir) by the Wadi Hammamat. He sunk wells to the
ground water in the dry stream beds, where water was regularly
sought by ancient travellers in the border deserts of the Mediterranean lands. In the Wadi of Gerar, Abraham and Isaac
dug wells for their flocks in southern Palestine, and in a similar
wadi bed of the arid Moab country Elisha dug ditches to provide water for the invading Israelite army.

Mediterranean rivers have a more stable volume where they
drain the rainy western side of mountain ranges, like the Achelous of Acarnania and the Arnus (Arno) of Etruria, or rise
in mountains whose summits are accessible to the rain-bearing
westerly winds, like the Eurotas River of Laconia or the Peneus
of Thessaly. All streams are perennial which have their sources
in high mountains of summer showers, lingering snows and
ample forest covering. Such were the Leontes and Orontes
draining the flanks of the Lebanon and Anti-Lebanon Mountains, and "the rivers of Damascus" which created the great
oasis on the desert's edge; such was "the ever-flowing Cratis" of
Herodotus, rising near to the summit of Arcadian Aroania
(Mount Khelmos 7,724 feet), and the persistent but fluctuating
Bagradas of the Atlas valleys.

Smaller perennial streams, invaluable for irrigation and domestic water supply through all the historical period, had their

source in unfailing kephalaria or "fountain-heads," outlets of underground karst reservoirs, like numerous small rivers crossing the Plain of Sharon in Palestine, the lower Kishon, the Ladon branch of the Alpheus, and many streams of Epiros and southern Italy. In Argolis, "thirsty Argos" of the ancients, only the little kephalaria brook Erasinus reaches the sea in summer, so that the ancients correctly regarded its fountainhead as the outlet of a katavothra lake in highland Arcadia. With this exception, the whole east side of the Peloponnesos from the Isthmus to the Eurotas River has only intermittent wet-weather streams, while the west-side rivers are all perennial, and even the brooks persist throughout the winter.[4] A similar contrast in abated form can be noted between the east and west sides of Judea, Phœnicia, Hellas, the Italian and Spanish peninsulas: penury of water on the sunrise fronts, husbanding of the meager supply during the summer drought, sanctification of the precious fountains, all marks of a rigid water economy; towards the sunset, massing of clouds in an angry sky, perennial brooks, ample streams for irrigation, unfailing fountains, and occasional navigable rivers.

EROSION AND DEPOSITION—The Mediterranean rivers, owing to local conditions of climate and relief, have always been active agents of erosion and deposition. So conspicuous were these processes that they impressed the ancient mind, and led to the deduction of sound physiographic principles surprisingly advanced in an otherwise unscientific age. Here was an intellectual response to stimuli emanating from the physical environment. The conclusions reached were sound because they were the scientific outgrowth of age-long efforts to cope with river erosion and deposition: scientific theory and technical practice went hand in hand.

Erosion and denudation are rapid and persistent in the Mediterranean lands. Torrents race down the steep slopes in approximately parallel courses, carving out V-shaped gorges till they emerge upon the narrow coastal plain. During the summer drought, when the streams shrink to shreds and patches along their pebbly valley-floors, the sun bakes and cracks their banks; the dry north winds blow a gale and reduce the soil of the adjacent fields to dust; the Sirocco from Africa grinds off rock surfaces with its wind-borne Saharan sands, which sting the face like a thousand fairy flagellants and gnaw away the south sides of temple columns, as one sees them at Girgenti (Agrigentum) today. Then come the autumn storms. They wash away this veneer of waste into the swollen streams, gully the freshly ploughed fields, and draw off the liquid mud. The torrents increase their erosive and transporting power with their volume, tear away clods from their cracked banks and add to their burden of silt. Hence classical references to "the yellow Scamander" of the Trojan plain, "the yellow Xanthos" of Lycia, "the muddy Axius" of the Macedonian border, "the tawny Tiber with its burden of sand," "the pebbly Hermus" [5] of Lydia, and the *turbidi torrentes* in general, all descriptive expressions for the suspended matter in the flood-time streams. The ancients recognized the connection between tillage and river-borne silt. According to Frontinus, the water of the Anio aqueduct was muddy and fit only to irrigate the gardens about Rome, because it was supplied by the Anio River which drained an agricultural valley.[6] Pausanias considered that the Achelous River of western Hellas carried less silt than most streams owing to the untilled condition of its upper valley in the highland of Ætolia, which was devoted chiefly to grazing; and for this reason the river had failed to advance the shoreline of Acarnania to the Echinades Islands, as had long been predicted.[7]

The ancients understood all the features of deposition: the accumulation of alluvium about the river mouth, the formation of sandbars and deltas, of low deposit islands and spits interspersed with marshes and lagoons, the shoaling of off-shore waters whereby vessels grounded far from the coast, the slow aggradation of the silted area to high flood level, and the gradual protrusion of the shoreline to enclose off-shore islands and tie them to the mainland. Strabo states the general principle that rivers are checked in the seaward advance of their silt deposits by the action of the tides, because the fluvial current ceases a short distance beyond the mouth; that the amount of silt deposited depends upon the rocky or "soft" character of the adjacent land and the number of the torrent tributaries. "The Scamander and Simois rivers, uniting in the plain of

Troy, bring down a great quantity of mud, bank up the sea coast, and form a blind mouth, salt lagoons and marshes." Strabo observed that the Meander River of Asia Minor dropped some of its silt along the shore and forced some of it out into the open sea; and that these depositions through the centuries had made Priene an inland city debarring it from the sea by a silt belt five miles wide.[8] The mouth of the Cayster River, which served as the port of Ephesos, was shoaled by accumulations of silt, till it was no longer accessible to large cargo vessels. Trying to remedy this evil, Attalus Philadelphus constructed a mole across the wide mouth of the Cayster; but he only made matters worse by accelerating the mud accumulations. Strabo observed that previously the slight ebb and flow of the sea had helped to clear the channel.[9]

Hecatæus of Miletos (500 B.C.) was the first to call Egypt "the gift of the Nile." Herodotus, with the Hellenic ear for the apt phrase, borrowed the expression and enlarged upon the underlying physiographic principle. Quoting the Egyptian priests, he stated that the Nile had filled an old bay with its alluvial plain, whose soil differed from that of the land on either side; he conceived that the Nile, diverted into the Red Sea, could fill up this gulf in ten to twenty thousand years, and convert it into a new Egypt. The Nile was to him a prototype of other land-building rivers like the Scamander in the Trojan plain, the Caicus, Cayster, and Meander of Asia Minor whose fertile lowlands supported rich cities.[10] In the same way, Aristotle surmised the probable silting up of the Palus Mæotis (Sea of Azof), because sixty years previously ships visiting its ports found deeper water than during his time, with the result that smaller vessels had come into use. He saw the process quite clearly: the coastal waters invaded by river sediment, their conversion into marshes and eventually into dry land.[11] Polybius describes scientifically the delta of the Danube, "which ejects its silt nearly 1,000 stadia into the Euxine as far as its current"; the river sandbars and deposit islands called "the Breasts," located a day's sail from the shore where ships strand. He predicted the eventual silting up of the whole Euxine and Propontis (Marmara) in the course of ages.[12]

The "tying" of inshore islands to the coast by fluvial de-

posits was a commonplace to the ancients.　Herodotus cites the
case of the Achelous River of Acarnania, whose silt had already
cemented half the Echinades Islands to the mainland,[13] and
Pliny reports that its deposits were fast enveloping another
island in his day.[14]　Strabo states that the Pyramus River of
Cilicia had advanced the coastline by its deposits, and that according to the oracle the river would one day extend its banks
to the island of Cyprus.[15]　Pliny mentions two islets cemented
to the Milesian coast, another to the Ephesian coast, while the
quondam Ionian island of Hybanda lay in his time 200 stadia or
23 miles inland.　Moreover, the hill citadel of Epidauros in Argolis was no longer an island, nor was Oricum in the Gulf of Avlona in Illyria.　So also Mount Circei, known to Theophrastus
as an island of Latium with a circuit of 80 stadia, by Pliny's
time had become attached to the plain of the Pontine marshes,[16]
after an interval of 380 years.　The ancients did not fail to
read aright the physiographic history of the promontories of
Populonia and Mount Argentarius as converted islands of the
Etruscan coast.　Pliny, however, in some cases erroneously
ascribed the conversion of these islands into peninsulas to the
recession of the sea.[17]　Such was the origin of the Acte promontory of Attica, in his opinion.

The ancients utilized with nice discrimination the various
parts of the silted districts.　They reserved the rich alluvium of
the drained portions for their exacting wheat crops, and used
the marshes as hay meadows or wet pastures during the summer droughts for the horses and cattle.　The lakes and lagoons
yielded a large revenue as preserves for fish and oysters, like
those of the Cayster which belonged to the temple of Diana of
Ephesos and in Strabo's time became the subject of a lawsuit
at Rome.　The river itself, whether single or multiple with
various distributaries, was generally a problem; it was prone to
shift its channel after every freshet, to the detriment of navigation and the confusion of farm boundaries.　Aristotle observed
that the Achelous River had often changed its course.[18]　The
Anser (Serchio) of Etruria at one time flowed into the Arnus
(Arno) just below Pisa, but in Strabo's day had an independent mouth; and there were indications that it had altered
its watery track more than once.[19]　The mouths of the Rhone

were variously stated at different times to number two, three, five, or even seven. For the Danube, two mouths were mentioned by Eratosthenes, five by Herodotus and Ephorus, seven by Strabo, Ovid and Pliny. The ancients spoke of the "mouths of the Meander," "mouths of the Axius," as the common feature.

RIVER FLOODS—Associated with these shifting, braided channels were the recurrent floods which characterized the Mediterranean rivers on every level stretch of their course, whether inland or coastal. This was their history from the Pyrenees to Palestine, as it is today. So long as they pour muddy waters down their deeply eroded valleys in the mountains, they do little damage; but when they emerge upon the plain, they overlap their low banks and spread their debris over the cultivated land. Stories of widespread inundations, coupled with efforts at flood control, were recorded for the Peneus River in the old lake plain of Thessaly, the Alpheus in Elis, the Clanis in Etruria, the Trebia and Ticinus in the middle Po valley, the Druentia (Durance) in southern Gaul, the Orontes in Cœlo-Syria, and countless others. Everywhere the physical conditions for such floods prevailed—bold relief, torrential run-off from the slopes, catastrophic winter storms, coincidence of spring rains with the melting of snow on the mountains, and in the plains constant deposition of silt which choked the outlets and retarded the flow-off.

Echoes of these floods permeate classical literature. The Jew, who often saw a single storm convert a trickling wadi into a raging river, adopted it as the symbol of overwhelming trouble, "the deep waters" of adversity. The terrifying voice of God "was like the sound of many waters," [20] the roar of the swollen torrent which announced the oncoming flood to some wayfarer trapped between the deep wadi walls. The power of God was ruthless, like a stream in flood. Jehovah saved the Israelites from defeat in the battle of the Kishon valley by a storm, which soaked the adhesive alluvium, mired the horses and chariots of Sisera, and overwhelmed his forces in the ensuing flood. "The River of Kishon swept them away, that torrent of spates, the river Kishon." [21]

The inundations were a recurrent danger during the whole

period of winter tillage, and they expended their devastating force particularly upon the scant but fertile alluvial plains with dire effects for the ancient Mediterranean farmer. "The swift-moving flood from a mountain stream overwhelms the fields, lays low the smiling crops, wipes out the work of the oxen, and sweeps the forest with it headlong," a catastrophe which Vergil had doubtless witnessed on his father's farm along the Mincio River.[22] He knew too the ominous accompaniment: "The roaring torrent gives forth a noise with its rocks and whirling eddy." [23] In like manner "the far-sounding Aufidus" of Horace, sweeping down from Mount Vultur (4,365 feet), trumpeted the impending flood to the farms and pastures of the Apulian plain, just as it does today. The ancients symbolized the River Achelous in flood by a roaring bull, and as a serpent with sinuous folds when the shrunken summer stream meandered through its deltaic flats.[24] They attributed to Heracles, engineer hero, the control of the flood waters of the Achelous by dykes and ditches, which reclaimed the fertile soil to tillage. Homer vividly describes the devastating work of the winter torrent, sweeping along tree trunks, gravel and silt, and depositing them around any obstacle in its course; but he also testified to the dykes and dams built even in his time to restrain the swollen stream within its banks.[25]

The annual floods of the Nile timed their coming by the punctual stars. They dominated all Egyptian life, which therefore represented a nearly perfect adjustment to the fluvial environment. Not so the floods of the Tiber, which reflected highly variable rainfall and temperatures. As the largest river of peninsular Italy with innumerable mountain tributaries, its capacity for destructive spates was impressive especially in the Latium plain about the Roman capital. Floods occurred twice in 215 B.C. when the Tiber inundated cropland, demolished houses, and caused great loss of human life and cattle. They came again in 204 B.C. and swamped the Circus Maximus,[26] which lay in the narrow valley between the Palatine and Aventine hills. In 105 A.D. violent winter storms and cloudbursts caused both the Tiber and Anio to overflow the adjacent lowlands when houses, furniture, farming implements and cattle went floating down the tawny tide.[27] Finally in the reign of

Tiberius, the Tiber floods had become such a menace to Rome, probably in consequence of increasing denudation of the Apennine forests, that the senate proposed to divert some of its tributaries as source lakes. But this scheme for flood control aroused protests from the nearby valleys. The city of Florentia objected to the River Clanis being turned into the Arno, which was already subject to floods. The town of Interamna protested that the alteration of the Nar river course would expose to inundation the richest plains of Italy, and Reate opposed for a like reason any stoppage of the outlet of Lake Fucinus.[28] The Emperor Claudius finally dug an additional channel for the lower Tiber to facilitate the discharge of water and thus prevent the inundations at Rome. The floods of the Arno frequently converted its valley floor into extensive swamps, like those in which Hannibal and his forces floundered for four days on his invasion of Etruria in 217 B.C. Hannibal unwisely began his march over the mountains before the advent of spring,—*jam ver appetebat*,—ignorant that the snows on the southern slope of the Apennines often melted in February, when the rains were still heavy.[29]

This recurrent danger in Mediterranean lands enforced a discriminating selection of house and town sites. In Palestine it was the custom to place a farm dwelling on rock foundations well above the stream, so that "when the rains descended and the floods came and the winds blew and beat upon that house, it fell not." It was the part of a fool to locate his building on the sand where the wadi opened out upon the plain, where the rising waters would undermine the foundations and sweep it away. Rome itself often saw the collapse of houses whose foundations had been weakened by the Tiber flood. Varro and Columella warn against placing farm house and buildings near a river, unless the stream has high banks and is distant from the hills, because a sudden shower may cause an overflow and damage the villa foundations.[30]

The same principle applied to cities in valley plains. Artificial mounds, constructed by war prisoners and criminals, lifted the Egyptian cities above the Nile floods; they resembled the Cyclades islands dotting the Ægean Sea. The nucleus of Larissa in Thessaly was a hill acropolis, 85 feet high, located on the neck of a river loop peninsula, which was too exposed to the Peneus floods for settlement; but the hill site was occupied from pre-Hellenic times, as the only spot protected from inundation and hostile attack.[31]   Such was the ridge site of Ilium above the plain of the lawless Scamander, whose numerous tributaries drained 25 miles of the Mount Ida range (5,740 feet) and were likely to put it in flood after every winter rain.   A heavy storm sufficed to inundate the city of Ephesos if the drains of the Cayster were obstructed, as was done by Lysimachus;[32] only its little citadel emerged, while the silting of ages long since covered the ruins of the temple of Artemis.   A similar fate met Olympia and its sacred precincts, despite a slightly elevated location above the Alpheus plain.   The broad flood plain of the Tiber River is flanked by rocky promontories running out into the low alluvium capped by ruins of old towns like Fidenæ which served as Etruscan bridge-head on the right Tiber bank 5 miles from Rome.   In the Bætis (Guadalquivir) valley of Spain there were no towns above Hispalis (Seville) on the oft-flooded south bank, which is low and offers no protected sites.   Hence the settlements edged back twenty miles or more from the Bætis to higher ground on the entrenched streams flowing down from the Sierra Nevada.

Valley roads tended to skirt the river plains and hug the piedmont rim in order to reach solid ground above the flooded alluvium.   Thus they linked the piedmont towns; but crossing the alluvial fans at the outlet of lateral valleys from the mountains, they were exposed to winter and spring freshets.   This flood state of the winter roads may partly explain the custom of restricting military campaigns to the summer.   Where wadi beds furnished the only trails, this reason was especially cogent. Homer's dramatic description of Achilles' struggle with the turbulent Scamander River applied to later wayfarers along this great trunk road between Asia Minor and Thrace.   The hero feared he might drown "like a swineherd boy whom a torrent sweeps downstream as he tries to cross it in a storm." For the Scamander, which has its sources "in many-fountained Ida," shows the immediate effect of a storm on that mountain, and has taken its toll of life for ages.   As the Persian army, in the spring of 480 B.C. marched along this route, they camped for the night under Mount Ida and experienced there a typical spring thunder storm, which "destroyed a considerable number of troops on the spot," Herodotus says, but evidently a freshet in one of its deep valleys did the damage. When the army reached the Scamander, the river was too low to provide drinking water for men and beasts.[33] The further route westward along the coast road of Thrace crossed several rivers which did not suffice for the army, among them the Nestus, though it drained from the Rhodope highland and often flooded the fertile Abdera plain.[34] Even the Hebrus (Maritza) proved fordable at this season. But "the great Strymon River" had an evil reputation on this coast, for Xerxes propitiated it by sacrificing white horses and previously had a bridge constructed across it above the river seaport of Eion.

All the Roman roads of Italy followed the valley piedmont and avoided the rivers, except at certain vantage points feasible for bridges. Such was the course of the *Via Latina* down the valley of the Trerus-Liris system to its junction with the Appian Way at Casinum in Campania, and of the *Via Æmilia*, which traced the Apennine piedmont of the Po basin from the Adriatic coast at Ariminum to Placentia, touching the various piedmont cities between. All of these were located on interfluvial spaces between the Apennine affluents of the Po or on minor streams, thus safeguarded from the floods, though their altitudes ranged only from 30 to 50 meters (100 to 165 feet). From Placentia, situated half a mile from the south bank of the Po between the braided courses of the Trebia and Nura, the Postumian Way branched north, skirting the lower rim of the sand and gravel deposits from the Alps, and led through Cremona, Verona, and Vicentia to Aquileia "by the roots of the Alps and encircling the marshes," according to Strabo.[35]

The coast road from the Gallo-Italian frontier to the Rhone and Iberia suffered from the torrents draining the rainy slopes of the Alps and Cevennes Plateau. They caused washouts even in summer. Therefore after the first rough track was converted into the Via Julia Augusta, it was still "muddy and flooded by rivers in winter and spring." Some of the streams were crossed by ferry boats and others by means of bridges.[36]

The construction and maintenance of bridges presented re-

current problems. These undoubtedly explain the admirable
technique developed by Roman engineers, and their discernment
in the selection of bridge sites in the lowlands. For instance,
the Via Julia Augusta swung far inland to cross the Rhone.
Though it passed through the market town of Arelate at the
head of the delta and therefore above the bifurcation of the
river, it turned eight miles farther north to find a feasible transit point for the bridge. There it found a rare combination of
geographic features. A low limestone ridge from the Provence
Hills crossed the moist plain like a natural causeway, lifted 16
feet above flood level. It was nicked in the middle by a narrow
trench where the Rhone had eroded a passage through. The
river thus constricted was easy to span, while the low limestone
bluffs on either bank formed perfect bridgehead sites, both for
construction and later for defence. Here grew up garrison
towns which persist today as Tarascon and Beaucaire. This
was probably the spot chosen by Hannibal for his passage of
the Rhone, "where the stream was single," at a distance of four
days' march from the sea. It not only offered a dry approach
for his army, but it also lay directly west of the point (Cavil-
lon) where he made his difficult crossing of the Druentia
(Durance).[37] That river combined all the evils of Alpine
streams. Swollen to immense volumes by the autumn showers,
its swift current, shifting channels, and its treacherous boulder-
strewn bed which offered dangerous footing, united to impede
the passage of Hannibal's troops.[38] The stately Pont du Gard
near Nîmes over a western affluent of the lower Rhone in the
same district survives today to show how effectively Roman
bridge-builders coped with the problem of spanning mountain
rivers with road and aqueduct.

It is significant of the toll of life collected by swollen streams
that the Romans regarded bridges as infringement of the rights
of the river god by depriving him of sacrificial lives of the
drowned. Hence Father Tiber was appeased by annual sacrifices offered by the Pontifex. Human victims were cast into the
river from the Sublician bridge in very early times, but later
effigies were substituted. This bridge, which linked Rome with
the Janiculum Hill fort on the right bank of the Tiber, was
swept away by a flood in 69 A.D.[39]

Greek bridges on the other hand were simple affairs, merely broad earthen dykes forming a causeway suited for inundated districts. The stream flowed away through culverts. This is the type which the traveller sees today across the four-mile outlet of the Sperchius River valley in eastern Hellas. The Greek river was usually small enough to be forded, especially at the sand and gravel reef which grew up every summer across its mouth. But when Greece was incorporated in the Roman Empire, the imperial government, with a view to rapid land communication, constructed great bridges in its new territories like the 1,000-foot bridge across the Acheron River of Epiros.[40]

DIVERSION OF RIVERS—The shifting channels of rivers in flood gave repeated object lessons in river diversion. Profiting by these lessons, the ancients practised the principles involved on a small scale in reclamation and irrigation, and on a larger scale in certain military operations. They understood the principle of *divide et impera* as applied to rivers. When the Lydian army under Crœsus invaded the Persian territory of Asia Minor in 546 B.C. they found the Halys River impassable; under the direction of Thales of Miletos, who had spent some time in Egypt, they diverted part of the river and made the channels fordable.[41] By the same device, Cæsar escaped from a predicament during his war with Pompey in northeast Spain. A flood, caused by a storm and sudden thaw in the Pyrenees, washed away the bridges over the Sicoris and Cinga flanking his camp, thus cutting him off from his foraging district and also from a new convoy of supplies from Gaul and Italy. Both rivers were too swift and deep to permit reconstruction of the bridges, especially under hostile attacks. To escape starvation, Cæsar began turning the Sicoris into an artificial channel to render it fordable.[42] The people of Croton succeeded in taking Sybaris (510 B.C.) by diverting the River Crathis and inundating the town.[43] When the city of Mantinea in Arcadia was built on the old lake plain, the little river Ophis was made to encircle the walls as a moat; but when the Spartans attacked the place in 385 B.C. they had only to flood the Ophis by a dam and thereby undermine the city walls so that they fell.[44] Xerxes saw the possibility of a parallel operation when he observed the outflow of the Peneus through the Vale of

Tempe, for he remarked upon the ease of damming the stream and submerging the Thessalian plain as a means of conquering the country.[45]

RIVER NAVIGATION—The Mediterranean rivers are not only handicapped by the climate, but they are dwarfed by the rugged relief, which parcels up the land already subdivided by bays or narrowed by deserts. Hence navigable systems comparable to the great intruding streams cannot originate within the region. The largest rivers, small at best, develop only in the troughs between distinct mountain systems, which provide ample catchment basins. Such are the Guadalquivir, Ebro, Po, and Maritza. Their trunk streams profit by the slow run-off in the valley plains, which not only conserves their water but also facilitates navigation. Hence all were commercial waterways in ancient times. They acquired importance because, like the Rhone and Danube, they opened up the colonial frontier districts of the Roman republic. The Bætis (Guadalquivir) was navigable for sea-going vessels 54 miles up to Hispalis (Seville), and for river boats 80 miles farther to Corduba (Cordova). It served to bring out the oil, wine, and various raw products of a fertile province and deliver them for export to the numerous ships in the river-seaports.[46] The Ebro was a busy thoroughfare in its navigable middle course for 250 miles below Vereia (Logrons),[47] but opened no waterway thence to the sea; because through the Catalonian coast mountains it traverses a hundred-mile gorge, so winding and narrow where it cuts through the lias and trias, that it was impassable for boats. Hence traffic avoided this stretch. It made a detour by the Roman road from the coast at Tarraco (Tarragona) and crossed the Catalonian range at 3,320 feet (1,012 meters) to Ilerda on the Sicoris (Segre), a tributary of the Ebro.[48] This detour of 59 miles made Tarraco the emporium of the whole Ebro basin,[49] though the town had no harbor, scarcely an anchorage, and lay forty miles north of the river mouth.

The Maritza River (Hebrus), whose basin is flanked by the snowy ranges of the Balkan and Rhodope Mountains, opened up Thrace, which was a frontier region for Greek and Macedonian enterprise, as later for the Romans. According to Strabo, it was navigable from its seaport Ænos for fifteen miles

up to Cypsela (Ipsala), possibly the limit for large boats, and
yet farther up nearly to Philippopolis in the Bessi country; [50] but this latter statement doubtless applied only to small
boats or rafts, for the river shifts its bed and forms sandbanks
in the Philippopolis basin. The river god Hebrus was represented on the coins of ancient Philippopolis with ears of wheat
or a horn of plenty or reeds in his hand, thus emphasizing his
irrigation of the soil rather than navigation.

The Po was the one wholly Mediterranean river navigable
on a considerable scale. It had an ample volume throughout
the year, owing to summer rains and melting snow, and flowed
with gentle current through its level plain; while its long
course, numerous lakes, navigable tributaries and canals constituted a complex system of inland waterways. Its several
mouths offered safe anchorage on an otherwise harborless coast,
and its broad deep channel carried ships 250 miles upstream to
Augusta Taurinorum (Turin), originally a Ligurian settlement. As early as 218 B.C. the Romans transported supplies
up the Po to their forces at Cremona during Hannibal's invasion of Cisalpine Gaul,[51] and later used it to bring out the raw
products of a fertile province. It was "the King of Italian
rivers," and "by its bounteous channel conveys the gifts of
all the seas" to a large inland region.[52] Spring and summer
small boats, laden with bee-hives and poled along its banks,
enabled the bees to pasture on its flowery meadows, Pliny
reports.

The limited group of navigable streams included also the
Tiber, which occupied no intermontane basin, but drew its tributaries from the longitudinal valleys of the Central Apennines;
it therefore drained a long stretch of well-watered highlands.
Even so, it had a slender volume by midsummer. The upper
course was then rendered navigable by means of dams and
sluices and its water was impounded sometimes for nine days,
unless a timely storm filled the channel and enabled boats and
rafts to float down the current. This method, common enough
on the logging streams of America, enabled the Clanis and
Teneas (Timia) to convey lumber and local produce to the
Tiber and Rome.[53] The Anio, another affluent, provided cheap
transportation for stone from the famous travertine quarries

of Tibur, twenty miles to Rome.   Many Roman edifices like
the Colosseum were built of material from this source.[54]   The
Tiber and its tributaries, as the only navigable river system of
peninsular Italy, greatly contributed to the strategic and commercial power of the great city which controlled its mouth.[55]

River navigation in the Mediterranean lands as a whole was
limited.   It was well developed only on the Nile; here it was
facilitated downstream by the current and upstream by the
Etesian winds, and it was stimulated by the strictly riparian
distribution of the Egyptian cities and the flood-plain location
of the farms.   It was active also on the Rhone, which with its
navigable tributaries of the Saône and Doubs (Arar and Dubis)
constituted a system of inland waterways, and gave access to
a large and productive hinterland, of contrasted climate and
culture.   Hannibal, for his passage of the lower Rhone in 218
B.C., was able to purchase numerous dug-out boats which were
used by the native inhabitants "in their extensive sea traffic."
In Roman times, vessels of heavy burden went up the Rhone,
Saône, and Doubs almost to the Belfort Gap.   Cæsar on his
Gallic campaigns regularly transported his supplies by boat up
the Saône,[56] probably from a commissary base in Lugdunum
(Lyons).   This city was the emporium for all the up-river valley and commanded abundant wheat and salt-pork from its
tributary districts.[57]   Therefore after the victory of Alesia,
Cæsar stationed garrisons at Matisco (Macon) and Cabillonum
(Chalon) on the Saône to safeguard the transportation of grain
for the winter camps of eastern Gaul.[58]   Traffic on the Saône
was so brisk owing to portage connections with the Rhine,
Moselle and Seine, that the neighboring Ædui and Sequani
fought over the right to collect tolls on vessels passing along
the river.[59]   Through traffic provided part of the cargoes.   In
Nero's time, when the middle Rhine was the scene of constant
military operations, L. Vetus proposed linking the Saône with
the Moselle by canal, to facilitate the conveyance of supplies
to the front.[60]   Local boatmen evidently handled the river
transportation, for the *nautæ Araris et Rhodani* are frequently
mentioned in inscriptions.   Even passenger travel was not excluded.   Vitellius on his return to Italy from the Rhine to be

crowned Emperor, journeyed down the Arar by boat, while his army proceeded by land.[61]

Upstream navigation on the Rhone was difficult owing to the swift current and the strong wind sweeping down the valley from the north, the modern mistral and the *Circius* of the ancients. Therefore merchants starting out with goods for the upper Loire and the Central Plateau of Gaul preferred to take their wares by wagon up the valley road to Lugdunum, where they turned off west to the highland. Thus they avoided breaking bulk and escaped the struggle against wind and current.[62] The Arar presented no such difficulty; it flowed down its old lake basin *"incredible lenitate,"* as Cæsar says.[63]

SMALL NAVIGABLE STREAMS—In contrast to these few big rivers with navigable courses ranging from 140 miles on the Bætis to 250 miles or more on the Po, the majority of the remaining Mediterranean rivers were fit only for log-streams. The largest and best of them, from the standpoint of human use, were perennial, and had a short lower course of gentle current, where they crossed a narrow coastal plain to the sea. There they dropped their burden of silt; and aided by the well-nigh tideless sea in front, they built up slender alluvial plains and deltaic flats, across which they trailed in a meandering but navigable course, feasible for the small boats of ancient times. The bar which formed at the mouth, and in summer often emerged to a barrier beach, served as a practicable ford across the stream, better far than points higher up.

At the head of navigation a few miles from the sea, native towns or foreign colonies sprang up in ancient times. They appropriated a site on the nearest hill or rocky ridge protruding from the piedmont into the moist alluvium. The location of these river seaports was rarely more than two to ten miles inland. Though determined by the head of navigation, it served the further purpose of protection against pirate raids so frequent on ancient Mediterranean shores. The elevated site provided an acropolis and lifted the town above the recurring winter floods. It commanded the tillage land and pastures of the coastal plain, the orchard land and forests of the piedmont slope. It also controlled the outlet of the mountain valley, which usually carried a trail and gave access to the trade of the rugged hinterland. Here was a combination of geographic advantages which ancient colonizers were quick to seize upon, and which gave rise to cities of moderate but stable development just so long as the river maintained a passage through the accumulating silt and debouchure marshes to the sea. But the story of these river ports is a struggle to maintain connection with the sea; and to this struggle many succumbed even in the short span of ancient history.

The ancient merchant was ready to utilize even a short stretch of river to reach his market, no matter what difficulties it presented, if that market were the staple place of a productive hinterland. The Syrian metropolis of Antioch, located at the elbow of the Orontes 14 miles from the coast, could be reached by river; but the ascent took a whole day,[64] and could have been accomplished only by small boats propelled by oars and poles, because the city lay on the plateau 262 feet (80 meters) above sea level. Therefore Antioch had to rely upon an inferior outport on the coast at Seleucia. This was an open roadstead, located five miles north of the Orontes mouth to avoid the silted shallows and reach deep-water. Seleucia's site too was typical. It occupied a spur running out seaward from Mount Coryphæus, the southern outlier of the Amanus range, and included a strong rock citadel connected by walls with a lower town on the shore, where the docks and markets were situated.[65] In 219 B.C. it had a population of 30,000 or more, estimated from its 6,000 free citizens, most of them seamen who were doubtless employed in lightering the cargoes of incoming vessels up the Orontes to Antioch. This break of bulk at the junction of sea and river route in the chief gateway of Syria must have severely handicapped the commerce of Antioch. A parallel development was presented by the lower Meander River of western Asia Minor. The marshy debouchure course had no settlement, but was flanked by Priene on the slope of Mount Mycale on the north, and by Myos three miles up the main distributary at the base of the Latmos Mountain on the south—both Ionian colonies and originally coast towns, but in Strabo's time marking the head of navigation for row boats.[66] The outport for the fertile Meander valley was Miletos, which faced the delta from a rocky promontory across the sheltered waters of

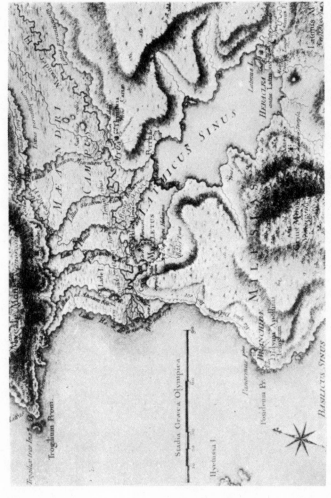

MAP 5—The progressive silting of the Meander River. Myos and Priene were inaccessible in the time of Augustus. The entrance to the Gulf of Latmicus and the harbors of Miletos has been closed in recent centuries.

the Latmic Bay; but even this mile-wide inlet succumbed in the Middle Ages to the massive silt deposits of the tawny Meander, which sealed up Miletos in a tomb of clay.

Another type of river port developed where the alluvial silt cemented rocky inshore islets to the mainland, and thus afforded citadels close to river and to sea. Such was the town of Mallus on the Pyramus River (Jihan) of lowland Cilicia, originally a pre-Hellenic settlement located on an isolated limestone hill, whose former insular nature was obvious to the ancients.[67] The other ports of the Cilician plain retreated from the marshy coastal belt to the skirts of the flanking mountains, where they found a solid base for a town between piedmont and sea. Such was the site of Tarsus, half a mile inland from the lagoon of the Cydnus River, which served as harbor with naval arsenal and dock yard.[68] Through the lagoon to Tarsus sailed the fleet of Cleopatra with purple canvas spread to meet her Antony, Plutarch tells us.

River and port conditions in the mountain-girt plain of Pamphylia on the southern coast of Asia Minor reproduced those of lowland Cilicia. Its rivers had the ample volume of streams in a limestone region, carved the typical limestone canyons down from the lofty ranges of the Taurus, and afforded difficult access to the hinterland; but they flowed with a full current through the coastal plain. The Cestrus was navigable seven miles up to the city of Perga, located on the lowest piedmont terrace mid irrigated fields and orchards, while its famous temple of Artemis looked down from a nearby hill. Similar was the site of Aspendos, an Argive colony situated on a high citadel seven miles up the navigable course of the Eurymedon River, scene of Cimon's naval victory over the Persians in 469 b.c.[69] The outer edge of the coastal zone was unfit for settlement—a belt of marsh pastures, of water-soaked alluvium, lagoons and sandbars, with a line of deposit islands marking the goal of the forward-creeping shore. Only at the eastern end of the plain, where the mountains dropped down to the sea, the Greek colony of Side found a foothold for its shipyards; and also at the western angle, on a travertine terrace deposited by the mountain torrents lay the old Hellenic colony of Olbia and the later Attalia.[70] This latter port flourished in ancient times, participated in the Levantine trade of the Middle Ages, and as the modern Adalia, is still a busy place, shipping wood to Egypt from the Taurus mountain forests, and exporting grain, cotton and leather from the moist Pamphylian plain.[71] Adalia survived as a port because it side-stepped the river mouths.

The western rivers of Asia Minor reveal the same story— the Xanthos River of Lycia accessible to lighters bringing merchandise a few miles upstream, the Calbis River of Caria with a deep navigable entrance which made Caunus a safe and busy port.[72] It preserved its depth doubtless because it flowed through a lake which served as a settling tank five miles back from the sea. The Sangarius, which drained north into the Euxine, was navigable for 35 miles from the sea, but it had no port, owing doubtless to the recent elevation of the coastal ranges and to the heavy floods which developed in all these Pontic streams of Asia Minor. Different was the Phasis, draining the trough between the Caucasus and Anti-Caucasus. A broad intermontane valley of gentle gradient and heavy rainfall made it navigable for 39 miles to Surium for large boats, and much farther for small ones; hence its hundred bridges.[73]

The ill-watered eastern side of the Grecian peninsula boasted only one small navigable stream; that belonged to the depression at the head of the Thermaic Gulf, gathering place of many waters and core of old Macedonia. Here the little Ludias River afforded a waterway fourteen miles up to Ludias Lake, where Philip II established his capital city Pella on an island hill.[74] The Axius, owing to the silted channels of its delta, was inaccessible to vessels from the sea, even in very ancient times.

The western side of Greece, blessed with a heavier rainfall and wider coastal plains, had a few streams available at least for local traffic. The little Pamisos of Messenia was navigable for a mile and a quarter, and it still carries out the produce from its fertile plain in boats able to cross the two-foot bar at its mouth.[75] The Alpheus was navigable for six miles into the lowland of Elis when the stream ran full in winter.[76] Farther north, the Achelous, the largest river of Greece, was navigable for twenty-three miles northward across the Acarnanian plain to Stratos, the capital of the state. This city lay on high ground where a line of rocky hills pinched the Achelous valley in a water gap. At this strategic point, moreover, another valley debouched from the northwest and linked southern Acarnania with the Gulf of Ambracia (Arta), completing a natural avenue of communication across the state, and emphasizing the importance of the lower Achelous as a navigable stream.[77] But Stratos paid for these local advantages, invaluable for an administrative center, by its frontier position, which exposed it to the depredations of Ætolian mountaineers, and also by a situation too far from the sea. Therefore, Stratos had its outport in Œniadæ on the coast, situated on a rocky hill rising like an island from a dead lagoon and maintaining connection with the sea by the river mouth.[78] It was unapproachable by land when the winter floods filled the marshes and restored the old island nature of its citadel. It was a genuine river seaport in 454 B.C. when unsuccessfully attacked by an Athenian fleet and army,[79] and again in 219 B.C. when Philip V of Macedon fortified its harbor and dockyard preliminary to making it his base of embarkation for the Peloponnesos.[80] Two centuries later the silting process had so advanced the shoreline that Strabo described old Œniadæ as lying twelve miles (100 stadia) from the sea, while a new port occupied a site only eight miles (70 stadia) above the river mouth.

In contrast to these short waterways of Asia Minor and Greece, the long rivers of Italy like the Po and the Tiber system assumed considerable economic importance. Many streams flowing from the Alps across the Venetian plain into the shallow Adriatic silted up their mouths and formed marshes and lagoons, through which the inhabitants opened canals to maintain connection with the sea; for the soil was productive, when reclaimed by dykes, and the populous river towns depended on the rivers to get their merchandise down to the coast for export to Rome and other parts of Italy. The thriving city of Patavium (Padua) communicated with the Adriatic by the Medoacus River (Brenta), navigable for thirty miles through the marshes, and sent out in Strabo's time manufactured goods, especially clothing of all kinds, from its seaport of Edron at the river mouth.

The eastward flowing streams of the Apennine peninsula were essentially mountain torrents as far as the plain of Apulia; but there the impetuous streams, like the "far sounding Aufidus," checked their currents, became navigable for ten miles from the sea, and carried out the wheat and cattle of a productive agricultural region.[81] Even the rainy western side of this peninsula developed few navigable rivers except the Tiber and its larger tributaries. The Arnus admitted vessels two miles upstream, but Pisa, its port, was finally compelled to establish an outport at Triturrita, nine miles south of the Arnus mouth, near the site of modern Livorno.

Farther west, the Apennines and Alps tracing the coast send down only torrents to the sea. Beyond lies the long navigable course of the Rhone, and the silted plain of Narbonne with its numerous streams flowing down from the Cevennes and the Pyrenees. Some of these carried small vessels up to their river towns, which formed therefore minor commercial centers; but the Atax (Aude) was navigable up to Narbo, a distance of twelve miles in Pliny's day.[82] In earlier times, the sea was doubtless nearer when Narbo was the chief emporium of this district. Most of the river towns lay well back from the coast, owing to the lagoons and marshes fringing the shore. Only the Massilian colony of Agatha found a safe site at the mouth of the Arauris (Herault) on an old volcanic hill,[83] a rocky islet "tied" to the mainland, where the traveller today sees the little French town of Agde; Leucate's very name describes its location on a white limestone headland, jutting out from a spur of the Corbières Mountains into a coastal lagoon.

The rivers of Spain tell the same story: mountains skirting the coast and curtailing the length of the streams, variable rainfall and variable volume in the torrents, active delta building and short navigable stretches on the few perennial streams. The Ebro was navigable, as it is today, twelve miles from the sea to the point where the river issued from the mountains. There lay Dertosa (Tortosa) on a hill site overlooking the rich campus of the Ebro and the coastal highway of Spain, which here crossed the river above the apex of the delta.[84] The next navigable stream was the ancient River of Malaga (Guadalhorce) which flows down from a longitudinal valley

north of the Andalusian Alps, cuts a passage through the
mountain barrier, and drops its burden of silt in an angle
of the shoreline, where it has built up its alluvial plain. It was
navigable for twelve miles across this plain to the ancient
Roman town of Cartima (Cartania), which marked the head
of navigation doubtless for small boats. Its active seaport was
the old Punic colony of Malaca on a typical Phœnician colonial
site at the eastern corner of the plain. There a deep harbor
protected by a low cape afforded the safest anchorage along
this littoral, while a hill (560 ft.) in the immediate background
provided a citadel on its summit and a town site on its slope
shelving down to the bay. Lifted above the reach of recurrent
floods, fortified against hostile natives, commanding the alluvial
garden land of the lower river and the hinterland route of its
upper valley, exploiting the natural salt pans of the lagoons
and the fisheries of the coast, Malaca enjoyed a rare combination of geographic advantages. It specialized in the export of
salted fish and was both buying and selling market for the opposite African coast. Its name was derived from *malac*, a
Punic term meaning "to salt," which suggests a salt trade with
its Iberian hinterland, and lends significance to its active eighteenth century salt trade with the American colonies.

Outside the Strait of Gibraltar, the heavy tides flooded not
only the rivers but the coastal creeks of southern Spain. According to Strabo, "the whole land is rendered navigable, thus
providing wonderful facility both for the export and import
of merchandise." But river navigation became difficult when
strong flood-tides met the current of the streams, and ebb-tides
often left vessels stranded on the shores. However, every
estuary had its cities and settlements, wherever it washed the
base of a rock outcrop, such as gave safe sites to ancient Esuris,
Onoba and Nabrissa. The ancient Hasta Regia or Eboro
probably occupied the hill which rises from the estuary of the
Bætis (Guadalquivir) and forms today the site of San Lucar
de Barrameda.[85]

CANALS AND LIGHTERS AT RIVER MOUTHS—Constant deposition, seconded by the impotence of tides in the Mediterranean Sea and the lack of their scouring action on river
mouths, impaired the value of these as harbors, and multiplied

the shallow shifting channels across the silted zone. Intercourse between sea and interior admitted only boats of light draft; heavy cargo boats were barred. In view of the barrier boundaries of mountains and deserts confining the Mediterranean region, this break at the normal junction of maritime and river routes handicapped ancient commerce and reduced the value of the few river highways. The littoral courses of the Mediterranean rivers have therefore attained slight economic or historical importance, though the mouth of a stream normally focuses the activities of all its basin.

But the ancients resorted to various means of counteracting these geographic disadvantages. To facilitate communication between sea and river, canals were constructed across the deltaic flats at an early date. This measure was doubtless part of that water control developed by Mediterranean peoples in their adjustment to their physical environment. The soft alluvium of the silted zone rendered the original construction easy, but its yielding character made maintenance difficult. Hence we hear of the constant reconstruction of these canals. Herodotus reports on the authority of the Egyptian priests that the Bolbitine and Bucolic distributaries of the Nile were artificial channels.[86] The Pelusiac mouth was silted up by 285 B.C. and its port barred from the sea by a belt of marshland. The other mouths were inaccessible to large vessels in 24 B.C. and necessitated the use of lighters. These were employed on numerous Mediterranean rivers as an alternative to canalization, notably on the Tiber.[87] The Rhone distributaries were impassable except for the native dugouts, so that Marius in 102 B.C. had to dig an artificial channel for boats conveying his troops inland for his campaign against the Cimbri. This canal was afterwards maintained as a toll waterway by Massilia. The whole Rhone delta was a waste in ancient times. The first market town to be met going up from the sea was Arelate (Arles), occupying a hill site at the apex of the delta.

The Po mouth shows an evolution of ancient ports similar to those of the Nile. Spina on a southern distributary was an early Grecian colony with wide overseas connections, but in Strabo's time it had declined to a village ten miles from the Adriatic. Adria, an old Etruscan port on the Tartarus mouth,

had a similar fate and was superseded by Ravenna, which was
built on piles near the southern outlet. This port prolonged
its life by a large canal, made by order of Augustus, which connected the city with the Adriatic at the naval station of Classis;
but Ravenna finally capitulated to the besieging sands, which
raised a rampart four miles wide between the old port and the
sea. But all through the imperial period a chain of canals ran
north and south through the blur of swamps, lagoons and winding distributaries, and connected Ravenna on the south with
the Atesis (Adige) and the Medoacus (Brenta) on the north.[88]
The maritime cities of Venetia province, located on the inner
edge of the coastal belt where the coarse detritus from the Alps
gave them solid foundations, maintained connection with the
Adriatic by canals across the marshy littoral.[89] They also
benefited by the faint tides which welled up along this coast
from Ravenna to Aquileia and flooded the river channels to the
depth of two feet. Procopius gives us the picture in 550 A.D.[90]

"For the city of Ravenna lies in a level plain at the extremity
of the Ionian Gulf, lacking two stades (400 yards) of being on
the sea; and it is so situated as not to be easily approached
either by ships or by a land army. Ships cannot possibly put
in to shore there, because the sea itself prevents them by forming shoals for not less than thirty stades (3.5 miles); consequently the beach at Ravenna, though to the eye of the mariner it is very near at hand, is in reality very far away by
reason of the great extent of the shoal water. . . . In that
place a very wonderful thing takes place every day. For early
in the morning, the sea forms a kind of river and comes up
over the land for the distance of a day's journey for an unen-
cumbered traveller and becomes navigable in the midst of the
mainland; and then in the late afternoon it turns back again,
causing the inlet to disappear, and gathers the stream to itself.
All those, therefore, who have to convey provisions into the city
or carry them out from there for trade or for any other reason,
place their cargoes in boats, and drawing them down to the
place where the inlet is regularly formed, they await the inflow
of the water. And when this comes, the boats are lifted little
by little from the ground, and the sailors on them set to work
and from that time on are seafaring men."

In all tideless basins river ports must advance coastward to meet the sea.[91]   In the Mediterranean, owing to the active erosion and deposition, they had to do more; they side-stepped the deltaic plain and the shoal waters off-shore.   Only thus did they secure deep harbors, maintain their sea connections unimpaired, enjoy freedom from inundation and immunity from malaria that bred in the marshes.   These considerations for a port site out-weighed the doubtful and declining benefit of a silted river channel, or the advantage of proximity to the valley highway, where the river was not navigable.   In contrast to the sick, moribund, dead and buried ports of the ancient Mediterranean, such as Pelusium, Tanis, Tarsus, Priene, Ephesos, Ostium, Pisa, and the Po River family of ports, which were stricken in succession as if by some hereditary disease, the immortal entrepôts of the Mediterranean Sea have been those which either side-stepped the fatal river mouths, or like Constantinople, Smyrna, Piræus, Brundusium, Naples, Trieste, Syracuse, Palermo, Genoa, Barcino (Barcelona), Tingis (Tangier), Hippo Diarrhytus (Bizerta) and Hippo Regius (Boné), took up their positions on deep protected harbors without river valley connections with the hinterland.

The side-step location of ports applies to rivers both small and great.   Atarneus, entrepôt for the fertile Caicus Valley, lay fifty miles north of the Caicus mouth.   The debouchment of the Hermus was flanked on the north by Phocæa and the south by Leucæ, each about ten miles away.   The delta of the Axius River had no settlement but was flanked east and west by Therma (Thessalonica, Saloniki) and Methone, twelve to twenty miles away; but even so the hill-rimmed harbor of Saloniki today is nearly blocked with silt, repeating the medieval history of Miletos.   In the same way Carthage and Utica were located on citadel hills a few miles either side of the mouth of the Bagradas (Mejerda), which offered no site for a town.   "The turbid Bagradas with sluggish current cuts through the sands and surrounds its meadows with shallow marshes." [92]   But its longitudinal valleys opened up the best wheat land of Africa.

The Nile, whose history reveals a succession of declining ports on its shifting distributaries, did not achieve a permanent entrepôt till Alexander the Great with a Greek eye for maritime possibilities, and with rare geographic insight, fixed upon the site of Alexandria. The city, built by Ptolemy I after Alexander's plans, lay quite outside the delta three miles west of the Canobic arm, where a limestone ridge a hundred feet high, extended towards the Nile from the Libyan plateau. It there-fore lay on Libyan and not on Nilotic ground. Moreover, a coastal current setting here from west to east carried the Nile silt toward Pelusium and away from the narrow islet of Pharos which sheltered Alexandria's port. Quite similar were the con-ditions which determined the permanence of the port of Mas-silia: a situation forty miles southeast of the Rhone mouth, parallel spurs of the Provence hills enclosing its harbor, deep water close inshore, sufficient proximity to a river highway opening up a productive hinterland, and again a coastwise current here setting westward and carrying off the Rhone silt toward the competing port of Narbo.[93] Ænos, a Greek colony on the coast of Thrace, was an exception to the rule. It was located at the mouth of the Hebrus River, served as entrepôt for its valley, and still survives as the modern Enos. The colony occupied a unique site on a southern spur of the Hieron Mountains (Kuru Dagh), running out between the Hebrus mouth and the Ægean. It lay beyond the zone of maximum silting, at the outer edge of the *liman*, and maintained its deep-water approach till recent times;[94] now it has been superseded by Dede Agach, the railroad terminus about fifteen miles to the northwest.

The Mediterranean rivers reveal a story of limitations, which explain their inconspicuous rôle in ancient Mediterranean life. River navigation bulked small. Only on the Nile did it assume significant proportions. Yet even so it had local importance because it helped to exploit the patches of alluvial land scat-tered through this region of prevailing mountain relief.

LEGAL CONTROL OF RIVERS—The Roman law, embodied in the digests of Justinian, epitomized the relation of the Medi-terranean peoples to their rivers. It stressed the importance of rivers for navigation and irrigation; hence it made provision for their control and the protection of their water supply, especially in summer when the supply ran low. Thus the law found its ultimate basis in the Mediterranean climate.

The law announced the general principle that a perennial or "public" river should not be diverted into a different channel from that which it occupied the previous summer; "i.e., when the water was low and the natural channel best defined." This edict of the judge provided that the river, whether navigable or not, should not be dried up by concessions or diversions of water, or its channel changed to the detriment of neighboring land-owners, who had water-rights in said stream. However, some lawyers held that an exception should be made where the alteration of the river's course was made for the purpose of strengthening its banks against inundations, to the common benefit.[95]

Navigable rivers were especially protected. The law provided that prætors should forbid water to be drawn off from a navigable river, if the process should make the river less navigable. The same ruling applied if through this stream some other river were made navigable. If water were drawn off from a river, so that it lost in volume and thus became less navigable; or if the river were spread out in several shallow channels, or if it were confined within narrow banks, and thus became less navigable, or if a footpath leading to the river were obstructed, so that the use of the river were impaired; then the edict of the prætor against the alteration applied. If a river were navigable or helped to make another river navigable, drawing off its water was forbidden by law. The edict of one prætor provided that "nothing should be done in the sea or on the shore, by which the port, anchorage or the navigable course should be impaired." [96]

Both perennial rivers and their banks were considered public property. Hence a man owning a house and land on both banks of a public river might not construct a private bridge across the stream. No one might build anything in a public river or on its bank which was likely to impair the anchorage or the navigable channel; [97] but he might construct riverine works as dykes to protect the bank or his fields along the banks, provided they did not interfere with navigation, because such works were a public benefit.[98] A public river was defined by law as a perennial stream, and river craft as boats and rafts.[99]

Rivers had the power of gods to benefit or destroy. Hence

the sources of larger streams were marked with altars or images of the river-god, like those at the springs of the Clitumnus in Umbria, to whom honors were paid.[100]   In an angry mood the river-god had to be appeased.   Wading rivers was a common practice in Greece, where the streams were small but subject to unexpected floods.[101]   Hence Hesiod advises the wayfarer: "Never cross the limpid stream of ever-flowing rivers with thy feet before thou shalt have prayed and washed thy hands with the clear water." [102]

Thus the ancients took Nature to their hearts.   "So much is certain: History lies not near but in Nature."

AUTHORITIES—CHAPTER VI

1. E. H. Mimms, *The Scythians and Greeks*, pp. 4, 445, 447.   Cambridge, 1913.
2. Aristotle, *De Mirabilibus*, IV.
3. Dio Cassius, 49, 37. Appian, *Illyrian Wars*, XXII-XXIII.
4. Philippson, *Der Peloponnes*, pp. 495-8.   Berlin, 1892.
5. Herodotus, I, 55.
6. Frontinus, *De Aquis Romæ.*
7. Pausanias, VIII, Chap. 26, 11.
8. Strabo, XII, Chap. VIII, 17.
9. Strabo, XIV, Chap. I, 24.
10. Herodotus, II, 4, 5, 7, 10-12.
11. Aristotle, *Meteorology*, I, 14.
12. Polybius, IV, 39-42.
13. Herodotus, II, 10.
14. Pliny, *op. cit.*, IV, 2.
15. Strabo, I, Chap. III, 7.
16. Pliny, *op. cit.*, III, 9.
17. *Ibid.*, II, 87.
18. Aristotle, *Meteorology*, I, 14, 1-20.
19. Strabo, V, Chap. II, 5.
20. *Ezekiel*, XLIII, 2. *Revelation*, I, 15; XIV, 2; XIX, 6.
21. *Judges*, V, 21.
22. Vergil, *Æneid*, II, 305.
23. *Ibid.*, VII, 566-7.
24. Sophocles, *Trachinæ*, 8-20.
25. *Iliad*, XII, 16-25.
26. Livy, *Historia*, XXIV, 9; XXX, 38.
27. Pliny the Younger, *Letters*, VIII, 17.
28. Tacitus, *Annales*, I, 79.
29. Polybius, III, 79. Livy, *Historia*, XXII, 2.
30. Columella, *De Re Rustica*, I, Chaps. 4-5. Varro, I, 11-12.
31. Pauly-Wissowa, Article, Larissa.
32. Strabo, XIV, Chap. I, 21.
33. Herodotus, VI, 31; VII, 42-43.

34. Herodotus, VII, 58, 108-109.
35. Strabo, V, Chap. I, 11.
36. Strabo, IV, Chap. I, 12. A. E. Mitard, "Pluviosité de la Bordure Sud-
    Oriental du Massif Central," *Rev. de la Géog. Alpine,* Vol. XV,
    pp. 8-9. 1927.
37. Polybius, III, 42.
38. Livy, *Historia,* XXI, 31.
39. Tacitus, *Historia,* I, 86. Compare *Odys.* V, 440-454 for river gods.
40. Pliny, *op. cit.,* IV, 1.
41. Herodotus, I, 75.
42. Cæsar, *Bello Civili,* I, 46-55.
43. Herodotus, VI, 1, 13.
44. Xenophon, *Hellenes,* V, 2.
45. Herodotus, III, 130.
46. Strabo, III, Chap. II, 1-6.
47. Pliny, *op. cit.,* III, 21.
48. Th. Fisher, Kirchoff, *Länderkunde von Europa,* Pt. II, p. 617. 1893.
49. Strabo, III, Chap. IV, 7.
50. Strabo, *Fragment,* 48.
51. Polybius, II, 16. Livy, XXI, 25, 57.
52. Vergil, Georgic I, 481.
53. Pliny, *op. cit.,* III, 9.
54. Strabo, V, Chap. III, 2.
55. Mommsen, *History of Rome,* I, pp. 59-60. New York, 1900.
56. Cæsar, *Bello Gallico,* I, 15.
57. Strabo, IV, Chap. III, 1.
58. Cæsar, *Bello Gallico,* VII, 90.
59. Strabo, IV, Chap. III, 2.
60. Tacitus, *Annales,* XIII, 53.
61. Tacitus, *Historia,* II, 59.
62. Strabo, IV, Chap. I, 14.
63. Cæsar, *Bello Gallico,* I, 12.
64. Strabo, XVI, Chap. II, 7.
65. Polybius, V, 59.
66. Strabo, XII, Chap. VIII, 17; XIV, Chap. I, 10. Vitruvius, IV, 1.
67. Strabo, XIV, Chap. V, 16.
68. *Ibid.,* XIV, Chap. V, 10.
69. *Ibid.,* XIV, Chap. IV, 2. Arrian, *Anabasis of Alexander,* I, Chap.
    XXVII. Thucydides, I, 100.
70. Strabo, XIV, Chap. IV, 1.
71. E. Banse, *Die Turkei,* pp. 159-161. Braunschweig, 1916.
72. Strabo, XIV, Chap. II, 2; Chap. III, 6. Diodorus Siculus, XX, 27.
73. Pliny, *op. cit.,* VI, 5.
74. Strabo, *Fragment,* 20.
75. Pausanias, IV, 34.
76. Pliny, *op. cit.,* IV, 6.
77. Bursian, *Geographie von Griechenland,* Vol. I, pp. 120-3. Leipzig,
    1862.
78. Strabo, X, Chap. II, 2 and 21.
79. Thucydides, I, 111; II, 102.
80. Polybius, IV, 65.
81. Strabo, IV, Chap. III, 9.

82. *Ibid.*, IV, Chap. 1, 6; Pliny, *Historia Naturalis*, III, 5.
83. L. de Launay, *Geologie de la France*, p. 171. Paris, 1921.
84. Strabo, III, Chap. 4, 6.
85. Pomponius Mela, III, 4.
86. Herodotus, II, 17.
87. Strabo, V, Chap. III, 5.
88. Pliny, *op. cit.*, III, 20.
89. Strabo, V, Chap. I, 5-8.
90. Procopius, *The Gothic War*, Bk. V, Chap. 1, 11-23.
91. Ellen C. Semple, *Influences of Geographic Environment*, p. 347. New York, 1911. Ratzel, *Anthropo-Geographie*, pp. 298-301. Stuttgart, 1899.
92. Silvius Italus, VI, 140-143.
93. Philippson, *Das Mittelmeergebiet*, p. 56. Leipzig, 1907.
94. Herodotus, VII, 58. Thucydides, VII, 57. Stanley Casson, *Macedonia, Thrace and Illyria*, pp. 11-12. Oxford, 1926.
95. *Digesta Just.*, Bk. 43, Chap. XIII, 1 (1), (3), (6); Bk. 39, Chap. III, 10.
96. *Ibid.*, Bk. 43, Chap. XII, 1, (14-15); Chap. XII, 2-3.
97. *Ibid.*, Bk. 43, Chap. XII, 1, (1), (12); Chap. XII, 3-4.
98. *Ibid.*, Bk. 43, Chap. XIII, 1, (7-8); Chap. XV, 1.
99. *Ibid.*, Bk. 43, Chap. XII, 1, (2-4), (14).
100. Pliny the Younger, *Epistolæ*, VIII, 8; Seneca, *Epistolæ*, 41.
101. Apollonius Rhodius, I, 9; Callimachus, *Hymn to Zeus*, 23-24.
102. Hesiod, *Works and Days*, 735-739. *Odyssey*, V, 440-460.

PART II

THE BARRIER BOUNDARIES OF THE MEDITER-
RANEAN REGION

CHAPTER VII

THE SOUTHERN BOUNDARIES

The location of the Mediterranean Region in the belt of young folded mountains and within the northern margin of the trade-wind tract gives it natural boundaries of mountains and deserts. The Mediterranean is essentially an enclosed sea. It is enclosed not only by the land, but by barrier forms of the land. Rarely are these barriers single. Range rises behind range to a snow-capped climax of highland; beyond mountain system or steep escarpment lies rugged plateau or desert.

NATURE AND EFFECTS OF THE BARRIERS—These barrier boundaries were serious obstructions to human movements in ancient times. The wide deserts to the south and east of the Mediterranean coastlands were crossed by shifting, uncharted tracks, where hunger and thirst threatened man and beast and where robber nomads lurked about the water-holes. The secret places of the Sahara were penetrated only after the advent of the Saracens, who came armed with the technique of desert travel developed in the arid regions of Arabia.

The mountains presented forbidding fronts difficult to cross. Forests on their rainy slopes were an additional obstruction, for the undergrowth yearly obliterated the blazed trail, till the century-long task of clearing and road making was accomplished. Moreover, the mountain forests with their oppressive gloom (*horrenda umbra*) held an element of terror for the ancients, who were accustomed to the open woods of the Mediterranean lowlands. Allusions to this forest fear run through all Latin literature. Through the dense tree-growth torrent beds afforded the only open lines of approach to the passes and the only easy gradients; but their boulder-strewn floors made travel slow and laborious. Road making was long postponed because population was sparse, poor and retarded. Itinerant merchant and marching army alike found it impossible to live off the mountain country, owing to the meager local food supply, and they had to restrict their bulky commissariat owing to the difficult and costly transportation.

Moreover, the passage of the great ranges was limited to the summer, when the snow had melted from the higher slopes and the swollen torrents had abated their violent flow. Otherwise the venture resulted in heavy loss of men, animals and equipment such as Hannibal experienced in his winter passage of the Alps in 218 B.c.,[1] and Cæsar in his winter ascent of the Cevennes highland to checkmate the Arvernian conspiracy,[2]—both of them surprise movements. Even in summer the rough trails were unsafe, for they were liable to washouts after every mountain storm. Furthermore, they were beset by the highland tribesmen who were driven to eke out their scant subsistence by attacking merchant pack-trains or armies crossing the passes, or who levied a transit tax on men and merchandise in lieu of plunder. This was their history from the Pyrenees [3] in the west to the Rhodope Mountains [4] in the east. Conquest of these predatory mountaineers was a long and costly operation, because they had the advantage of strategic position in the fighting, and impregnable strongholds in case of retreat, as the Romans found in the subjugation of Iberia.[5] Therefore not only the mountains but also their inhabitants contributed to the barrier character of the highlands enclosing the Mediterranean region.

These barrier boundaries exercised a strong influence upon Mediterranean history. They long held apart the continental interiors from the stirring events on the Mediterranean rim. Many inland peoples first stepped upon the stage of history when they emerged from some dim hinterland upon the Mediterranean shores. They sought out every natural opening in the encircling barriers and followed the rough paths which nature had made. If they were still nomadic and retained their primitive mobility, they straggled across mountain passes in detachments and arrived in successive groups, like the early Hellenic tribes in Thessaly, and the Celtic tribes in the Po valley. Wide gaps admitted larger, more frequent hordes, and became recognized as danger spots on the Mediterranean frontiers. But through all these breaches the surrounding continents exerted their influences upon the Mediterranean lands, contributing diverse race elements, barbarism or civilization, raw materials or the fine products of native workshops.[6] After the Christian era migrant tribes arrived in increasing masses from the distant interiors and overwhelmed the ancient lands; for the breaches had become thoroughfares and the weakened Mediterranean states no longer planted guards at their gates.

These barriers also helped to confine Mediterranean history for a surprisingly long time within the limits of the Basin, except where the few breaches facilitated intercourse between coast and continental hinterland. Trade first sought out these natural openings because they provided a common place for exchanges between two regions of contrasted production. Colonization, conquest or political negotiations followed to secure strategic positions on these obvious trade routes. The intensity with which these breaches were exploited depended both upon their physical character, affording easy or difficult communication, and also upon the economic demand, with the attendant profit, from either side. The passway through the barrier might be easy, but the market beyond possess scant purchasing power; or the passway might be difficult, but the chance of profit great. Where the breaches became avenues of invasion from the continental interiors, conquest from one side or the other became inevitable. Here the roots of Mediterranean history penetrated far into the hinterlands, so long as the Mediterranean states could hold their own against the barbarian interiors.

One breach in the Mediterranean rim belongs to the Sea as a whole. This is the Strait of Gibraltar, link between the interior basin and the open Atlantic, neck of the Mediterranean bottle. It was probably discovered in the eleventh century B.C. by Phœnician merchants who, alive to its strategic location, planted their trading stations about the outside bay, the *Sinus Emporicus*, the Atlantic vestibule beyond the Gate of the Pillars. These discerning pioneers appropriated vantage points which have retained their significance through historical times. Onoba, outlet for the copper mines of the Rio Tinto, was the colonial ancestor of Huelva; Gades, forerunner of Cadiz, was entrepôt of the productive Bætis (Guadalquivir) valley; Carteia near the present Algeciras, Calpe at Gibraltar, Abila at Ceuta, and Tingis at Tangier occupied strategic sites for the control of the Strait. The earliest trading station, apparently a native Iberian town, was Tartessus, located near the mouth of the "silver-bedded River Tartessus" or Bætis. It was visited by Greek vessels from Samos and Phocæa in the seventh century B.C.,[7] but the Tyrians effected a monopoly of its trade.[8] Finally it was superseded by Gades, which occupied a safer site and absorbed the colonists of Tartessus.

Movements through the Gibraltar breach were wholly outward, no counter-movement eastward came from the untenanted waste of the Atlantic. The homing voyage of the Phœnician ships sent out by Necho II of Egypt from the Red Sea to circumnavigate Africa [9] brought the only arrivals who had not started from the Strait. All other ventures moved outward, either north along the Atlantic coast to the tin mines of the old Bretagne Plateau and Cornwall,[10] or south along the African coast in the interest of exploration and trade, like that of Hanno about 520 B.C. All were Phœnician enterprises, except the westward voyage of the Massiliot Pytheas, who must have been endowed with the guile of Ulysses to elude the jealous guardians of the Strait and follow the uncharted track to the tin land of Britain. These first Atlantic voyages brought the first vague reports of Britain, Ireland and the Canary Isles.[11] The latter were woven into Hellenic mythology as the Islands of the Blest; but the mines of Cornwall became the objective of overland trade and eventual conquest. Thus the Strait of Gibraltar afforded a detour around the barrier of the Spanish Meseta and its bordering ranges to the north, and around the forbidding Rif Mountains of old Mauretania to the south.

THE SOUTHERN BARRIER BOUNDARIES

THE ATLAS FRONT OF AFRICA—The broad belt of the Atlas Mountains and the deserts which stretch across North Africa effectually enclosed the Mediterranean Region on the south. It called a halt to Mediterranean enterprise even when directed by energetic Carthage or militant Rome, except where the Nile valley opened a pathway far into the interior. The physical barrier did not operate alone. The nomads of the Sahara and the interior valleys of the Atlas Mountains were inveterate robbers; they raided the fringe of the coast settlements and were generally hostile to trade. They had little purchasing power, owing to poverty of natural resources, and made small demand for Mediterranean products. They had horses but no camels till after the Christian era, and hence they were poorly equipped to carry on a middleman trade between the seaboard and the Sudan. Their land itself repelled conquest. Hence ancient Mediterranean civilization tarried on the African coastland, and left no impress on the shifting sands of humanity beyond.

The African front of the Mediterranean suffers the double handicap of an inhospitable coast and inaccessible hinterland. A long geological history of elevation has given it sinuous shorelines, forming shallow bights or coves exposed to the north winds which prevail during the summer season of navigation. Only where sharp subsidence shattered the eastern end of the Atlas ranges does a deeply indented coast afford sheltered harbors. Here alone in ancient times arose a great maritime power, Carthage—a power based on its overseas trade and the land beneath its feet, not on the big continent at its back. This African coastland of the Mediterranean is poor and limited in area, despite certain scattered districts of local fertility and despite its length of about 3,200 miles; for its depth is slight. It is confined by the desert behind, at once its jailor and its prison wall. Its history has been dominated by these geographic conditions. It bred no great race, raised no native empire, originated no national movement. "It won transitory importance only when foreign civilizations were transplanted here" by Phœnicians, Greeks, Romans, Saracens or French.[12]

This statement takes no account of Egypt; for Egypt in its soil, its water, its great perennial river, is an exotic in tradewind Africa. Only its sky is Libyan. Everything else that goes to make up the land of Egypt had a far-away origin in the highlands and lakes of Equatorial Africa and was imported thence. Therefore the ancients with some right considered Egypt as no part of Africa, and the Nile valley merely as the eastern boundary of the continent.[13]

THE ATLAS BARRIER—The whole Mediterranean coast belt of Africa borders an inaccessible hinterland, yet it presents a sharp geographical contrast in its western and eastern halves in point of relief and the climatic differences due to relief. From the Red Sea to the Atlantic Ocean extends the desert plateau belt, 1,200 miles wide, reinforced on its Mediterranean side from the Sicilian Strait west to the Atlantic by the triple rampart of the Atlas system, 200 to 300 miles wide and 1,200 miles long. These highlands, which the natives call "the Island," appear as a vast excrescence attached to the edge of the older African plateau, alien both in relief and climate. One series of longitudinal ranges traces the African shore. In the Rif Mountains it rises directly from the sea to forbidding heights, but drops eastward to a chain of mountains and hills, broken at intervals by local subsidences or cut through by streams which give access to a succession of fertile longitudinal valleys lying between the parallel ranges. This is the productive Tell, with its filled valley-plains about thirty miles wide and of varying length, well watered by mountain streams and winter rains, the garden of North Africa. The series of Tell valleys receive annually from 36 to 16 inches of rain, the amount declining from east to west, or a little less than the seaboard; but the heaviest precipitation comes in March and is protracted into April and even into May, so it is well timed for grain crops and vineyards. The autumn rains get a good start in October and reach their maximum in December.[14]

The bold coast has been carved into typical crescent-shaped coves by the wind-driven surf; but a few inlets approach the pouch-form indicative of local subsidence. These afforded some protection to shipping behind their flanking capes,[15] and in ancient times were the site of frequented ports like Hippo Regius (Bône), Saldæ (Bougie) and Portus Divini (Oran), which however scarcely mitigated the general evil of scant harborage along a vast length of coast.

Inland from the Tell valleys the massive earthfolds mount higher in the Tell Atlas (5,100 to 7,500 feet, or 1,600 to 2,300 meters), and again farther south in the Saharan Atlas (5,500 to 7,800 feet, 1,700 to 2,400 meters), which enclose between them a broad elevated longitudinal trough, from 50 to 100 miles wide and about 3,000 feet above sea level. This is the Highland of the Shotts or salt lakes, barred from the coastal rains, powerless to send its weak streams out to the sea, capable of supporting irrigated grainfields here and there along its piedmont, but better adapted for grazing. Hence from the earliest times it was associated with nomadism and desert Africa rather than the tillage lands and cities of the coastal belt. Beyond it the Saharan Atlas, the *Transtagnenses* of the ancients, sink sharply to the Sahara and send down short drainage streams to nourish a zone of oases at their base. This piedmont zone and the Highland of the Shotts were inhabited by the barbarous Gætuli nomads, who met on the summer pastures of the intervening ranges.

At its two extremities the Atlas system runs out endwise into the sea and loses much of its barrier character. Along the Atlantic the ranges spread out fan-wise and enclose silted valley plains which get only 13 to 17 inches of rain but are well watered by irrigating streams from the high western Atlas. These fertile valleys bordered the old *Sinus Emporicus* and provided a productive though retarded hinterland for the Phœnician trading stations on the coast.

SUBSIDENCE OF THE EASTERN ATLAS MOUNTAINS—The eastern Atlas ranges had a different geological history, with contrasted economic and political results. Broken off by subsidence at the Sicilian Strait and subjected to repeated elevation and depression, they protrude into the Mediterranean Sea as bold headlands, sheltering deep bays between. Their longitudinal valleys open eastward and seaward between the flanking promontories; they head westward to low watersheds, which afford easy passes to the chain of Tell valleys, and they receive tributary valleys from the south which open up the highland interior of the Shotts Plateau. The southward bend of the Mediterranean coast for a distance of 400 miles gives access to the Saharan flank of the Atlas and its piedmont settlements. The whole region in its geographical features is a child of Europe rather than of Africa. Here Mediterranean trade and colonization found it easy to penetrate where nature had opened the gates and smoothed the valley paths. Elsewhere they scarcely passed beyond the Atlas threshold of the African continent.

This is the Africa of Punic Utica and Carthage, of Rome

and the Vandal Kingdom, a Berber or Libyan province glossed over in turn by Semitic, Italic and old Teutonic civilizations, till it was recovered by a Semitic power in the person of the all-conquering Saracens and Mohammedanized. The expansion of French rule from Algeria over Tunisia in 1871 restored it to a genuine Mediterranean power. This power entered by a back door from the west, be it noted. Otherwise all civilization came to the Atlas lands from the east, and entered by the wide-open portals which faced the rising sun.

Here the barriers of Africa, both mountain and desert, recede farthest from the coast; here the continent affords the territorial base for a Mediterranean state like Carthage resting upon an economic foundation of agriculture and maritime trade. Conditions of climate, soil and tillable area were good. The district included the fairly broad Bagradas valley with the hill and dale country of the Byzacium coastal plain to the south. Owing to low rainfall the soil retained its precious alkalies, but adequate drainage and moderate evaporation insured against excessive accumulations like those in the Shotts plateau.[16] The drought hazard was always imminent, owing to location near the trade-wind belt. Rainfall decreased rapidly along this coast from north to south, as the series shows: Bizerta (Hippo Diarrhytus) with a rainfall of 25.3 inches, Tunis and Carthage 17.8 inches, Sousse (Hadrumetum) 16 inches, Kairuan 13.5, and Gabes at the head of the Syrtis Minor 7.2 inches. The district received in normal years enough precipitation for the fine winter wheat of Byzacium, except at Gabes where irrigation was necessary for all tillage. About Tunis and Carthage the March rains were doubtless heavy as now, and continued with slight diminution into April, so that the maturing crops were fortified against the early summer drought. But Carthage reveals the variable precipitation characteristic of its location, with a maximum of 22.8 inches and a minimum of 11 inches.[17]

The ancient Phœnician colonists responded to these favorable geographic conditions by abandoning their traditional *pied e terre* policy, and adopting a system of wide territorial expansion under the leadership of Carthage. They stretched their frontiers to the limit of steppe and desert suitable only

for pastoral nomads,[18] increased the productivity of the fertile
soil by improved methods of tillage and reclaimed semi-arid
land by irrigation. They pushed up the valley of the Bagradas
River (Majerda) westward into Numidia, whence they drew
the cavalry for their armies, and southward into the mountains
where a Majerda tributary opened a rocky way to Theveste
(Tebessa) 200 miles inland. Thus far they were able to maintain routes of communication and exercise their authority.

The Atlas presented obstacles to conquest not only in its
physical difficulties but also in the character of the inhabitants.
Sustained resistance to conquest and readiness for revolt at the
first sign of weakness in the government appeared equally under
Carthaginian, Roman, Vandal, Byzantine, and Saracen rule.
The Aurasius Mountains, forming the eastern massif of the
Saharan Atlas, were a constant hotbed of disturbance on the
borders of Numidia and Carthaginian Africa (Byzacium). Its
unruly tribes, organized under their own chiefs and frequently
assisted by the nomads of the Shotts Highland, recurrently
pillaged the cities of valley and coastal plain. Their method
was swift raids and swifter retreats into their mountain fast-
nesses, whither pursuit was difficult and costly.[19] Political efficiency, aided by two river valleys, enabled the Romans to push
their control across Numidia from Cirta to the irrigated piedmont of the Aurasius Mountains, where they built the city of
Tabunæ (Timgad), and to run a road through a pass across
the western flank at *Aquæ Herculis* (El Kantara) down to Bes-
cera (Biskra) on the border of the Sahara. Here alone, where
the Atlas contracts to a width of 150 miles, did the Romans
span the highlands.

Elsewhere the Atlas ranges held Carthage and Rome at bay.
Strabo's account of Mauretania reveals how little the early imperial rule penetrated beyond the Tell valleys, and Pliny's account shows negligible progress a century later. They describe
the coast settlements and the exuberant fertility of the Tell,
but they know of the interior by hearsay as a region of mountains and deserts, infested by monster beasts and inhabited by
nomads.[20]

Below the Hermæan Promontory the southern ranges of the
Atlas decline eastward to a coastal plain of steppe and salt lake

from 30 to 60 miles wide. In relief and climate it represents a transition to the African platform of horizontal strata, monotonous relief, sinuous shoreline and meager rainfall. It gives evidence of subsidence only in the Syrtis Minor; this depression can be traced inland for 300 miles along the southern foot of the Atlas, through the shallow trough of the Saharan Shotts, which sinks 101 feet (—31 meters) below sea level in the Shott Melrir (*Libyca Palus*). After the first subsidence a later arching of the coast severed the bay from its inland extension by an isthmus 20 miles wide, and left the Shotts as a series of salt incrustations, transformed into lakes of liquid mud for short periods when the drainage streams of the Saharan Atlas run full enough to reach them.

THE PLATFORM FRONT OF AFRICA—At the head of the Syrtis Minor the mountains merge into the African platform; the steppe and desert coast of the continent begins, stretching 1,600 miles to the Nile. Here the Mediterranean rim presents a sharp contrast to that of the Atlas littoral. Indentations take the form of shallow bights like the two Syrtes.[21] Headlands are rare and peninsulas are lacking; except for the blunt protrusion of the Barca Plateau. Even for the small boats of ancient times harbors were few and poor, mere exposed roadsteads. The best were found where rocky capes or inshore islets, typical of an abrasion coast, afforded shelter on their leeward side from the strong northwinds of summer. The ancient port of Œa (Tripoli) was protected by a triangular cape and a string of islets stretching along for a mile or more. Anchorage might be found in the opening of the numerous lagoons which lined the shelving shores, but its connection with the sea was precarious.

This north African coast was in ill repute among ancient Mediterranean seamen. Long stretches between the Syrtis Major and Egypt were scantily supplied with ports, anchorages, villages and watering places,[22] so that coastwise voyages, which depended on frequent stops for food, water and trade, were most difficult. The old sea route from Greece to Egypt which followed this inhospitable littoral was "long and vexatious," according to Homer.[23] Navigation of the two Syrtes was dreaded owing to extensive shoal waters, strong on-shore winds, and the flood and ebb tides which left vessels stranded in the quicksands, whence they were rarely recovered.[24] According to legend, Jason in trying to round the Peloponnesos with his good ship *Argo* was driven by a northeast storm into the shallows of the Syrtis Minor before he could discern the land, and was extricated only by divine help.[25] These were the quicksands feared by St. Paul on his perilous October voyage from Palestine to Rome; [26] and again by Marcus Cato in the autumn of 47 B.C. when he preferred to march his army around the shore of the Syrtis Minor and north to Utica, subjecting them to heat and thirst, rather than expose them to shipwreck in these dangerous waters.[27] Yet the Carthaginians, skillful navigators and keen merchants, sailed into the Syrtis Major as far as Charax, to trade their cargoes of wine for the Cyrene silphium, a medicinal root in great demand. The abundant littoral sea life of these shallow waters attracted sponge fishermen and sailors seeking the purple-yielding murex which supplied the Punic dye factories along the Syrtis Minor coast.[28]

This section of the Mediterranean rim presents a sharp contrast to the well watered climatic island of the Atlas Mountains. Its sharp southward recession brings it into the arid domain of the trade-winds; low relief further restricts the rainfall, except where the Barca peninsula lifts its bold front in natural terraces 2,000 feet above the sea and where the steep escarpment of the interior plateau, 1,800 to 2,000 feet high, approaches within 50 miles of the Tripolis coast. Only in these two limited districts does the mean annual rainfall reach twelve to eighteen inches. But the Barca Plateau is a faulted over-drained highland of permeable limestones, without interbedded clay layers to hold up the water for wells and springs. Hence the ground as a whole is so porous that the rain water sinks beneath the surface and flows off to the sea or to the low-lying oases in the desert to the south. Tripolis, though lower, stores in its underlying silts and sands the water flowing down from the nearby escarpment, while the adjacent sea is too shallow to facilitate free drainage from the well soaked coastal plain.[29] Hence the abundant wells and extensive olive groves of ancient and modern Tripolis. In Cyrenaica the coastal belt, given over to towns, orchards and grainfields, was only about 25 miles wide, but it also exploited a dry inner zone 35 miles wide producing the wild silphium.[30]   In Tripolis the belt of sedentary population, both urban and agricultural, was necessarily narrower, except for scattered oases of tillage on the highland escarpment.   Elsewhere along this Libyan seaboard a mean annual rainfall of eight inches or less supported a hem of winter grassland, reverting to desert during the seven months of summer drought, and maintaining a breadth of thirty miles between the Sahara and the sea.

THE NOMAD POPULATION OF STEPPE AND DESERT—Here the Mediterranean borderland shrinks to a mere strip, supporting a sprinkle of nomad population, while a thousand miles of desert bar the distant hinterland.   But this strip has had a history all its own.   It forms an isthmus of seasonal grassland, washed by the blue sea of the Mediterranean on the north and fringed by the yellow sea of the Saharan sands on the south; it extends from the Nile Delta westward to the "island" of the well watered Atlas.   Through all time it has bridged the space between the southwest corner of Asia and the eastern gateways of the Atlas valleys.   Traffic, migration and conquest have moved east and west along this Mediterranean rim, because mass movement into the interior was blocked by the desert barrier.   Carthage traded and expanded eastward to the border of Grecian Cyrenaica, excluding all rivals, pushing her frontier step by step. In her wake centuries later came the Romans, then the Vandals. In like manner Egyptian rule, from the seventeenth to the thirteenth century B.C. stretched west to the Syrtis Major, and again in the sixth century B.C. under Persian direction.   Saracens swarmed along this bridge from Egypt to Spain.   Landbred peoples like the Egyptians and Persians naturally preferred the littoral highway to the perilous coastwise voyage to the west.   But even the nautical Carthaginians sufficiently prized the road along the Tripolis coast to construct a causeway on which to carry it through some marshes east of the Cinyps River.

Besides the coast road from the Nile delta to the Syrtis Major, there was an alternative inland route leading off west, approximately along the 29th parallel, from the populous district about Memphis and Lake Mœris (Fayoum).   Its course was determined by a chain of basin oases scattered along an old subsidence zone which defined the base of the Libyan platform (120 to 150 meters in altitude) and the Barca Plateau, and resembled a long silted marine inlet, a fact observed by the ancients.[31] The springs or wells of the oases are fed by water which percolates through the porous limestone highlands on the north and is gathered on the underlying Nubian sandstones, here only a few meters beneath the surface. This depression ran southeast from the Wadi El Fareg near the Syrtis Major as a long winding valley, expanding at intervals into barley fields and date plantations, shrinking to saline basins where the springs were scant or intermittent. It included the ancient oasis of Augila (Aufila, 92 feet) which the Nasomenes of the coast visited in summer to harvest their dates;[32] the larger oasis of Ammon (Siva, —98 feet) with its famous temple whence Alexander the Great returned by this inland route;[33] the Oasis Minor 130 miles southwest of Lake Mœris and the deep fertile basin of the Fayoum (—141 feet), which is fed by a channel from the Nile.

Both oasis and coast routes linked Egypt with Cyrenaica but not with Tripolis to the west, because a 200-mile belt of desert flanks the Syrtis Major and cuts off the Augila oasis from the highlands of Tripolis, where springs and wadi wells again occur. This wedge of desert has obstructed communication through all time. It drew the settled or agricultural frontier of Cyrenaica at Berenice (Hesperides) and checked Carthaginian coastwise expansion at *Aræ Philænorum*, 200 miles to the southwest. The intervening seaboard belonged to the Nasomenes nomads, and was apparently traversed only by silphium smugglers from Cyrenaica, who were drawn by the profits of a contraband trade to the markets on the Carthaginian frontier. It is shunned today by the Egyptian caravan trail, which swings north from Augila to Bengazi, the old Berenice.

This chain of oases was known to Herodotus from Egyptian reports, and was traced by him west to Cydamus (Ghadames), the desert focus of the Garamantes. The inhabitants were Libyans and represented the desert outposts of the nomad tribes occupying the steppes northward to the Mediterranean.

All alike reared herds of cattle, horses, asses and sheep, and carried on some tillage by irrigation, where spring or wadi made it feasible; but in general they had been excluded from the arable lands of the coast by intruding Phœnician and Grecian colonies. They assimilated certain social and religious customs from their Egyptian and Hellenic neighbors with whom they traded; but in turn they taught the Greeks the use of four-horse chariots.[34]

These steppe nomads of the Libyan tableland became middlemen in the fitful desert trade from the Sudan, but they operated only along the last lap of the route from the oases of Ghadames, Fezzan and Augila, where they received the goods delivered by the interior tribes. Through traffic was impossible, owing not only to geographic conditions but to social and economic retardation of the hinterland. The northern nomads relied for their transport on horses, asses and slave carriers, as they imported black slaves from the south for the Carthage market. Camels, though used in Egypt before the Exodus,[35] were apparently unknown in North Africa till quite late. They were first reported in 47 B.C. during the civil war of Pompey and Cæsar when twenty-two camels figured in the booty taken from King Juba.[36] They were still scarce, for that same year Cato the Younger employed asses to carry water for his army on the long march from the Syrtis Minor north to Utica. Once introduced, camels multiplied to meet a growing demand. In 366 A.D., 4,000 of them were commandeered from the cities of Tripolis for a punitive campaign against the raiding desert tribes.

OVERLAND TRADE TO THE SUDAN—It was the seaboard of the two Syrtes that first developed something like a systematic overland trade to the south. The venturesome expedition of the Nasomenian youths to explore the desert interior and the direction of their journey westward, probably by the oasis of Ghadames, seems to indicate a clearly defined purpose, as if they were doing scout duty for older and wiser heads, spying out some rumored trade route. Behind the two Syrtes the Atlas barrier fell away. The desert barrier, owing to the southward recession of the gulfs, narrowed to fifteen degrees of latitude, and further reduced the difficulties of travel by a happy distri-

bution of oases along a straight north-south line leading from
Leptis Magna to Lake Chad, and again along a southwest line
from Tacape (Gabes) at the head of the Syrtis Minor through
Ghadames to the great north bend of the Niger River.

The trans-Saharan trade was limited in quantity and variety
because it was necessarily restricted to articles of small bulk
and large value. The Sudan sent out gold-dust from the Niger,
ivory, ostrich feathers, ebony, skins of wild beasts, and negro
slaves. It took in return dates from the northern oases, salt,
and certain manufactured wares from the coast cities such as
cheap textiles, ornaments and metal goods made in quantity by
the Phœnician colonists.[37] Despite the small purchasing power
of the hinterland tribes, the Mediterranean markets evidently
derived big profits from the trade. This can be inferred from
the fact that Sidonians at an early date planted colonies along
the Tripolis seaboard, where Leptis Magna, Œa, and Sabrata
long maintained an independent and flourishing commercial fed-
eration; that Carthage about 514 b.c. with the help of the local
Libyans rooted out a Spartan colony from the Cinyps valley
where it had maintained itself for two years; and that later
(c. 450 b.c.) Carthage extended her dominion over the Syrtis
Minor littoral to absorb the market of Tacape (Gabes),[38] annexed the old Punic settlements on the Tripolis coast, and
finally erected her boundary stone in the Syrtis Major. Thus
she monopolized the Mediterranean termini of the shortest
oases routes to the south, dislodged the Greek settlements or
trading-posts existing there in the time of Herodotus,[39] and
excluded the Cyrenaican Greeks, restricting them to land trade
with Egypt and their immediate nomad neighbors. The coast
strip thus secured by Carthage had little value apart from the
murex fisheries and the inland trade, because the arable area
was small, although certain favored spots yielded crops of
wheat and olives.

Some authorities consider that the commercial prosperity of
both Carthage and Cyrenaica was based largely upon the Sudan
trade;[40] but this opinion is hardly justified by the facts. The
Libyan trade of Carthage bulked small in comparison with her
maritime commerce with other countries. Cyrenaica's wealth
rested chiefly on the grainfields and pastures of the Barca Pla-

teau, the monopoly of the wild silphium which grew nowhere except in the adjacent steppes, on the trade in dates with the nearby oases, and the live-stock and wool supplied by the nomad tribes. Its immediate hinterland was sufficiently large and productive to make the Greek colony independent of the overland trade, inasmuch as the silphium crop alone yielded large profits at monopoly prices.

The old Phœnician and Greek cities along the Libyan coast cooperated with their nomad neighbors, for these alone facilitated traffic with the oases. The tribesmen learned to prefer orderly profits to the booty of border raids, though they indulged at times in such depredation. But the Romans, who annexed this territory between 106 and 96 B.C., became involved in a series of wars with the nomads which may have arisen from increased rivalry in the desert trade due to the introduction of the camel. The Romans possibly wished to eliminate the nomad middleman and deal directly with the oases by means of camel caravans, for they carried their military campaigns a twelve days' journey into the desert to Fezzan and Ghadames. The latter, which lay 300 miles south of Tacape, was conquered by Cornelius Balba in 43 B.C. Its perennial springs, grain fields, date and fig plantations, made it an ideal outpost cantonment. These Saharan campaigns began in the time of Augustus and continued under the later Emperors; they secured control of the oases, which not only protected the frontier but also stimulated traffic from the interior.[41]

The first symptoms of decline in the Roman Empire were registered in the recession of this Saharan frontier. The desert again dropped its curtain on the drama of the Libyan hinterland. The momentary lift had given at best only a glimpse of the scene behind. Strabo discerned hardly as much as Herodotus: never again did that stage reveal against its shadowy background the Pygmies guiding the five Nasomenian explorers through the morasses of Ethiopia to their settlement beside the great river flowing from the west.[42] To the Romans of the enlightened Augustan Age the Libyan interior was an unfamiliar country, vast, sandy, barren. "The people inhabiting Libya," wrote Strabo, "are for the most part unknown to us, as it has rarely been entered either by armies or adventurers.

But few of the inhabitants from the farther parts come amongst us and their accounts are both incomplete and unreliable." [43] Though the best of the ancient authorities, he could speak with certainty only about the Mediterranean littoral. He made only conjectures about the country 50 miles back from the coast, and he was dubious about the breadth of the silphium district which began 25 miles inland. Pliny the Elder, who wrote a century later (d. 79 A.D.) had little or no further information. The withdrawal of Roman rule when the Vandals conquered North Africa left the Saharan barrier unimpaired until the Saracens appeared, masters of the meager desert economy, equipped by training in the arid spaces of Arabia to cope with the great difficulties of the Sahara. They occupied the Libyan oases and the overland routes, to spread Mohammedanism and a veneer of civilized wants beyond the desert rim. [44] Thus they became the voice of one crying in the wilderness, preparing the way for the civilization now advancing across the sands under the guidance of French engineers.

Africa, as the ancients knew and viewed it, was a very limited territory, offering limited opportunities. Their Libya ended at the margin of the Nile trench. Beyond that ribbon of green to the east lay not Africa but the Arabian Desert, part of that Arabia flanking the Red Sea or *Sinus Arabicus* on the other side. It extended south to the Second Cataract, where it bordered on Ethiopia. [45] The Nile valley had neither soil nor relief in common with Africa, but it shared much that was characteristic of Asia. These were great irrigating streams like the Tigris and Euphrates with their long stretch of deltaic flats built up on the edge of a tideless sea, or smaller alluvial valleys like the silted plains of Troy, the Caicus, the Cayster and Meander Rivers. [46]

The rift valley of the Red Sea was a vast fissure across the surface of Arabia, dividing it into the Arabian Desert attached to the Nile side, and peninsular Arabia attached to the Asian side; the Nile valley had once been a long pouch-shaped gulf like the Red Sea, extending from the Mediterranean south to the Theban district, as the *Sinus Arabicus* penetrated from the Indian Ocean northward till it almost perforated the slender barrier built up by the Nile silt. [47] The learned Egyptian priests with whom Herodotus talked had seen the two rift valleys linked by canal for over a thousand years, pursuing a common history as they continued to pursue it for two thousand years more. The Nile River breach and the Red Sea breach were not to be divorced.

AUTHORITIES—CHAPTER VII

1. Polybius, III, 50-53.
2. Cæsar, *Bello Gallico,* VII, 8.
3. Plutarch, *Sertorius,* Chaps. VI, VII.   Polybius, III, 40.
4. Tacitus, *Annals,* II, 64; IV, 46-51.   Strabo, VII, Chap. V, 12.
5. Diodorus Siculus, V, 2.   Livy, XXI, 60-61; XXII, 22.
6. E. C. Semple, *Influences of Geographic Environment,* pp. 75-84.   New York, 1911.
7. Herodotus, I, 163; IV, 152.   Strabo, III, Chap. II, 11-14.
8. *Ezekiel,* XXVII.
9. Herodotus, IV, 42.
10. *Ibid.,* III, 115.
11. Strabo, III, Chap. III, 13.
12. H. Helmolt, *History of the World,* Vol. IV, p. 220.   New York, 1911.
13. Herodotus, II, 12, 16.   Pliny, *Historia Naturalis,* V, Chap. 1, 1.
14. J. Hann, *Klimatologie,* Vol. III, p. 46, 70.   Stuttgart, 1911.
15. Philippson, *Das Mittelmeergebiet,* p. 89.   Leipzig, 1907.
16. K. Glinka, *Die Typen der Bodenbildung,* pp. 150-151.   Berlin, 1914.
17. J. Hann, *op. cit.,* Vol. III, p. 79.
18. Strabo, XVII, Chap. III, 15.
19. Tacitus, *Annals,* III, 20, 21, 74; IV, 23-25.   Procopius, *Bello Vandalico,* I, Chap. VII, 5; II, Chap. XII; 29 and Chap. XIII, 1-13, 18.
20. Strabo, XVII, Chap. III, 1, 4-5, 8-13.   Pliny, *Hist. Nat.,* I, 1; V, 1.
21. Strabo, II, Chap. V, 33.
22. Strabo, XVII, Chap. III, 18, 20, 22.
23. *Odyssey,* IV, 481.
24. Strabo, XVII, Chap. III, 20.
25. Herodotus, IV, 179.
26. *Book of Acts,* XXVII, 17.   Revised version.
27. Plutarch, *Cato Minor,* 56.   Lucan, IX, 320, 374.
28. Strabo, XVII, Chap. III, 17-18; 20.
29. J. W. Gregory, "Cyrenaica," *Geog. Jour.,* Vol. 47, pp. 330-333.   1916.
30. Strabo, XVII, Chap. III, 23.   Pliny, *Hist. Nat.,* V, 5.
31. Strabo, I, Chap. III, 4.
32. Herodotus, IV, 172.
33. Arrian, *Anabasis of Alexander,* III, 3.
34. Herodotus, IV, 168-183, 186.   Strabo, XVII, Chap. III, 19.
35. *Exodus,* IX, 3; *Leviticus,* XI, 4.
36. Mommsen, *Provinces of the Roman Empire,* Vol. II, pp. 370-371. 1887.
37. E. Speck, *Handelsgeschichte des Altertums,* Vol. III, pp. 180-182.   1905.
38. Herodotus, V, 42.
39. Strabo, XVII, Chap. III, 17, 20.

40. H. Helmolt, *op. cit.,* Vol. IV, p. 221.
41. Mommsen, *op. cit.,* Vol. II, pp. 342-344. 1887.
42. Herodotus, II, 32.
43. Strabo, II, Chap. V, 33; XVII, Chap. III, 23-24.
44. Th. Fischer, *Mittelmeerbilder,* p. 36. Leipzig, 1905.
45. Herodotus, II, 12.
46. *Ibid.,* II, 10-11.
47. *Ibid.,* II, 11.

CHAPTER VIII

THE NILE AND RED SEA BREACH

Nature barricaded the Mediterranean front of Africa from the Strait of Gibraltar to the Nile, a shoreline of 3,200 miles. She made it barely accessible from the sea, and virtually inaccessible from the hinterland. Then an abrupt change followed. At the northeast corner of Africa she crowded together two major breaches in the barrier, merging into one another,—the rift valley of the Red Sea which in late geological times reached the Mediterranean, and the rift valley of the Nile extending south to Keneh, where the River Joseph splits off from the Nile as a companion stream.[1] One forms a river highway and fluvial oasis crossing the African desert south to the Equator. The other forms the Red Sea passage which in historical times diverged from the old Nile distributary in the Wadi Tumilat. It now runs tangent to the northeast coast of Africa for 1,600 miles. From the outlet of the Gulf of Suez the two rift valleys maintain a course nearly parallel southward to the First Cataract and the Red Sea port of Berenice. This fact had an important effect upon the ancient Nile River and Red Sea trade routes. It kept them closely linked together from early times till the opening of the Suez Canal (1869), because it permitted cargoes to be shifted from one to another by caravan across the intervening stretch of desert, which was not more than 150 miles wide. Moreover this break of bulk was made imperative by sailing conditions in the Red Sea.

As national highway and source of fertility, the dominance of the Nile was reflected in all phases of ancient Egyptian life. The river stimulated the priests to make a study of the stars as the time-keepers of the floods, and to master the principles of mathematics and surveying in order to restore the farm boundaries obliterated by the annual inundations. In each district or nome the temples were orientated to the sunrise at the summer solstice, when the floods began, on the date when each

temple was constructed. The Nile permeated religious observances, both ritual and festivals. It was reflected in the term
"downstream" which meant north, and "upstream" which meant
south. The Egyptians were amused to discover that in Mesopotamia, where Tigris and Euphrates took the place of the
Nile, the meaning of these two terms was reversed.

The Nile was the most cogent argument for a stable and
orderly government. Under such rule the Nile spread out
through irrigation canals to the border of the flanking deserts,
and under political collapse the desert crept forward to the
banks of the Nile. Yet the long narrow form of Egypt lacked
the compactness necessary for a stable, centralized government.
Excessive length weakened the arm of authority, despite easy
river communication, so that collapse was always threatening a
country 750 miles long and less than ten miles broad. The shift
of the ancient capital from Memphis near the Delta to the
medial location of Thebes was a geographical move to facilitate
centralization.[2]

THE NILE HIGHWAY—The Nile opened a straight passage
from the Mediterranean 750 miles to the First Cataract, where
the river crossed a granite dyke and met a serious obstruction
to navigation. This began at ancient Syene or Elephantine
Island, the modern Assuan. It was taken by the ancients as
the traditional southern boundary of Egypt,[3] though the
Pharaohs occasionally pushed their frontier 140 miles farther
south to the Second Cataract or *Cataracta-Major* above Sycaminos, a far more difficult obstacle. To reach Sycaminos it was
necessary to tow boats for four days up the First Cataract.
Hence the oracle of Jupiter Ammon said: "All are Egyptians
who dwell below the city Elephantine and drink of the Nile." [4]

Elephantine was a typical border market, a common dwelling
place of Egyptians and Ethiopians with a frontier police force
from Egypt.[5] In the twenty-sixth century B.C., and again
in the twentieth century, it was a fortified trading station, controlled by a nobleman who was made "Keeper of the Door of
the South." His duty was to suppress the turbulent tribes attacking the frontier and to protect the trade coming down the
river, bringing gold, silver, ostrich feathers, ebony logs, panther skins and ivory tusks from the Sudan. Oriental products

6 *

from Punt and more eastern lands, consisting of myrrh, gums, resin and fine woods, came hither by the Red Sea route and the upper Nile.[6] When the Romans assumed control of Egypt in 31 B.C. they established a frontier guard here to ward off Ethiopian attacks.[7] Apollonius of Tyana, visiting Sycaminos in the reign of Emperor Titus, found there a quantity of un-coined gold, linen, various roots, myrrh and spices, all lying about. There Egyptians and Ethiopians bartered their products. The borderland inhabitants were a half-breed population, darker than the Egyptians and lighter than the Ethiopians.[8] Hence the debatable frontier evidently extended from the First to the Second Cataract.

Above Sycaminos lay the Ethiopian Desert with the great bend of the Nile and its four cataracts. These were avoided by a caravan route straight across the bend to Meroë above the confluence of the Atbara, the first permanent tributary of the Nile, and below the Blue Nile flowing down from the highlands of Abyssinia. The Nile has its sources in the Equatorial Lakes of Africa, in a region of 40 to 80 inches rainfall drained by the White Nile. This stream maintains the level of the main river in Egypt. It also brings down sand and deposits it in bars at the head of the Delta. This forms the underlying soil. The floods are due to the monsoon rains, blowing in from the Indian Ocean and the Atlantic to the Abyssinian Highlands, where their moisture is condensed, flooding the Atbara, the Dinder and the Blue Nile, and inundating Egypt from about June 22nd to November. From the great cap of volcanic rock covering the Abyssinian Highlands the rains wash off the fertile red soil and deposit it in Egypt as a light top dressing to the underlying sand.

About 70 miles below the First Cataract the Nile reaches the nummulitic limestone, in which it broadens its trench and forms a flood plain from six to nine miles broad, accessible to the fructifying waters. Here from very early times the stream was bordered by large cities or agricultural villages maintained by canal, shaduf and well irrigation. The villages, raised on artificial mounds and wreathed in date palms, appeared like the Cyclades Islands above the tawny flood-plain during the period of inundation. All lay near the great river, which was an ad-

mirable commercial highway.   The Nile distributed not only
the imports from the Sudan, but also the far more abundant
local products, especially those seeking the Mediterranean coast
for export.   It enabled the builders of the pyramids to employ
the red granite of the First Cataract, the Assuan dyke, for
their various structures at Memphis and for the obelisk at
Heliopolis.   The abundant wheat of Egypt, canvas for sails,
and fine linen for garments from the irrigated flax fields went
down the river to the Delta coast for export; fine wines from
the Ægean isles, purple and saffron dye, lumber from the
Taurus, Lebanon, and Mount Amanus, copper and malachite
from Mount Sinai, came upstream from the Mediterranean seaboard to meet various Egyptian needs.

Nile navigation was easy.   The steady north winds which
blew most of the year in Egypt carried the sailing vessels upstream.   In calm weather it was necessary to use oars or to
tow boats by shore.   The types of boats were various and river
transportation evidently reached considerable efficiency.   Vessels 170 feet long were known in 2900 B.C.   The luxurious boats
of the nobles were equipped with awnings and many oars.
Skiffs for fishing and duck shooting were made of the papyrus
growing in the river.   These were evidently the boats of the
poor, made of local raw material in a treeless land.

DEFECTIVE CONTACT BETWEEN MEDITERRANEAN AND NILE—
Egypt's grave handicap was the lack of ready communication
between the Nile and the Mediterranean.   From the earliest
times the country suffered from this drawback, which discounted many advantages of the river highway—a fact which
the ancients recognized and deplored.   Diodorus Siculus states
that on a 600-mile stretch of coast, from Parætonium in Libya
to Joppa in Syria, there was no safe harbor except the island
of Pharos which sheltered the port of Alexandria.   Moreover,
the shore abounded in rock reefs and sandbars not discernible
by seamen, who were therefore shipwrecked when they tried to
land.   The low Delta surface could not be distinguished from
the marshes in which the boats ran aground, nor the main distributaries of the Nile from numerous blind channels in which
the seamen wandered about.[9]   The Egyptian voyage was there-

fore dreaded from Homeric days, especially as river pirates found this coast suited to their purposes.[10]

A broad belt of these lagoons and marshes bordered the seaward side of the Delta from the Canobic arm of the Nile and Lake Mareotis on the west, to the Pelusiac arm and Lake Sirbonis on the east.[11] It varied in width from 10 to 35 miles, and it was always changing. Breasted thinks that it was broader in ancient times than at present. Sir William Willcocks attributes its present great width to the Saracens who destroyed the out-fall canals draining the lower Delta.[12] The nature of this amphibious coast was sufficient to keep the ancient Egyptians at arm's length from the Mediterranean. Only a few of the seven main distributaries of the Nile crossing this coast zone were navigable from the sea, because their mouths could admit no big vessels, but only lighters; [13] hence contact was slight.

The coastal belt of the northern Delta must always have had a barren soil marked by salt and alkali deposits. At the apex of the flood, which was also the peak of the Etesian winds, the north onshore storms drove the saline waters of the Mediterranean on to the tillable land and choked with wind-driven sand the out-fall canals, which would have kept the basins drained and their soil sweet.[14] Salts in the marine deposits at slight depths were brought to the surface by capillarity and evaporation. Hence owing to the low elevation of less than seven meters, and to lack of drainage, salts and alkali must have ruined the soil for tillage.[15] This was doubtless the long history of the Delta as it slowly protruded northward with the accumulation of silt, for this is the story of soil deterioration on its northern rim today. Soils came into use only in the southern and higher part of the Delta as this section attained an elevation sufficient for drainage. The commercial cities and temporary capitals of the coastal belt, like Pelusium, Tanis, Mendes and Canobus, were located on its inner edge, and undoubtedly derived their food from upstream districts. We do not find here the thickly strewn rural villages that characterize the upper Delta both in ancient and modern times.

Hence the Mediterranean coast of Egypt discouraged enterprise on the sea, and offered contact to only a few of its inhabitants. It bred a stay-at-home race, indifferent to nautical adventures; but its more passable channels, like the Canobic and Pelusiac arms, which developed ports near their mouths, were penetrated by maritime Phœnician and Greek traders whose rugged homelands provided a scant food supply, and who therefore sought the Egyptian grain markets. They spread a veneer of Mediterranean culture and Greek speech over the Delta. This district became the seat of steady maritime activity, however, only when the old Milesian factory at Naucratis on the Canobic arm was converted into the one open treaty port of Egypt by Psammeticus about 620 B.C.; [16] and again after 330 B.C. when Alexander the Great built the Greek city of Alexandria on the western rim of the Delta beyond the reach of Nile silt.[17] But this active port was wholly Greek with a large cosmopolitan population; it was in no sense Egyptian. Its maritime enterprises were directed by the Greek dynasty of the Ptolemies. The Phœnicians penetrated up the Pelusiac arm of the Nile. We read of the "Tyrian camp" with its temple of the foreign Venus or Astarte at Memphis.[18] The Egyptians in general remained sea-shy. When their rulers wished to launch big maritime enterprises, like Necho's scheme to circumnavigate Africa, they employed these Phœnician and Greek aliens for the task.

ISOLATION OF THE NILE VALLEY—Egypt suffered from excessive isolation which laid upon it the stamp of excessive conservatism. This fact both Herodotus and Strabo recognized. Attributing the national peculiarities to the distinctive climate and economic conditions imposed by the Nile, Herodotus says: "They have adopted customs and usages different in almost every respect from the rest of mankind." Again, "They observe their ancient customs but acquire no new ones," and "They avoid using Grecian customs and in a word those of all other people whatsoever." [19]

Strabo emphasizes the isolation and protection of strong natural boundaries—the harborless coast inaccessible to strangers, the deserts to east and west, the morasses of Pelusium and the Desert of Tih on the northeast, and the broad band of desert and cataracts on the south.[20] To the progressive and enterprising Greek, the sea was the natural field of adventure. Therefore Herodotus comments with surprise that the Egyptians had no divinity like Poseidon or the Dioscurii, the saviors of seamen.[21] Hence Egypt exercised slight influence upon other peoples of the Mediterranean, except the Greeks, Ionians and Phœnicians who came to the Nile, and who learned there the principles of astronomy, mathematics and architecture. Early Cretan raiders and traders also from an early date took back elements of Egyptian culture to their island home.

Only under the urge of dire necessity did the Egyptians leave their own confines to get anything, as when they sent ships to Cyprus and Lebanon for cedar and pine logs under the early dynasties, before Phœnicians took over the carrying trade of the Levantine Sea. The Pharaohs learned too well the lesson of their environment and long maintained a strict system of territorial isolation. Moreover, Egypt's neighbors were all very remote. Apart from its policy of exclusion, the country was in no location to enjoy stimulating contact with other peoples. Its African neighbors had little to offer either in the way of commodities or ideas, because their social-economic life was based on pastoral nomadism or meager sedentary agriculture. Moreover, Egypt was nearly self-sufficing owing to its generous resources. It therefore had little incentive to aggression to extend its boundaries and its contacts; it restricted its imports to a few luxury articles besides the lumber and the metals like copper and manganese which the country did not produce. Consequently control of the one great passway across Africa to the Equator produced limited results, owing to a combination of adverse geographic conditions.

CONTACT OF EGYPT THROUGH THE RED SEA WITH THE ORIENT—On the east Egypt made commercial contacts that were more stimulating. Before any report of Oriental trade was recorded, goods from India and South Asia found their way to Egypt—myrrh, indigo dyes used in mummy clothes, bronze and tin called by the Sanskrit name of Kastira. This term to designate tin appeared also in the Aramaic Semitic speech and in Arabic; [22] and in the tongue of the trading Phœnicians, the great metallurgists of their time, it spread over the Mediterranean lands and became attached to the tin-mining coast of Cornwall as the Cassiterides Islands. Tin appeared in

Egypt as an imported article as early as 4000 B.C. It seems reasonable to assign its origin to the Peninsula of Malacca, because some centuries later it was followed by bronze weapons of Oriental design which provided models for the early Ægean cultural region. The traveller who visits the Malay museums of Singapore and Java today stands amazed at the similarity of form and decoration to be seen in the old Malay bronze daggers and in the famous sword of Mycenæ. These weapons seem to link the tin mines of Malacca with the palace of Agamemnon, by way of the Red Sea.

These untraced commodities of early Oriental commerce may have passed by the short laps of primitive trade to the Indian or Arab middlemen of the lower Red Sea, and found their way thence by caravan along the piedmont of Abyssinia to the Atbara River and the Nile, a distance of over 250 miles from the port of Suakin to *Premis magna* or Meroë. Big profits lured the Egyptians to track these goods to their nearest source of supply. Hence, where the Nile makes an eastward bend in the latitude of Coptos and Thebes and approaches within a hundred miles of the Red Sea, they opened a caravan route with wells and stations from Coptos up the Wadi Hammamat to a little wadi port on the Red Sea near the later Greek *Leucos Limen* (modern Kosseir).[23] Here in the Fifth Dynasty they began building ships with sails and oars, and Sahure, a Pharaoh of this period, in 2750 B.C. sent out a fleet to Punt or Somaliland at the Strait of Bab-el-Mandeb, where Arab middlemen handled the trade from India. Sahure's fleet brought back electrum, ebony, gums, myrrh, and resins needed for ointments and incense. One very early official boasted that he made the voyage to Punt eleven times,[24] for traffic once started kept up.

The removal of the Egyptian capital from Memphis to Thebes in the Twelfth Dynasty (1935 to 1887 B.C.) gave fresh impulse to the Punt trade, and doubtless from this time Thebes acquired the great reputation for wealth which it enjoyed in Homeric days.[25] The Coptos-Red Sea route involved a caravan journey of five or six days, but the road was kept in excellent condition. The wells in the wadi floor were constantly cleaned out to prevent their being choked by the sand.[26] The Punt trade expanded to include ivory, gold, perfume, cinnamon, cassia, muslin and sandalwood from India, apes and peacocks, and finally live myrrh trees from Yemen for planting. It evidently soon acquired all the features which Herodotus depicts in his vivid account—the rafts of the Sabean Arabs plying back and forth across the ten miles of strait between Ocelis and African Punt, the huge birds (ships) which brought the rolls of cinnamon bark from unknown shores; and the terrifying stories told by the Arab middlemen to discourage all visitants from seeking out the sources of this rich trade and introducing competition.[27]

The Punt trade flourished with slight variations through all ancient history. It was more active under vigorous rulers in Egypt like the Rameside Dynasty, progressed rapidly under the maritime Ptolemies, and expanded to an Indian commerce under the Romans. It failed to give Egypt broader human contacts and the stimulation connected with such; but it brought to the Nile increased wealth and new luxuries, and multiplied Egypt's contribution to Mediterranean trade.

THE RED SEA WIND SYSTEM AND THE TRADE WITH THE EAST —The outbound and homeward voyages in this Punt trade were strictly controlled by the winds of the Red Sea. These were sufficiently regular and favorable to facilitate navigation. Northwest winds prevail in the northern part of the Red Sea down to 19° N. Lat. and blow over the entire marine basin from June to September, when they withdraw from Bab-el-Mandeb up to 16° N. Lat. South of this the winds are variable for a while. In the southern part of the basin southeast winds prevail in winter, with east winds in the Gulf of Aden or deflected northeast monsoons.[28]

Vessels bound from the Egyptian ports of Myoshormos, Leucos Limen or Berenice to southern Arabia or African Punt set sail in September and were carried by the northwest wind of the Red Sea down to the Strait of Bab-el-Mandeb. Those bound on the longer voyage to India and Ceylon left earlier, in July, sailed with the northwest wind down to the Gulf of Aden, where they caught the southwest monsoon to carry them across the Arabian Sea to the Malabar Coast or to Barygaza[29] near the site of the later Surat. The first voyage of exploration undoubtedly followed the coast of the Arabian Sea, but the regularity of the monsoons enabled the Greek seamen from Ptolemaic Egypt to strike straight across the basin to the coast of India. The return voyage to the Red Sea relied on the northeast monsoon, which became steady in late November or early December on the coast of India. Nearchus, exploring the voyage from the Indus River mouth to the Persian Gulf for Alexander of Macedon, found this wind still variable during November.[30]

At the Strait of Bab-el-Mandeb the northeast monsoon, deflected by the high relief of the Red Sea coast to a southeast wind, carried the homing ships up the Red Sea to 19° N. Lat.; but from that point they had to use their oars to force their way up to Berenice (24° N. Lat.) or yet farther to Leucos Limen (26° N. Lat.). Only the last stretch of the homebound voyages was therefore difficult. But the traffic had to bear the heavy cost of breaking bulk at a wretched Red Sea port of Egypt, and of caravan transportation across the desert by camel for five or six days from Leucos Limen, or eleven days from Berenice to the Nile. Only goods of small bulk and large value seeking a high-priced market could have stood these heavy charges. Hence it is natural that the Egyptians, who were the Mediterranean middlemen in this trade, should have early sought to remedy the most obvious leakage in the system by establishing water communication between the Nile and the Red Sea.

NILE AND RED SEA CANAL—The two rift valleys of the Nile and Red Sea, when formed in the Quaternary Period, were long marine inlets branching off at an acute angle from the southeast corner of the Mediterranean, which at that time was connected with the Red Sea by a Suez strait. This passage, however, was not permanent. Two physical forces set to work to obliterate it. One was the filling in of the Nile rift by rapid deposition, till the old inlet disappeared. The bay at its mouth was converted into the fan-shaped protrusion of the Nile Delta, which blocked the Suez strait on its Mediterranean side with a belt of alluvium forming an isthmus. The other process was the slow elevation of the Red Sea coasts, with long pauses between rises, recorded in old sea strands; till finally the old Suez strait survived in vestigial form in the line of the Bitter Lakes,

which still constituted a northern extension of the Gulf of Suez
in early historical times. The traveller on the Red Sea today,
whose voyage is perforce a coasting voyage, feasts his eyes on
the vast terraces that rise from the foaming coral reefs along
the shores up to 1,000 feet or more. These look as if some
Titanic Rodin of immortal genius had sculptured the escarpment into a gigantic *scala sancta*, mounting from the lowly

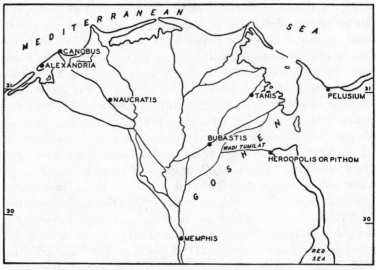

Map 6—The Nile Delta showing the eastern distributary of the Wadi
Tumilat and the northward extension of the Red Sea through the Gulf
of Heroopolis.

earth up to the high altar of some local deity, like the seat of
Jehovah upon Sinai.

Land under the old strait of Suez emerged only enough to
form a narrow sand and gravel plain of low relief. Across this
the Gulf of Suez or Gulf of Heroopolis penetrated half way
or nearly to the Wadi Tumilat, the southern distributary of
the Nile, extending east from Bubastis on the Pelusiac arm.
The physical character of the isthmus obviously suggested deep-
ening the Wadi Tumilat and extending it by canal through the
soft alluvium to the Gulf of Heroopolis, thus gaining a waterway to the Red Sea from the Nile and the Mediterranean.

The first canal was projected and constructed by Sesostris II (1900 B.C.) of the Middle Kingdom. It extended east from the Nile to the Egyptian town of Pithom (Heroopolis) located 23 miles west of the present Ismailia near the western end of Lake Timsah, the most northern link in the later chain of the Bitter Lakes, and 43 miles northwest of the present Gulf of Suez. Here the Pharaoh built underground storehouses for grain which was to go down the Red Sea to Yemen, to pay the Arabs for the products of their myrrh terraces and for the imports from India. Pithom was the staple place for the fertile land of Goshen, watered by the Wadi Tumilat.

The Punt fleet of five vessels sent out by Queen Hatshepsut about 1500 B.C. went down the Nile from Thebes to the Wadi Tumilat, passed through the canal to the Red Sea, and thence to Punt. Later it returned to Thebes by the same route, laden with "fragrant woods of God's Country," with myrrh and live myrrh trees, ebony, ivory, gold, cinnamon, incense, eye cosmetic, baboons, monkeys, dogs, skins of southern panther, natives and their children.[31] This was a profitable cargo, but a hundred years later, by the time of Rameses III, this canal had fallen into disuse; the Punt trade had resumed the old caravan route from Leucos Limen to Coptos, where goods were transferred to Nile boats and forwarded to the new capital in the Delta.

A succession of Nile-Suez canals were built through the centuries, but they were left unfinished at the supposed warning of some oracle; but in general they were unable to compete with the rival route by caravan across the desert from the Red Sea ports to Coptos on the Nile. These canals were made by:

1. Sesostris II in 1900 B.C.
2. Seti I in 1380 B.C.
3. Necho in 609 B.C.
4. Darius of Persia in 520 B.C.
5. Ptolemy II in 285 B.C.
6. Trajan's new channel from Nile to Wadi Tumilat, 98 A.D.
7. Arab Canal in 640 A.D., closed in 767 A.D.

The question is: why were these canals allowed to lapse? Seti's canal may have been simply a project to clean out the previous canal, which had become silted up with Nile mud or blocked by drifting sand. Since that canal was 30 miles long, 150 feet wide and 17 feet deep, the task was sufficient to make Seti claim the honor of reconstruction. Necho's canal proposed to extend the older canal southward from Lake Timsah to the Gulf of Suez; it was possibly abandoned owing to an adverse oracle, but completed almost a century later by Darius the Persian, who commemorated the event by monuments erected at various points between Pithom and the present Suez (Clysma). His object was to connect his new territory in the Indus valley of India with the grain fields of Egypt.[32] Ptolemy Philadelphus reconstructed the canal, from Phacusa on the Nile about twenty miles below Bubastis to the Gulf of Suez at Arsinoë, where he built locks to exclude the salt water.[33] But he no sooner completed this enterprise before he reopened the old caravan road from Coptos to Leucos Limen and surveyed a new one that ran an eleven days' journey southeast to Berenice on the Red Sea.[34]

SAILING CONDITIONS IN THE GULF OF SUEZ—The explanation is to be found in the difficult and dangerous sailing conditions which prevailed in "the recess of the Gulf," or Gulf of Suez and the northern part of the Red Sea for the sailing vessels of ancient times.[35] The shape of the Suez and Akabah gulfs gives rise to marked tidal circulation of the water. This is further complicated by transverse currents that move down from the two gulfs, driven by the strong or even violent winds, —northwest winds in the Gulf of Suez and north or northeast winds in the Gulf of Akabah. Winds and currents meet at the apex of the Sinai Peninsula during all the season of navigation. Moreover, when the southwest monsoon is blowing in the Arabian Sea, it draws out the water from the Gulf of Aden and causes the sea level at the head of the Red Sea to be depressed three feet, thus complicating still further the currents there. Nor is this all. The shores of the Red Sea are deeply fringed with coral reefs of the Quaternary Period. These reefs, showing all degrees of submergence, narrow the already slender form of the Gulf of Suez, and leave a navigable channel so constricted that shipwreck is almost inevitable for vessels sailing before the high winds of the inlet.[36]

Egyptian navigators were hardly efficient enough to cope with these conditions, which from time to time must have entailed heavy losses. Therefore King Solomon, though he evidently pushed his frontier south to include the port of Ezeongeber at the head of the Gulf of Akabah with the purpose of sharing in the Red Sea trade to the Orient, combined with Hiram of Tyre in fitting out an expedition to Ophir, the land of gold. The Tyrians furnished the seamen, while Solomon provided port and probably some of the capital. The voyage lasted three years, after the leisurely sailing methods of the Phœnicians described in Homer; but it evidently reached India and brought back a valuable cargo. The apes, sandalwood and peacocks, the latter with a Sanskrit name among the Hebrews, all point to India as a place of origin.[37] This Semitic maritime enterprise seems not to have been repeated. But the "goodwill visit" of the Queen of Sheba to King Solomon from her capital in Yemen may have aimed to divert him from the farther voyage, and persuade him to employ her Arab middlemen established conveniently at Muza (Mocha), Ocelis and Adana on the Strait of Bab-el-Mandeb.

Navigation in the narrow gulfs at the head of the Red Sea remained difficult enough to terrify dauntless seamen. The Roman expedition of Ælius Gallus, which set out from the Gulf of Suez to the Gulf of Akabah and the land of the Nabatæans in 23 B.C., was disastrous. It resulted in the loss of 150 vessels out of a fleet of 300, or half the total.[38]

Hence under Greek and Roman rule in Egypt the Oriental products continued to move overland from Leucos Limen or Berenice to Coptos on the Nile, and thence by river down to Alexandria, whence they were exported to all coasts of the Mediterranean.[39] Aside from the costly carriage by donkey or camel caravan from the Red Sea, traffic charges by this marine and river route were heavy; they included transit duties on all goods entering and leaving Egypt, and customs *ad valorem* imposed at the frontier of the various nomes or provinces, where custom houses were maintained or a bridge of boats blocked the passage.[40] These irksome tolls and duties burdened and delayed traffic all during the Middle Ages, when Venice exploited the Egyptian trade from Alexandria,[41] and furnished a cogent

argument for the exploration of the outside sea route to India.
It was a human invention, the application of steam to navigation, that finally enabled vessels to defy the dangers of the
Gulf of Suez. A British steamer from Bombay reached Suez
in 1830. In 1859 De Lesseps began to cut the Suez Canal and
finished it in 1869, utilizing the old Suez breach and making a
new adjustment to geographic conditions, superior to the earlier Nile Canal.

AUTHORITIES—CHAPTER VIII

1. Suess, *The Face of the Earth,* Vol. IV, p. 278. Compare Herodotus,
   II, 10-12.
2. Sir Norman Lockyer, *The Dawn of Astronomy,* pp. 230, 240. J.
   Breasted, *History of Egypt,* pp. 7, 143, 147, 150. 1911.
3. Herodotus, II, 30. Strabo, XVII, Chap. I, 3-5, 48.
4. Herodotus, II, 18.
5. Herodotus, II, 30.
6. Breasted, *op. cit.,* pp. 135-138. 1911.
7. Strabo, XVII, Chap. I, 12, 48, 49, 54.
8. Philostratus, *Life of Apollonius of Tyana,* VI, 2. Loeb's Classical
   Library, London, 1912.
9. Diodorus Siculus, Bk. I, Chap. III. Strabo, XVII, Chap. I, 19.
10. *Odyssey,* IV, 485.
11. Strabo, XVII, Chap. I, 18-21, 24.
12. W. Willcocks and J. I. Craig, *Egyptian Irrigation,* Vol. II, pp. 453-4.
    London, 1913. Breasted, *op. cit.,* p. 5.
13. Strabo, XVII, Chap. I, 18.
14. Willcocks and Craig, *op. cit.,* p. 454.
15. W. F. Haine, "Character of the Soils of Egypt," *Comité International
    de la Pedologie,* IV. *Commission* No. 6. Helsingfors, 1924.
16. Herodotus, II, 178-179.
17. Th. Fischer, *Mittelmeerbilder,* p. 4. Leipzig, 1908.
18. Herodotus, II, 112.
19. Herodotus, II, 35, 79, 81.
20. Strabo, XVII, Chap. I, 18-21, 53.
21. Herodotus, II, 43, 50.
22. E. Speck, *Handelsgeschichte des Altertums,* Vol. I, pp. 193-194.
    Leipzig, 1900.
23. John L. Myres, *The Dawn of History,* p. 56, 1911. For Wadi Ham-
    mamat, see Baedeker's *Egypt.*
24. Breasted, *op. cit.,* pp. 127-128, 142, 153, 183.
25. *Odyssey,* IV, 125.
26. Breasted, *op. cit.,* pp. 153-154, 182-183.
27. Herodotus, III, 106.
28. Hann, *Klimatologie,* Vol. III, p. 90. 1911.
29. *Periplus of the Erythræan Sea,* 14, 24, 56-57. Translated by W. Schoff,
    London and New York, 1912.
30. Arrian, *Indica,* Chaps. 21-29. Translated by E. Chinnock, London,
    1893.

31. Breasted, *op. cit.*, pp. 276-277, 486. *Ancient Records of Egypt,* Vol. II, paragraphs 247-248, 263, 265, 272. Chicago, 1906.
32. Herodotus, II, 138; IV, 42, 44.
33. Strabo, XVII, Chap. I, 25-26.
34. Strabo, XVI, Chap. IV, 5.
35. Strabo, XVII, Chap. I, 45.
36. Article "Red Sea," *Ency. Brit.*
37. I *Kings,* IX, 26-28; X, 11-12, 22; XII, 48-49. W. Götz, *Die Verkehrswege im Dienste des Welthandels,* pp. 100-101. Stuttgart, 1888.
38. Strabo, XVI, Chap. IV, 23.
39. Strabo, XVII, Chap. I, 7; XVI, Chap. IV, 24.
40. Strabo, XVII, Chap, I, 13, 16, 41-42.
41. Horatio Brown, *Studies in the History of Venice,* Vol. I, pp. 352-354. London, 1907.

CHAPTER IX

THE EASTERN BARRIER BOUNDARY AND ITS BREACHES

The complex Eastern Basin of the Mediterranean spans the Asian front from the head of the Sea of Azov to the Isthmus of Suez, a north and south stretch of nearly 1,200 miles. Behind this front lie various barriers to human movement—deserts, young folded mountains like the Caucasus and Taurus, an inland sea like the Caspian, dissected plateaus like the highland of Judea, and steep block mountains like the Lebanon and Anti-Lebanon. Generally a succession of barriers necessitate long and devious routes to reach the productive and civilized interior of southwest Asia from the Mediterranean front.

Even the seaboard is not hospitable except along the Ægean littoral of Asia Minor. Elsewhere Nature seems to throw open the gateways of the land, but soon puts up the bars again and excludes the migrant, whether he be explorer or caravan leader or general with an army at his back. In ancient times Greek traders and colonists penetrated to the head of the Sea of Azov, where the Don River opened a path eastward towards Asia; but beyond its mouth the land was forbidding. The Volga River formed for the ancients a barrier of braided streams and marshes, thirty miles wide, where it flowed down into the Caspian Depression. The barrier was worst moreover in summer, when the snows were melting about the river sources in northeastern Europe. Beyond the Volga lay the endless Kirghiz steppes, always the home of pastoral nomads, restless and uneasy neighbors, with small purchasing power and a preference for loot rather than trade.

There are several such initial openings on the coast of the Eastern Basin, but rarely are these combined with a feasible hinterland route into the interior of Asia. At the eastern end of the Black Sea the Caucasus Trough, the deep furrow between the Caucasus and Anti-Caucasus, opened a way eastward from the ancient Euxine ports of Dioscurias and Phasis in Colchis, which were much frequented for local products. The track led from the Euxine up the Phasis River to its elbow, then a five days' journey over a mountain pass (altitude 3,116 ft.[1]) to the Cyrus (Kura) River forty miles above the present site of Tiflis, then down this navigable stream to the Caspian; the route continued across the Caspian by an eight days' sail, thence through Bactria to the Oxus River, up the Oxus to the Pamir Plateau and over the Plateau to the Tarim Basin of Central Asia. This was a difficult route suited only for goods of small bulk and large value. For the Greek colonists of the Euxine coast this was the way to Serica, the land of silk, and to the gold fields of the Altai Mountains and Tibet, inhabited by the Issedones who monopolized their profitable trade by stories of "the gold-guarding griffins." Intermediaries in this trade were the bald Kalmucks of the Caspian steppes who were frequently visited by the Scythians and occasionally by the Greeks of the Pontic coast.[2]

A little trade in silk and gold doubtless trickled through the Caucasus Trough while the Persians controlled it [3] and the Bactrian road to the Oxus from the 7th century B.C. till the time of the Macedonian conquest. But the silk trade increased only when the Chinese conquered the Tarim Basin from 101 B.C. to 60 B.C., and again from 72 A.D. to 90 A.D.[4] However, Constantinople never quite lost the tradition of this silk trade, and was finally responsible for the introduction of the silkworm into Europe during the reign of Justinian about 550 A.D.

THE ASIA MINOR LAND BRIDGE—Asia Minor served as a land bridge from Armenia and the mountain rim of northern Mesopotamia to the Thracian Peninsula along its Bosporus and Hellespontine shore; but nowhere did it present a breach in the eastern barrier. On the contrary it involved a devious journey across mountains and over steppes or deserts, which made travel difficult even for a well organized army like that of Xerxes or Alexander. Only pastoral nomads with flocks and herds to provide food found movement easy. Therefore through all time Asia Minor has been the route of nomad invasion from the steppes of Asia to the nearby Thracian Peninsula.

The high folded mountains that rim the northern and south-

ern sides of the Anatolian Plateau greatly impede access to
the interior. Their torrent valleys repel traffic. The Pontic
ranges rise abruptly from the Euxine. Owing to heavy precipitation, their northern location (41° to 42° N. Lat.) and northern outlook, the winter snows linger till late summer on the high
passes, some of which reach an altitude of 10,000 feet. Heavy
forests and robber tribesmen [5] formerly impeded travel during
the short period when the mountain trails were open. The
southern coasts and southern hinterland were also barely accessible, the former haunted by pirates and the mountain trails
beset by robber nests through the whole length of the Taurus
system.

The western front of Asia Minor presents a sharp contrast
to its northern and southern flanks. The subsidence which
formed the Ægean Sea broke up the coast into a multiplicity
of bays and inlets, back of which lie parallel subsidence belts,
like the graben of the Meander and Hermus rivers, opening
well graded routes up to the rim of the central Anatolian Plateau. Farther north the Sangarius River opened a valley
path into the high hinterland of the Propontis. The sources of
all three spread out along the border of Great Phrygia and
Bithynia,[6] where they linked with the piedmont roads defining
the inner base of the Pontus ranges on the north and the
Taurus system on the south.

Since the Pontic coast range receives the heavier rainfall, it
sends down fuller irrigation streams, like the Sangarius, Halys
and Iris, than the rivers draining the inner slope of the Taurus
Mountains. Therefore, the main road eastward through Asia
Minor in ancient times followed approximately the 40th parallel, traversing belts of irrigated land and running through
Ancyra (Angora) and the ancient Hittite capital of Pteria.
Thence it turned southeast through Cappadocia across the high
watershed (5,000 ft.) between the Halys and the upper Euphrates to Melitene (Malatia), and thence south to Samosata
where the Euphrates issues from a mountain gorge upon the
piedmont plain of northern Mesopotamia.[7] An alternative
route crossed the Euphrates near Melitene to the sources of
the Tigris and followed this river down stream to northern
Mesopotamia not far from Nineveh at Rezabde.

The route up the Meander valley from the Ionian coast of Asia Minor linked also with the southern piedmont route to the east. It ran through Laodicea or Apamea Cibotus to the lake country of southern Phrygia and passed through the broken line of towns and irrigated fields dotting the inner base of the Taurus Mountains to Tyana in southern Cappadocia; thence it crossed the Taurus southeastward, dropping down through the Cilician Gates (*Pylæ Cilicæ*, 3,805 ft.) [8] to Adana in the coastal plain of lowland Cilicia. The southern piedmont was subject to constant raids by the Taurian mountaineers of Pisidia, Isauria and Rugged Cilicia (Cilicia Trachea) [9] who therefore must have imperilled all commercial travel along this piedmont route. A more serious drawback, however, was the fact that this route had its natural terminus in the Bay of Issus (Alexandretta) at the northeast corner of the Levantine Sea. It therefore necessitated further travel across the eastern barrier boundaries of the Levantine Sea in order to reach the fertile hinterland of Mesopotamia, whose products supplied the markets of the Levantine coast and contributed largely to the commerce of the Eastern Mediterranean.

Since the Asia Minor bridge involved a difficult journey of a thousand miles or more from the Ægean coast, it presented no easy opening through the eastern barrier; but it did afford land routes competing in part with the marine route of the Levantine Sea. These routes were preferred by the nomadic hordes that moved from Europe into southwest Asia, or from southwest Asia into Europe, and also by the expanding Assyrians and Persians whose native mountain environment afforded them no experience in nautical activity, but equipped them for rough travel through the highlands of Armenia and Anatolia. The Persians, who were masters of orderly administration, pushed the road development of Asia Minor, converted the original piedmont route of the Pontic ranges into the Imperial Post Road at the service of armies and post runners,[10] and conquered the Ægean seaboard whose ports formed the natural termini of the land routes.

THE HITTITE POWER AND ITS LOCATION IN ASIA MINOR— Asia Minor became the seat of the native Hittite or Hatti empire about 2200 B.C. This embodied allied or tributary states

and extended at its greatest expanse from the frontier of the
Ægean seaboard on the west to the north-south course of the
Euphrates on the east.[11] Its capital Pteria (Borghaz Keui)
lay on a bend of the Halys River at the crossroads of the old
Pontic Piedmont route between east and west, and the north-
south track from Sinope, the best harbor on the Euxine coast,
leading down to Tyana and the Cilician Gates through the
Taurus Mountains to Adana on the Sarus River plain of
Cilicia.[12] The distribution of Hittite ruins and monuments indicates the limits of their territory; the lack of any remains on
the Ægean coast emphasizes the fact that they were conservative mountaineer landsmen and used their littoral neighbors as
middlemen in the Ægean trade.[13]

A period of expansion from 1500 b.c. to 1225 b.c. carried
the conquering Hittite arms across the Amanus Mountains
and up the southern Orontes River valley to Hemesa (Homs),
where they came into conflict with the Egyptians about 1400
b.c.;[14] and across the plain of northern Syria to the great
bend of the Euphrates, where they encountered the expanding
forces of Assyria about 1300 b.c. The Hittites had met the
Assyrians several centuries earlier, from 1700 to 1600 b.c.,
where their frontiers marched along the upper Halys River.
There they had borrowed many features of Assyrian art and
passed these westward through Asia Minor to the Ægean coast
of Ionia, where they were appropriated by the Hellenic colonists. Mesopotamian characteristics appear in the ribbed or
pleated underskirt of the Hera of Samos now in the Louvre.
They appear also in the ivory-carved figurines dating from
about 700 b.c. found in the Temple of Ephesos, in their form
more reminiscent of Astarte than of the chaste Diana or proud
Hera, though they were the products of Ionian craftsmen.[15]
Centuries later the images of Diana called forth the fulmina-
tions of St. Paul[16] because they were made in the likeness of
the nature goddess Astarte of Arbela and encouraged her obscene cult. In a previous century this degraded Artemis worship had aroused the censure of Plato and Demosthenes. The
distribution of this oriental style of art all the way from Arbela
and Nineveh through Asia Minor to the Ionian coast indicated
the Anatolian bridge as the route of transmission. However,

Phœnician seamen, trading with the coast of Caria and Ionia, may also have shared in this dissemination of Asiatic art and religion.[17] From the Asiatic Greeks the art crossed the Ægean and reappeared in all archaic Hellenic sculpture,[18] as in the charioteer of the Delphi Museum.

The location of the Hittites in central Asia Minor exposed them to the victorious inroads of the Aryan Phrygians (about 1200 B.C.) who swept from the Thracian Peninsula into the fertile lands east of the Propontis and Hellespont,[19] secured the control of the northern and southern piedmont trade routes, and gained thereby great wealth, which made the name of Midas, official title of their kings, a synonym of riches. They brought with them the patriarchal society and the Father God Zeus, but absorbed the art and in part the religion of the Hittites,[20] whose name and empire they blotted out. Later came the Æolian, Ionian and Dorian Greeks to the Ægean coast and islands of Asia Minor, barring the Mysians, Phrygians and Lydians from the seaboard. All these Indo-European elements in the complex ethnography of Asia Minor came in from the west.[21] They were followed, 710 to 675 B.C., by the Cimmerians of Crimean and the Scythian plains, who probably entered *via* the Bosporus and Thrace, overwhelmed Phrygia and northern Lydia, and then vanished by the end of the 7th century B.C.

Asia Minor was the obvious land route westward for the Persian armies in their advance to the Balkan Peninsula. Cyrus moved across this bridge in 546 B.C. to the conquest of Lydia. Soon the Hellenic littoral was overcome by the Persians, who in 512 B.C. spread over the Thracian Peninsula and in the next three decades attempted to conquer Greece; but Cilician, Phœnician and Egyptian fleets furnished the Levantine Sea connection for the Persians, who required a navy for the conquest of maritime Greece.

THE SYRIAN SADDLE AND ITS HINTERLAND CONNECTIONS

Along the northeast coast of the Levantine Sea, between the Gulf of Issus (Alexandretta) and the Orontes River mouth, the Mediterranean approaches nearest to the productive and civilized countries of southwestern Asia. A hundred-mile belt of territory intervenes between this littoral and the great western bend of the Euphrates River, which marks the beginning of Mesopotamia. Access from this littoral strip to the Euphrates bend is not difficult; a natural gateway here facilitates communication between the coast and the fertile Mesopotamian hinterland, whose resources were developed for centuries under the stimulus of irrigation by the series of ancient states occupying this territory. Mesopotamia ends on the south where the Persian Gulf and the Gulf of Oman cut back 900 miles (1,500 kilometers) from the Arabian Sea, and make a broad isthmus of the intervening territory between the mouth of the Tigris and the Orontes.

THE TRANSIT LAND OF MESOPOTAMIA—The recurrent operation of geographic factors in history is nowhere more strikingly evinced than in the policies of commercial and territorial expansion directed backward and forward between the Levantine Sea and the Mesopotamian Basin. Through the ages a long succession of Asiatic, European and Egyptian powers have tried to control this natural transit land between East and West. Ancient Chaldean, Babylonian and Assyrian kings pushed their frontiers from the Tigris west to the Mediterranean. Persian conquerors like Cyrus and Darius, incorporating in their expanding empires the coastland of the Levantine Sea, anticipated by many centuries the design of the British power in India to control this great diagonal land-route from the Persian Gulf to the Mediterranean. History shows a like recurrent outreach from the West. Phœnicia, when Sidon was young, began the *Drang nach Osten* with the peaceful penetration of trade and the establishment of commercial colonies in Mesopotamia. The Pharaohs of the Eighteenth Dynasty, the Hittite power of Asia Minor, and the Greeks under Alexander the Great marched eastward as conquerors to the Euphrates bend and the Tigris. Rome's expansion over her military road through northern Mesopotamia anticipated the economic outreach of modern Germany over this strategic region. Nisibis was the easternmost outpost of the Roman Empire, and in 1918 it was the eastern terminus of the German-made Bagdad Railroad.

What are the geographic factors in this recurrent historical development, the drama which returns with monotonous action

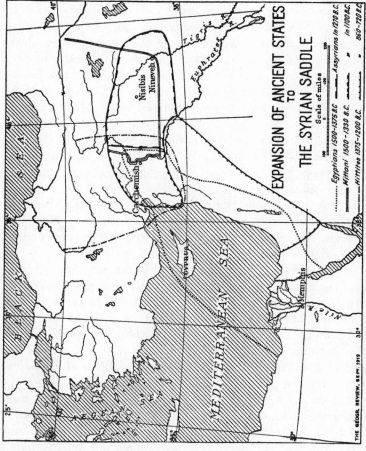

MAP 7.—Location of the Syrian Saddle between the western bend of the Euphrates and the nearby Mediterranean Coast.

and theme, though the actors change in race, nationality, and civilization from one age to another?

The valley of the Tigris and Euphrates rivers occupies a vast geographical trough extending diagonally across southwestern Asia from the Persian Gulf almost to the Mediterranean. It lies between the massive folded mountains of Persia and Armenia on the northeast, and the plateau of the Syrian and Arabian Deserts on the southwest. Thus it forms a natural passway, flanked by two regions inhospitable to travel and transportation. It finds its eastern outlet through the Persian Gulf to the Indian Ocean, and its western outlet to the Mediterranean through a breach in the barriers of mountain and desert which forms the eastern rim of the Levantine Sea. Except the Red Sea-Suez route, it has no effective competitor in the communication between East and West. The commercial significance of the Mesopotamian passway lies in the fact that it links now, as it did 5,000 years ago, two regions of contrasted climates, contrasted products and civilizations—the temperate European countries of the Mediterranean Basin and the tropical Asiatic lands of the Indian and Pacific Oceans.

THE EASTERN BARRIERS OF THE LEVANTINE SEA—Access from the Mediterranean to the Mesopotamian passage is difficult, except at one point. The Levantine Sea faces on the east a multiple barrier which rises behind an inhospitable coast, with scarcely a harbor worthy of the name in a stretch of 440 miles between the Egyptian frontier at Rhinocolura and the head of the Gulf of Issus. The Maritime Plain of Palestine, comprising the plains of Philistia and Sharon, owes its origin to a Tertiary uplift of the old sea floor. Not a single nick breaks its smooth shoreline from the Egyptian border to Haifa. North of Mount Carmel, along the coast of Phœnicia and Syria, the roots or buttresses of the Lebanon and Bargylus Mountains run out to form inferior ports, protected slightly by inshore reefs, a few hundred yards from shore, which the enterprising Phœnicians converted into breakwaters.

Overlooking this unpromising littoral is a line of mountains and plateaus, stretching from the Amanus range in northern Syria to the towering massif of Sinai (8,530 feet or 2,600 meters) in the south. These highlands are nearly everywhere steep and lofty enough, as in the Alpine heights of Lebanon, or repellent enough, as in the rugged limestone plateau of Judea, to constitute serious barriers. Immediately behind the coastal highlands runs a long, narrow trough which sinks in the Jordan Valley and Dead Sea 682 to 1,293 feet (208 to 393 meters) below ocean level. From the brink of this rift valley a second system of highlands rises parallel to the first, maintaining a mean elevation of about 2,500 feet (800 meters) in the south, but rising to imposing heights in Mount Hermon (9,020 feet or 2,750 meters) and the long wall of the Anti-Lebanon. East of Palestine this inner range is formed by the abrupt scarp of the Arabian Plateau. Though it rises to only moderate heights, it is a serious barrier, because the deep canyons of its drainage streams obstruct rather than facilitate the ascent from the Jordan trough. Beyond this second mountain system stretch the Syrian and Arabian Deserts, quite to the flood plain of the Euphrates.

The Levantine Sea is therefore cut off from its eastern hinterland by double mountain walls with a moat between. Passage across this country is a series of ups and downs. The railroad from Jaffa up to Jerusalem (2,600 feet or 792 meters) stops on the summit, blocked from further progress by the deep descent to the Dead Sea and the sharp ascent beyond to the heights of Gilead and Moab. The railroad from Haifa follows a feasible route eastward up the faulted plain of Esdraelon, along the track of an ancient highroad, to an elevation of 260 feet (80 meters), then drops down the canyon of the Jalud to the Jordan River, which it crosses at 815 feet (249 meters) below sea level, mounts the Yarmuk canyon to Derat at 1,886 feet (575 meters), and turning northward to its natural goal at Damascus, it ascends at Kisweh to 2,425 feet (739 meters) before reaching its destination in the great desert metropolis at an elevation of 2,266 feet (691 meters).[22] The Beirut-Damascus railroad mounts the steep slope of the Lebanon Mountains from the sea by twenty miles of rock-and-pinion track, crosses the summit of the range at 4,880 feet (1,500 meters), drops to the intermontane trough at Reyak at 3,500 feet (1,070 meters), crosses the Anti-Lebanon at an elevation of 4,610 feet (1,405 meters), and finally descends nearly 2,400 feet to the plain of

7

Damascus.[23]   After all the vicissitudes of up-and-down transportation, with its attendant heavy costs, these transverse railroads come out on the economic void of the Arabian Desert, save where the old volcanic soil of the Hauran and the oasis of Damascus offer limited areas of tillage.

The eastern barrier of the Levantine Sea has, however, a breach at each extremity, which in all times has admitted traffic from the Mediterranean. To the south the barrier shrinks and drops to the Suez Isthmus, which affords a short and level passage to the Red Sea, but in ancient times carried comparatively little traffic even in the palmy days of the Roman Empire.

Between the Isthmus of Suez and the Gulf of Issus the highland barrier overlooking the Levantine Sea is pierced at only two points. One is the faulted plain of Esdraelon which was followed by an ancient highway leading from the seaports of Haifa and Acre (Akka) eastward to the canyon of the Jalud River, and thence by a devious route to Damascus. The other is the valley of the Eleutheros River (modern El Kebir or "great river") which marks the division between the Lebanon and Bargylus Mountains. This stream rises on the inner slope of the Lebanon range and opens a pass 1,755 feet high which was utilized for an ancient route connecting the early Phœnician seaport of Simyra or the later city of Tripolis with the busy crossroads town of Hemesa (Homs) in the upper Orontes valley of the Lebanon trough. This was the route taken by the Egyptian army of Rameses II when in 1272 b.c. he advanced to block the Hittite invasion of Syria. Shortly before 1914 it was adopted as the route of a branch railroad connecting the trunk railroad of the Lebanon trough with the coast at the busy port of Tripoli. It was built to restore to Tripoli some of the traffic which was diverted south to Beirut when the Beirut-Damascus line was opened.

THE SYRIAN SADDLE—A far more frequented route was that leading from the Levantine Sea through the northern breach in the barrier to the natural highway of the Tigris and Euphrates valley, and thence to the Persian Gulf. Where the Gulf of Alexandretta, the ancient Gulf of Issus, drives a marine wedge fifty miles back into the coastline of northern Syria, the mountain barrier contracts and drops to the single, relatively low range of Mount Amanus, which forms a saddle connecting the tall and massive highlands to the north and south of it.   This structural saddle, whose crest rises in general to 5,000 feet (1,530 meters), was crossed in ancient times by three pass routes.   One led from the Cilician plain eastward up a tributary of the Pyramus River (modern Seihun) to the *Pylæ Amani* or modern Bogtche Pass at about 3,000 feet, dropped thence down to the ancient Hittite town of Sendjerle near the modern settlement of Islahiya, whence it proceeded southeast over the plain to Chalyb (Aleppo).   This is the route of the modern Bagdad Railroad which pierces the pass by a three-mile tunnel.

As originally projected, the railroad was to follow the second route over the Amanus Range, which was the ancient path of travel.   This route left the Bay of Issus at Myriandros near the later Alexandretta, crossed the range by the *Pylæ Syriæ* or Beilan Pass at an altitude of 2,395 feet (730 meters), and descended thence to the plain of Aleppo at 1,215 feet altitude on the east.   This was Alexander's route after the battle of Issus in 332 B.C., and the most direct line of access to the Mediterranean for any modern railroad.   The Macedonian army, approaching it from Cilicia along the narrow coastal road at the western foot of the Amanus Range, met the Persians drawn up to block their advance.   The military Germans who built the railway saw in imagination this coast road bombarded by British ships, and hence made the railroad take a long detour to the Bogtche Pass to the north.

Forty miles south of Alexandretta the Amanus Range is cleft by the gorge of the Orontes River, which cuts a passage to the sea.   To the ancient Greek road-builders this offered a feasible route of easy grade, only 17 miles long, from the Mediterranean up to the plain of Antioch at 227 feet elevation.   Early settlements, probably of Phœnician origin, at both entrances to the gorge indicate that a rough track must have penetrated this passway in very ancient times.   But it was the great pass city of Antioch and its port Seleucia Pieria which exploited their geographical position as the natural western termini of the great trade route to the East.   Some day they may revive as railroad termini.

Behind the Amanus Range, where the Levantine mountain rampart is thus pierced and shrunken, the moat of the rift valley disappears; the inner mountain system runs out into low hills; and the last barrier formed by the Arabian and Syrian deserts is superseded in this more rainy northern tract by a grassy plain, which with the Amanus Range fills the scant hundred-mile stretch between the Mediterranean and the great western bend of the Euphrates River. This plain receives from 10 to 20 inches (250 to 500 mm.) of rain, enough to maintain ample herbage for the camels and horses of passing caravans, and to support winter crops of wheat and barley. Moreover, it is furrowed by small streams flowing down from the Taurus foothills on the north, whose waters have for ages irrigated the orchards and gardens of the big market towns scattered over this plain. Hence the ancients called it the Naharain or "land of rivers."

This northern district of Syria therefore lowers the bars between the Mediterranean and the Euphrates. It may properly be called the Syrian Saddle, because here the multiple barrier of mountains and desert is reduced to a single low passage, which gives access to the great valley of the twin rivers, stretching away southeastward for 800 miles (1,300 kilometers) to the Persian Gulf.

The Tigris-Euphrates trough varies in width from 200 miles (330 kilometers) in the south to nearly 400 miles (600 kilometers) in the north, where the rivers emerge from the Taurus Mountains upon the plain. Except along its highland rim on the north and east, it has a rainfall so scant as to induce steppe or desert conditions over all its area. The alluvial tract of the lower valley was reclaimed to tillage and settlement only by irrigation. Northern Mesopotamia was a grassland in winter and early spring, and a desert the rest of the year. The question now is: Where lay the main route of travel through this broad but semi-arid trough?

THE EUPHRATES ROUTE—At first glance the Euphrates River seems to afford the shortest and most obvious line of communication. And sure enough, from the gray dawn of history (3000 B.C.) the river was utilized for the transport of cedar, cypress and pine timber from the wooded slopes of Mount

MAP 8—Relation of the Piedmont Route to the Antioch outlet of the Orontes, and the *Pylæ Syriæ* of the Amanus Mountains. Chief towns along the Piedmont Route. Lower sketch shows the relation of the Piedmont Route to the middle Tigris and Euphrates Rivers.

Amanus and Lebanon,[24] and fine building stone and asphalt from upstream points, down to Hit at the head of the treeless delta, and thence by canal over to the Tigris towns.[25] These bulky commodities were floated down the Euphrates on rafts buoyed up by inflated skins, like those depicted on ancient Babylonian and Assyrian monuments. The Euphrates, however, is a poor waterway, and doubtless always has been. Gathering its main supply of water in its long mountain course in Armenia, it becomes navigable for rafts in the flood season from April to August. But when the short winter rains are over, when the spring floods due to the melting of the mountain snows subside, when summer heat and irrigation further deplete the volume of water, the Euphrates reaches so low a stage between August and late November that navigation is constantly interrupted by shallows and reefs.[26]

Ancient traffic on both the Tigris and Euphrates moved exclusively down stream.[27] The means of transportation were rafts and round wicker boats plastered with bitumen.[28] Such craft was unsuited to up-stream navigation, especially in view of the swift current which above the deltaic lowland runs four miles an hour in flood time. This was the season of navigation, because the awkward boats were swept down stream to their destination by the rapid current and escaped the danger of shipwreck on the rocky reefs. Herodotus indicates that the Euphrates River was a common route for passenger traffic from the Mediterranean to Babylon. In Pliny's time it took ten days to make the voyage down the river from a point near the mouth of the Balikh to Ctesiphon, the Parthian capital.[29]

The Euphrates has never invited the development of a highway along its banks. It flows through Mesopotamia but does not water it. Its swift stream lies at the bottom of a narrow, cliff-faced intervale, hardly accessible to the nomads on the plains above. Occasionally where the cliffs recede and admit a broader strip of alluvium along the banks, within reach of irrigation from shaduf and water wheel, villages with cultivated fields and date-palms appear. The sparse sedentary population along the Euphrates, the meager products of the arid country, the scant local commissariat for caravan or army, and the constant danger of nomad attack or blackmail [30] combined to discourage ancient travel along the river above the delta, which marked the beginning of the dense population.

Among all the military campaigns conducted by would-be conquerors between Babylonia and the Syrian coast during 2,000 years or more, only one, so far as we have been able to discover, followed the route along the Euphrates. That was the expedition of Cyrus the Younger (401 B.C.), who took the shortest road to Babylon, in order to surprise Artaxerxes before he had news of the revolt. The description of that journey in Xenophon's *Anabasis* shows this to have been no route for armies which had to live off the country. On the desert stretch below the mouth of the Khabur River, a thirteen days' march, many of the baggage animals perished from hunger, and some of the soldiers subsisted entirely upon the meat of the antelopes and wild asses grazing on the plains. At times it was necessary to prolong the day's march in order to get water and fodder.[31] A Roman campaign, which was planned in 242 A.D. to invade Parthia by the Euphrates route and capture Ctesiphon, proved abortive owing to the lack of food. The army reached Circesium at the mouth of the Khabur River, but, failing to find there the store of provisions which it had expected for the long desert march, it mutinied and turned back.[32]

Caravans, carrying their own food supply, followed a variant of this route many miles east of the river. They must have been confined to winter and spring, when their camels could find forage. Possibly the caravan traffic of the cooler months was supplemented by river traffic during the hot summer, when navigation was good but desert travel particularly bad. In the time of Augustus, "the road of the merchants," as Strabo calls it, to Ctesiphon or Seleucia on the lower Tigris started from the Euphrates bridge at Europos (Hittite Carchemish and modern Jerablus) and led thence for twenty-five days southeast through the steppes and deserts of the nomad *Scenitæ*, or tent-dwellers, who gave the caravans safe passage for a moderate transit duty and furnished them with water drawn from local wells or brought from a distance.[33] The route along the river was avoided because of the exorbitant dues exacted by the tribes dwelling along the stream. At a later date (51 A.D.) a Parthian king evidently succeeded in suppressing or controlling this evil, because he attracted to his entrepôt of Vologesia and other towns on the lower Euphrates the trade which reached the upper river from Damascus. This Syrian metropolis maintained connection with the Euphrates by a desert track running through a series of oases strung along the foot of a ridge to Tadmor,[34] and thence east to Birtha (modern Deir) near the mouth of the Khabur River, or north to Sura, located on the Euphrates between Thapsacus and the mouth of the Balikh. During the second and third centuries A.D. Palmyra or Tadmor, as way station between the Euphrates and Middle Syria, enjoyed a short-lived prosperity which rose and declined with this caravan trade to the Persian Gulf.[35]

Traffic on a small scale doubtless dribbled into Babylon and Damascus straight across the desert ever since those early days when "the Princes of Kedar" brought in lambs and rams from their meager pastures for the markets of ancient Tyre. The nomads were the natural middlemen and carriers in this desultory trade. In their normal course of life, they drifted down to the marsh meadows of the lower Euphrates in summer, when their water-holes were dried up and their pastures burnt bare, then back again to the desert when the winter rains revived the herbage, and on to towns of the desert fringe like Damascus and Bosra,[36] to barter the products of their herds and their slender stock of Babylonian merchandise for grain and arms— the wheat of Bosra and the steel of Damascus. The desert junction of Petra, which traded with Gaza and Egypt, imported nothing from Babylonia, so far as the evidence shows, but only the rare products of Arabian Yemen together with the Indian and African commodities brought to Aden (Adana) and Mocha (Muza). These goods were carried from the southern ports up the Red Sea to Leuce Come (24° N. Lat. near the modern Janbo) on the Arabian coast during autumn and winter, when the southeast monsoon was blowing. There they were transferred to caravans for transportation to Petra. The route probably followed approximately the line of the Hejaz Railroad from Maan to Medina. It was impracticable for an army; so the Nabataean guide maintained who advised that the Roman campaign against this country in 25 B.C. should move by sea. The guide was made the scapegoat of an unsuccessful expedition and charged with treachery by Strabo,[37] who with biased judgment reasoned that the route was feasible for large caravans and therefore for an army of 10,000 men. Only this trade in aromatics, goods of small bulk and large value like frankincense, myrrh, cinnamon, and perfumes,[38] could stand the heavy cost of desert transportation. Fodder and water had to be purchased all along the way; and transit dues had to be paid in addition to the imperial Roman customs. Guards had to be employed then as now to protect the caravan against the robber nomads. Pliny reckoned the total cost of carriage for a camel's load of frankincense from Leuce Come to Gaza at 688 denarii, or $150.[39] Only the wealth and luxury of the Roman Empire could have supported this caravan trade on a large scale; and even so it must be remembered that the major part of these oriental luxury articles reached Mediterranean ports by the Red Sea and Nile route to Alexandria.[40]

Diligent research discloses no evidence that the desert routes ever forwarded a large amount of trade, or were ever traversed by an army. The nearest approach to such a venture was that of the Babylonian prince Nebuchadnezzar in 605 B.C. He was in southern Palestine about to pursue the forces of Pharaoh Necho into Egypt, when he learned that his father Nabopolassar had died. Fearing a pretender might arise, he hurried, to save time, across the Arabian Desert to Babylon with a small band of followers; but he sent his army by the circuitous route around by the Naharain, the western bend of the Euphrates and northern Mesopotamia by which he had come.[41] Countless conquerors before him had travelled this road, whether they marched east or west.

THE PIEDMONT ROUTE—This was the route of Alexander the Great. Moving north after his conquest of Egypt and Phœnicia, he crossed the Euphrates at Thapsacus in August, 331 B.C., for the invasion of Mesopotamia, struck north up the Balikh valley and then east along the piedmont of the Taurus foothills to the Tigris River, because this route offered the easiest line of march, provisions for his men, and fodder for his animals; so Arrian, his chronicler, tells us.[42] In Mesopotamia a food supply big enough for a large army and its transport in late summer pointed to irrigated fields, a sedentary population, and considerable towns. These conditions attracted ancient armies and traders to this route. They attracted also the German promoters and engineers who projected the modern Bagdad Railroad.

As far back as we can penetrate into the remote past, we find that the main line of communication from the Persian Gulf to the Mediterranean followed a land road east of the Tigris along the base of the Persian highlands north to Assur or Nineveh near modern Mosul, ran thence westward along the piedmont of northern Mesopotamia to the great western bend of the Euphrates, which it crossed by ford or ferry according to the place and time of the year. Thence it continued west past Chalybon (Aleppo) to the Mediterranean by the Amanus passes, or by more devious and difficult tracks farther south. From Aleppo eastward to Mosul this is the route of the Bagdad Railroad, which between Mosul and Bagdad follows the level west bank of the Tigris to avoid engineering difficulties and reduce operating expenses. Many of the stations on or near the railroad, like Nisibis, Ras-el-Ain (Resaina), Harran, Jerablus (Carchemish), and Aleppo meet us at the beginning of history. They have seen the encampment of royal Babylonian armies 2000 or 3000 B.C., and they have watched the sheik Abraham pitch his tents by their wayside waters, as he drifted westward with his clan towards the land of Canaan.[43]

This ancient route between the Syrian Saddle and the Tigris highway finds its explanation in the climatic and physiographic conditions of northern Mesopotamia. These have determined the distribution of settlements and the main lines of travel in this semi-arid land. Mesopotamia is a region of meager winter rains and long summer droughts. The dry season falls in the hottest part of the year, when great heat prevails over the plains and evaporation is intense. The precipitation from May to November is practically nil, and even in the cold season it is scant. The plains from the Persian Gulf north to the 36th parallel get less than 8 inches (200 mm.) of rain.[44] From this line northward precipitation increases owing both to the more northern location and the higher elevation of upper Mesopotamia. The increments, however, are very small. The line of

10 inches (250 mm.) annual rainfall describes an arc subtended
by the 36th parallel, with one extremity 30 miles (50 kilometers) southeast of Mosul and the other at Aleppo, while the
curve runs up the Tigris River and along the crest of a series
of highlands which form an outlier of the Taurus system and
wall in the plains of Mesopotamia on the north.

These highlands consist of the Tur Abdin (ancient Mount
Masius), a long narrow plateau of 3,300 to 4,000 feet elevation (1,000 to 1,200 meters) with a steep escarpment to the
south; and the Karaja Mountains (ancient Mount Izala) an
old volcanic massif which maintains a general altitude of about
4,100 feet (1,250 meters), but rises to 6,068 feet (1,850
meters) in its culminating peak, only to sink westward towards
the Euphrates bend in an undulating upland 2,600 feet (800
meters) above sea level.[45] These massive foothills of the
Taurus are high enough to wring some moisture from the reluctant clouds. In winter they accumulate on their upper
slopes snow enough to form a considerable reservoir of moisture; and in the spring they drop a fringe of slender torrents
down on the plain. Their irrigating streams through the ages
have reclaimed the northern border of the Mesopotamian steppe
from pastoral nomadism, and stretched a piedmont belt of
towns, surrounded by well-watered gardens, orchards, vineyards
and fields, to link the settlements on the Tigris with the western
bend of the Euphrates and the Syrian Saddle.

The breadth of this urban belt, the density and prosperity
of its population, has generally depended upon the strength
and sanity of the ruling governments, whether in Babylon,
Nineveh, Antioch, Rome or Bagdad. Its northern edge in ancient times, as in modern, was pushed well up into the highlands
to an altitude of about 2,000 feet (600 meters), at Urhai or
Edessa (modern Urfa), at the ancient Babylonian Tela near
the later Roman Constantia and modern Veranshehr, and at
the ancient Armenian capital of Tigranocerta, whose mound
of ruins lies beside the modern Kojhissar; but at Marde (modern Mardin) it climbed the steep slope of Mount Masius to
3,050 feet (930 meters). These upper towns enjoyed comparative immunity from nomad raids from the steppes, while they
commanded numerous springs and a fairly sure water supply.

However, in Mardin in the 12th century every house had its
cistern for storing rain water; [46] ancient cisterns everywhere
indicate the economy practiced.

The down-stream settlements of this urban belt, like Harran
or Carrhæ, Resaina or Ras-el-Ain, and Nisibis, lay only about
1,400 or 1,500 feet above sea level; though more precariously
located as to water supply and nomad attack, they nevertheless occupied a better position for trade. They were stations
on the great piedmont route between Tigris and Euphrates,
which was a type of all such roads in semi-arid lands. It
marked the nice adjustment between the farthest encroachment

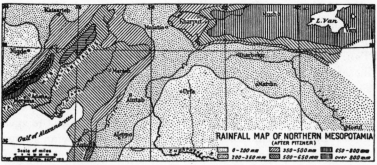

MAP 9—The rainfall of Northern Mesopotamia in relation to the Piedmont Route.

of the desert up-hill in the dry season, and the farthest assured
reach desertward of the irrigation streams from the mountains
behind. North of this line, where the slope from the marginal
highlands was steeper, the deeper valleys cut by the swift
drainage streams and the more rugged character of the country
presented obstacles to transportation.

It must not be supposed, however, that the ancient route
never deviated from this line; that would be contrary to the
nature of primitive roads in grasslands. In the late summer,
when the interfluvial spaces were parched and the water holes
dry, especially when a succession of almost rainless years had
expanded the domain of the desert, then army or caravan
would take a parallel path farther north, near the upper edge
of the urban piedmont belt. It would cross the Euphrates at
Biredjik, one of the chief crossing-places of the river from time

immemorial, site of the Greek Zeugma or bridge,[47] and turn thence east to the ancient Greek Edessa and yet more ancient Aramaic Urhai.   Then, passing numerous villages, now heaps of ruins except for their ancient cisterns which still serve travellers till late summer, it would go eastward through the upper hill towns till it reached ancient Marde.   This upper track, maintaining a general level of 2,000 feet, was nearer the springs that fed the streams and offered better pasturage for pack animals.   From Marde, however, it dropped down to Nisibis which lay on the Gargar, the last perennial stream.   Few of these piedmont rivers outlive the summer drought and the tax of irrigation.   The Gargar, which still waters the gardens and fields of Nisibis, is sometimes 20 feet wide in August and too deep to be crossed except at fords.[48]   Nisibis was therefore always a station on the piedmont route.

In the dry season, the track continued eastward, hugging the foot of the Tur Abdin escarpment with its fountains and wells all the way to the Tigris gorge at ancient Bezabde (modern Jezira-ibn-Oman).   This was the road taken by Alexander the Great in the summer of 331 B.C.   An eclipse of the sun fixes the date when he crossed the Tigris as September 20th, the climax of the dry season.[49]   However, after the winter rains had carpeted all northern Mesopotamia with grasses and flowers, the main route turned southeastward, about 20 miles east of Nisibis, and struck out straight towards Nineveh across an arid stretch of 30 miles (50 kilometers), until it met the wadis draining northeastward from the Singar Mountains to the Tigris.   This is the path of the Bagdad Railroad from Nisibis to Mosul.   So stable is the geography of communications in these semi-arid lands.   Yet another variant, feasible in spring for armies, turned west from Nineveh and followed the southern base of the Singar Mountains, whose barrier was high enough to make the passing winds pay a toll of water; then bent north through a gap in the range to Nisibis,[50] crossing the sheaf of wadis which united to form the Saocaras River.   This route was better for armies than for caravans because it was exposed to nomad raids.

MOVEMENT OF ARMIES AND COMMERCE ALONG THE PIEDMONT ROUTE—Historical evidence shows that the Mesopotamian piedmont was the chief link between ancient Babylonia and the West. This is indicated by the persistent trend of Babylonian and Assyrian expansion westward along this piedmont, especially after 1500 B.C., when we begin to get reliable accounts of the wars for the control of northern Mesopotamia. The need of lumber in the treeless lands of the delta was the original motive which induced the early kings like Sargon of Akkad (2500 B.C.) to conquer the well-wooded mountain district fronting the Mediterranean and to extend their dominion over "the lands of the Sunset Sea," [51] as the cuneiform records call the Mediterranean. The Euphrates River may have been the original outward line of exploration, as it undoubtedly brought down to Babylon the bulky exports from the Amanus and Lebanon forests; [52] but the piedmont route early begins to emerge in the movement of armies, the spread of commerce and religions. The names of its cities appear in early Babylonian history—Assur, Singara, Nisibis, Tilli or Tela and Harran.[53]

Harran or "Road Town," located on the Bilechas River (Balikh), on the trunk route of northern Mesopotamia and at the focus of tracks radiating fanwise to the several fords of the Euphrates elbow, was the most important city of all this region.[54] Of unknown origin, reputed by tradition to be the first town after the Flood,[55] it became the western outpost of Babylonian civilization. By the 10th century B.C. it was a capital of Assyria co-equal with Assur itself. It was the seat of the ancient moon cult, which spread thence to Babylonia at an early date, and which later colored the religious life of Assyria to the east and Phœnicia, Syria and Palestine to the west.[56] Many of the foreign cultural influences apparent in Syria and Palestine emanated from Harran rather than from Assyria, to which they have been attributed. On the other hand, many occidental influences which can be discerned in the cults of Babylonia spread to the lower Tigris by way of Harran. The Syrian weather god Rammon is domiciled in Babylon by 2000 B.C., and he is worshipped in Assur on a par with the local god Assur in 1800 B.C. The goddess Ishtar, or Astarte, or Astaroth, was chief deity of Nineveh and Arbela in Assyria. Her worship spread thence westward along the piedmont to Phœnicia, Cyprus, and western Asia Minor along the routes of Phœnician traffic in the second millennium B.C.[57]

Phœnicia early secured trade connections with the piedmont belt, because this opened up her most productive hinterland.[58] She did this by means of inland colonies or trading stations, located at strategic points along established routes. Laish or Dan, a Sidonian colony of the 15th century B.C., situated at the sources of the Jordan River, gave access to the old military road which led north through the Lebanon trough [59] to the Euphrates bend. Hamath (Hama), of supposed Phœnician origin, was a station on the Orontes road, and Thapsacus at the Euphrates ford commanded the trading advantages at the crossing of the river. Nisibis, claimed as a Phœnician foundation because of its name,[60] was probably rather the seat of a Phœnician commercial factory, which introduced there the wares and religions of the West. Harran participated actively in the markets of Tyre in Ezekiel's time,[61] and doubtless much earlier when it was an important independent city and middleman between West and East. Syria and Palestine evidently regarded the piedmont route as their chief line of communication with Babylonia and Chaldæa. According to Jewish legendary history, it was from Harran on this old trunk road that Abraham and his nomad tribe moved westward to Canaan.[62]

FOCUS OF ROUTES IN THE NAHARAIN—The Mesopotamian piedmont of town and highway extended west to the great bend of the Euphrates. There it joined the populous plain of Naharain and the Syrian Saddle, which together were the focus of trade routes radiating north, west and south. One well-travelled road led up from Egypt along the narrow land-bridge between the Mediterranean waste of water and the Arabian waste of desert sands. Another ran northwest across the Cilician plain and over the Cilician Gates in the mighty Taurus range to the Hittite country in Asia Minor, where it connected with tracks leading west to the Ægean Sea. Yet another ran north from Harran through Urfa and Samosata at the passage of the Euphrates to Melite (Malatia), where it connected with the main road through Asia Minor to the Hittite country. Besides these land routes, dissolving Medi-

terranean trails, whose sign-posts were the stars, brought
Phœnician cargo ships from Egypt, Crete and other Ægean
lands, and contributed rare overseas products to this focal
market region.

The commodities meeting here for exchange were varied—
pearls, jewels, and spices from India; embroidered garments
and imitation lapis lazuli from Babylonia; gums, perfumes,
drugs and frankincense from Arabia; linen, goldwork and in-
laid ivory from Egypt; horses, cattle and metals from Armenia
and the northern mountains; sheep, goats, fruits and wine
from the piedmont towns of Mesopotamia; olive oil, wines,
copper and Tyrian purple from the Mediterranean lands, besides the beautiful manufactured wares of the Phœnician cities.

All these routes with their richly laden caravans converged
upon the cities strung along the western bend of the Euphrates
from Thapsacus to Samosata, and those scattered over the
plain between the river and the foot of Mount Amanus. Each
city became a market because it was a necessary stopping
place. It commanded a ford or ferry across the Euphrates,
which involved a halt until all the long caravan should have
safely crossed; or it supplied water to the merchant and his
transport from the stream which irrigated its gardens and
orchards. This was a desirable district. It offered big profits.
to the trader and big revenues to the government. Its towns
were inhabited by merchant princes. Azaz, Arpad, Pethor,
Chalybon (Aleppo) and Carchemish yielded rich booty to the
conqueror.[63]

THE SYRIAN SADDLE AS GOAL OF EXPANSION—Hence this
whole region early became the object of conquest from every
side, while the Mesopotamian piedmont belt, which linked it with
the tropical East, was hardly less the goal of expansion. Every
contiguous power, no matter how small or unorganized, tried to
set up its toll gate on this great highway. A map of the series
of conquests in this region from 1600 B.C. to the Crusades, and
again through the modern period shows all the great historical
episodes to have been cast in the same mold; and this mold in
turn was fashioned by the geographic conditions. The artifi-
cers were in turn of all races, tongues, religions, and cultural

development; but their hands knew only the one cunning when it came to turning out historical events in this region.

Babylon, as we have seen, claimed suzerainty over the Syrian Saddle and the piedmont belt from about 3000 B.C. From the time Sargon of Akkad made his expedition against the Amorites of the Orontes valley in 2500 B.C., Babylonian influences were strong throughout northern Syria,[64] disseminated there by caravans travelling either by desert trails, the Euphrates track from Babylon, or by the piedmont route. The Mesopotamian route apparently got most of the traffic. The Babylonian king Kadashman-Kharbe (c. 1450 B.C.), finding himself excluded from the piedmont road by Assyria's occupation of northern Mesopotamia, undertook to open a road across the Syrian Desert. He subdued the nomad Suti dwelling about the mouth of the Khabur River, made wells, erected military posts, and established Babylonian settlements along the way, which probably ran through Tadmor to Damascus. By this route, which was shorter and avoided the long detour to the north, he hoped to divert the western trade from Assyria, which was expanding along the piedmont to secure this very trade.[65] The desert road was apparently a failure, for soon Babylonia is again fighting Assyria for the control of northern Mesopotamia, and keeps up the conflict for centuries.[66]

Assyria, owing to her geographic location, had a dominant interest in the traffic which moved along the piedmont belt to and from the Mediterranean ports. The cities of Assur and Nineveh, situated on the upper course of the Tigris at the head of regular navigation, were the eastern termini of the piedmont route. There goods were transferred from caravan to *kelek* for transportation downstream to Babylonia; or they went north to the fertile Lake Van district (Lake Thospitis) of Armenia by a road up the Tigris valley and over the Taurus Mountains by the Bitlis Pass (5,000 feet), the route followed later by Xenophon's retreating army. Yet other wares went east through Arbela and over the passes in the Zagros Mountains to Media.[67] Thus Nineveh, like Carchemish on the Euphrates, was a river town at the focus of land routes. Geographical location made it the natural middleman between East and West, stimulated commercial and territorial expansion, and impelled it especially to secure control of the piedmont route to the west. Hence Nineveh drove out all competitors and monopolized the profits. Finally, she seized the fords of the Euphrates at the great bend and controlled the highroads to the Phœnician ports. The process of western conquest went on for seven centuries with alternating success and failure; but it was not relinquished until Nineveh fell to Median attacks in 607 B.C.

"The land of the city of Assur," the original Assyria, was a colony or vassal state of Babylon; [68] but it developed differently owing to geographic conditions. It was poor in irrigable plough land, and for this reason turned to commerce. Its more northern location, its relatively cold winters and prevailing mountainous relief tended to produce a more enterprising and energetic population than was to be found on the low alluvium of Babylonia. Moreover, the people were probably a pure Semitic stock, unmixed with the Sumerian blood which diluted the Semitic strain in the deltaic lowland. Hence Assur developed a different type of people with different interests.[69] It became a typical colonial frontier state, with a natural tendency to political defection born of remoteness, contrasted conditions, and divergent interests. So it set up an independent government some time between 1800 and 1500 B.C. When the kingdom of Assyria expanded, it spread westward along the lines of least physical resistance and greatest commercial opportunity. It never for any length of time transcended the Zagros Mountains to the east or the main Taurus range to the north. Its military campaigns in these directions seem to have been primarily defensive or punitive, designed to protect its own borders, while those towards the west reveal a sustained policy of expansion which had for its goal the eastern littoral of the Levantine Sea. The cost of these campaigns was amply covered by the enormous booty, ransoms, and tributes secured from the piedmont cities which studded the main line of march from the Assyrian frontier to the Phœnician ports.[70] The treasure in these cities, varied and abundant as it was, could not have been derived from the meager local resources of the district, and therefore bears evidence to immense profits procured from the passing trade.

For the seven centuries of her westward advance, Assyria ran the gauntlet between enemies on the north and south who wished to get a foothold in the piedmont belt. From the south came repeated attacks from Babylon, several of which between 1300 and 960 B.C. succeeded in temporarily recovering Mesopotamia.[71] Moreover, the nomads of the grasslands were prone to encroach on the better-watered territory of the piedmont and constantly had to be expelled.[72] A decline of Assyrian power after the death of Tiglath-Pileser I enabled the Aramæan tribes of the Syrian Desert to push north and northeast into the Mesopotamian piedmont and the Naharain. They were drawn thither by the prospect of trade, for such nomads are natural middlemen. Hovering about the fringes of the cultivated land, they probably furnished camel transport for the piedmont commerce or took a hand in the caravan commerce down the Euphrates to Babylon. Now they established little independent states on the lower Khabur River, the Balikh and on both banks of the Euphrates below Carchemish. Chief of these was Bit-Adini near Harran on the Balikh.[73] There they sought to maintain their independence against the attacks of Assyria, who tried to crush every rival middleman on the piedmont route. They were sustained by Babylon, who always hoped to reassert her claim to northern Mesopotamia; and they found a powerful champion and leader in Damascus, who, with the assistance of the nomads as well as the settled tribes, gravely threatened the western piedmont. When Assyria revived under Assurnazipal (885-860 B.C.) it absorbed these little states, together with the Euphrates city Sura, river terminus of the desert route from Damascus *via* Tadmor.[74]

The piedmont belt was more seriously threatened from the north. It was repeatedly conquered in whole or in part by a succession of states which rose to power in the highlands of Armenia and the mountain ranges northwest of the great bend. These kingdoms, condemned by their rugged environment to backward economic development, based their meager national wealth on the raw products of forest, pasture, field and mine. They wanted a frontage on the busy thoroughfare of the plain, in order to exchange their raw products for manufactured wares, and share in the lucrative trade between East

and West. This they achieved by conquering from time to time
a section of the Mesopotamian piedmont, setting themselves up
as middlemen, and levying transit dues on the through traffic.
Such were the Mitanni, an Aryan people of the Armenian highlands, who about 1500 B.c. pushed their frontier southward
over the rim of Mount Masius, and occupied the piedmont belt
from Nineveh on the Tigris through Nisibis and Harran to the
bend of the Euphrates.[75] Thus they got astride of the piedmont road and cut off Assyria and Babylon from the western
trade.[76]

In 1330 B.c. Assyria inaugurated her westward movement
by expelling the Mitanni from northern Mesopotamia. In 1270
B.c. Shalmaneser I consolidated the previous conquests, extended the frontier west to the Balikh River, if not to the
Euphrates, and incorporated the city of Harran as his western
capital on a par with Assur itself, to emphasize the union of
the two states.[77] In order to secure the piedmont belt from
attack, he conquered the Amida (modern Diarbekir) basin of
the upper Tigris, advanced his frontier up to the main range
of the Taurus on the north, which served as a border rampart,
and planted Assyrian colonies through the newly acquired territories as outpost defenses of Mesopotamia.

This history repeated itself again in the reign of Tiglath-
Pileser I (1170 B.c.), who pushed his way to the Mediterranean,[78] and with slight variations many times thereafter.
Assyria during centuries of struggle for an open road to the
western sea had constantly to beat back these mountaineers
who threatened the right flank of her advance. Her main line
of march was a corridor running along the base of their highland. Defeat involved withdrawal along this corridor, constantly exposed to flank attack. The semi-arid land south
of the piedmont offered a difficult line of retreat in summer and
a doubtful one in spring, when fodder indeed was abundant
but the widely flooded streams impeded the progress of an
army. For military strategy this piedmont belt presented
much the same problem as the Venetian plain of northern Italy,
between the Austrian Alps and the Adriatic, for an Italian
army advancing from the Piave River to the Carso saddle.
Therefore a mountain campaign in lower Armenia was the pre-

liminary to every movement of Assyrian expansion along the piedmont belt.

This is the principle which emerges out of the fragmentary and confused accounts of the wars from the 14th to the 7th century B.C. The highland campaign usually started from Nisibis, which controlled a road leading northward through an easy pass in Mount Masius to the basin of the upper Tigris and thence west into the Hittite country of Asia Minor.[79] The offensive often had to be pushed as far west as the Melitene district of Cappadocia and the Commagene country; because these mountain states enclosed on the north the strategic district of converging highways west of the Euphrates bend. They commanded the passes and roads leading down to the plain of Naharain, which in turn commanded the Mediterranean outlets of the piedmont road. The temptation to encroach was irresistible, because a few months of sovereignty there yielded a big revenue in transit dues and commercial profits. Hence these little mountain states often risked the wrath of Nineveh. In the time of Tiglath-Pileser III (745-727 B.C.) they combined with the Armenian state of Urarta and extended their conquests to include Carchemish and Arpad, until the Assyrian forces drove them back again.[80]

Assyria's progress along the piedmont was a halting one, an alternating advance and retreat, owing to these constant flank attacks. Difficulties increased, however, as she approached the Syrian Saddle. The strategic importance of this district as focus of the converging western roads made it the object of attack from all sides. Here competitors multiplied, a recurring crop which had to be cut down. Prior to the Assyrian advance, while the Mitanni were establishing themselves in the Mesopotamian piedmont, Thutmose I of Egypt (1530 B.C.) inaugurated a policy of territorial expansion northward to the Syrian Saddle, in order to eliminate the western middleman from the Babylonian trade, which had already assumed importance for Egypt. He and his successors secured their hold on the Naharain and the Euphrates bend, dominated the trading town of Carchemish at the middle passage of the river, and established peaceful relations with their Mitanni neighbors, as the interests of trade demanded.[81]

The Egyptians held this strategic district 150 years, till 1375 B.C., when they were dislodged from it by the Hittites, who had gradually been advancing southward from their mountain seat in eastern Asia Minor. The Hittites combined with their kinsmen, the Khati, who occupied the rugged mountains between the upper Pyramus River and the Euphrates above the great bend, invaded the Syrian Saddle district, and got astride of the Euphrates bend east to the Khabur River at the cost of the Mitanni.[82] From this base they pushed their conquests up the Orontes valley, which formed the southern approach of the Syrian Saddle. Thus they gathered into their hands the whole traffic between Babylonia on the east, and Egypt and Phœnicia on the west. Hittite remains have been found all along the route of the Bagdad Railroad from the Mount Amanus tunnel to the Khabur River, at Sendjerle, Aleppo, Jerablus (Carchemish) and Ras-el-Ain; [83] the ancient stations are the modern stations. Remains also at Alexandretta indicate that this excellent harbor was the Hittite sea terminus of the piedmont road, as it is today the Mediterranean terminus of the Railroad.

The Hittites had to defend their position in the Syrian Saddle against repeated attacks by the Egyptians, who suffered by their exclusion from the piedmont trade, and under Rameses II from 1288 to 1271 B.C. made a last sustained but futile effort to regain their lost advantage.[84] Soon afterwards the Hittites were assailed on the east by the rising power of the Assyrians, who for centuries battled to get and maintain their hold on the Syrian Saddle. They found it necessary to expand over the Amanus Mountains into Cilicia,[85] in order to control the northwestern approaches through the Cilician Gates and other Taurus passes of Asia Minor. Assyria was forced also to dominate the Phœnician littoral, which made large contributions to the piedmont trade, in order to reap the full profits of her position.

THE PHOENICIAN PORTS AND THE PIEDMONT ROUTE—The distribution of the ancient Phœnician cities in relation to the Mesopotamian piedmont reveals a significant interplay of geographic factors; geographical isolation and security operated versus geographical proximity and accessibility to an estab-

lished trade route, a location which gave protection versus a
location which gave profits. According to every law of geographical probability, the Phœnician settlements spread originally all along this coast from Mount Carmel to the head of
the Gulf of Issus. Mövers maintains such a distribution on the
basis of place names, religious cults, mythology and legend,
even for cities like Tarsus and Mallus, which have been attributed to later Greek colonists.[86] It is just around the Gulf
of Issus, with easy access to the Syrian Saddle and fair harbors
at Alexandretta and the mouths of the Cilician rivers, that we
should have expected the Phœnicians to place their commercial
ports. On the evidence adduced by Mövers, so they did.

The persistent aggressions of the Babylonians, Hittites and
Assyrians, however, from 3000 to 605 B.C., jeopardized especially the northern seaboard towns which lay near the Mediterranean outlet of the piedmont route. The Amanus and Bargylus Mountains afforded no adequate bulwark to settlements
along their coast against rear attacks. Relative security could
be found only along the littoral of the broad and lofty Lebanon
Range. There the great and enduring Phœnician cities grew
up, protected by their geographical location—Tyre, Sidon,
Berytus, Byblus, Bothrys, Tripolis, Arka and Simyra near the
northern end of the Lebanon Range. The location of all these
cities was the resultant of two divergent geographic forces; it
combined sufficient proximity to the piedmont road for participation in its trade, and sufficient remoteness combined with protected sites to insure the peace necessary for early industrial
and commercial development. The sole exception to the rule
is the conspicuous proof. That was the city of Arvad or
Aradus, situated on a little island two miles off the Bargylus
Mountain coast, about 30 miles (50 kilometers) north of Tripolis. When no war clouds hung on the land horizon, its citizens
occupied a twin settlement on the coast called Antaradus, and
cultivated their terraced gardens while they gathered in oriental merchandise from the inland trade routes. But when
the Assyrian wolf pack burst through the passes in the mountains, the people scurried into their boats and took refuge in
their rocky island; there Manhattan-wise, they stored themselves away in their ancient sky-scrapers.[87] An Assyrian at-

tack on the coast settlement of Aradus was the signal to the
south Phœnician cities to mobilize their forces for defense.
Conquest was followed by a period of tribute-paying, then by a
period of successful revolt and independence, because the long
reach from Nineveh to Tyre weakened the arm of Assyrian
authority.

The Gulf of Issus, before the Greek period, was not permitted
to breed on its shores the goose that might lay the golden egg
of maritime commerce. Undoubtedly the goose was hatched
again and again, built its nest, and then was destroyed. The
easy seizure of the Phœnician city of Myriandros, located on
the Amanus littoral near the foot of the *Pylæ Syriæ* (Beilan
Pass, 2,395 feet), when Cyrus the Younger marched through
in 401 B.C., shows how exposed was the location.[88] Alexander
the Great planned Alexandretta on the basis of a unified political control from the Mediterranean to the Persian Gulf. We
are forced to think with Mövers that very ancient Phœnician
towns occupied the approximate locations of Antioch and
Seleucia, which the Seleucids built as the Mediterranean outlet
of the piedmont road. Situations so promising could not have
been overlooked. They were apparent to Antigonus who built
the town of Antigonea five miles upstream from the later Antioch,[89] near the site of the old Phœnician Heraclea. Seleucia
also occupied the exact site of an earlier settlement,[90] and it
faced across the little Bay of Antioch at the foot of Mount
Casius the ancient port of Posidium, probably of Phœnician
origin. On this marine inlet lay the city of Kundu in 670 B.C.,
an ally of Sidon and undoubtedly the seat of a Phœnician factory, which was seized by Esarhaddon for Assyria.[91] Thus
these northern Phœnician settlements were destroyed or overlaid by Greek colonies, while the southern ones proved the law
of the survival of the fittest, geographically speaking.

The Seleucid kingdom succeeded Alexander's rule in this transit region between the Mediterranean and the Persian Gulf, and
it fattened on the trade which streamed along the piedmont
road and out to the sea by Antioch and its port Seleucia Pieria.
Like previous incumbents of the Syrian Saddle, it had to defend its strategic position against attacks from several sides;
but it enjoyed this advantage, that Antioch and "the land of

the rivers" formed the center and not the periphery of its domain, as was the case with the ancient Egyptian, Hittite, and Assyrian possessors of this focal district.

Egypt never through the ages lost her interest in the Syrian Saddle; nor has any modern dynasty or power, native or foreign, which has fallen heir to the throne of the Pharaohs. Control of the Suez or the Nile-Red Sea route to the Orient seems to have aroused a desire to control the Mediterranean outlet of the competing Mesopotamian route. The effort of the Eighteenth Dynasty to get astride of the Euphrates bend was repeated by Necho in 605 B.C., and this ambition colored the Asiatic policy of Egypt in the intervening centuries. It animated also the Ptolemies in their attacks upon the Seleucid power in Palestine, Syria and Cilicia. Ptolemy II in 246 B.C. captured Antioch and its port Seleucia, Syria, Cilicia "and the upper districts across the Euphrates." [92] He was unable long to hold all this territory, but significantly enough he kept the seaport Seleucia Pieria in his grasp for twenty-five years. [93]

The declining power of the Ptolemies ceased to threaten the Seleucid state, which was also declining. At the beginning of the first century B.C. it had withdrawn to the west of the Euphrates before the advance of the reviving Persian or Parthian kingdom, and soon was forced to defend its frontier along the Euphrates bend against a new enemy. The rising kingdom of Armenia, under its king Tigranes, had pushed its frontier south over the rim of its highland, and incorporated the Mesopotamian piedmont belt from Nineveh and Nisibis in the east to the old Carchemish district in the west. [94] It thus duplicated the territorial expansion of the Mitanni kingdom fourteen centuries before, and with the same purpose,—to get a frontage on the piedmont road. To emphasize the new outlook, the king built a new capital, Tigranocerta, up in the foothills of Mount Masius about 40 miles northwest of Nisibis; and he settled a tribe of Arab nomads in the Harran and Edessa (Urfa) districts, where they commanded the piedmont route and the chief fords or ferries of the Euphrates bend, so that they might collect transit dues for him. [95] To get outlets to the Mediterranean, he seized Antioch, northern Phœnicia and eastern Cilicia, but failed to hold them long. When Lucullus with his

Roman legions pushed the Mithradatic war into Armenia in
69 B.C., and captured Tigranocerta and Nisibis, he found there
treasure [96] which recalls the riches of the piedmont cities in ancient Assyrian days.

The Roman advance eastward, like the Assyrian advance
westward, had to push its way between the enemy of the mountains and that of the plains, Armenians and Parthians, who
came to make common cause against the Roman intruder.
Every Roman offensive began with a campaign in highland
Armenia, which automatically threw the piedmont belt into
Roman hands. Highland Armenia, after its conquest, was allowed to fall away; but the piedmont was retained and therewith the great traffic route between East and West. The Euphrates fords or ferries, Carrhæ (Harran), Resaina and Nisibis
became familiar to Roman merchants traveling to and from the
east, Roman customs officials, and Roman armies bound towards
the Tigris road on their way to Ctesiphon; for Parthian attacks were incessant. Nisibis was a Roman frontier fortress
from 115 to 363 A.D. and the regular base of operations against
the Parthian capital on the lower Tigris.[97] As the Empire declined, her eastern frontier fell back only a few miles behind
Nisibis. The Patriarchate of Antioch reached from the Mediterranean to the Khabur River in 638 A.D. when the Saracens
came.[98]

After the Saracen conquest of Syria and Mesopotamia, traffic moved busily east and west along the piedmont road. The
Arab geographers of the tenth and twelfth centuries describe
with enthusiasm its thriving cities with their irrigated fields,
gardens, orchards and vineyards, their crowded mosques and
markets, as these existed under the Seljuk Turks in 1100 A.D.[99]
Then the Crusaders came. With purpose more commercial
than religious, they aimed directly for control of the Syrian
Saddle. From 1098 to 1268 we find one noble house of Crusaders established in the Principality of Antioch, extending
from the Bay of Alexandretta and Laodicea east across the
Orontes valley nearly to Aleppo. This principality marched
on the northeast with the County of Edessa (1098 to 1144)
which stood fairly astride of the Euphrates bend, the upper
Balikh and the upper Khabur, embracing the old district of

Carchemish, Edessa, and the northern ford of the Euphrates at Samosata. The Crusader's County of Tripoli included all the old Phœnician coastland from Aradus south to Berytus (Beirut).[100] There was keen competition among the Knights of the Cross for these profitable gateways to the East, but the throne of Jerusalem went begging.

It was Egypt again, under the rule of the Mameluke Sultans, who next occupied the Syrian Saddle. By 1268 they held Antioch and Aleppo to the Euphrates bend, and gradually controlled the whole Saddle. For over two hundred years it was theirs, while they advanced their frontier over Cilicia to the Taurus crest, as a defensive boundary against the Ottoman Turks on the northwest. Very significantly, the Venetians, who since the Turks got astride of the Dardanelles (1356) were concentrating their trade at Alexandria and developing the Nile-Red Sea commerce with the Orient, in 1489 occupied Cyprus, apparently for nearer access to the competing piedmont route, whose outlets now were also in the hands of the friendly Egyptian government.

It is a notable fact that all through history designs upon the Syrian Saddle, whether commercial or political or both, have been inaugurated or accompanied by the acquisition or occupation of Cyprus. England in 1876 purchased the controlling interest in the Suez Canal stock through the agency of Disraeli; through the diplomacy of the same statesman she secured Cyprus in 1878, and thereby control of the sea approaches to the possible Mediterranean termini of any future Bagdad Railroad. The very outline of Cyprus suggests a hand pointing a pistol at the Bay of Alexandretta and the Orontes mouth.

AUTHORITIES—CHAPTER IX

1. Tiflis sheet, R. G. S. I: 1,000,000 map.
2. Herodotus, IV, 13-15, 24-27.
3. *Ibid.*, III, 97.
4. E. Speck, *Handelsgeschichte des Altertums*, Vol. I, pp. 171, 172, 178, 180, 290. Leipzig, 1900.
5. Strabo, XII, Chap. III, 18.
6. D. G. Hogarth, *Ionia and the East*, p. 65. London, 1909. J. L. Myres, "The Marmara Region," *Scott. Geog. Mag.*, Vol. 40, 1924, pp. 128-150.
7. J. Garstang, *The Land of the Hittites*, pp. 132, 141-148, 364-366. London, 1910.
8. R. Kiepert, *Karten von Kleinasien*, 1: 400,000.
9. Strabo, XII, Chap. VI, 2, 4-5; Chap. VII, 2-3; XIV, Chap. V, 6-7, 10.
10. Garstang, *op. cit.*, pp. 37-38.
11. *Ibid.*, pp. 132, 141-148, 154.
12. W. M. Ramsay, *Historical Geography of Asia Minor*, pp. 28-35. London, 1870. Garstang, *op. cit.*, pp. 24-25, 162-164, 366. For Sinope harbor, E. Nowack, "Northern Anatolia," *Geog. Rev.*, Vol. 21, pp. 80-81. 1931.
13. Hogarth, *op. cit.*, pp. 45-48, 75. Garstang, *op. cit.*, pp. 1-3, 52-53.
14. Eduard Meyer, *Geschichte des Altertums*, p. 619. Stuttgart, 1909. Garstang, *op. cit.*, pp. 16-17, 52-53.
15. Eduard Meyer, *op. cit.*, pp. 640-650, 655.
16. *Acts of the Apostles*, XIX, 23-38.
17. Hogarth, *op. cit.*, pp. 55, 59-63, 99-100.
18. Garstang, *op. cit.*, pp. 12, 142.
19. Strabo, XII, Chap. VIII, 4.
20. Garstang, *op. cit.*, p. 53.
21. Eduard Meyer, *op. cit.*, p. 613. 1909.
22. Baedeker, *Palestine and Syria*, pp. 151-152, 235-237. Leipzig, 1906.
23. *Ibid.*, pp. 296-298, 300.
24. F. Hommel, *Geschichte von Babylonien und Assyrien*, pp. 325-330. Berlin, 1885. Hugo Winckler, *Geschichte Babyloniens und Assyriens*, pp. 43-44, 56. Leipzig, 1892.
25. E. Speck, *Handelsgeschichte des Altertums*, Vol. 1, p. 289. Leipzig, 1900.
26. Meyers, *Konversations—Lexikon*, article, *Euphrat*.
27. J. L. Myres, *The Dawn of History*, pp. 95-96. New York, 1911.
28. Herodotus, I, 185, 194.
29. Pliny, *Historia Naturalis*, V, 26, 89.
30. Strabo, XVI, Chap. I, 27.
31. Xenophon, *Anabasis*, I, 4, 5.
32. Mommsen, *The Provinces of the Roman Empire*, Vol. II, pp. 98-99. New York, 1887.
33. Strabo, XVI, Chap. I, 27.
34. Hogarth, *The Nearer East*, p. 135. London, 1902. E. Huntington, *Palestine and Its Transformation*, pp. 337-340. Boston, 1911.
35. Mommsen, *op. cit.*, Vol. II, pp. 50, 69, 101-102, 106.
36. *Ibid.*, Vol. II, pp. 169-170.
37. *Ibid.*, pp. 316-317, footnote 2.

38. Strabo, XVI, Chap. IV, 19, 23, 24.
39. Pliny, *Historia Naturalis*, XII, 14, 65. Periplus of the Erythræan Sea, 19.
40. Strabo, XVI, Chap. I, 24.
41. Maspero, *The Passing of the Empires*, p. 518. New York, 1900. George Rawlinson, *The Five Great Monarchies of the Ancient Eastern World*, Vol. III, p. 49, footnote 16. New York, 1870.
42. Arrian, *Anabasis of Alexander*, Bk. III, 7.
43. *Genesis*, XI, 31; XII, 4-5.
44. R. Fitzner, *Niederschläge in Klein-Asien,Petermanns Mitt. Ergänzungsheft No. 140*, 1896, p. 90, rainfall chart.
45. Hogarth, *The Nearer East*, pp. 62, 91, 97. E. Banse, *Die Turkei*, pp. 256-260. Braunschweig, 1916.
46. Guy Le Strange, *The Lands of the Eastern Caliphate*, p. 97. Cambridge, 1905.
47. Strabo, XVI, Chap. I, 23.
48. Max von Oppenheim, *Vom Mittelmeer zum Persischen Golf*, Vol. II, pp. 26, 31, 256. Berlin, 1900.
49. Arrian, *op. cit.*, Bk. III, 7.
50. Maspero, *The Struggle of the Nations*, p. 643. New York, 1897.
51. E. Meyer, *op. cit.*, Vol. I, pp. 420, 519-520.
52. Hommel, *op. cit.*, pp. 328-330.
53. Maspero, *The Struggle of the Nations*, p. 26.
54. R. W. Rogers, *A History of Babylonia and Assyria*, Vol. I, pp. 445-446. New York, 1915.
55. Le Strange, *op. cit.*, p. 103.
56. E. Meyer, *op. cit.*, Vol. I, pp. 420, 519-520, 606. Winckler, *op. cit.*, pp. 148-149.
57. Winckler, *op. cit.*, pp. 163-171.
58. Wilhelm Götz, *Die Verkehrswege im Dienste des Welthandels*, pp. 95-97. Stuttgart, 1888. Maspero, *The Struggle of the Nations*, pp. 193-194.
59. *Judges*, XVIII, 7 and 28. F. C. Mövers, *Die Phœnizier*, Vol. II, pp. 136, 160. Berlin, 1850.
60. Mövers, *op. cit.*, pp. 161-165.
61. *Ezekiel*, XXVII, 23.
62. *Genesis*, XI, 31; XII, 5.
63. Rogers, *op. cit.*, Vol. II, pp. 64-65 and 75, footnote 2. A. H. Sayce, *The Hittites*, pp. 46-47. London, 1890.
64. E. Meyer, *op. cit.*, pp. 389, 601-604.
65. Winckler, *History of Babylonia and Assyria*, pp. 82-83. Translated and edited by J. A. Craig. New York, 1907.
66. *Ibid.*, pp. 84-85; 93-94.
67. Winckler, *Geschichte Babyloniens und Assyriens*, pp. 147-148.
68. *Ibid.*, pp. 144, 153-154. Maspero, *The Dawn of Civilization*, pp. 564. New York, 1901.
69. Rogers, *op. cit.*, Vol. II, p. 308.
70. *Ibid.*, Vol. II, pp. 64, 65, 75-76, 81, 96-97 and 225.
71. *Ibid.*, pp. 93, 101, 103.
72. *Ibid.*, p. 104. Strabo, XVI, Chap. I, 26.
73. Rogers, *op. cit.*, Vol. II, p. 28.

74. *Ibid.*, Vol. II, pp. 57-62, 74. Winckler, *Geschichte Babyloniens und Assyriens*, pp. 176-188.
75. E. Meyer, *op. cit.*, pp. 672-673.
76. J. H. Breasted, *History of the Ancient Egyptians*, p. 212. New York, 1916.
77. Winckler, *Geschichte Babyloniens und Assyriens*, pp. 154-161, 165.
78. *Ibid.*, pp. 172-175. Maspero, *The Struggle of the Nations*, pp. 643-647.
79. Maspero, *The Struggle of the Nations*, pp. 364-365.
80. Rogers, *op. cit.*, Vol. II, pp. 114-118.
81. Breasted, *op. cit.*, pp. 212-234.
82. Maspero, *The Struggle of the Nations*, pp. 364-366, 368.
83. D. G. Hogarth, article "Hittites," *Enc. Brit.* 11th edit., 1910.
84. Breasted, *op. cit.*, pp. 280-285; 428-430.
85. Winckler, *Geschichte Babyloniens und Assyriens*, pp. 192-198, 223-226, 241-244, 255-258.
86. Mövers, *op. cit.*, Vol. I, p. 404; Vol. II, pp. 50-51, 166-174.
87. Strabo, XVI, Chap. II, 13, 14.
88. Xenophon, *Anabasis*, Bk. I, 4.
89. Diodorus Siculus, Bk. XX, 47. Strabo, XVI, Chap. II, 4.
90. Strabo, XVI, Chap. II, 8.
91. Rogers, *op. cit.*, Vol. II, pp. 223-225.
92. J. P. Mahaffy, *The Empire of the Ptolemies*, pp. 34-35, 82, 87, 197, 200. London, 1895.
93. Polybius, Bk. V, 59-60.
94. W. R. Shepherd, *Historical Atlas*, p. 33, map 2. New York, 1911.
95. Mommsen, *The History of Rome*, Vol. IV, pp. 315-317 and footnotes. New York, 1905.
96. *Ibid.*, Vol. 4, pp. 339-341.
97. Mommsen, *History of the Provinces of the Roman Empire*, Vol. II, pp. 72-73, 84-85, 94-95, 98.
98. Shepherd, *op. cit.*, p. 52, map.
99. Le Strange, *op. cit.*, pp. 87-108.
100. Shepherd, *op. cit.*, p. 68, map.

CHAPTER X

THE NORTHERN BARRIER BOUNDARY OF THE MEDITERRANEAN BASIN AND ITS BREACHES

The barriers enclosing the Mediterranean Region on the north consist of the young folded mountains stretching across southern Europe from the Pyrenees to the Caucasus, supplemented by the old Cevennes Plateau, the Rhodope Massif, and the Anatolian Highland. These barriers have always separated two regions of contrasted climates and contrasted civilizations, though in ancient times the cultural contrast was more striking than now and more closely linked with the contrast in climate.

These contrasted regions comprised: I. the borderland of the Midland Sea, with its sub-tropical climate and sub-tropical earth products like the fig and olive, almond and citron; its advanced tillage and varied agricultural products, its wines and perfumes made from the fruits and flowers of the earth; its artistic gold and silver ornaments, its textiles and pottery, all which surpassed anything produced farther north. II. The middle and northern European region, stretching from the Bay of Biscay to the lower Volga, with its mild to cold temperate climate, its raw products of forest, field and pasture marking a backwoods civilization; with its tin from Cornwall, probably too from Corbilo near the lower Loire, and possibly from the crystalline rocks of the Bohemian basin; its amber from the North Sea and the Samland coast of the Baltic; its sturdy slaves from the Scythian plains and its fair slaves from Germany and England.

This vast backward region of northern Europe furnished a market for the finished products of the Mediterranean region, which in turn drew upon the raw materials of the north. Here were the conditions for very active exchanges, and for a steady stream of men and merchandise using all the breaches in the barrier. Moreover, the northern or European hinterland of the Mediterranean was far more productive than the southern or

African hinterland; and it was potentially more productive and extensive than the eastern or Asian hinterland, which consisted largely of deserts and steppes from the Khirgiz plains in the north to the arid plateau of Baluchistan and Arabia in the south.

FIVE BREACHES IN THE NORTHERN BARRIER—The northern barrier, in contrast to the southern and eastern, had five breaches, well distributed with fairly equal intervals between, and connected with inland highways or navigable rivers opening up the interior of Europe. In early times when forests covered most of this hinterland, both the number of the breaches and their inland connections were a great natural advantage. The breaches moreover were characterized by surprising variety. They comprised:

I. The Bosporus-Hellespont marine passage leading to the Black Sea and the rivers of southeastern Europe.

II. The Vardar-Morava furrow, connecting the north Ægean Sea with the middle Danube by a low pass linking two rivers.

III. The Carso Plateau gap in the Alpine barrier, connecting the head of the Adriatic with the Save branch of the Danube by a short, direct route over a fairly high pass.

IV. The intermontane valley of the Rhone, leading north to a group of low passes, which connect the navigable course of the Rhone with radiating rivers and give access to the North Sea through the Rhine, the English Channel through the Seine, and the Atlantic through the Loire. Canals now link the Rhone with all these rivers.

V. Gap of Carcassonne, a low intermontane valley between the navigable Aude and Garonne, connecting the Mediterranean with the Bay of Biscay by a barge canal since 1681. A naval ship canal is projected for the future through this breach.

These breaches had each its distinctive character, owing to its different relief or elevation, its different starting point from the Midland Sea, and its different hinterland connection which determined the destination of the route into central Europe. Hence each enacted a different historical rôle in the great Mediterranean drama. Each facilitated in a different degree the spread of Mediterranean culture into northern Europe, though the character of the inland peoples and of their country decided whether this transplanted culture should take root or die—whether it should flourish, as did the Roman civilization among the agricultural Gauls west of the Rhine, or should be wiped out, as was the older Hellenic culture of the Scythian coast by nomadic inroads from the Asian deserts.

While a few high and difficult passes in the Alps or Pyrenees permitted a little local intercourse and a modicum of trade, these more hospitable breaches, which were low and wide, focused upon themselves through all time the historical events of wide areas. They crowded into their channels streams of commerce, migration, colonization and conquest; they drew these from remote sources and directed them to equally remote destinations. The earliest transit route across ancient Gaul, from Massilia in the lower Rhone valley north to the Paris Basin and the lower Seine, is followed today by the busiest railroad and heaviest freight trains of modern France. The Hellespont delivers the wheat of the Scythian steppes within reach of Mediterranean lands as it did in the days of Themistocles, but it carries coal and oil besides. The breaches have increased their importance with the increase of international trade and human intercourse.

The Mediterranean is enclosed on the north by a mountain rampart measuring 2,330 miles from the folded ranges of Spanish Granada to the massive Taurus system, where it looms above the Bay of Alexandretta. The huge oblong of the Asia Minor Peninsula confines the Levantine Basin of the Mediterranean on the north for a distance of 560 miles (900 kilometers). Its rigid billows of land, mounting higher from west to east, merge into other highlands extending far into Asia. Any attempts to round them on the east involves a toilsome journey over the ranges of Armenia, whose valley floors lie nearly 6,000 feet (1,800 meters) above sea-level.

THE BOSPORUS-HELLESPONT BREACH—This barrier peninsula sinks on the west beneath the Ægean Sea; but its folded ranges, lifting their peaks as rocky islands, emerge again in the corrugated highlands of the Balkan Peninsula. The blunt northwest corner of Asia Minor dips so slightly that the Bos-

porus and Hellespont form only a wet scratch across its surface. But that scratch is enough. It makes a breach in the
mountain wall. Through it the Mediterranean penetrates into
the Euxine Basin; there it faces other mountain obstructions
encircling this marine alcove on all but its northwest coast.
The extensive subsidence between the lower Danube plain and
the Crimea breaks the continuity of the barrier earth-folds
between the Balkans and the Caucasus. The Caucasus, also,
is nipped in two by the Kertch Strait, which severs the Yaila
Mountains of the Crimea from the parent range, and admits
the Euxine waters into the Sea of Azof. This local depression
is companion-piece of the Gulf of Odessa. Only in these two
inlets of shallow water does the Mediterranean penetrate beyond its normal mountain barriers into the low accessible plains
of Eastern Europe.

The marine breach of the Bosporus and Hellespont conferred
a conspicuous benefit upon the Eastern Mediterranean because
it provided its coasts with admirable fishing grounds near at
hand. It admitted the shoals of mackerel and tunny to the
Scythian rivers, flowing full in summer and bringing down
abundant food for the spawning fish, just when the other Mediterranean rivers were beginning to dry up. Aristotle observed
that the tunny grew rapidly in the Euxine owing to the large
rivers discharging there.[1] The fish arrived to spawn in May or
June, and were caught from that time till they left the Hellespont. The mackerel migrated from the Euxine from August
22nd to September 22nd and the tunny from September 22nd to
October 22nd, at the end of the sailing season. They followed
a regular course in the Euxine, keeping the coast of Asia Minor
on the right going in, and on the left when outward bound,
swimming close inshore to avoid the mid-sea current setting
towards the Bosporus. The shoal fish were caught in greatest
quantity as they left the Euxine, crowding through the Strait
which Homer calls "the fishy Bosporus." [2] The strong out-
current of the Bosporus, rebounding from the Asian shore at
Chrysopolis, carried the fish diagonally across the Strait to
the Golden Horn, which got this name from the profits of the
fishing industry there.[3] The mackerel was caught at its best

in the Propontis, before it was depleted by the spawning process.

These northern fisheries early attracted the Phœnicians, who were always searching for sources of food supply. Their earliest fishing station seems to have been Lampsacus on the Troad coast near the northern entrance to the Hellespont; but they can be traced by local legends and religious cults at Pronectus on the Bithynian coast of the Propontis, and along the whole southern shore of the Euxine.[4] Euripides in his *Iphigenia in Tauris* attests their fishing stations in the caves of southern Crimea, where their Astarte worship long lingered. The Phœnicians were followed by Greek seamen, who exploited the fisheries of Byzantium and established their fishing stations and colonies on the Crimean and Scythian shores of the Euxine. They also seized upon every advantageous site for a colony along the Asia Minor coast of the Euxine, whether it offered a hinterland route like Heraclea Pontica, or boxwood forests like Cytorus, or the iron of Pontic mines from various points.

Though the Bosporus-Hellespont breach opened a marine passage through the mountain barrier and therefore facilitated the cheap water transportation of the bulky products from the Euxine coasts, it did not make navigation easy for northbound vessels. The swift current passing through both straits from the higher water-level of the Euxine, and the violent north winds of summer delayed all northbound traffic. Ships entering the Hellespont from the Ægean found great difficulty in rounding Cape Sigeum, for the current here rushed out along the Asian shore with great velocity all through the summer, even when not intensified by a strong Etesian wind. This fact doubtless explains the abiding importance of Troy, with its nine successive cities on the same site. Small boats, which found it impossible to beat up the Strait against the combined force of current and wind, disembarked in a small bay behind the Isle of Tenedos about eight miles south of Cape Sigeum, and carried their goods by road or canal across the Troad Peninsula to the Hellespont. The acropolis of Troy commanded this isthmian route, kept up canal and road, and levied a toll on all who used them [5]—Greeks, Phœnicians, and the nearby peoples of Asia Minor. The Trojan War was a great struggle for the key to commercial supremacy in the Euxine and Ægean. The Greeks wanted to put an end to the tribute levied by Troy on the trade of the Hellespont, which was the secret of Troy's greatness. Troy drew her allies, as enumerated in the *Iliad*, from both sides of the Hellespont and Propontis, and from the Ægean coast of Asia Minor south to Lycia; for all these peoples were beginning to fear Hellenic expansion, both territorial and commercial. They looked to Troy as their leader, because she kept open for them the trading fields of Thrace and the Euxine shores. When Troy fell, she lost her grip on the Hellespont. None was left to stem the tide of the Greek deluge.[6]

Where the north wall opens its gates at the Bosporus and Hellespont, the Mediterranean reached out and drew the coastal plains of Russia into its field of history from the seventh century before Christ till the control of the Straits passed to the intruding Turks in 1453. The elements of this history were in general peaceful: commerce and colonization. Greek trading-stations and colonies at an early date began to line the Pontic shores,[7] and to send out lumber from the well-forested Caucasus, summer wheat from the Crimean plains, hides from steppe pastures, and fish from the tunny spawning-grounds.[8] Ancient Athens, poor in plowland, came to depend chiefly upon Pontic wheat to supply her market,[9] and the Scythian tribes of the Dnieper grassland came equally to depend upon Greek wine as the luxury of their meager fare. These are the chief exchanges today between the two localities. With every threat of interruption to communication through the Bosporus and Hellespont the price of wheat went up in Attica and Miletos, till finally Athens drew all the coastal fringe of Pontic cities and the Straits themselves into her maritime empire, and guaranteed the security of her grain trade by an unrivaled navy.

This marine breach in the mountain barrier enabled the Greeks to weave a border of Hellenic blood and culture upon the northern Euxine shores. Owing to successive streams of nomad hordes from Western Asia which flooded the adjoining plains, however, Mediterranean civilization left there no permanent impress. Nevertheless, Russian traders and marauders from northern Slav principalities like Kiev, Smolensk, and commercial Novgorod, took the Dnieper River route to the Black

Sea and Constantinople in the ninth and tenth centuries, and carried away the elements of Byzantine art and religion to the untutored north.

THE BALKAN BARRIERS AND THE MORAVA-VARDAR FURROW— West of the Bosporus and Hellespont the border barriers of the Mediterranean reappear, faintly at first, as the worn-down hill country of eastern Thrace. This affords an easy land road through the Maritza Valley between the Ægean and the Black Sea, and thus reinforces the marine communication through the nearby straits. The Thracian hills, however, soon rise and merge into the broad, compound barrier formed by the steep Balkan folds and the ancient crystalline mass of the Thraco-Macedonian Highlands. This old dissected mountain region, rising to heights of 9,000 feet or more in the Rhodope and Perim ranges, but sinking elsewhere to broad, undulating uplands and deep river valleys, serves to cement the young Balkan system to the multiple ranges of the Dinaric Alps. These run north and south through the western part of the Peninsula, from the head of the Adriatic to the rocky headlands of the Peloponnesos, in a forbidding succession of bold limestone ridges, which rise to jagged crests 6,500 feet (2,000 meters) above the sea. Communication between the Adriatic coast and the interior is excessively difficult. No thoroughfare is offered by the rivers Narenta and Drin, which break through the ranges in wild, impassable gorges. Travel across the country is a succession of ups and downs over gray, stony ridges and gray, barren valleys, for rarely does a saddle nick the high sky-line of the chains. Width, height, and lack of passes make the Dinaric system maintain in a pre-eminent degree the barrier nature of mountains.[10]

In all the 700-mile stretch of mountains between the Maritza Valley and the Gulf of Trieste there is no real breach, but only a few passes which are approached by long, often devious, routes across the highlands. The Morava and Vardar rivers, the one flowing north and the other south from a low watershed, the Scubi or Uskub Pass (460 meters or 1,508 feet), in the heart of the Peninsula, together cut a valley furrow of gentle slopes across the mountains from the Danube near Belgrade to the northwest corner of the Ægean Sea. This furrow has from ancient times determined the north-and-south line of communication. The land route which it opens is easy but long, because it crosses a mountain mass over 300 miles wide. Moreover, travel on it is not assisted by river transportation. The Vardar, choked by sand in its passage across its swampy, deltaic plain to the Gulf of Salonica, and broken by rapids in its upper course, affords no water-way to the interior, while the Morava is navigable for only seventy miles from the Danube.[11]

The mountains about the head of the Vardar, inhabited by robber tribes from remote times, served to discourage Macedonia's expansion northward, even under Philip and Alexander the Great and Philip V in 217 B.C.[12] Roman dominion did not overstep this barrier till 29 B.C., or a hundred and fifteen years after the conquest of Macedonia, when the Morava Valley, under the title of Upper Mœsia, was embodied in the Empire. Even then the mountain watershed remained the provincial boundary, and was never crossed by a Roman road between the two valleys.

The great Roman highway of the Peninsula ran between the capital at Constantinople and the middle Danubian frontier—between the military center and the exposed border. It left the Morava Valley at Naissus (modern Nish) and followed a diagonal furrow across the high valleys between the Balkan and Anti-Balkan mountains through Serdica (Sofia), and then by the Trajan Pass (843 meters, or 2,765 feet) reached the upper Maritza Valley. Thence it led past Philippopolis and Adrianople to Constantinople. This route took a long and devious course to avoid the great highland mass of the Peninsula, and thereby became the historic highway from Central Europe to the Byzantine bridge and Asia Minor; it was essentially a land route from west to east, rather than a transit route across the mountains from north to south.

This rôle fell to the Morava-Vardar groove, and was a later development so far as historical record goes; but doubtless it played its part in the prehistoric drift of the Greek peoples from the northwest southward into Macedonia, Thessaly, and Hellas. This was the route traversed by the Ostrogoths in 473 A.D. in their invasion of Northern Greece.[13] It was the line of expansion of the Servian kingdom under the great Stephan

Dusan (1336-56), whose inland domain needed an outlet on the Ægean;[14] and also the line of expansion with the same objective in the Gulf of Salonica, that was the aim of Servia in the Balkan War in 1912.

Servia's location in the Morava Basin made it custodian of these main routes south and east across the Balkan Peninsula. For this reason the Turkish sultans of the fifteenth century saw that they must first occupy Servia, if they were to realize their purpose of conquering the rich fields of Hungary; and Hungary rushed to the support of Servia when the Turkish onslaught came, in order to guard the avenue leading to its own frontier. The Turks secured the control of Servia. They found its thoroughfare so necessary to them in their long wars with Hungary, that they kept a tighter grip upon Servia than upon Moldavia and Wallachia, and immediately upon its conquest in 1459 made it an integral part of their empire.[15]

From the early eighteenth century, when the Turks began their slow recessional in the Balkan Peninsula and the Austrian power its advance, the country holding the Morava highway was again the bone of contention. Between 1718 and 1739 Austria drove a wedge of occupation up the Morava Basin nearly to Nish. From the time of Emperor Joseph II (d. 1790) the domination of Servia was a fundamental principle of Austrian statesmanship. The object was twofold: to guard this open highway which gives access to the middle Danube from two directions; and to gain for the vast inland empire of Austria-Hungary an outlet to the Ægean and the Bosporus.

PASSES OF THE JULIAN ALPS AND THE KARST—Near the Italian and Yugoslav frontier at the head of the Adriatic, the broad and corrugated highlands bordering the western side of the Balkan Peninsula contract and dip as they merge into the Karst Plateau and the Julian Alps. Farther north again towers the mighty system of the Alps, rising range beyond range, up to the high, white levels of eternal snow. The Julian Alps are a slender southeastern offshoot of the main system. They attain in the north an altitude of 9,394 feet (2,864 meters) in the peak of Terglon, but from this they shelve off southward into a rugged limestone platform of low altitude, fractured to a marked degree and step-faulted down to the

Adriatic. Such is the Carso Plateau. Presenting toward the
west a steep and forbidding escarpment, crossed by narrow

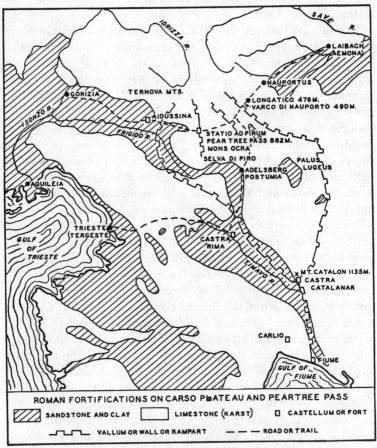

MAP 10—The strategic region of the Carso Plateau between the head of
the Adriatic Sea and the navigable course of the Save-Danube System. A
major breach in the northern barrier of the Mediterranean Region. Hence
the necessity of Roman fortifications beginning with the military colony
of Aquileia. This map of Roman fortifications across the Peartree Pass
Route is authoritative, though the author is not at liberty to disclose its
origin.

ridges, pock-marked by numerous sinks and potholes, guiltless
of visible drainage streams, this Karst Plateau extends along
the base of the Istrian Peninsula as far as the Gulf of Fiume

and the eastward-flowing Kulpa River. It merges beyond into the high, folded ranges of the Great Capella Mountains, which effectively cut off their hinterland from the sea.

Northeast of the Adriatic, therefore, for a stretch of 46 miles (75 kilometers), the mountain barrier of the Mediterranean Basin is partially breached. At one point it narrows to the width of 30 miles (50 kilometers) between the low Venetian plains and the deep re-entrant valley of erosion cut back into the highland mass by the upper Save River and its headstreams. Moreover, at this narrowest point the barrier sinks to the level of 2,897 feet in a limestone plateau known to the ancients as the *Mons Ocra*, and to moderns as the Peartree Range. Two rivers, the Frigidus or Wipbach on the western slope, and the Laibach on the eastern, issue from limestone caverns, after the manner of streams in a karst country, traverse a belt of sandstone or alluvium, and carve out paths down the opposite sides from the plateau above to the plains below. Here, therefore, the Alpine barrier *et largius patentem et planissimum habet ingressum*, says the historian Paulus (720-800 A.D.), who from his boyhood had known this broad and easy entrance, and had seen a barbarian horde burst through it as through an open door.[16]

There were other routes across the mountain saddle, but this was the best, and from very ancient times it became a well-trodden path. Here concentrated the traffic of a far-reaching hinterland. The geographical reasons are plain enough. The Peartree Pass afforded the shortest and easiest transit route to the interior in the 1,300-mile stretch of mountains between the Bosporus and the Rhone Valley breach. It lay between two natural thoroughfares, the level plains of Northern Italy and the wide plain of the Danube, which cannot be separated geographically or historically from the nomad-breeding steppes of Southern Russia. The Drave and Save rivers, tributaries of the Danube, drain the longitudinal valleys of the eastern Alps and open avenues of easy grade far up the eastern slope of the dividing range. Moreover, this dip in the mountain wall was located between the head of the Adriatic, an old sea-lane of maritime enterprise, and the head of navigation on the Laibach-Save-Danube system. For the little Laibach can carry a barge soon after it issues from its cavern. It springs full grown from the mountain's womb, such strength has it gathered in its underground life, fed by a whole arterial system of hidden rivers.

The historical importance of passes increases with their facility of transit; with their command of valley thoroughfares and water approaches, either navigable rivers or seas; and with the contrast between the regions of productions, both in point of climate and of industrial development, which such passes serve to unite and whose trade they forward. All four of these advantages were possessed by the Peartree Pass in a high degree. Its claim to the first two has been indicated. Through all ancient and medieval times it connected the civilized and industrial Mediterranean lands with a vast hinterland of barbarism, with shifting tribes of nomadic herdsmen and seminomadic agriculturists. It facilitated the exchange of artistic manufactured products in bronze, pottery, linen and woolen fabric for raw materials from forest, pasture, and mine.

The contrast in climate is almost as marked. The Julian Alps and Carso Plateau are a thermal divide. On their slopes the warm temperate climate of the Mediterranean Basin meets the cold temperate climate of Central Europe. The January isotherm of 0 degree C. (32 degrees F.), which marks the dividing line, nowhere else approaches so near to the Mediterranean proper as here. It runs through Bremen, Munich, along the watershed of the Carso, then turns southeast into the heart of the Balkan Peninsula. A similar contrast of winter temperatures in an equally short space appears on opposite sides of the Caucasus windshield, along the Black Sea littoral. The Peartree Pass, which is located approximately on the forty-sixth parallel of latitude, looks down upon the olive trees and rice fields of the warm Venetian plains. Here Italy revealed her fatal gift of beauty to the barbarian hordes who pushed up the Danube highroad to the half-open gate of the Hesperian Garden.

The ancient *Mons Ocra* route left the Adriatic at Aquileia, a Roman river port located four miles up the navigable Aquilo, accessible to the sea but somewhat protected from the chronic piracy of the Adriatic. Turning eastward, the road crossed the Sontius (modern Isonzo) and led up the fertile valley of the Frigidus (Wipbach) to the summit of the *Mons Ocra* plateau. There the easiest path across must have run past a wild pear tree, whose white blossoms made a conspicuous landmark against the green of the surrounding forest when spring re-opened traffic on the road.   At any rate, the Roman road-makers called the station at the summit *Ad Pirum.*   This name survives in the Peartree Pass and the Birnbaumer Wald, the German name of the old *Mons Ocra* plateau.   From the summit (2,897 feet) the road dropped down to Nauportus (modern Ober-Laibach, at 970 feet) on the Laibach River, where naviga-tion began on the Save-Danube system.   Strabo states that the distance between Aquileia and Nauportus was variously esti-mated from 350 to 500 stadia, or 40 to 57 miles.[17]

The Romans knew of another track over the *Mons Ocra,* leading up from Tergeste (Trieste) to *Lacus Lugeum* (Lake Zirknitz), and thence to Nauportus.[18]   This route had marked disadvantages.   It ascended the plateau by no long valley of approach like that of the Frigidus, but mounted the steep escarpment overhanging the Gulf of Trieste.   Though it may have found a lower gap than the Peartree Pass, it had to tra-verse the plateau at its greatest width and therefore to cross the successive hill ranges that corrugate its surface.   More-over, the plateau is almost devoid of water, which everywhere seeps through the porous limestone to some impervious stratum of clay or sandstone.   None remains on the surface to carve out a river valley of easy travel for the wayfarer.   Therefore this route seems early to have been abandoned in favor of the Peartree Pass.   Centuries later it was partially revived when Aquileia and the other ports along the low Venetian coast were silted up by the deposits of muddy Alpine torrents, and were therefore superseded by the deep mountain-rimmed harbor of Trieste.   This harbor was the geographical determinant which made the modern railroad follow the plateau route and grapple with the problem of mounting its bold escarpment.

This second *Mons Ocra* route lacked early historical im-portance also because it did not debouch upon the fertile Vene-tian plains.   It was therefore generally neglected by invading hordes from the Danube, whose objective was the rich cities of Cisalpine Gaul. The barbarians preferred as alternatives two routes to the north of the Julian Alps. These were approached by the valley highways of the upper Drave and Save rivers, and crossed the mountains by a high saddle between the Julian and Carnic Alps. The eastern starting-point for both was the ancient Santicum (modern Villach), located at an altitude of 1,665 feet, in a broad and lake-strewn basin at the head of navigation on the Drave. It had a situation similar to that of Nauportus. From this point one track led south over the Col di Tarvis and the difficult Predil Pass, called the "Thermopylæ of Carinthia" (3,810 feet or 1,162 meters), to the head of the Sontius Valley (Isonzo), which opened a way down to the coast near Aquileia.[19] The Predil Pass was too difficult to attract a military road in ancient times, though it was the route of the invading Lombards in 568 A.D. A few miles to the west of it, through the Pontebba or Pontafel Pass (2,615 feet or 797 meters), ran the other route from the Col di Tarvis, which connected on the Italian slope with a headstream of the Tiliaventus River (Tagliamento). In the days of the Empire a Roman military road followed this route over the Alps, and connected Aquileia with the navigable course of the Drave,[20] but for the trader it involved a long detour from his market.

THE AMBER ROUTE—The ancient amber route from the Baltic, one of the earliest trade routes of Europe, doubtless reached the Mediterranean by all these passes, especially in its primitive stages, when it was trying all the paths to find the easiest. This is the evolutionary history of all the pioneer roads. The amber route started from the famous amber fields of the southeastern Baltic, especially those of the Samland, and led up the Vistula or Oder River to the Moravian Gate, a broad geological gap between the Carpathian and Sudetes mountains, which was once a passage of the Eocene Sea. The route led thence down the March River to the Danube, thence across the spreading spurs of the eastern Alps to the Save Valley, the shrunken barrier of the Julian Alps, and the Mons Ocra Pass. According to Pliny, amber was brought by the Germans to Pannonia (Carinthia and Carniola), and purchased from them by the Veneti living on the north Adriatic coast. He mentions the amber necklaces worn by the women of this region, not only as an ornament, but as a protection against sore throat.[21]

So regularly did the Baltic amber emerge here upon the horizon of Mediterranean commerce that the myth of Phaëthon's sisters, transformed into poplar trees and weeping tears that turned into amber, associated the precious commodity with the mouth of the Po River,[22] showing that the trade must have reached back into exceedingly ancient times. Herodotus reports its supposed origin at the mouth of a stream flowing into the northern sea,[23] the Eridanus, a name which later came to be identified with the Po. He also clearly indicates a route of communication from the far northern land of the Hyperboreans, which emerged at the head of the Adriatic and passed down this sea to Epirus. The offerings to Apollo's shrine at Delos which he describes as taking this long journey were probably forwarded down the Adriatic by the trading ships of Corcyra and Epidamnus, which nearly three centuries before had been colonized by Corinth for the purpose of exploiting the commerce of this basin. The inland trade from the head of the Adriatic was appropriated at an early date by the Etruscans, and pushed with an assiduity which suggests that besides amber, other valuable northern products, like gold and tin from mines in the Archean rocks of the Bohemian massif, may have reached the Mediterranean by the Peartree route.

According to a tradition reported by Pliny, the Argonauts sailed up the Danube and Save to the head of navigation on the Laibach, and there built a settlement which they called Nauportus, because from there they carried their ship "Argo" across the mountains on men's shoulders to the Adriatic. The feat is not impossible, in view of the elevation of Nauportus (970 feet), only 2,000 feet below the pass; the probable presence here of stalwart mountain packers, such as are found in all pass regions of the world; the desire of such poverty-stricken mountain tribes to make money by this service and by levying tolls on the traffic over their mountain trails; and especially in view of the small vessels of this legendary period. The Homeric Greeks had boats of only twenty oars. The large penteconter of fifty oars hardly came into use before the eighth century B.C., and it appears in the later Homeric poems as a masterpiece of sea-craft. When one considers that the Bolivian Indian carries 150 pounds of rubber over the Andean watershed, and that the tea-packer of western China shoulders a burden of 300 pounds for the arduous ascent of the Central Asiatic Plateau, a twenty-oared boat carried on "the shoulders of men" across the Peartree Pass seems an easy undertaking for a group of mountain porters. It may be the first historical mention of the watershed "portage" or "carry," which is a regular feature of primitive inland navigation the world over. The portage is a commonplace of the Indian canoe routes in the Western Hemisphere, in the pioneer exploration and fur trade of Canada, the United States, Russia, and Siberia. Isthmian portages were familiar to the Greeks from very ancient times on the Isthmus of Corinth, in Eastern Crete, and probably on the narrow Dalmatian islands.[24]

In the case of Pliny's story, what probably happened was that some enterprising Greek inland traders may have found their way up the Danube to the Laibach, made their "carry" to the Isonzo River and Adriatic, and after long years their bold exploit was embodied into the tradition of the Argonautic expedition. Such was the process of accretion by which the *Odyssey* grew. The use of this portage path for boats may have given rise to the persistent impression among the ancients that there was river connection between the head of the Adriatic and the Danube.[25]

Strabo emphasizes the value of the Mons Ocra route for forwarding military supplies to the Roman armies engaged in war with the Dacians on the lower Danube. But this was only part of the traffic. Merchandise in large quantities was carried by wagon from Aquileia to Nauportus, and thence by boat to Segestica (Sisek), an important distributing point at the confluence of the Save and Kulpa rivers. There was an active trade between Italy and the barbarians of the upper Danube. The exchanges were the usual ones between two regions of different climates and contrasted economic development. The barbarians sent over the pass cattle, hides, slaves captured in their incessant border wars, gold from the Alpine mines, resin, pitch, and other forest products. They received in return the oil and wine of Italy, fine fabrics of Mediterranean make, glass,

and pottery.[26] The emporium for all this trade was the forti-
fięd town of Aquileia, at the head of the Adriatic.

BARBARIAN INVASION THROUGH THE CARSO BREACH—The location of Aquileia was not altogether a fortunate one, however.
Here on the eastern land frontier of Cisalpine Gaul lay the
weak spot in the Alpine frontier of Italy. Here, therefore, at
the eastern extremity of the big province lay the local capital,
Aquileia, in a position of opportunity, but also of danger. The
city was founded in 181 B.C., soon after the Roman conquest of
the region, as a fortress against intrusive Celtic peoples, who
were already beginning to threaten this vulnerable frontier.
Their first detachment came in 186 B.C., quietly enough, though
they could muster 12,000 fighting men, Livy tells us.[27] They
were bent upon peaceable settlement, so they arrived with "all
their property which they had brought with them or driven
before them." The road which they took across the forested
mountains was previously unknown to the Romans, but it lay
at the very head of the Adriatic. They emerged from this unknown pass upon the Venetian plain, and set to work building
their villages in the vicinity of the later Aquileia. But they
were ordered out by the Roman proconsul.

The Senate, finding the Alps in this region not the "almost
impassable barrier" that they had supposed them to be, established Aquileia as a Latin colony to protect the border. The
new settlement was a peculiarly remote outpost of the military
frontier. The nearest Roman colonies, which marked the line
of continuous settlement and of assured civil government in
the young province of Cisalpine Gaul, were Bononia, Mutina,
Parma, and Placentia. All were located at the northern foot
of the Apennines along the new Via Æmilia, and all had been
built within the four previous decades. Then only two years
after the founding of Mutina, Aquileia was established over a
hundred and fifty miles away, an ethnic island, dropped down
in a sea of Veneti allies. A sudden protrusion of the frontier
like this means that the expansion is necessitated by danger or
suggested by opportunity. The situation evidently required
peculiar inducements, for the 3,000 militia colonists who were
assigned to Aquileia received extraordinary allotments of land,
50 *jugera*, or 32 acres, to every foot soldier and 140 *jugera*,

or 87 acres, to every horseman.[28] This was eight or ten times
the usual allowance. Some 1,500 families were added in
169 B.C.

The border cantonment was established none too soon. In
179 B.C. came another Gallic band of 3,000, pushing across
the Alps and asking for land. More serious seemed the threat
of Philip of Macedon to lead a horde of his mountain barbarians into Italy by this convenient northeast frontier. So
the Romans, preparing for all emergencies, conquered the Peninsula of Istria in 177 B.C. to extend their scientific mountain
boundary, to secure their sea communication with Aquileia, and
to suppress Illyrian piracy in the upper Adriatic.[29] The appearance of the migrating Cimbri at the approaches to the
eastern Alps in 113 B.C. summoned the Roman army to the
heights near Aquileia in order to protect the passes, but the
barbarians withdrew, only to find their way by the upper
Danube and the Burgundian Gate to the Rhone Valley approach to the Mediterranean. (See map of Roman fortifications on the Carso Plateau.)

The policy of the Romans on this northeast frontier was
quiescent and defensive. The Peartree Pass was the back door
of Italy; the Danube Valley, on which it opened, was a back
street of the continent. Italy and the Tiber Valley fronted on
the western Mediterranean. This was the result of the eastward
curve of the Apennines, which threw the large populous plains
and valleys on the sunset side of the peninsula, and centered
their interests on the western sea. Therefore Rome's inland
expansion first sought the Rhone Valley breach to the north,
though the Peartree Pass route had been known to the Etruscans, the most ancient commercial expansionists of Italy.
Genuine expansion beyond this mountain boundary began in
the time of Augustus with an effort to police this frontier, a
common first forward step. Depredations of the mountain
tribes behind Istria upon Tergeste and Aquileia in 35 B.C.
necessitated the conquest of all the highland hinterland.[30] In
10 B.C., the process had to be repeated in order to teach the
predatory tribes of the Julian Alps respect for property, and
especially to open up the Peartree Pass route for merchandise
and armies bound for the new Danubian provinces. Ere long a

Roman road crossed the Mons Ocra to the colony of Æmona, where Laibach now stands.

During the *Voelkerwanderung* the danger of invasion was always imminent. The towns of Venetia were the first to glut the barbarians' greed for massacre and rapine, because the Danube avenue, immemorial highway for the packs of human wolves from the Russian and Asiatic steppes, led straight to the mountain door of the Venetian plains. The first historic invader to cross the Peartree Pass and spread his tents upon the banks of the Sontius was the emperor Theodosius the Great. In 388 A.D. and again in 394 A.D. he advanced from Constantinople up the Danube to interfere in the turbulent affairs of decadent Rome. Siscia on the lower Save, Æmona, and Aquileia saw his formidable army, and the battle of the Frigidus River below the Peartree Pass determined the conquest of the Roman Empire of the West by the Roman Empire of the East.[31]

The Visigoths, who participated in the campaign of Theodosius, learned how easy was the road to Italy and how weak were the defenders. Under their leader Alaric in 402 they invaded Italy. Taking the route through Pannonia to the Julian Alps, they pushed aside the guardians of the pass and descended rapidly to the siege of ill-fated Aquileia. Alaric overwhelmed Venetia and the neighboring Peninsula of Istria; but, defeated by the Roman general Stilicho at Verona and Pollentia, he retired from Northern Italy, checked but not broken. The Romans found him an enemy to be conciliated, for they appointed him *magister militæ* or commander of the Roman armies throughout Illyricum, which included Pannonia and Dalmatia. Thus they utilized his barbarian forces as a border defense on a weak and exposed frontier, as nations have been wont to employ their nomadic or semi-nomadic neighbors in all times and all parts of the earth.[32] Alaric now held a strategic position. He fixed his camp at Æmona, where the Peartree Pass road reached the Save River. From that base he demanded the pay due himself and his men for their services, and when he failed to get it from the disorganized government, he again invaded Italy in 408. Once more the Peartree Pass led him over to the siege of Aquileia and the other Venetian towns,[33] and the ancient Etruscan route from the Po over the Apennines guided his forces to Rome. After the siege and sack of the capital, Alaric demanded territory for his Visigoths in Venetia, Dalmatia, Pannonia, and Noricum, and the office of *magister militæ* for himself, so that he might again command the important line of communication between Italy and the Danube. His sudden death put an end to this demand, but his victorious followers moved westward out of Italy into southern Gaul, where they received an allotment of land.

The departure of the Visigoths from the territory of Illyricum left a vacant border. This meant that the gate of the Julian Alps was thrown open to other rude visitants. East of the previous Visigothic settlements in Pannonia lay the empire of the Huns, who for a century had been pushing up the Danube Valley. In 452 Attila led his savage hordes by the undefended road of the Julian Alps to the walls of Aquileia. Having sacked and destroyed that city, he laid waste the Venetian plain,[34] whose refugees sought an asylum in the coastal lagoons and marshy islands to the west, and there gave rise to the terror-haunted beginnings of Venice. Attila withdrew to his home beyond the Danube, but the destruction which he wrought in the Po Valley had not been repaired before the Ostrogoths under Theodoric, in 488, moved westward from their capital, near the present city of Belgrade, up the valleys of the Save and Drave to the Julian Alps. They dropped down the valley of the Frigidus and pitched their camp by the Isonzo.[35] Here, on this chronic battlefield, they defeated the Roman army of the emperor Odovacar.

Eighty years elapsed before the teeming hive of the Danube plain threw out another swarm. The next to mount the Julian barrier were the Lombards, in 568. In the course of long migrations they had drifted from the mouth of the Elbe River southward to Pannonia, and after a temporary halt they moved up the Save Valley through Æmona to the Peartree Pass and Venice.[36] This seems their probable route, though according to one authority they reached the Venetian plains by the higher and more difficult Predil Pass from the upper Drave Valley to the head of the Isonzo.[37] It is quite possible that the large and motley horde, incumbered by wagons, their families, flocks, and herds, found it necessary to use both routes in order to make a sudden descent upon the Venetian plains. From this base they ravaged all Italy, and eventually gave their name to the plain west of the Adige and north of the Po.

The easy approach up the long inland slope of the Julian Alps, the march across the low passes, and the swift descent down the steep seaward slope of the ranges was an historical event that must easily repeat itself. This was apparent to the new Lombard conqueror. Hence he opened a new chapter in the history of Northeastern Italy. He erected all the Venetian plain between the Mincio River, the Po, the Carnic Alps on the north and the Julian on the east, into the border Duchy of Friuli, with Forum Julii as its capital. To its Duke he intrusted the hazardous and responsible task of guarding the mountain passes leading to the Danube. The Duke stipulated for the noblest, most valorous Lombard clans to form his soldiery and the finest brood mares to sustain his border cavalry.[38] Thus was established here a typical frontier principality of defense, after the order of the German *Mark*. A hundred years later its chief was called a *Markgraf;* and from this time for five hundred years, so long as the human cauldron on the Danube seethed and boiled and overflowed, there was always a *Mark* of fluctuating boundaries and varying name that rested upon the Julian Alps.

This Lombard frontier state took its name from its capital, Forum Julii (modern Cividale), originally a market built by Julius Cæsar in the foothills of the Julian Alps. It was a typical pass town, located on the northeast margin of the Venetian plains where it could command the trade which the Peartree, Predil, and Pontebba passes brought over from Pannonia and Noricum. As a base for guarding these passes, the site offered better facilities than Aquileia, which never recovered from the Hun's attack and retained only ecclesiastical importance. The frontiers of the Duchy probably reached north to the summit of the Carnic Alps, east to the crest of the Julian Range and the Karst, south to the Adriatic coast, and west to the Tagliamento River. It therefore had natural or scientific boundaries on its exposed sides. On the north its Bavarian neighbors were giving evidence of aggression.

Slovenians, an advance guard of the great southern Slav migration, occupied the eastern slope of the Julian Alps. They were a small detachment of herdsmen and farmers, who in reality served as a border outpost of defense against the dreaded Avars and other intrusive peoples of Mongolian stock occupying the middle Danubian plain.

The mere presence of these nomadic hordes in the nearby pasture lands was a threat. In about 610 the Avars swept across the Julian or Carnic passes from the Save and Drave. They spread desolation among the Lombard cities of the Duchy of Friuli, much as the Lombards had done a few decades before among the Roman cities of this fertile but exposed province. After the raid they retired, only to return again in 663, this time by the Peartree Pass. In the chronic battlefield of the Frigidus Valley they defeated the Duke of Friuli, ravaged the Duchy, and again withdrew.[39] The Slav neighbors on the eastern slopes of the Julian Alps were probably impoverished by the Avar raids; for a few years after (688-700) they resorted to systematic cattle-stealing—the ancestral occupation of barbarian mountaineers—crossed the border and despoiled the herds in the Friulian pastures. Punitive expeditions to stop these depredations only served to incite the warlike spirit of the Slovenians. They invaded the Duchy by the Predil Pass, and defeated the Duke's forces in the valley approach below.[40] Gradually, however, they became assimilated, through constant intercourse, to the higher civilization of the Duchy of Friuli. Their territory, which received the Slav name of Krajena or Krain, or "frontier," [41] occupied the mountain country between the Kulpa River on the south and the Karawanken Alps hemming in the Save Valley on the north. It was conquered by the Duke of Bavaria in 772, and in 788 was embodied in the Frankish Empire by Charlemagne, who thus secured the strategic portion of the old Roman Pannonia for the defense of his wide dominion, and erected it into the *Mark* or March of Friuli.

THE FRONTIER MARCH ON THE CARSO PLATEAU—During the ninth century, the Karling kings of Italy strengthened this weak frontier. They extended the March of Friuli west to the Adige River and reinforced it by the March of Istria, thus giving it command of the whole stretch of the Julian Alps and Karst Plateau down to the present Gulf of Fiume. Beyond the crest, on the eastern slope, they had an additional defense in the Krain, or March of Carniola, which formed a frontier state of the east Frankish Kingdom or German Empire.

During the ninth century these three Marches served as outposts against the migrant Avars. At the end of this period they faced a new enemy from the Danubian plains. These were the Magyars or Hungarians. For a long time they had been moving along the broad highway of migration across Southern Europe, pressing on the rear of the Slavs and Avars, till they occupied the present territory of Hungary. The exposed duchies of the German Empire threw out a series of defensive vassal states, endowed with unusual privileges and unusual responsibilities, as buffers and bulwarks against the enemy. It was a political process of thickening the hide of the Empire, so to speak. It was a process as natural as that of protective coloring in plants and animals, and it is one that has been developed on exposed boundaries the world over, and the ages through.[42]

These German border states established to ward off Hungarian aggression were the March of Moravia, the March of Austria, the March of Carinthia, the March of Styria, and the March of Carniola. Behind the last lay the Italian March of Friuli, which was also of Teutonic origin. The *Markgraf*, or ruler of a March, had the legal status of the older counts, but he controlled a much larger territory and enjoyed far greater independence, as his dangerous frontier location demanded. He exercised justice, maintained a standing army, and had the right to call out militia from his population; but in return for this enlarged authority he assumed the grave responsibility of defending the border state.[43]

The proximity of Italy tempted the first inroads of the Hungarians. In 899 or 900 they descended from the mountain rim of Friuli, "the most harmful door left open by nature to chastise the faults of Italy," and ravaged as far west as Pavia.[44] They came again in 921, and yet again in 924 at the request of King Berengar, who was on friendly terms with the Hungarian chief, but was threatened by his rebellious Lombard vassals. These facts suggest steady intercourse, probably commercial, between the Italian cities and the barbarians, by way of the Julian Alps and the Karst passes. The desolating raids became almost annual, spreading farther and farther—to Apulia in 922, to Rome in 926, and to Capua in 937. They emerged upon the horizon of Italy somewhere in the Friulian or Venetian plains, *per ignotas vias*, the chronicler says; [45] but they had no connection with the numerous Hungarian incursions along the upper Danube Valley into Bavaria, Swabia, and Alsace. These facts seem to justify the assumption that they came by the old eastern passes, especially since the northern passes had long been guarded by the Bavarians. When the German king, Otto the Great, became overlord of Italy in 952, he transferred Friuli, now called the March of Verona, and the March of Istria to the Duke of Bavaria, who at the same time ruled over Carinthia and the March of Carniola. Thus he effectively closed the way to Italy against Hungarian raids.[46] A little later, in 976, Carinthia was erected into a duchy, ruling over the vassal Marches of Friuli, Istria, and Carniola, and served as chief of the border police.

These frontier provinces were transferred so often and so arbitrarily by the politician emperors of the Middle Ages in payment for votes in the imperial elections that any geographical law in the combinations became obscured. However, one or two principles emerge out of the chaotic changes. The March of Carniola, because of its location across the sunny path to Italy, retained longest (till 1254 or later) the March constitution and privileges which at once facilitated and repaid the task of defending the frontier. There seems to have been a recognition of the fact that this border state on the eastern slope of the Julian Alps was only part of a geographical whole; therefore a recurrent tendency is revealed to combine it with Istria and Friuli,[47] and thus to round out the geographical whole comprised in the wide frontier zone of defense.

The growing Republic of Venice during the twelfth and thirteenth centuries gradually absorbed most of the coastal belt of the Istrian Peninsula. This brought a turning-point in the history of Carniola. The March acquired nearly all the territory that was left of the old March of Istria, and for the first time (c. 1250) it had a small littoral of its own on the Gulf of Trieste and the Gulf of Fiume. Moreover, it extended to the lowlands of the Isonzo, though not to the river. In other words, the March of Carniola was astride the Julian Alps and the Karst Plateau, with a foot resting on the Adriatic shore. This location gave it an entirely new significance and value. It was no longer merely a strategic border state, but a border state with a sea front, and as such it became a goal to the inland states.

Carniola was momentarily acquired between 1269 and 1276 by King Ottocar of Bohemia and Moravia, who had managed to annex all the old belt of March lands between Istria and the head of the Vistula and Oder rivers in the Moravian Gates. Since he had shortly before founded the city of Koenigsberg on the coast of East Prussia,[48] his long-strung possessions comprised most of the old amber route. This was "the seacoast of Bohemia." Ottocar was forced by the emperor Rudolph of Hapsburg to renounce his recent acquisitions, all of which except Carinthia and Carniola went to found the fortunes of the House of Hapsburg. Later another Bohemian king endeavored to secure this important corridor as a passway to Italy.[49] His plans were frustrated by the growing power of Austria, which also felt a vital need of stretching its frontier to Italy and the sea, and which in 1335 acquired Carniola.

This marchland of Carniola, which had originated on the eastern slope of the Julian Alps as an outpost of successive Italian powers, now faced about westward. It became Austria's exposed frontier toward expanding Venice, and gave to inland Austria its first narrow foothold upon the sea. While its eastern border never changed, thus evidencing the equilibrium between pressure and counter pressure of nations in the Danube Valley during the later Middle Ages, on the west Carniola gradually acquired the valley of the Isonzo River and the base of the Istrian Peninsula. Thus it comprised all the weak highland barrier which it served to defend. Its western frontier toward Italy constantly fluctuated; but throughout its subsequent history from 1335 till 1807 it managed to keep some strip of seaboard on the Adriatic, at Trieste or Aquileia or on the littoral between, besides a coastal *pied de terre* on the Gulf of Fiume. This it accomplished despite the century-long efforts of the Venetian Republic to exclude Austria from the Adriatic, and to get closer access to the trade routes leading over the Peartree and Pontebba passes. By these routes Venice fed her products into backward Austria. During the Middle Ages 40,000 packhorses came yearly from the north down to Istria to take back Venetian salt to the Austrian Empire.[50]

When the fall of Constantinople let loose another flood of barbarians into the flat Danube plains, Carniola again became the fighting marchland. Under the hot blast of Turkish attack Hungary shriveled up like a dead leaf. Its frontier rolled back within forty or fifty miles of the old Austrian Marches. Across this narrow buffer territory poured the Turks into Carniola, in 1463, 1472, 1473, 1493, 1521, and again in 1559.[51] Laibach saw the Mongol cavalry around its walls.[52] Once more the migrants of the Danubian plains stormed this half-open door of Italy. Once more the geographical location of Carniola made her the mountain warden of Venetian Italy until, in 1683, the Turkish advance spent itself and gave place to a century-long retreat.

During the Napoleonic Wars these lines of easy communication between Austria and Italy were the scenes of marching and counter-marching. Napoleon, in 1787, erected a new Illyrian state out of Carinthia, Carniola, Goerz, Istria, the coast of Dalmatia, and Croatia, to be "a guard set before the gates of Vienna," he said.[53] With true geographical insight he was reviving the old March of the Julian Alps and the Karst Plateau with somewhat extended boundaries.

The accessible nature of the Julian Alps and the Karst Plateau is evidenced also by the distribution of population in these highlands, and by its ethnic elements. Nowhere else in the whole semicircle of the Alps does the density of population exceed one hundred to the square mile (forty to the square kilometer) across the summit of the mountains, except along the French and Italian Riviera, where the Maritime Alps sink down to the Mediterranean. Moreover, there the density decreases to half this number a few miles back from the coast, whereas it is maintained across the Karst Plateau in a broad belt from Goerz to Laibach, extending south to Fiume.[54]

Ethnology also reveals the breachlike character of the Julian Alps. Throughout the Venetian plains today, as far west as the Mincio River, the inhabitants are distinguished by a tall stature, rare among pure Italians. Their underlying stock is a lowland offshoot of the tall Illyrian race which is found today in Bosnia, Montenegro, and Albania, and which has given some additional inches to the later Slav immigrants.[55] As the Julian Alps were no barrier to the tall Illyrians, neither were they to the Slovenians, who, in the seventh century, pushed up the Save Valley from the east, and today cover the intervening territory down to the Isonzo. All this region up to the summit of the Julian Alps formed part of *Italia irredenda*. Its recovery gave the peninsular kingdom a scientific frontier and deprived Austria of her advantage in offensive and defensive warfare on this border.

THE RHONE VALLEY BREACH—Different from the low Karst saddle and the marine passage of the Bosporus and Hellespont is the third breach in the mountain barrier, formed by the Rhone-Saône-Doubs groove. Like the other two, it connects with the Mediterranean Basin a region of strongly contrasted climatic conditions and, during ancient and medieval times, of contrasted economic and industrial development. Remote from the early eastern centers of urban life and progress in the Ægean and the Levantine basins, this Rhone breach came much later upon the historical stage than did the Bosporus-Hellespont. It assumed an important rôle only after the Roman Republic had transferred the big dramatic events of Mediterranean history to the western basin by encircling that basin with a rim of Roman lands. To compensate for this tardy appearance, it has played a peculiarly important part in the history, not only of the Mediterranean, but of all Northwestern Europe. It made Gaul, and later France, one great transit land. Through it Roman civilization penetrated into Gaul, and spread from the radiating passes at the head of the Rhone-Saône Valley west and north over all that province into Britain, and finally eastward over the Rhine into Germany. The location of the Alpine barrier and the Rhone breach combined to retard the dissemination of Roman culture into Germany, and at length admitted it only in a Gallicized form. During the decline of the Roman Empire, the Rhone breach became in turn the passway for German tribes migrating south. The local population there today reveals in its fairer coloring and tall stature the ethnic infusion of the blonde giants of the north. Linked geographically with the north, the valley became linked ethnically as well with the Teutonic peoples who had drifted along the shelving coastal plains of Germany and France.

Thus the Rhone Valley breach performed the great historical service of uniting the mature civilization of the warm Mediterranean lands with the budding civilizations around the colder thalassic basins of the English Channel, the North Sea, and the Baltic. These northern seas, in turn, distributed to all their shores the germs of culture brought up from the south. Through the instrumentality of Flemish, Dutch, German, Hanseatic, and English traders they raised the *niveau* of civilization in these retarded northern lands. The similar seed of Greek culture, planted early and thickly on the southern shores of Russia, found no such favorable conditions for transplanting to the Russian north. Many were destroyed by nomadic invaders from Western Asia before they had taken root on the Scythian coast. The few that were disseminated northward to the chill plains of Central Russia lost their vitality. Far from the vivifying contact with the sea, impoverished by the lack of fresh accessions, they did not breed true to their type, but languished in dwarfed and flowerless form on the monotonous steppes. The ultimate environment of the Bosporus breach is found in the Valdai Hills, the Volga plains, and the Caspian desert, as that of the Rhone breach is found in the shores of the northern seas.

While the Bosporus-Hellespont breach dates back only to Quaternary times, the Rhone groove has an old geological pedigree. It is not a mere river valley of erosion, though erosion has carved out some of its minor physiographic features; but it traces back its ancestry to a marine inlet which in Eocene and Miocene times penetrated northward through a narrow belt of depression between the young folded ranges of the Alps and Jura on the east and the steep escarpment of the old

Cevennes Plateau on the west. This sea-arm filled the present valleys of the Rhone, Saône and Doubs to the granitic Vosges massif. The slow elevation of the later Miocene left the broad gap between the Jura and the southern face of the Vosges, while the Rhone-Saône depression was converted into a long, pouchlike inlet of the sea. Finally, in the Pliocene, the Rhone-Saône emerged as it is today, a great river flowing through a narrow plain, fed by the big streams that drain the western slopes of the Alps and Jura, and the torrents which at close intervals scar the long front of the Cevennes escarpment.[56]

The Rhone system opens a navigable highway straight north from the Mediterranean for 340 miles (550 kilometers), half-way across the base of the Gallo-Iberian peninsula. At its northern end lies the chief hydrographic center of Western Europe. Here it connects with a group of navigable rivers which radiate from its low encircling watershed, and open routes of communication to the Bay of Biscay, the English Channel, the North Sea, and even the Black Sea through the nearby head streams of the Danube River. Scarcely a tidal wave of invasion that swept the western shores of the Black Sea failed to spread up the Danube Valley also, and to reach in its ultimate wash that old geological gap between the Vosges and the Jura.

This is the famous Pass of Belfort, known in ancient and medieval times as "The Burgundian Gate," a broad gap about 18 miles wide (30 kilometers) lying only 1,138 feet (347 meters) above sea-level. It unites the Rhone groove with the long, fertile rift-valley of the northward-flowing Rhine. Together these formed the chief historical highway of ancient and medieval times between the Mediterranean and the North Sea. Migrant hordes, with their wagons and cattle, moving westward from the upper Danube Valley or southward along the Rhine trough from the chill Baltic plains, converged upon this open gateway leading to the sunny shores and rich cities of the Roman Mediterranean. They beat out tracks which were later transformed into Roman roads. Centuries later a canal from l'Isle, the head of navigation on the Doubs, connected that river with the Ill at Muelhausen and the Rhine at Basel.

Meantime a long chain of cities, united by commercial interests, had grown up along the Rhone, Saône, Doubs, Rhine, and the network of channels in the Rhine Delta to expedite the trade between two contrasted regions of production. The North Sea lands, located on the far outskirts of the ancient civilized world, retarded in their economic and cultural development by geographic remoteness and relatively harsh climatic conditions, commanded nevertheless the abundant raw materials of new, unexploited countries. As growing civilization and trade pricked the desire for luxuries, these raw materials enabled them to purchase the varied products of that subtropical and industrial Mediterranean world. Therefore Holland and Flanders, lying at the outlets of this Rhine-Rhone highway, were the first states of Northern Europe to feel the concentrated effects of Mediterranean culture, and to produce on these northern shores a replica of Mediterranean Venice, Pisa, and Genoa. In their splendid art, the rich fabrics of their looms, their brocades and tapestries, fine silverwork, printing, and map-making, we trace the Mediterranean lineage of their models.

Geographical companion pieces to the Burgundian Gate are found in the series of low passways which penetrate the hill country filling the older and broader geological gap between the Archean massif of the Vosges and that of the Cevennes Plateau. The long, sluggish Saône, which is navigable up to this hill country in the so-called Monts Faucilles, affords easy access to these watershed passes. They, in turn, have from the earliest times offered a wide choice of routes for intercourse between the Saône and the diverging rivers of France which drain outward to the North Sea and the Atlantic. Early migration, conquest, and trade sought them out and used them all. The easiest tracks beaten out by migrant barbarians traversing these uplands or the ones offering the shortest connection with tin-bearing Britain were later followed by Roman roads. Yet later most of them were utilized for water carriage by the system of canals projected by Sully in the sixteenth century. All combined to cement together the various parts of France.

The Saône connects with the Moselle near the great French

fortress of Epernal by a broad, open pass, 1,135 feet (or 346 meters) high, between the Vosges and the Monts Faucilles. So low is the barrier that it has never presented an appreciable obstacle to communication between northern Burgundy and southern Lorraine. Here today one finds the same provincial accent, the same peculiarity of geographical names ending in -ey, the same type of rural house, and the same character of inhabitants on both sides of the low watershed.[57] Thirty miles to the west an easy pass route between the Mont de Fourches and the Plateau de Langres connects the Saône with the Meuse Valley; and yet another crosses the Plateau of Langres at 1,550 feet (473 meters), where canal and railroad now link the Saône with the Marne. This was the route of the chief Roman road leading northward to the Lower Rhine. It crossed the summit at the ancient town of Andematunnum (Langres), but turning thence across the upland to the Moselle at Tullum (Toul), it followed the valley of this river past modern Metz and Trier, and then continued north to the Rhine at Colonia Agrippina, the modern Cologne.

The Roman road to the Seine, which was probably the main route of the tin trade, was important because of this trade and also because the Seine offered the best navigation of all the northern rivers except the Rhine. The road left the Saône or Arar at the Æduan town of Cabillonum (Chalons-sur Saône), turned west past modern Chagny, and mounted the plateau rim now known as the Côte d'Or to the ancient Æduan fortress of Bibracte, later to the nearby Roman town of Augustodunum (Autun). Thence it turned northwest, avoiding the granite massif of the Morvan Plateau, and followed the Yonne Valley across the Auxois plain down to the southern elbow of the Seine. The modern route from the Saône to the Auxois upland leaves the valley at Dijon and turns up the gorge of the Ouche, which is now traced by highway, the Burgundian Canal, and railroad. But the old road goes back beyond the memory of man. It was the route taken by Cæsar in 58 B.C., when he turned aside from his pursuit of the retreating Helvetians to seek the big Æduan town of Bibracte, eighteen miles away, where he hoped to find provisions for his soldiers.[58] Limestone buttresses running out from the base of Mont de

Rome-Château, which overlooks the route, preserve for us today ruins of bygone habitations or forts, and testify to the importance of this ancient thoroughfare.[59]

Thus the upper Saône and Doubs command a semicircle of transmontane connections. Midway between these headwater passes and the Mediterranean is the confluence of the Saône and Rhone. Here lay the ancient city of Lugdunum (Lyons), which for centuries was the heart of Roman Gaul. It commanded not only the whole length of the Rhone-Saône breach, but also the east course of the Rhone, which opens a narrow and difficult route between the Jura and Savoy Alps to Lake Geneva and the lake plateau of Switzerland. This is the passage which the migrating Helvetians attempted to force in 58 B.C., and which Cæsar defended.[60] The swift and often turbulent current of this mountain course of the Rhone, its difficult navigation, and its gorgelike valley afforded a fairly good barrier boundary to the young Roman *provincia*, whose limits had shortly before been pushed northward to the Rhone and Lake Geneva.

This history of the Rhone Valley begins with the founding of the Greek colony of Massilia (Marseilles) about 600 B.C. The site of the settlement was well chosen. Like many ports designed to exploit the commerce of big river systems, it was located, not at the mouth of the stream, but off to one side, where the constant deposition of deltaic mud could not silt up its harbor and spring floods threaten it with inundation. Such a location Massilia found where the hills of Provence run out as headlands into the sea east of the Rhone mouth. These afforded an acropolis for the city and a deep port, protected on the north by the long promontory of the l'Estagne from the destructive blasts of the *mistral*. Small inshore islets to guard the approaches to the harbor, sunny hillsides for vineyards and olive orchards, and the nearby river for inland commerce added all the other elements considered desirable for a Greek colony.[61] The region yielded poor wheat crops, however, so the colonists were compelled to "trust more to the resources of the sea than of the land, and avail themselves, in preference, of their excellent position for commerce," as Strabo tells us.[62]

APPROACHES TO THE RHONE VALLEY BREACH—The southern
approach to the Rhone Valley breach was made either by sea or
by land. The shallow waters of the Gulf of Lyons, the weak
tides of the Mediterranean, and the heavy burden of silt transported by the swift-flowing Rhone and Durance, all combined
to build up a large deltaic plain, through which wind the
tortuous courses of the Rhone distributaries. Like the outlets
of the Nile, these varied in number from two to five at different
periods and shifted their location.[63] Access to them was difficult. The flat, alluvial shore was often difficult to discern in
bad weather, as it lacked the bold sea-marks on which the
Mediterranean sailor was wont to rely. The debouchment
channels were constantly obstructed by the mud deposits at
their mouths. As early as 101 B.C. Caius Marius, who probably took his troops by sea from some northern Roman port
for the campaign against the Cimbri, found it necessary to
construct a navigable channel through the lagoons and half-
silted distributaries from the eastern outlet of the Rhone to a
point above the delta, where the road crossed the river.[64]
These *fossæ Marianæ* he gave to the people of Massilia in return for their aid against the invaders. The city made revenue
out of the canal by levying a toll on all boats using it.[65] But
the silting process in time impaired its usefulness, and threatened once more to block the entrance. Further obstacles to
navigation were found in the powerful current of the Rhone,
and the *mistral*, called by the ancients "the black north," which
swept down the valley.

Ancient traffic on the Rhone seems to have been considerable,
despite the difficulties of navigation. The Massilians were not
the only ones engaged in this river commerce. When Hannibal
in 218 B.C. crossed the Rhone on his march from Spain to
Italy, he was able to buy numerous dugout canoes and boats
from the natives, who used them in their extensive sea traffic.[66]
Massilia was the distributing center for the tin which found its
way southward across Gaul from Britain [67] and probably also
from mines in the Vilaine Valley of southeastern Brittany,
where ancient workings have been found.[68] Diodorus Siculus
states that the tin of Cornwall was collected for export on a
small inshore islet of the British coast, a typical maritime

market place.   There it was purchased by merchants who took
it over to Gaul, and transported it on horses, a thirty days'
journey across the country, to the mouth of the Rhone.[69]   The
Massiliots set up mercantile factories in the Gallic towns to
forward the British tin to the coast, together with the raw
products of the interior.   In exchange, they supplied the back
country with fish, salt, olive oil, wine, bronze utensils, and
pottery,[70] some of which undoubtedly found their way to that
indented Cornwall peninsula first known to the ancients as the
Cassiterides Islands.[71]   Through the Rhone Valley breach the
cruder elements of Hellenic civilization thus trickled into
Northern Europe, while the Greek language, alphabet, and
economic methods were disseminated among the neighboring
Gauls of the long Massiliot littoral.

The Rhone Valley breach is approached also by two land
routes, one from Italy and one from Spain,[72] which respectively turn the mountain barrier where the Maritime Alps and
the eastern Pyrenees run out into the Mediterranean.   These
narrow passways between mountain and sea have always opened
lines both of trade and of attack.   Hence Massilia fringed
them with her subsidiary colonies.   She lined the Gulf of Lyons
from Emporiæ and Rhoda (modern Rosas) on the Spanish
coast of the Pyrenees, around to Olbia (Eoube) and the Iles
d'Hyeros on the east; farther on, Antipolis or Antibes, Nicæa
or Nice, and Portus Monœci or Monaco, strung along the rocky
seaboard of the Maritime Alps, opposed the depredations of
the mountaineers and maintained the connections of Massilia
with its ally Rome.[73]

These routes became important also to the Romans after
their acquisition of Spain from Carthage in 201 B.C.   Hence
their first systematic campaigns against the Alpine tribes and
their conquest of the Rhone Valley were both inaugurated by
attacks on the mountaineers flanking this route, the valiant
Salluvii of the Maritime Alps and their Ligurian neighbors of
the western Apennines.   Like all highland tribes, they took
advantage of their strategic location to maintain a system of
pillage by land and sea, to block Roman traffic with Massilia
and Spain, and even to obstruct the passage of Roman armies.
The geographical relief of the country fought for them.   It

enabled them to maintain a guerilla warfare in intensity and duration out of all proportion to their numerical strength, after the manner of primitive mountain people the world over. In 125 B.C., after a conflict of eighty years, all that the Romans could force from the barbarians was a coastal strip, averaging a little over a mile in width, for purposes of a highway.[74] The ceded strip was transferred to the Massiliots, who undertook to construct and maintain the coast road, since it united their settlements. Beginning at Genoa, where it connected with the Via Aurelia, the road ran west across the roots of the Alps between mountain and sea as far as the modern Frejus (Forum Julii). There it left the coast, which runs out southward into a blunt peninsula, and turning up the valley of the Argeus River, continued westward along a longitudinal groove between parallel hill ranges. Where it emerged upon the alluvial plain of the Rhone, just north of Massilia, the Romans built the garrison town of Aquæ Sextiæ (Aix) to guard the road.[75] This Massiliot highway was later replaced by the Via Julia Augusta in the early days of the Empire. Centuries afterward, in 1807, it was revived by Napoleon in the famous Cornice Road, which he built to connect France with his short-lived Kingdom of Italy. Thus geography turned back to the history of the imperial Cæsars for a page to insert in the history of the great French Emperor.

From the military base at Aquæ Sextiæ, which commanded land and sea connection with Italy, began the Roman conquest of the Rhone Valley in 125 B.C. First the Salluvii between the Durance River and the sea were subdued, then their northern neighbors, the Vocontii, and finally in 122 B.C. the powerful Celtic tribes of the Allobroges, who inhabited the rich valley of the Isara (Isère) and the country north to Lake Lemanus (Geneva). The powerful Averni of the Cevennes Plateau, who had lent assistance to Allobroges, were forced to cede to Rome all the short southeastern slope of their highlands to the Rhone and the Mediterranean as far west as Tolosa (Toulouse) on the Garonne River, a territory comprised in the later French province of Languedoc. Thus practically all the Rhone Valley, north to the Saône confluence and to Lake Geneva, was comprised in the Roman province, except the coastal strip tributary to its ally Massilia. The geographic reasons are clear. The valleys of the Durance and Isère opened avenues of approach to the only two practical passes over the western Alps, the Mons Matrona or Mont Genevre at an altitude of 6,080 feet (1,853 meters), and the Little St. Bernard at 7,075 feet (2,157 meters). The latter was the unguarded door, hardly feasible for an army, which probably admitted Hannibal's forces into Italy, though it collected a frightful toll of life from his men and animals. Hence Hannibal's line of march, by the Pyrenean coast road, the valleys of the Rhone and Isère, and the Little St. Bernard Pass, determined with some accuracy the limits of early Roman expansion into Gaul.

On this point the first Roman road-building across the Rhone is instructive. From Arelate (Arles) at the head of the delta, or Tarusco (Tarascon), where the passage of the river was easiest and where therefore the Massiliot road had its terminus, the Romans ran the Via Domitia westward around the Gulf of Lyons, through Narbo (Narbonne), capital of the new province, and thence southward over the last spur of the Pyrenees into Spain. Here the massive form of the Pyrenees, stripping off its surplus folds before plunging into the sea, thrusts out an arm to the Mediterranean. This arm is the Alberes range, a single bold ridge deeply notched by the Col du Pertus (951 feet or 290 meters), which opens a low passway between the maritime plains of Roussillon in France and those of Ampurdan in Spain.[76] The sea-front of the Pyrenees forms a series of mountain headlands towering high above the fretting waves. It was enough to daunt the Roman road-builders, for it taxed the skill of the modern engineers, who by means of tunnels and galleries put through the coast railway here in 1880. The ancient gate of the Pyrenees lay, therefore, 7 miles back from the sea. Massilia had seen danger in this open door, and therefore planted along its southern approach several outpost colonies as bulwarks against Iberian invasion. Rome had seen it too, when the Carthaginians began to establish a new empire in Spain, and in 225 B.C. exacted from the Carthaginian governor a pledge that he would make the Ebro River the northern limit of his conquests in Spain.[77] But when Hannibal invaded Italy, he crossed the Pyrenees by the Col du Pertus,[78] traversed southern Gaul, and was already over the Rhone before the Roman army under Publius Scipio had landed in Massilia. From this time on through ancient and medieval history the Col du Pertus was a passway for migration and conquest.

THE RHONE VALLEY BREACH AND THE CONQUEST OF GAUL— It is significant of the purely Mediterranean outlook of the Roman Republic that it began its inland expansion up the Rhone Valley breach only under the spur of necessity. The century-long rivalry with Carthage kept it facing seaward, and forced it out of its peninsular isolation into wide maritime contact and dominion. Its great historical events were staged on the coasts. The hinterlands of the three surrounding continents as yet counted for nothing. Conquest of the lower Rhone Valley, the initial step of inland expansion, was begun only after the annexation of Carthage in 146 B.C. had made the western Mediterranean basin a Roman lake, and after the Adriatic, the Ionian, and Ægean seas with their bordering lands had likewise been incorporated in the empire of the Republic. Moreover, the *Provincia Romana* of Gaul, located between the western Alps, the Cevennes escarpment, and the Pyrenees, was Mediterranean in its climate, its natural products, and to some extent in its civilization, owing to the strong Hellenizing influences which for nearly five centuries had been emanating from Massilia. The Province was organized and annexed in 121 B.C. Further expansion beyond the climatic limit defined by the Rhone elbow at the Saône confluence had to wait till 58 B.C., or over sixty years.

Meantime the *Provincia* was having the typical experiences of a border district on an exposed frontier. While other Roman provinces like Sicily and Spain suffered from local revolts against an oppressive government, this one alone suffered from foreign incursions. Therein it anticipated by some five hundred years the similar historical events of Pannonia and the Julian Alps, growing out of similar geographic conditions. It became in effect a Marchland, after the order of the later German *Mark;* and it duplicated the history. First a border district of defense, it passed suddenly to a more brilliant rôle as a base for conquest and expansion. Often a geographical handicap may be converted into a geographical opportunity. It is a matter of tipping the scales.

Rome secured her end of the Rhone Valley breach not a moment too soon. Immediately she began to encounter here a persistent stream of Germanic expansion, which selected this easy path to the sunny Mediterranean lands. Hither, in 109 B.C., came the Cimbri, who four years earlier had been ordered off from that half-open door of the Julian Alps. The door was wide open here, so they defeated the Roman army somewhere in the Rhone Valley. They returned in 105 B.C., hurled aside the Roman army stationed at Arausio (Orange) on the lower Rhone to obstruct their course, and passed on victorious by the nearby Pyrenean gate into Spain. They wandered in Spain and Gaul for two or three years, but were soon back, nosing like hungry dogs about the doors of Italy.[79] This time (102 B.C.) the Cimbri found a way to the Po Valley by the Brenner Pass (4,470 feet, 1,362 meters) over the Central Alps; but their allies, the Teutons and Ambrones, came down the Rhone Valley. Caius Marius, Rome's great general, four times elected consul in anticipation of this danger on the Rhone, was sent to oppose them. He let the barbarians trek past his camp on the lower Isère, where he had taken his stand to head them off from the western Alpine passes; but near Aquæ Sextiæ (Aix), at the entrance to the Massiliot coast road to Italy, he stopped their advance by a crushing defeat in 101 B.C.

The real points of danger for Rome lay in that semicircle of passes crossing the watershed of the upper Saône and Doubs. The country between the Saône and the Rhine was held by the Sequani, who thus commanded the Burgundian Gate; that between the Saône and the plateau course of the Loire and Seine systems was occupied by the Ædui, who thus controlled the western passes. Rivalry existed between the tribes, because each claimed exclusive right to the Saône and especially to the tolls levied on passing vessels.[80] The Romans, stretching their sphere of influence to this strategic locality where lay the keys to the Rhone Valley door, made an alliance with the Ædui, and enabled them to exclude the Sequani from the profitable Saône commerce. The Sequani, in turn, invited in Ariovistus and his German horde who dwelt just across the Rhine, and in 62 B.C.

by their assistance defeated the Ædui. The bars of the Burgundian Gate were down. The Germans kept pouring into Gaul and settling in the Sequani land. Ariovistus had a German province there by 58 B.C., when Cæsar, adopting an aggressive policy, moved up the Saône Valley to prevent the Helvetian invasion. This accomplished, he prepared to attack the Germans, who showed no inclination to withdraw from their newly acquired territory. He advanced up the Doubs Valley and seized the Sequanian fortified town of Vesontio, which occupied a strong location within a circular loop of the Doubs and which survives today as the great fortress of Besançon. From this town as a military base he attacked the Germans near the Rhine and drove them across the river out of Gaul. That autumn the army of Cæsar went into winter quarters in the Sequanian territory.[81] Rome held the Burgundian Gate.

Thus began the conquest of Gaul. The significance of the movement for the Romans lay in the complete control of the Rhone Valley breach and its inland approaches; in the protrusion of the frontier far beyond the danger line found in that semicircle of watershed passes; and in the inland extension of Roman trade routes. For the world at large it meant the advance of historical events beyond the narrow rim of the Mediterranean Basin to the contrasted Atlantic lands of Europe.

The conquests of Cæsar checked for a time the streams of barbarian invasion. The decline of the Empire saw them surging on again. The Germans repeated the history of Ariovistus and his hordes. They settled first in the elbow of the Rhine, then moved across the river and through the Burgundian Gate into the Doubs and Saône valleys. Others followed the course of the Cimbri, moved westward by the Belgian plain to the Meuse and then up its valley to the Saône passes. In the fifth and early sixth century the Burgundians occupied all the old Sequanian and much of the Æduan territory; in fact all the basin of the Saône and middle Rhone. There, strong in their strategic location, their mountain barrier, and their geographic unity, they maintained themselves as an independent kingdom for nearly a hundred years, till in 534 they were conquered by the Franks.[82]

THE RHONE VALLEY AND THE KINGDOM OF BURGUNDY—
The threefold division of the Carolingian Empire by the treaty
of Verdun (843) is explicable only in the light of the Rhone
Valley breach. This geographical fact is the key to what
otherwise appears to be an arbitrary and erratic allotment
of territory to the three heirs. The division left to Charles
the major part of what we are wont to call France, or the
kingdom of the West Franks; to Louis, the kingdom of the
East Franks, which might be called the big nucleus of modern
Germany; to Lothair it gave Italy and "a long narrow strip of
territory between the dominions of his Eastern and Western
brothers," Freeman states, and then adds in explanation: "Between these two states the policy of the ninth century instinc-
tively put a barrier." [83]

Geography admits no place for instinct in its interpretation
of history. It looks for concrete and tangible causes. In this
particular case it observes that the problematical strip of
Lothair's territory comprised the whole Rhone-Saône-Doubs
Valley, the Burgundian Gate with the elbow of the Rhine, the
two northern passes of the hill country of the Monts Faucilles
and Mont des Fourches to the Moselle and the Meuse, all the
country drained by these two rivers, and the valley of the
Rhine below the confluence of the Moselle at Coblenz. In other
words, Lothair, to compensate himself for the small territory
of Northern and Central Italy, secured the whole stretch of
that natural transit belt which crossed Europe from Marseilles
northward to Cologne, Aix, and the mouths of the Rhine, the
Meuse, and the Scheldt. This he held in its entirety except
at two points. The West Frankish kingdom retained the
Langres Pass, where the original Roman road had crossed the
watershed; and it also thrust its frontier across the Saône at
Chalon-sur-Saône in order to keep the valley terminus of the
ancient Æduan and Roman highway down from Autun. But
Lothair's strip, in compensation, bent sharply west from Lyons
far up on the Cevennes Plateau, in order to include the city of
Roanne (Rodumna) on the Loire, terminus of the old Roman
road which ran west to Bordeaux on the Garonne estuary.
Though these ancient Roman highways had undoubtedly de-

generated into mere tracks, they still sufficed to direct the commerce of the Middle Ages.

A traffic zone hardly furnishes a sound basis for a political territory, though it may yield a generous revenue. This transit strip constituting the continental part of Lothair's kingdom proved its artificial character by its rapid dissolution.[84] The northern half, comprising the valleys of the Meuse, the Moselle, and the Rhine, was absorbed by the East Frankish kingdom. Out of the remaining ruins emerged once more, in 887, the independent kingdom of Burgundy, a geographical unit with natural boundaries of mountain and sea to protect its frontiers; with the Rhone-Saône-Doubs system penetrating every part of its area, like a great artery, to unify its national life; with the control of the Burgundian Gate, the northern passes, and the Alpine coast road to Italy, to give it weight in the political councils of Western Europe. Its strategic location tended to compensate for its lack of area. It stood in the center of the balance and could throw its weight on one side or the other. Through this power it was able to maintain its independence till 1032, when it became a fief of the German Empire. Then the whole stretch of the Rhone-Rhine groove was politically united. The influence of the through commerce is indicated by the rise here of numerous free cities, Besançon, Lyons, Orange, Arles, and Marseilles, which controlled all the foci of trade till the fourteenth century, and maintained the importance of this vassal state of Burgundy. Until 1365 the medieval German kaiser went to Arles to be crowned king of Burgundy, as he went to Rome to be crowned emperor of the Holy Roman Empire.

The later history of Burgundy recites the gradual absorption of this "middle kingdom," as the old chronicles called it, by the modern kingdom of France. Early in the fourteenth century its voracious western neighbor began to gnaw at its western frontier, taking a bite here and there, till by 1378 it had swallowed the southern Rhone Valley from the Mediterranean to Lyons. The northern part of Burgundy, which was more closely linked with Germany through the Burgundian Gate and the Lorraine passes, was able longer to resist French expansion. Nevertheless, in another hundred years, by 1477, it had shrunk to the free County of Burgundy or the Franche Comté, a small territory comprising the valleys of the upper Saône and Doubs, which passed to the expanding France of Louis XIV.[85]

The Rhone Valley breach facilitated the expansion of the French kingdom to the Mediterranean coast and enabled it to round out its territory to its natural frontier. It gave this stretch of coast a unique importance as the only littoral in the western Mediterranean commanding easy connection with a continental hinterland, and as the southern outlet of a great plexus of northern land routes.

Marseilles, which long overshadowed its medieval rival Arles, is the only seaport of the Rhone Valley. It has therefore concentrated upon itself the exports of Northwestern Europe which seek the market of Africa, the Levant, Eastern Asia, and Australia; it gathers in return the wheat of Russia, the oil seeds of India and Africa, the wines and dried fruits of the Mediterranean, the teas and spices of the Far East.[86] The variety of products from distant sources which pass through the harbor of Marseilles is symbolic of the peoples, tongues, and civilizations that have moved along the Rhone Valley thoroughfare since the dawn of history.

The Gap of Carcassonne—Another breach opens westward from the Rhone mouth and links the Gulf of Lyons with the Bay of Biscay, the Mediterranean with the open Atlantic. This is the Col de Naurouse or the Gap of Carcassonne, a broad saddle of low elevation (620 feet or 189 meters) which occupies the watershed between two navigable rivers,—the large Garonne system flowing into the Bay of Biscay and the little Aude debouching into the Gulf of Lyons at the ancient seaport of Narbo (Narbonne). The two rivers and the saddle between occupy an old subsidence belt which in the early Tertiary Period opened a strait between the two seas, and which today forms a broad zone of contact between the *Massif Central* of France on the north and the folded Pyrenees on the south.

The resulting passage resembles physically that between the French Alps and the Cevennes Plateau, though its plain is broader and lower; but it has never yet attained a like historical significance, for obvious geographical reasons. It was

the route of an old Roman road, a passway for migrating peoples and conquering armies, a route for a barge canal constructed between 1672 and 1681, and for a projected ship
canal to facilitate the union of the Atlantic and Mediterranean
fleets of France.   Towns and cities bordering its plain show
the survival of old walls and moats, like the picturesque fortress
of Carcassonne.[87]

The Mediterranean outlet of this passage was marked by
Narbo situated just above the mouth of the ancient Atax
(Aude).   It was a very ancient place, mentioned by Hecatæus
who lived in 520 B.C.; it became the chief commercial and maritime city on the *Sinus Gallicus* or Sea of Narbo (Gulf of
Lyons).   It commanded two bays or lagoons protected by
inshore islands, the navigable course of the Aude, and the Gap
of Carcassonne.   These advantages led to its selection as the
site of the first colony of Roman citizens in 111 B.C.   But these
advantages were not all, for it rapidly grew to be chief emporium of this coast and attracted a great number of foreign
visitors.[88]   The chief factor in this preëminence seems to have
been the wealth of gold and silver, mined by the native Gallic
tribes on the slopes of the Pyrenees and the Cevennes Plateau,
and especially the tin which here reached the Mediterranean
coast.

The tin (*stannum*), which was in constant demand for the
manufacture of bronze, came in part from several localities of
the Meseta in northwest Spain; but more was brought from
the island of Britain to the continent, and transported from the
coast on horses across Gaul to Massilia and Narbo.[89]   Some of
the tin may have come from the old mines on the southern
margin of the Armorican Plateau between the Vilaine and the
Loire.   The port of the Loire was Corbilo.   On this point a line
from Polybius is significant.   He says, "There was once an
ancient emporium named Corbilo on this river (Liger or
Loire); but none of its inhabitants nor those of Massilia or
Narbo could give Scipio any information worth mentioning
about Britain when questioned by him, though they were the
most important cities in that part of the country."[90]   This
Scipio seems to have visited Narbo, Massilia and Corbilo in the
fourth century B.C., inquiring about centers of trade open to

9 *

Rome in rivalry with Carthage,[91] and especially about the northern sources of tin. It is possible that the Phœnicians first came to know of the tin of Gallicia and Britain on this coast, and later sought out the sea way thither in order to establish direct trade, reap larger profits, and establish a monopoly in the trade on the coast of Cornwall.[92]

The gold and silver of the Pyrenees and Cevennes slopes also appealed to the Romans. The Tectosages, who controlled the hinterland of Narbo to Tolosa at the head of navigation on the Garonne River, about 50 miles from the Mediterranean coast, had immense stores of gold and silver bullion stored up in the temple treasuries and sacred tanks at their capital Tolosa (Toulouse).[93] The Romans acquired the Narbo district from the Cevennes to the Pyrenees and west to the Garonne River in 121 B.C. by the defeat of the Arverni and Allobroges, with whom the Tectosages were allied. The chief object of the Romans, however, was to secure the land route between the Rhone and Spain.[94]

The Biscay shores of this western breach was a sandy, unproductive country, though the western Pyrenees had valuable gold mines. The port of Burdigala (Bordeaux) at the tidal head of the Garonne River faced the stormy Bay of Biscay; it had only a drop-in trade from Phœnician vessels coasting northward to the tin mines of the Vilaine valley or Cornwall. A limited hinterland restricted the development of Burdigala and Narbo, though the Mediterranean port maintained its rivalry with Massilia till its harbor was silted up in the fourth century A.D. by the deposits of the Aude River and the mud carried westward from the Rhone mouth by a current along this coast.

The expanding Franks, advancing south from the plains of northern Gaul, swung around to the west of the Cevennes Plateau in 511 A.D., conquered all Aquitaine to the Gap of Carcassonne and thus controlled this western breach though they failed to get access to the Mediterranean, because this coastal strip was held by the Visigoths while the stretch from the Rhone delta eastward was held by the Ostrogoths. But by 536 Clovis and his Franks annexed all Provence and therefore controlled both the Rhone valley and the whole passway of Carcassonne.

Tolosa, by reason of its central location on the Garonne at the head of navigation, was again and again a capital city; but in time it declined before the centralization of commerce at Bordeaux and Marseilles, and the concentration of railroad traffic at Paris. Only the projected ship canal can some day revive the importance of the Gap of Carcassonne.

SUMMARY—The effects of the barriers encircling the Mediterranean were numerous and significant. They tended to keep the Mediterranean peoples as a whole within the coast lands of the Midland Sea and therefore to give them for many centuries the impress of its stimulating contact. Since these barriers helped to prevent dispersion over the continental hinterlands, they led to marked concentration of national life within each segregated district, as seen in Attica, Lesbos, Etruria or Latium, and to the persistent exploitation of local resources. The result was improved economic processes, as in agriculture and industry, and progressive adjustment to the natural environment.

Another effect was to protect the Mediterranean people from the overwhelming inroads of barbarians. These were admitted through the few breaches in necessarily small groups, who were easily resisted or easily absorbed by the local population, until the period of the *Voelkerwanderung* let loose unprecedented hordes. The exclusion of the barbarians, who proved to be powerful solvents of the Mediterranean civilization, and the confinement of that civilization within the barrier boundaries which kept it in constant touch with the interior sea, had the effect of unifying Mediterranean culture. Traders, colonists and fishing fleets carried the elements of that culture from shore to shore, amplifying it, enriching it, till the drama of Euripides was at home in Sicilian Syracuse, the art of Praxiteles familiar to Rome, the philosophy of Plato to Massilia and the religion of Christ to Athens and Constantinople.

AUTHORITIES—CHAPTER X

1. Aristotle, *Historia Animalium*, VI, 16-17. Pliny, *Hist. Nat.*, IX, 19.
2. Aristotle, *op. cit.*, VIII, 12-14.
3. Polybius, IV, 43. Aristotle, *op. cit.*, VIII, 16. Pliny, *op. cit.*, IX, 20.
4. Kenrick, *Phœnicia*, pp. 90-91. London, 1855.
5. V. Bérard, *Les Phéniciens et l'Odyssie*, Vol. I, pp. 79-82. Paris, 1902.
6. See Walter Leaf, *A Study in Homeric Geography*, New York, 1913, for full discussion. Also Dörpfeld, *Troja und Ilion*.
7. J. B. Bury, *History of Greece*, pp. 90-93. New York, 1909.
8. Strabo, XI, Chap. II, 3-4.
9. Herodotus, IV, 17; VII, 147. Demosthenes, *De Corona,* ¶ 73 and 87. Xenophon, *Hellenes*, V, 4, 61. Diodorus Siculus, XV, 34.
10. Based upon personal observation during a motor trip through Dalmatia, Bosnia, Herzegovina and Montenegro in 1912.
11. D. G. Hogarth, *The Nearer East*, pp. 23, 24, 238. London, 1905.
12. Polybius, V, 97; XXVIII, 8.
13. Hodgkin, *Italy and Her Invaders*, Vol. III, pp. 31-32 with note and map. Oxford, 1880.
14. William Miller, *The Balkans*, p. 273. New York, 1907.
15. *Ibid.*, p. 293.
16. Paulus, quoted in Hodgkin, *op. cit.*, Vol. V. Bk. VI, note p. 160.
17. Strabo, IV, Chap. VI, 10; VII, Chap. V, 2. For modern road in detail see Walter Kröhn, *Beiträge zur Verkehrs-geographie von Krain*, pp. 61-62. Königsberg, 1911. Also Agostini, *Carta Venezia Giulia*, 1: 250,000, Novara, 1920.
18. Mommsen, *History of Rome*, Vol. III, pp. 427-428. New York, 1900. For modern road, see P. von Canstein, *Die oestlichen Alpen*, pp. 235-258. Berlin, 1837.
19. For modern road see Baedeker, *The Eastern Alps*, pp. 441-442, Leipzig, 1888, and Norbert Krebs, *Länderkunde der oesterreichischen Alpen*, pp. 401, 409. Stuttgart, 1913.
20. W. R. Shepherd, *Historical Atlas*, p. 27. New York, 1911.
21. Pliny, *Hist. Nat.* XXXVI, 2, 11.
22. Aristotle, *De Mirabilibus*, Chaps. 81 and 104. Diodorus Siculus, V, 22. Pliny, III, 30.
23. Herodotus, III, 15; IV, 33.
24. H. Rudolphi, "Tragelaetze und Schleppwege." *Deutsche Rundschau für Geographie*, Vol. 34, p. 66.
25. Aristotle, *Hist. Animal.*, VIII, 13. Strabo, IV, Chap. IV, 9. Pliny, III, 22. Apollonius Rhodius, IV, 283. Supported also by Hipparchus and Theopompus.
26. Strabo, IV, Chap. VI, 9, 12; V, Chap. I, 8; VII, Chap. V, 2.
27. Livy, *Historia*, XXXIX, 22, 45, 54.
28. *Ibid.*, XL, 34; XLIII, 1, 17. A *jugerum* is .623 acre.
29. W. E. Heitland, *The Roman Republic*, Vol. II, pp. 141-142, 1909.
30. J. B. Bury, *History of the Roman Empire*, pp. 95-98. New York, 1909.
31. T. Hodgkin, *op. cit.*, Vol. I, Bk. I, pp. 159-169.
32. E. C. Semple, *Influences of Geographic Environment*, pp. 233-235. New York, 1911.
33. Hodgkin, *op. cit.*, Vol. I, Bk. I, pp. 250-258, 280-282, 317.
34. *Ibid.*, Vol. II, Bk. II, pp. 164-170.

35. *Ibid.*, Vol. III, Bk. IV, pp. 202-211.
36. P. Villare, *Barbarian Invasions of Italy*, Vol. II, p. 279. 1902.
37. Hodgkin, *op. cit.*, Vol. V, Bk. VI, pp. 158-169.
38. *Ibid.*, pp. 160-161, Vol. VI, Bk. VII, pp. 38-44.
39. *Ibid.*, Vol. VI, Bk. VII, pp. 50-64, 286-287.
40. *Ibid.*, pp. 328-331.
41. *Enc. Brit.*, article "Carniola."
42. E. C. Semple, *op. cit.*, pp. 233-234.
43. Waitz, *Deutsche. Verfassungsgeschichte*, Vol. VII, pp. 84-94. 1876.
44. Paulus, quoted by W. R. Thayer, *Short History of Venice*, p. 32. 1905.
45. J. Marquart, *Osteuropaeische und ostasiatiche Streifzuge circa* 840-940, pp. 156-158. Leipzig, 1903.
46. Alfons Huber, *Geschichte Oesterreichs*, Vol. I, p. 136. Gotha, 1885.
47. *Ibid.*, pp. 218-220.
48. E. A. Freeman, *Historical Geography of Europe*, p. 319. London, 1882.
49. William Coxe, *History of the House of Austria*, Vol. II, pp. 105-106. London, 1847.
50. W. R. Thayer, *op. cit.*, p. 93.
51. Abbot, *Austria, Its Rise and Fall*, pp. 70, 71, 75, 83, 146, 147. Alfons Huber, *op. cit.*, Vol. IV, p. 13. Gotha, 1892.
52. Louis Leger, *History of Austro-Hungary*, pp. 154, 258. London, 1889.
53. R. W. Seton-Watson, *The Southern Slav Question and the Hapsburg Monarchy*, p. 26. London, 1911.
54. Norbert Krebs, *op. cit.*, p. 413. Diercke, *Schulatlas*, maps pp. 89, 129. 1909.
55. W. Z. Ripley, *Races of Europe*, pp. 255-268. New York, 1910.
56. Chamberlin and Salisbury, *Geology*, Vol. III, pp. 277, 319. New York, 1906.
57. Vidal de la Blache, *Géographie de la France*, pp. 234-42. Paris, 1903. Compare Tacitus, *Annales*, XIII, 53.
58. Cæsar, *De Bello Gallico*, I, 23.
59. Vidal de la Blache, *op. cit.*, p. 240.
60. Cæsar, *op. cit.*, I, 2-10.
61. Vidal de la Blache, *op. cit.*, pp. 341, 344, 345.
62. Strabo, IV, Chap. I, 5.
63. *Ibid.*, IV, Chap. I, 8.
64. Heitland, W. E., *op. cit.*, II, 372.
65. Strabo, IV, Chap. I, 8.
66. Polybius, *Histories*, III, 42.
67. Strabo, III, Chap. II, 9.
68. Vidal de la Blache, *op. cit.*, pp. 20-21.
69. Diodorus Siculus, V, 22.
70. Ernst Curtius, *History of Greece*, Vol. I, p. 482. New York.
71. Strabo, III, Chap. V, 11.
72. N. Bergier, *Histoire des Grands Chemins de l'Empire Romain*, Vol. I, p. 493. Brussels, 1728. Mommsen, *Provinces of the Roman Empire*, Vol. I, p. 80. New York, 1887.
73. Strabo, IV, Chap. I, 5.
74. *Ibid.*, IV, Chap. VI, 3.
75. *Ibid.*, IV, Chap. I, 5.
76. Vidal de la Blache, *op. cit.*, pp. 355-356.

77. Heitland, *op. cit.*, II, 223.
78. Polybius, *op. cit.*, III, 9; XVI, 23, 24.
79. Heitland, *op. cit.*, II, 363-366, 372-373.
80. Strabo, IV, Chap. III, 2.
81. Cæsar, *op. cit.*, I, 31-54.
82. Hodgkin, *op. cit.*, III, pp. 357-358, 592.
83. Freeman, *op. cit.*, p. 140.
84. Lavisse, *Histoire de France*, Vol. II, Part II, p. 4.   Paris, 1901.
85. Freeman, *op. cit.*, pp. 141, 148, 150, 194; map plates XVIII-XXV.
86. George G. Chisholm, *Compendium of the Geography of Europe*, I, p. 429.   London, 1899.
87. Vidal de la Blache, *op. cit.*, Vol. I, pp. 353-354.
88. Strabo, IV, Chap. I, 6, 12.
89. Diodorus Siculus, V, 38.   Vidal de la Blache, *op. cit.*, pp. 19-21.
90. Polybius, XXXIV, 10.
91. E. S. Schuckburgh, Translation of *Polybius*, Vol. II, p. 488, note.   London, 1889.
92. E. Speck, *Handelsgeschichte des Altertums*, vol. I, p. 502.   Leipzig, 1900.
93. Strabo, IV, Chap. I, 13.
94. Mommsen, *History of Rome*, Vol. III, p. 419.   New York, 1900.

PART III

VEGETATION AND AGRICULTURE.

CHAPTER XI

ANCIENT MEDITERRANEAN FORESTS AND THE LUMBER TRADE

A study of existing Mediterranean forests throws light on the various climatic and physiographic factors which have aided their survival, either in their pristine extent or as mere fragments of former widespread woodlands. Chief among these factors have been the amount of the rainfall and the duration of the rainy season. Bound up with these have been location in the more arid Eastern Basin as opposed to the moister Western Basin; location south or north of the fortieth parallel of latitude; location on high mountains with summer showers and winter snow-cover which conserves moisture; exposure to rain-bearing winds from the west, northwest or southwest in the Mediterranean Sea proper, and from the north and west in the Euxine. Inaccessible location remote from centers of population has tended to preserve forests, owing to heavy charges for transportation. Soil also has been a factor. Ancient forests have been more likely to persist on soils of disintegrated sandstone and crystalline rocks, especially when mingled with clay, and on volcanic soils and volcanic ash, because these are retentive of moisture. The porous limestone soils, which are very arid, when once deforested never recover in the dry sections of the Mediterranean lands, but deteriorate into a *maqui*. In the rainy karst of the Carso Plateau, however, forests have held their own against the depredations of man, but in the karst of Montenegro and Dalmatia they have not survived the onslaughts of goats, sheep and cattle.[1]

CLIMATE AND VEGETATION IN THE MEDITERRANEAN REGION —The Mediterranean Basin as a whole is distinguished not only by a common type of climate, but by a type of vegetation whose common physiognomy reflects the prevailing climatic conditions. Thus the ancients described it, and thus we find it today. Trees, shrubs, herbs and grasses in their structure and life course show a close adaptation to their environment. Many of them which were immigrants from northern Europe and central Africa became modified to suit Mediterranean conditions of climate and soil.

Like the Mediterranean climate, Mediterranean vegetation shows a series of graduated transition forms. On the north it merges into the plant life of Middle Europe with its dense forests, abundant deciduous trees, juicy grasses and weeds, which are amply watered by the rains all year round, grow during the summer heat, and rest during the winter cold. On the south it gradually passes over into steppe and desert vegetation adapted to arid conditions—a sparse growth of thorny or spiny shrubs armed to resist the prevailing drought and to conserve the meager store of water which they get during the winter showers. Mingled with these shrubs is an equally sparse growth of grasses and herbs which spring up in moister districts after the winter rains, hasten through their few weeks of life, and die down under the parching summer heat. In desert and steppe alike the growth is thin; each plant stands apart from its fellows in an effort to monopolize a maximum space for its thirsty roots.

In type and in location the Mediterranean vegetation stands between these two contrasted groups of plant life. It knows neither the blessing of perennial rains, nor the curse of Saharan aridity, but it has a taste of the latter in the long summer drought, while in the winter rains it gets the abundant moisture of the north, combined with sufficient warmth to keep its life processes going. In winter and spring, therefore, it has its period of growth, and in summer its period of rest. To these natural conditions it has adapted itself, and under them it has spread over Mediterranean lands as far as Mediterranean climatic influences penetrate. It finds its limit not far from the sea itself, because this body of water is the main reservoir of the winter moisture. At a relatively short distance back from the coast the typical Mediterranean vegetation gives place to steppe vegetation in Africa, central Spain and Asia Minor. In the mountains, where the winters are colder and the summers moister, it merges into a highland vegetation which closely resembles that of Middle Europe, and in higher altitudes it passes

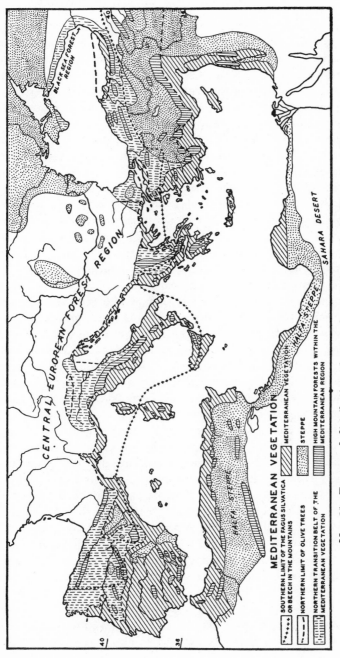

MAP 11—Types and distribution of natural vegetation in the Mediterranean Region.

MEDITERRANEAN VEGETATION

✕✕✕✕	SOUTHERN LIMIT OF THE FAGUS SILVATICA OR BEECH IN THE MOUNTAINS	MEDITERRANEAN VEGETATION
	NORTHERN LIMIT OF OLIVE TREES	STEPPE
	NORTHERN TRANSITION BELT OF THE MEDITERRANEAN VEGETATION	HIGH MOUNTAIN FORESTS WITHIN THE MEDITERRANEAN REGION

BLACK SEA FOREST REGION

CENTRAL EUROPEAN FOREST REGION

SAHARA DESERT

HALFA STEPPE

HALFA STEPPE

over into Alpine types. The genuine Mediterranean vegetation, therefore, belongs to low slopes and the vicinity of the coasts. It is most typical in the middle zone of rainless summers found in southern Spain and Italy, in Greece and Palestine. It constitutes the fragrant flowery *maqui*, an evergreen shrub vegetation which forms extensive thickets on crystalline rock soil, and poor, thin growth on dry limestone soil. Its characteristic plants are myrtle, laurel, arbutus, cistus, juniper, evergreen oak, and wild olive, which appears both as shrub and dwarfed tree.

In this broad transition zone, cereals and other grasses, having superficial roots and hence depending on the surface moisture in the soil, sprout during the warm rains of autumn, grow slowly during the winter, rapidly during spring, and reach maturity in early summer. After this they dry up in the drought and heat. Tuberous, bulbous and annual plants, likewise dependent upon surface moisture, are reawakened to life by the first warmth of spring, grow and blossom and seed while the soil is still damp, thus completing their life processes before the summer drought. To these groups of plants belong the chief crops of cereals and vegetables raised by Mediterranean agriculture. Therefore, from time immemorial winter has been the period of tillage for most native crops, spring or early summer the harvest time, and middle or late summer a season of comparative leisure for farm labor.

Plants and trees that weather the long summer are equipped to resist drought. Many have elaborate root systems, which enable them to gather in moisture from a large area and especially from the deeper layers of soil. Their leaves are commonly narrow, often needle-shaped, so that they present the least possible surface to the sun. Some take the form of spines and thorns, which indicate approach to desert conditions. The leaves have a dark green or gray color, with a polished or resinous surface above and a silvery coating of hairs beneath. All these are nature's devices to diminish evaporation and conserve moisture in the plants. Many species of trees are dwarfed and gnarled, with stocky trunks and low branches hugging the ground, where rest the moister strata of air; for the higher the trees, the more they are exposed to the drying action of the winds. Others that grow tall, like the cypress, spring up into a slender spire of dark green, presenting little surface to the sun. Trees and shrubs at sea level are evergreen or nearly so. Even deciduous trees lose their leaves for only a brief space, because they need both the winter rain and summer heat to complete their life functions.

DISTRIBUTION OF FORESTS—Mediterranean forests reflect the vicissitudes of their life conditions embodied in the long summer drought. The dense continuous forests which stretch across middle and northern Europe under the influence of an ample and well distributed rainfall reach their southern limit just within the northern border of the Mediterranean Basin. Beyond this margin, life conditions fluctuate or fail; the summer water supply is inadequate. Each tree, therefore, appropriates a large area with its spreading roots in order to get sufficient moisture. Consequently Mediterranean forests are usually sparse woodlands or savannahs, open plantations into which the light penetrates. Genuine forests of the European stamp are found only on the northern rim of the Basin and on high mountains which are able to condense moisture from the summer clouds. They are ample on the Pyrenees, Alps, northern Apennines, the Macedonian highlands, and the mountain coasts of the Black Sea. In southern districts they occur as islands of green foliage on lofty mountains, like the peaks of Sicily, Arcadia, Crete and Cyprus, and especially on westward facing slopes like Mount Amanus and Lebanon. Palestine, even in very early times, knew no forests except the pine woods of Mount Hermon, firs and cedars of Lebanon, and the oak groves of Bashan or Gilead. Scarcity of timber made tall trees conspicuous landmarks and even objects of worship. In the southern lowlands forests degenerate into poor scrub growth, or shrink to detached groups of trees about a spring pool, or contract to a ribbon of foliage along a wadi bed, or are replaced by irrigated plantations of domestic trees as in Egypt, or they succumb to the power of the desert.

The mountains of the Mediterranean Basin show climatic zones of altitude with their appropriate tree growth. On lower slopes the forests consist of maritime pine and evergreen oaks, up to an altitude of 2,000 or 3,000 feet. Above that height grow deciduous trees, like the oak, elm, chestnut and beech; at this elevation they get enough rain to survive the summer, and also get more heat than the winter affords. The chestnut grows at altitudes from 2,000 to 5,000 feet according to the latitude; above it is the beech, and higher still are firs and cedars. Deciduous trees increase in abundance from lower to higher altitudes and from south to north. This is also the ancient distribution described by Theophrastus and Pliny. Theophrastus found the water-loving plane-trees lining the banks of the perennial rivers of Greece; [2] and today the modern traveler, tramping through the Vale of Tempe along the swift-flowing Peneus, enjoys their grateful shade.

The dense forests that covered the mountains along the northern rim of the Mediterranean Basin undoubtedly intensified their barrier nature in ancient times, and helped to discourage invasion by the pastoral nomads of the Eurasian grasslands. The wooded heights of the Caucasus, Balkans and Carpathians probably deflected many a migration away from Asia Minor and Greece, and turned it westward over the open plains of the lower and middle Danube towards Italy and Gaul. But these thick border forests once passed, the early peoples who pushed their way into Mediterranean lands found easy going for themselves and their wide-horned cattle through the open woodlands of the valleys and coastal plains. When they halted to make permanent settlements, they had only thin forests to clear before sowing their crops. This consideration must have been an important factor in territorial expansion in the days when stone and bronze axes were the only weapons of attack upon hardwood trees. Indeed, history hints that the primeval forests of Cyprus and Corsica were a deterrent to the earliest Greek and Roman settlements on these islands.[3]

EARLY LUMBER TRADE—The relative paucity of trees in the lowlands and coastal strips, just where population settled thickest, resulted in a rapid denudation of the forests about the ancient cities and towns. This in turn gave rise to early importation of various woods from better timbered regions to deforested districts like Attica, and to forestless areas like Philistia and Egypt, whose local species of trees yielded little or no lumber. The result was the early development of the

lumber trade. This supplied the demand for fuel, building materials, cabinet woods and ship timber; the latter included special kinds of lumber for keel, hull, decking, masts and oars.

The active demand for ship supplies in all the coastal cities
of the Mediterranean and the irregular distribution of the forests resulted in early government control of the lumber trade.
The object was to guarantee ample provision for the home
state, and to cripple rivals by excluding them from the best
lumber markets. Athens prohibited by law the export of ship
timber, pitch, wax, cordage and flax—all materials for building
and equipping fleets. Even states with abundant lumber permitted its export only by treaty agreement. Amyntas II of
Macedonia allowed the towns of the Chalcidice Peninsula to
export pitch and various kinds of house lumber, but timber like
pine and fir fit for shipbuilding might be exported only for the
use of the state, and then only after conference with the royal
officials. Even so, the Chalcidians had to pay export duties on
such materials. Archelaus of Macedon (died in 399 B.C.) permitted Andocides, a wealthy merchant, to export all the oak
timber for oars he pleased, owing to friendship between the latter's father and the king.[4] Ship timber and oak for oars were
important resources of Chalcidice. Pharnabazus, Satrap of
Phrygia, wishing to strengthen Sparta against Athens, invited
the Spartans to rebuild their shattered fleet in 411 B.C. from
the forests of Mount Ida and gave them money for the work.[5]
When Æmilius Paulus in 167 B.C. conquered Macedon, he stipulated that no ship timber be cut or exported. Ten years before
this, Perseus of Macedon had given a quantity of ship timber
to Rhodes for its fleet, both to seal friendship with the island
and to strengthen Rome's chief rival in the Ægean Sea.[6] In
the "Characters" of Theophrastus, the Ostentatious Man of
Athens pretends that he has secured the costly license for the
export of lumber from the city.

Owing to the diminution of rainfall from north to south, from
west to east, and from highland to lowland, these were exactly
the directions in which the chief lumber traffic moved. Exceptions occurred mainly where choice woods from a limited area
of production gradually acquired wide use, as in the case of the
tall pines of the Caucasus and the unsurpassed cedars of Leb-

anon. The ebony and teak imported from India over the eastern rim of the Basin met a demand in all the capital cities.

The wide distribution of mountains within and around the Mediterranean Basin made the highlands the predominant source of lumber from the earliest historical times. In the *Iliad*, Achilles sent mules and wood cutters to Mount Ida to bring oak for the funeral pyre of Patroclus down to the Trojan plain. Later Priam got the fuel for the pyre of Hector from the same source.[7] Mount Pelion furnished the shaft of ash for the spear of Achilles.[8] Sarpedon fell in battle "as falls an oak or silver poplar or a slim pine tree that on the hills the shipwrights fell with whetted axes, to be timber for ship-building." The roar of conflict about the dead Sarpedon was "as the din of woodcutters in the glades of the mountains." [9]

The scant rainfall of the Eastern Basin except on the highlands emphasized the value of the mountain forests. Therefore the ancients had a sharp eye for this source of their lumber supply. Homer speaks of "the topmost crest of wooded Samothrace"; [10] Hesiod knew "where on the mountain the oak trees bear acorns on their tops," [11] and Aristophanes "the woodcrowned summits of the lofty mountains." [12] Theophrastus, discussing the tree life of the Eastern Basin, alludes to the woodlands of the plains, but discourses at length on the important forests of Lebanon and Taurus mountains, Mount Tmolus of Lydia, the Mysian Olympos, Mount Odynnos of Lesbos, Phrygian Ida, Mount Cytorus and the other Pontic ranges of Asia Minor, Hæmus and other Thracian mountains, the Macedonian highlands, Thessalian Olympos, the high wooded ridges of Magnesia, certain ranges of northern Hellas, Mount Parnassos and certain peaks of Eubœa, Mount Cyllene and the Arcadian highlands in general, Mount Ida of Crete and the Leuca ranges in the western part of that island.[13] He repeatedly emphasized the general superiority of mountain woods for timber purposes, even where a given species of tree grew alike in highland and lowland and reached a taller growth in the more fertile soil of the plain. In the case of mountain trees, he discriminated in favor of forests covering the high level stretches or terraces of plateau and range, as against the stunted timber of the lofty summits.[14] It is a striking fact also that Theophrastus constantly cites the classification, nomenclature and description of trees current among the people of Phrygian Ida, Macedonia and Arcadia.[15] All these were mountaineers, backward in the culture prized by the Attic Greeks, but evidently recognized authorities in everything pertaining to forestry and lumbering.

Pliny, who enumerated the lumber resources of the whole Mediterranean Basin, also noted that the quality of trees depended upon their place of growth. According to him, the best Italian timber came from the Alps and Apennines, the best Gallic woods from the Jura and Vosges ranges. The Gallic lumber was doubtless floated down the Rhone and Saône to the Mediterranean. Other well-known lumber regions which he enumerated were all mountainous—Corsica, the Pyrenees, Bithynia, Pontus, Macedonia, Arcadia, Crete, the Lebanon district of Syria, and the coast ranges of Roman Africa which yielded the famous Atlas cedars.[16]

As the mountains of the Mediterranean Basin rise almost everywhere directly from the sea, the logs were floated down the drainage streams in flood time to the nearest harbor, whence they were exported. Ancient writers frequently emphasize the accessibility of the timber supply to the coasts. Tyre and Sidon were great lumber ports from early times. When King Hiram made a contract with Solomon to furnish the wood for the new temple of Jerusalem, he sent his expert lumbermen up into the Lebanon ranges and collected the cedar and pine logs (translated "fir" in the Bible) at Tyre. There he made them into rafts and had them towed down the coast to Joppa.[17] Both Tyre and Sidon furnished cedars for the rebuilding of the Jewish temple after the Babylonish captivity, and transported them by sea to Joppa.[18] The woods of Mount Ida in Phrygia reached Mediterranean trade through the lumber port of Aspaneos and also Antandros, located near the head of the Adramyttene Gulf.[19] Forests which did not command easy transportation to the coast long escaped the woodman's axe, or supplied merely local needs unless general scarcity of timber intensified the demand. After the Macedonian conquest of Cyprus, the Greek kings of the island began to conserve the valuable cedars of their mountains when it proved to be a losing business to pay the freight charges from the interior to the coast.[20]

LUMBER TRADE OF THE EASTERN BASIN—The Mediterranean lumber trade was more active in the Eastern Basin than in the Western, because of the irregular distribution of forests and the meager tree growth around the Levantine and Ægean seaboard. The chief importers of lumber were the populous maritime cities surrounding the Ægean, who wanted it for their big merchant marine and various domestic purposes. They used the woods of coniferous trees, like fir, various pines, juniper and cedar primarily for ships,[21] but employed them also extensively in the construction of buildings. Cypress, laurel, box, olive, poplar, maple, wild fig, larch, chestnut, walnut, beech, oak, elm, ash, mulberry, plane and holly were used for carpentry and cabinet work.[22] Keels of ships were occasionally reinforced with oak for greater strength,[23] or with beech when they had to be hauled.[24] The modern is often amazed at the ancient use of woods for manufacturing or building purposes which are now regarded fit only for fuel or wood pulp.

Many woods were widely distributed over the Mediterranean Basin, like the box, olive, fig, various oaks and conifers. Some were found chiefly in southern lands, like the cypress in Cyrene, Crete, Rhodes and Lycia,[25] and the palm in the desert belts. Those which supplied the best and most abundant lumber grew on the western slopes of high mountains or in the northern zone of the Mediterranean Basin.

The whole African coast of the Eastern Basin was practically lacking in timber, owing to the semi-desert conditions. The Egyptians cut short planks three feet long from the local acacia trees for constructing their river transport boats,[26] and they utilized the wood of the olive, sycamore (*Ficus Sycamorus*), *balanos* and doum-palm for cabinet and carpentry work in lieu of anything better.[27] The paucity of their wood supply is indicated by their skiffs made of bundles of papyrus reeds, after the manner of the balsa boats of Lake Titicaca in Peru, and by the use of the papyrus root as fuel. The highland oasis of Cyrenaica had olive, lotus and cypress trees, of which only the last could be used primarily for lumber.[28] The thuya or thyon tree (*Callistris quadravalvis*), a juniper related to the cypress, grew abundantly in Cyrenaica and the oasis of Ammon in the fourth century B.C. It furnished material for roofs in very ancient times, but as the wood was fragrant and proof against decay, it was valuable for cabinet work.[29] It entered into the trade of the eastern Mediterranean by way of Crete or Egypt. Homer makes Calypso burn it with cedar and larch to perfume her grotto, and the Book of Revelation, written in the latter part of the first century A.D., alludes to it as a choice wood of commerce.[30]

The absence of forests and paucity of timber trees made these regions of lowland north Africa importers of lumber. The same conditions held in Palestine and the low Philistian coast. Their nearest source of supply lay in the cedar forests of Lebanon, the pine woods of Mount Amanus, and the wooded heights of Cyprus. Hence these forested districts were national possessions envied by all the countries around the Levantine Sea. The timber of Mount Amanus and Lebanon occasioned the repeated conquest of these ranges by Egypt and especially by Babylonia in the arid southeast, which had imported thence building material for its temples since 3000 B.C. or earlier.[31] It supplied wood for the Phœnician export trade in cedar and pine logs to Palestine and Egypt,[32] and for countless Phœnician fleets. Tyre secured ship timber also from the coniferous forests of Mount Hermon, whose great height (9,020 feet or 2,750 meters) insured summer showers, and it imported oak for oars from Bashan.[33]

The mountain forests of Cyprus, together with the copper mines, doubtless furnished the motive for the Phœnician conquest of the island in the eleventh century B.C. Even at this early date the necessity of conserving the Lebanon timber may have become apparent, since the pine groves of Amanus had long before this been seriously invaded. Forests renewed themselves with difficulty under the climatic conditions of the Eastern Mediterranean. For centuries the Cyprian ranges furnished excellent cedar for ship-building; the Greek kings after the Macedonian conquest began to conserve the forests, which were evidently declining in extent and retreating from the shore.[34] Theophrastus states that in his time (313 B.C.) the Syrians and Phœnicians made their triremes of cedar because they had no fir and little pine timber, but that the Cypriots generally preferred Aleppo pine for this purpose because it grew abundantly on the island and was superior to their other woods.[35] Strabo, on the authority of Erastosthenes, states that the forests of the Cyprian plain were once so dense that they formed an obstacle to tillage; that though they were invaded for fuel to smelt the copper and silver from the local mines, and for timber to build whole fleets of ships, nevertheless, consumption did not keep pace with the growth of the forests until, by legal enactment, the act of clearing the land was made to convey title to it.[36] So dense a mantle of trees would indicate a heavier rainfall in Cyprus than the meager 15 to 23 inches recorded in recent decades. Erastosthenes' account, however, may be based upon traditions of the Bronze Age, when the people of the island had imperfect tools for clearing even their woodlands, and moreover, devoted their energies to mining rather than to agriculture. Yet even in Strabo's time a forest covered the western promontory of Acamas, which was exposed to rain-bearing winds.[37]

The high Taurus Mountains, which wall in the coast of Cilicia Trachea, Pamphylia and Lycia in Asia Minor, get today from 30 to 40 inches of rain (75 to 100 centimeters) from the southwestern storms. The Pisidian Taurus range, back of the Gulf of Adalia, abounded in forests in ancient times. It was drained by the Eurymedon and Melas rivers, which were apparently used as log streams to float lumber down to the coast; because between them lay the seaport of Side, where the Cilician pirates placed their shipyards.[38] The Cilician and Lycian Taurus produced fine cedars,[39] which the pirates used for their swift-sailing boats. The Persians also utilized these timber supplies in the shipyards which they maintained on the Cilician coast. There Artaxerxes in 460 B.C. built three hundred triremes for an attack on Egypt.[40]

After the Roman conquest the chief lumber port of this coast was Hamaxia,[41] near the site of modern Alaja. Just behind this town the Taurus Mountains rise to 10,266 feet (3,130 meters) and therefore get ample precipitation for forests, though the seaboard receives less than 20 inches. All this region was comparatively near Egypt and desirable to her for

its timber.   Hence that country, whose palm trees yielded poor
lumber and whose irrigated fruit trees were too valuable for
that purpose, maintained sovereignty over all or part of this
forested mountain coast for nearly three hundred years after
the break-up of Alexander's empire (323 B.C.).   In 300 B.C. the
Ptolemies owned Cyprus and the whole southern coast of Asia
Minor from Rhodes and Lycia to Issus, but by 218 B.C. their
possessions had shrunk to Cilicia Trachea and Cyprus.[42]   These
were retained till 67 B.C. and 58 B.C., respectively, when they
were conquered by Rome; but later Mark Antony assigned
Hamaxia and the neighboring coast of Cilicia Trachea to Cleopatra to furnish wood for the Egyptian fleet.[43]   In the thirteenth century Hamaxia had a successor in the port of Alaya,
where the Seljuk Turks had shipyards for their navy.[44]   So the
Cilician forests persisted.

LUMBER RESOURCES OF THE EUXINE COASTS—It was especially the northern mountains of the Mediterranean Basin, with
their heavier rainfall and denser forests, which yielded the most
ample and varied supply of timber, and which, therefore, furnished the chief cargoes for the lumber fleets of ancient times.
These cargoes included other ship supplies besides woods,
namely, pitch for caulking the seams of vessels, and wax for
the encaustic painting of the hulls to make them impervious to
water.   It is a significant fact that wax and honey invariably
figure as forest products in ancient Mediterranean trade, because numerous flowering trees and shrubs like myrtle, laurel,
oleander, tamarisk, hawthorn, lime or linden, wild apple and
pear mingled with other forest growth and provided honey
pastures for the bees.   The rainy slopes of the Caucasus Mountains overlooking the Euxine yielded various timbers, especially
those suitable for ship-building, besides wax and pitch in great
abundance.   These forest products were conveyed down the
River Phasis to Colchis, whence they were exported.[45]   They
equipped the navies of Mithradates.   Pontic pines, famous for
ships, besides other woods used by builders and wheelwrights,
were imported into Italy from the Caucasus forests during the
last century of the Roman Republic.[46]

Along the northern shore of Asia Minor, from Colchis to
Heraclea Pontica and Calpe [47] in Bithynia, the high Pontic

ranges facing the Euxine winds were mantled with forests of excellent ship timber, besides oak, elm, chestnut, ash, maple and a superior variety of box. These woods could be easily conveyed away, Strabo tells us. They entered the Mediterranean trade through the ports of Cerasos or Pharnacea, Amisos, Sinope and Amastris.[48] The walnut wood exported from Sinope was a fine variety used for making table tops. Box trees grew in such perfection and abundance on the Cytorus range [49] in the coastal belt of Paphlagonia that they became proverbial and gave rise to the saying "carrying boxwood to Cytorus," equivalent to the English "carrying coals to Newcastle." The box yielded a very hard close-grained wood, almost proof against decay, used for the manufacture of sacred images, carpenters' tools, flutes and combs.[50] It was evidently imported into Italy for these purposes, for its fame is sung by Vergil, Catullus and Ovid, who always specify the Cytorian or Phrygian variety of box.[51]

In western Bithynia the mountains decrease in height, the rainfall of the Asia Minor coast declines to 28 inches (700 mm.), but the summer showers suffice for the forests. Near the Propontis, the Mysian Olympos rises to the height of 8,300 feet in the face of the Pontic winds, and receives enough precipitation (over 32 inches or 800 mm.) [52] for large, diversified forests.[53] In ancient times its export timber was floated down the Rhyndacus River to the sea,[54] and probably marketed through the Milesian port of Cyzicos. Mysian Olympos and Phrygian Ida furnished to the Ægean world varied and abundant timber, but little that was suitable for ship-building, according to Theophrastus.[55] The fir and pine forests of these ranges were probably approaching exhaustion in his time, 313 B.C. Mount Ida's proximity to the fertile Trojan plain and the nine successive cities on the site of Ilium would suggest long exploitation of its best lumber. The process went on as late as 424 B.C. after the Athenian conquest of Lesbos, when refugees from the island occupied Antandros on the mainland near by, and planned to build a fleet from the forests of Mount Ida, for the purpose of harassing Lesbos and the neighboring coast cities of the Athenian league.[56]

The Ægean front of Asia Minor receives an average rainfall

of 25 inches in the lowlands (Smyrna 26 inches or 650 mm.).
This is scant allowance for forests, especially in view of the almost rainless summers. The whole region, however, from the
Troad to Caria and Rhodes is crossed by numerous short mountain ranges in close proximity to the sea; their peaks, rising
from 3,500 to 4,100 feet and receiving about 30 inches or
750 mm. of rain,[57] doubtless offered in ancient times sufficient
timber for the needs of the early Phœnician and Greek colonies
along this coast. Forested promontories and island peaks, like
Mimas (3,803 feet or 1,190 meters), Mycale (4,150 feet or
1,265 meters), Mount Atabyrios in Rhodes (4,067 feet or 1,240
meters) and Mount Pelinnæos in Chios (4,147 feet or 1,264
meters), were probably one attraction to settlers who sought
the deep-running inlets for their new homes. The ranges were
neither long nor very high, however, and had evidently lost
much of their forest covering by the Christian Era. Theophrastus mentions only the woods of the Phrygian Mountains,
which lie farthest north, and those of the Tmolos Mountains in
Lydia, which, however, yielded no ship timber.[58] In Strabo's
time, the bold sea-washed ridges of Mycale and Mimas were still
well forested and harbored abundant game, while the hill country of Ortygia near Ephesos had woods of various trees, especially cypress groves.[59] The latter doubtless furnished the
famous doors of the temple of Diana, but the cedar planks for
its roof [60] were undoubtedly imported from Crete, Lycia, Phœnicia or Cyprus. The early exhaustion of the local supply of
ship timber forced the big trading cities of this coast to search
for it abroad. Miletos, which required much timber for her
merchant marine, may have established her Pontic colonies of
Sinope, Amisus, Cerasus and Trapezos partly for the purpose
of controlling her own ship supplies. Even Cyzicos could furnish timber from Mysian Olympos.

IMPORTS OF LUMBER INTO GREECE—The busy maritime cities
of eastern Greece, located in the rain shadow of the Grecian
highlands, were even more dependent upon imported lumber, because their local hills and mountains, according to Theophrastus, yielded only inferior woods. Megara, when she founded
the colony of Heraclea Pontica on the Euxine, selected a spot
which today, as the modern Eregli, has the reputation of being

unusually rainy and well timbered.[61]   Heraclea was therefore
designed to exploit for Megara's benefit the forests of the
Pontic ranges as well as the abundant yield of the coast fisheries there.   Athens, whose local mountains were practically
denuded of their forests in the time of Plato,[62] brought lumber
from great distances, both for naval purposes and for building.
Even fencing and beams for the Laurion mines came from over
sea.[63]   The construction of lumber rafts equipped with sails
was familiar to the Greeks.   Athens occasionally secured ship
timber from Phœnicia or Cyprus, and undoubtedly organized
her vast Pontic trade in the days of her maritime empire with
a view to the importation of Pontic lumber.   She drew also
upon the forest supplies of the west.   The speech of Alcibiades
revealing to the Spartans the Athenians' motives for the Sicilian
Expedition specifies the control "of the ship timber which Italy
supplies in such abundance," [64] and points to an established
lumber trade with the Greek colonies of Magna Græcia and
Sicily.   A century later Theophrastus shows so detailed a
knowledge of Italian woods [65] as to indicate their presence in
the Athenian market, whither they had come in exchange for
manufactured Greek wares.   "The tall pines and crested oaks"
of Sicily had been famous from Homeric days.[66]

The nearest and most abundant supply of good ship timber
for the cities of eastern Greece was found in Thrace and Macedonia,[67] where a northern location, moderate summer showers
and extensive mountain ranges insured considerable forests.
The best watered and therefore the best wooded section lay between the Strymon and Hebrus rivers.   The coastal plain here
receives about 25 inches (625 mm.) of rain annually, but the
great Rhodope highland forming its hinterland has 30 to 40
inches or more (750 to 1,000 mm.).[68]   There at the mouth of
the Strymon River lay the important Athenian colony of Amphipolis, founded only after repeated efforts, owing to the hostility of the local tribes.[69]   Significantly enough, its site had
previously been selected by an abortive colony from Miletos.[70]
Contiguous to this region, less rainy, but offering protected
sites for coast settlements, was the Chalcidice Peninsula, colonized by Chalcis, Eretria, Andros and Corinth.   All these cities
doubtless counted chiefly on the forest products among the raw

materials which were the natural exports of a new and backward region.

Theophrastus recognized the general superiority of the
northern timber.[71] The woods imported into Hellas· for building and carpentry work he graded according to quality, as follows: Macedonian, Pontic, Mysian-Olympian, Ænianian from
the high slope of the Œta (7,078 feet or 2,158 meters) and
Tymphrestus ranges (7,606 feet or 2,319 meters) in northern
Hellas, down to the poor knotty timber from Mount Parnassos
and the Eubœan ranges. Wood of variable quality was also
brought from highland Arcadia,[72] where the peaks have considerable forests even today. All the maritime cities made a
steady demand for the strong, light, durable Macedonian fir,
which was used for oars, masts and sailyards. Athens imported this timber through her colony of Amphipolis, which
commanded the forests of the Strymon River basin. Therefore
she was dealt a heavy blow when this town and its port of Eion
were captured by the Spartans in 424 B.C. during the Peloponnesian War, since her navy needed constant replenishing.[73]
Later the expansion of Macedon over·all this coast as far as the
Hellespont excluded Athens from her nearest and surest lumber
supply, and jeopardized her sea connection with the Caucasus
and Pontic forests, until her incorporation into Philip's empire
again opened these sources of supply. Athens revolted from
Cassander in 305 B.C. and forfeited her right to use the Macedonian forests. Then she turned to Demetrius of Syria and
was promised timber for a hundred war ships.[74] The wood
doubtless came from the Lebanon range.

The Macedonian forests long remained the chief source of
lumber for the Ægean states.[75] In 158 B.C. we find Rome pro-
hibiting the export of ship-timber from Macedon, evidently as
a measure to cripple the commerce of Rhodes,[76] which was then
the great middleman of the Ægean. These forests were not exhausted in Strabo's time, because the town of Datum near the
mouth of the Strymon River on the Strymonic Gulf had dockyards for ship building,[77] evidence of accessible timber. But it
must be remembered that this river drains an extensive highland region, which, owing to its elevation and northern location,
gets a moderate rainfall in summer.

10

Deciduous trees, especially timber growth like the oak, ash, beech and chestnut, were widely distributed in northern and western Greece; but on the dry eastern side of the peninsula, where the rainfall rarely exceeds 25 inches, and in many localities falls far below, these trees were generally restricted to the mountains. The chestnut tree, still found in groves on Mount Olympos and the Pindus range, grows in Hellas at altitudes of 2,000 to 4,000 feet (600-1,300 m.), but declines in size and abundance farther south. Theophrastus calls the sweet chestnut (*Castanea vesca*) the "Eubœan nut." It grew on the Mysian Olympos and the Tmolos range of Lydia, whence it was called "the nut of Sardis," but was more abundant on the mountains of Eubœa and the Magnesian Peninsula of Thessaly.[78] Near the foot of Mount Pelion, which still has its chestnut trees [79] was located the Magnesian seaport of Castanea, mentioned by Herodotus and Strabo.[80] Thence probably the nutritious nuts were shipped to the large Greek cities, and took their name from the place of export, like the modern Brazilian nut. Today the best chestnuts are brought to Athens from the mountains of western Crete, where an altitude of 7,500 feet or more compensates for the southern latitude. This island, owing to its mountainous relief and its exposure to rain-bearing winds, was well wooded in ancient times [81] and supported a variety of trees, especially cypress [82] and cedar.[83] These helped to maintain the navies of King Minos and the fleets of the Cretan pirates, and met a steady demand for architectural purposes both in Athens and Rome. The finest and most abundant tree was the cypress, which grew very tall on the Cretan mountains. It yielded a superior building and cabinet wood almost proof against decay.

MOUNTAIN FORESTS OF ANCIENT GREECE—Oak and beech groves were widely distributed over the mountains of Greece, and furnished mast for large herds of wild and domestic swine. Oaks especially grew on Mount Olympos and Pelion. They covered the low Calledromos range of eastern Locris [84] and Mount Ptoon in Bœotia.[85] They flourished on the Arcadian highlands and covered the heights of the Parnon range on the boundary between Argolis and Laconia.[86] The Laconian side of the high Taygetos Mountains, especially about the peak of

Taletum, had forests in the second century A.D.[87] which were presumably fir and vallona oak groves such as Leake found there a century ago.[88] The Taygetos Mountains now turn a bare rocky front to the Eurotas valley, except where the gulches retain soil and moisture. But the slopes, now washed bare of their humus or converted into terraced vineyards, were once mantled in oak trees which Theophrastus found characteristic of Laconia.[89] The modern traveler who motors from Sparta to Tegea in Arcadia, across the mountains forming the northern boundary of Laconia, finds these highlands (pass at 3,065 feet or 940 meters) covered with a poor oak brush, preyed upon by goats, which represents the degenerate successor of the pristine oak forests.

Western Peloponnesos presents even today a pleasant contrast to the bald eastern escarpment of Arcadia, which is located in the rain shadow of the central highland. The half of Greece lying west of the mountain backbone of the peninsula, formed by the Taygetos, Arcadian, Corax, Tymphrestos and Pindus ranges, has 30 inches (750 mm.) or more of rain a year. From the Gulf of Ambracia (Gulf of Arta) northward, the broad belt of coastal highlands is yet better supplied, and gets over 40 inches (1,000 mm.) annually; moreover, slight summer showers revive its vegetation, and these increase in frequency from Illyria northward.[90]

This western front of classical Greece had sufficient rainfall to maintain considerable forests, remnants of which still survive the depredation of the goats, where located far from human habitations. In ancient times even the plain of Elis had its oak groves and woods of wild pine.[91] Forests large enough to harbor abundant deer, wild boar and antelope covered the low hill country near Olympia and the higher Phœlœ Plateau,[92] which defined the boundary between Elis and Arcadia. There Xenophon and his sons used to range the forests for game before the crowds assembled for the Olympic Games.[93] The towering peaks of western Arcadia, which overlook the Elian plains, were well forested in ancient times. Mount Lycæus was mantled in maples and oaks, and therefore was sacred to Zeus.[94] On Mount Erymanthos was staged the famous boar hunt of Hercules, which bears witness to mast groves of beech and oak.

These trees grow on its slopes today, interspersed with planes; and in spring their tender green makes a background for the white blossoms of the wild pear tree.[95]

The northern flank of mighty Erymanthos belongs to Achaia, which today has the amplest forests of oaks and conifers to be found in all the Peloponnesos, and in ancient times must have been even more abundantly supplied.[96] The ancient province occupied the northern and northwestern escarpment of the Arcadian plateau, and sloped down from a succession of lofty peaks like Erymanthos (modern Olonos, altitude 7,300 feet or 2,225 meters), Panachaicos (Voidhia, 6,320 feet or 1,927 meters), Aroanio (Khelmos, 7,724 feet or 2,355 meters) and Cyllene (Ziria, 7,790 feet or 2,375 meters). These mountains today have oak woods on their middle zone and fir forests on their upper reaches,[97] owing to the rain-bearing winds that sweep through the Gulf of Corinth. In ancient times they undoubtedly furnished convenient supplies of timber to the shipyards of Corinth and Sicyon, because they offered a choice of cedar,[98] fir and oak.[99]

Across the Corinthian Gulf the mountainous coasts of western Hellas still have scattered woodlands which bear testimony to ancient forests. Parnassos, towering to the height of 8,070 feet (2,460 meters) behind the Crissæan Bay, has beautiful pine woods at 3,000 feet elevation; and its western slope is covered with a thriving, young growth of beech, oak, and conifers, through which the modern automobile road runs from Delphi north to Gravia. Groves of cypress and pine near Oeanthia in Locris in ancient times faced the Gulf of Corinth from this northern shore.[100] Naupactus, the important seaport and naval station of this coast, lay only ten miles from the Evenos River (modern Phidari) of Ætolia, whose valley was clothed in oak forests when Leake visited it a century ago.[101] This stream flows out to sea between mountains over three thousand feet high, and reaches the coast between the sites of Homeric Calydon and the ancient Corinthian colony of Chalcis.[102] It doubtless brought down wood to build the Calydonian fleet which sailed for the Trojan War, and centuries later, ship timber to be exported to the treeless city of Corinth. All the mountains fronting this north coast of the Gulf of Patras were well wooded on their upper slopes a century ago, though cleared for cultivation below. Oak trees growing there were big enough to furnish the dug-out boats used in the navigation of the shallow Lagoon of Mesolongion between the mouth of the Evenos and the Achelous (Aspropotamo).[103]   The Achelous River opened up the well-wooded mountains of Acarnania, which faced the rain-bearing winds from the west.

To the forests of the Ionian Islands Homer himself bears witness. He was familiar with "wooded Zacynthos," the tree-grown slopes of showery Ithaca, and the wind-swept woods of Neritos.[104]   Abundant timber was one factor in the nautical development of all these western islands and coastlands from Zacynthos north to Epidamnos (Dyrrachium or Durazzo) on the Illyrian seaboard. Moreover, the numerous colonies planted by Corinth on these coasts in Corcyra (Corfu) Ambracia, Leucas and Epidamnos [105] suggest that the mother city, poorly provided with wood, wished to assure her supply of ship timber for her navy and merchant marine from these western sources. From these she could not easily be cut off by great commercial rivals like Ægina, Eubœan Chalcis, and Athens, which lay on the Ægean side of the Isthmus, while Corinth could import the western lumber through her port of Lechæum on the Gulf of Corinth.

The mountains surrounding the Gulf of Ambracia (Arta) a hundred years ago still abounded in large oaks and conifers well suited to naval construction. In 1788 and for seven years thereafter ship timber from these slopes was regularly exported from Prevesa to the French navy-yard at Toulon.[106]   When Augustus Cæsar planted the important naval base of Nicopolis at the entrance of the Gulf of Ambracia,[107] he chose the location with remarkable insight. This big inlet marked the southern border of Epiros and of the area of heavy rainfall with occasional summer showers, which characterized the Adriatic front of the Balkan Peninsula.[108]   The forests of western Hellas culminated in the mountains of Epiros. There the famous oak grove of Dodona formed the earliest sanctuary of Zeus, the Thunderer. Beyond Epiros lay the rainy coasts of Illyria and Dalmatia, whose forests supplied the pirate fleets infesting these shores from ancient times.

According to the evidence, the crying need of eastern Mediterranean lands was for ship timber. A multitude of fishing smacks, naval vessels, merchant ships, and coastwise transportation boats kept up the demand for fir, pine, cedar and minor woods which entered into their construction. The coniferous forests were therefore constantly levied upon; and they were further depleted by the steady demand for pitch, tar and resin. Traffic in these usually accompanied the lumber trade, and emanated from the same sources of supply. Pitch and tar were doubtless procured from pine and fir trees in all parts of Greece, but the chief output came from the Caucasus, Phrygian Ida, and Macedonia, especially from the extensive coniferous forests on the northern slopes of Mount Olympos and Mount Pieros in southern Macedonia.[109] In Syria pitch was distilled from terebinth and Phœnician cedar,[110] and was exported thence to Egypt, where it was used, among other things, for treating the surface of the bulrush boats.[111]

The demand for all products of resinous woods was relatively greater in antiquity than now. They were employed for the preservation of ship wood and all ship equipments, for coating the interior of earthenware wine jars, and for the preparation of volatile oils, salves and ointments, which were almost universally used in ancient times. Resin and tar were the chief basis of cough medicines prepared by Greek physicians, and were ingredients of salves for external use. Oil of cedar, distilled from the Syrian cedar, was regularly used for these purposes, because its antiseptic or cleansing qualities were recognized.[112] It was exported from Phœnicia to Egypt where it was needed for embalming the dead.[113] The Romans used it for soaking wood as a protection against decay and insect attack.[114] This was the ancient forerunner of the modern creosoting process.

LUMBER TRADE OF THE WESTERN BASIN—The western Mediterranean Basin, owing to more ample and protracted rains, was fairly well supplied with timber in nearly all its parts. This was true even of its African coast, because the high Atlas ranges tracing this littoral extract rain from the prevailing north winds. Hence they supported forests of big trees in ancient times.[115] The woods on the mountainous Rif

coast of western Mauretania in places came down close to the
sea, and clothed the promontory of Mount Abila at the Strait
of Gibraltar with a mantle of great trees.[116]   These doubtless
furnished timber for the ships of the Rif pirates who for two
thousand years sallied out from that rugged littoral.   The
highest peak of the western Rif range, the modern Beni-Hassan,
rises to an altitude of 7,216 feet or 2,200 meters, and lies only
about twelve miles from the sea so that its timber was readily
accessible.   Farther east, in Algeria (ancient Mauretania Cæ-
sariensis and Numidia) the rainfall varies along the coast
ranges from 24 to 32 inches (600 to 800 mm.), but exceeds this
maximum in the great highlands of the Grand and Little Kabyle
(ancient Byrinus Mons) where peaks towering to 7,000 feet
or more get 60 inches (1,500 mm.).[117]   This was essentially the
region of the famous *Atlantis silva*,[118] or forests of a tree known
to the Romans as the *citrus*, but quite distinct from the *citrus
Medica* or citron.   The tree was related to the cypress, and
yielded a beautifully variegated wood, which was imported into
Italy for the manufacture of fine furniture and coffered ceilings.[119]   Pliny identifies it with the thyon or thuya tree of the
Greeks, which is still a product of Moroccan and Algerian forests, and is used by the Turks in their mosques as the choicest
material for ceilings and floors.   Among the ancient Romans
the wood was highly prized and very costly.   Tables of it sometimes measured four and a half feet in diameter, and sold in
Cicero's time, before the days of degenerate luxury, for a million sesterces or twenty thousand dollars.[120]   Martial reflects
the popular estimate of the wood when he writes:

> Accipe felices, Atlantica munera, silvas:
> Aurea qui dederit dona, minora dabit.[121]

Some commentators identify this *citrus* with the *cedrus* or
cedar tree of the Atlas Mountains, which Pliny rated as high
as the cedars of Lebanon.[122]   Vitruvius, who was an authority
on architectural materials, made the same estimate of this
wood.   It was abundant in ancient times, and was exported to
Rome.   Beams of Numidian cedar used in the construction of
the Temple of Apollo at Utica [123] when the city was founded

undoubtedly came from these forests. We must look to the same source for the ship timber which for centuries built the Carthaginian fleets.[124] Cork and tanners' bark have through the ages contributed to the trade of Saldæ (Bougie) and Hippo Regius (Boné).

Owing to the more general distribution of forests in the Western Mediterranean Basin, the lumber trade seems never to have reached the development which it attained in the Levantine and Ægean Seas. In the days of Rome's splendor it brought building materials and choice cabinet woods from various regions to the rich and growing capital, and furnished ship supplies for the maintenance of the navy. Italy itself included the districts of heaviest rainfall and therefore of the best forests of ship timber, but certain other ship supplies, such as tar, pitch and wax, were economically produced elsewhere. Their bulk was small in relation to their value; so transportation charges were an almost negligible element in their market price.

Pitch was a regular article of commerce, procured from regions of ample coniferous forests; it was usually coupled with ship timber, resin, honey and wax. The Sila Mountains of the southern Apennines, today as in ancient times an important lumber region,[125] produced the famous Bruttium pitch of the Roman world.[126] This was evidently exported through the harbor of Narycium, the old Greek Epizephyrii, for Vergil couples the pitch-yielding forests with that city.[127] Gades (Cadiz) in southern Spain used the local ship timber for her own merchant marine, but supplied to Mediterranean commerce pitch, honey, wax and quantities of kermes berries or cochineal,[128] which point to oak forests. Cadiz and its vicinity get about 30 inches (750 mm.) of rain a year; but to the east rises the great Sierra de Volox with a peak 6,530 feet (1,960 meters), and from this range forest products were doubtless obtained. The still higher Sierra Nevada, culminating in the peak of Mulhaden (11,418 feet or 3,481 meters), and the northeastern extension of these highlands in the Sierra de Segura, rising in the Sierra Sagra to 7,872 feet (2,400 meters), were called by Strabo the mountain chain of the Bastetani, and described as thickly wooded with gigantic trees.[129] This was probably an exaggeration in view of the moderate rainfall of

20 to 30 inches, but the forests were ample enough to supply the Phœnician coast colonies of Malaca (Malaga), Mænaca, and Abdera. New Carthage probably drew the ship supplies for its busy port from Sierra Sagra by way of the Tader River (Segura), which rises on these high slopes. All the eastern Spanish littoral, except the Pyrenean coast, has a rainfall of 16 inches or less (400 mm. or less),[130] and therefore was compelled to import its timber from the mountains or from overseas. The juniper beams in the temple of Diana at Saguntum were said to have been brought by the original Greek colonists from Zacynthos.[131]

Southern Sicily has a meager rainfall, but Ætna and the mountains along the northern coast get sufficient precipitation for moderate forests. Early Greek legend represented it as well wooded, abounding in stately oak groves and open forest glades where cattle pastured.[132]   Odysseus found this island of the Cyclops covered with trees, among them "tall pines and crested oaks." [133]   Evidence of local ship timber is found in the big fleets maintained for centuries by the tyrants of Syracuse and other Sicilian cities. These enterprising rulers drew their main supply from the ample forests of Ætna; and they also tapped the resources of the Sila Mountains across the Strait of Messina, in those periods when Syracuse extended its control over Bruttium.[134]

FORESTS OF THE ALPS AND APENNINES—Italy was the chief seat of the lumber trade in the Western Mediterranean, owing to the considerable rainfall (30 to 40 inches or more) on the Alps and Apennines. The eastern littoral, lying in the rain shadow of the Apennines, was poorly provided with timber; but the western and northern plains, even near sea level, had a goodly covering of forests as late as the end of the fourth century B.C. Both the hills and plains of Latium were well supplied with timber. Pliny and Livy mention numerous ancient woodlands in the vicinity of Rome.[135]   Theophrastus considers Italy one of the important sources of ship timber accessible from the Mediterranean.[136]   He praises the fir and pine of Latium, but finds them excelled by the tall coniferous forests of Corsica. He mentions the fine beech groves of the Latin plain from which the Etruscans got long planks for the keels of their ships, and comments on the abundant growth of oak, laurel and myrtle on the promontory of Circei.[137]

Hence during Italy's early centuries of retarded economic development, when she furnished only raw materials to commerce, one of her chief items of export was ship timber.[138] It is probable that firs and other woods from the northern Apennines figured in the early commercial dealings of the Etruscans with the Carthaginians, for the domestic timber of the latter was comparatively limited in variety. Greece, as we have seen, probably drew upon Italian lumber, both from the mainland and from Corsica. The forests of Corsica reached down to the shore; they were therefore readily accessible and made the island an object of conquest. At some very early date timber was cut there by the Romans, and conveyed away on rafts provided with sails. One of these was broken up by a storm and lost.[139] It was probably these wooded shores of Corsica which gave the island a high repute far away on the Ionian coast of Asia Minor, and which induced the ancient colonists from Phocæa to settle there. The Etruscans expelled the strangers from this choice forest reserve, and for centuries after exacted a tribute of pitch, honey and wax from the island.[140] Later the Romans exploited its fine boxwood, for box trees grew there to extraordinary height.[141] The familiarity of Theophrastus with this particular Corsican product[142] suggests that it was imported into Greece, where the hard, close-grained wood was used in carving images of the gods.[143]

The early Etruscans sought timber far afield because of some peculiar fitness for their purposes, like the long beech logs of Latium,[144] or because of its superior accessibility. They had ample wood at home, owing to the northern location of their district and its numerous mountain ranges. The Ciminian forest covering the hill range of Mount Ciminius in southern Etruria was, in 310 B.C., considered as frightful and impassable by the Roman army as were the vast German forests centuries later. Not even a trader with his pack mule dared to traverse it.[145] In the Second Punic War a fleet of thirty ships was contributed by the Etruscan cities to the navy of Rome. The timber was donated by Volaterræ, Clusium and Perusia, all located in the hills of Etruria, and Rusellæ on the coast, which com-

manded the fir forests of the Umbria River basin.[146] The Tiber
River and its tributaries Clanis, Tinia, Nar and Anio, tapped
the Apennine forests of Etruria, Umbria, and the high Abruzzi
Plateau of the Sabine country, and brought thence the immense
supplies of lumber required by the growing capital of Rome.
From .these sources came the longest and straightest planks
used in Rome to build its villas, palaces and temples during the
time of Augustus.[147]

Where the Apennines bend westward and trace the Ligurian
coast, they get over 50 inches of rain a year. Their rain-
drenched slopes were therefore covered with dense forests in
ancient times. Trees grew there to immense height and sometimes measured eight feet in diameter. Much of the wood was
very superior, beautifully veined, and equal to cedar for cabinet
work. This, together with excellent ship timber, was exported
through the port of Genoa.[148] The Roman naval base of Luna,
located in a deep bay (Bay of Spezia) on the southern edge
of the Ligurian Apennines, undoubtedly drew thence its abundant ship supplies. This choice timber of the northern Apennines had once been employed in constructing the vessels of the
Etruscan pirates; later it built the triremes of ancient Pisa for
her long wars against the Ligurian pirates,[149] and later still
the growing fleets of Rome. In the Middle Ages it equipped the
merchant marine and navy of both the Pisan and Genoese Republics, when competing for the trade of the Mediterranean and
fighting Saracen pirates.

Northern Italy had abundant timber also on the Alpine
slopes and in the Po valley, but these supplies were in general
too remote from the big centers of population in the south for
the export of crude lumber, unless in response to a special demand. Larch trees which were found chiefly in this northern
district and which furnished very long, straight timbers, were
transported from the Alpine valleys by the Po River to Ravenna, and distributed thence along the neighboring coasts as
far south as Ancona; but they could not stand the costly haul
to Rome.[150] However, Tiberius Cæsar, needing long beams for
the construction of a bridge over his *naumachia*, ordered larch
trees to be cut on the Rhætian Alps and brought to Rome. One
of these large logs was 120 feet long.[151] The finest bird's eye

or "peacock" maple to be found anywhere came from the Rhætian Alps and the hill ranges of the Istrian peninsula. It
ranked with the famous citrus wood in point of beauty, and
was so valuable for cabinet work [152] that it could bear the heavy
transportation charges to distant Rome.

Ship timber from the eastern Alps was undoubtedly floated
down to the Adriatic in very early times to build the Etruscan
merchant ships at Adria and Spina, and later to equip the
transport and naval vessels of the Romans in the ports of
Aquileia and Pola. On a larger scale, however, forest products
of small bulk, such as resin, pitch, honey and wax, were contributed by the tribes of the eastern Alps to Mediterranean
commerce in exchange for foodstuffs, and were shipped from
Aquileia and other Adriatic ports.[153] Fine resin used in medi-
cine came from the foothills of the Italian Alps.[154] Cisalpine
Gaul had extensive pitch works, and manufactured huge wooden
wine casks lined with pitch, which aroused the admiration of
Strabo.[155] This cooperage business was coupled with an active
and long established pork-packing industry, for the abundant
mast in the oak, beech and chestnut groves of the Po valley
supported large herds of swine.[156]

The Mediterranean coast of Transalpine Gaul and its Rhone
valley hinterland, owing to its northern location, had ample
forests. These furnished timber for the rafts and dugout boats
which forwarded native traffic on the river; [157] and also equipped
the merchant marine of the Greek traders of Massilia from the
sixth century B.C.[158] An ancient export trade in ham and bacon
from the Rhone valley to Rome indicates mast groves in this
district, while a similar trade from the eastern Pyrenees points
to forests there.[159] The conifers of the Pyrenean hinterland of
the Mediterranean, nourished by a rainfall of 30 inches (750
mm.) or more, undoubtedly maintained the merchant fleets of
the ancient Greek colonies of Emporiæ and Rhoda, western outposts of the Massiliot settlements, while the woods of the Maritime Alps equipped the ships of the eastern outposts, Antipolis,
Nicæa, and Portus Monœi, as likewise of the native pirates who
raided Massilian commerce.

All this northern timber belt of the Western Mediterranean
lies within the limits of the middle-European forests. In an-

cient times it produced finer, more varied and abundant timber
than was generally to be found in the southern districts. Moreover, the stretch from the Pyrenees to the Julian Alps long remained a colonial frontier of Rome, and hence served as a forest
reserve after the good timber of Latium and other densely populated districts of the Peninsula had been exhausted.

DENUDATION OF THE MEDITERRANEAN FORESTS—The denudation of the Mediterranean forests progressed rapidly in
antiquity, especially in the Eastern Basin, which was more
scantily provided with timber, and developed big centers of
population and advanced civilization earlier than the Western
Basin. Therefore its supply was small and the demand was
great. Plato, in the fifth century B.C., deplores the reckless
destruction of the forests and the consequent failure of springs
and streams in Greece, owing to the rapid run-off of the rain
from the bared hillsides. He also indicates that the Greeks for
a long time had been turning their attention to raising forest
trees by cultivation,[160] probably in an effort to maintain a local
supply of timber for minor local needs. A century later
Theophrastus complained that the supply of ship timber in the
Eastern Basin was very limited, and that only the forests of
Macedonia and Thrace remained fairly abundant.[161] In the
same period the cedar groves of Cyprus were retreating from
the coasts into the mountain interior of the island, though the
woods of the Lebanon range still survived, owing to the elevation and westward exposure of the mountains. One is led to
surmise also that those expert Phœnician woodsmen, who were
commended by King Solomon, may have understood the fundamental principles of forestry and therefore have intelligently
exploited their timber supplies. The small copses and meager
woodlands of ancient Palestine were unable to stand the onslaughts of civilization. Therefore for Abraham and other ancient sheiks it was an act of merit to plant even a solitary tree
by a pool or spring.[162] The Jews cultivated walnut and fig
trees for the wood as well as for the fruit.[163] They regarded
the destruction of their groves by fire as a visitation from on
high,[164] and the wanton destruction of fruit trees in war as a
heinous offense.[165]

In the Western Mediterranean, the recession of the forests

became very apparent, but at a later date. Though the lumber trade of Italy was active enough to supply the large demand, ancient Roman farmers, as indicated by Cato's treatise on Agriculture, early began to raise plantations of various trees on their estates by irrigation, and thus supply their immediate needs for timber by local production. Under the Empire arboriculture was practiced on all Roman farms, as indicated by the instructions of Vergil, Varro, Columella and Pliny. The steady demand for *citrus* wood for the roofs of temples, palaces and fine buildings greatly reduced the supply, for the best trees grew only in Mauretania, Crete, Syria and Cilicia.[166] In Pliny's time the superb forests of this wood on Mount Ancorarius in Hither Mauretania were already exhausted.[167] Even before this, Roman lumber ships sought the far-away Caucasus ports. Denudation of the forests made such inroads upon the wood supply of Italy that by the fifth century Roman architectural technique had become modified to meet the growing scarcity and increased price of wood.[168]

Clearing for tillage land and the legitimate consumption of wood as lumber and fuel were only part of the process of destruction. The long dry summers and the resinous character of Mediterranean *maqui* shrubs made forest fires frequent and disastrous, while the high winds of the hot season fanned the flames. Such fires were a commonplace in ancient Palestine. Isaiah describes one in a metaphorical passage: "It shall devour the briers and thorns, and shall kindle in the thickets of the forest, and they shall mount up like the lifting up of smoke." [169] Homer knows the effect of protracted drought and strong summer winds upon such a conflagration. "Through deep glens rageth fierce fire on some parched mountain side and the deep forest beneath, and the wind, driving it, whirleth everywhere the flame." [170] The Greeks were familiar with the spontaneous origin of such fires in the mutual attrition of branches or trees in the dry season.[171]

Fires were often started, either intentionally or accidentally, by the herdsmen who ranged the mountain forests with their sheep and goats in the dry season. Burning improved the pasturage, because the ashes temporarily enriched the soil, and the abundant shoots from the old roots furnished better fodder.

The forests once destroyed were hard to restore. Goats clipped the young growth from the hillsides as with shears. Trees which depended on deep root systems for their moisture could not survive the summer drought; saplings with shallow roots could not get a start. Moreover, there was no shade to help conserve the surface moisture in soil and root, at a season when the dry atmosphere was especially pervious to the sun's light and heat.

The chemical decomposition of rocks has always proceeded slowly in Mediterranean lands, owing to the lack of sufficient moisture for abundant plant life. Mechanical disintegration has also been slow, owing to the lack of intense cold. Hence both weathering processes have been weak, with the result that soil has accumulated by infinitesimal degrees, and has spread in a very thin mantle over the slopes. Except in the small silted valleys the rocks lie near the surface. Alluvial plains of considerable extent are rare; plains of loess or glacial clay are wanting.[172] The rock skeletons of Mediterranean lands are everywhere prone to thrust through the meager envelope of soil.

When the mountains were denuded of their forests, the violent autumn storms with their sudden downpour of rain scoured off the thin covering of earth from the steep declivities. The shield of foliage was no longer there to break the impact of the rain; the network of roots no longer held the light humus to the slopes. The *maqui*, rooted in shallow pockets of earth, succeeded the denuded forests which formerly conserved and distributed moisture in the dry season, and preserved large areas for cultivation by irrigation. Under the assault of the goats, the *maqui* even has grown shorter and thinner, exposing ever larger spaces to the scouring action of rain in winter and wind in summer, till mountains have become quite bare, as in parts of Greece and Spain. In many sections of the Mediterranean a single deforestation has meant denudation of the soil also and hence, the permanent destruction of the forests.[173]

Hence all Mediterranean lands today show a low percentage of forested area, despite the predominant mountain relief which would naturally be devoted to tree growth. Spain has 20.8 per cent of her area in forests, Portugal 5.2 per cent, Italy

15.7, Greece 9.3.   These are much lower percentages than are
to be found in Germany, Switzerland, Norway or Japan; yet
even these probably represent in part a low scrub and not genuine forests.

AUTHORITIES—CHAPTER XI

 1. For general character of Mediterranean vegetation see
     Philippson, *Das Mittelmeergebiet.* Leipzig, 1907.
     Theobald Fischer, *Mittelmeerbilder.* Leipzig, 1908.
     Neumann and Partsch, *Physikalische Geographie Griechenlands.*
        Breslau, 1885.
     Deecke, *Italy.* Translated from the German. London.
     R. Fitzner, *Niederschlag und Bewölkung in Kleinasien,* Peterm.
        Geogr. Mitt. Ergänz, Vol. XXX, No. 140. Gotha, 1903.
     F. Trzebitsky, *Niederschlagvertheilung auf den Sudost-Europaischen
        Halbinseln,* Peterm. *Geogr. Mitt.,* Vol. 55. Gotha, 1909.
     E. Banse, *Die Turkei.* Braunschweig, 1919.
     A. Grisebach, *Die Vegetation der Erde nach ihrer klimatischen
        Anordnung.* Leipzig, 1884.
     Isaiah Bowman, *Forest Physiography.* New York, 1911.
     M. Newbigin, *The Mediterranean Lands.* London, 1924.
     ——*Modern Geography.* New York, and London, 1911.
 2. Theophrastus, *De Historia Plantarum,* IV, Chap. V, 6.
 3. Strabo, XIV, Chap. VI, 5.   Theophrastus, *op. cit.,* V, Chap. VIII, 2.
 4. A. Boeckh, *Public Economy of the Athenians,* pp. 75-76.   Translated
        from the German.   Boston and London, 1857.
 5. Xenophon, *Hellenica,* I, Chap. I, 24-25.
 6. Livy, XLV, 29.   Polybius, XXV, 4.
 7. *Iliad,* XXIII, 118-121; XXIV, 663.
 8. *Iliad,* XIX, 390-392.
 9. *Iliad,* XVI, 482-484; 634-636.
10. *Iliad,* XIII, 13.
11. Hesiod, *Works and Days,* 233-235.
12. Aristophanes, *Clouds,* 281.
13. Theophrastus, *Hist. Plant.,* Bk. III, Chap. II, 5, 6; Chap. III, 2-4;
        Chap. V, 1; Chap. IX, 5; Chap. X, 6; Chap. XV, 5; Chap. XVII,
        3-6, 13; Bk. IV, Chap. I, 2-3; Chap. V, 2-7.
14. *Ibid.,* Bk. III, Chap. III, 2.
15. *Ibid.,* Bks. III, IV and IX, *passim.*
16. Pliny, *Historia Naturalis,* Bk. XVI, Chap. 15, 16, 18, 29; Bk. XIII,
        Chap. 15, 16.
17. II *Chronicles,* II, 16; I *Kings,* V, 5-12.
18. *Ezra,* III, 7.
19. Strabo, XIII, Chap. I, 51.   Xenophon, *Hellenica,* I, Chap. I, 24-25.
     Vergil, *Æneid,* III, 5-8.   The Turkish port on site of Antandros still
     exports planks and logs from Mount Ida.   Walter Leaf, *Troy,* p.
     203.   London, 1912.
20. Theophrastus, *Hist. Plant.,* Bk. V, Chap. VIII, 1.
21. *Ibid.,* Bk. IV, Chap. V.   Bk. V, Chap. 7-8; Chap. VII, 1-3, 5; Chap.
     VIII, 1-2.
22. *Ibid.,* Bk. V, Chap. III, 1-7; Chap. IV, 1-2; Chap. VII, 4-8.

23. *Ibid.*, Bk. V, Chap. IV, 3; Chap. VII, 6.
24. *Ibid.*, Bk. III, Chap. X, 1. Bk. V, Chap. VII, 2.
25. *Ibid.*, Bk. III, Chap. I, 6; Chap. II, 6. Bk. IV, Chap. III, 1; Chap. V, 2.
26. Herodotus, II, 96.
27. Theophrastus, *Hist. Plant.*, Bk. IV, Chap. II, 2, 6-9.
28. *Ibid.*, Bk. IV, Chap. VIII, 4.
29. *Ibid.*, Bk. V, Chap. II, 7.
30. *Odyssey*, V, 60. *Revelation*, XVIII, 12.
31. F. Hommel, *Geschichte von Babylonien und Assyrien*, pp. 328-330. Berlin, 1885.
32. J. Breasted, *History of Egypt*, pp. 95, 114-115, 127. New York, 1909.
33. *Ezekiel*, XXVII, 5, 6.
34. Theophrastus, *Hist. Plant.*, Bk. V, Chap. VIII, 1.
35. *Ibid.*, Bk. V, Chap. VII, 1.
36. Strabo, XIV, Chap. VI, 5.
37. Strabo, XIV, Chap. VI, 2. Compare C. W. Orr, *Cyprus under British Rule*, pp. 136-140. London, 1918.
38. Strabo, XII, Chap. VII, 3; XIV, Chap. III, 2.
39. Theophrastus, *op. cit.*, Bk. III, Chap. II, 6. Pliny, *Hist. Nat.*, XVI, 32.
40. Diodorus Siculus, XI, 60, 75, 77.
41. Strabo, XIV, Chap. V, 3.
42. E. A. Freeman, *Historical Geography of Europe*, Atlas, Maps VI, VIII, IX. London, 1882.
43. Strabo, XIV, Chap. V, 3. Compare Banse, *Die Turkei*, pp. 160-167. 1919.
44. Guy Le Strange, *Lands of the Eastern Caliphates*, p. 142. Cambridge, 1905. Compare Banse, *op. cit.*, p. 160, for present lumber export from Alaya to Egypt.
45. Strabo, XI, Chap. II, 15-18.
46. Vergil, Georgic II, 440-445. Horace, *Carmina*, I, 14, 11.
47. Xenophon, *Anabasis*, Bk. VI, Chap. IV, 4, 5.
48. Theophrastus, *Hist. Plant.*, Bk. IV, Chap. V, 3-5; Bk. V, Chap. VII, 3. Strabo, XII, Chap. III, 10, 12, 15. Compare Banse, *op. cit.*, pp. 81-90, for present lumber trade.
49. Pliny, *op. cit.*, XVI, 16. Theophrastus, *Hist. Plant.*, Bk. III, Chap. XV, 5.
50. Theophrastus, *Hist. Plant.*, Bk. I, Chap. V, 4, 5. Bk. V, Chap. III, 1, 7; Chap. IV, 1, 2; Chap. VIII, 8.
51. Catullus, IV, 3. Vergil, Georgic II, 438. Ovid, *Metamorphoses*, IV, 311.
52. R. Fitzner, *op. cit.*, pp. 78-80, rainfall map, p. 91. *Pet. Geog. Mitt.*, *Ergänzungsheft*, Vol. XXX, No. 140. Gotha, 1902.
53. Theophrastus, *Hist. Plant.*, Bk. III, Chap. II, 5; Bk. IV, Chap. V, 3. Strabo, XII, Chap. VIII, 3, 8.
54. Theophrastus, *Hist. Plant.*, Bk. V, Chap. III, 1.
55. *Ibid.*, Bk. IV, Chap. II, 5.
56. Thucydides, IV, 52.
57. R. Fitzner, *op. cit.*, rainfall map, p. 91.
58. Theophrastus, *Hist. Plant.*, Bk. IV, Chap. V, 3, 4.
59. Strabo, XIV, Chap. 1, 12, 20, 33. Banse, *op. cit.*, pp. 141, 149.
60. Vitruvius, *De Architectura*, II, IX, 13. Pliny, XVI, 79.

294 FORESTS AND THE LUMBER TRADE

61. R. Fitzner, *op. cit.*, p. 80. E. Banse, *op. cit.*, p. 83.
62. Plato, *Critias*, Chap. V, p. 418. Translated by Henry Davis. London, 1870.
63. A. Boeckh, *The Public Economy of Athens*, p. 138. Translated from German. Boston, 1857.
64. Thucydides, VI, 90.
65. Theophrastus, *Hist. Plant.*, Bk. IV, Chap. V, 5.
66. *Odyssey*, IX, 112-120, 186.
67. Xenophon, *Hellenes*, VI, I, 11.
68. F. Trzebitsky, *op. cit.*, *Pet. Geog. Mitt.*, Vol. LV, pp. 186-187. Gotha, 1909.
69. Thucydides, I, 100; IV, 102. Herodotus, V, 23.
70. Herodotus, V, 124-126.
71. Theophrastus, *Hist. Plant.*, Bk. I, Chap. IX, 2.
72. *Ibid.*, Bk. V, Chap. II, 1.
73. Thucydides, IV, 108.
74. Plutarch, *Lives*, Demetrius, X.
75. Theophrastus, *Hist. Plant.*, Bk. IV, Chap. V.
76. Mommsen, *History of Rome*, Vol. II, pp. 358, 364. New York, 1872. Polybius, XXV, 4.
77. Strabo, *Fragments*, 33, 36.
78. Theophrastus, *Hist. Plant.*, Bk. IV, Chap. V, 4.
79. Leake, *Travels in Northern Greece*, Vol. IV, p. 393. London, 1835.
80. Herodotus, VII, 183, 188. Strabo, IX, Chap. V, 22.
81. Strabo, X, Chap. IV, 4.
82. Theophrastus, *Hist. Plant.*, Bk. III, Chap. 1, 6; Chap. II, 6; Chap. III, 3, 4.
83. Vitruvius, Bk. II, Chap. IX, 13.
84. Herodotus, VII, 218.
85. Pausanias, Bk. IX, Chap. XXIII, 4.
86. *Ibid.*, Bk. VIII, Chap. XI, 1; Chap. XII, 1; Chap. LIV, 5. Bk. III, Chap. XI, 6.
87. *Ibid.*, Bk. III, Chap. XX, 4.
88. Leake, *Travels in the Morea*, Vol. I, pp. 128, 132, 251. London, 1830.
89. Theophrastus, *Hist. Plant.*, Bk. III, Chap. XVI, 3.
90. Philippson, *Das Mittelmeergebiet*, p. 121, maps III, IV. Leipzig, 1907.
91. Pausanias, Bk. V, Chap. VI, 4.
92. Strabo, VIII, Chap. III, 32.
93. Xenophon, *Anabasis*, Bk. V, Chap. III, 9-12.
94. Pausanias, Bk. IX, Chap. XXIII, 4.
95. Leake, *Travels in the Morea*, Vol. II, p. 232. London, 1830.
96. Pausanias, Bk. VII, Chap. XXVI, 10.
97. Leake, *Travels in the Morea*, Vol. II, pp. 112-117. London, 1830.
98. Theophrastus, *Hist. Plant.*, Bk. III, Chap. II, 5; Bk. IV, Chap. 1, 2.
99. Pausanias, Bk. VII, Chap. XXVI, 10.
100. Pausanias, Bk. X, Chap. XXXVIII, 9.
101. Leake, *Travels in Northern Greece*, Vol. I, p. 108. London, 1835. Neumann and Partsch, *Physikalische Geographie Griechenlands*, p. 361. Breslau, 1885.
102. Thucydides, I, 108.
103. Leake, *Travels in Northern Greece*, Vol. I, pp. 113-114. 1835.

FORESTS AND THE LUMBER TRADE 295

104. *Iliad,* II, 361, 632. *Odyssey,* I, 246; XIII, 243-6; XIV, 1-2.
105. Thucydides, I, 24, 30, 80.
106. Leake, *Travels in Northern Greece,* Vol. I, pp. 163-6, 172, 181-2; Vol. IV, pp. 47-50.
107. Strabo, VII, Chap. VII, 5-6.
108. F. Trzebitsky, *op. cit.,* pp. 186-7.
109. Vergil, Georgic III, 450. Pliny, *Hist. Nat.,* XIV, 20. Theophrastus, *Hist. Plant.,* Bk. IX, Chap. II, 3-4; Chap. III, 1-4.
110. Theophrastus, *Hist. Plant.,* Bk. IX, Chap. II, 2, 3; Bk. IV, Chap. VI, 1; Bk. III, Chap. XV, 4.
111. *Exodus,* II, 3.
112. Neumann and Partsch, *op. cit.,* pp. 376-377.
113. Herodotus, II, 87. Pliny, *Hist. Nat.,* XVI, 11.
114. Vitruvius, *De Architectura,* II, 9.
115. Pliny, *Hist. Nat.,* V, I.
116. Strabo, XVII, Chap. III, 4, 6.
117. Vidal de la Blache, *Atlas,* map 2, p. 79. Paris, 1906.
118. Lucanus, X, 144.
119. Horace, *Carmina,* IV, 1, 20. Pliny, *Hist. Nat.,* XXXIII, 146; XVI, 231.
120. Strabo, XVII, Chap. III, 4. Pliny, *Hist. Nat.,* XIII, 15, 29. Lucanus, IX, 416. Cicero Verres, IV, 17, 37.
121. Martialis, XIV, Ep. 89; X, 98, 6.
122. Pliny, *Hist. Nat.,* XVI, 39.
123. *Ibid.,* XVI, 40.
124. E. Speck, *Handelsgeschichte des Altertums,* Vol. III, Part I, ¶ 522. Leipzig, 1905.
125. Pliny, *Hist. Nat.,* III, 5. W. Deecke, *Italy,* pp. 428-430. London, 1904.
126. Strabo, VI, Chap. I, 9. Pliny, *Hist. Nat.,* XV, 7.
127. Vergil, Georgic II, 438.
128. Strabo, III, Chap. II, 6.
129. Strabo, III, Chap. IV, 2.
130. Philippson, *Das Mittelmeergebiet,* p. 119, map III. Leipzig, 1907.
131. Pliny, *Hist. Nat.,* XVI, 40.
132. Diodorus Siculus, IV, 5.
133. *Odyssey,* IX, 112-113, 186.
134. Strabo, VI, Chap. II, 8. Diodorus Siculus, XIV, 41, 42.
135. Livy, *Historia Romæ,* I, 30, 33; II, 7. Pliny, *Hist. Nat.,* XVI, 10, 15
136. Theophrastus, *Hist. Plant.,* Bk. IV, Chap. V, 5.
137. *Ibid.,* Bk. V, Chap. VIII, 1-3.
138. Mommsen, *History of Rome,* Vol. II, p. 255. New York, 1906.
139. Theophrastus, *Hist. Plant.,* Bk. V, Chap. VIII, 2.
140. Diodorus Siculus, V, 13.
141. *Ibid.,* V, 1. Pliny, *Hist. Nat.,* XVI, 16.
142. Theophrastus, *Hist. Plant.,* Bk. III, Chap. XV, 5.
143. *Ibid.,* Bk. V, Chap. III, 1, 7.
144. *Ibid.,* Bk. V, Chap. VIII, 3.
145. Livy, *Hist. Romæ,* IX, 35-36.
146. *Ibid.,* XVIII, 45.
147. Strabo, V, Chap. II, 5; Chap. III, 7.
148. Strabo, IV, Chap. VI, 2. Diodorus Siculus, V, Chap. 39, 1-4.

149. Strabo, V, Chap. II, 5.
150. Vitruvius, *op. cit.*, Bk. II, Chap. IX, 14-17.
151. Pliny, *Hist. Nat.*, XVI, 39-40.
152. *Ibid.*, XVI, 15.
153. Strabo, IV, Chap. VI, 9-10; V, Chap. I, 8.
154. Pliny, *Hist. Nat.*, XVI, 11.
155. Strabo, V, Chap. I, 12.
156. Polybius, II, 15. Varro, *Rerum Rusticarum*, II, 4.
157. Polybius, III, 42. Livy, *Hist. Romæ*, XXI, 26.
158. Strabo, IV, Chap. I, 5.
159. Strabo, III, Chap. IV, 11.
160. Plato, *Critias*, Chap. V, p. 418. Translated by Henry Davis. London, 1870.
161. Theophrastus, *Hist. Plant.*, Bk. IV, Chap. V, 5.
162. *Genesis*, XXI, 33.
163. G. Adam Smith, *Historical Geography of the Holy Land*, pp. 80-81. New York, 1897.
164. *Isaiah*, X, 18-19.
165. *Deuteronomy*, XX, 19.
166. Vitruvius, *op. cit.*, Bk. II, Chap. IX, 13. Ivan Muller, *Handbuch der Klass. Altertumswissenschaft*, Vol. IV, 2, Part II, pp. 117, 124-125. Munich, 1911.
167. Pliny, *Hist. Nat.*, XIII, 15.
168. Personal communication, Professor Kingsley Porter, Harvard University.
169. *Isaiah*, IX, 18; X, 17-19.
170. *Iliad*, XX, 490-492. Also XI, 154-157; XXI, 340-349.
171. Thucydides, II, 77.
172. Philippson, *op. cit.*, pp. 142-144.
173. *Ibid.*, pp. 144, 154.

CHAPTER XII

PASTURES AND STOCK-RAISING

"It is weather rather than soil that determines the harvest" in Mediterranean lands, said the Greek Theophrastus. It was climate which determined the pasturage there, causing its mediocre quality, its limited quantity and its seasonal distribution through the year. The scant endowment of this region with good grazing revolutionized the economic life of all those pastoral tribes who pushed into the Mediterranean Basin, from the well-watered Danube valley on the north and the vast undulating grasslands on the east. Here Nature offered for their occupancy only limited areas, whose boundaries were drawn by the "unpastured seas," to use Homer's expression. Here steep mountain barriers discouraged nomadizing, while the low valleys and narrow coastal plains provided fodder only half the year. Therefore from the arrival of the Israelites and other Semitic hordes in Palestine to that of the shadowy Pelasgians in Greece and Italy, these conditions forced a more or less rapid decrease in the flocks and herds of the pastoral invaders, and hastened the advance from nomadism to sedentary agriculture. The Jewish Scriptures, the *Iliad* and *Odyssey*, the traditions, customs and religious institutions of primitive Latins, Celts and Iberians, all point to a former preponderance of stock-raising gradually superseded by tillage. Grazing survived, but hardly as an adjunct of tillage. It evolved along lines alien to the rainy lands of the north and to the semi-arid lands to the east. It developed the semi-nomadic summer shift to highland pastures, familiar in the Swiss Alps and the Scandinavian mountains, but arising from quite different geographic causes, and attended by quite different economic results.

Stock-raising in the ancient Mediterranean world bore the unmistakable impress of its environment. It was conditioned primarily by the summer drought. This destroyed pasturage in the lowlands for two to six months, according to the latitude, and permitted the shallow-rooted herbage to survive only on swampy coastal belts, deltaic flats and mountain-locked lake basins in which the ground-water table was high. Such choice but limited spots furnished the wet meadows or marsh pastures, which the ancients reserved for their brood mares, horses and fine cattle, and which they sometimes guaranteed against failure in exceptionally dry seasons by artificial irrigation. Yet even these grassy areas shrank to mere patches of green as the summer advanced, unless the streams which watered them flowed down from high mountains with lingering hoods of snow.

EFFECT OF RELIEF UPON MEDITERRANEAN PASTURAGE— The Mediterranean lands made some compensation for the summer drought by their prevailing mountain relief, which provided summer pastures on the heights. The great altitude of the young folded ranges and massive horsts which almost surround the Mediterranean and its Black Sea alcove, their extensive distribution from the Rif Atlas to the densely wooded Caucasus, and their immediate proximity to the vapor-yielding seas, all combined to sprinkle the Mediterranean lands with lofty climatic islands of persistent verdure, wherever the slopes rose high enough to take a toll of moisture from the passing clouds. Here the lowly herbage of the sod flourished the summer through, screened from the sun by the deciduous forests of the upper slopes, nourished by the bed of moist humus about their roots. The summer pastures of the Mediterranean highlands, however, did not offer the variety of grasses and nutritious herbs found in the Alpine meadows farther north; nor did they wear so long the covering of snow which subjects the soil to a slow process of saturation and promotes growth through the ensuing months of sunny days. Therefore, except on the high Alpine rim of the Mediterranean Basin, the flocks and herds grazing on the mountain pastures have always eked out their grass diet by the fresh shoots and accessible twigs of the deciduous trees. This supplementary fodder was undoubtedly more abundant and varied in ancient times than now, when the forests are the thin and deteriorated residue left by centuries of denudation. Moreover, the original forest covering conserved the moisture in the soil of the slopes, and thereby maintained a richer pasturage of herbs and grasses than exists there today.

The quality of the mountain pastures declined from north to south and from west to east within the long flattened ellipse of the Mediterranean lands, and it fell off rapidly from the more rainy western flank of mountainous coastland or peninsula to the rain-shadow on the eastern side; for in these directions the summer drought increased in length and intensity. The northern mountains, whose rainfall approximated the all-year precipitation of middle Europe, had good and reliable summer pastures which supported herds of horses, cattle and mast-fed pigs, besides flocks of sheep and goats. The southern mountains, located below the 40th or 41st parallel, were covered up to 2,000 or 3,300 feet (600 to 1,000 meters) with the typical thorny and leathery Mediterranean vegetation, varied by occasional groups of deciduous trees growing in deeper pockets of soil, where humus and moisture collected. These lower slopes furnished pasturage fit only for sheep and goats, except in spring and the warm rainy autumn when the short-lived grasses lifted their green stalks.

Above this limit the less fastidious flocks found ampler and better pasturage. Cattle and horses, however, which needed succulent herbage, found suitable grazing only in high level valleys or lake basins which combined deep soil with summer showers, like the lake-strewn highlands of ancient Arcadia and Epirus or the longitudinal valleys of the Apennines. In the more arid southern zone, the best summer pastures were located on westward-facing ranges, like the western Apennines, the mountains of Elis, and the high valleys of "many-fountained" Ida, whose cattle pastures in Homeric days reflected the location of this Mysian mountain between rain-bearing winds from the Ægean Sea and those from the Propontis or Marmara. Mountains or limestone plateaus which barely attained the critical elevation of 3,300 feet (1,000 meters), like the Judean Plateau or the Barca Plateau of northern Africa, yielded ephemeral grasses even on their summits. These countries, therefore, had to restrict the raising of horses and cattle to the scant water-soaked or irrigable lowlands at their base, or draw on the stock of the pastoral nomads along their steppe borders.

Only sheep and goats, led about by some boy shepherd of the hills, could thrive. on these uncertain upland pastures.

RELATION OF STOCK-RAISING TO SEDENTARY AGRICULTURE— Conditions of climate and relief in Mediterranean lands greatly restricted stock-raising as an adjunct of sedentary agriculture. In fact, the two industries were almost divorced. The flocks and herds fed in winter on the untilled lands, the lowland meadows, and stubble fields of the home farm; but before the advent of summer they were driven out for their half-year on the highland pastures. This is the rule also today. The author has seen sheep feeding on the crest of the Cithæron range (elevation 2,800 feet or 850 meters) between Attica and Bœotia in early April, while 100 miles farther north the flocks were still grazing on the lake plain of Thessaly, because the middle and upper slopes of the Olympos massif were covered with snow. This divorce of stock-raising from tillage had a marked influence upon the latter. For six months the manure of the flocks and herds was lost to the home fields. To replace it the ancient Mediterranean farmer had to exercise a Chinese-like economy in devising other fertilizers, even to the plough-ing-in of green crops as early as 400 B.C.; [1] but he probably never compensated the soil for the moisture-conserving qualities of the animal manures.

Owing to the lack of home pastures, moreover, animals kept on the farm were restricted to the imperative needs of agri-cultural labor, and were stall-fed throughout the year. Their feeding, moreover, called for the utmost economy. The arable land, scant at best because of the predominant mountainous relief, was carefully apportioned to field crops, gardens, fruit orchards, olive plantations and vineyards, according to its suitability for each. Meadows for hay or forage crops could be maintained through the summer only by irrigation; but irrigable fields were scarce and valuable. Natural meadows were confined to wet lands too low for drainage,[2] and were usually of small extent, except in the deltaic flats of the peren-nial rivers or along the sea edge of coastal plains. The an-cients discriminated between the choice lowland pastures suited to milk cattle and horses and the scant forage of the mountain range whose typical Mediterranean vegetation, *macchia* and *phrygana*, yielded poor grazing for sheep and goats; for their pigs they valued in turn the mast found in the hardwood forests of chestnut, oak and beech clothing the higher ranges or rainy western slopes. Various native clovers they grouped under the generic name *lotos*, which grew in moist meadow, especially the wild strawberry clover (*Trifolium fragiferum*).[3] This was the lauded herbage of the Homeric poems and the "swift-growing clover from the meadows of Juno" which fed the steeds of Zeus and the stags of Artemis,[4] perhaps familiar to poet Callimachus in some spring pasture of Cyrene. These were mingled with various wild grasses [5] and nutritious flowering herbs which had the merits of mixed forage. Even red clover (*Trifolium pratensis*) occurred in natural hay meadows.[6]

FODDER CROPS—Fodder crops of great excellence were raised, but forage was doled out to the work animal with a skimping hand.[7] The ancient farmers cultivated various fodder legumes by irrigation during the dry season, reaped several harvests therefrom where the water sufficed, and let the fields serve for green forage during the winter.[8] Various clovers and beans, vetch, various peas and lupines were native to the Mediterranean lands and were widely cultivated.[9] Cytisus (*Medicago arborea*), a shrubby lucerne raised extensively in Greece and the Cyclades Islands but little in Italy, provided excellent fodder for sheep, oxen, horses, swine and fowl; as feed for cows it increased the quantity and improved the quality of milk; and its flowering fields were lauded by Democritus of Abdera (b. 460 B.C.) as food for bees.[10]

Medic clover (*Medicago sativa*) or lucerne, known in America by its Moorish name of alfalfa, was introduced into Greece by the invading Persians in 490 B.C. However, like cytisus, it received only a passing allusion from Theophrastus,[11] but Amphilochus of Athens devotes a whole book to lucerne and cytisus,[12] while Aristotle also recognized its feed value.[13] If we accept the argument *de silentio*, alfalfa did not reach Italy till after the long sojourn of the Roman armies in Greece incident to the conquest of that country in 146 B.C. It was unknown to Cato who died in 149 B.C., but was described in 28 B.C. by Varro,[14] who had been a gentleman farmer for many of his 88 years. It was mentioned as an important irrigated fodder crop

by Vergil about a decade earlier.[15]   An alfalfa field lasted ten
years from one sowing and yielded four to six harvests a year.[16]
To free it from weeds, it was cut close to the ground each
spring. The weeds thereby perished, but the alfalfa survived,
owing to its deep root system.[17]

During the *Voelkerwanderung* lucerne seems to have vanished
from the Mediterranean lands except from Spain. There it
survived with the careful irrigation tillage of the Saracens who
wanted the alfa-alfa or "the best of all fodders" for their Arab
horses. In the slow recovery of European agriculture, lucerne
spread from Spain into France, taking the obvious route up
the Rhone valley from the Saracen area of occupation in
Languedoc in the 16th century. About this time it was called
the "Burgundian hay," pointing to a new center of distribution
near the hydrographic center of eastern France. The people
of Provence received lucerne from Italy and named it from the
Italian place Clauserne, from which they derived it. The cultivation and name of alfalfa went to Mexico in the 16th century with the Conquistadores, who took it with them to feed
their Arab barbs. Doubtless the irrigated basin around the
Mexican capital was purple in spring when the alfalfa fields
came into flower. From old Mexico its cultivation spread
northward into California in the hands of Junipero Serra and
the other brothers who instructed the Indians in Spanish methods of tillage around their various missions. But not till this
fodder was introduced from Chile into the San Francisco district of California in 1854 was it extensively raised to supply
cattle for the growing population of the gold rush period.
The center of distribution in the Great Salt Lake Oasis, where
it was called lucerne, points to a north European origin in the
hands of the Mormons and Joseph Smith.

Barley and spelt, an inferior wheat, were the feed grains for
stock throughout the Mediterranean Basin. Rye and oats,
which required a moist climate, were for a long time scarcely
known. Oats were regarded as a weed by Theophrastus and
even Vergil,[18] but a few decades later Columella mentions them
as a fodder crop.[19] Rye was raised only in the moister northern parts of the Mediterranean region. . Thracians and Macedonians planted it in the 2nd century,[20] and probably earlier,

in the 4th century B.C., if Theophrastus is correct. The ancient Taurini, who occupied the upper Po valley about Turin and whose name indicates a cattle-raising folk, raised rye in their well-watered territory.[21] Pliny mentions mixed fodder crops of spelt or barley with vetch and beans,[22] a combination which shows how far the Roman farmers had advanced in the art of feeding cattle, after the enormous grain importations into Italy caused field agriculture to be superseded by stock-raising.

KINDS AND DISTRIBUTION OF THE ANIMALS RAISED—The character of Mediterranean pasturage determined the kind, number and distribution of the animals raised. Pigs were associated with the rainier districts of the north and west, where mast-yielding forests abounded; they were eliminated by climatic conditions from Palestine, Syria, and the semi-arid interior of Asia Minor. In all these regions the climatic inhibition was echoed in a religious taboo. Sheep and goats represented the survival of the fittest for Mediterranean pasturage, and therefore began their successful competition with other kinds of stock at an extraordinarily early date. On the dry fields of Palestine they alone could nibble a living from the poor, thin herbage. Though exempt from farm labor, they furnished milk, cheese, leather, wool and hair for textiles. When slaughtered for meat, their small size was an advantage in iceless homes and in a region where the winter cold rarely sufficed to freeze meat.

Cattle and horses, on the other hand, which required good feeding, were associated even in the time of Homer and Solomon with advanced sedentary agriculture, the possession of marsh meadows, and the maintenance of fodder crops through the dry season by means of irrigation. Their presence reflected quite accurately the geographic possibilities of good or fair summer pasturage. They were therefore rare in Palestine but relatively abundant in Italy, whose long narrow peninsular form, high relief and more northern location curtailed the dry season and insured occasional summer showers, while its extensive plains of moist or swampy alluvium provided conditions for wet pastures in the Po, Arno and Adige valleys and certain coastal lowlands. These conditions also permitted Italy to

abandon field agriculture, as opposed to horticulture and viticulture, and to resort to stock-raising on a large scale, when
Rome's over-rapid territorial expansion and the enormous importation of foreign grain had ruined the small peasant.

MEAT DIET IN MEDITERRANEAN LANDS—The pasturage conditions were further reflected in the amount and kinds of meat
used as food in the ancient Mediterranean world. While the
flood-plain of the Nile supported cattle, sheep, goats and pigs
in relative abundance and supplied meat to the tables of the
well-to-do, everywhere else the meat diet was restricted, just
as it is today. In Palestine and Greece, a religious festival
attended by the sacrifice of a ram, lamb or kid was the chief
occasion for the appearance of meat on the table of the common
people. These conditions held in Palestine from the earliest
times and emphasized the importance of olive oil as a substitute,
as revealed all through the Scriptures. The consumption of
beef decreased from north to south and from west to east.
Except in Italy, it declined also from the earlier to the later
epochs with the deterioration of the mountain pastures and the
growing pressure of population upon the irrigable lands of the
plains. The sustaining food of beef and swine meat which characterized Homeric Greece was greatly attenuated by the 7th
century B.C., and by the 5th century came rarely on the daily
table. A goat or a pig was the treat for a festival in Athens,
and beef was enjoyed by the common man only at public banquets on the occasion of public sacrifices.[23] Lucky people like
the Thessalians and Bœotians, who had good pastures and fat
kine in their old lake basins, were scorned as gluttons but were
none the less envied. If Solon forbade the sacrifice of an ox for
a funeral feast as a sumptuary law in the interest of economy,[24]
this prohibition may reflect the increasing price of cattle in
Attica, a land poor in pastures.

Meat was a luxury for feast days also in the early Republic
of Rome; but with the rapid acquisition of more ample and nutritious pastures, as the northern Apennines and the Po valley
were conquered and annexed, and with the transition to large-
scale stock farming following the Second and Third Punic wars,
beef became a more common article of food; lamb, mutton and
goat's meat were cheap, and every form of *porcina* or hog meat

was in general demand.[25] Meat figured conspicuously as food among the large patrician and official classes of the capital, where wealth was centralized, and therefore doubtless occasioned the sharp advance in the market price of all cattle which made the older Cato rank stock-raising as the most remunerative branch of tillage ; [26] but among the growing proletariat and the vast number of slaves, salt-fish, supplemented by the poorer grades of olives and olive oil, probably took the place of meat, as it did among the common people of Greece.[27] In the early centuries of the Roman Republic, when a balanced system of agriculture prevailed, and at all times elsewhere in the Mediterranean world an immense impulse was given to the ancient fisheries by the need to supply the place of meat. The wide sea ventures of the ancient tunny fleets, therefore, may be regarded as the joint effect of ample coastlines and meager pastures. And when the early Christian church imposed meatless days or fasts upon the Greek and Roman adherents within the Empire, the restriction worked little hardship to the mass of the people, whose dietary stand-by was salt fish. This reflection leaves us with the query how far climatic conditions may discount the merit acquired by certain religious observances.

The scrupulous economy of the grazing and meadow lands in the ancient Mediterranean world reveals itself in various secondary or derivative effects of geographic conditions. Cows and oxen were raised at a minimum cost on the out-pastures of the mountains and marshes, and brought to the home farm when old enough to work. There they were employed for agricultural labor in preference to the horse, which had fewer economic uses and yet required the best feed. We read of ox-wagons and horse-carts in Athens, used to transport building materials to the Acropolis in the time of Pericles,[28] but mules and oxen were more generally employed as draft animals.[29] The unassuming ass was the pack-animal for the rough mountain paths and ill-made tracks which prevailed in the Mediterranean world before the expansion of the imperial road-builders of Rome.

THE HORSE IN MEDITERRANEAN LIFE—In most Mediterranean lands, horses appear as luxury articles from very early times. Only in the northern and rainy parts of the region, where good pastures were found, did horses become a common-place. Owing to the cost of raising and maintaining them, they were the luxury of the rich, the special privilege of nobility and royalty, whether among the Jewish kings and princes of ancient Palestine,[30] or the Greek and Trojan chieftains warring on the plains of Ilium,[31] whether among the landed aristocracy of the *Hippobotæ* or "horse feeders" of Greek Eubœa, or the wealthy class of *Hippes* who constituted the small equestrian order of Athens in the 7th and 6th centuries B.C.,[32] or the *nouveau riche* of Rome who formed the order of the *equites* or knights, among whom the gold ring, the purple-bordered toga and the prancing steed, were the badge of all their tribe. The Eupatrid family of the Alcmæonides of Athens, like other noble clans of the commonwealth, acquired riches, raised horses on their landed estates, won prizes in the four-horse chariot races in the Olympic Games, and thus arrived at distinction.[33] Vergil specifies the raising of fine sleek-coated horses as the congenial occupation and conspicuous characteristic of the Trojan and Roman nobles.[34]   When the poet describes the equestrian evolutions of the Trojan lads at the *Ludus Trojæ* or funeral games of Anchises in Sicily, he makes it clear that only the little aristocrats of Æneas' exile band participated in this miniature cavalry display.[35]   Does some such fact as this explain the patrician beauty and noble bearing of the mounted boys in the frieze of the Parthenon?   No beggar ever got on horseback in the Mediterranean region: that edifying spectacle was reserved for rainier lands.

Cavalry and chariot service in war became the obligation of the rich, and made horses the concomitant of war throughout the Mediterranean.[36] Aside from their appearance in religious processions, sacred games and races, war was their essential use. The amount of cavalry which each country could command depended upon the supply of wet meadows and therefore often fluctuated with the expansion and contraction of the national frontiers, as the boundaries included or excluded such natural pastures. The few states with abundant and superior pastures became famous for their cavalry and were sought as allies in war; from them horses were purchased or mounted troops were hired by commercial states of large revenue like

Athens, which in the days of its wealth could import horse feed. Horses, like cattle, were scarce in Athens, where climate, relief and the composition of the soil were all adverse to good pasturage. Therefore the Athenian cavalry was always small, only 100 to 300 horsemen originally—a negligible force at the Battle of Marathon—and never numbering more than a thousand, who were occasionally reinforced by mounted Scythian bowmen.[37] Hence the Athenian state, in the protracted wars with its rivals, always sought the alliance of the few Greek commonwealths which had a numerous cavalry.

The prevailing rugged relief of the Mediterranean lands tended to restrict the employment of cavalry and chariots in war, and in some districts quite inhibited their use. It dictated the choice of broad and level battlegrounds by generals with strong mounted forces, who therefore manœuvred for place. Thus the northern Syrians and Philistines, who had numerous chariots, drew the horseless Israelites into battle in the lake-plain of Merom and the plain of Esdraelon.[38] The Persian invaders of Greece in 490 B.C. selected the plain of Marathon for their decisive battle, by the advice of the traitor Hippias, and later the plain of Platea, because the defending forces were weak in cavalry and the Persians were strong.[39] Attica was not a country whose terrain permitted the free operation of mounted troops, but Bœotia was;[40] hence the significance of the battle fields of Chæronea and Coronea, located in lake and valley plains of Bœotia, for the Macedonian conquest of Greece. Hannibal, on his invasion of Italy, could employ his Numidian cavalry to an advantage in the broad Po lowlands at Ticinus and Trebia, the lake plain of Trasimenus and the coastal plain of Apulia at Cannæ. When caught by the Romans in a mountain valley where his cavalry was useless, he escaped from the trap by strategy.

ECONOMY OF PASTURES AND IMPROVEMENT OF ANIMAL BREEDS —The paucity of the Mediterranean pastures necessitated their intelligent and economic use. This requirement led to the improvement of the animal breeds by artificial selection at an early period, in Egypt even under the old Empire in 3000-2500 B.C.[41] Selected breeding was a commonplace to the Greeks from the time of Theognis of Megara (570-490 B.C.)

and Polycrates of Samos (died 520 b.c.); it developed into a broadly applied system in Italy and Sicily, and appeared in Cyrene, Africa and Spain. The process was fostered by the early live-stock trade, due to the uneven distribution of pasturage, which sprang up between districts of good and poor grazing. Surplus animals from all the pastoral hinterlands reached the Mediterranean markets where they were exchanged for grain or manufactured commodities. Occasionally they came as tribute; and since the kind and breed of animals were generally specified by the law imposing the tributes, such animals were probably the best of their kind. This was particularly true in the case of horses. Overseas trade in live-stock was facilitated by the early development of horse transports as a branch of the merchant marines of both Phœnicia and Greece. Aside from the imperative need of transporting cavalry for war, which was well established by 490 b.c.,[42] the risk and expense of taking animals on long voyages in small boats must have been prohibitive except for choice specimens which would command high prices; and these would naturally be used for breeding purposes. We hear of Venetian horses in Sparta in the middle of the 7th century b.c.[43] Fine horses and mules of racing stock were brought from African Cyrene and various cities of Sicily as early as 494 b.c. to compete in the sacred games of Greece at Corinth, Delphi and Olympia.[44] It is easy to imagine that the sacred precincts of the games became the scene of busy horse trading after the prizes had been awarded, and that thus various strains were mixed and eventually improved.

The evidence points to a very early importation of the superior Thracian horses into Italy. Vergil would hardly have dared to make Æneas find Thracian horses the property of the local kings in Sicily and Latium,[45] if the anachronism had been all too violent. The fact that the Carthaginians employed horse transports in 488 b.c. in a military expedition to Sicily [46] suggests that they may have earlier imported choice animals from Phœnicia to stock their big landed estates in Africa, as is indicated in the Æneid when Dido presents the boy Ascanius with a fine Sidonian steed.[47] The nature of the horse as a luxury article and its highly specialized use for chariot races and war, requiring speed and endurance, doubtless contributed to the early improvement of the equine strains through artificial selection, and therefore to a peculiarly discriminating trade in the animal. The horse breeds were improved also by superior feeding, by the reservation of the best green pastures for mares and colts, and by the maintenance of stud-farms at great distances, wherever natural pastures afforded green fodder all year round. This was noticeable among Macedonian, Greek, Sicilian, and Roman nobles and plutocrats.

Regions of export for selected breeds of horses and cattle were characterized by marsh-meadows, heavy rainfall with summer showers, or by the moist soils of lacustrine basins surrounded by high mountains. Such regions were Egypt and the Cilician lowland; Thrace, Thessaly, Messinia, Arcadia, Elis, Argos and Epirus in Greece; Apulia, the Po valley, and Venetia in Italy, together with Sicily. In the Iberian peninsula only the Guadalquivir lowlands or Bætica had attained a sufficiently advanced economic development to yield superior breeds.

The best sheep and goats were sought for breeding purposes in regions of dry pasturage near old industrial centers famous for their textiles, like Miletos, Megara, Athens, Tarentum, Corduba and Gades. These districts had selected their breeds for the fineness, length and color of their wool or hair; and further to improve the quality of the fleece, they covered the sheep with skins.[48] Diogenes said that the children of the Megarans ran about naked, while their sheep were clothed. This trade in improved strains began very early. We read, for instance, that Polycrates of Samos (532 b.c.) imported goats from the islands of Naxos and Scyros, sheep from Attica and Miletos, and swine from Sicily.[49] The demand for wool and goat's hair for textiles was imperative. Cotton was as yet unknown to the Mediterranean farmers, and the cultivation of flax for fibre was practically restricted to Egypt for centuries, for it required moist alluvial soil. Such soil was found in other Mediterranean lands in limited quantities, and seldom could be spared from the more important wheat, especially since both Hebrew, Greek, and Roman farmers knew that flax exhausted the ground.[50] Therefore flax culture came late into Italy and

then was centered in the alluvial plains of the Po valley.[51]
Linen was sparingly used for clothing even in the first century
of the Empire, when it was a luxury article for the Cæsars
and the rich.[52] In contrast, every rocky island unfit for tillage
supported flocks of goats, while goats and sheep flecked every
mountain side in summer, and drifted over every plain and hill
in winter.

Let us now examine the various Mediterranean countries in
the light of these general principles, and get the picture of
stock-raising in each from the data which we command.

STOCK-RAISING IN EGYPT AND NEARBY ASIA—Ancient Egypt
had cattle and horses in abundance both for home use and
export. In time of famine they were exchanged for the government grain under Joseph's rule.[53] To the Greeks the Nile
was "the stream where graze the goodly kine." [54] Compare
the vision of Pharaoh before the seven year's famine: "There
came out of the River seven well-favored kine and fat-fleshed,
and they fed in a meadow." [55] The inundations of the Nile
irrigated an area large enough both for plough land and pasture. Moreover, the marshes of the Delta, which remained unreclaimed long after the river valley proper had been brought
under cultivation and which were in part unreclaimable, furnished natural pastures when the fodder supply in the farm
land ran low, prior to the summer flood. Thither the cattle
were driven from the south every year, and were entrusted to
the local marsh-men. These were an uncouth people but pro-
fessional herdsmen; they still persisted as such in the time of
Marcus Aurelius (180 A.D.), when the Romans called the
marshes of the Delta the *bucolia* or cattle pastures.[56] The
Nile valley furnished various irrigated forage crops, which fed
the home cattle and horses penned up in the mound villages
during the summer floods.[57] Under these favorable geographic
conditions, Egypt from 3000 B.C. maintained a careful system
of cattle-breeding, which resulted in several varieties of ordinary and humped cattle; [58] and it supported the horse-breeding
industry which supplied an export trade to Palestine, Syria and
the Hittite country of Asia Minor.

The Egyptian horses were carefully bred and were evidently
superior to the native stock of southwestern Asia, because they

commanded high prices in export.   The large number of chariots and cavalry in the Egyptian armies from the 14th century
B.C. indicates horse-raising on a big scale.   This was rendered
possible by the ample grain and fodder crops of the Nile valley, and in turn it rendered possible the broad artificial selection which improved the breed.   The original equine stock came
in with the Hyksos invaders (1700 B.C.), but it was probably
improved by crossing with the fine horses of the Libyan tribes,
who began pushing into the western margin of the Delta from
the 13th century.   These nomads, like the later Bedouins, apparently developed an animal distinguished by speed and endurance, in response to the requirements of thinly scattered pasturage, desert warfare and border raids.   The excellence of this
Libyan breed reappeared in the race horses of Cyrene, which
frequently carried off the prizes in the Olympic Games.[59]

Palestine, because of its climate, geology, relief and the deep
Jordan rift which makes the highland over-drained, has always
had scant natural grazing for cattle and horses, though sheep
and goats can find enough forage of a poor kind.   But flocks
and herds alike suffered from the frequent droughts or half-
droughts which visited the land, when cow and ewe, like the
hart, "panted for the water-brooks."   The ancient breed of
sheep was undoubtedly the broad-tailed variety, which probably came from arid Asia by way of Arabia.[60]   It was fortified
against a season of poor pasturage by the store of fat in the
immense tail, translated "rump" in the Bible but now given as
"fat tail" in the revised version.[61]   The limestone plateau of
Judea and the lower Negeb to the south were covered with
herbage after the March rains, and furnished a nutritious but
transitory pasturage.   Here in the spring grazed "the cattle
upon a thousand hills" of which the psalmist sang[62] with more
religious fervor than scientific accuracy.   By midsummer all
was parched and brown.   Earlier still faded the belt of green
to the east and south, the short-lived "pastures of the wilderness."[63]   The flood plain of the lower Jordan, which the sheik
Lot selected for his portion of Palestine because it was well-
watered, was indeed saturated with moisture after the melting of
the snows on high Hermon (9,020 feet or 2,750 meters) to the

north; but its grass soon perished in the furnace heat of the deep rift (1,293 feet or 394 meters below sea-level).

Only on the narrow coastal plain of Sharon and the valley floor of Esdraelon did the grass never wholly fail in summer. These were the chief natural pastures for the cattle of King David.[64] Both districts are fed by springs from the porous limestone plateau and have a high water-table which ensures a modicum of moisture to the soil. Sharon extends 50 miles from Joppa to Carmel, with a varying width of 6 to 12 miles. Swamps half a mile wide border its streams, whose outlets are obstructed by the coastal dunes, and many small lagoons are strung along its shore. Sharon is today a district of pastures and scattered farms, between which stretch belts of evergreen oak, the remnant of the forest described by Strabo and Josephus.[65] Much of it was under cultivation in ancient times, but the remainder yielded the best pasturage of Palestine and nourished superior cattle, which are praised in the *Talmud*.[66] The old lacustrine plain of Esdraelon, surrounded by Mount Carmel and the hills of Samaria and Galilee, located farther north than Sharon and better watered, is a natural meadow land. Its broad, smooth floor lies so little above sea-level and has such a slight drainage slope that much of it is marshy during winter and spring, so that the modern road crosses it on a dyke. This is the plain where Sisera and his 900 war chariots got mired during a battle when the Lord sent a sudden storm to assist the Israelites.[67] The value of these wet meadows was recognized in ancient Palestine. "Blessed are ye that sow beside all waters, that lead out thither your ox and your ass." The Bible gives a picture of poor and uncertain grazing for the larger animals elsewhere west of Jordan. Allusions to "fat pastures" and "large pastures" occur only when the prophets, in rare moments of optimism, indulge in hyperbole to describe the material blessings promised to a repentant Israel [68] by an irascible deity, whose moods varied with the weather, not as an effect but as a cause.

East of Jordan, the plateau belt of Gilead, Golan and Bashan rises 2,600 to 4,400 feet (800 to 1,300 meters) above the sea, and receives from 16 to 24 inches (400 to 600 mm.) of rainfall in Golan, but less in Gilead to the south.[69] This sufficed in ancient times, as today, for good or even excellent grasslands,[70] over which cattle wandered in a half-wild state in charge of nomadic herdsmen. Such were the "bulls of Bashan" and the herds whose yield figured in the tribute paid to the kings of Israel and Judea, and in the produce sent to the western markets. This district furnished booty in the form of cattle to the Israelite conquerors; [71] and it was appropriated by the tribes of Gad who were essentially herdsmen.[72]

The small natural meadows of ancient Palestine seem to have been reserved for the cows and oxen which performed the farm labor of ploughing and treading out the grain, and which served also for food and religious sacrifices. There is little evidence of efforts to improve breeds. Cows were kept to maintain the supply of oxen; their milk-giving ability was small, owing in part to the inferior pasturage and their constant labor. For the same reasons the cattle were small and short-limbed, but tolerant of the harsh conditions.[73] The regulations of Leviticus, which exacted victims without blemish for sacrifice in the temple, may have been an adroit priestly method to encourage discriminating breeding; but this was possible only to a limited degree, since the majority of the stock ran free on the highland or lowland pastures.

HORSES IN PALESTINE—Nowhere else were horses so great a luxury as in Palestine. Before the Jewish conquest, the Philistines of the coastal plain had numerous horses and chariots,[74] and so had the Canaanites who occupied the plain of Esdraelon and the moist lake-basin of Merom; [75] but the native tribes of the upland seem to have had none. When the Israelites invaded Palestine and established themselves on the rugged Judean plateau, they saved the cattle taken in their conquest, but were instructed to hamstring the horses,[76] because the land afforded no suitable pasturage. The earliest laws, embodied in the book of *Deuteronomy*, were the result of about three centuries of practical experience in Palestine. They forbade the kings to breed horses or to import them from Egypt for breeding purposes.[77] But later, when David and Solomon had extended the frontier of their domain from the Mediterranean coast to the Arabian Desert, and northward to the great bend of the Euphrates, the pasturage situation was improved, because the kingdom included the plains of Sharon, Esdraelon, and Cœle-Syria, the broad fertile valley between the Lebanon and Anti-Lebanon Mountains, which provided both natural and irrigable meadows.

David deviated from the old rule after his victory over the northern Syrians by reserving from the booty horses for a hundred chariots [78] or probably three hundred animals. All the rest he disabled. Solomon went into horse-breeding on a large scale and made it a royal monopoly.[79] He received both horses and mules as tribute, doubtless from Gilead and Damascus, where the kings had chariots [80] and also from the northern Syrians; and he imported from Egypt droves of horses at a cost equivalent to $100 per head, to supply the cavalry and chariot corps of his army,[81] which was enlarged to protect the wide frontiers of the new Empire. From this time horses were royal beasts, associated with war. They were chiefly stall-fed on barley and straw.[82] The temporary expansion of the Jewish kingdom to the Mediterranean gave Solomon control of the great caravan route along the maritime plain, and made him the sole middleman in the horse trade between Egypt and the Syrian and Hittite kings of the north.[83] The Tel Amarna letters indicate that these rulers made an active demand for the Nile horses, which were doubtless a superior breed. Solomon also purchased stallions from Cilicia, probably to sell them again to Egypt to improve the strain there.[84] Lowland Cilicia, located between Mount Amanus and the Taurus system, was a broad, well-watered alluvial plain, abounding in marsh meadows. As its tribute to Darius the Persian in 500 B.C. consisted of 360 white horses,[85] it had developed a pure equine breed by artificial selection. After the division of the Jewish kingdom, the plains of northern Palestine or Israel continued to raise horses, but rugged Judea had to rely on importations from Egypt, despite the protests of the prophets.[86]

Narrow, rugged Phœnicia, with its terraced mountain sides devoted to gardens and orchards, offered limited pasturage for animals, and little opportunity for their employment. Hence cities like Tyre and Sidon imported sheep and goats from the nomad tribes of Kedar in northern Arabia, and wool from Damascus. From Armenia (Togarmah) they bought war

horses and mules,[87] which they probably sold again farther south
in Palestine or Egypt. Armenia was a famous horse-breeding
region in ancient times and used to pay to the Persian kings an
annual tribute of 20,000 foals [88] which fed on its high Alpine
pastures in summer, and in winter on the produce of its fertile
valleys, as the horses of the wandering Kurds do today. The
hinterland of the Phœnician seaboard was Cœle-Syria or the
Lebanon trough, which afforded the largest and best pasture
area of all Syria. The trough, which forms a broad U-shaped
valley of gentle gradient, is drained by the Leontes and Orontes
rivers, which rise in a swampy, indeterminate watershed near
Baalbek at an altitude of 3,500 feet. The Orontes, the longer
stream, takes a leisurely course northward through an almost
level plain, and at intervals spreads out in broad marshy
pools,[89] which in ancient times created extensive meadows for
horses and cattle. Reclaimed in part for irrigated fields, the
plain fed the ancient populations of Kadesh, Hemesa (Homs),
Hamath, Apameia and Antioch.[90] After Alexander's conquest
of Syria, the wet meadows formed by the Orontes near the city
of Apameia were selected for the royal Macedonian stud-farm,
which kept 30,000 brood mares and 300 stallions.[91] This is
part of that Syria whose chariot and cavalry forces wrought
havoc among the armies of the Kingdom of Israel.

Asia Minor, owing to its more northern location, its peninsula form and high elevation, had a well assured rainfall along
its coasts, especially on the west and north where the precipitation ranged from 25 to 40 inches (625 mm. to 1,000 mm.). In
the mountain rimmed interior of the plateau, steppes and salt
deserts prevailed, where cattle, wild asses and sheep roamed at
large over dry or saline pastures,[92] or in summer ascended the
inner valleys of the encircling mountains as they do today.[93]
The products of this semi-arid hinterland were probably one
source of the fine wool which through the ages has sought the
industrial cities of the Ægean littoral and supported their textile industries. Phrygia Major, which lay just east of Lydia
at the head of the mountain valleys opening westward to Ægean
winds, got hardly less rain than the coastal belt (400-500
mm.),[94] and therefore, Herodotus says, was famous for its wheat
and cattle among the ancient Greeks of Ionia and the Carian

seaboard. Cappadocia comprised the high eastern portion of
Anatolia, 3,300 feet or 1,000 meters, and included in its area
the lofty *massif* of Mount Argæus (13,000 feet or 4,000 meters), an old volcano, whose lower slopes and piedmont, covered
with a rich soil of weathered trachyte, tufa, and lava, merge
into the fertile fields and meadows of Cæsarea.[95] This region
produced the immense number of horses, mules and sheep sent
yearly as tribute to the Persian kings, and the famous Cappa-
docian race-horses of the Roman Circus.[96] The latter developed lung power on these high pastures.

Western Asia Minor was a part of the ancient Ægean world,
so far as its broad embayed littoral was concerned. Its early
activities in stock-raising are therefore interwoven with those
of the Greek people, by whom it was colonized. In the *Iliad* and
Odyssey, horses and cattle belonged to sedentary agriculture,
which presupposed irrigated fodder crops and wet meadows,
and they therefore shared the honor due to the highest civilization of Homeric times.[97] But their distribution around the
Ægean circle of lands shows a close connection with geographic
conditions. Saturated river lowlands, deltaic flats, and lacustrine basins seem to produce horses and cattle as naturally as
the reeds growing in the marshes. In such places were found
the flowery meadows and level stretches of rich soil which the
Homeric Greeks loved for their cattle and horses.[98] Beside
every green pasture was the meandering brook or reedy pool,
recalling the *prata recentia rivis* of Vergil.[99] "The kine that
are feeding innumerable in the low-lying land of a great marsh"
give us the typical picture,[100] or the horses of Achilles "cropping clover and parsley of the marsh" on the Troad coast.[101]
Of a Trojan prince we are told, "Three thousand mares with
their colts had he, that pastured along the marsh meadow,"
where the Simois and Scamander rivers had deposited their silt
on the flat coast,[102] forming swamps and lagoons about their
obstructed outlets.[103] Enops tended "his herds near the banks
of the Satnioïs," where this stream watered another meadow for
the horse-taming Trojans.[104] Farther south on the Ægean
coast of Asia Minor, Homer observes "the wild geese or cranes
or long-necked swans on the Asian meadow about the streams

of Cáyster," [105] where the river meanders through its alluvial plain to the sea.

The Troad and Phrygia Minor to the north, located between the Ægean and the Propontis or Marmara, receive rain-bearing winds from both seas. Especially the Pontic clouds condense on the successive tiers of east-and-west ranges, which increase in altitude towards the high crests of Mount Ida and the Mysian Olympos in the south. A rainfall of 32 inches (800 mm.), fertile valley floors of alluvium, rich moist meadows, and swampy lakes formed by the streams dammed by the coastal hill ranges, combined to make admirable conditions for tillage and stock-raising here in ancient times as today.[106] Therefore Abydos and Percote on the Hellespontine shore had "pastures for swift mares" and for oxen; [107] and the Adrasteia plain, through which the Granikos flowed, was a natural pastureland praised by Homer. Near by "many-fountained Ida," [108] exposing a long flank to the Pontic winds and rains, was wont to echo with "the lowing of herds and the bleating of sheep." [109] Farther east Asia Minor presents a continuous front of high forested mountains to the Pontic winds; but wherever a longitudinal trough like the Salon valley of northern Bithynia provided a level surface, or a river like the Iris or Phasis had built a small delta on this steep coast, and supplied nature's irrigation during the summer drought,[110] there we hear of highly valued pastures for cattle and horses, of cows famous for their milk,[111] and of choice cheeses which entered the markets of the Mediterranean world.[112] So rare were good pastures that they were never overlooked by the ancients, even though small in area. Significant is the fact that these ancient meadows are districts of cattle production today. Such is the ancient Salon or modern Boli valley of Bithynia.[113]

STOCK-RAISING IN THRACE AND GREECE—Thrace was famous for its horses from Homeric times. The great Quaternary plain of eastern Thrace was probably too dry in the summer, as it is today, to provide proper pasturage for horses. However, the long southern littoral from Lake Stentoris and the mouth of the Hebrus River (Maritza) west to the Axius (Vardar) was a succession of lakes, lagoons, marshes, and brackish pools, and of alluvial lowlands, flooded at intervals by the mountain streams draining from the lofty Rhodope highlands,[114] and possessing every geographical feature for wet pastures. Diomedes, whose horses figured in the Trojan War and in the adventures of Hercules, ruled over the plain of Lake Bistonis with its city of Abdera, a region lying so low that Hercules was able to flood it by cutting a canal to the sea.[115] The horses of the Thracian Rheseus were the finest, swiftest and whitest ever seen by Trojan or Greek. Two herds of chestnut horses formed part of the dowry of a daughter of King Cotys of Thrace in the 4th century B.C.[116] Cavalry constituted an important feature of the Thracian army from the time of the Peloponnesian War down to that of the Roman Cæsars, and made it a valuable ally in war.[117] In Strabo's time the Thracian cavalry numbered 15,000, and the infantry 20,000, an unusual proportion.[118] Thracian horses were early imported into Italy and Sicily, and the peculiar markings of the Thracian breed were well known.[119] White horses were brought to Rome for sacrifices and also to carry the victorious consuls in the public triumphs. After the Macedonian conquest, Thracian cavalry was incorporated in the mounted forces of Philip the Great, which were already strong. For Macedon has ample meadows in the broad alluvial plain of the Axius River, and excellent summer pastures in the northern mountains, whence came the Pæonian cavalry. Moreover, Philip imported 20,000 fine mares (*Nobilium equarum*) from the lower Danube Plains to improve his stock and probably introduced Thracian, Thessalian and Epirote strains for the same purpose.[120]

In Greece proper only a few localities afforded suitable pastures for horses and cattle, especially in the more arid eastern part of the peninsula, which was cut off by mountain ranges from the rain-bearing winds from the west. In this populous and progressive eastern flank, cattle or their products were imported from the steppes of far-away Scythia, Africa and from Macedonia [121] to supply the local demand. The best and largest pastures were to be found in the broad lacustrine basin of Thessaly, which was alternately flooded and drained by the Peneus River system. Here the invading Persians found the best horses of Greece, but inferior to the Persian steed. This region repeatedly furnished cavalry for Athens from the days

of Pisistratus,[122] and provided horsemen for Alexander's army
in his conquest of Asia. In all Greek wars its alliance was
sought because of its mounted troops. The Thessalian horse
was a superior animal, the product of good feeding, of broad
artificial selection made possible by large numbers, and of free
movement over wide plains, whether he was grazing, training
for races, or practising in cavalry manœuvers. Therefore
Sophocles makes Orestes enter the Pythian Games with a span
of Thessalian steeds. A Thessalian stud-farm at Pharsalus,
on the southern margin of the lacustrine basin, bred Alexander's famous horse Bucephalus.[123] Aristotle in his Politics attributed the strong oligarchy which always ruled Thessaly to
the adaptation of the country to horse-breeding, and the consequent concentration of cavalry forces in the hands of rich
landowners. Homer praises "the oxen, horses and harvests of
deep-soiled Phthia" [124] whose pastures bred the steeds of Achilles. This region comprised the shelving coast of the Pegasæ
Gulf and the alluvial valley of the Sperchius River, whose broad
flats along the sea, always soaked and always growing by annual accretions of silt out into the Malic Gulf, must have furnished excellent wet meadows for the ancient war-lord as for the
peasant of today. Across these fens of the Sperchius the modern carriage road runs for five miles on the top of a dyke,
pierced at intervals to let the distributaries flow out to the sea,
whose low shoreline is faintly visible several miles to the east.
The growth of the half-fluid soil went on in Homeric times as
today and provided perennial meadows. The scene embossed on
the shield of Achilles may have been taken from his home country. It depicted a herd of kine: "lowing they hurried from the
byre to pasture beside a murmuring river, beside the waving
reeds," invariable marks of swamp vegetation.[125]

Aside from the Sperchius valley plain, which was the borderland of ancient Thessaly, Hellas proper could show only one
region of excellent pasturage, and that was the moist lacustrine
basin of Bœotia. Its early preëminence in horse breeding was
based upon the rich pastures of "grassy Haliartus" on the
reed-grown margin of Lake Copais,[126] and "Graia and Mycales-
sos with their wide meadows" in the valley of the River Asopus.[127] Therefore Bœotia was chief "of all the lands far-famed

for goodly steeds." [128]   This reputation, voiced by Sophocles, is repeated three centuries later by Dicæarchus.[129]   And Thucydides states that only Bœotia, Phocis and Locris furnished the cavalry of the Spartan allied forces during the Peloponnesian War.[130]   Phocis comprised the northern portion of the fairly broad valley of the Cephissus River, which continues southward as part of the Bœotian plain.   It is rather a significant coincidence that the author, in a recent motor trip through Greece, met groups of horses only in Bœotia, the Cephissus valley of Phocis, and in Thessaly.   The cavalry of Locris must have depended upon the small but fertile coastal plain of Opous along the Eubœan Sound.   The location of these cavalry states was ominous for Greece.   At the battle of Platæa, as described by Herodotus, the allied Hellenic states had no mounted troops, because the invading Persians conquered or conciliated all the "horse" country to the north through which they marched.[131]   Attica, as we have seen, had no good pasture land and very slowly developed a limited force of cavalry.   The conquest of the lower Asopus plain from Bœotia and the acquisition of the island of Eubœa with its good pastures, once famous for their horses and cattle,[132] may have helped Athens maintain its thousand horsemen.

The Peloponnesos contained little territory suited to cavalry movements.   This fact partly explains the scarcity of mounted troops in the peninsula, whose wars were largely border conflicts along the high mountain boundaries of the several states. Such were Sparta's wars with Messenia, Argolis and Arcadia. "Argos pasture land of horses," which comprised the small silted plain at the head of the Argolic Gulf, and the valleys of Homeric Sparta, which included both Laconia and Messenia, were famous for their meadows and their equine stock.[133]   The boy Telemachus, coming from the rugged isle of Ithaca, admired Sparta's "open plains where clover is abundant, marsh-grass and wheat and corn and white-eared barley," [134] and he received from King Menelaus a pair of horses as a gift.   But the valley plain of the Eurotas River contains only about 50 square miles of level land "lying low amid the rifted hills"; it is shut off from the sea by a broad limestone ridge through which the little stream has cut its course to the Laconic Gulf.   This plain had to suffice for both plough and pasture land for the Spartans of the historical period, till they conquered Messenia about 600 B.C.

It is easy to see the growing pressure of population upon the limits of subsistence in this secluded valley, the consequent substitution of hoplites or spearmen for cavalry as the main force of the Spartan army,[135] and the conquest of Messenia as a piece of necessary territorial expansion, all at about the same time. Consider the further fact that the Eurotas valley, lying far south and in the rain-shadow of the lofty Taygetos Mountains, receives 32 inches on only 82 days, endures four months of summer drought and eight arid months. Significant is the fact that the first Messenian war arose from a border quarrel, evidently about some pastures on a high, water-soaked moor (a common Alpine phenomenon), located west of the Taygetos crest, where the Spartans had set up a shrine or temple to Artemis Limnates or Artemis of the Marshes,[136] possibly to sanction their encroachment on Messenian territory. This Artemis was a goddess of fertility, worshipped in swampy or moist alluvial spots made conspicuous by their succulent green herbage in the dry brown landscapes of the Greek summer.[137]

Messenia's extensive lacustrine basins, alluvial plains and her location on the windward side of the Taygetos range insured for her fairly abundant moist meadows. Here were "grassy Hira, divine Pharæ, and Antheia deep in meads" all located on the deltaic flats along the Messenian Gulf.[138] The modern Kalamata, on the site of ancient Pharæ, gets an annual rainfall of 34 inches (841 mm.) on 92 days,[139] and occupies a plain irrigated by the Nedon River, draining from the Gomo peak (4,165 feet or 1,277 meters) of the Taygetos range. Therefore ancient Messenia was famous for its cattle and horses.[140] We even hear of its selling a shipload of horses to Egypt in the third century B.C.[141]

Messenia shared the advantage of an ampler rainfall, coupled however with a long summer drought, with all western Peloponnesos and Hellas north to the Gulf of Ambracia (Arta) and the borders of Epiros where summer showers begin. The broad Tertiary plain of Elis, watered by the Alpheus and Peneus rivers, and dotted with lagoons along its coastal belt, contained the best lowland pastures of the Peloponnesos;[142] it was always more pastoral than agricultural. Here grazed the cattle from the stables of King Augeus and the famous horses of Nestor of Pylos,[143] the king who in a cattle raid on the neighboring city of Elis drove off 50 herds of kine, 50 flocks of sheep, 50 flocks of goats, and 150 mares with their foals.[144] There followed a punitive expedition by mounted Eleians and a battle in which horses and chariots were part of the booty,[145] fought out on the level plain of the Alpheus. When Philip V of Macedon invaded the Peloponnesos in 218 B.C. and violated the sanctity of sacred Elis, he secured an immense amount of cattle.[146] Today, the little town of Gastouni near the mouth of the Peneus, only six miles from the ancient capital city of Elis, is the chief cattle market of the Peloponnesos. Thus closely does the prosaic present link itself with the heroic past. Thus persistently operate the geographic factors in history.

The highland core of the Peloponnesos, the plateau of Arcadia, contained several small lake basins with katavothra drains, subject to flooding after winter rains and spring thaw of the snow on the surrounding mountains. These afforded fine meadows, as the central pool contracted with the continued drought of summer, leaving a girdle of verdure behind. The lake plain of Orchomenus was mostly mere,[147] owing to the drainage from the surrounding heights; on the plain of Pheneus, according to tradition, Odysseus kept his mares on pasture.[148] All Arcadia became famous for its sheep, asses, horses and cattle.[149] Rugged mountain relief excluded horses and cattle from the small islands of Greece, but admitted sheep, goats and swine, where the forest yielded mast. Telemachus describes his native Ithaca as having "no open runs, no meadows, a land for goats and pleasanter than grazing country. Not one of the islands is a place to drive a horse, none has good meadows of all that rest upon the sea."[150] Therefore Odysseus pastured his goats and some of his swine on the home island, but sent his twelve herds of cattle and his flocks of sheep to pasture on the moist alluvial lowlands of Acarnania and Ætolia on the opposite mainland.[151] An Ithacan nobleman kept a stud-farm of twelve mares across the strait in Elis, where he bred mules.[152]

Farther north on this western front of Greece lay Epiros,

with high lake plains tucked away between its wooded mountain slopes, receiving 40 inches of rain (1,000 mm.) or more annually and getting thunder storms till mid-summer. Though located on the sunset side of Greece, far from the morning foci of Hellenic culture, the fame of its pastures and herds penetrated eastward, because it contained the Pelasgian sanctuary of Dodona. So Hesiod sang: "There is a land Ellopia with much glebe and rich meadows, abounding in flocks and shambling kine. There dwell men who have many sheep and many oxen. . . . And there upon its border is built a city Dodona." [153] The sanctuary lay on the southern margin of the katavothra pool, Lake Ioanina, which in ancient as in modern times was bordered by wet meadows, while the whole valley of Ioanina, 20 by 7 miles in extent, was one immense plain of pasture,[154] free from the encroachments of a too dense population. The cattle of Epiros were the finest of Greece, better than those of Italy, and therefore they were exported to improve the strains on Roman farms.[155] Aristotle states that "Epiros raised very large cows which gave one and one-half amphora from each pair of teats or 6 gallons and 7 pints of milk daily"; and that these cows, which required much pasture, could be changed to fresh grazing every season of the year, so abundant and excellent was the meadow land.[156] The oxen too were very large. Epiros pastured also the King's herds of huge Pyrrhic cattle which could not live, or more probably deteriorated, when removed to other countries.[157] Today the pasture lands of Epiros, still excellent and much extended by deforestation, support a considerable cattle and horse-raising industry.[158]

Goats and sheep were regular adjuncts of ancient Greek farms like the homestead of Odysseus; but in summer they went to "the high meadows of the pasturing flocks." [159] The shepherd in Sophocles' *Œdipus Rex*, when asked where he dwelt, replied: "Now 'twas Kithæron, now on neighboring heights." And again: "He needs must know when on Kithæron's fields, he with a double flock and I with one, I was his neighbor during three half-years, from spring until Arcturus rose; and I in winter to my own fold drove down my flocks, and he to those of Laios" (in Thebes).[160] These mountain pastures were inter-state boundary zones, where shepherds and flocks from the two sides mingled every season. Here it was easy to spirit away a child across the border to an asylum in some shepherd's cot beyond, as was done with the infant Œdipus, rather than incur the moral responsibility of exposing him to the wolves.

The breeds of sheep and goats were selected for the improvement of the wool and hair. Cattle rearing too was conducted in Greece on scientific principles. Choice animals were reserved for breeding purposes, and the strain was improved by the importation of superior foreign kinds.[161] Aristotle states that the oxen and sheep of Greece were smaller than those of Egypt, though he seems to make an exception of the Epirote cattle.[162] In this connection, the fact is significant that Xerxes found the Thessalian horses, which were the best of all Greece, distinctly inferior to the Persian animals.[163] This may mean that horse-raising in Greece suffered from small numbers and excessive inbreeding, which frequently results in dwarfing; while the stud-farms of Babylonia comprised enormous numbers of animals. The cob type of horse depicted in the frieze of the Parthenon may be the far-off artistic effect of a geographic cause.

STOCK-RAISING IN ITALY—The location of Italy farther west and north than the lands of the Eastern Mediterranean Basin insured the peninsula a heavier rainfall and therefore better grazing.[164] Its relatively extensive coastal lowlands and river plains afforded larger areas for wet meadows than were found farther east, except in Egypt. The Alps, with their frequent summer showers and big forests of deciduous trees, furnished excellent highland pastures in the hot season. The Apennines, owing to their ample precipitation (35 to 50 inches), their long western slope facing the rain-bearing winds, and the top dressing of volcanic soil covering much of their valley floors, yielded fair or even excellent grazing for horses and cattle during the summer droughts, and thus supplemented the winter pastures on the plains. Geographic conditions in Italy therefore favored the development in ancient times of organized pastoral husbandry on a big scale, many phases of which have persisted to the present, despite the deterioration of the Apennine pastures in consequence of forest denudation. Before the Punic Wars, as now, flocks and herds were driven every spring from the plains of Apulia to the public grazing grounds in the mountains

of Samnium;[165] and in autumn they descended again to the lowlands, to feed upon the meadows, reviving with the fall rains,
or upon the stubble of the grain fields. In these seasonal migrations through the centuries they beat out broad, grassy
tracks, the ancient *calles publicæ,* which survive in the modern
tratturi used today by the nomad herders.

During the last two centuries of the Roman Republic, stock-
raising on big mountain estates (*saltus*), varying in size from
800 to many thousand *jugera* (500 acres up) began greatly
to overshadow tillage.[166] The term *saltus* came to be applied
indifferently to a highland pasture and a mountain range or
massif,[167] like the *Saltus Ciminius* of Etruria and the *Saltus
Vescinus* on the border between Latium and Campania. The
animals raised were chiefly sheep, goats, and swine; in a less
degree cattle, horses, mules, and asses, for whom suitable pasturage was in general less abundant.[168] However, the brushwood and leafage of the hill pastures, where groves of deciduous
trees abounded, made a welcome and wholesome change to horses
and cattle from the grass of the lowlands, and constituted one
advantage of the transfer from the winter grazing land.[169] Another factor in the improvement may have been the escape from
the mosquitoes and flies of the plains.

Cattle, horses, and mules of inferior breeds were raised in
the Ligurian Apennines, where a rainfall of 50 inches (1,250
mm.) insured unfailing pastures, and were sold in Genoa whence
they were exported to Rome.[170] In the extreme south of Italy,
the crystalline *massif* of the Sila Mountain stretching through
the length of Bruttium rises high enough (Sila Forest 6,330
feet and Aspromonte 6,420 feet) to get a rainfall rivalling that
of the Alpine piedmont (43.3 inches at Cosenza).[171] It was
therefore covered with forests and pastures, frequented by
flocks and herds. "On mighty Sila feeds the lovely heifer,"
sang Vergil.[172] The cheese of the region was famous, "recalling
by its taste the fragrant herbs on which the cattle browsed." [173]
On the eastern slope of Sila Forest, in the valley of the Neæthus
(modern Neto), Theocritus staged the meeting of neatherd
and rustic in his fourth idyl. Today thousands of horses,
cattle and sheep crop the summer herbage of the Sila pastures,[174] tended by rougher herdsmen than those who piped to

the Greek Theocritus. Sicily presented a happy combination of upland pastures and moist, lowland meadows,[175] which made it a home of horse-breeders and cattlemen from early times. Horses and mules from Syracuse, Ætna, Acragas and Kamarina took prizes in the Sacred Games of Greece from 494 B.C.,[176] and cavalry forces were always at hand for the Tyrants of Syracuse.[177] The Roman conquest saw the whole interior of Sicily converted into vast grazing estates. The official plunder of the Proconsul Verres comprised "herds of the noblest mares." [178]

Italy had numerous wet pastures unreclaimed or unreclaimable for tillage, like the Fenland of England and the polders of Holland. The depressed area of northern Apulia, located between the Apennines and Monte Gargano, was a lake-strewn lowland of immature drainage underlain by hard limestone, which was impenetrable to the roots of trees.[179] Useless for orchard or vineyards, and flooded by the Apennine torrents from October to June, it served well for pasture land.[180] Greek legend associated the region with Diomedes, the great horse-fancier, and told of his attempts to control the inundations by cutting a canal through the lowland to the sea. The founding here of Argos Hippium or "horse-breeding Argos,"[181] which survived as the Roman town of Arpi, coupled with the legend of Diomedes, points to marsh pastures, which Greek colonists exploited and drained by ditches during the winter floods. Here arose the Apulian breed of horses,[182] which was famous among the Romans.

Similar geographic causes and economic effects existed in the extensive marshes about the head of the Adriatic, which in summer afforded wide stretches of wet meadows. There the flood season was protracted long after the winter rains, owing to the slow melting of the Alpine snows; and there in a region of marshes, lagoons, braided streams, meandering rivers and deltaic distributaries, lived the ancient Veneti, from remote times famous for their horses. They let their equine herds pasture at large on the wet meadows, but branded each animal with its owner's name. Certain fine breeds of horses became established, and acquired a reputation even in Greece. The grazing was so excellent, that Dionysius, Tyrant of Syracuse, (d. 367 B.C.)

kept his stud of race horses on these Venetian plains.[183] Similar conditions obtained over much of the well watered Po valley, where abundant irrigating streams, high water table, and occasional summer showers combined to keep the meadows green. There, on his father's Mantuan farm, Vergil knew the "wide pastures by the brimming river, where moss abounds and green herbage lines the banks"; and where brood mares and cows found the best grazing. There was the grass, the willow leaves, the marsh sedge and the standing grain which made the best fodder for growing oxen.[184] Countless irrigation streams, fed by Alpine rivers, kept the lush grass green throughout the hot season, and maintained the herds of cattle and the famous cheese industry of antiquity, much as they do today.

Wet meadows on a smaller scale were found in many longitudinal valleys of the Apennines, where the drainage was imperfect. Horace, on his frequent journeys to his Sabine farm in the Anio valley, must have often seen these "grassy meads with winding streams and willows of the marsh."[185] He had one on his own estate which needed diking, because the winter or spring floods were sometimes excessive.[186] The Sabine country comprised also the Reate district with its excellent pastures, where Varro located his stud-farm and where the famous Rosea breed of horses originated.[187] It lay in an old lake basin where converging streams debouched upon the intermontane plain. Constant deposition of travertine by the River Velinus, whose waters were impregnated with carbonate of lime, tended to dam the outflow, kept the valley floor too wet for tillage, and finally flooded the Rosea pastures.[188] This necessitated a series of drainage canals, constructed through the centuries from 271 B.C., to reclaim the Rosea plain for grazing.[189] In summer, the mules and asses of Reate were driven up into the neighboring mountains,[190] probably to release the Rosea meadows for hay crops. Similar valleys of immature or arrested drainage in Etruria and Umbria, like the lake-strewn course of the Clanis River and swampy course of the lower Arno in Etruria, must have provided the excellent meadows which, supplemented by the Apennine pastures, explain the good cattle and sheep, and the famous cheese of these districts.

The out-pastures of the mountains and marshes were abundantly supplemented by hay, clover, alfalfa and other fodder crops, maintained by irrigation through the summer for the winter keep of the stock, especially the horses and work animals. Meadows were located preferably in rich valley or plain land. The soil, whether light and loose or stiff and heavy, was carefully tilled and regularly manured, especially on hillside fields. Marshy land, if in meadow, was drained by ditches and then irrigated at will.[191] Pliny urged that rain water from public highways should be diverted to the meadows, evidently because it contained soluble manure from the droppings of passing animals. After ploughing, the meadow was sown with seed which had fallen in the hay loft or manger because such seed was ripe; then it was harrowed. The hay field was not watered the first year, probably to stimulate deep rooting; nor was it grazed by cattle till after the second hay harvest, lest the blade should be bruised or torn up by the roots. When well established, hay and clover fields were irrigated about May eighth, mowed in early June, then irrigated, mowed and irrigated again in August or September. The grass grew again during the mild and rainy autumn and afforded admirable grazing for the flocks and herds on their return from the mountain pastures.[192]

If meadows gave signs of deterioration after several years of cropping, they were manured and weeded.[193] This operation was especially important for non-irrigated meadows, and was performed shortly before the vernal equinox when the weeds were sprouting in the warm, moist soil.[194] But if hay needed more drastic measures, it was renovated by sowing on it a crop of beans or rape or millet, followed the next year by wheat, and then it was left the third year for hay again, when cultivation had eradicated the weeds. Most hay fields yielded three crops a year. But in the Interamna district of Umbria the farmers got four hay harvests annually and that without irrigation,[195] because Interamna lay, as its name indicates, in a flood plain between two rivers, at the confluence of the Nar and a small tributary, which were fed by the spring and autumn rains of the Central Apennines.

The various legumes raised in Italy for fodder were occasionally supplemented by green barley [196] and by rape, the green tops of which were choice feed for cattle.[197] The roots were evidently reserved for human use, though they attained enormous size and in the Po valley yielded large harvests. The importance of legumes is indicated by the explicit directions given by Latin writers for their cultivation. Some legumes gave better provender for some animals, others for others, according to the discriminating practice of the ancients.[198] But for the Roman farmer the Medic clover was the preëminent fodder crop. It found in the prevailing limestone soils of Italy its chief requirement in the way of plant food. Its entire cultivation by the ancients, both as to selection and preparation of the soil, work, weeding, planting, irrigation and harvesting tallies with the practice of American farmers today. In Cæsar's Italy as in modern California, the alfalfa field had to be well manured, well watered but well drained. It yielded always four crops annually, sometimes six, and was harvested when it bloomed. One planting lasted ten years or more. The deep roots of the Medic clover protected it against the weeding hook and the plough when these were necessary to eradicate the weeds. Along with cytisus, Medic clover held "the very foremost place among the fodders." [199]

Further evidence of how far the Roman farmers had advanced in the art of feeding cattle is found in their mixed forage crops. These consisted of spelt or barley mingled with vetch and sown very thick; or of several kinds of fodder planted together and cut green before the frost; or of various legumes, to which some Greek oats were occasionally added, all sown together.[200] Such crops reproduced the mixed feed of the natural pasture and economized not only labor but the plant nutriment in the soil.

Even with this careful provision for fodder, animals were most economically fed. Cato recommended that the green leaves of elm, poplar, fig and oak trees, so long as they were available, should be fed to cattle and sheep, if hay were scarce; [201] that the straw of all grains, also of beans, vetch and lupines should be stacked in the barn for fodder, and grape husks preserved in jars for the same purpose; that the mast gathered in the forests be soaked in water and fed to the oxen.[202] Chaff also, preferably that of millet or barley, was used as feed.[203] Moreover the allowance of oxen for tillage land was small, only one yoke for every 80 or 100 *jugera*,[204] despite the numerous ploughings both of fallow and crop fields. Cattle-raising was an important branch of stock-farming in Italy, because cows or oxen yielded various products (meat, milk, hides and horns) and served as the chief work animals. Horses and mules were extensively used as draft animals, more than in Greece and Asia Minor; because land travel was better developed in Italy, luxury had reached a higher point,[205] and the supply of animals was greater, owing to more abundant pasturage. Nevertheless, the effect of the summer drought in restricting the supply of horses remained apparent. From 200 to 50 B.C. the export of horses from Italy was forbidden by law. Certain Gallic envoys from Istria and the neighboring Alps in 170 B.C. received special permits to export ten horses each,[206]—proof of the rigid control. The importance of the unfailing northern pastures for horse-raising is evidenced by a fact cited by Mommsen, namely, that in the Imperial Roman army the cavalry was Celtic, recruited preëminently from Trans-Alpine Gaul, with Gallic men, whose manœuvers and technical terms were Celtic.[207]

Swine production, which in the ancient Mediterranean world depended chiefly on mast-yielding forests, flourished in Italy, because climatic conditions permitted beech, oak and chestnut groves in nearly all parts of the peninsula. Pigs were raised on every landed estate.[208] They were fed mainly on the mast of the home woodland or the mountain forests,[209] and then fattened on barley and other grains to give the meat various flavors.[210] Beechnut bacon was a commonplace in Rome. No other country slaughtered so many pigs, for sacrifices, family use and the army commissary, according to Polybius. The chief supplies in his time (150 B.C.) came from the Po valley, whose northern location and encircling mountains ensured the late spring and early summer rains necessary to maintain abundant mast forests.[211] With the expansion of Roman power into Farther Gaul and the growing demand of the populace for imported food supplies, this well forested province began shipping salt pork not only to Rome but to other parts of Italy. That from the Sequanian country at the head of the Saóne

valley had a great reputation.[212]   The wooded slopes of the
Pyrenees and rainy Cantabrian Mountains of northern Spain
also supported herds of swine, which furnished the basis for a
lucrative native export trade in hams.[213]

Sheep-raising was widely distributed in ancient Italy, and
it was semi-nomadic in its character, the flocks vibrating between the plains in winter and the Alps and Apennines in summer.   The sheep producing the choicest wool, both as to softness, fineness and natural colors (white, black and tan), grazed
on the leeward slopes of the Alps and Apennines, where the
pastures were relatively dry.   They were found in the south
in ancient Apulia about Luceria and Canusium, in Calabria
about Tarentum and Brundusium, in eastern Lucania and the
nearby valleys of the Sybaris and Crathis.[214]   Their superiority
in this district may be attributed in part to the fact that they
belonged to the fine Greek breeds imported by the original
colonists of Magna Græcia.[215]   In northern Italy also the finest
fleeces came from the rain-shadow sides of the Apennines and
Alps; from the *Campi Macri* in the northern Apennines between
Parma and Mutina, whose fine toga wool ranked with that of
Tarentum; [216] from western Liguria at the eastern foot of the
Alps about Pollentia; and from the Venetian plain about
Altinum, whose product ranked next to that of Apulia and
Parma.[217]   All the Po valley pastures produced coarse wool
and goats' hair suitable for weaving rough cloth for mantles
and slaves' dress.   The finer yields were evidently a late de-
velopment,[218] synchronous with the advance of civilization and
movement of population into this colonial frontier district of
Roman Italy.   Significantly enough, all these regions of fine
wool production have maintained their leadership into the
present.[219]

THE IMPROVEMENT OF BREEDS—At a time when the rainy
lands of middle and northern Europe knew only uncontrolled
stock-raising on the open range, Italy, like Greece, secured the
largest financial returns from its relatively limited pastures
by improving its stock through artificial selection.[220]   It laid
great emphasis upon the choice of the best strains for breeding purposes.   Horned cattle were imported from the Po valley
and Epiros to improve the local breeds,[221] especially large cows

from the Pyrrhic herds, which had a great reputation in Italy.[222] The Italian cattle, which were bred primarily for work animals, were strong but gave little milk. Hence it became usual to import good milk cows from the Alpine regions.[223] Significantly enough, the same thing is done today on a big scale to exploit the wet meadows along the Po River, which are devoted to dairy cattle. Swiss cows are imported since they yield more milk when fed on these irrigated pastures for ten months than do the native Italian kine,—700 as opposed to 550 gallons. This large milk production explains the modern export trade in Parmesan, Gorganzola and Stracchino cheese which emanates from this region.[224] In ancient times the Apennines of Umbria, Etruria and Liguria were the chief districts of cheese production,[225] but the Alpine cheese of Narbonensian Gaul was the best, according to Martial.[226]

But the improvement of stock was not restricted to cattle. Fine mares of racing blood were imported from Thrace, Thessaly and Epiros,[227] asses for breeding purposes from Arcadia,[228] fine sheep from Attica and other parts of Greece,[229] and rams for covering from the Guadalquivir valley of Spain.

Narbonensian Gaul formed a connecting link geographically and economically between Alpine Italy and Pyrenean Spain, owing to location, relief and climate. The valley plain and deltaic flats of the Rhone furnished moist pastures [230] till July, just as they do today,[231] while the neighboring Alps and Cevennes Plateau furnished summer grazing. The abundance of cattle about Massilia was reflected in the low price paid for sacrificial oxen and young bullocks in the fourth century B.C. at the local Carthaginian temple, whose tariff of charges has been preserved; [232] and it explains the ancient cheese export from Nemausus (Nîmes) and the district of the Gabali,[233] famous for its cheese today.

STOCK-RAISING IN SPAIN AND MEDITERRANEAN AFRICA—In the rainy mountains of northern Spain, swine raising and the pork-packing industry were supplemented in the rugged provinces of Asturia and Gallacia by the breeding of sumpter mules, which answered the local need of transportation and were also exported to Rome.[234] On the steppes of the semi-arid Iberian plateau, large herds of wild horses pastured at

large. They were fine swift animals, and explain the superiority of the native Iberian cavalry.[235] Hannibal had large numbers of African horses in Spain in 219 B.C., and he invaded
Italy with 12,000 cavalry, chiefly Numidian but partly Spanish.
In time, the Spanish breeds were greatly improved, because
Spanish race horses competed in the Roman Circus with Cap-
padocian, Parthian and Armenian steeds in the first century
of the Empire. Martial praises the horse racing at Bilbilis,
on the northeastern rim of the Meseta.

The economy of the highland tribes was primitive, based
chiefly on a half-migratory agriculture and goat-herding,
which was suited to their dry grasslands. Cattle-raising as
an adjunct of sedentary tillage meets us only in Bætica in the
tidewater plains of southwestern Spain, where Phœnician colonists early established themselves. There, in a region of scant
rainfall (12 to 15 inches), the belt of littoral between the
multiple mouths of the Guadalquivir and the Guadiana afforded
natural meadows, which were watered both by meandering distributaries and flood tides. Those near Cadiz seem to have
been communal pastures, probably owned by the city. The
cattle grazing there were fat and yielded rich milk, but they
were occasionally overwhelmed by the incoming tides.[236] The
dry pastures of the Guadalquivir valley supported excellent
sheep, whose wool was famous in the Roman world for its
softness and color, especially the reddish-tan wool of the
Corduba (Cordova) district.[237] The folded mountain ranges
which enclose this valley on the south received enough rain
for extensive forests of oak and other trees. These apparently
supported herds of swine, for Strabo tells us that Mellaria
(modern Tarifa) produced salted provisions and exported them
to Tingis (Tangier) in Mauretania.[238] These salted provisions undoubtedly comprised pork products, though they may
have included also salt fish.[239] On the northwest side of the
Iberian Peninsula, where exposure to the Atlantic winds insured unfailing rains, there was ample pasturage all year
round, both in the plains of the Tagus and Duoro and on the
neighboring highlands. This is indicated by the abundance
and cheapness of oxen, calves, pigs and sheep in ancient Lusi-

tania (Portugal),[240] where the grazing conditions resembled those of northern Italy.

North Africa reproduces the climatic conditions of interior Spain and the Guadalquivir valley, with their attendant effects upon stock-raising. In the territory of ancient Carthage, cattle and horses were associated with tillage in the irrigable plains near the coast. There in the moist alluvial valley of the Bagradas (Majerda) River the invading army of the Sicilian Agathocles (4th Century B.C.) saw cows, oxen and sheep grazing in the irrigated meadows, while "in the nearby marshes there were vast numbers of brood-mares." [241] The interior grasslands, lying in the rain-shadow of the Atlas ranges, were pastured by big herds of horses and cattle belonging to the nomads of Numidia and Mauretania.[242] These supplied the Numidian cavalry which formed an important part of Hannibal's forces in the Second Punic War, and constituted the major part of Massinissa's army, Scipio's ally, in the Roman campaign in Africa.[243]

Farther east, on the Cyrenaican coast of Africa, the plateau of Barca (elevation 2,000 feet or 610 metres) was high enough to condense winter rains in this otherwise arid belt, and therefore to support good but ephemeral pastures for horses and cattle back to the margin of the desert.[244] Springs issuing from the escarpment and base of the limestone highland irrigated fields and hay meadows. Hence the Greek colony of Cyrenaica enjoyed a great reputation for horse breeding in antiquity.[245] Its kings frequently won the chariot races in the Greek Games and became the theme of many a Pindaric ode.[246] The colonists doubtless purchased horses from the neighboring nomads, whose route to the coast ran right past the city of Cyrene,[247] and then improved the animals by good feeding and training.

Horses and cattle, sheep and goats, formed the chief wealth of the nomads who hung on the semi-arid outskirts of the Mediterranean lands, and ranged widely in search of grass. Their animals drifted into the markets and stockfarms of the sedentary Mediterranean peoples in various ways,—by purchase at border trading-post or town, by capture during nomadic invasions or in the subsequent punitive expedition of the farmer nations, or by the employment of nomad cavalry as allies or mercenaries in war. This was especially the case with horses and cattle whose importation when full-grown worked an economic saving in countries of limited pasturage. As a corollary, this saving was usually greater in eastern Mediterranean lands than in western.

The sources from which such imports were drawn were not limited to the semi-arid regions to the south and east of the Mediterranean; they included the European steppes bordering the Black Sea and the well watered districts north of the Alpine barrier. Cattle, hides and wool were regularly purchased by the ancient Greek traders from the Scythians of the Euxine coast,[248] and they were also imported into Italy from the upper Danubian plains by the passes of the Julian Alps and Carso Plateau.[249] Marine transportation of live animals presented no problem, as has been shown.

Thus the economic history of the Mediterranean lands can never ignore the factors of climate, relief, and the uniting force of the *Mare Internum*.

336 PASTURES AND STOCK-RAISING

AUTHORITIES—CHAPTER XII

1. Xenophon, *Œconomicus*, XVII, 10.
2. Theophrastus; *Historia Plantarum*, Bk. IV, Chap. VIII, 13. Aristotle, *De Animalibus*, VII, Chap. 23, 8. Neumann and Partsch, *Physikalische Geographie Griechenlands*, p. 404. Breslau, 1885.
3. Theophrastus, *Hist. Plant.*, VII, Chap. VIII, 3.
4. Callimachus, *Hymn to Artemis*, 164-166.
5. Theophrastus, *Hist. Plant.*, VII, Chap. VIII, 3; VII, Chap. XIII, 5.
6. Neumann and Partsch, *op. cit.*, p. 405.
7. Hesiod, *Works and Days*, 558-562.
8. Pliny, *Historia Naturalis*, Bk. XVIII, Chap. 30-43. Columella, Bk. II, 7 and 10; Bk. V, 12.
9. Cato, 28.
10. Pliny, XIII, 47. Columella, V, 12.
11. Theophrastus, *Hist. Plant.*, VIII, Chap. VII, 7; IV, Chap. XVI, 5.
12. Pliny, XVIII, 43, quoting Amphilochus.
13. Aristotle, *De Animalibus*, III, 21; VIII, 8.
14. Varro, R. R., I, 42.
15. Vergil, Georgic I, 214-216.
16. Columella, II, 10, 24-28. Pliny, XVIII, 43.
17. Aristotle, *History of Animals*, III, 21; VIII, 8. Strabo, XI, Chap. XIII, 7. Pliny, XVIII, 43.
18. Vergil, Georgic I, 77. Pliny, XVIII. Theophrastus, *Hist. Plant.*, VIII, Chap. 9, 2.
19. Columella, II, 19, 32.
20. Galen, VI, 514.
21. Pliny, Bk. XVIII, 40.
22. Varro, I, 31, 5. Columella, II, 7, 2. Pliny, XVIII, 41, 42. Cato, 54, 60.
23. E. Speck, *Handelsgeschichte des Altertums*, Vol. II, pp. 537-8. Leipzig, 1901. W. S. Davis, *A Day in Old Athens*, p. 180. Boston, 1915.
24. Plutarch, *Solon*, XXI.
25. H. Blümner, *Die Römischen Privataltertümer*, pp. 174-175. Munich, 1911.
26. Cicero, *De Officiis*, II, 25.
27. E. Speck, *op. cit.*, Vol. II, p. 477. Leipzig, 1901. Boeckh, *Staatshaushaltung der Athener*, Vol. I, pp. 127-130. Berlin, 1886.
28. Plutarch, *Pericles*, XII.
29. A. E. Zimmern, *The Greek Commonwealth*, p. 270. Oxford, 1911.
30. II *Samuel*, XV, 1; I *Kings*, I, 5; *Jeremiah*, XVII, 25.
31. J. D. Seymour, *Life in the Homeric Age*, p. 349. New York, 1907.
32. Herodotus, V, 77. Plutarch, *Pericles*, XXIII. Aristotle, *Politics*, VI, 7.
33. Herodotus, VI, 125. E. Curtius, *History of Greece*, Vol. I, p. 369. New York, 1867.
34. Vergil, *Æneid*, VI, 653-655.
35. *Ibid.*, V, 558-570.
36. *Ibid.*, I, 444; III, 539-543; VI, 653-655. *Proverbs*, XXI, 3.
37. A. Boeckh, *op. cit.*, Vol. I, pp. 330-333. Berlin, 1866.
38. *Joshua*, XI, 4, 5. I *Samuel*, XIII, 5. *Judges*, IV, 3; V, 19-22.

39. Herodotus, VI, 102.
40. Herodotus, IX, 13.
41. Erman, *Life in Ancient Egypt*, pp. 436-438. London, 1894.
42. Herodotus, VI, 95; VII, 87, 97.
43. E. Speck, *op. cit.*, Vol. II, p. 483. Leipzig, 1901.
44. Pindar, *Odes*, Pyth., I, II, III, VI; Olym., I, III-VI; Nem., IX.
45. Vergil, *Æneid*, V, 565-567.
46. Diodorus Siculus, Bk. XI, Chap. II.
47. Vergil, *Æneid*, V, 571.
48. H. Blümner, *Gewerbe und Kunst bei Griechen und Römern*, Vol. I, pp. 91-98. Leipzig, 1875.
49. Athenæus, XII, 57.
50. H. Vogelstein, *Landwirthschaft in Palästina zur Zeit der Mischmah*. Berlin, 1894. Columella, II, 10, 17. Theophrastus, *De Causis Plantarum*, IV, V, 4.
51. Pliny, XIX, 9.
52. H. Blümner, *Die Römischen Privataltertümer*, p. 241. Munich, 1911.
53. Herodotus, II, 37. *Genesis*, XLVII, 15-18.
54. Æschylus, *The Suppliants*, 834.
55. *Genesis*, XLI, 2.
56. A. Erman, *Life in Ancient Egypt*, pp. 439-444. London, 1894. Mommsen, *Provinces of the Roman Empire*, Vol. II, p. 284. New York, 1887.
57. Diodorus Siculus, Bk. I, Chap. III, 36.
58. A. Erman, *Life in Ancient Egypt*, pp. 436-438. London, 1894.
59. Otto Keller, *Die Antike Tierwelt*, Vol. I, pp. 219-221. Leipzig, 1909. W. Ridgeway, *Origin and Influence of the Thoroughbred Horse*, pp. 216-223. Cambridge, 1905.
60. Herodotus, III, 113.
61. *Exodus*, XXIX, 22. *Leviticus*, III, 9. Hastings, *Dictionary of the Bible*, article "Sheep." Edinburgh, 1900.
62. *Psalms*, L, 10.
63. *Joel*, I, 18-20.
64. I *Chronicles*, XXVII, 29.
65. General Staff map. No. 2,321, Jaffa sheet. Banse, *Die Turkei*, p. 371. 1919.
66. Hastings, *Dictionary of the Bible*, article "Sharon." *Isaiah*, XXXV, 2; LXV, 10.
67. *Judges*, IV, 3, 13; V, 19-20.
68. *Ezekiel*, XXXIV, 14; *Isaiah*, XXX, 23.
69. E. Banse, *Die Turkei*, pp. 361-362. 1919.
70. Libbey and Hoskins, *The Jordan Valley and Petra*, Vol. I, pp. 107-108. New York, 1905.
71. *Deuteronomy*, III, 7-8.
72. *Numbers*, XXXII, 1-5, 33.
73. Hastings, *Dictionary of the Bible*, article, "Food."
74. *Judges*, I, 19.
75. *Joshua*, XI, 4-7.
76. *Joshua*, XI, 9, 14.
77. *Deuteronomy*, XVII, 16.
78. II *Samuel*, VIII, 3-4.
79. I *Kings*, X, 25-26.

80. II *Kings*, IX, 16, 20; V, 9.
81. I *Kings*, X, 28-29; II *Chronicles*, IX, 28.
82. I *Kings*, IV, 28.
83. I *Kings*, X, 28-29.
84. Maspero, *Struggle of the Nations*, pp. 215-216, 739-740. New York, 1897.
85. Herodotus, III, 90.
86. *Isaiah*, XXXI, 1; *Ezekiel*, XVII, 15.
87. *Ezekiel*, XXVII, 14, 18, 21.
88. Herodotus, V, 49.   Strabo, XI, Chap. XIV, 4, 9.
89. E. Banse, *Die Turkei*, pp. 315, 333-338. 1919.
90. Mommsen, *Provinces of the Roman Empire*, Vol. II, p. 148.
91. Strabo, XVI, Chap. II, 10.
92. Strabo, XII. Chap. II, 7, 9; Chap. III, 8; Chap. VI, 1.
93. Banse, *op. cit.*, pp. 98-114.
94. *Ibid.*, p. 114.
95. *Ibid.*, pp. 98-114.
96. Strabo, XI, Chap. XIII, 8; XII, Chap. II, 7-10. O. Keller, *Die Antike Tierwelt*, Vol. I, p. 225. Leipzig, 1909.
97. A. G. Keller, *Homeric Society*, pp. 20-21, 33-37. New York, 1902.
98. E. Buchholz, *Homerischen Realien*, Vol. II, pp. 137-139. Leipzig, 1881.
99. Vergil, *Æneid*, VI, 674.
100. *Iliad*, XV, 630-632.
101. *Iliad*, II, 775.
102. *Iliad*, XX, 221-222.
103. Strabo, XIII, Chap. I, 31, 36.
104. *Iliad*, III, 250; XIV, 443.
105. *Iliad*, II, 460-461.
106. Banse, *Die Turkei*, pp. 65-71.
107. *Iliad*, II, 819; XV, 546.
108. *Iliad*, XIV, 283.
109. Sophocles, *Niobe*, quoted in Strabo, XII, Chap. VIII, 21. *Iliad*, II, 749; V, 315; XXI, 448.
110. Strabo, XII, Chap. III, 5.
111. Aristotle, *De Animalibus*, III, Chap. XVI, 17.
112. Strabo, XII, Chap. V, 9. Pliny, XI, Chap. 97.
113. Banse, *Die Turkei*, p. 80.
114. Herodotus, VII, 58, 109, 124.
115. *Iliad*, XIV, 225-227. Strabo, *Fragment*, 48.
116. Athenæus, IV, 7.
117. Mommsen, *Provinces of the Roman Empire*, Vol. I, p. 226.
118. Strabo, *Fragment*, 48.
119. Vergil, *Æneid*, V. 585. A regiment of lancers in the modern Italian cavalry is mounted on white horses, which recall the ancient Thracian breed.
120. O. Keller, *Die Antike Tierwelt*, Vol. I, p. 227. Leipzig, 1909.
121. Herodotus, IV, 1-12; VII, 126. Polybius, IV, 38. Blümner, *Greek Home Life*, p. 496. London, 1895.
122. Herodotus, V, 63. Thucydides, I, 102, 107; II, 22.
123. Arrian, *Anabasis of Alexander*, V, Chap. 19, 5.
124. *Iliad*, I, 154.

125. *Iliad,* XVIII, 573-576.
126. Theophrastus, *Historia Plantarum,* IV, Chap. X, 7. *Iliad,* II, 503. Strabo, IX, Chap. II, 18.
127. *Iliad,* IV, 499. Strabo, IX, Chap. II, 10-11.
128. Sophocles, *Œdipus Colonus,* 668.
129. Quoted in J. G. Frazer, *Pausanias,* Introduction, p. XLV. London, 1898.
130. Thucydides, II, 9.
131. Herodotus, IX, 19-29.
132. *Ibid.,* V, 77.
133. *Iliad,* III, 74; IV, 530.
134. *Odyssey,* IV, 602-604.
135. J. B. Bury, *History of Greece,* p. 129. London, 1909.
136. Tacitus, *Annals,* IV, 43. Pausanias, III, Chap. VII, 4; IV, Chap. XXXI, 3.
137. M. P. Nilsson, *Griechischen Feste,* pp. 214-216. Leipzig, 1906.
138. *Iliad,* IV, 291. Strabo, VIII, Chap. IV, 1, 5.
139. A. Philippson, *Europa,* p. 284. Leipzig, 1906. Mariolopoulos, *Le Climat de la Grèce,* Table of rainfall. Paris, 1925.
140. Strabo, VIII, Chap. V, 6.
141. Polybius, V, 37.
142. Theocritus, *Idyls,* XXV.
143. *Iliad,* XXIII, 202-203.
144. *Iliad,* XI, 671-680.
145. *Iliad,* XI, 707-723, 739-747.
146. Polybius, IV, 75.
147. Pausanias, VIII, Chap. XIV, 1-4.
148. *Ibid.,* VIII, Chap. XIV, 5-6.
149. Varro, II, Chap. 1, 14; Chap. IV, 12; Chap. VI, 2; Chap. VIII, 3.
150. *Odyssey,* IV, 604-608; XIII, 241-246.
151. *Odyssey,* XIV, 13, 99-103. Strabo, VIII, Chap. VIII, 1.
152. *Odyssey,* IV, 634-635.
153. Hesiod, *Catalogue of Women and Eoiœ,* 97. Loeb Lib., London, 1914.
154. W. Leake, *Northern Greece,* Vol. IV, pp. 131-135, 168-173, 184-200. London, 1835.
155. Varro, II, Chap. V, 10. Strabo, VII, Chap. VII, 5, 12.
156. Aristotle, *De Animalibus,* III, Chap. XXI.
157. *Ibid.,* VIII, Chap. VII.
158. Philippson, *Thessalien und Epirus,* p. 279. Berlin.
159. Sophocles, *Œdipus Rex,* 1103.
160. *Ibid.,* 1127, 1135-1139.
161. Blümner, *Home Life of the Ancient Greeks,* p. 497. London, 1895.
162. Aristotle, *De Animalibus,* VIII, Chap. XXVII, 5.
163. Herodotus, VII, 196.
164. Strabo, III, Chap. V, 1.
165. Varro, II, Chap. 1, 16; Chap. II, 9.
166. Mommsen, *History of Rome,* Vol. III, p. 74. New York. 1905.
167. Catullus, XXXIV, 11. *Prato* on modern Italian maps means mountain pasture. *Alp* in Switzerland means mountain or summer pasture.
168. E. Speck, *Handelsgeschichte des Altertums,* Vol. II, Part II, p. 240. Leipzig, 1901.

169. Varro, II, Chap. II, 10.
170. Strabo, IV, Chap. VI, 2.
171. W. Deecke, *Italy*, pp. 82, 428-431. London, 1904.
172. Vergil, Georgic III, 219.
173. *Cassiodori Variæ*, II, 9-13.
174. Gael-Fells, *Unter-Italien*, p. 721.
175. Theocritus, Idyls, *passim*. Strabo, VI, Chap. II, 3.
176. Pindar, *Odes*, Olym., I, III-VI; Pyth., I, II, III, VI. Diodorus Siculus, XIII, 82.
177. Thucydides, VI, 20.
178. Strabo, VI, Chap. II, 6, 7. Cicero, *Verres*, II, 7, 20.
179. Deecke, *Italy*, p. 401.
180. Columella, VI, Chap. XXVII, 2. Pliny, VIII, 154.
181. Strabo, VI, Chap. III, 9.
182. Varro, II, Chap. VII, 1. Columella, VI, Chap. XXVII, 2.
183. Strabo, V, Chap. I, 4, 5, 6.
184. Vergil, Georgic III, 143-144; 175-176.
185. Horace, *Odes*, Bk. II, V, 1.
186. Horace, *Epistles*, Bk. II, XIV, 29.
187. Varro, II, Chap. VI, 1-2; Chap. VII, 6; Chap. VIII, 3.
188. Deecke, *Italy*, p. 102.
189. Mommsen, *History of Rome*, Vol. II, p. 85.
190. Varro, II, Chap. VIII, 5.
191. Cato, *De Re Rustica*, VIII, XXVIII, LIII. Columella, II, Chap. 2, 17, 18. Varro, I, 29.
192. Pliny, XVIII, 67. Columella, II, 18. Varro, I, 31, 33. Vergil, Georgic I, 104.
193. Varro, I, 29. Columella, II, XVIII.
194. Cato, *R. R.* 40.
195. Pliny, XVIII, 67.
196. Columella, II, Chap. VII, 10.
197. Pliny, XVIII, 34.
198. *Ibid.*, XVIII, 30-40.
199. Compare Varro, 1, 42. Pliny, XVIII, 43. Columella, II, 11 with Farm Bulletin No. 339, J. M. Westgate, Alfalfa. Washington, 1908.
200. Cato, 54, 60. Columella, II, 7, 2. Varro, I, 31, 5. Pliny, XVIII, 41-42.
201. Cato, *R. R.*, V, XXV. Pliny, XVIII, 74.
202. Cato, *R. R.*, XXX, LIV.
203. Pliny, XVIII, 72.
204. Cato, *R. R.*, X. Varro, I, Chap. XIX, 1.
205. Blümner, *Die Römischen Privataltertümer*, p. 460-465.
206. Livy, XLIII, 5. E. Speck, *Handelsgeschichte des Altertums*, Vol. III, Part II, p. 284.
207. Mommsen, *Provinces of the Roman Empire*, Vol. I, p. 116.
208. Cicero, *De Senectute*, XVI, 56. Columella, XVII, 9.
209. Vergil, Georgic II, 72, 520.
210. Varro, II, Chap. IV, 3. Pliny, VIII, 209.
211. Varro, II, Chap. IV, 10-11. Polybius, II, 15. Strabo, V, Chap. I, 12.
212. Strabo, IV, Chap. I, 2; Chap. III, 2; Chap. IV, 3.
213. Strabo, III, Chap. IV. II.
214. Horace, *Carmina*, Bk. III, XV, 13. Columella, VII, Chap. 11, 3; Chap. IV, 1. Pliny, VIII, 190.

215. Blümner, *Die Römischen Privataltertümer*, p. 237. Munich, 1911.
216. Columella, VII, Chap. II, 3.
217. Martial, XIV, 155.
218. Columella, VII, Chap. II, 3.
219. L. W. Lyde, *Continent of Europe*, p. 94. London, 1913.
220. Vergil, Georgic III, 156-161.
221. Varro, II, Chap. V, 9-10.
222. Pliny, VIII, 176.
223. Columella, VI, Chap. XXIV, 5. Pliny, VIII, 179.
224. G. C. Chisholm, *Commercial Geography*, p. 337. London, 1904.
225. Pliny, XI, 97.
226. Martial, XIII, 30, 31.
227. Vergil, Georgic I, 59; II, 90.
228. Varro, II, Chap. VIII, 3. Columella, VII, 1.
229. Varro, II, Chap. II, 18. Columella, IV, 1.
230. Strabo, IV, Chap. I, 7.
231. E. Reclus, *Europe*, Vol. II, pp. 99-102. New York, 1883. Also personal observation, 1922.
232. A. Boeckh, *Die Staatshaushaltung der Athener*, Vol. I, p. 95.
233. Pliny, XI, 97.
234. E. Speck, *Handelsgeschichte des Altertums*, Vol. III, Part II, p. 283. Leipzig, 1901.
235. Strabo, III, Chap. IV, 15.
236. Strabo, II, Chap. II, 4, 5, 6; Chap. V, 4.
237. Blümner, *Die Römischen Privataltertümer*, p. 240. Munich, 1911.
238. Strabo, III, Chap. I, 8.
239. Strabo, III, Chap. II, 6.
240. Polybius, XXXIV, 8.
241. Diodorus Siculus, XX, Chap. I, 8.
242. Strabo, XVII, Chap. III, 7, 9, 19. Mommsen, *Provinces of the Roman Empire*, Vol. II, p. 368.
243. Polybius, III, Chaps. 35, 65, 68, 71, 72, 113, 114, 117; XV, Chaps. 3, 5, *et passim*.
244. Arrian, *Indica*, Chap. 43.
245. Strabo, XVIII, Chap. III, 2.
246. Pindar, *Odes*, Pyth., IV, V.
247. E. Curtius, *History of Greece*, Vol. I, pp. 486-487. New York, 1867.
248. *Ibid.*, Vol. I, pp. 440-441.
249. Strabo, V, Chap. I, 8.

CHAPTER XIII

GRAIN PRODUCTION AND THE GRAIN TRADE

EARLY IMPORTANCE OF THE MEDITERRANEAN GRAIN TRADE
—The grain trade of the Mediterranean region assumed peculiar importance from very early times. This was due to several causes. Population tended to concentrate on or near the coasts, where maritime conditions encouraged trade and fisheries. There population outgrew the local means of subsistence; for except in a few favored districts, the supply of breadstuffs was inadequate or was subject to fluctuations which made imports necessary. The predominant mountainous relief, thin soils of weathered limestone, the paucity of alluvial valley lands and coastal plains, the practical restriction of grain crops to the winter or rainy season, the elimination of summer grain crops to compensate for scant harvests from the autumn sowing, the unreliability of the fall and spring rains on which the success of the crops depended, especially in the Eastern Basin,—all combined to make the geographical distribution of grainlands a vital factor in early Mediterranean history.

This was especially true of wheat. According to the ancient writers, wheat required rich, humid earth, preferably deep valley alluvium with plenty of ground water, or fertile volcanic soils retentive of moisture, like that about Naples and Syracuse.[1] Wheat was also fastidious as to its rain supply in the period of germination; this made the exact date for fall sowing a constant problem for the ancient Mediterranean farmer, who saw his hopes of harvest blasted if the autumn showers held off a few days after he had "consigned his seed to the unwilling earth," as Vergil expresses it. The same thing is true today; the result of the harvest still depends upon the timely advent and the duration of the fall and spring rains.[2]

Barley was far less exacting both as to soil and weather, and therefore better adapted to Mediterranean conditions. Hence

342

it was widely cultivated, from sea level up to 1,500 meters (4,900 feet). As barley cake and barley broth, it constituted a food staple for the common people, except where the local wheat was ample or the foreign sources of grain accessible to an active merchant marine; for the cost of land carriage was generally prohibitive for this bulky commodity. The price of barley was only one-half or two-thirds that of wheat.[3] This fact reflects the wide distribution of soils and climate suited to barley production, the limited total area of the wheat lands, their uneven distribution which involved heavy marine freight charges to get the product to the best markets, and finally the relatively greater demand for the choicer grain with the advance of civilization. Barley was the earlier and probably the aboriginal cereal in the Mediterranean lands. Wheat is mentioned only three times in the *Iliad* and six times in the *Odyssey* a century or more later; but barley in many varieties is frequently mentioned in Homer.[4] The early worship of Demeter at Eleusis in the only fertile alluvial plain of Attica and at Pyrasus in the old lacustrine basin of Thessaly point to the introduction of wheat culture in those districts.[5] The sacrificial bread in religious ceremonies of Greece and Rome was always barley cake, evidence of the primitive use of barley as opposed to wheat. In the time of Cato, however, the cereals cultivated in Italy were chiefly spelt (*far* or *ador*) and wheat, with some barley and millet.[6]

Oats and rye were unsuited to Mediterranean tillage owing to insufficient moisture, though fodder crops of rye were raised in a few northern localities with ampler rainfall and abundant ground water. Millet and panic, which required both heat and moisture, found ideal conditions in the irrigated fields of the Nile valley and the Cilician lowland,[7] where they were grown extensively. In other parts of the Mediterranean basin they were spring crops; were planted at the vernal equinox, throve with a little irrigation, and matured after a short growing period.[8] Millet and panic, the grain of poor backward peoples, kept well and were used for bread or porridge, to a limited degree in ancient Greece,[9] but more extensively in Cisalpine Gaul, because the water supply and frequent summer showers of the Po valley insured abundant millet crops.[10]

Owing to conditions of climate and relief, and to the geological composition of the soils, wheat lands were sparsely distributed and, with a few exceptions, limited in area. Narrow alluvial valleys or lacustrine plains yielded enough wheat for the local demand where the population was small, as in ancient Bœotia, or was satisfied with a predominant barley diet, as in the retarded parts of Greece and Italy. Regions of large wheat production were widely separated, while population tended to pronounced concentration around the big industrial and commercial cities of the Mediterranean littoral, whose advanced culture was associated with fastidious palates demanding wheat as opposed to the widespread plebeian barley. The grain trade was therefore mainly wheat trade. Rarely were generous wheat lands and dense populations contiguous; but markets for the one and breadstuffs for the other were provided by the navigation early developed in this enclosed sea by a fortunate combination of geographic conditions. The districts of big wheat production were Egypt and the Scythian coastlands, which lay outside the Mediterranean climatic region, the highland of Hauran, lowland Cilicia, Thrace, Sicily, parts of Italy, Spain, Numidia and Carthaginian Africa. These raised a sufficient surplus to maintain an export trade, which fluctuated with crop conditions in other parts of the Mediterranean Basin.

Local production of wheat, however, was everywhere common. It utilized small fertile fields or even mediocre soils, where the seed had to be thinly planted and the harvest was correspondingly meager. This was due to the fact that the chief importing centers got their foreign wheat from overseas, and that the period of navigation, when such imports could be made, was limited to the four and a half months between early May and the fall equinox. Even this short term was sometimes curtailed by the early advent of autumnal storms. Moreover communication along the sea-lanes was liable to interruption in time of war, as when the Spartan fleet during the Peloponnesian War seized the Bœotian grain ships, laden with Thessalian wheat, as they emerged from the port of Pagasæ;[11] or when Sparta in the Peloponnesian War and Philip in the Macedonian wars intercepted the foreign wheat cargoes bound from various points to Athens; or when Agathocles of Syracuse in 310 B.C.

undertook to break up the importation of wheat into the rival state of Carthage from Sicily and Sardinia.[12]

Piracy also was a recurrent threat to the wheat trade. This threat was particularly ominous to small islands like Rhodes and Ægina, which constantly took a hand in the suppression of piracy, not only to save their commerce but to supply the home grain markets. Even Rome suffered. For years before Pompey's dictatorship of the Mediterranean in 67 B.C., the depredations of the pirates on the Roman grain ships caused serious scarcity of provisions in the capital and other parts of Italy which relied upon foreign wheat. Circumstances of weather or war, therefore, which cut off the oversea supply of wheat, encouraged the production of home-grown grains to serve in an emergency. Moreover the cost of sea transportation left the local grain a margin of profit, which probably covered the cost of labor and fertilizer necessary to maintain the productivity of the home fields; for the transport vessels were small, the crews were large owing to the need of oarsmen to propel the ship when the course lay in the teeth of the Etesian winds, the voyages were long and slow, and the interest on borrowed capital for such ventures was high, in Athens often 30 per cent.

In the Eastern Basin of the Mediterranean, about the Levantine Sea, the grain trade originated at a very early date, owing to the scant and uncertain rainfall. The Nile valley raised irrigated crops of wheat and barley, and, by 1500 B.C., probably durra or black millet [13] far beyond the needs of the local population. Therefore Egyptian wheat figured in the caravan trade with Palestine from patriarchal times during the not infrequent years when drought brought famine or scarcity to Judea and Israel. Palestine raised barley on its infertile limestone highlands; but it seems to have drawn its wheat chiefly from the abundant supplies of the Hauran, the ancient Bashan. This is a high plateau (600-700 meters elevation) east of the upper Jordan and the Lake of Galilee. The west winds from the Mediterranean bring it an average of 400 mm. of rain in winter and early spring, just enough for wheat, supplemented by the considerable dews. In antiquity, judging from numerous ruins of aqueducts and reservoirs, the inhabitants conserved the water draining from the lofty Mount Hauran (1,800 meters) on the east, and in dry years distributed it by irrigation canals over the tilled land, as the people do today.[14] The Hauran is an old volcanic district; its soil consists of disintegrated lava, rich in plant food and retentive of moisture, overlying the limestone which elsewhere in Palestine forms the surface rock.[15] The Hauran was therefore the granary of Syria, probably the source of the wheat which in ancient times was exported from Palestine to Tyre [16] and even to Greece.[17]

The terraced slopes of Phœnicia were better adapted to gardens, vineyards and orchards than to field agriculture. Hence the populous commercial cities of the Lebanon coast drew upon the wheat of the Nile valley in their extensive exchanges with Egypt, and probably also from the wide and well watered alluvial plain of lowland Cilicia, where they seem to have maintained colonies at an early date, till dislodged by the expanding Greeks. Cilicia was famous for its grain fields in the time of Xenophon,[18] and today it raises cereals as winter crops on its 1,200 square miles of tilled land.[19] Nearby Cyprus, which in antiquity had a reputation for fertility, produced enough wheat on the alluvial floor of its intermont valley to supply the local demand in the time of Strabo, and occasionally in rainy years for export, for Athens bought Cyprian grain.[20]

The western front of Asia Minor, which took so active a part in ancient Hellenic life, had grain enough and to spare. The old Ægean folded mountains of Mysia and Hellespontine Phrygia, and the crystalline mass of Lydia and northern Caria are all overlaid with late Tertiary deposits and volcanic outflows, which have contributed elements of fertility to the silted floors of the subsidence valleys penetrating inland from the embayed coast.[21] The alluvial plains of the Scamander, Caicus, Hermus, Cayster and Meander rivers all had a reputation for fertility in ancient times [22] which made them constant objects of conquest.[23] They yielded wheat crops which were further aided by a favorable climate.[24] The Ægean winds distribute moderate rains (500 to 650 mm.) for 60 miles inland.[25] Caria south of the Meander valley floor is a mountainous land of bare crystalline rock, poor thin soil, and a pronounced Mediterranean climate with six months of summer drought. The inhabitants of this coast were forced to seek foreign foodstuffs and to follow commercial vocations; [26] hence the maritime trade of Cnidos and Halicarnassos. The mountain land of Lycia is dissected by gorges, which open on the coast into deltaic flats at the head of protected bays. These small alluvial areas and certain limited lacustrine basins of late Tertiary deposits far up in the mountains furnished the rich "wheat-bearing tilth" of Lycia which Homer praised.[27] It was a self-sufficing land, condemned to isolation, which was reflected in the characteristically detached life and peculiar culture of the people.

The populous Hellenic cities, distributed along the Ægean coast and off-shore islands of Asia Minor, absorbed the surplus grain of the inland states, when they could get it, and reached out overseas for more. They occupied narrow coastal strips, small islands and peninsulas with limited area and mountainous relief. Only Naxos, Samos and Lesbos had a little level land which gave them a reputation for fertility.[28] The island cities at times, by a recognized law of anthropogeography,[29] acquired territory on the coast to extend their land base, as did Samos, Rhodes, Chios and Mytilene.[30] Chios secured a foothold on the Mysian littoral by a shady transaction which gave it Atarneus,[31] market for the grain of the fertile Caicus valley. Mytilene levied on this same Caicus wheatland during the Persian War.[32]

The Hellenic cities, however, were often excluded from the neighboring grain markets by wars waged by the alien inland powers of Asia Minor for the conquest of the Ægean littoral. Hence in their food quest, which was always combined with various commercial enterprises, they turned their ships to the wheat fields of Egypt, the Pontic coastlands of Scythia (Russia), the broad Quaternary plain of eastern Thrace, and the volcanic soils of Sicily. On the coasts of these corn countries they planted colonies as export points for the productive hinterland. In some cases the Greek colonists helped cultivate the land; in others, they bought the produce of the native population. They also established settlements at strategic points along the sea routes to the grainlands to maintain the line of communication. These way-stations developed a middleman grain trade, owing to the great length of the sea routes and the short duration of the sailing season.

Looking at the evidence, we find that eleven Hellenic cities of the Asia Minor littoral and offshore islands participated in the trading colony of Naucratis on the Canobic arm of the Nile. These cities were Mytilene, Phocæa, Chios, Clazomenæ, Teos, Samos, Miletos, Halicarnassos, Cnidos, Rhodes and Pharselis, besides the Greek island city of Ægina.[33] The Æolian settlements of this coast, whose land enjoyed an exceptional reputation for fertility,[34] had only one representative in the Egyptian enterprise, namely Mytilene, which shared the island of Lesbos with five other city-states. Mytilene was also interested in the Pontic fields, whence it imported wheat.[35] It occupied and fortified Sigeum at the entrance to the Hellespont as early as 600 B.C.,[36] and later built Ænos near the mouth of the Hebrus River [37] (Maritza), which was the Ægean port for the Thracian wheatlands.

The Ionian Miletos, a populous industrial city, took the lead in colonizing the remote Pontic wheatlands by founding Olbia near the confluence of the Bug and Dnieper rivers, and Panticapæum on the Crimean Bosporus.[38] On the opposite shore of the Strait, Ionian Teos founded Phanagoria. To secure her lines of communication with the Pontic markets, Miletos planted colonies along the Hellespont and Propontis, either alone or assisted by other Ionian towns like Clazomenæ, Phocæa and Erythræ.[39] Clazomenæ regularly imported its wheat,[40] and doubtless the others did also. On the Thracian shore of the Propontis, Samos founded a colony at Perinthos, as export point for Thracian grain. The islands of Rhodes, Chios and Cos were especially active in the Pontic trade, and therefore participated in all Hellenic movements, military or political, to maintain a free passage for merchant ships through the Bosporus and Hellespont.[41] Rhodes turned also to the grain fields of distant Sicily, and founded there the colony of Gela on the margin of a river plain,[42] about 688 B.C. After the Roman conquest of Sicily, Rhodes secured a permit to export annually 150,000 bushels of Sicilian wheat.[43] It is a significant fact, too, that the Ionian cities of Asia Minor, when threatened with destruction by the Persians, discussed a recurring project to abandon their homes and settle in Sardinia.[44] They were undoubtedly attracted by the security of an island location; but their anticipations of a prosperous future in Sardinia were probably based upon mariners' accounts of the rich valley soil and excellent wheat land of the island.

THE LIMITED GRAIN LANDS OF GREECE—Greece was scantily supplied with wheat land, owing to its small area, rugged relief, narrow alluvial valleys, and prevailing infertile soils produced by the weathering of Cretaceous limestones and crystalline rocks. The later Tertiary deposits, whose easily weathered marls made good tillage land, were limited in extent, but they contributed much to the fertility of the lacustrine valleys of Laconia, Messenia and Elis.[45] The rivers of Greece, being mostly torrents, deposited in their deltaic plains chiefly coarse detritus unfit for tillage. Only a few longer streams, with a well developed lowland course, afforded the alluvial flats of deep soil suitable for wheat fields; yet even these strike the modern traveller as pitiably small. The river plain of Argos, praised by Homer, comprises about 30,000 acres, yet it offered the only local wheat land for three cities,—Argos, Mycenæ and Tiryns, besides the seaport of Nauplia. On the other hand, barley, which yielded a fair crop even from poor soil, was widely cultivated, and formed the main diet of the people. Barley bread and barley stew, supplemented by cheese, fruit and wine, constituted the public meals at Sparta in the time of Lycurgus.[46] Wheat bread was a delicacy served as dessert. In early Attica it was eaten only on feast days, till the development of maritime trade made it a commonplace.[47]

Laconia, "lying low among the rifted hills," as Homer described it, was a rugged country suited chiefly for barley culture. Its wheat, which was light in weight and poor in food value,[48] was grown only in the Sparta Basin of the Eurotas, 70 square miles in area, planted also in vines. Messenia, which comprised an upper lacustrine basin of rich loam soil and the broad fertile Macaria plain at the head of the Messenian Gulf, was accessible to the rain-bearing winds from the west and was watered by numerous streams. Its soil, described by a Spartan poet as "good to plant and good to ear," enjoyed a rare reputation for productivity from very early times.[49] This aroused the cupidity of over-crowded Sparta, which in the seventh century B.C. annexed Messenia after a series of wars, and thereby supplied three thousand young Spartans with new land allotments.[50] Yet wheat remained scarce, and even the local barley crops yielded no margin for times of stress. During the Peloponnesian War, Sparta relied on wheat from Sicily. Athens, to check this trade, sent a fleet in 427 B.C. against Syracuse, the chief export point.[51] During the war of Agesilaus of Sparta against Persia, a flotilla of wheat transports bound from Egypt to Laconia was intercepted in 395 B.C. by the Athenian fleet, then an ally of Persia.[52]

Elis doubtless supplied the local demand for grains from its ample coastal plain, which was overlaid by late Tertiary marls,[53] enriched by the alluvial deposits of the Peneus and Alpheus Rivers, and adequately watered by the western rains; for the Elians seem to have taken no part in the grain trade. Achaia, on the other hand, which occupied the northern escarpment of the Arcadian highland and had only fragmentary alluvial flats along the Corinthian Gulf, was early driven to colonize Zakynthos, famous for its fertility,[54] and also the small but rich alluvial plains of Sybaris and Metapontum in Southern Italy, where essentially agricultural states developed.[55] The deltaic lowland of the Cratis River at Sybaris gave the largest yield of wheat *per jugerum* in all Italy,[56] and with the Metapontum fields was perhaps the first part of Italy to raise grain for export.[57] Corinth,[58] Megara[59] and Ægina, owing to small area, poor soil and rugged relief, despite careful methods of tillage, were forced to import grain, though little Ægina raised good crops of barley.[60] Therefore Corinth, expanding early, occupied points in southern Acarnania along the Achelous River, whose alluvial plain, abounding in grain and timber, supplied the most urgent needs of this populous commercial city.[61] Corinth also colonized Potidæa on the Pallene peninsula of southern Macedonia, accessible to a region which produced grain, fruit and timber.[62] Megara secured a colonial foothold near the Sicilian grain fields at Megara Hyblæa, and near those of Thrace by founding Selymbria on the Propontis. She anticipated Miletos in seeking the Pontic wheat markets, for as early as 660 B.C. she insured her access to the Euxine by colonizing Calchedon and Byzantium, the two warders of the Bosporus. The grain ships which Xerxes in 480 B.C. saw sailing through the Hellespont "on their way to Ægina and the Peloponnesos" were probably destined in part for Megara and Corinth.[63] Ægina's imports from Egypt through the station at Naucratis doubtless included Nile valley wheat, as well as some of the small wares which she hawked about the Eastern Mediterranean.

Hellas or Central Greece had a poor reputation among the ancients for fertility,[64] and Northern Greece was little better. In Homeric times rugged Epiros, inhabited by the Thesprotians, drew supplies from "the grain fields of Dulichium," probably Zancynthos or one of the deposit islands near the mouth of the Achelous River.[65] Wheat lands existed only in small detached districts, as in the Achelous lowland and the valley plain of the Sperchius River, which was considered fertile in Homeric times. The plain of Opuntian Locris and the Crissian plain of rugged Phocis were fertile, but minute. The latter, which would make a good-sized American farm, was dedicated to the shrine of Apollo at Delphi; but it was so rare a bit of tillage land that the neighboring hill-towns of Crissa and Amphissa could not resist the temptation of cultivating it for their own use, and thus brought on the Sacred Wars.[66]

Attica had the poorest soil of all Greece. The land was so unproductive that it attracted no invaders, Thucydides tells us.[67] The little plain of Thias, 38 square miles in area, sacred to Demeter, who here introduced the cultivation of cereals,[68] a few districts in the valley of the Cephisus, and the small (10 square miles) alluvial Marathon plain alone could claim fertility. These must have produced Attica's meager wheat crop. According to the Eleusinian inscription of 328 B.C. the average yield of wheat was only one-tenth that of barley.[69] The wheat moreover was light and poor in food value.[70] The barley was excellent; it was the only cereal that could thrive on the porous red soil (*terra rossa*) of weathered limestone and the residuum of weathered crystalline rock, which covered the surface of the Mesogæa or "Midlands" with mediocre soil.[71] A meager average rainfall of 408 millimeters (16 inches), which drops at times to 325 millimeters (13 inches), further reduced the productivity of this ungenerous land.

Athens like Sparta undertook at an early period to despoil

her neighbors of their best grain land; but these territorial acquisitions were necessarily small. In 506 B.C. she took from Chalcis the fertile Lelantine plain on the neighboring coast of Euboea, and settled there 2,000 Athenian colonists to secure her hold; about the same time she seized from Eretria the little deltaic plain of Oropus at the mouth of the Asopus River. This little garden spot had long been a bone of contention between Eretria and Boeotia, whose border it adjoined; and it came to be a chronic cause of enmity between Boeotia and Athens.[72] The small area of these acquisitions emphasize the urgency of Attica's need. The Lelantine wheat fields were vital to Athens as her nearest source of supply. Hence during the Peloponnesian War, the occupation of Decelea by the Spartans in 413 B.C. enabled the invaders to control the road across northern Attica, and thus crippled Athens by cutting its communication with Oropus and the Euboean granary.[73] The great Athenian expansionist Alcibiades [74] urged the expedition for the conquest of Sicily (415 B.C.), on the ground of the abundant wheat, barley and other food-stuffs of the island. Nicias, arguing against the expedition, said:—"The Sicilians have a numerous cavalry and grow their own wheat instead of importing it; in the last two respects they have a great advantage over us." [75] To the Athenian statesmen, the inadequate grain supply was a constant handicap. This weakness had to be counterbalanced by the development of extraordinary strength in other directions. Climate, soil, small area, a long indented coast line, and a commanding central location in the Eastern Basin of the Mediterranean, all combined to force Athens into a brilliant industrial and maritime development. This enabled the state in the age of Pericles to support a population of 250,000, one-half of them slaves, on its scant 700 or 750 square miles of area.[76] Boeckh's estimate of half a million population is excessive, because he grossly overestimates both the fertility and arable area of Attica.[77]

Only two states of Greece, Thessaly and Boeotia, raised an adequate supply of wheat; Thessaly alone produced a margin for export.[78] Its extensive lake plains were famous for their fertility from Homeric times.[79] The large area and abundant resources of the land were the geographic foundation of Jason's ambition to make himself master of Greece and the neighboring countries.[80] Generous nature enabled the inhabitants to display a munificent hospitality and develop voracious appetites; "a Thessalian mouthful" was proverbial in Greece.[81] Bœotia was a small state, but it had productive wheat fields and gardens bordering the lacustrine plains of Lake Copais and Lake Hylica and along the valley of the Cephisus. Fertile soil made the Bœotians a nation of farmers, unenterprising and stolid, but the best fed people of Hellas.[82] The Athenians regarded them with scorn, not unmixed with envy, because of their voracity; and indeed this characteristic made them the butt of the comic writers of Greece. One such humorist, when asked what sort of people the Bœotians were, replied that "they spoke just as vessels might be expected to speak if they had a voice, telling how much each of them could hold." [83]

The Bœotian wheat, a hard spring wheat, was the heaviest and best of the whole Mediterranean region, superior to the Libyan, Pontic wheat of winter, Thracian, Syrian, Egyptian and Sicilian, which in turn was the heaviest of all imported wheats. In proof of this contention, Theophrastus adduced the fact that the Bœotian athletes, who at home ate scarcely three pints of the native wheat a day, easily consumed five pints of Attic wheat when they were staying in Athens.[84] The Athenian wheat therefore ranked low in food value. The superiority of the Bœotian wheat persisted; when later it entered the grain market of Rome, probably as tribute, it yielded only to the very best Italian product, according to Pliny. There is no evidence, however, that the Bœotian grain was exported even across the border into Attica. Theophrastus distinguished two kinds of Pontic wheat, "the hard wheat crops of spring and the soft wheat of winter, for soft kinds are very light. For two sowings of all wheats are made there alike, it seems, one in winter and one in spring." [85]

EARLY DEVELOPMENT OF THE GREEK GRAIN TRADE—Poverty of wheat land in Greece necessitated importation of breadstuffs from the earliest times. Even the most fertile districts, owing to small area, had no surplus for emergencies. These emergencies, moreover, recurred, owing to the variable rainfall and frequent wars between the city-states, with the consequent devastations of the fields in the spring campaigns and interruption to tillage by military service. During the Peloponnesian War, Bœotian Thebes sent ships to Pagasæ to buy Thessalian wheat, because for two years its land had remained uncultivated.[86] Preliminary to its revolt from Athens in 428 B.C. Lesbos made extensive importations of grain and other supplies from the Pontic coasts.[87] When the Persian invasion threatened Greece in 480 B.C., Gelon of Syracuse, foreseeing that the Pontic and Egyptian wheat ships bound for Greece would be intercepted by the enemy's fleets, offered to supply Sicilian grain for the entire Hellenic army, and to send a large naval and military force, on condition of his getting the supreme command of the allied forces.[88] This offer points to a long established wheat trade between Sicily and Greece. It also suggests a fact which impresses the investigator in this subject,— namely, that in the ancient Hellenic world wheat was the most important contraband of war.

Constant concern for their breadstuffs, especially wheat, harassed all the Greek states of the mainland and islands except Bœotia, Thessaly and backward mountain communities like the Arcadian commonwealths, whom nature had long disciplined to an abstemious contentment with the local barley and acorns. This concern stimulated the maritime trade and colonial enterprises of all the distinctly commercial states, whose development was determined by the pull of ready access to the sea and the push of meager tillage land at home.[89] Their governments became the chief *entrepreneurs* in the grain business, because private capital, nervous over the big risks taken by the grain fleets, was limited, and therefore voracious as to profits; transportation facilities were restricted and unreliable; and food supply at any crisis became a national question.[90] Foreign grain markets had to be kept open by reciprocity treaties, and distant grain lands linked with Greece by seaboard colonies. These colonies duplicated the types which emanated from the Hellenic cities of the Asia Minor coast. They were agricultural, like Achean Sybaris and Metapontum on the delta lands of the South Italian littoral, and the Athenian Thurii near the earlier Sybaris, where the people "could eat bread without measure"; [91] or strategic way-stations and middlemen ports, like the Athenian Sestos and Cardia on the Hellespont.

No other Greek state was so dependent upon foreign grain as Athens.[92]   Even the Attic farmers relied on it in part, owing to the sterility of their fields.[93]   The literature of Athens therefore yields abundant historical material on the extent and control of the grain trade, and shows what probably happened also in other Greek states which carried similar geographical handicaps, but failed to leave behind so ample a record.   Grain was brought to the Piræus from the Pontic coast, especially the Crimea, from eastern Thrace, Syria, Egypt, Libya, Sicily,[94] and occasionally from the island of Cyprus.   The Libyan wheat was doubtless the product of Cyrenaica, which had excellent grainland [95] and sufficient rainfall on the Barca plateau (1,800 feet) for winter crops; but owing to the semi-arid climate and variable precipitation, the country probably raised a margin of wheat for export only in exceptional years.   The same was doubtless true of Cyprus.   This island, which normally raised only enough for local consumption, sent grain fleets to Athens in the time of Andocides [96] (468-400 B.C.), probably during the Peloponnesian War, when wheat commanded high prices.

Egyptian wheat was brought to the Piræus not only by Athenian merchants, but also by foreign grain dealers from Rhodes, Miletos, Phœnicia and Egypt itself.[97]   Rhodes and Miletos probably bought wheat beyond their own needs at Naucratis on the Nile, and sold the surplus to their sister state Athens.   During a period of scarcity in 445 B.C., the king of Egypt sent a present of 40,000 medimni of wheat to be divided among the Athenian citizens.[98]   The dependence of Athens upon Egyptian wheat was marked.   After the Macedonian conquest of the Nile valley, Cleomenes, governor of Egypt, worked great hardship against Athens and other Greek states by controlling the export of Egyptian wheat, both as to price and destination. He imposed high export duties and sent the grain to the best market.[99]   Sicily was a resource for Athens when grain exports from Egypt failed, owing either to a low Nile or to excessive manipulation of the market, as in the case cited.   The familiarity of Nicias and Alcibiades with the Sicilian wheat supply in 415 B.C. indicates that Athens, like Sparta, had long imported breadstuffs from that island. The Sicilian spring wheat, sown in February, was the heaviest brought into Greece, and ranked just below the native Bœotian product.[100] Hellenic grain ships sought the markets not only of the Greek colonies in eastern Sicily, but visited also the Phœnician ports in western Sicily. "The great advantages and profits" which they drew thence [101] can be attributed in part to dealings in grain, for this district exported wheat to Carthage.

The Thracian wheat which Theophrastus was familiar with in Athens probably came chiefly from the Strymon Valley and the neighboring coastal plain as far as the Nestus River. This district was known in ancient as in modern times as fertile and well watered; it was rich in grain fields, forests, and gold mines.[102] Athens seized the coast fortress of Eion near the Strymon mouth from the Persians in 475 B.C.; tempted by the local resources, it made an unsuccessful effort in 465 B.C. to plant a colony at the bridge of the Strymon just above Eion, where thirty years later Pericles established the thriving emporium of Amphipolis.[103] That grain formed one of the exports of Amphipolis is suggested by the fact that about 286 B.C. the king of Pæonia, a country of the upper Strymon and Axius valleys, presented 10,000 Attic medimni of grain as a gift to the Athenian citizens.[104] Other Thracian wheat may have come to Athens from its allies Selymbria and Perinthos, either direct or through the market of Sestos. The East Thracian fields, which were very productive,[105] were probably cultivated by the Hellenized natives who maintained commercial relations with the coasts, because most of the Thracians were engaged in herding in the time of Herodotus.[106]

IMPORTANCE OF THE PONTIC MARKETS—The northern coastlands of the Pontus Euxine became Attica's chief source of wheat, though other Hellenic states were the pioneer traders on those remote shores. The Hellespontine policy of Pisistratus indicates that Athens began her commercial ventures there at the beginning of the sixth century B.C. Her maritime empire established in the age of Pericles drew all the Hellenized shores of the Euxine into her alliance, and opened every port to her trade. Pericles toured this northern sea to consolidate commercial and political relations by a display of Athenian naval power;[107] for the growth of Athens necessitated increased grain and wood imports from the Pontic shores. In the time of Demosthenes, Leucon, King of the Crimean Bosporus, supplied Athens yearly with 400,000 medimni (600,000 bushels), or nearly half its total annual import of grain.[108] The total import was therefore over 800,000 medimni or 1,200,000 bushels. One year, however, probably in 360 B.C. during the famine of the 105th Olympiad when, as Demosthenes implies, the grain shipments from Theodosia were extraordinarily large, Leucon shipped to Athens 2,100,000 medimni or 3,150,000 bushels.[109]

While the official dealings of Athens were largely with the Crimean grain market of Theodosia, wheat was brought to the Piræus by foreign merchants from the wide plains of the Dnieper (Borysthenes) and Bug (Hypanis). On the peninsula formed by the confluence of these two rivers stood a temple of Ceres, a seamark on this low coast pointing the way to the grain market of Olbia, which was founded by Miletos and became a wealthy city like the modern Odessa. The Greeks considered the Dnieper district comparable to the Nile valley in productivity.[110] On the Dniester they founded the colony of Tyras,[111] doubtless as a wheat port. The work of tillage was done by Scythian nomads, who became partly Hellenized and settled down to cultivate land for the Greek grain fleets.[112] This Pontic wheat included a hard spring wheat and a soft, light winter wheat. Theophrastus states that both a winter and spring sowing of all grains were made in that country; but as he describes the Pontic wheat in general as very light, importations of winter wheat must have predominated.[113] It therefore came chiefly from the southern and western grain fields of the Pontic littoral, for these are the only sections which today have enough snow to blanket the winter fields.

The Pontic coast lands offered profitable fields of trade to the industrial and commercial cities of the Ægean. They were a sparsely populated region of raw production, abounding in the produce of forest, field, pasture and fishing grounds. They yielded not only cereals in abundance, but cattle, hides, wool, salt fish, and timber from the Caucasus. For these the Greek city-states, commanding at home scant wheatlands, scant forests, scant pasturage, exchanged the finer products of the south,—olive oil, wines, potteries, woolen goods and clothing. Ships sailed with full cargoes on outbound and homebound voyages, and earned big profits. The Pontic shores, owing to a cold climate and to a backward civilization, afforded better selling markets than Egypt or Sicily; for Sicily, after three centuries of colonization was Hellenized on the eastern side by the time of the Peloponnesian War.

ATHENIAN CONTROL OF THE PONTIC TRADE ROUTE—Forced by her geographic conditions into a precocious industrial and commercial development, Athens early recognized her need of these Pontic markets. About 600 B.C. she seized Mytilene's fortress of Sigeum at the entrance to the Hellespont,[114] probably with the purpose of interfering with Megara's trade in Pontic wheat. In 535 B.C., Pisistratus inaugurated a regular Hellespontine policy aiming at access to the Euxine, and from this policy Athenian statesmen never thereafter deviated. It consisted in augmenting Athenian influence and multiplying Athenian colonies along the Hellespont, Propontis and Bosporus, in order to control this whole strategic passage. The Delian League gave her eventual possession of Lemnos, Imbros and Tenedos, which commanded the Ægean approaches to the Hellespont, and on these islands she rarely loosened her grip. Her line of communication as far as Lemnos was maintained by control of Eubœa, which safeguarded the marine Broadway of the Eubœan Sound, and by the possession of the islands of Sciathos, Peparethos and rocky Halonnesos. The latter had no value except as an island way-station on the voyage to the Hellespont, though in hostile hands, like those of Philip of Macedon, it threatened the wheat track.[115]

The economic and political life of Athens depended upon her ability to maintain this line of communication; of this fact the state was vividly aware. At the close of the Persian War, Athens sent its fleet to the Hellespont and drove the enemy from Sestos (478 B.C.), which controlled the narrows of the strait, thus clearing the way for future ascendancy there.[116] Two years later, when the Spartan Pausanias occupied Byzantium and Sestos, an Athenian fleet under Cimon promptly dislodged the intruder from both positions. After the maritime empire of Athens was established by Pericles, her enemies came to see that her vulnerable spot lay in the straits where her communication with the Pontic grain fields and forests could be most effectually interrupted. Therefore in the latter years of the Peloponnesian War, naval engagements multiplied in the Hellespont, as Athens made a fight for her life. Finally her fleet was wiped out by the Spartans in the battle of Ægospotamos near Sestos in 405 B.C. Ernst Curtius surmises that this battle occurred in summer, not later than August, at the peak of the season when the Pontic grain ships were hurrying south, in order to reach their home ports before the September storms should stop navigation.[117] The Spartan Lysander probably selected the critical moment to close the Hellespont, and that with dramatic effect. The Athenian sacred galley escaped from the battle and carried the news to Athens. Xenophon describes the scene which ensued. "At Athens, on the arrival of the Paralus in the night, the tale of their disaster was told; and the lamentations spread from the Piræus up the long walls unto the city, one man passing on the tidings to another; that night no man in Athens slept." [118]

Ten years later, when Athens revived and established the Athenian Confederation (395 B.C.) to operate against Sparta, she first secured the alliance of Lemnos and Imbros, island warders of the Hellespont. In 389 B.C. she began to get control over the sea route to the Euxine by drawing into her alliance Samothrace, Lesbos, various Hellespontine cities, Byzantium and Calchedon, and raised a revenue by imposing tolls on merchandise passing through the Bosporus. Again the straits became the scene of hostilities between Athenians and Spartans, till in 387 B.C. the Athenian fleet was blockaded in the Hellespont and the Pontic grain vessels were cut off from the Ægean.[119] The second Athenian Confederacy (378 B.C.) comprised Byzantium, various Thracian cities, Lesbos, and most of the Eubœan towns, all stations on the sea route to the Euxine, besides Rhodes and Chios, who as small island states were vitally interested in the Pontic trade. This time the Spartan fleet did not go so far as the Hellespont, but hovered about Ægina, Andros and Ceos, on the sea approaches to the Piræus. There they blocked the advance of the grain ships, which had reached the southern end of Eubœa, and prevented their rounding Cape Sunium, till the Athenians fitted out an emergency fleet, defeated the Spartan triremes, and brought in the grain to their starving populace.[120] The approaches to the Saronic Gulf offered many strategic points for intercepting the Athenian grain ships. Therefore Athens made Sunium a fortified naval base during the Peloponnesian War to protect this last perilous thirty-mile stretch up to the Piræus.[121] The outer seagate to the Saronic Gulf had the island of Andros and the seaport of Carystus in south Eubœa as its keepers. In order to safeguard the strategic passage, therefore, almost the first act of the Delian League was to reduce Carystus in 471 B.C., and force its entry into the confederation.[122] When Athens converted the League into an empire, she took the further precaution of settling cleruchies or out-colonists in Andros to secure the loyalty of that island (447 B.C.).[123]

Whoever fought Athens had to strike at her overseas grain trade. Therefore her next rival, Thebes, was forced out of her normal character as a land power and assumed the novel rôle of a sea power; built a hundred triremes, and sent them to the Propontis to prey upon the Pontic grain ships (364 B.C.). While Athens from her base at Sestos endeavored to defend these, the Theban admiral adopted the obvious policy of stirring up the Hellespontine cities of the Chersonnesos against Athens, and alarming King Cotys of Thrace with predictions of Athenian conquests. Cotys seized Sestos and nearly the whole Chersonnesos in 360 B.C. His death soon after and the decline of Thebes enabled Athens to recover control of the Hellespont in 357 B.C., when she again drew Eubœa into her alliance.[124] Thus, with her old possessions Lemnos and Imbros, she restored the security of the grain track from the Propontis to the Piræus, and fortified herself for her next big struggle.

Philip of Macedon was the next rival to Athens. The chief actor in the drama changes, but not the scenes or the dramatic episodes. These recur with historical monotony due to the same controlling geographic conditions. There was the same old struggle for the control of the Bosporus, the Hellespont and the wheat emporiums of the Thracian coast,—Byzantium, Selymbria, and Perinthos. Macedon, like Thebes, was forced to become a naval power. She let loose her triremes to capture

Athenian wheat transports in the north Ægean and to harry
Lemnos, Imbros, and Eubœa. There the Macedonian forces
seized Eretria and fortified Oreus at the northern end of the
island, in order to dominate the stormy and dangerous entrance
into the Eubœan Sound.[125] Philip's land campaigns aimed at
the conquest of Thrace, from Byzantium to the tip of the Chersonnesos, where Athens was most vulnerable. He endeavored to
conquer Athens in Thrace, as Napoleon endeavored to conquer
England in Egypt. The arguments of Demosthenes to arouse
Athens to the gravity of the danger paralleled those used in the
British Parliament for the continuance of the French war.
Demosthenes, enumerating his provisions for Athens' safety,
gives a digest of the geography and the strategy of the war.
By the recovery of lost Eubœa he protected the Attic seaboard
and the grain track through the Eubœan Sound. Effecting the
release of Byzantium, the Chersonnesos and Halonnesos from
Macedonian dominion, he opened the Hellespont and Bosporus
for the passage of the Pontic grain ships, and provided for
their conveyance along a friendly coast all the way to the
Piræus. He persistently exhorted the citizens to expand and
strengthen the navy, with which to guard these overseas connections.[126]

Athens was the Britain of the ancient Mediterranean. Its
navy alone guaranteed the full loaf of bread. Fleets had to
police the Pontic wheat track against the Caucasus pirates,
and suppress other sea-robbers who recurrently infested the
routes to Egypt and Sicily. A strong navy was necessary to
check sporadic depredations on the merchant ships by rival
powers even in time of peace. Calchedon, embarrassed by an
empty treasury, once utilized its location on the Bosporus to
plunder some vessels going north into the Euxine,[127] doubtless
loaded with manufactured goods with which to pay for the return cargo of wheat and fish. While Philip of Macedon was
besieging Selymbria in eastern Thrace, his fleet captured twenty
Athenian grain ships passing through the Propontis to the
Hellespont *en route* to Lemnos, because the Macedonian admiral suspected that the supplies were meant for the besieged
city.[128] Again early in the reign of Alexander the Great, Pontic ships were arbitrarily seized by the Macedonians and held

up at Tenedos, though freedom of the seas and security of ships against seizure had been pledged by Alexander's recent treaty with Greece. Athens' prompt equipment of a large naval fleet led to the release of the captured vessels.[129]

In time of war, naval convoys attended not only the wheat fleets of Athens but those of any member of the Athenian Confederacy. For this protection an annual tribute was paid.[130] Hostile attacks were not limited to the mere seizure of food vessels. When Demetrius of Macedon was besieging Athens about 300 B.C., he captured a wheat transport bound for the Piraeus, and hanged the captain together with the pilot. This treatment so terrified the merchants that they stayed away and let Athens starve till she surrendered to Demetrius.[131]

At all times the gloved hand of diplomacy aided the mailed fist of the navy. In the age of Pericles, and again in the time of Demosthenes, the international policy of Athens was dominated by the economic interests of the State. In the Euxine Athens held the friendship of the Greek towns by giving them support against barbarian attacks. With the reigning house of the Cimmerian Bosporus she maintained close relations based upon reciprocity of trade. Leucon, prince of Panticapæum from 393 to 353 B.C., exempted Attic ships from the export duty, allowed them to purchase grain ahead of other ships, and fixed a market for them in the excellent port of Theodosia near the Crimean wheat fields.[132] Athens convinced him that she was his best customer, and conferred honors upon him. She also cultivated friendship with the powers of the Thracian Bosporus and Propontis; with the Persian satrap of Hellespontine Phrygia, who by reason of geographical location could imperil or police the southern strait; with the barbarian kings of eastern Thrace; and with the free cities of Byzantium and Perinthos,[133] who not only occupied strategic positions, but were themselves wheat emporiums.

Byzantium grew rich on her Pontic trade. It was an obvious policy for the cities of the Propontis and straits to accumulate grain, either by direct importation from the Euxine or by the levy of port dues and Bosporus tolls, paid in kind [134] on passing ships; they could then resell it to merchants who were unwilling to make the long voyage to the Crimea, or who arrived near the end of the sailing season and wished to return home before the autumn storms. Thus we read that Heraclea, located on the Thracian coast north of the Chersonnesos, sent forty ships to the Crimean Bosporus to buy wheat and other supplies.[135] Sestos was called in Athens "the wheat-bin of the Piræus," [136] a term applicable only to a grain emporium. Its strategic location at the narrows of the Hellespont made it not only a base for military control, but also like Byzantium a natural toll station which Athens sometimes used for collecting transit dues, levied in kind, if we may judge from Leucon's export taxes on the Pontic wheat. Athens showed persistent friendship for Egypt and Cyprus by assistance rendered to these states when revolting against Persian dominion. Her motive may have been partly her old hostility to the Great King, but partly also her need of Egyptian and Cyprian grain.

GOVERNMENT CONTROL OF THE ATHENIAN GRAIN MARKET— The grain market of the Athenian Agora, despite all government measures to insure a steady supply of wheat and barley, was sensitive to every political movement in Scythia and Thrace, to every disturbance in the towns of the Bosporus and Hellespont. Prices fluctuated according to the seasons, as these were favorable or unfavorable to crops and to navigation; they fluctuated as importations increased or diminished, as export duties were raised or lowered in the grain emporiums of the Mediterranean, and as the markets were cornered both within and without Attica and prices arbitrarily raised. War and piracy always made the grain business in the Piræus feverish. The fluctuations, however, were not excessive except during a siege or sudden threat of war. In the time of Pericles and Socrates, the medimnus of prepared barley cost normally two drachmæ or 34.2 cents, and wheat was probably a third more. In 396 B.C. wheat sold for three drachmæ or 51.3 cents, and fifty years later in the time of Demosthenes for five drachmæ or 85.5 cents.[137] Prices in other Greek states were about the same. At Lampsacus the normal price for a medimnus of wheat in Aristotle's time was four drachmæ or 68.4 cents, but this was arbitrarily advanced by the State to six drachmæ, or $1.02 at a threat of war, doubtless as a hint for conservation.[138]

The cheapest and best market in which the Athenians could

buy was that of the Crimean Bosporus. There excellent rates
were given even in time of scarcity. At Olbia on the Dnieper
estuary, prices were variously two, four and eight drachmæ or
34.2 cents to $1.37 in the first or second century B.C., but they
must have been lower in the fifth and fourth centuries B.C.
Prices in Egypt were low, reflecting the fertile soil, large arable
area, cheap labor, and the relative certainty of harvest under
irrigation tillage. In the time of the Ptolemies the normal
price for spelt and wheat was about two drachmæ or 34.2 cents
the medimnus, and in times of scarcity it increased hardly three-
fold. Shortly after the founding of Alexandria, however, under
the satrap Cleomenes, the wholesale price of wheat rose to ten
drachmæ or $1.71 in a time of scarcity. Sicilian grain was
doubtless cheap prior to the Roman conquest of the island. In
74 B.C., the price of wheat there was fixed at an equivalent of
91.2 cents and barley at 45.6 cents the medimnus.[139]

The vicissitudes of the grain trade, due largely to geographic
conditions, necessitated governmental control. Even Egypt
found it necessary in years of reduced crops to prevent exports,
either by direct inhibition or by imposition of enormous export
duties.[140] Selymbria, though located in a wheat-growing district of Thrace, prohibited grain exports in time of scarcity.[141]
Athens during the Peloponnesian War employed her control of
the Bosporus and Hellespont to allow no grain exports from
the Euxine or Byzantium, except by permission as to destination and annual amount.[142] She thus waged an economic war
against her ill-fed enemies like Corinth, Megara and Sparta,
and used her command of the Pontic grain as a means to hold
the allegiance of her restless insular allies, like Rhodes, Cos,
Chios and Lesbos.

At all times the grain trade of the Piræus was closely controlled, as was also the sale of lumber and ship supplies; otherwise the commerce of Athens was free. The exportation of
native grain from Attica was prohibited by law. Furthermore,
two-thirds of every cargo of foreign grain entering an Attic
port had to remain in the country. No inhabitants of Attica,
whether native or alien residents, might transport grain to any
other but Attic ports; nor might they so much as loan money
on the security of a vessel, unless such vessel should return to

Athens with a cargo of grain or other commodities. The object of these measures was to compel importations of foreign grain. Furthermore Athens like Teos appointed certain officials who kept account of the imported grain, and saw to it that two-thirds of the supply should be brought to the city from the ports. She provided public storehouses for the state-owned grain, and also for the stock of private dealers. Government commissioners purchased grain for the state, while yet others received and measured it.[143] Thus a reserve was at hand in time of emergency, to be sold to the populace at a moderate figure and to stabilize prices. Probably some of it was given to the citizens. Measures were also adopted to prevent dealers from cornering the market. Retailers might sell only at the advance of one obolus, or about three cents on the cost price of a medimnus, though in time of dearth they ran up the prices and sold at six times the legal profit. Eager to profit by every fluctuation in the market, the grain dealers spread alarming rumors to send up the price of wheat, saying that the grain ships had been wrecked in the Euxine or captured at sea by the Spartans, that commercial treaties had been violated and the grain ports closed against Attic merchantmen, with the result that the nervous populace was willing to buy at any price. To curb these enemies within the state, Athens imposed a death penalty for any effort to establish a grain monopoly.[144] The same punishment was imposed at Teos for the same offense, as we learn from a fragment of Sophocles. The free foreign dealers regularly bought grain in the cheapest market and sold in the highest, and with this purpose they scoured the Ægean, the Euxine and the Sicilian coasts.[145] Athens made every effort to attract them to the Piræus market; this rich and populous state was in a position to pay well for the needed breadstuffs, but it encouraged competitive selling.

It is reasonable to suppose that other states, possessing similar geographic conditions to those of Attica, and therefore compelled to import overseas grain, adopted similar foreign and domestic policies to maintain a balance of breadstuffs and population. The abundant literature of Athens enables us to reconstruct in considerable detail the constant efforts of the state to fill its grain-bins. Megara, located astride of the

Isthmus of Corinth with a port on each side, maintained connection with the Sicilian fields as well as with the Pontic wheat lands, as indicated by her colonies both in Sicily and on the Bosporus. Corinth early in the eighth century B.C. established trade relations westward with Syracuse and other Sicilian wheat markets. Mountainous Achaia, located on the marine highway of the Corinthian Gulf [146] and having easy access to the west, imported grain from Sicily and doubtless also from her Italian colonies in the fertile plains of Sybaris and Croton. The island states of the Ægean, like Rhodes, Chios and Cos, seem to have relied chiefly on the Pontic grain. They therefore rushed to the support of Athens whenever the Euxine connection was jeopardized. Their interests were identical, and therefore they were nearly always members of the various Athenian confederacies. After the decline of Athens, Rhodes became the chief maritime power of the Ægean. In 228 B.C., we find her heading all the states interested in the Pontic trade in a war against Byzantium, which had got astride of the Bosporus by the acquisition of territory on the Asian side, and was levying a toll on all goods brought from the Pontus.[147] As Rhodes and her island confederates assisted Athens and Byzantium against the expanding power of Philip of Macedon, in 340 B.C., in his effort to control the straits, so in 201 B.C. the Rhodian League joined the King of Pergamos and the Romans to prevent Philip V from attaining a like purpose.[148]

WHEAT PRODUCTION AND WHEAT TRADE IN WESTERN MEDITERRANEAN LANDS—In the lands of the Western Mediterranean, geographic conditions were more favorable to wheat culture than in the Eastern Basin, apart from the Pontic and Egyptian fields, which lay outside the Mediterranean climatic region. The rainfall was in general greater, more reliable, and lasted longer. Hence crops were less jeopardized by failure of the autumn and spring rains. Tertiary and Quaternary plains, though no larger, were more evenly distributed. In Sicily and parts of Italy disintegrated lava, tufa, and volcanic ash lent exuberance to the fertility of the soil; and enabled it to retain the moisture necessary for the maturity of the crop during the dry period before the harvest. Sicily was an important granary from very ancient times, and produced wheat that almost equalled the Bœotian grain in nutritive quality. Theophrastus attributed the heavy crops to the frequent spring showers of Sicily.[149]   Strabo states that its wheat, honey and saffron surpassed that of Italy.[150]   Its grain exports went to Greece certainly at the beginning of the fifth century B.C., and probably earlier.   During the time of Agathocles of Syracuse, about 310 B.C., Carthage imported wheat and other provisions from Sicily and Sardinia, securing this traffic by her control of the sea.   Agathocles, at war with his Punic neighbor, planned to break up this grain trade and equipped a fleet for the purpose.[151]

Rome imported Sicilian wheat from the beginning of the Republic.   Ordinarily the fertile plains of the lower Tiber and Anio sufficed for the agricultural communities which constituted the ancient Latin League and the early Roman state; but during periods of drought which destroyed the harvests, or of sustained war, which interrupted tillage and devastated the growing crops, importations of wheat and spelt were necessary. Frequently these came from the fertile volcanic region about the Bay of Naples.   The moist black earth of Capua and the famous Phlegræan fields about Cumæ were considered standard wheat lands by the ancients,[152] and their choice product could be readily transported by sea along the coast to the Tiber mouth.   Rome's nearer neighbors, the Hernici of the broad and fertile Trerus River valley, and the Volscii of the upper Liris valley and the Latium coastal plain, possessed good wheat land, and at times they seem to have sold grain to Rome; but they were victims of Roman wars of expansion and therefore generally refused to sell to their ambitious neighbor in her hour of need.[153]   Rome therefore often drew upon the abundant grain resources of Etruria, whence wheat could be transported either down the Tiber or along the coast.   Etruria is an old volcanic region of rich heavy soil.   Its streams drain hills overlaid with trachyte, tufa and basalt, and deposit in the valley plains soil rich in potash, soda and phosphoric acid,—all important articles of plant food.[154]   Pliny considered the wheat of Clusium, grown in the lake-strewn basin of the upper Clanis River (Chiana), the best in the world.   It weighed twenty-five per cent more than Bœotian wheat.[155]

In the early interstate grain trade of Italy, Rome figured as a frequent importer. During a protracted period of famine in 490 and 489 B.C., it purchased grain all along the Etruscan and Campanian coasts and in Sicily. Etruscan grain was also brought down the Tiber, probably from the rich Clusium fields.[156] In 474 B.C., during a scarcity due to a prolonged war with Veii, Rome imported wheat from Campania; [157] in 437 B.C., when evidently a general drought had reduced the harvests, she "sent out embassies by land and sea to all the neighboring states to purchase grain, with little result except that a small quantity was procured in Etruria." [158] In 409 and 408 B.C. Rome was forced by famine and pestilence to import grain from Etruria, the upper Tiber cities and Greek Sicily. She could get none from Campania because the fertile district of Capua and Cumæ had just been conquered by the mountain Samnites, who refused to aid their rival neighbor.[159] Etruria continued to be the chief Italian source of supply [160] until Rome established her naval power sufficiently to ensure importations of overseas wheat. The importance of this nearby reliable supply of Etruscan wheat may be inferred from the fact that in 210 B.C., when the grain fields of Campania were in Hannibal's hands, and those of Sicily had been devastated by five years of continual war, Rome's granaries were so depleted that a medimnus of Sicilian wheat sold in Rome for the high price of 15 denarii, or $2.56.[161] At this junction Rome renewed an old alliance with Egypt, and secured the support of its grain ships to feed Italy and the legions.[162] On the restoration of peace in Sicily, she made extraordinary efforts to revive agriculture in the island for the sake of the wheat.

TERRITORIAL EXPANSION AND THE ROMAN GRAIN TRADE— This Second Punic War, which gave Rome command of the sea, demonstrated to the government the possibility of maintaining Italy and her army by wheat from Sicily and Egypt. Then followed a disastrous competition between the small Italian farms and the vast slave estates in the rich wheat lands of Sicily, Sardinia, Numidia, Carthaginian Africa, and the Guadalquivir valley of Spain.[163] Field agriculture in Italy declined as the country was flooded with foreign grain. Sea transportation of wheat from Sicily and Sardinia was as cheap as land transportation from Etruria and Campania. The extensive alluvial plain of the Po valley, especially Gallia Transpadana, yielded fine wheat in large quantities,[164] but it was too far from the capitāl to compete with Sicilian and Sardinian grain. Hence in 150 B.C. wheat sold there for four oboli or twelve cents the medimnus, and barley for two oboli or six cents,[165] owing to lack of a market. The farmers found it more profitable to feed their grain to hogs, fattening the mast-fed pigs till they rivalled modern Berkshires and exporting the hams and bacon to Rome.[166] Meanwhile Sicilian and Sardinian wheat sometimes sold in Rome for the freight charge.[167] The conquest of Spain, especially the fertile Guadalquivir valley, in the Second Punic War placed the Iberian grain at the disposal of Rome. Even in 203 B.C. the government drew wheat both from Spain and Sicily to supply Scipio's army in Africa, while that army, immediately after landing on Carthaginian soil, gathered in the grain from the broad and productive fields of the Bagradas River valley.[168] At the close of the war Rome was selling its citizens Spanish and African wheat at 12 to 24 asses (20 to 40 cents) a medimnus.[169] It procured the grain by tribute and purchase. The Roman army fighting in Macedonia in 170 B.C. was supplied by Carthage with 250,000 bushels of wheat and 125,000 bushels of barley. Numidia sent it an equal amount of wheat which the Roman government bought.[170]

After the annexation of Carthaginian and Numidian Africa and the conquest of Egypt, both the tribute and purchase grain increased in amount, in proportion to the productive area and fertility of these countries. In the time of Augustus, Egypt furnished one-third of the grain consumed by Rome, Africa another third, while Sicily, Sardinia, Spanish Bætica, and Italy's own reduced yield supplied the final third. The grain of Egypt and Africa was so vital to Italy and the Imperial City that these countries became the key to the control of Rome itself. Conquest of either one was equivalent to the conquest of Italy, a fact that was not lost upon the later adventurous aspirants to the throne of the Cæsars.[171]

The immense area of the Roman Empire, which finally included all the Mediterranean wheat lands, was the politico-geographical factor which stimulated grain importations into

Italy and discouraged native agriculture. Italy's focal location in the Mediterranean Sea was a second geographic factor operating to the same end. It facilitated maritime movements of grain from all the big areas of production and on a scale impossible in a land empire in ancient times. Italy's location was comparable to that of the Attic peninsula in the Eastern Basin, and was conducive to similar economic effects. The maintenance of these systematic importations depended upon the security of the sea-ways between the wheat countries and the Roman markets, and therefore upon the efficiency of the navy. The decline of Roman sea power from 102 to 67 B.C. fatally weakened the marine police. Pirates so infested the grain tracks that between 75 and 67 B.C. imports ceased, and the price of wheat at Rome soared to 120 sestertii or $4.65 the medimnus, or about ten times the market price in Sicily.[172] Therefore when Pompey was appointed dictator of the sea in 67 B.C., his first act was to clear the waters about Sicily, Sardinia and Africa, in order to restore the movement of wheat from those provinces to Italy; his next was to suppress the Cilician pirates, who issued from their convenient lairs along the Taurus Mountain littoral and infested the wheat route from Egypt passing their doors.

Imperial Rome and Athens owing to quite different causes were both singularly dependent upon overseas grain lands. The vulnerable spot of Athens' sea empire lay in the Hellespont; that of Rome's land empire lay in Africa and Egypt. While Athens was constantly fighting rival Greek commonwealths, whom she was powerless to conquer because of her small land base and the nature-made individualism of the Greek states, Rome eliminated her foreign enemies by the *pax Romana*, but left sea pirates who captured her grain ships, and political pirates who seized the imperial throne by possessing themselves of her chief grain lands. There was perhaps never a time that ancient Italy could not have fed itself from its home fields, except in the rare years of drought. There was never a time that Athens could have fed itself, unless it established a maritime power supported by some measure of political power, as evinced in the various Athenian confederacies. Rome's expansion aimed always at more territory; an imperial parasite, she lived off the newly acquired lands as Athens never lived off Eubœa or Thrace or Crimea. Therefore Rome's grain lands became a bludgeon in the hands of candidates for the imperial throne.

AUTHORITIES—CHAPTER XIII

1. Vergil, Georgic II, 217-224. Columella, II, 9.
   Theophrastus, *Historia Plantarum*, Bk. VIII, Chap. IX, 1, 2.
2. A. Philippson, *Das Mittelmeergebiet*, p. 167. Leipzig, 1907.
3. Polybius, Bk. II, 15; Bk. XXXIV, 7, 8. Boeckh, *Public Economy of the Athenians*, pp. 128-131. Translated from the German. London, 1857.
4. T. D. Seymour, *Life in the Homeric Age*, p. 328. New York, 1907.
5. *Iliad*, II, 695. *Hymn to Demeter* in the *Homeric Hymns*.
6. Mommsen, *History of Rome*, Vol. III, p. 66. New York, 1905.
   R. Grademann, *Der Getreidebau in Altertum*, pp. 32-39. Jena, 1909.
7. Xenophon, *Anabasis*, Bk. I, Chap. II, 23.
8. Theophrastus, *De Causis Plantarum*, Bk. IV, Chap. VII, 2. *Hist. Plant.*, Bk. VIII, Chap. I, 1-4; Chap. VII, 3; Chap. XI, 1.
9. Neumann and Partsch, *Physikalische Geographie Griechenlands*, p. 446. Breslau, 1885.
10. Strabo, V, Chap. I, 12.
11. Xenophon, *Hellenes*, Bk. V, Chap. IV, 56.
12. Diodorus Siculus, Bk. XXI, Fragment 12.
13. A. Erman, *Life in Ancient Egypt*, p. 434. London, 1894.
14. Ewald Banse, *Die Turkei*, pp. 353, 357, 358. Braunschweig, 1919.
15. D. G. Hogarth, *The Nearer East*, pp. 66, 136, 188. London, 1902.
    E. Huntington, *Palestine and Its Transformation*, pp. 31, 230-235. Boston, 1911.
16. I *Kings*, V, 11; *Ezekiel*, XXVII, 17.
17. Theophrastus, *Hist. Plant.*, Bk. VIII, Chap. IV, 3. Varro, I, 44.
18. Xenophon, *Anabasis*, II, 23.
19. E. Banse, *op. cit.*, p. 176.
20. Strabo, XIV, Chap. VI, 5.
21. E. Banse, *op. cit.*, pp. 124-140.
22. Herodotus, I, 149.
23. Strabo, Bk. VIII, Chap. IV, 6; Bk. XII, Chap. IV, 4; Bk. XIII, Chap. IV, 2, 5, 13.
24. Vergil, Georgic I, 103. Herodotus, I, 142.
25. E. Banse, *op. cit.*, pp. 124-125.
26. *Ibid.*, pp. 125, 142.
27. *Iliad*, XII, 314-315; XVI, 672-673, 682.
28. Herodotus, V, 31. Strabo, Bk. XIV, Chap. I, 14, 15.
29. E. C. Semple, *Influences of Geographic Environment*, pp. 252-253, 444-445. New York, 1911.
30. Herodotus, III, 39; I, 160. Strabo, XIV, Chap. I, 33; Chap. II, 2. Thucydides, III, 50; IV, 52.
31. Herodotus, I, 160; VIII, 106. Xenophon, *Hellenica*, III, Chap. II, 11.

32. Herodotus, VI, 28.
33. Herodotus, II, 178.
34. Herodotus, I, 149.
35. Thucydides, III, 2.
36. Herodotus, V, 94.
37. Strabo, Fragment 52.
38. Strabo, Bk. VII, Chap. III, 17; Chap. IV, 4.
39. J. B. Bury, *History of Greece*, p. 92. London, 1909.
40. Aristotle, *Economics*, Bk. II, Chap. XVII.
41. Polybius, IV, 46, 47, 52. Bury, *op. cit.*, pp. 722-723.
42. Herodotus, VII, 153. A. E. Zimmern, *The Greek Commonwealth*, p. 66. 1911.
43. Polybius, XXVIII, 2.
44. Herodotus, I, 170; V, 124.
45. Neumann and Partsch, *op. cit.*, pp. 347-348. Breslau, 1885.
46. Plutarch, *Lycurgus*, VIII.
47. W. Richter, *Handel und Verkehr der wichtigsten Völker des Mittelmeers im Altertum*, p. 94. Leipzig, 1886.
48. Theophrastus, *Hist. Plant.*, Bk. VIII, Chap. IV, 5. A. Philippson, *Der Peloponnes*, p. 238. Berlin, 1892.
49. *Odyssey*, III, 495. *Tyrtæus in Strabo*, Bk. VI, Chap. III, 3. *Euripides in Strabo*, Bk. VIII, Chap. V, 6. Philippson, *Der Peloponnes*, p. 378.
50. Ernst Curtius, *History of Greece*, Vol. I, pp. 227-230. New York, 1872.
51. Thucydides, III, 86.
52. Bury, *History of Greece*, p. 539. 1909.
53. Neumann and Partsch, *op. cit.*, p. 348.
54. Pliny, *Historia Naturalis*, IV, 54.
55. Bury, *History of Greece*, pp. 103, 105. 1909.
56. Varro, Bk. I, 44.
57. Mommsen, *History of Rome*, Vol. I, p. 171. New York, 1905.
58. Strabo, Bk. VIII, Chap. VI, 23.
59. A. Philippson, *Der Peloponnes*, pp. 16-18. Berlin, 1892. Strabo, Bk. IX, Chap. I, 6.
60. Herodotus, VII, 147. Strabo, Bk. VIII, Chap. VI, 16.
61. Strabo, Bk. X, Chap. II, 3, 4. E. Curtius, *History of Greece*, Vol. I, p. 290.
62. Livy, XLV, Chap. 30.
63. Herodotus, VII, 147.
64. Herodotus, III, 106.
65. *Odyssey*, XIV, 335. Strabo, Bk. X, Chap. II, 13-19.
66. Bury, *History of Greece*, pp. 159, 724-725. 1909.
67. Thucydides, I, 2, 5.
68. Homeric Hymns, Hymn to Demeter.
69. T. D. Seymour, *Life in Homeric Greece*, p. 328. New York, 1907.
70. Theophrastus, *Hist. Plant.*, Bk. VIII, Chap. IV, 5.
71. Neumann and Partsch, *op. cit.*, p. 347. Pauly-Wissowa, *Real-Encyl. der class. Altertumswissenschaft*, article, *Attica*.
72. Bury, *op. cit.*, pp. 217-218.
73. Thucydides, VII, 27, 28; VIII, 95, 96.
74. Plutarch, *Alcibiades*, XVI.
75. Thucydides, VI, 20.

76. Bury, *op. cit.*, p. 378; note, p. 870.
77. Boeckh, *Public Economy of the Athenians*, pp. 50-57, 107-114. London, 1857.
78. Xenophon, *Hellenes*, Bk. V, Chap. IV, 5, 6; Bk. VI, Chap. I, 11.
79. *Iliad*, II, 695. Thucydides, I, 2, 3. Strabo, Bk. IX, Chap. V, 2, 19.
80. Xenophon, *Hellenes*, Bk. VI, Chap. I, 8-18.
81. *Ibid.*, Bk. VI, Chap. I, 3. Athenæus, X, 12.
82. E. Curtius, *History of Greece*, Vol. IV, pp. 349-352.
83. Eratosthenes, quoted in Athenæus, X, 11.
84. Theophrastus, *Hist. Plant.*, Bk. VIII, Chap. IV, 5.
85. *Ibid.*, Bk. VIII, Chap. IV, 5.
86. Xenophon, *Hellenes*, Bk. V, Chap. IV, 56.
87. Thucydides, III, 2.
88. Herodotus, VII, 158.
89. E. C. Semple, *op. cit.*, pp. 15, 268.
90. W. L. Westerman, "Decline of Ancient Culture," *Amer. Hist. Review*, Vol. XX, p. 736. 1915.
91. Bury, *op. cit.*, p. 380.
92. Demosthenes' *Orations*, On the Crown, and Against Leptines. Xenophon, *Hellenes*, Bk. VI, Chap. I, 11. Diodorus Siculus, I, 2.
93. Livy, XLIII, 6.
94. Theophrastus, *Hist. Plant.*, Bk. VIII, Chap. IV, 5.
95. Strabo, Bk. XVII, Chap. III, 21; Pliny, *Hist. Nat.*, V, 5.
96. Boeckh, *Public Economy of the Athenians*, p. 76. London, 1857.
97. *Ibid.*, pp. 110, 117.
98. Plutarch, *Pericles*, 37.
99. Aristotle, *Economics*, II, 34; Demosthenes, *Contre Parmenis*, *Œuvres Complettes*, Vol. IV, p. 229. Translated by Abbé Auger. Paris, 1777.
100. Theophrastus, *Hist. Plant.*, Bk. VIII, Chap. IV, 3.
101. Herodotus, VII, 158.
102. Strabo, Bk. VII, Chap. VII, 5; Fragment 36. Apollonius Rhodius, *Argonautæ*, Bk. I, lines 796, 826. Pliny, XLV, 30.
103. Bury, *History of Greece*, pp. 336, 382. 1909.
104. Boeckh, *Public Economy of the Athenians*, p. 124. 1857.
105. Aristotle, *Economics*, II, 27.
106. Herodotus, V, 6.
107. Plutarch, *Pericles*, XX.
108. Demosthenes, *Contre Leptines*, *Œuvres Complettes*, Vol. III, p. 9. Paris, 1777.
109. Strabo, Bk. VII, Chap. IV, 6.
110. Herodotus, IV, 53, 78. Strabo, Bk. VII, Chap. 3, 17.
111. Herodotus, IV, 51.
112. Herodotus, IV, 17, 18.
113. Theophrastus, *Hist. Plant.*, Bk. VIII, IV, 5.
114. Herodotus, V, 94, 95.
115. Demosthenes, Oration on Halonnesos.
116. Herodotus, IX, 114-118.
117. E. Curtius, *History of Greece*, Vol. III, p. 591, note XI. 1872.
118. Xenophon, *Hellenes*, Bk. II, Chap. II, 3.
119. Bury, *History of Greece*, pp. 546, 550-552. Xenophon, *Hellenes*. Bk. V, Chap. I, 28.

120. Xenophon, *Hellenes*, Bk. V, Chap. IV, 16-61.
121. Thucydides, VIII, 4.
122. Bury, *History of Greece*, p. 337.
123. Plutarch, *Pericles*, XI.
124. Bury, *History of Greece*, pp. 615-617, 682-683.
125. Demosthenes, Oration on the Chersonnesos, and First Philippic.
126. Demosthenes, Oration on the Crown.
127. Aristotle, *Economics*, II, 11.
128. Demosthenes, Oration on the Crown, and the Letter of Philip.
129. Demosthenes, Treaty of Alexander.
130. Demosthenes, Oration on the Chersonncsos.
131. Plutarch, *Demetrius*, XXXIII.
132. Demosthenes, *Contre Leptines*, *Œuvres Complettes*, Vol. III, pp. 19-20. Paris, 1777.
133. Demosthenes, Letters of Byzantium and Perinthos in the Oration on the Crown.
134. Xenophon, *Hellenes*, Bk. I, Chap. I, 22. Polybius, IV, II, 46.
135. Aristotle, *Economics*, II, 9.
136. Aristotle, *Rhetoric*, III, 10.
137. Boeckh, *Public Economy of the Athenians*, pp. 128-129. 1857. Demosthenes, Oration against Phormion. A Grecian medimnus, which was variable in size, equalled about two and a half bushels.
138. Aristotle, *Economics*, II, 8.
139. Boeckh, *Public Economy of the Athenians*, pp. 130-132.
140. Aristotle, *Economics*, II, 34.
141. *Ibid.*, II, 17.
142. Boeckh, *Public Economy of the Athenians*, p. 78.
143. *Ibid.*, pp. 78-79, 114-116, 121-123. C. Scheffler, *De Rebus Teiorum*, pp. 63-66. Leipzig, 1882.
144. Lysias, *Contre les Commercans de Blé*, *Œuvres Complettes*, pp. 304-305. Translated by Abbé Auger. Paris, 1783.
145. Xenophon, *Œconomicus*, XX, 27-28.
146. Theophrastus, *Hist. Plant.*, Bk. VIII, Chap. IV, 5.
147. Polybius, IV, 39, 46, 47, 50.
148. Mommsen, *History of Rome*, Vol. II, p. 411. 1905.
149. Theophrastus, *Hist. Plant.*, Bk. VIII, Chap. IV, 4; Chap. VI, 6.
150. Strabo, Bk. VI, Chap. II, 7.
151. Diodorus Siculus, XXI, Fragment 18.
152. Vergil, Georgic II, 217-224. Columella, II, 8. Strabo, Bk. V, Chap. IV, 3, 4, 8.
153. Livy, II, 34.
154. W. Deecke, *Italy*, pp. 64, 96, 376. New York, 1904.
155. Pliny, *Hist. Nat.*, XVIII, 7.
156. Livy, II, 34.
157. Livy, II, 52.
158. Livy, IV, 12, 13.
159. Livy, IV, 52.
160. Livy, XXVIII, 45.
161. Polybius, IX, 44.
162. Mommsen, *History of Rome*, Vol. II, p. 315. 1905.
163. Strabo, Bk. III, Chap. II, 6; Bk. V, Chap. II, 7. Pliny, *Hist. Nat.*, XVIII, 10.

164. Pliny, *Hist. Nat.*, XVIII, 7.
165. Polybius, II, 165.
166. Strabo, Bk. V, Chap. I, 12.
167. Livy, XXX, 38.
168. Livy, XXX, 3.
169. Mommsen, *History of Rome,* Vol. III, p. 76. 1905.
170. Livy, XLIII, 6; XLV, 13.
171. Mommsen, *Provinces of the Roman Empire,* Vol. II, pp. 260, 366-7. 1887.
172. Cicero, *Verres,* 92, 214.

CHAPTER XIV

SOWN AND PLANTED CROPS

GEOGRAPHIC CONDITIONS OF ANCIENT TILLAGE—Ancient Mediterranean agriculture had to adjust itself to a complex group of geographic conditions. It found a simple combination of climate, soil, and relief over a large area only in a few places like Egypt and the Po River valley. In other districts the combinations were manifold within a small extent of country. Mountains dropped down to plains; a gravel-strewn soil bordered a fertile alluvium; a highland section of heavy rainfall sent down its streams to a semi-arid lowland; a limestone plateau, covered with a thin veneer of earth, overlooked a valley of deep rich soil; rainy winters alternated with long periods of summer drought, and the amount of the rainfall was unreliable. Agriculture was stimulated by the necessity of adjusting itself to these varied geographic conditions, and hence attained a precocious development which in many respects anticipated the best modern achievements.

Owing to the prevailing mountain relief, the Mediterranean countries suffered from a paucity of level land adapted to tillage. Young folded systems with steep slopes, narrow valleys, and eroded canyons alternated here and there with old highlands of gentler slope. Coastal plains and interior lowlands were small and rare. Nearly the whole region was broken up into a series of narrow valleys opening out into deltaic flats, enclosed on three sides by hills or mountains. These were the garden spots of the Mediterranean. Here population concentrated, living off the produce of the small but fertile area, and securing its luxuries by sea-borne commerce. But population early outstripped the local means of subsistence. The home fields were compelled to produce more by improved methods of cultivation. Mountain-sides were terraced to extend the arable area. Retaining walls protected the new-made fields from erosion, and constant manuring kept up the fertility of these shallow shelves of land. On the durable valley fields every method was applied to increase the yield; repeated fertilization of the soil, careful tillage, intelligent selection of crops suited to climate and soil, importation of foreign seed and foreign plants, painstaking seed selection, all combined to constitute a precocious form of intensive tillage.

The Mediterranean climate, by reason of its sub-tropical temperatures, winter rains, and summer droughts, caused winter to become the chief season of tillage, and summer a period of relative rest. For the sown crops of winter, which were aided by the mild winter temperatures, the rains usually sufficed; but owing to the variability of the annual precipitation and to the uncertain duration and intensity of the long summer drought, the Mediterranean peasant had to adjust his tillage to the constant threat of inadequate rainfall. Hence he resorted to dry farming methods, which involved an alternate year of crop and fallow, elaborate plowing and working both of the fallow and the crop land, and careful discrimination in the use of soils, those which were dry and those which were retentive of moisture. The method of soil improvement resulting from this pressure of climatic conditions was a form of intensive agriculture.

The summer drought, which increased in length and intensity from north to south and from west to east in the long ellipse of the Mediterranean lands, necessitated irrigation for the cultivation of summer crops. These included many legumes, all vegetables, and also monsoon fruits which, in the course of time, were imported from the Orient and which required for their growth both heat and moisture. Irrigated tillage was also a form of intensive agriculture. It involved an expenditure of labor and capital in the construction of reservoirs and conduits; it necessitated frequent manuring of the irrigated fields which could be cropped all the year round; and it encouraged selection of seeds and plants in order to secure a fair return upon the valuable irrigated land. The mild winter temperatures of the Mediterranean region provided a long growing season which repaid tillage and therefore was an incentive to increased effort. The definitive checks upon the crops which might be raised were the amount of rain or available irrigation water and the quality of the soil.

Soils—The ancient farmers recognized the importance of soils and distinguished many varieties. Interest in the quality of soil meets us in the earliest Greek literature. Odysseus, in the Isle of the Cyclops, observes that "the land might yield a very heavy crop and one always in season, for the subsoil is rich." [1] Homer in the *Iliad* speaks of "deep-soiled Troyland," "deep-soiled Thrace," "deep-soiled Phthia," and "goodly Elis," [2]—a broad plain of loose Tertiary materials, overlaid by alluvium washed down from the Arcadian Highland. He knows "the fresh plowed field of rich tilth and wide," where "the upturned soil shows black." [3] One would have enjoyed touring Greece with that observant poet before the light of his eyes went out. Herodotus sweeps Egyptian land with the discerning glance of a farmer; he describes the soil of the Nile flood plain as "black and crumbling as if it were mud and alluvial deposit, brought down by the river from Ethiopia; whereas we know that the earth of Libya is reddish and somewhat more sandy, and that of Arabia and Syria is more clayey and flinty." [4] Libya and Arabia defined respectively the western and eastern borders of the Nile flood plain, which alone constituted the Egypt of his time.

The ancients judged the fertility of soil by its color, according as it was black, dark, red, grey, or white; by its texture as fat or lean, heavy or light, dense and sticky or loose, compact or friable, gravelly, chalky or sandy, loamy or clayey; by its water content as wet, miry, moist, dry and parched; and finally by its natural vegetation.[5] They recognized various combinations of these qualities, as light loose, warm soil or cold, dense clayey soil, or rich friable soil. At an early date they appreciated the value of mixed soils, in regard not only to fertility but also to mechanical composition. Theophrastus apparently questioning many of the two thousand students who attended his lectures in the Lyceum of Athens, summarized the agricultural practice which they had observed in their widely scattered native localities. "They tell us to mix contrasted kinds of soils, heavy with light and light with heavy; thin soil with rich, and also the red (*terra rubra*) with the white; and all contrasted kinds with rich soil. For the mixture not only remedies defects, but also adds strength, no matter what kind it was. If you will mix with another soil that which is exhausted and unsuited to grains, it will bear again as if renewed." [6]

The ancients distinguished soils also by their location in valleys, at the base of mountains, or on the middle or upper slopes; [7] they recognized the relation of fertility and soil depth to the terrain, and therefore gave more manure to hillside fields than to valley land. [8] Moreover, they sowed thickly or scantily according to the quality of the soil. [9] "A fat good soil can bear heavier seeding than one which is sandy and light. However, they say that the same piece of land can take up more seed at one time and less at another time." [10] Rainfall, snow, exposure, winds, dew, sun, and especially cultivation were all recognized as affecting the yield of the soil. [11] Xenophon found nothing more profitable than to buy poor neglected farm land, renovate it by judicious cultivation, and sell it at an increased price. [12] Pliny dissented from a current opinion that the land of Italy was worn out, although the deterioration of field agriculture in his time was generally acknowledged. [13] As a matter of fact, these and other soils of the region have shown marked durability and powers of recuperation.

The soils of the Mediterranean region were in general young soils. They were allied in origin for the most part to the black earths of southern Russia. Conditions of climate and relief and the presence of widespread limestone formations combined to maintain the youth of these soils. The moderate or meager rainfall characteristic of large parts of the basin and its seasonal distribution tended to reduce the evil of leaching and hence to conserve the scant humus content of the soil. The limey constituents in the soil contributed to the same end by furnishing abundant supplies of calcium carbonate, which counteracted the natural tendency to acid formation and deflocculation; for a flocculated soil tends to preserve its fertility indefinitely. The limey content was constantly renewed from the underlying rock or it was supplied by the wash of earth on the ever present slopes. Moreover, the prevailing mountain relief produced a slow rejuvenation of the soils by the steady transportation of fresh soil materials from the higher to the lower slopes, from mountain to piedmont, and from piedmont to valley or coastal plain. This process was accelerated by the erosive power of the wet weather streams, which carried off waste from the slopes and banks all the more effectively because the earth was baked and cracked by the summer drought.

The Tertiary terraces flanking many Mediterranean highlands consisted of weathered limestone, sandstone, marl, and clay, veneered with alluvium. They therefore provided successive levels of deep arable soil extending far up the mountains. But numerous slopes of pure Cretaceous or Tertiary limestones were covered with only a thin mantle of earth. These furnished considerable areas of shallow soil, poor and arid, because the rain water percolated through the porous underlying rock; and where precipitation was heavy, as in the karst districts of Italy, Illyria, Greece, Epiros, and the summit of the Judean Plateau, these conditions combined to develop the *terra rossa* or *terra rubra* of the ancients, infertile red clays, from which all alkalies had been leached out and the scant humus content had vanished. In contrast, the black earth soils of Scythia were vast in extent and inexhaustible in their alkaline content, owing to low rainfall of 12 to 18 inches.[14]

Another factor indirectly encouraged ancient Mediterranean tillage. This was the enclosed sea which everywhere opened up avenues of communication; along these Greek and Phœnician colonists and traders carried improved methods of tillage from old cultural centers in the east to the pioneer regions of the west. Agricultural exchanges characterized the maritime commerce from earliest times. Import and export of foodstuffs figured equally in the trade of ancient Palestine and ancient Spain. The result was the practice of propagating new seeds and new plants from oversea lands. It was a trial and error method, but brought about a great diversification in the crops raised.

The ancient farmer learned by experience that climate and soil were big factors in the differentiation of fruits and grains; that a vine stock from Lebanon, for instance, gave a different grape on the slopes of Vesuvius or in the plain of the Rhone Valley. He became an experimental farmer, observing the results of every agricultural venture and drawing his conclusions accordingly. He was weak in theory but strong in practice. His methods were warranted to produce results, his result, the best yield possible for his particular type of climate and of soil. Hence he watched his neighbors' crops and was guided by their experience.[15] In our common parlance, he was a good "dirt farmer."

Conditions of climate and relief gave rise to an elaborate system of land utilization. Plains were used for grain, hills for vineyards and orchards, mountains for forests and summer pasturage.[16] Undrained land in deltaic swamps or water-soaked lowlands were reserved for wet meadows, where hay was mown or cattle were grazed in summer.[17] Other undrained fields were planted to asparagus, to osiers and willows which provided material for baskets and wagon bodies.[18] Rich, moist valley lands were reserved for wheat, flax, and cabbage;[19] poor level soils were planted in various legumes which required little nutriment, like snail clover.[20] Red soil or *terra rossa* of the weathered limestone would yield good lupine and lentil crops.[21] All ancient authorities stress the importance of selecting certain soils for certain crops. Limestone or crystalline rock slopes with thin stony soil, like the hills of Judea and Caria, were suited for figs and olives. They produced small trees but excellent fruit.[22] Mountain-sides of better soil, like volcanic ash overlying Tertiary deposits of limestone and clay, were reserved for vineyards, which climbed the southward slopes up to 1,000 feet or more, as on Mount Massicus in Italy and Tmolos in Phrygia.[23]

The base of a mountain range, where the land was enriched by the wash of the highlands behind, was considered the best site for a farm; here the soil was young and the fields were accessible to irrigation streams from the highlands, while the farm itself was protected from floods by its elevated site. A southward facing piedmont was the best.[24] Here the sun's heat was most effective by reason of insolation and the mountains behind warded off cold winds from the north, while air drainage protected orchards against untimely frosts. This was the general practice in the land utilization system of the ancients, but many exceptions to these rules were caused by local conditions of climate and soil.

SEASON OF TILLAGE—The distribution of rainfall made the mild Mediterranean winter the season of vegetative growth and the dry summer a period of rest, unless irrigation could supply the requisite moisture. Consequently for the ancient farmer, the winter half-year was preëminently the season of work. Most of the ploughing, harrowing, sowing, and planting had to be crowded into the ever shortening days between the autumn equinox and the winter solstice. The summer, after the early harvest in May or June, was the normal season of leisure. Hesiod, writing in the eighth century B.C., advised the Greek peasant to rest during the heat of the dog days and feast.[25] Therefore, ancient Mediterranean farm life, before the introduction of summer irrigated crops, presented a sharp contrast in its season of rural activity to ·the Tigris and Euphrates basins, where tillage depended upon the river floods caused by the spring and summer melting of the snows in Armenia; and it presented a like contrast to central and northern Europe, where the summer heat determined the season of tillage. But it accorded with Egypt, for the Nile floods, caused by the summer rains in the Highlands of Abyssinia, did not recede till autumn and therefore threw the big crops into the winter.

Autumn was the sowing season throughout the Mediterranean Basin; it was called "the seed-time" in Greece and Italy. "The yearly cry of the crane from the cloud," winging his way southward, was the sign of approaching winter with its rains, and warned the farmer that all hands "must plough and sow early and late, on wet days and dry, that the grain lands may be full," says Hesiod, and "a bounteous harvest come with the white blossoms of spring."[26] To delay this autumn labor was to invite disaster. On the Roman farm the fall equinox was "the time to urge on the belated ploughs, while the dry soil allows it, while the clouds hang aloft."[27] The later advent of the autumn rains in Greece postponed the date of ploughing and sowing to October, and in Phœnicia and Palestine to November, when the first showers softened the soil preliminary to the heavy rains which began a month later. At the first sign of rain it was customary to "begin and sow the barley fields right into the showery skirts of frost-bound winter."[28] Greater caution had to be exercised with the wheat, which required immediate showers for its germination, but no excess moisture; therefore it was sown after the barley, at successive intervals during the autumn to insure at least some yield.[29] In Greece, "all farmers look wistfully to the sky to see when the gods will send rain and allow them to sow." The rural maxim was: "Sow not on dry soil"; and the losses of impatient farmers pointed its moral.[30] In the eastern part of the Mediterranean Basin, where the growing season was short at best, the harvest was reduced or ruined if the autumn showers preceding the rains were tardy, or if the rainy season failed to end in late spring showers, which fortified the crops for their last period of growth. These were "the former and the latter rains" of the Bible for which the Hebrew farmer prayed.[31]

The crops grew quickly through the warm humid autumn, slowly during the winter, but matured rapidly under the increased warmth of spring. "Abundant harvests come with abundant heat" is Vergil's generalization for Italy; and in Greece Hesiod tells the farmer "to gather the ripe grain, when the snail seeks the shade of a leaf to escape the heat of the sun." [32] The harvest fell in May or June, according to the locality, and had ideal conditions of warm, drying weather. The ripe crops were never jeopardized as in lands of summer rains.

Less common was spring wheat or "three-months wheat," so called because it matured in three months after sowing in February or March. It was grown in Alpine Italy, Thrace, Sicily, southern Euboea and Boeotia, and was known to yield a hard, heavy grain as opposed to the light, soft winter wheat, which however was generally preferred for food.[33] On the Scythian plains of the Black Sea, both kinds were raised. The spring wheat of Thrace was attributed by the ancients to the severe winters of that northern region, though the lingering spring rains may have been a factor. The heavy Boeotian wheat was doubtless spring-sown, as it is today, on the margin of the Lake Copais basin as the winter flood waters gradually receded and Lake Copais contracted. The rich lacustrine soil and high water table explained the superior quality of the grain.[34]

Millet and panic also were raised in various parts of the Mediterranean lands. As they required both heat and moisture, they found proper conditions in the irrigated fields of the Nile Valley and the Cilician lowland, where they were extensively cultivated. In other districts they were planted at the vernal equinox, throve with a little irrigation, and matured after a short growing season. They were raised on a large scale as summer crops in the Scythian plains, in Campania of Italy, the northern part of the Po valley and in southern Gaul,—all regions of summer showers or irrigation streams.

Besides cereals, several minor field crops which could stand the winter cold were planted in autumn and harvested in summer. But in the northern districts of the region where the winters were rather severe but summers showery, and irrigation was easy, these were set out in the spring. Various legumes like lupines, beans, kidney-bean, various peas, chick-pea, vetch and lentils were usually sown in the autumn in Greece and peninsular Italy; but if they missed this seed time for any reason, they might be sown in the spring. Peas and lentils, which could ill endure the cold, were usually spring sown.[35] Vergil, whose principles of agriculture were reminiscent of his father's farm in the Mincio valley north of the river Po, advocated spring as the best seed time for beans, as frequent summer showers and abundant ground water provided all the moisture necessary, while irrigation was feasible at the critical blossoming time.[36] Sesame, like millet and panic, was a summer crop in both Greece and Italy and all three throve best by irrigation.[37]

Flax, which in time was widely cultivated, required a rich moist soil, which it was known to exhaust.[38] Soil, therefore, was the chief factor in its distribution. It was raised in Egypt for linen from the earliest times; in Palestine before and after the Jewish conquest,[39] where owing to its exhausting effects on the soil, tenants' contracts permitted it to be sown only once in seven years.[40] It flourished in the alluvial plain of the Phasis River in the land of Colchis, where Herodotus surmised that the culture had been introduced by Egyptian colonists.[41] It was known in Homeric Greece only by the imported fiber; later fine crops were grown in the fertile Tertiary plain of Elis,[42] but in general the climate and soil of Greece were too dry.[43] Flax was raised extensively in the Po Valley and the east coast

of Spain where it gave rise to a finished linen industry.[44] It was
sown in spring in northern Italy and probably in Colchis where
summer rains were bountiful; but in autumn in Egypt and other
semi-arid lands of the Eastern Mediterranean. The fiber was
used for various grades of linen, and the flaxseed for food both
in Greece and Italy.[45]

DRY FARMING—The annual rainfall in most Mediterranean
lands usually sufficed for the winter crops, but owing to wide
variations in amount and in duration of the rains, tillage early
developed dry farming methods. Records of recurrent drought
and famine meet us in the ancient history of Palestine, Syria,
Cyprus, Crete, Asia Minor, Greece, Cyrenaica and Italy.
These were often due to curtailment of the growing season.
Amos makes Jehovah say: "I have withholden the rain from
you when there were yet three months to the harvest." [46] This
meant cessation of the rains in February and consequent death
to the standing grain. Modern precipitation records of Jerusalem tell the same story. The "former rains" may begin any
time between October 4th and November 28th, the first date
promising a long growing season with timely germination of the
seed in a warm soil, and the latter a short season and imperfect germination in ground chilled by winter cold. Moreover,
the "latter rains" may cease any time between April 1st and
May 27th, the former date meaning imperilled crops and the
latter a full harvest. Italy, in 1922, lost so much of her wheat
harvest, because the rains stopped early in May before the
grain was filled out, that she had to lift the import duty on
wheat. The amount of the rainfall is equally unreliable. At
Jerusalem it fluctuates between 13 and 43 inches from a mean
annual of 26 inches; at Athens, between 4.5 and 22.5 inches
from a mean annual of 16 inches; in the Tunisian or Carthaginian district, between 13 and 26 inches from a mean annual
of 17.75 inches; at Syracuse between 10 and 43 inches from an
average of 25 inches.

These fluctuations are recognized by modern climatologists
as normal phenomena on the margin of the arid belts; and they
were taken into account by the ancient farmers. Dry farming
methods were developed to a surprising degree, in Palestine
and Greece in the ninth century B.C. or even earlier. Fields

were regularly allowed to lie fallow in alternate years.[47] The effect was not only to rest the land, but also to accumulate in the soil a whole year's supply of moisture for the next crop. To accomplish this end, the idle field was kept constantly under cultivation; for working the fallow removed weeds and rendered the soil lighter and moister.[48] Three ploughings were considered imperative, and a fourth or even fifth was advocated. Hesiod calls the fallow "the guardian against death and ruin."[49] He mentions "a thrice-ploughed fallow in the fertile land of Crete."[50] Homer frequently mentions "the thrice-ploughed fallow," which seems to have been the early standard.[51] For the thin dry limestone soils of Palestine, the Hebrew *Proverbs* advise a fourth or mid-winter ploughing: "The sluggard will not plough by reason of the winter; therefore he shall beg in harvest."[52] Besides the three ploughings between spring and fall, Theophrastus advocates winter ploughing for light dry soils in order to enrich and moisten them.[53] Theocritus observes it was the custom in ancient Elis to "sow the seed in fallow land thrice, aye, four times broken by the plough."[54] Italy's best practice was the same: "That field yields best which twice has felt the summer's heat and twice the winter's cold.[55] Pliny advised five ploughings for dense soils; nine were needed to break up the hard clay land of Etruria.[56] The ancients regarded the fallow as a means of accumulating all the resources of the soil, of which water was "the chief aliment."[57] "Fruitful fields in turn now yield to man his yearly bread upon the plains, and now again they pause, and gather back their strength," says Pindar.[58]

The fields destined for fallow were ploughed first in September in time to catch the autumn showers; the second time in mid-winter to make the soil hospitable both to the winter rains and to the frost; the third time in spring before the last showers of the rainy season; and a fourth time in mid-summer.[59] This last ploughing, which was emphasized by all ancient authorities, had the effect of breaking up the surface enough to prevent loss of moisture by capillary attraction; it was rarely followed by harrowing. The standard was a bare, clean fallow. A field overgrown with thorns and weeds proclaimed the owner a slothful man, void of understanding, indulging in "a little sleep, a little slumber, a little folding of the hands to sleep," but destined to bitter poverty.[60] Xenophon urges ploughing in spring and repeatedly during the summer, in order to eradicate weeds and turn up the fallow to the sun.[61]

Ploughing moreover had to be thorough. Theophrastus and Cato considered it the essence of good tillage.[62] The first furrows were run in straight lines and others were drawn obliquely across these to level the ridges.[63] A field was considered well ploughed when it was scarcely possible to detect in which direction the share had last gone.[64] Moreover, all clods were regularly broken up with the mattock, rake or hoe,[65] till no harrowing was necessary for the summer fallow or even for the sown field in autumn except to cover the seed, according to most authorities. Varro and Columella advise harrowing only in case of poorly tilled land.[66] On hillsides, furrows were drawn horizontally in order to prevent washing and to hold the moisture for the plant roots.[67]

The depth of the ploughing was determined by the nature of the land. In Syria and Palestine, where the underlying rock came near the surface, the native farmers used small ploughshares which made a shallow furrow, "lest the earth burnt by the sun, refuse a crop." [68] The Greeks appreciated the value of deep culture. It was customary in Megara every five years to dig down deep and turn up the subsoil as far as the water penetrated, because the rain carried the fertile elements down beyond the reach of the roots. The peasants of the rich lake plains of Thessaly had a digging implement called a *mischum* which did the work of a subsoil plough, turning up the earth from a considerable depth.[69] The comment of Ulysses on the subsoil of Sicily suggests that even the Homeric Greeks may have practised deep cultivation. The Romans considered that grain land had to be rich and well tilled for two feet down, not merely on the surface. Hence the fallow was ploughed deep, in order that the roots of the crop might readily penetrate.[70]

Deviation from this alternate fallow system was considered permissible only when the winter grain crop was followed by a winter legume crop, which after an early harvest was turned under as a green manure.[71] But this three-field system had to be applied with caution. On a farm of 200 *jugera*, 100 *jugera* were sown in autumn; if a spring crop was raised, it was limited to 30 *jugera* so that nearly half of the land remained fallow. Only rich, moist, volcanic soils, like those in the Neapolitan district where the ground water was high, were cropped every year.[72]

The fallow system persists in modern Greece. "Grain or fallow" or "grain or forage crop" describes the use of farm land there today, even in the excellent sandy loam of the Marathon plain.[73] In the Peloponnesos, the cropland lies fallow every second or third year, except in a few very fertile districts which are irrigated for gardens or used for currant plantations.[74]

The yield per acre was moderate, despite all efforts at soil improvement through tillage and fertilization. Herodotus and Pliny cite returns of a hundred fold or more, but these were obviously exaggerations. The same applies to the sixty and thirty fold of the Bible, an impossible yield even for the scant sowing practised then as today on the poor soil of the Judean Plateau. According to reliable authorities, the maximum return known in Roman Italy about 50 B.C. was eight to ten fold. This was the yield of winter wheat from rich volcanic soils in eastern Sicily, and it amounted to 20 or 24 bushels to the acre.[75] A yield of fifteen fold or 36 bushels of wheat to the acre was quite extraordinary and restricted to a few favored spots.[76] Old Cato, who a hundred years earlier tilled a farm of average soil in the Sabine hills near Rome, was content with five fold, which meant 10 bushels of wheat or 12 bushels of barley to the acre. This average fell to 8 bushels of wheat or less in the time of Columella (60 A.D.), when field tillage declined in Italy owing to excessive competition of foreign grain.[77]

ORCHARD AND VINEYARD CULTURE—Hardly less important than field agriculture was the orchard and vineyard culture of the ancient Mediterranean world. Every farm normally combined both branches of tillage in order to provide its own bread, olive oil and wine. This was the rule from the earliest times. To the ancient Jews, vineyards and orchards were essential features of sedentary agriculture as opposed to pastoral nomadism.[78] Every son of Israel wanted to sit under his own vine and his own fig tree.[79] Solomon purchased building materials for the Temple with wheat, oil and wine, all products of Palestine.[80]   Grain fields, vineyards and orchards characterized the princely estates of the Homeric age in Greece.[81]   Each farm, each district was practically self-sufficing.

But as maritime trade developed, as centers of population increased in size and multiplied, natural grain regions like Egypt and the Scythian plains became the dominant sources for bread-stuffs, though every small district and especially inland localities maintained some cereal culture against emergency times of war and piracy, when oversea supplies of grain became unreliable.   With the curtailment of home-grown wheat fields, orchard and vineyard culture spread.[82]   From the time of Solon, Attica was famous for its olive groves, the only remunerative crop on that poor limestone soil; Lesbos and Chios were noted for their vineyards.   In the last decades of the Roman Republic, Italy looked like one great orchard,[83] while its mountains were mantled in vineyards.   These branches of tillage yielded a big profit.   They increased in regions of dense population or small arable area, where large returns from the soil were imperative.   Such were the islands of the Ægean Sea and countless mountain-rimmed valleys, like that of Sparta. Certain localities, adapted by soil and climate to superior varieties of fruit or vine, specialized accordingly.

Ancient farmers made a radical distinction between sown and planted crops.[84]   The latter were assigned to the hills, but were developed by close adaptation to conditions of prevailing winds, soil, exposure and air drainage.   Their place in the complex system of land utilization was formulated in 313 B.C. by the Greek Theophrastus, but the practice was centuries older. Theophrastus says: "Use your rich soils for grains and thin soils for trees.   Grains and all other annuals take the nutriment from the surface soil, which therefore ought not to be thin or of a quality to be quickly exhausted, as happens in a shallow layer of earth.   But trees, equipped with long and strong roots, draw their nourishment from the depths.   In rich soils, trees run to wood and foliage, but yield little or no fruit.   Hence a thin soil is superior from both standpoints; it produces a balanced foliage and fruitage." [85]   But this lean hillside soil required constant spadework to render it permeable by the roots, and manuring to provide plant food for the trees.[86]

The olive, fig, and vine, held a conspicuous place in ancient Mediterranean tillage. They seem to have been indigenous throughout the region, as they were equipped by nature to withstand the summer drought; but their intensive cultivation, by which wild forms were domesticated and superior varieties were produced, spread from the eastern to the western end of the basin through the distributing agencies of trade and colonization. Vines and olive and fig trees survived the summer drought by reason of their elaborate root systems which penetrated down to the moisture conserved in the deeper layers of soil, and moreover spread out widely to gather in the maximum amount of moisture during the rainy season. The olive figured large in the domestic economy of the ancients. Its oil supplied the place of butter which was excluded by the poor pasturage of the Mediterranean lands, and it furnished the chief ingredient in the unguents and ointments for the skin which the strong dry winds of the Mediterranean summers made a necessity. Bread, oil, wine, figs, and grapes, eaten either fresh or dried as raisins and fig cakes, formed staple articles in the ancient Mediterranean diet. Wine was the universal beverage except for the beer used in Egypt and the mead consumed by the retarded mountaineers of central Spain.[87]

Orchards and vineyards flowered in early spring and produced their fruit in late summer or autumn. In ordinary seasons, they weathered the summer drought without irrigation, but in semi-arid regions or in especially dry years they demanded some artificial watering. Egypt, which is a special province of the Mediterranean region both from the climatic and physiographic standpoint, produced fruit trees and vines only by irrigation.[88]

Everywhere in the Mediterranean region these plants had to begin their life in nursery beds in order to develop an adequate root system, their prime requirement, before they should be set out in the fields. These nursery beds were carefully prepared. Generally a trench was dug two or three feet deep and about as wide; stones or boulders were placed at the bottom for drainage, and covered with soil enriched with the proper kind of manure. The soil of the nursery bed and its exposure both to sun and prevailing winds was similar to that of the field into which the young trees or vines should be transferred,[89] "lest a sudden change of mother estrange the young plant," says Vergil. Shoots selected for propagation were the best varieties which could be found adapted to the local soil and climate.[90] They were irrigated morning and night until they had made a good start, and thereafter they were tended two to five years before being transplanted. Then they were removed with great care and rapidity to avoid mutilation of the roots and to prevent their getting dry.[91] Months or even a year before this important operation, holes were dug in the orchard or vineyard deeper than the trench of the nursery bed in order to facilitate the downward growth of the young roots.[92] Moreover, the young plant was then set out in the field with its south side indicated by a chalk mark, facing south, and its back to the north;[93] because, says Vergil, "so strong is the habit of infancy."[94] Vine stocks and trees set out in a rich plain were placed close together, because the abundant fertility of the soil would support the close planting;[95] but on the thinner soils of hillsides or mountains, they were given more room.[96]

Olive and fig trees were known to have especially wide-spreading roots.[97] For this reason, a law in ancient Attica prohibited a farmer from planting these trees within nine feet of his neighbor's boundary line, lest the roots should encroach upon the next estate.[98] The interval between olive trees in Italy measured from twenty-five to thirty feet according to Cato,[99] but the distance varied elsewhere according to the locality. Mago of Carthage prescribed an interval of seventy-five feet each way between the olive trees, or of forty-five feet where the soil was poor and exposed to winds.[100] This wide spacing undoubtedly reflected the low rainfall—10 to 14 inches—in the coastal plain of Tripolis, a region long famous for its olive groves, and in Mago's time (500 B.C.)[101] already in the Carthaginian sphere of influence. The trees there and also in the Atlas coast valleys were very large, because the soil was rich and ground water high. They were large also and widely spaced in the orchards of the Guadalquivir Valley; but there the interval may have been due to fertile soil and low rainfall, or to leave room for the grain crops regularly sown in the olive groves. The reach of the branches was considered the proper guide for the spacing.[102] The interval between pomegranates and myrtle was at least nine feet, and more for apples, pears, almonds and figs. Declivities required smaller intervals between the trees because the spread of the branches was less.[103] On windy sites it was found advisable to plant the trees close together for protection.

It was a general principle, recognized by Theophrastus and other writers, that barren trees lived longer than fecund ones, and those bearing scant fruit than those yielding much.[104] The cultivation of the orchard, however, aimed at production of fruit, and not at the vigor of the tree. To achieve this purpose the ancients developed an elaborate system of pruning, thereby diverting the nutriment of the tree into the fruit. It was usual to keep the tree low and compact, since a tall growth involved waste of nutriment.[105] But in starting the young tree on its life course, climatic conditions forced the consideration of the woody growth until the tree was established. Experience taught that autumn pruning encouraged the vegetative growth and spring pruning the development of fruit. Hence it was the rule to prune the poor, meager vine in the autumn and the strong healthy vine in the spring. Moreover, the vine quicksets were cut down almost to the ground at the end of the first year and again at the end of the second year in order to develop/ roots and to encourage vigorous branching.[106]

The application of this principle meets us in Palestine among the Jews, who probably learned it from the resident Canaanites, a people already advanced in agriculture. The Bible instructs the Jews to plant all kinds of fruit trees but forbad them to eat the fruit of the tree till the fifth year of its growth. For the first three years, the yield was declared unclean; that of the fourth year was sacrificed in the Temple, but that of the fifth might be eaten.[107] The effect of this religious taboo was to discourage all pruning for fruitage and to encourage pruning for tree growth. The experience of American farmers in the interior of Washington teaches that hot, dry summers with intense sunlight stimulate premature fruiting.[108] This evil under similar climatic conditions in ancient Palestine was checked by autumn pruning. But the orchards once established were made to give as large a crop as possible, because of the relative paucity of good arable land and gentle slopes. The Bible for-

bad the Jews to destroy olive trees in war time, either wantonly
or to use the wood in besieging a city, because they were an
asset for the conquerors.[109]

The chief problem in the ancient Mediterranean orchard was
to get the root system of a tree established. Young trees with
shallow roots were at a disadvantage unless they were accessible to irrigation streams; but artificial watering often impaired the quality of the fruit. Hence grafting early became a
feature of ancient fruit culture. A tree once established with
a strong root system, such as wild olive, wild pear or wild
apple, could be utilized by a fine grafted shoot.[110] According
to Theophrastus, it was thus possible to upset the laws of nature, since the vine-dresser could produce black, white, and red
bunches on the same shoot and could develop seedless grapes.[111]
Experience also taught the ancients that grafted branches gave
a yield true to type, while seedlings tended to revert to the wild
variety or bear inferior fruit.[112] Grafting enabled the farmer
to render barren trees productive and to introduce superior
varieties.

OLIVE ORCHARDS—A large proportion of the orchard land
apparently was devoted to olives. This was true in ancient as
in modern times.[113] Pliny mentions fifteen varieties of olives,
distributed from Syria to central Spain, and from the base of
the Alps to Africa. Italy raised the best fruit; Istria and
the Guadalquivir valley of Spain (Bætica) ranked next. Roman
Africa "has been all but deprived of oil and wine," because both
climate and soil were better adapted to grain production.[114]

Olive trees throve on a dry calcareous soil like that of Attica
or Judea, or on a tenacious clay covering a slope, or on a mixture of clay and sand with a gravelly sub-soil.[115] Drainage
was imperative. "Stubborn land and ungracious hills, fields
of lean marl and pebbly brushwood welcome the long-lived
groves of Pallas Athene," says Vergil,[116] speaking from the
standpoint of the Alpine piedmont with its ample rainfall.
Cato and Varro, familiar with the dry summers of Latium, ad-
vocate a dense warm soil for eight specified varieties of olive
trees.[117] In the Guadalquivir valley, with a fifteen inch rainfall, the orchards needed rich soil to retain moisture; but they
yielded an excellent fruit in the Venafrum hill country of Cam-

pania, where the soil was gravelly and the rainfall amounted to
30 inches.[118] Hence it was a question of soil in relation to climatic condition. But exposure also came into the problem.
The site of the olive grove might vary; but a location near the
sea which reduced the frost hazard, and a westward facing
slope were always preferable.[119]

Olive orchards required only moderate cultivation, because
they were inured to the dry summers. It was necessary to
prune, to manure, to plow or dig about the trees each year,
and occasionally to bare the surface roots and clean away the
suckers.[120] Improved methods of tillage which developed in
course of time greatly curtailed the interval between planting
the slow-growing orchard and reaping a crop. Hesiod said
that a man who planted an olive grove would never live long
enough to eat its fruit; but young trees raised for five years in
the nursery bed and cultivated after transplanting could be
made to yield in seven years. But this was only under the
best climatic conditions; in many localities the interval was
longer.[121]

FIG ORCHARDS—Figs ranked next to olives as an article of
food. They were grouped with bread and oil in the diet of the
common people throughout the Mediterranean lands.[122] Farm
slaves were fed chiefly on figs in Attica and Italy from the summer solstice, when the first crop came in, till late autumn.[123]
Dried figs were eaten by the country folk all winter in Italy,[124]
they were welcome as army rations in ancient Palestine,[125] and
once served instead of grain for the forces of Philip of Macedon
in western Asia Minor,[126] doubtless owing to their sugar content.

Fig trees were adapted to a semi-arid climate, owing to their
numerous spreading roots [127] and their scant leafage,[128] which
lost little moisture by evaporation. They thrived best where
the rainfall was light and the summer drought long; they preferred a sunny, well drained site on a hillside and a thin dry soil
of weathered limestone or chalk, mingled with gravel or rocks.[129]
Hence districts offering these natural conditions raised famous
figs,—Caria and Phrygia in southwest Asia Minor where the
"Smyrna figs" are raised today,[130] the island of Chios and even
Paros with its soil of weathered marble,[131] and Attica which forbad the export of its figs, needing to conserve all its scant

home-grown food supply.[132]   Theophrastus must have had the
infertile land of Attica in mind when he advocated a low or
valley site for fig and olive orchard.[133]   Italy, which acclimated
many imported fig trees, planted one kind in a light chalky soil,
and another in a rich or well manured soil.[134]   Only the Me-
garean and Laconian fig were improved by irrigation, which
was detrimental to all other kinds.[135]   Hence the numerous varieties, twenty-nine in Pliny's time,[136] finally extended the possible selection of fig orchard sites; but lean hillsides held the
preference.

Fig trees yielded their crop in June and again in September.
The late fruit hung on the trees all winter to be harvested at
will.   The failure of the crop was a serious matter.   Yet the
domestic trees, except the varieties grown in middle Italy, and
the Isthmus of Corinth, frequently made a diminished yield
owing to the dropping of the immature fruit.   A remedy for
this evil was assiduously sought, Theophrastus tells us, and
was found in caprification.   This consisted in attaching to the
branches of the domestic trees, which bore only female flowers,
the fruit of the wild fig or caprifig, in order that minute gall
wasps, *psenes*, which were generated therein, might crawl into
the half-developed edible fruit of the domestic fig.   The time
for the operation was in late June and again in September,
when the wild figs contained abundant male flowers with their
pollen, and the insects were ready to emerge.[137]   This natural
process was properly interpreted by Theophrastus as cross fertilization of the fig fruit by an insect.[138]

The ancient Greeks thus improved upon nature's method,
while following nature's example; they had doubtless learned
from older cultivators of the fig in Syria and Asia Minor to tie
bunches of the wild fruit on the domestic fig tree in order to
insure a short journey for the insect to its destination.   However, a like purpose was achieved by planting caprifigs in the
fig orchards, the early variety near the early, and the late near
the late kind, if the wild trees were set out on the windward side
of the orchard so that the breezes might aid the flight of the
little insects to the domestic trees.[139]   This method was less
troublesome but also less reliable, especially in late summer
when the strong north winds might sweep the insects quite

away.[140] These pollen-carriers were necessary to save the figs which were best adapted for drying; and caprification also improved the flavor of the fruit. Hence the insects were made the subject of careful study by the ancients. The *psenes* were found to have an enemy in the *cynipes*. The Greeks discovered a corrective for this pest in *cancri* (literally crabs) which preyed upon the *cynipes* and which therefore were applied to the trees.[141] The *cynipes* and *cancri* have not been certainly identified, but the *psenes* are known to moderns as the *blastophaga grossorum*. They were colonized in California from Caria after Smyrna fig trees were introduced into that state between 1880 and 1890. There, also, the immature fruit dropped until caprification was practised.

A similar method was used to fertilize palm trees and prevent their dropping the immature dates. It consisted in cutting off the spathe of the male palm and shaking out its pollen over the flower of the female tree. From its resemblance to caprification, this treatment of the palm was called *olynthazein* or "the use of the wild fruit." "In the latter case it was a genuine marriage; in the former, the same result was achieved in a different manner," says Theophrastus, anticipating Darwin by 2,165 years.[142]

What the fig and olive were to the northern and eastern coast lands of the Mediterranean, the date palm was to the hot southern rim. It furnished nourishing fruit, cakes, wine, fiber and inferior wood. The Arab saying that the date palm flourishes with its head in fire and its feet in water indicates the conditions for its cultivation: tropical heat, aridity, saline soil, and irrigation. Though the tree grew at certain places on the European coast, it was either sterile or yielded immature dates.[143] The northern limit of its growth in ancient Ægean lands ran through Chios, Delos, Tenos and the southern end of Eubœa, where it runs unchanged today.[144] The palm was fecund in Libya, Egypt, Phœnicia, Syria, Cyprus, and Crete; but yielded dates suitable for drying only in the Dead Sea-Jordan Valley.[145] This depression, 682 to 1,293 feet below sea level in the rain-shadow of the Judean Plateau, insured torrid heat and an arid climate with a scant eight-inch rainfall. Springs breaking out along the step-faults of the Jordan rift

provided irrigation water. Hence the excellence and fecundity
of the date plantations were unsurpassed, and made Jericho
famous as "the city of the palms." [146]

VINEYARD CULTURE—The culture of the vine presented many
problems of adjustment to geographic conditions. Maturing
its fruit in August and September, it had to run the gauntlet
of the dry summer months. Vineyards were planted on low
moist ground in the semi-arid districts like Attica,[147] but on fertile slopes of hills and mountains in the better watered parts of
the region.[148] There was a choice also in the exposure. Most
authorities advise a southerly aspect for the vineyards. Vergil
condemns a western exposure,[149] but in some localities it was
preferred to an easterly one. In northern sections, as in the
Po valley, another motive came into play owing to possible
frosts. There vineyards regularly faced north or northeast;
this exposure proved advantageous,[150] because the blossoming
was retarded beyond the frost limit. Some planters selected
the exposure according to the humidity of the locality. In a
dry section, they faced the vineyard east or north to conserve
the moisture in the plants, but in a humid region they planted
the vineyard on a southward slope. Vines and trees to which
dews were injurious were given an eastern exposure, that the
sun might quickly evaporate the moisture; but those helped by
the dew were made to face west or north in order to retain the
precious moisture as long as possible.[151]

The training of vines also was adjusted to climatic conditions. Where the ground moisture was abundant or where
rare showers relieved the summer drought, vines were grown on
posts or trellis or they were festooned from tree to tree in an
arbusta.[152] The latter method of training was found chiefly
in northern regions like Latium, Etruria, the Po valley, and
western and northern Hellas, where exposure to the winds did
not dry out the moisture of the plants. In arid regions like
Africa, southern Spain, Sicily, southern Greece, Palestine,
Syria, and parts of Asia Minor, the vines were allowed to trail
on the ground, and only the grape-bearing shoots were supported by short forked sticks.[153] The advantage was obvious.
Plants spreading out over the field presented the greatest possible surface to the heavy dews of high slopes; owing to their

low position they were little exposed to the desiccating summer winds, and their foliage shaded the soil about their roots. This was the method of planting in ancient times and it may be seen today in such districts.

The vines suffered, however, from the depredations of field mice and foxes, "the little foxes that spoil the vines" mentioned in the Song of Solomon.[154] Varro said that in the island of Pantellaria each vine thus planted needed a mouse trap and a fox trap.[155] Æsop who wrote the fable of the Fox and the Sour Grapes lived in Phrygia in the sixth century B.C. He was accustomed to the ground-grown vineyards of southern Asia Minor and also to grape-eating foxes. Therefore the thirsty marauder of the fable was disappointed when he came upon a trellis vine, doubtless a novelty introduced by Greek colonists from northern Hellas; for the fox expected to find the grapes lying on the ground within his reach. Theocritus in one of his Sicilian idyls gives us a charming description of such a vineyard.[156] It is twilight. A little lad sits on the rough wall guarding the vines, which are laden with fire-red clusters; for it is summer when the springs have dried up and wild animals are thirsty. Below him two foxes are skulking; one goes along the fine vine rows to devour the juicy grapes, and the other is eating the lunch in the wallet which the boy has dropped on the ground at his feet. For the little lad, perched on the vineyard wall, is absorbed in plaiting a pretty locust cage from stalks of asphodel; and less care of his wallet has he, and of the vines he was sent to guard, than delight in his interesting task.

Vineyards were allowed to sprawl on the ground also in Liguria on the slopes of the Apennines and on the Mediterranean coast of the Rhone lowland; but the climatic reason here was different. The low situation was a protection against the fierce *mistral* or Circius wind, which swept down from the heights of the Cevennes Plateau with irresistible violence.[157] This method of planting may be seen in Languedoc and Berry today, where the vine rows are generally protected also by a wind-break of cypress trees. The severe summer winds of north Africa provided an additional reason for the ground planting there. Moreover the shoots were pruned away above the first branches and the vine stock thus kept low.[158] This ground planting had the further advantage of economy, because it avoided the cost of props and trellis. Altogether, differences in soil, climate and location, determined the method of cultivation. Wherever the soil was damp, the vine was by preference grown high, for the grapes when forming needed plenty of sun and the vine shoots by natural inclination climbed up the highest trees, where they were supposed to yield the finest juice.[159]

The vine-dresser also helped to conserve the moisture in the vine. He ploughed deep and cut away the surface roots of the plant in early spring in order to force the development of the lower roots running down to the underground moisture.[160] He pruned also to throw the strength into a few shoots and increase the yield of fruit,[161] but in so doing he also reduced the surface of evaporation. The same end was accomplished also by the habit of thinning out the leaves as the summer advanced and the vintage approached.[162] The remaining leaves in time shriveled in the dry heat and ceased their function of transpiration; but even this was not enough. At the end of August, when the summer's heat and drought reached their maximum, and evaporation was most intense, the soil of the vineyard was regularly reduced to a powder; the dust was tossed up into the air and allowed to settle all over the vines as a protection against the sun.[163] This process, which was called *pulveratio*, checked evaporation from the grapes, leaves, and from the earth about the roots, by preventing capillary attraction of the underground water. This same method was applied in Megara during the September heat to cucumber and squash plants. The fruits were made far sweeter and more tender by this natural conservation of moisture than by the alternative measure of irrigation.[164] In the hot regions of north Africa and southern Spain the vine-dressers covered the grapes with straw to protect them from sun and wind. On the other hand, in northern parts of the Mediterranean region, where the vintage came late and the grapes were occasionally caught by the September showers, the vine-dressers stripped the leaves from the vine to expose the grapes to the intermittent sunshine, and thus hastened their ripening, lest they should rot on the vines.[165]

DRY FARMING IN VINEYARDS—The cultivation of the ancient Mediterranean vineyards represented a thorough system of dry farming, designed to conserve the moisture in the soil and in the plant during the whole period of growth. This involved constant hoe and spade work during spring and summer.[166] Vergil's instructions required unremitting labor in the vineyards, frequent plowings, banking up the earth repeatedly against the vine stocks, loosening the soils "thrice and again," breaking up the earth with hoe or mattock, "wheeling the steaming oxen between the vineyard rows." [167] That nothing might interfere with constant cultivation, all authorities from the Bible to Vergil advised against the planting of other crops between the vine rows. A system of clean culture was necessary. "Thou shalt not sow thy vineyard with divers seed, lest the fruit of the vineyard be defiled," says the author of *Deuteronomy*.[168] The purpose of this injunction was to facilitate constant cultivation of the vineyard soil, and to let the vine absorb all the moisture and nourishment in the ground. Columella sanctioned only the interculture of a short-lived green-manure crop, to be ploughed in.[169] A cover crop of legumes is common today in vineyards in Mediterranean regions which command sufficient water for irrigation; more common is a companion crop (*culture intercalaire*), planted for its own sake, which in Italy greatly reduces the yield of the vineyards.[170]

The ancients considered viticulture one of the most profitable branches of husbandry.[171] The yield of the vineyards seems to support this opinion. Some parts of Italy yielded 300 amphora of wine to the *jugerum* or 3,100 gallons to the acre, equivalent to 19,000 bottles. This was the return in the Faventia district at the northern base of the Apennines near Bologna. The Ager Gallicus on the Adriatic coast of Umbria yielded 200 amphora to the *jugerum* or 2,000 gallons to the acre.[172]

It was the wine-making connected with the vineyard culture which gave the large profit. Hence this twin industry was highly developed on small mountainous islands and peninsulas, and there it produced famous wines. Some of the best wines of the Grecian world came from Chios, Melos, Lesbos, Thasos, Ikaros, Andros, Naxos, Peparetos, Cyprus, and the Cnidos peninsula. All these islands had a large export trade.[173] In Italy the famous Falernian wine grew on the southward facing slopes of Mount Massicus, where a thick soil of weathered vol-

canic rock overlay limestone strata. Vesuvius and Ætna, the
Alban Mountains, and other volcanic districts produced superior wines.[174]

The earliest wine of great celebrity, lauded in the *Odyssey*,
came from the vineyards on the seaward slope of the Ismarus
range, which traces the southern coast of Thrace. It was red
and "honey-sweet" with a fine bouquet, and so strong that it
had to be diluted with twenty parts of water.[175] This same
district in Pliny's time produced a wine that could stand dilution with eighty times its volume of water.[176] Phœnician seamen, half traders, half pirates, put into the ports of Homeric
Greece and sold choice wines from vineyards spread like a car-
pet over the Mediterranean slope of the Lebanon Mountains.
These were the solace of the tired farmer, as Hesiod sings their
praise. "At the height of summer when the grasshopper sounds
his shrill note, when the heat is greatest and the skin is parched
and dry, under a shady ledge of rock with a bowl of Byblian
wine, three-fourths water, let me rest by an ever-flowing
spring." [177]

AUTHORITIES—CHAPTER XIV

1. *Odyssey*, IX, 136.
2. *Iliad*, III, 73; XX, 485; IX, 328; XI, 685, 697.
3. *Iliad*, XVIII, 541-548.
4. Herodotus, II, 12.
5. Xenophon, *Œconomicus*, XVI, 4. Herodotus, IV, 198. Theophrastus, *Historia Plantarum*, Bk. VIII, Chap. II, 8; Chap. VI, 2-6; Chap. VII, 5-7. Cato, *De Re Rustica*, 34. Varro, *Rerum Rusticarum*, Bk. I, Chap. IX, 2-7. Columella, *De Agricultura*, I, 2, 15; II, 9. Vergil, Georgic II, 177-258. Pliny, XVII, 3, 4.
6. Theophrastus, *De Causis Plantarum*, Bk. III, Chap. XX, 3.
7. Theophrastus, *Hist. Plant.*, II, Chap. V, 7.
8. Columella, II, Chap. V, 1; II, Chap. X, 6. Palladius, X, 1, 2.
9. *Leviticus*, XXVII, 16. Xenophon, *Œconomicus*, XVII, 8-11. Columella, II, 9. Varro, I, Chap. XLIV, 1. Pliny, XVIII, 55.
10. Theophrastus, *Hist. Plant.*, VIII, Chap. VI, 2.
11. *Ibid.*, VIII, Chap. VII, 2, 6; IV, Chap. III, 7.
12. Xenophon, *op. cit.*, XX, 22-26.
13. Pliny, XVII, 3.
14. Glinka, *Typen der Bodenbildung*, pp. 62-64. Berlin, 1914.
15. Xenophon, *op. cit.*, XVI, 3. Cato, VI, 1, 4. Varro, I, 44, 1.
16. Varro, I, Chap. VI, 2-6; Chap. XXIII, 1-4.

17. Theophrastus, *Hist. Plant.*, IV, Chap. VIII, 13.   Aristotle, *De Animalibus*, VII, Chap. 23, 6.   Neumann and Partsch, *Physikalische Geographie Griechenlands*, p. 404.   Breslau, 1885.

18. Cato, VI, 4; IX.

19. Vergil, Georgic II, 203-225.   Varro, I, Chap. XXIII, 3.

20. Varro, I, Chap. XXIII, 2.

21. Cato, 34 and 35.   Columella, II, 10.   Pliny, XVIII, 36.

22. Theophrastus, *De Causis*, III, Chap. VI, 6-8.   Vergil, Georgic II, 179-183.   Columella, V, Chap. X, 9.

23. Strabo, V, Chap. IV, 3, 8; XIV, Chap. I, 15.   Vergil, Georgic II, 97, 143.

24. Cato, I, 3.   Varro, I, Chap. XII, 1-3.

25. Hesiod, *Works and Days*, 582-595.   Loeb Lib. Edit.

26. *Ibid.*, 448-450, 458-461.

27. Vergil, Georgic I, 213-215.

28. *Ibid.*, I, 210-211.

29. Xenophon, *Œconomicus*, XVII, 4-6.   Theophrastus, *Hist. Plant.*, VIII, Chap. VI, 1; *De Causis*, IV, Chap. IV, 7.   Vergil, Georgic I, 219-226.   Pliny, *Hist. Nat.*, XVIII, 60.

30. Xenophon, *Œconomicus*, XVII, 2.

31. *Deuteronomy*, XI, 14.

32. Hesiod, *Works and Days*, 570-574.

33. Columella, II, Chap. VI, 38.   Pliny, XVIII, 12, 20.

34. Theophrastus, *De Causis*, IV, Chap. IX, 5.

35. Theophrastus, *Hist. Plant.*, VIII, Chap. I, 3-4; Chap. VI, 5.   Pliny, XVIII, 30, 31, 33, 36, 37.

36. Vergil, Georgic I, 214-216.

37. Theophrastus, *Hist. Plant.*, VIII, Chap. I, 1; Chap. VII, 3.   Pliny, XVIII, 22.

38. Theophrastus, *De Causis*, IV, Chap. V, 4.   Columella, II, Chap. X, 17.

39. *Joshua*, II, 6; *Hosea*, II, 9.

40. H. Vogelstein, *Die Landwirthschaft in Palästina zur Zeit der Mishnah*, p. 50.   Berlin, 1894.

41. Strabo, XI, Chap. II, 17.   Herodotus, II, 105; IV, 74

42. Pausanias, V, Chap. V, 2; VI, Chap. XXVI, 4.

43. H. Blümner, *Griechische Privataltertümer*, pp. 107-108.   Freiburg, 1882.

44. Pliny, XIX, 2.

45. Thucydides, IV, Chap. XXVI, 8.   Pliny, XIX, 3.

46. *Amos*, IV, 7.

47. Vergil, Georgic I, 71-72.   Varro, I, XLIV, 3.   Pliny, XVIII, 49.

48. Theophrastus, *De Causis*, III, Chap. X, 1.   Xenophon, *Œconomicus*, XVI, 11-15.

49. Hesiod, *Works and Days*, 464.

50. Hesiod, *Theogony*, 971.

51. *Iliad*, XVIII, 542.   *Odyssey*, V, 127; XIII, 32.

52. *Proverbs*, XX, 4.

53. Theophrastus, *De Causis*, III, Chap. XX, 2, 6-7.   *Hist. Plant.*, VIII, 5.

54. Theocritus, *Idyl*, 25.

55. Vergil, Georgic I, 42-49.   Compare Theophrastus, *De Causis*, III, Chap. XX, 6-7.

56. Pliny, XVIII, 49.   Pliny the Younger, *Letters*, Bk. V, 6.

57. Pliny, XIX, 59. Theophrastus, *Hist. Plant.*, IV, Chap. III, 7; *De Causis*, II, Chap. II, 1; Chap. V, 2; Chap. VI, 3.
58. Pindar, *Nemean Odes*, VI, 10-12.
59. Varro, I, 29-32.
60. *Proverbs*, XXIV, 30-34; *Hosea*, X, 12; *Jeremiah*, IV, 3.
61. Xenophon, *Œconomicus*, XVI, 12-14.
62. Cato, 61. Theophrastus, *De Causis*, III, Chap. X, 6.
63. Vergil, Georgic I, 9.
64. Varro, I, 9. Columella, II, 4-5.
65. *Hosea*, X, 11; *Isaiah*, XXVIII, 24-25. Vergil, Georgic I, 164. Varro, I, 29.
66. Columella, II, 5.
67. Pliny, XVIII, 49.
68. Pliny, XVII, 3. Theophrastus, *De Causis*, II, Chap. XX, 5.
69. Theophrastus, *De Causis*, III, Chap. XX, 4, 8.
70. Columella, II, 2, 23.
71. Varro, I, 44. Theophrastus, *Hist. Plant.*, VIII, Chap. I, 4; *De Causis*, III, Chap. XX, 7.
72. Strabo, V, Chap. IV, 3.
73. Cyrus Hopkins, Univ. Ill., Agri. Exp. Sta. Bull., 239. Tables on pages 442, 444, 456. (1922.)
74. A. Philippson, *Der Peloponnes*, pp. 540, 561-562. Berlin, 1892.
75. Cicero, *In Verrem*, III, 47, 116.
76. Varro, I, 44. Pliny, XVIII, 55.
77. Columella, III, 3-4.
78. *Jeremiah*, XXXV, 6-10.
79. I *Kings*, IV, 25; *Isaiah*, XXXVI, 16.
80. II *Chronicles*, II, 10, 15.
81. *Iliad*, XVIII, 564-565. *Odyssey*, XXIV, 241-246. Hesiod, *Works and Days*, 610-617.
82. Suetonius, *Augustus*, 42; *Domitian*, 7.
83. Varro, I, Chap. II, 6.
84. Xenophon, *Hellenica*, III, Chap. II, 10. Cicero, *De Re Publica*, V, 2.
85. Theophrastus, *De Causis*, II, Chap. IV, 2-3.
86. Theophrastus, *Hist. Plant.*, II, Chap. VIII, 1.
87. Diodorus Siculus, V, 34.
88. Xenophon, *Œconomicus*, XIX, 3-10. Pliny, XVII, 14, 16. Vergil, Georgic II, 348 *et seq.*
89. Cato, 45, 46, 48. Theophrastus, *De Causis*, III, Chap. VI.
90. Theophrastus, *Hist. Plant.*, II, Chap. V, 1.
91. Cato, 28, 45.
92. Mago quoted in Pliny, *Hist. Nat.*, XVII, 16. Cato, 43. Columella, V, 10.
93. Theophrastus, *Hist. Plant.*, II, Chap. V, 1.
94. Vergil, Georgic II, 272.
95. Vergil, Georgic II, 274-277.
96. Theophrastus, *Hist. Plant.*, II, Chap. V, 6.
97. Theophrastus, *Hist. Plant.*, I, Chap. VI, 4; II, Chap. V, 6. Palladius, IV, 10-25. Pliny, XVII, 88.
98. Plutarch, *Solon*, 23.
99. Cato, VI, 2.

404 SOWN AND PLANTED CROPS

100. Mago quoted in Pliny, *Hist. Nat.*, XVII, 19.
101. J. P. Mahaffy, "The Work of Mago on Agriculture," *Hermathena*, Vol. VII, pp. 29-35. London, 1890.
102. Pliny, *Hist. Nat.*, XVII, 17.
103. Theophrastus, *De Causis*, III, 8.
104. *Ibid.*, II, Chap. XI, 1-3.
105. *Ibid.*, I, Chap. XVI, 3-5; III, Chap. VII, 6, 10; *Hist. Plant.*, II, Chap. VII, 2. Cato, 50. Columella, V, Chap. 10, 10.
106. Pliny, XVII, 35.
107. *Leviticus*, XIX, 23-25. Josephus, *Antiquities of the Jews*, IV, Chap. VIII, 19.
108. L. H. Bailey, *The Pruning Book*, pp. 182, 185, 188. New York, 1914.
109. *Deuteronomy*, XX, 19.
110. Aristotle, *De Plantis*, I, 6. Cato, 40-42, 45. Varro, I, 40. Columella, V, 2, 8.
111. Columella, *De Arboribus*, IX. Theophrastus, *De Causis*, V, Chap. III, 1; I, Chap. XXI, 2.
112. Theophrastus, *Hist. Plant.*, II, Chap. II, 4-6; *De Causis*, II, 24.
113. For Italy and Spain, International Year Book of Agricultural Statistics, Tables 38, 39, pp. 98-99. Rome, 1922. For Greece, Report on the Industrial and Economic Situation in Greece. London, 1927.
114. Pliny, *Hist. Nat.*, XV, 3-4.
115. Columella, V, 8.
116. Vergil, Georgic II, 179-183.
117. Cato, 6. Varro, I, Chap. XXIV, 1-2. Theophrastus, *Hist. Plant.*, II, Chap. V, 7.
118. Pliny, XVII, 3.
119. Cato, 6. Varro, I, Chap. XXIV, 1.
120. Columella, V, 9, 15.
121. Pliny, XV, 1.
122. *Judges*, IX, 8-13; *Habakkuk*, III, 17. *Odyssey*, XXIV, 243-246. Plutarch, *Lycurgus*, XI.
123. Aristophanes, *Pax*, 1248-1250. Cato, 56.
124. Columella, XII, 14.
125. I *Samuel*, XXV, 18.
126. Polybius, XII, 10.
127. Theophrastus, *Hist. Plant.*, I, Chap. VI, 3-4.
128. Pliny, XVII, 18.
129. Columella, V, Chap. X, 9. Palladius, IV, 10, 25-26.
130. E. Banse, *Die Turkei*, pp. 143-144. Berlin, 1919.
131. Athenæus, III, 6-9.
132. Plutarch, *Solon*, XXIV.
133. Theophrastus, *De Causis*, III, Chap. VI, 6.
134. Cato, 8, 1; 40, 1. Varro, I, Chap. XLI, 4. Pliny, XV, 19.
135. Theophrastus, *De Causis*, III, Chap. VI, 6.
136. Pliny, XV, 19.
137. Aristotle, *De Animalibus*, V, 146. Theophrastus, *Hist. Plant.*, II, Chap. VIII, 1-2; *De Causis*, II, Chap. IX, 3, 6-15. Columella, XI, 2, 56.
138. Theophrastus, *Hist. Plant.*, II, Chap. VIII, 4.
139. Theophrastus, *De Causis*, II, Chap. IX, 5-6.

140. Aristotle, *De Animalibus,* V, 146.   Theophrastus, *Hist. Plant.,* II, Chap. VIII, 1.
141. Theophrastus, *Hist. Plant.,* II, Chap. VIII, 3.
142. Theophrastus, *Hist. Plant.,* II, Chap. VIII, 4; *De Causis,* III, 18, 1. Pliny, XIII, 7.
143. Theophrastus, *Hist. Plant.,* III, Chap. III, 5.   Pliny, XIII, 6.
144. Neumann and Partsch, *Physikalische Geographie von Griechenland,* pp. 410-411.   Breslau, 1885.
145. Pliny, XIII, 6.   Theophrastus, *Hist. Plant.,* II, Chap. VI, 2, 5, 8, 9.
146. *Deuteronomy,* XXXIV, 3.   *Judges,* I, 16; III, 13.   Pliny, V, 15.
147. Theophrastus, *Hist. Plant.,* II, Chap. V, 7.
148. *Isaiah,* V, 1-2; *Jeremiah,* XXXI, 5.   Vergil, Georgic II, 36-37, 184-194.
149. Vergil, Georgic II, 298, 357.
150. Pliny, XVII, 2.
151. Pliny, XVII, 3.
152. *Iliad,* XVIII, 564-565.   Varro, I, Chap. VIII, 3, 5.   Pliny, XIV, 3; XVII, 35.
153. Varro, I, Chap. VIII, 1, 5-7.
154. *Canticles,* II, 15.
155. Varro, I, Chap. VIII, 5.
156. Theocritus, Idyl I.   Compare also Idyl V.
157. Pliny, XVII, 2.
158. Pliny, XIV, 3.
159. Varro, I, VIII, 7.
160. Columella, II, 2.
161. Theophrastus, *Hist. Plant.,* II, Chap. VII, 2.
162. Xenophon, *Œconomicus,* XIX, 18.   Vergil, Georgic II, 400.
163. Theophrastus, *Hist. Plant.,* II, Chap. VII, 5; *De Causis,* III, Chap. XVI, 3.   Columella, IV, 28, 1; XI, 2, 60.
164. Theophrastus, *Hist. Plant.,* II, Chap. VII, 5.
165. Columella, XI, Chap. II, 61.
166. *Isaiah,* V, 6.   Hesiod, *Works and Days,* 572.   *Odyssey,* XXIV, 224-226, 241-246.   Cato, 33.   Columella, IV, 28.
167. Vergil, Georgic II, 398-400.
168. *Deuteronomy,* XX, 9.
169. Columella, XI, Chap. II, 60.
170. International Yearbook of Agricultural Statistics, Tables 34 and 37. Rome, 1922.
171. Columella, III, 3.
172. Varro, I, Chap. II, 7.
173. Pliny, XIV, 4, 9.
174. Strabo, V, Chap. III, 1; Chap. IV, 3; XIII, Chap. IV, 11.
175. *Odyssey,* IX, 208.
176. Pliny, XIV, 6.
177. Hesiod, *Works and Days,* 582-595.

CHAPTER XV

MANURING AND SEED SELECTION

The essence of ancient Mediterranean agriculture was the improvement of the soil, both in its mechanical and chemical composition. Working the land accomplished the first; manuring, the second; the biennial fallow contributed to both ends, while conserving the precious moisture in the soil.

Despite the fallow, overcropping was a persistent danger owing to the highly specialized utilization of the land, which arrested the development of crop rotation; owing also to the limited arable land rendered available by conditions of climate and relief. Olive groves were made to support a grain crop in alternate years; the *arbustum* field often yielded a second harvest between its vine-draped trees. Irrigated land with its summer and winter crop was doubly taxed and had to be doubly compensated; for the soil sends in its bill for every pound of plant food which is taken out.

MANURING—Hence the ancients developed the art of manuring to a surprising degree, in order to get a maximum yield from the limited tillage land and to replenish the nutriment in exhausted fields. In Palestine during the Mishnah period, irrigated land which was cropped twice annually was manured a second time before the summer seeding.[1] Everywhere irrigated hay meadows, which were mown three or four times a year, and alfalfa fields which yielded four or five harvests had to be amply fertilized at the sowing.[2] Moreover, in years of heavy rains when soil moisture was abundant, the farmer found he could avoid the economic waste of the fallow by judicious fertilization and some rotation of crops.

Without science the ancients evolved a scientific system of manuring, which became a conspicuous feature of their intensive tillage. They discriminated between various manures as to strength, and relative value for different crops and different soils. Without chemistry they learned to conserve the important chemical elements of farm manure; and without bacteriology they learned how to get the maximum result from the bacteria in their compost heaps and legume crops. They apportioned the amount of the manure to the quality of the soil, and in their gardens they practiced "head-fertilizing" (*kopfdüngung*) like the modern Japanese, feeding the individual plant rather than enriching the whole field.

Burdened with the labor of conserving the nutriment and moisture in the soil, the ancients looked with envy upon the easy tillage processes of Babylonia and Egypt. In the Tigris alluvium, "cultivation of the land consists in letting the water lie on it as long as possible, so that it may deposit much silt." [3] Herodotus considered that the Egyptians of the Delta garnered the fruits of the earth more easily than all other people, for they escaped the endless toil of plowing, harrowing, hoeing and fertilizing which other men had to perform to obtain a crop of grain.[4]

The first lesson in soil compensation was forced upon the peasants' notice. Stone Age cultivators burned the forests to clear the land, because their blunt axes made slow work of felling hardwood trees. Ashes were found to enrich the ground and adopted as the first obvious fertilizer in the Mediterranean countries as elsewhere. The ancient Jews set fire to briers, thorn bushes and other scrub growth.[5] It was a common practice everywhere to burn the stubble of the previous crop on the land to clear the fields and destroy the weeds.[6] However, this was an uneconomic method of converting the vegetable waste into fertilizer, because it dissipated the volatile elements like nitrogen and moisture; so most of the straw was utilized in other ways. But Cato advised the vine-dresser to burn the prunings of the vineyard on the spot and plough in the ashes to stimulate growth.[7] The advice was sound since wood ashes supply lime, potash and phosphoric acid to the soil; and it is exactly the small shoots and twigs which contain these chemicals in great amount.[8]

The principle of applying various animal and vegetable refuse to the soil originated with the beginning of migratory agriculture. The droppings of the flocks and herds about the nomad camp or in the open pasture revealed their power

to enrich the land.   The invention of manuring was ascribed
to various gods and heroes, notably to King Augeas of Elis and
to Hercules,[9] whose labor of cleansing the Augean stables by
turning a river through them might be interpreted as the
simultaneous application of irrigation and barnyard manure,
a common practice among the ancients.   The dunghill meets
us in the courtyards of Ulysses and Laertes his father; [10] it
was very ancient among the Jews who probably learned its
value from the local Canaanites.[11]   They carried all the manure
of Jerusalem from the city by the Dung gate to the gardens
outside.[12]   The power of dead bodies to fertilize the ground
after a battle or execution was known to the Greek Archilochus
by 700 B.C.[13] and even earlier to the Jews.[14]   Jeremiah emphasized the value of bone-dust,[15] and *Deuteronomy* directed
the blood of slaughtered animals to be poured out on the
ground, a practice which persisted for centuries.[16]   The tragic
fertility of old battle-fields distinguished the spot where Caius
Marius wiped out the Teutonic horde at Aquæ Sextiæ in 102
B.C.   "They say that the soil, after the bodies had rotted and
the winter rains had fallen, was so fertilized and saturated with
the putrefied matter which sank into it, that it produced an
unusual crop the next season." [17]   This effect was doubtless
observed wherever men fought and tilled the land, from Megiddo
to Flanders field.

> I sometimes think that never blows so red
> The rose as where some buried Cæsar bled.

FARMYARD MANURES—The main source of animal manures
was in the flocks and herds, whose value came largely from the
dung to enrich the soil, according to Varro.[18]   To maintain
a proper balance between live stock and crops was difficult for
the Mediterranean farmer, because the long summer drought
necessitated keeping his animals for five or six months every
year on the mountain pastures.   Hence nearly half their manure
was lost to the home farm.   The amount available for the
fields was limited to that provided by the few stall-fed oxen,
asses and mules kept on the farm as work animals during
summer; and by the returning flocks and herds which pastured
during winter on the home land.   It was customary to fold them

at night on the meadows, shifting them systematically, so that their droppings were evenly distributed. Their fresh manure insured a good stand of grass.[19] This method of applying the manure saved waste of organic material and of labor, but was best suited to meadows. For grain crops old rotted manure was best. The dunghill possessed special importance in dry countries like Palestine, Syria, Asia Minor and Greece, because it supplied humus to the soil. This element of plant food is always scant in clean-cultured fallow fields and in the thin herbage of semi-arid soils. To husband his manure was the farmer's first duty. Xenophon criticized peasants who failed to collect dung.[20] Gathering it from stall and sheepcote was a regular task of the farm of Ulysses in Ithaca.

Greeks and Romans employed human excrements and the dung of cows, horses, asses, sheep, goats, swine, poultry, pigeons and various other birds. The Jews used the manure of these animals and also that of camels, but from human sources only the urine, which was applied in diluted form to the land.[21] These several animal manures were known to possess various degrees of efficiency, because they had been tested for ages and their relative values estimated, as Pliny states.[22] The surprising fact is how closely the ancient estimates agree with the results of chemical analyses made in modern agricultural laboratories, though the ancient authorities differed in details from each other.

Theophrastus ranks manures in point of richness or concentration as follows: (1) human excrements, (2), that of swine, (3), of goats, (4), of sheep, (5), of cows and oxen, (6), of beasts of burden or horses, mules and asses. He adds that these are different from one another and need to be differently applied.[23] He explains that manure of beasts of burden is "bad because it is most apt to lose its moisture." [24] This was true if the manure was placed only half rotted in a dry soil during a dry season, such as Attica provided.

The Roman authorities considered bird and chicken manures the richest, especially the droppings in dovecotes and aviaries; but they ranked low the excrements of ducks and geese,[25] a significant evidence of their close observation. In this opinion modern agricultural chemists concur. Poultry manure combines the solid and liquid elements with a minimum loss of the latter, which contains most of the nitrogen, while the solid matter contains large percentages of potash and phosphoric acid. Pigeons' manure is the richest; hens' manure stands next. Much lower comes ducks' manure, and that of geese ranks far down in the scale.[26] The differences are largely the result of different feeding; pigeons and poultry have concentrated food. The ancients, too, recognized that the feed of animals affected the quality of the manure. For instance, cytisus or snail clover, a legume fodder lauded by Columella, was thought to enrich all animal excrements.[27]

Varro's list, quoted from Cassius (40 B.C.) who probably relied on Mago, is as follows: (I) Manures of birds and fowls. (II) of human beings. (III) That of goats, sheep, swine and asses. (IV) That of horses and draught animals fed on barley. This, however, was the best for meadows, because it stimulated the herbage.[28] Columella accepted this classification as to groups; but for farm dung he ranked the ass first, sheep second, goats and horses third, and swine lowest.[29] Modern experiments corroborate these ancient estimates, especially for swine dung and human manure. The former is rich in phosphoric acid but poor in nitrogen, the element most needed by Mediterranean soils; the latter contains high percentages of nitrogen and phosphoric acid. It was so concentrated that Columella advised its being diluted or mixed with farm refuse, lest it burn the soil. When properly handled, it was excellent for vines and fruit trees, which therefore ought to be planted near the bagnios. In undiluted form it was good for poor sandy land.[30]

The chief dependence of the ancient farm was the manure pile. Therefore it received the best care. It was kept preferably in a water-tight cemented pit covered over to prevent loss of its moisture by drainage, leaching or evaporation, and was kept a year to rot before being placed on the land.[31] Straw, leaves, weeds from the fields, reeds and sedges from swamps or willow plots were bedded under the farm animals,[32] and when trodden down added to the bulk and humus value of the manure,[33] besides conserving the urine. Isaiah speaks of "straw trodden down for the dunghill." [34] Into the compost heap went every form of organic refuse—chaff, husks, pods, dead leaves, ferns, bean stalks, lupine straw. Columella added to this list weeds from the hedgerows, ashes, sewage and every kind of waste; and he emphasized the value of vegetable refuse on farms without cattle.[35] Xenophon found that weeds gathered from the fields and allowed "to rot in stagnant water made good manure to gladden the field." [36] To these various organic ingredients of the compost heap salt was added in Palestine. "Salt that has lost its savour is fit neither for the land nor for the dunghill." [37] Its value lay in its power to retain moisture, retard decomposition, and react on certain inert compounds, so that their lime and potash were more available.[38]

When the contents of the compost heap were well rotted, they were carted out, spread on the land, and ploughed in promptly to conserve moisture. This was done in Italy after a rain in September for an autumn crop, and for a spring crop in late winter when the ground was still wet.[39] There was a period when the manure was at its best. If too new or imperfectly rotted, it burnt the seed and the roots of trees; [40] if kept longer than a year it lost strength.[41] Concentrated manures, if undiluted or applied in excess, were likely to burn and dry out the soil. "The dung most recommended is that which is mixed with litter," is the generalization arrived at by Theophrastus; [42] for the ancients like the moderns recognized the effect of litter in diluting manure,[43] and they apparently adopted a rule for the proportion of bedding to be used. "Where sheep furnish a cartload of manure, the larger cattle should furnish ten loads; otherwise it is clear proof that the husbandman has littered his animals badly." [44] A standard bulk gave a standard strength, so far as this was affected by the litter and not by the kind of dung. Very rich manures, like human excrements, which ferment quickly, were regularly diluted.[45] Bird and pigeon guano was powdered and thinly strewn over field and garden,[46] as it is today for the same reason.

A study of the treatment and application of animal manures by the ancients reveals a painstaking adjustment to climatic conditions, especially to the long summer period of warmth and drought, when the soil contains insufficient moisture for the decay of organic matter. Stable manure rots with great difficulty on or in land which contains scant moisture, because the necessary bacteria do not develop in sufficient amount to produce the proper chemical changes in the manure. Unrotted manure keeps the soil open, allows its precious moisture to escape, and burns the crop. For this reason many dry farmers in semi-arid America do not use stable manure.[47] The ancients met this difficulty by composting the manure for a year to insure its complete decay, soaking it with its own fluids or with water when it became too dry, and turning it frequently to admit the air.[48] The final product of this organic decay was humus or mould, which might be seen "passed through a sieve like so much flour, and perfectly devoid, through lapse of time, of all bad smell or repulsive appearance." [49]

AMOUNT OF MANURE—From motives of economy and concern for a successful crop, the ancient farmer used no more manure than was absolutely necessary. "They tell us to manure a thin soil abundantly and a rich soil sparingly, both on account of the fertility of the soil and because the muck brings more nutriment than the land is able to take care of." Thus Theophrastus reports the general practice of farmers who feared the consequences of excessive manuring.[50] "It is better to manure little and often than in excess" was the Roman motto.[51] Therefore after a fallow season, when the ground would have partly recuperated its strength, manures were applied only to very poor land or to exacting crops like beans, hemp, alfalfa and barley.[52] "Flax, oats and the sleep-giving poppy exhaust the soil, but it is easy to sow them in alternate years, provided you do not fail to soak the dry earth with rich muck and scatter foul ashes over the exhausted fields," says Vergil.[53]

The amount of manure customarily used under average conditions of soil and weather is specified by Columella. For a *jugerum* of hillside land 24 loads of 80 *modii*, or 492 bushels, sufficed; this equalled 788 bushels to the acre. On level land only 18 loads per *jugerum* or 525 bushels per acre were required, though the larger amount was used on a field prepared for a bean (*faba*) crop immediately after a grain crop.[54]

But weather conditions modified both the amount of manure

and the method of its application; because a timely rain abated the danger attending excess. In an average autumn it was customary to manure the field just after a rain, then sow it, plough in seed and dung together, and then ridge and harrow;[55] but some farmers preferred to cast the manure and seed together.[56] The interval left between the two operations was always short, because the dung was known to loosen and warm the soil, thereby stimulating germination.[57] Some farmers spread the manure between the upper and under soil, where it was easily reached by the rain and carried down to the roots of the plants, but where it was protected from the desiccating heat of the sun.[58] This method preserved not only moisture but also the important chemical constituents in the fertilizer. Cato advised scattering pigeon guano over meadow, garden or sown field, further to enrich the land.[59] Where the regular manuring had been omitted, it was necessary to spread the land with aviary dust just before the mid-winter hoeing.[60] At that season the rains would carry this rich fertilizer down to the roots as a tonic to the crop.

Always loomed the danger of excessive manuring. This was known to kill trees and grain crops, unless they got a saving shower. Therefore in rainy localities, frequent and abundant manuring was safe and efficacious; but in arid districts or in thin dry soil a moderate application was the wise course,[61] and the avoidance of highly concentrated manures. To obviate all difficulty in a hot dry region, it was customary to fill the furrows or trenches with water and allow three days for its absorption, then throw the manure on this saturated soil, then plant and cover.[62]

Rich, concentrated manures, whose plant food was quickly available, were generally used in gardens and orchards which needed quick feeding; but to obviate the danger of burning, they were applied in diluted form or were combined with regular irrigation. In the Ægean lands night soil and swine dung were applied with irrigating water to pomegranate and almond trees to improve the flavor of the fruit and reduce the size of the seed or nuts.[63] In Italy, pomegranate trees were watered four times yearly with diluted human urine at the rate of one *amphora* or seven gallons to the tree.[64] Columella advises this treatment for vines and various fruit trees to improve the flavor and aroma of the fruit.[65]   All the waste from the olive oil presses, the amurca and the rotted lees were applied in the same way to fruit trees and vegetables;[66] and therefore Columella advised that gardens and orchards be located near the poultry yards, bagnios and olive waste receptacles.[67]   But Theophrastus advised great discrimination in the selection of manures, "for the same manure is not equally suited to all kinds of trees. The age of the tree also makes a difference."[68] Even the organic waste from the currier's shop consisting of wool, hair and leather scraps was used for vines and fruit trees; but as this material was rich and rotted slowly, it too was combined with irrigation.[69]

Vegetables were equally avid of rich diluted manure. Theophrastus laid down the principle that all plants needing much nutriment needed also much water. Most vegetables germinated quickly, within five to ten days, and grew rapidly; hence their demand for food and ample water.[70]   "All the pot-herbs are lovers of water and dung."[71]   Both were necessary to cucumber and squash.[72]   When applied to cabbages in small quantities, they produced heads of the finest flavor; but in larger amounts, they produced larger heads of inferior flavor.[73]   The truck gardens and olive groves about Athens were enriched by the sewage of the ancient city. The main *cloaca* or sewer ran across the city and through the Dipylon to a reservoir outside, from which square or cylindrical brick-lined canals carried the contents to the intensively cultivated plain of the Cephisus valley, with its orchards and farms. One of these canals seems to show a device for regulating the flow, and suggests that the sewage was sold to the farmers.[74]

MINERAL FERTILIZERS—All this sounds modern and scientific. Still more does the ancient use of mineral fertilizers. These were found in their native state, either as earths like marl, or as deposits of alkaline salts like carbonate of lime and nitrate of potassium (nitre). Mixing different kinds of earth was first advocated by Theophrastus as "a means of remedying defects and adding heart to the soil."[75]   Such mixtures improved both the chemical and mechanical composition of the soil, for the added ingredients were either direct or "indirect fertilizers." The value of alkaline earths was early recognized, notably in prehistoric Ægina, where their use became a theme of mythology. On this small and populous island the surface stratum of poor freshwater limestone was underlaid, one or two yards below, by a stratum of fertile marl. So the inhabitants pierced the sterile veneer, dug out the marl, mixed it with the soil above, or even spread it on the bare rocks to create a field.[76] This habit of burrowing underground and using the excavations as dwellings fastened on the early Æginetans the name of Myrmidons or ants.[77] Likewise in nearby Megara, where a poor surface soil was underlaid by thick strata of various marls,[78] the same thing was done with good effect.[79]

The Romans imitated the practice of the Greeks and Gauls in the use of marl. They distinguished several varieties, and applied them to grain and meadow lands, but they found the tufaceous and calcareous kinds the best for cereal crops. Like the modern farmers, they spread it very thinly on the ground to avoid burning, and found one such treatment sufficient for many years, though not fifty, as Pliny says. The white variety, if procured in the vicinity of springs (calcium carbonate) "rendered the soil immeasurably fecund for grain." [80]   Columella advocated spreading marl on a gravelly soil or of mixing gravel with a dense calcareous soil, "as I have seen my uncle do.   Thus he raised fine cereal crops and beautiful vineyards." [81]   This uncle was a gentleman farmer, a Roman colonist in Spain, who cultivated his estate near Corduba (Cordova) on the Guadalquivir River.

Lime was added to the soil in other forms, either as broken or powdered limestone, which was applied to orchards, vineyards and olive groves,[82] or as pumice stone and shells.[83]   It was also provided by wood ashes, which were widely used as fertilizer in all parts of the Mediterranean region,[84] and which supplied phosphoric acid and potash as well as lime. Lime from the limekilns proved excellent for olive trees.[85]   Some farmers living north of the Po and having superfluous dung from their big herds of cattle, burned part of the manure by preference and applied the light ashes to the field.[86]   Lime in any form was used to correct an acid soil. Sand was frequently mixed with a heavy clay or chalk soil to improve its mechanical composition in gardens and orchards,[87] and occasionally to facilitate drainage where the land had become saline.[88] Pliny disclaims any virtue in such a mixture, even when a red or black or white sand was combined with a rich earth.[89]

Sometimes the soil needed other elements. Nitre (nitrate of potassium) and salt were found beneficial to certain vegetables; therefore they were either sprinkled over the garden plots or applied in solution to the plants.[90] Radishes, beets, rue and asparagus were among the vegetables so benefited both in flavor and growth.[91] Nitre removed the excessive pungency of radishes, and increased the size of beans.[92] Palm trees, which were known to require a saline soil, were treated with salt or brine about their roots.[93]

GREEN MANURE CROPS—The drawback of these mineral fertilizers was their failure to supply humus, which was especially needed on arid soils and on clean-cultured fallow land. Hence the ancients scarcely relied on them to take the place of animal manures; but they devised instead by 400 B.C. or even earlier a system of green manure crops, which was also an improvement on the old fallow field system. Xenophon states that a green crop ploughed in enriches the soil as manure does,[94] but he does not specify the kind of crop. Theophrastus, however, reports that the farmers in Thessaly and Macedonia raised a bean crop and turned it under when it was in flower; because the bean (faba vicia) reinvigorated the soil, even when it was sown thickly and produced much grain. The reason he assigned for this effect was that "the plant was of loose growth and decayed quickly." [95] In his later book he makes the generalization that legumes do not take strength from the cultivated land but rather give it new strength. He made an exception however in the case of chick peas, because they required rich black soil and only served to exhaust the land.[96] In this opinion Cato concurred, specifying field beans, lupines and vetch as the best green manures for grain crops.[97] For thin soil Varro advocated ploughing in snail clover or beans before they began to pod.[98] Columella enumerated lupines, beans, vetches, lentils, chick peas and other pea varieties as renovating crops, provided they were ploughed in as soon as the green fodder crop was harvested, before the fresh roots should become dry and withered. Clover and alfalfa, after they had yielded fodder for their appropriate number of years, were turned under when the crop began to deteriorate.[99]

All the ancient authorities agreed however that the most economical and satisfactory green manure crop was lupines; it would thrive on dry, sandy, or gravelly soil or on *terra rossa*,[100] gave food for man and beast, was cheap to seed, quick to grow, blossomed three times; and to enrich the ground should be ploughed in just after the third flowering, or if planted on sandy soil, after the second flowering.[101] Moreover it was so vigorous that it competed successfully with weeds and underbrush.[102] Green lupine stalks enriched the soil exceedingly.[103] This ancient estimate of lupines as a green manure crop is sustained in every point by modern scientific agriculture.[104]

By age-long experiment the ancients learned the power of legumes to open up and mellow the soil by their thick, deep-running roots; to keep down weeds by their thick cover growth and deeper roots; to put more nutriment into the soil than they took out of it; to increase the farm income by substituting a food crop for an idle fallow which demanded constant tillage; and especially the great economic profit in growing legumes like lupines or vetch, which would thrive on poor dry soils, as compared with chick peas which required a rich heavy loam. The ancients reveal a deep understanding of the manurial value of green legume crops, when they raised mixed fodder crops of legumes and grains;[105] and especially when they "found it very profitable to sow garlic and onions between the rows of cytisus or snail clover,"[106] thereby anticipating the interculture of vegetables and legumes practiced today in intensive Japanese horticulture.

The ancients achieved results, without chemistry and bacteriology, which revealed the nitrogen-gathering bacilli harbored by the roots of legumes. These fix the free atmospheric nitrogen and incorporate it in the soil in the form of nitrates; thus they capture the most valuable and elusive element of plant food. The successful cultivation of legumes in all Mediterranean lands from earliest times indicates that the necessary bacteria were widely distributed. But the mixing of soils of different kinds, advocated by Theophrastus, may have owed its efficacy, so far as legumes were concerned, to the inoculation of the field with the necessary bacteria. This method of preparing land for clover crops has been practised in Kentucky for a hundred years or more, by borrowing a few barrels of soil from a neighbor's clover field; and it is now advocated by the United States Department of Agriculture.[107] Finally the ancients did not plough in the legume crop till the plants gave signs of podding; they postponed the operation till the critical date, taught only by long experience and observation. Modern laboratory experiments show that legumes of all kinds take nitrogen from the air in largest proportion as they approach maturity; so the ancients had sound basis for their practice.[108]

Rotation of crops was apparently inaugurated by the alternate planting of grains and legumes. Rye was the only other crop definitely used to enrich the soil; but its use for this purpose came in late and was restricted to the upper Po valley where the grain found a favorable rainfall.[109] But Pliny also indicates the ploughing in of millet and panic in the Alpine piedmont to fertilize the soil; he states that this was done just as the stem began to develop or had put forth two or three leaves.[110]

Otherwise, rotation of crops made limited progress. Varro advised that, in lieu of the fallow, the land be planted lightly with some other crop less exhausting than grain.[111] The fertile Neapolitan plain was cropped all year round, once with panic, twice with spelt, and occasionally a fourth time with vegetables,[112]—a series not calculated to conserve plant food. Pliny gives another rotation suited to black, friable soil of the kind described by Cato as "tender";[113] first barley, then millet, then rape, and finally barley again or wheat, with no cultivation between beyond ploughing when the seed was sown. Yet another rotation was spelt succeeded by a four-months' winter fallow, then spring beans, then winter beans.[114] This series provided amply for the compensation of the soil. The Romans had an effective system to renovate a worn-out meadow. After thorough ploughing, the field was planted in beans, rape, or millet, the next year in wheat, and the third year in some

hay crop like clover or grass.[115]   An old tenant's contract of
Palestine in Mishnah times provided that barley should be
raised the first year, onions the sixth of the Sabbatical cycle,
and flax one year between; but beyond this it indicated no system of rotation.[116]   Greek authorities mention only the alternation of legumes and grain.

Despite Vergil's generalization that "the fields rest by a
change of crops," [117] rotation was little practised.   This was
the weak spot in ancient agriculture.   It may have resulted
from the conservative allocation of crops to selected terrains
and soils, combined with the prevalence of small, naturally
defined districts, in which exchange of crops between different
fields was difficult or economically impossible.   Consequently
the persistent discrimination in the use of certain soils for certain crops tended to crystallize into a rigid system.   Rotation
was restricted before it could advance.   General farming, with
balanced stock-raising and diversified field agriculture on a
fairly ample scale, developed only in regions of low relief and
abundant water, like the Nile and Po valleys; or in smaller
districts of moderate relief and high fertility, like the hill-and-
dale country about the old volcanoes of Etruria and Sicily,
or like the productive lake basins of Greece.   Moreover, the
large area in all Mediterranean lands devoted to permanent
plantations of orchards and vineyards contributed to this fixa-
tion of crops by restricting the arable land susceptible of rotation.   The fallow system worked to the same end by halving
the amount of land available at any one time for field agriculture.   The result was the constant danger of over-cropping,
and the steady evolution of manuring to safeguard the soil from
exhaustion.

SEED SELECTION—The principle of seed selection was early
advocated by the ancient farmers as a prime means of improving crops; and in the first decades of the Roman Empire
it reached a development which has only recently been attained
in America.   This gospel, now preached by agricultural col-
leges, was adumbrated in the Hebrew Scriptures.   The biblical
injunction, "Thou shalt not sow thy field with mingled seed" [118]
was evidently intended to make the Judean peasant scrutinize
his seed corn and eliminate adulterations, in order to get a

clean crop. It was a kind of precautionary weeding. But the sorting process inevitably led to the rejection of imperfect specimens of the desired grain, and hence was an initial step in seed selection. The injunction, which is found in *Leviticus*, dates back to the eighth or ninth century B.C., and like other agricultural methods was probably borrowed from the local Canaanites; for the early folk tale of Ishobeth describes the door-keeper of the Israelite prince, drowsing in the noonday heat over his task of cleansing wheat for his master.[119] The practice was still current in the time of Josephus; [120] and in the New Testament the sowing of "good seed" is stressed.[121]

Jewish farmers, in the first and second centuries of our era, planted seed beds for the purpose of getting a superior quality. The plain of Jericho was divided up into numerous small plots of wheat and barley; for the soil was rich on this old river terrace of the Jordan, and irrigation from spring or reservoir insured sufficient water. Elsewhere whole fields were cut up into beds, each planted with a different seed. The Jews carried on a trade in seed-corn and made purchases by tested seed or by samples, much like the little trays of wheat carried about the market by the grain merchants of ancient Athens. They tested seed by planting a few in an earthen pot or a manure bed, and judged the vitality by the rapidity of germination.[122] This method recalls the miniature "gardens of Adonis," offered to the youthful god of spring throughout Syria from remote times. They consisted of seedling grains or vegetables raised in earthen pots by some forcing process, and may possibly have been either cause or effect of early experiments in seed testing.

The principle of seed selection emerges more clearly among the ancient Greeks. Aristotle observed that a good plant was not likely to grow from a bad seed, nor a bad plant from a good seed,[123] under proper conditions of climate and soil. Theophrastus voiced a general opinion of Hellenic farmers that seeds of herbs and vegetables collected from plants in their prime showed their superior vitality by rapid germination. Hence when the plants were at their best it was customary to gather the seed and dry them, since well cured seed were known to produce more fruit.[124] Theophrastus also stressed the importance of the youth of the seed: for all crops, whether grain or vegetables, the seed of the year was considered the best; next best was that of the previous year, and poorest that of the third year before. Beyond this the seed was likely to be sterile, though still suitable for food. Some exceptions to this rule depended upon the locality of production and preservation; for in high, windy regions seed seemed to retain their vitality longer.[125] Age affected the rapidity of germination also in garden plants. Fresh seed in general sprouted more quickly, though celery, beet, coriander, parsley and some others came up more promptly from older seed.[126] Moreover, the Greek farmers discovered that all vegetables were greatly improved in size and quality by transplanting; therefore they took special care to transplant those reserved for seed collection.[127] A similar tendency to coddle seed nurseries prevailed in Italy. Pliny states that cabbage plants intended for seed were never cut.[128] Cato devoted great care to his seed-plots.[129]

The Greeks experimented with choice seed from different countries, in consequence of the extensive importation of oversea grains, fruits and vegetables. For instance, a three-months Sicilian wheat was tried in Achaia, where it failed to yield a crop; but it was raised successfully in the southern part of the island of Euboea, which was exposed to the warm, rainy south wind (Notos) of spring. Experiments with seeds from various climates and soils about the Mediterranean shores led to an interesting generalization formulated by Theophrastus: "Each seed of the several seed kinds is adapted to the natural conditions of its native habitat, both genera as compared with genera and the different species of the same genus. It is wise to transfer seed from a warm region to one a little less warm, and from a cold region in the same way. . . . Those which are transplanted from far northern lands to a hot district unfold their flower so late that they are caught by the summer drought, unless they are saved by the late rains of spring. Wherefore, according to the general opinion, care should be taken to prevent them from becoming mixed with the local variety, unless they come from similar climatic conditions; for otherwise they are hardly suited to the new region in regard to their time either of sowing or sprouting." [130] In regard to soil he says: "Seed, like fruit trees, ought to be brought from

similar or poorer land, so that the change made is none at all
or for the better. However, they maintain that seed sprung
from good soil are more vigorous and maintain this virtue for
two years. But differences of climate must also be considered.
Seed sprung from a sunny, warm region should not be sown
in a late chilly region, nor vice versa. The former come out
too early and are nipped by the lingering cold; the latter too
late, and perish in the heat and drought." [131] Most of these
instructions anticipate the modern practice.

The Romans fell heir to the Greek attainments in the art of
tillage, and carried the principle of seed selection yet farther.
They recognized it as the chief means of keeping a crop true
to type. "Seed though long chosen and carefully approved
still degenerate unless the largest are selected year after year
by the hand of man," says Vergil.[132]   Siligo, a choice winter
wheat, was broadly planted in the moist alluvium of Italy; but
across the Alps it remained constant to type (*pertinax*) only
in the fertile soil and mild climate of the middle Rhone and
Isère valleys. Elsewhere in Gaul it reverted after two years to
the common local variety, unless only the heaviest grains were
selected for sowing.[133]

Large and heavy seed were known to be the best. Moreover
these had to be fresh, clean, free from alien admixtures.[134]
Therefore wheat and barley grains which by reason of their
weight settled to the bottom of the threshing floor or cleansing
sieve were reserved for seed. "This is very necessary because
all cereals tend to degenerate." Moreover, only the largest and
best ears of wheat and other grains were reserved for seed
corn.[135] "Ears of the finest and best grain should be taken
to the threshing floor and kept separate from the rest, so that
the farmer may have the best possible seed." [136] Ears with
vacant spaces between the grains were rejected. This is the
modern "ear selection." Moreover, the grains themselves were
tested by color, outside and in, especially for the red and the
white wheat.[137] There was a special test for lentil seed, which
were often eaten by weevils, even in the pod. Therefore after
the lentils were threshed they were thrown into tubs of water.
The empty or weevil-eaten ones floated, and those which sank
to the bottom were dried in the sun and kept for seed.[138]

The amount of seed sown to the *jugerum* varied according to the soil, location, exposure to wind and sun, time of sowing and also according to the kind of seed. A good rich soil could stand heavier seeding than a poor, thin, sandy soil; [139] for the latter if too thickly sown, yielded a small and empty ear.[140] The average amount broadcast on medium soil was 5 *modii* of wheat, 10 of spelt, and 6 of barley per *jugerum*, or 8, 16 and 10 pecks respectively to the acre.[141] These figures correspond fairly well with the modern English practice but exceed the American requirements when the seed are put in with the drill. The ancients themselves recognized that all seed made better growth when set or planted, than when scattered; [142] and hence employed the more careful method in their seed-beds, using fewer to the plot.[143] As opposed to the average 5 *modii* of wheat per *jugerum*, 4 *modii* sufficed on loose, fertile well-drained land, but 6 *modii* were required for the less productive, dense, cretaceous soil; because a rich soil made the grain stool freely and so yielded a thick crop for a light sowing.[144] The thrifty Mediterranean farmer was always ready to save his seed corn; but he knew it was poor economy to "rob the harvest" by under-seeding his field on which much labor had been spent.[145] Moreover, the seed was sown thick if put in early in the autumn, because it had to wait some time for the rains before germination and would not stool abundantly; when put in later just in time for the rains, it was sown thinly "to prevent it from being suffocated," because the plants were large and thick.[146]

Indirect testimony to the intensive character of ancient Mediterranean tillage is furnished by certain maxims that embodied old agricultural standards. The ideal was the small freehold estate, cultivated with infinite care under the master's personal supervision. The Judean national dream was every man established on a bit of land where he could rest "under his own vine and his own fig-tree," when the day's work was over. "He that hath a little garden and fertilizes it and digs it, and enjoys the produce is far better off than he who works a large garden on shares," was an ancient rabbinical comment on freehold versus tenant farming. Another was a precept for personal supervision: "He that inspects his field daily will find a stater in it." [147] Later Cato paraphrased this motto when he said that on a farm "the master's forehead is of more use than his back." [148]   So also Mago of Carthage, who formulated Phœnician tillage practice in the fifth century before Christ, stated that a person buying a farm ought to sell his town house and live in the country.[149]

Size of Ancient Farms or Estates—In the Homeric poems, the cultivated estates of princes and kings were of moderate size, though they were supplemented by broad pasture lands which were frequently communal.   The reward promised to Meleager by the people of Caledon for a great public service was "a fair demesne of 50 *guai*, the half thereof vineyard and the half open plough-land" located in the fertile Calydonian plain.[150]   The garden of Alcinous in the little island kingdom of Scheria comprised four *guai*, laid out in vineyard, orchard, and vegetable plots.[151]   The question is the size of the *gues*, which apparently corresponded to the yoke of the Hebrews and the *jugerum* of the Romans, or the area ploughed by a single yoke of oxen in one day or rather half a day.   It has been variously estimated as approximately half an acre by Seymour [152] and as four-fifths of an acre by Ridgway; [153] but Seebohm would cut the latter estimate in half.[154]   Hence the garden of a great king comprised only two acres, and Meleager's estate measured from 20 to 40 acres, in a time when Greece was sparsely populated.   The peasant holdings in Bœotia in the eighth century B.C. were apparently very small, because Hesiod wanted only one son, that he might inherit the entire farm.

The scale of land holdings in Attica under Solon (594 B.C.) corresponds with that of the legendary period in general.[155] (I) The great land owner, judging from the yield of his farm, had 75 to 125 acres of grain land, or 20 to 25 acres of vineyard, or 50 to 75 acres of mixed lands.   (II) The Knights forming the second class of big proprietors owned 45 to 75 acres of grain land, or 12 to 15 acres of vineyard, or 30 to 45 acres of mixed lands.   (III) The Zeugites or medium proprietors owned 30 to 50 acres of crop land, allowing for the alternate years of fallow, or 7 to 10 acres of vineyard, or 25 acres of mixed lands.   (IV) The Thetes had 22 acres at most if he raised grain, or 6 acres of vineyard, or 15 acres at most

if he carried on mixed farming.[156]   Thus the maximum estate
in Attica was small, when the people were groaning over the
appropriation of the land by the plutocrats.   A century and a
half later the sub-division of farm land had progressed.   The
paternal inheritance of Alcibiades was only 300 plethra or 70
acres of mediocre soil though he was accounted rich.   The
recorded sales of estates indicate many small plots or dwarf
farms under 14 acres.   The few large holdings were located on
the frontier remote from Athens or in the mountains where
the land was rough and fit only for forest.[157]   One such, which
became involved in a lawsuit in the time of Demosthenes, is the
largest reported, and comprised about 778 acres.   It had about
300 acres in barley and 50 acres in vineyards, but it also drew a
large revenue from the wood carried daily to the city by six
asses.[158]   Public opinion opposed the concentration of real
estate, as indicated by Plato in his *Laws*, where the maximum
property should not contain more than four single lots.[159]

It was on these small farms that the Attic farmers practised
agriculture as Theophrastus observed it.   The pressure of poor
soil and meager rainfall is revealed in the intensive methods
there developed.   Add to this the pressure of a dense urban
population engaged in trade and industries, and relying on the
local farmers for fresh vegetables, fruits and flowers, even
though most of the breadstuffs came from overseas.   Similar
conditions held in various other parts of Greece and in the
Ægean Islands, with similar effects upon land holdings [160] and
tillage methods.

In contrast to Greece and Palestine, ancient Egypt at the
zenith of its power doubtless approximated the arable area of
12,000 square miles which the country commands today.   Land
tenure on a big scale prevailed, owing both to the geographic
conditions of ample fertile soil and abundant water for irrigation, and even more to the social organization of the state.
But the very fecundity of the Nile Valley induced a density of
population which became excessive and therefore enforced careful tillage, especially the extension of the irrigable area,
against periods of famine in years of "low Nile."

In Italy again, where typical Mediterranean conditions of
climate and relief prevail, tillage adjustment is apparent in the

small freehold farms which were the rule, so long as the Roman territory was small. Prior to the Second Punic War, the land allotments of the free peasants were variously two, three, seven, ten, and fourteen *jugera* of tillage land with the right of pasturing cattle on the public domain. Cincinnatus was ploughing his four-*jugera* estate on the Vatican Hill, when called to be dictator in 458 B.C. A farm of seven *jugera* or four and a half acres was considered ample for an industrious peasant by conservative Romans.[161] This was the plebeian allotment in the early Republic and it was confirmed by the Consul Curius Dentatus in 289 B.C.[162] It corresponds to the "four acres and a cow" warranted by rural enthusiasts to support the modern farmer, if he practises scientific agriculture and locates near a big urban market.

The small farm, cultivated with intelligence and industry, remained the agricultural ideal of the Romans long after rapid territorial expansion and protracted military service had undermined the little peasant freehold in old peninsular Italy. Colonial allotments did not exceed ten *jugera* or six and a quarter acres till the time of Tiberius Gracchus (133 B.C.), except in Latin colonies planted on remote, exposed frontiers. In such cases larger land grants compensated the settlers for the danger incurred. Bononia was founded as a fortified colony in 189 B.C., among the recently conquered Boii, to guard the only direct road across the Apennines by the Futa Pass, maintaining connections between Rome and the Po valley. Hence the infantry received 50 *jugera* or 31 acres each, and the cavalry 70 *jugera* or 43 acres.[163] Similar large allotments were made at other danger points, like Aquileia at the foot of ominous Carso,[164] and Luna which was meant to police the Ligurian raids from the Apennines.[165]

The agrarian law of Gracchus provided land grants of 30 *jugera* or 18.7 acres for about 80,000 Roman citizens, and thus inaugurated a larger scale of land holding for the masses. August Meitzen, on the basis of all colonial allotments in ancient Italy, concludes that Roman citizens with full privileges held estates of 30 to 70 *jugera* or 18 to 44 acres, and that plebeian farms ran from 7 to 20 *jugera* or 4.5 to 12.5 acres.[166] These were probably the general conditions familiar to Cato, though as a big landed proprietor of this century (died 149 B.C.) he considered a 100 *jugera* vineyard (62 acres) and a 240 *jugera* olive grove (150 acres) a reasonable estate.[167]

Yet the little peasant farm tended to revive on fertile soil in populous districts, where careful garden and fruit culture would give the proprietor a living. When a distribution of the public land about Capua and the Stellas Plain in Campania was contemplated in 59 B.C., Cicero said the land could not support more than 5,000 colonists, "so as to give them 10 *jugera* apiece," [168] as if that amount would suffice. On this area of 50,000 *jugera* some 20,000 citizens were settled later, according to Suetonius. Figures like these, compared with colonial grants in modern Africa and the Americas, illuminate the whole question of agricultural methods and arable area in the Mediterranean lands.

All efforts to check the decay of tillage in Roman Italy stressed the old standards of intensive cultivation. "Praise big estates but cultivate a small one" was Vergil's advice.[169] Pliny quotes the ancient adage that it was wiser to sow less and plough more.[170] Columella applied the Greek maxim of "measure in all things" to land holdings, as he enunciated the economic principle that a large farm poorly cultivated yielded less profit than a small one well tilled; and he fortified his opinion by a precept of Mago of Carthage, that a husbandman ought to be more than a match for his farm, so that when he grappled with its problems he should come out ahead in the encounter.[171]

Nature gave the ancient farmer the privilege of the struggle. Under the influences of climate and relief was evolved a system of tillage, which produced: (I) Winter grain crops maturing in spring or early summer. (II) Planted crops of olives, figs and grapes ripening in autumn without artificial watering. (III) Widely distributed summer crops of fruits, vegetables and fodder plants raised by irrigation, wherever springs and perennial streams were available. The immediate material gain of this triple system was a larger and more certain total harvest and a more varied food supply than the single seasonal cultivation could have yielded. More important, however, was the economic gain, because it meant improved economic methods.

It involved increased application of capital for seed, manures and the construction of irrigation canals; and it demanded an elaborate and sustained system of farm work, in consequence of which the labor power of the community was kept employed all the year round.

The economy of national wealth and the gain in national efficiency were incalculable. There was no economic leakage incident to supporting the rural labor in idleness during half the agricultural year; for Mediterranean conditions of climate and relief rendered possible a vegetative year of twelve months. Therefore Varro and Xenophon show the ancient farmer with his slaves hurrying from one urgent agricultural task to another.[172] Harvest followed fast upon harvest all through summer from April to October; and the October harvest crowded upon the heels of the autumn ploughing and sowing. The days of plenty predicted by the prophet Amos, "when the ploughman shall overtake the reaper and the treader of grapes him that soweth seed," [173] describes the ideal of productive activity in farm life, not only in Palestine but in other Mediterranean countries. Thus under the prick of Nature's goad, primitive society in these lands began early to develop a capacity for sustained labor, which was at once evidence and guarantee of rapidly advancing civilization.

AUTHORITIES—CHAPTER XV

1. H. Vogelstein, *Landwirthschaft in Palästina zur Zeit der Mishnah*, p. 24. Berlin, 1894.
2. Cato, *De Re Rustica*, 40. Varro, *Rerum Rusticarum*, I, 29. Pliny, *Historia Naturalis*, XVIII, 43 and 67.
3. Theophrastus, *De Historia Plantarum*, VIII, 7, 4.
4. Herodotus, II, 14.
5. *Exodus*, XXII, 6; *Isaiah*, IX, 18.
6. *Isaiah*, V, 24. Xenophon, *Œconomicus*, XVIII, 2. Vergil, Georgic I, 84.
7. Cato, 37.
8. W. P. Brooks, *Agriculture*, Vol. II, p. 282. Springfield, Mass., 1905.
9. Pliny, XVII, 6.
10. *Odyssey*, XVII, 297-299; XXIV, 225.
11. I *Samuel*, II, 8; II *Kings*, XIX, 37.
12. *Nehemiah*, II, 13.
13. Plutarch, *Marius*, XXI.
14. *Jeremiah*, IX, 22; XVI, 4; II *Kings*, IX, 37.
15. *Jeremiah*, VIII, 1-2.
16. *Deuteronomy*, XII, 16, 24; XV, 23. Vogelstein, *op. cit.*, p. 19.
17. Plutarch, *Marius*, XXI.
18. Varro, *R. R. Præfatio*, 4.
19. Cato, 30. Columella, *De Agricultura*, II, 15, 9. Pliny, XVIII, 53. Vogelstein, *op. cit.*, pp. 19-21.
20. Xenophon, *Œconomicus*, XX, 10. Cato, 5.
21. Vogelstein, *op. cit.*, pp. 18-20.
22. Pliny, XVII, 6.
23. Theophrastus, *Hist. Plant.*, II, 7, 4.
24. Theophrastus, *De Causis Plantarum*, III, 9, 2; *Hist. Plant.*, VII, 5, 1.
25. Varro, I, 38; III, 7. Columella, II, 15.
26. W. P. Brooks, *op. cit.*, Vol. II, pp. 233-234.
27. Pliny, XVII, 6.
28. Varro, I, 38.
29. Columella, II, 15.
30. Columella, I, 6; II, 16; V, 10. Pliny, XVII, 6.
31. Columella, I, 6. Pliny, XVII, 8.
32. Cato, 5 and 37.
33. Theophrastus, *Hist. Plant.*, VII, 5, 1.
34. *Isaiah*, XXV, 10.
35. Vogelstein, *op. cit.*, p. 19. Cato, 5 and 37. Columella, II, 15.
36. Xenophon, *Œconomicus*, XX, 11.
37. *Luke*, XIV, 35.
38. W. P. Brooks, *op. cit.*, Vol. II, 315.
39. Cato, 5. Pliny, XVIII, 53.
40. Pliny, XVII, 46.
41. Columella, II, 15.
42. Theophrastus, *Hist. Plant.*, VII, 5, 1. Compare Xenophon, *Œconomicus*, XVIII, 2.
43. W. P. Brooks, *op. cit.*, Vol. II, 208.
44. Pliny, XVIII, 53.
45. Theophrastus, *Caus. Plant.*, III, 9, 2; *Hist. Plant.*, VII, 5, 1.

46. Cato, 36. Varro, I, 38. Pliny, XVIII, 53.
47. Wendell Paddock and Orville B. Whipple, *Fruit Growing in Arid Regions*, p. 197. New York, 1914.
48. Columella, I, 6.
49. Pliny, XVII, 6.
50. Theophrastus, *Caus. Plant.*, III, 20, 2. Compare Pliny, XVIII, 53.
51. Columella, II, 16.
52. Columella, II, 5, 10, 21, 23, 27, 31; XI, 2.
53. Vergil, Georgic I, 77-81.
54. Columella, II, 5, 16. Palladius, X, 1, 2.
55. Columella, II, 10.
56. Theophrastus, *Hist. Plant.*, VII, 5, 1.
57. *Ibid.*, VIII, 7, 7.
58. Theophrastus, *Caus. Plant.*, III, 6, 1.
59. Cato, 36.
60. Pliny, XVIII, 53.
61. Theophrastus, *Caus. Plant.*, III, 9, 2.
62. *Ibid.*, III, 6, 2.
63. Theophrastus, *Hist. Plant.*, VII, 51; *Caus. Plant.*, III, 9, 3. Columella, V, 10.
64. Pliny, XVII, 47.
65. Columella, II, 15.
66. Cato, 93.
67. Columella, I, 6.
68. Theophrastus, *Caus. Plant.*, II, 9, 5; *Hist. Plant.*, II, 7, 3-4.
69. Pliny, XVII, 46.
70. Theophrastus, *Hist. Plant.*, VII, 1, 3.
71. *Ibid.*, VII, 5, 1.
72. Pliny, XIX, 24.
73. Pliny, XIX, 41.
74. Article, "Cloaca," Smith, *Dictionary of Greek and Roman Antiquities*, and Pauly-Wissowa, *Real-Encyclo. des Alterthums*. Stuttgart, 1901.
75. Theophrastus, *Caus. Plant.*, III, 20, 3.
76. Neumann and Partsch, *Physikalische Geographie Griechenlands*, p. 348. Breslau, 1885.
77. Strabo, VIII, Chap. 6, 16.
78. A. Philippson, *Der Peloponnes*, p. 16. Berlin, 1892.
79. Theophrastus, *Caus. Plant.*, III, 20, 4.
80. Pliny, XVII, 4, 6-8.
81. Columella, II, 16.
82. Pliny, XVII, 4, 47.
83. Vergil, Georgic II, 348-350.
84. Vogelstein, *op. cit.*, 19-20. Pliny, XVII, 5, 47. Vergil, Georgic I, 80.
85. Pliny, XVII, 6.
86. Pliny, XVII, 5.
87. Vogelstein, *op. cit.*, 19-20. Article on Horticulture in *Jewish Encyclopedia*.
88. Theophrastus, *Caus. Plant.*, III, 6, 3.
89. Pliny, XVII, 3.
90. Pliny, XIX, 41. Luke, XIV, 35. Theophrastus, *Caus. Plant.*, III, 7, 8.
91. Pliny, XIX, 59.
92. Pliny, XIX, 26. Vergil, Georgic I, 194.

93. Theophrastus, *Caus. Plant.*, II, 5, 3; II, 7, 1-4.
94. Xenophon, *Œconomicus*, XVII, 10.
95. Theophrastus, *Hist. Plant.*, VIII, 7, 2; IX, 1.
96. Theophrastus, *Caus. Plant.*, IV, 8, 1-3.
97. Cato, 37 and 54.
98. Varro, I, 23, 2-3. Pliny, XVIII, 30.
99. Columella, II, 10 and 14.
100. Theophrastus, *Hist. Plant.*, VIII, 11, 8; *Caus. Plant*, IV, 7, 3.
101. Columella, II, 10; XVII, 6. Pliny, XVIII, 36.
102. Theophrastus, *Hist. Plant.*, I, 7, 3; VIII, 11, 8.
103. Columella, II, 15. Pliny, XVII, 6.
104. W. P. Brooks, *op. cit.*, Vol. II, 360.
105. Varro, I, 31. Pliny, XVIII, 41-42.
106. Pliny, XIII, 47.
107. *Farmers' Bull.*, No. 339, "Alfalfa," pp. 17-18. Washington, 1908.
108. W. P. Brooks, *op. cit.*, II, 365.
109. Pliny, XVIII, 40.
110. Pliny, XVIII, 49.
111. Varro, I, 44, 2.
112. Strabo, V, 4, 3; Pliny, XVIII, 29.
113. Cato, 151.
114. Pliny, XVIII, 52.
115. Pliny, XVIII, 67.
116. Vogelstein, *op. cit.*, p. 50.
117. Vergil, Georgic I, 82-83.
118. *Leviticus*, XIX, 19; *Deuteronomy*, XXII, 9.
119. II *Samuel*, IV, 5-6 (revised version).
120. Josephus, *Jewish Antiquities*, Bk. IV, Chap. VIII, 20.
121. *Matthew*, XIII, 24-30.
122. Vogelstein, *op. cit.*, 38-41.
123. Aristotle, *De Plantis*, I, 6; II, 6.
124. Theophrastus, *Hist. Plant.*, VII, 3, 3-4.
125. *Ibid.*, VII, 5, 5; VIII, 11, 5. Compare Pliny, XVIII, 54.
126. Theophrastus, *Hist. Plant.*, VII, 1, 6. Compare Pliny, XIX, 35.
127. Theophrastus, *Hist. Plant.*, VII, 4, 3; VII, 5, 3.
128. Pliny, XVIII, 62; XIX, 41.
129. Cato, 40.
130. Theophrastus, *Hist. Plant.*, VIII, 8, 1.
131. Theophrastus, *Caus. Plant.*, III, 14, 1-2; Pliny, XVIII, 54.
132. Vergil, Georgic I, 197.
133. Pliny, XVIII, 8.
134. Varro, I, 50.
135. Columella, II, 9.
136. Varro, I, 52.
137. Pliny, XVIII, 54.
138. Columella, II, 9.
139. Xenophon, *Œconomicus*, 8-11. Theophrastus, *Hist. Plant.*, VIII, 6, 2.
140. Pliny, XVIII, 55.
141. Columella, II, 9.
142. Theophrastus, *Hist. Plant.*, VII, 5, 3.
143. *Ibid.*, VII, 4, 3.
144. Pliny, XVIII, 55.

145. Cato, 5.
146. Pliny, XVIII, 54.
147. Article on Agriculture in *Jewish Encyclopedia.*
148. Cato, 4.
149. Mago quoted in Pliny, XVIII, 7.
150. *Iliad,* IX, 578-581.
151. *Odyssey,* VII, 113.
152. *Odyssey,* XVIII, 370-377. T. D. Seymour, *Life in the Homeric Age,* pp. 245-246. New York, 1907.
153. W. Ridgway, *Jour. of Hell. Studies,* Vol. VI, pp. 321-326. 1885.
154. F. Seebohm, *Customary Acres,* pp. 194-202. London, 1914.
155. Plutarch, *Solon,* XVIII.
156. G. Glotz, *Ancient Greece at Work,* p. 247. New York, 1926.
157. A. Boeckh, *Public Economy of the Athenians,* pp. 88-91. Translated from the German. Boston, 1857.
158. Demosthenes, Oration against Phænippus, Vol. IV, pp. 290-303. Translated by C. R. Kennedy. Bohn Lib., 1901.
159. Plato, Laws.
160. H. Blümner, *Life of the Ancient Greeks,* p. 493. Translated from the German. London, 1895.
161. Livy, *Historia,* V, 30.
162. Valerius Maximus, IV, Chap. IV, 6-7.
163. Livy, Bk. XXXVII, 57.
164. Livy, Bk. XL, 34.
165. Livy, XXXIX, 1, 2; XL, 38, 41.
166. August Meitzen, *Siedelung und Agrarwesen,* Vol. I, p. 255. Berlin, 1895.
167. Cato, 2 and 10.
168. Cicero, *Litteræ ad Atticum,* A., II, 16.
169. Vergil, Georgic II, 412.
170. Pliny, XVIII, 7.
171. Columella, I, 3.
172. Varro, I, 29-36.
173. *Amos,* IX, 13.

CHAPTER XVI

IRRIGATION AND RECLAMATION IN THE ANCIENT MEDITERRANEAN REGION

The early date at which irrigation appeared in the Mediterranean lands is proof of its necessity. In Egypt it goes back to 5000 B.C.; in other sections of the region it is described, often minutely, in the most ancient literatures or records of ancient travelers and traders. It developed in response to condition of climate and relief, and therefore of old was as widespread as today in these same lands. It supplemented the winter rains in dry years when the tantalizing clouds held tight their burden of moisture; it saved the ripening fields of wheat and barley when late spring showers quite failed; it rendered possible all the quick-growing summer crops which required intense heat and ample moisture; and it was regularly applied with animal manures, in order to make these beneficial and not deleterious to the crops.

Furthermore, irrigation was bound up with reclamation projects designed to increase the arable area of the Mediterranean countries. It pushed forward the verdant line of vegetation into the arid southern margin of the Mediterranean region; it was connected with the reclamation of wet lowlands by means of dykes and canals, for drainage ditches at proper levels were readily converted into irrigation conduits; and it became an adjunct to dams or reservoirs for flood control of mountain torrents, when these flashed into spate during winter storms and scoured the bordering fields.

Fertile, moist alluvium, always at a premium in this region of predominant mountain relief, was found only in valley floors, small lacustrine basins, and silted coastal plains. Here the soil was best and ground water abundant, but such lands were exposed to inundation during the winter rains and spring thaws on the highlands. Where they took the form of extensive deltaic flats on low coasts, the sluggish run-off left them water-logged, fit only in their natural state for wet summer pastures. To reclaim this productive soil, the ancient farmers early adopted measures of flood control. Their first step was to build dykes for the protection of the tilled fields; the next was to divert the excess water to nearby districts needing more moisture; and the final step was to impound the flood waters of the winter for summer distribution.

Irrigation in the Mediterranean countries had therefore either the single motive of conducting water to arid lands, like the streams of Anti-Lebanon to the flowery oasis of Damascus, or the double motive of drainage and distribution. Wherever practised, it stimulated intensive tillage. Irrigable land was generally limited in extent and high in value. As an economic proposition, it had to make a return commensurate with the outlay of capital and labor expressed by the water tax.

CROPS RAISED BY IRRIGATION—The crops requiring irrigation were numerous. They included various legumes, like bean, pea, lentil, vetch, and chick-pea, which were sown in the spring and watered when in bloom but rarely afterwards;[1] hay meadows, watered after each mowing, which usually occurred three times during the summer;[2] fodder crops, especially alfalfa or medic clover, which was harvested from four to six times annually and as often irrigated;[3] panic and millet, raised as summer crops on irrigated land, which in dry regions like lowland Cilicia and Greece was covered with a network of conduits.[4] But panic was given water in moderation, because an excess made it lose its leaves.[5]

One notes that the ancient farmers practised irrigation with caution and with economy of water, to get the best results. According to Vergil, in the Po valley water was shut off from a young meadow as soon as the grass had put forth a stem, though irrigation streams were abundant.[6] All plants accustomed to a dry soil and climate received an absolute minimum of water in summer, both in Greece and Italy. Fruit trees and deciduous shade trees, when being propagated in nursery beds, were frequently irrigated; but when mature, they were irrigated only in the intense drought of late July and August, and then only sparingly because much water was found to injure the roots. Moreover, the amount was proportioned to the age of the trees, saplings with their scant foliage receiving less.[7] This caution in application of water may partly explain the rare mention by ancient writers of saline or alkaline accumulations on irrigated soils, though high relief and rapid drainage also contributed to this healthy condition.

The ancient Jews and Greeks regarded summer tillage and irrigation as inseparable. Homer describes the irrigation of plantations, orchards, and gardens in Ithaca and Sheria (Corfu), both islands on the rainy western side of Greece.[8] Theophrastus states that vines and pomegranates loved water and derived thence their chief nutriment;[9] but the irrigation of vineyards was generally confined to dry districts like the eastern, rain-shadow slope of the Taygetos Mountains in Laconia,[10] and the arid, over-drained soil of Palestine. Ezekiel, in his rich figurative speech, describes a vine "planted in good soil by great waters, that it might bring forth branches and that it might bear fruit."[11] Pliny mentions the irrigation of vines in the high Sulmo valley of the Central Apennines, as a method of improving the harsh flavor of the local wines;[12] but water was so abundant in the Sulmo district that grain fields also were irrigated in spring.[13]

Even olive groves were not everywhere exempt from irrigation. They yielded the best oil when cultivated by dry-farming methods; but if large fruit was the object, they were watered in mid-September to stimulate the growth of the berries.[14] But the poor limestone soil and dry climate of Attica necessitated pungent manure and moderate watering for the olive orchards.[15] The sacred grove of Pallas Athene in the Academy, which was irrigated by the parcelled streams of the Cephisos River, served as a public park; its "deep impenetrable shade" lauded by Sophocles[16] indicates a dense foliage due to ample watering, for olive trees usually afford scant protection from the searching rays of the Mediterranean sun, as any one familiar with Greece well knows. It was in regions with little surplus water for irrigation, like Syria, Palestine, Cyrenaica, Attica, Sicyon, and Corinth that oil rather than fruit formed the chief product of the olive orchards.[17]

Fruit trees and shrubs from the monsoon countries of Asia and the river oases of Persia and Mesopotamia were gradually introduced along the maritime track from the Orient, as articles of commerce or prizes of the Macedonian and Roman conquest of the Near East. Such were the apricot, peach, various plums, cherries, pomegranates, and finally the citron. These trees, which required both heat and moisture for fruition, gave fresh impulse to orchard culture by irrigation. Hence they were planted near the base of the mountains,[18] where springs broke out along old fault lines and kept the soil damp through infiltration or supplied water for irrigation. Such conditions were found along the edges of the Eurotas valley in Laconia, where the traveler today sees orange groves. Associated with these plantations were doubtless the orchards of pears and apples native to the region, but requiring mid-summer irrigation to develop the fruit.[19] Varieties of both were numerous, but the only good ones came from the cooler districts of the region. The best were raised in an Alpine village near Aquileia and exported to Rome; the next best grew near Gangra far up in the highlands of Paphlagonia.[20]

The Mediterranean region produced in spring bulbous or tuberous plants and countless herbs. Found in their native state, they were small and undeveloped, but when their growing period was prolonged into summer by artificial irrigation, they afforded an excellent and varied vegetable diet. Therefore, the well watered vegetable garden became a feature of ancient Mediterranean tillage. It was worked with the utmost care, manured and irrigated;[21] bulbs and seedlings were regularly transplanted to stimulate growth.[22] Interculture of garlic or onion with some companion crop of legumes was practised.[23] Hardly a feature of modern intensive cultivation was omitted. The great cities of the ancient world, like Jerusalem, Thebes, Athens,[24] Alexandria, Carthage, and Rome[25] were surrounded by these truck gardens, which sent their fine produce daily to the urban market throughout the summer, and that with excellent profit. Columella describes the gardener's return from the city, his pockets jingling with coin and his head soaked with wine from repeated celebrations of a prosperous day.[26] Certain small plots of land planted with artichokes, in the vicinity of Carthage and of Corduba in Spain, yielded a yearly income of $124.00,[27] thus rivalling the famous artichoke fields in the Carmel River floodplain of California. Megara so depended upon her export of onions and cucumbers to Athens, fifteen miles away across the Gulf of Salamis, that her market gardeners faced bankruptcy when in 444 B.C. Athens prohibited the trade. Rich Athenian epicures got their earliest vegetables from the nearby islands, where the warm spring stimulated growth.[28]

In addition to these various summer crops, irrigation was required by nearly all agriculture on the southern and eastern margins of the Mediterranean region, where the desiccating trade winds held sway. The Nile valley was a fluvial oasis; other wadi oases fringed the African front. The rivers of Damascus and the slender streams of Moab stretched long green fingers into the tawny desert of Syria. Farther east similar conditions of long summer droughts and scant winter rains prevailed in the plain and piedmont of the Tigris-Euphrates valley, where again irrigation became the basis of agriculture. Its principles, there perfected, may have penetrated from the Mesopotamian hinterland westward by way of Syria, Phœnicia, and Palestine; or they may have spread from Egypt around the circle of the Mediterranean coasts. They found vehicles of dissemination at hand in commerce, colonization, conquests and especially the slave trade which distributed skilled cultivators all around the ancient Mediterranean shores.

THE ANTIQUITY OF IRRIGATION—However, irrigation may have been a native discovery made independently in several parts of the Mediterranean Basin in response to climatic conditions. This was possible wherever the uncertain rainfall brought a lean harvest in dry years. While geographic conditions set the problem of supplementing the inadequate precipitation, they also gave the cue to the solution. Everywhere the recurrent floods of swollen winter streams suggested the method of distributing the fructifying waters to the thirsty fields. Nature presented the object lesson, and repeated it year after year with pedagogical fidelity. The theory of independent discovery receives support from the development of irrigation elsewhere in widely separated regions like China, the Melanesian islands, Mexico, and Peru. In all these imitation seems excluded. On the other hand, irrigation stretched across

15

Eurasia in an almost unbroken belt from Spain to India and Java in very early times; here imitation is not excluded.

Legendary history names some of the distributors in the Mediterranean lands. Danaus and his fifty daughters, leaving the old matriarchal community of Egypt, established their clan in Grecian Argos and there introduced tillage by irrigation. Phœnicia, which was dominated alternately by Babylonian and Egyptian influences, and early acquired the principles of irrigation, sent out countless colonists whose trail was marked by water conduits and pools, from Asia Minor to Spain. Cadmus, the Phœnician, in the very act of founding Bœotian Thebes, introduced irrigation; and his descendants doubtless carried this along with the other useful arts which they communicated to Attica.[29] The Greek Heracles, borrowed from the Phœnicians, was the practical benefactor of mankind, teaching the control of water for irrigation. The Etruscans of semi-Asiatic stock apparently taught in Latium principles of irrigation which their colonial ancestors had learned on the Asia Minor coast from Tyrian and Sidonian settlers; irrigation again followed in Spain and Africa on the arrival there of Phœnician colonists.

While the seasonal distribution of the rainfall made irrigation desirable, the prevailing mountain relief of the Mediterranean lands made it possible. High folded ranges rising to 5,000 or 7,000 feet and peaks towering to 9,000 feet or more retained their snow until midsummer. The Sierra Nevada of Spain, Mount Ætna, Mount Olympos of Thessaly, the peaks of Lebanon and Mount Argæus in the eastern Taurus system showed white patches in shady gorges till late August. The northern ranges, like the Alps, Pyrenees and Rhodope massif, had yet deeper snows owing to heavier precipitation, and kept them longer owing to cooler summers and reduced evaporation.[30] All the highlands were therefore reservoirs of moisture, whose supply in former days was conserved by the forest covering and renewed by the occasional summer showers. These highlands fed their melting snows and their rain into the drainage streams, and thence into the farmer's irrigation ditches, which thus ran full during the growing season of the summer crops, even if they dwindled at harvest time.

Irrigation water was supplied also by the copious springs which issued from the lower slopes of chalk and limestone ridges, especially where the limestone rested on sandstone or crystalline rock. Subterranean reservoirs of the widespread karst provided a steady flow of water, and therefore were a safer and surer source than the variable mountain stream, which often threatened inundation to the plotted garden or tilled field. The same advantage belonged to the wells sunk to ground-water in valley, lacustrine basin, or coastal plain. These, however, entailed the labor of lifting the water to the surface by well-sweep or wheel pump worked by oxen or asses, as the traveler sees them today in the Tell valleys of the Atlas amid the low-growing vineyards, or in the orchards about Gaza and Ascalon in the Tertiary coastal plain of Palestine. A rainfall of 16 to 35 inches (400 to 900 mm.) in the Tell valleys and of 8 to 16 inches (200 to 400 mm.) in southern Philistia, reinforced by drainage and infiltration from the nearby slope, supplied enough moisture for winter crops; but during the summer drought irrigation from the numerous wells was imperative then as now.[31] The ancients preferred spring and well water for irrigation because it was cool and fresh, and also because it brought no weed seed to the fields, as did the irrigation ditches fed by drainage streams. On the other hand, wells sunk too near the coast were likely to contain brackish water, which was bad for the purpose.[32]

Fluctuating seasonal rainfall and limited arable area together put the screw upon the ancient Mediterranean farmer, and forced him to his obvious national task of extending his tillage land into desert, swamp and mountain slope. Under state or community direction, he undertook costly reclamation enterprises into which irrigation entered. On the arid margin, east and south of the Mediterranean region, he pushed forward "the line between the desert and the sown," wherever the fructifying waters were available. The soil brought under tillage was rich in phosphorus and potash, which are leached out in rainy lands; the irrigating streams contributed a top dressing of silt to the land and other plant food in the form of mineral salts held in solution. The result was big crops and reliable crops up to the regular limit of the water supply. This was the encouragement to extension of irrigation in ancient Egypt, Syria, Palestine, Carthaginian Africa, and Spain. This explains the flowering orchards and gardens spread out fan-wise in the fluvial oasis of Damascus, which seemed to the weary eyes of Mohammed a Paradise on earth.

IRRIGATION OF TERRACED LANDS—Irrigation was often associated with the reclamation of mountain slopes by terracing, which contributed to water conservation. The districts commanding a reliable summer water supply were necessarily limited owing to both climate and relief, except in the Nile valley and along the northern rim of the Mediterranean climatic region. They were found elsewhere sparsely scattered over the mountain sides where springs appeared, as on "the slopes of many-fountained Ida," or closely distributed at the base of the ranges, where streams and piedmont springs issued upon the valley floors. Both situations suggested terraces and contour ditches in order to expand the arable area accessible to the irrigation streams, to conserve the water supply (whether natural or artificial) by checking the run-off, and finally to prevent surface erosion. Hence terrace agriculture was constantly associated with ancient irrigation, especially in those Mediterranean lands which were formerly more populous than now.[33] It meets us in ancient Phœnicia, where the whole country was atilt and where irrigation had been reduced to an art; in Palestine, where "shoulder-stones" of old retaining walls are scattered over the mountains of Carmel, Gilboa and Samaria, once famous for their fertility.[34] Ruins of ancient terraces, designed for barley fields or olive orchards, are found lining the steep valley slopes of Moab and the arid Negeb in southern Judea,[35] where occupancy depended upon the control of springs.[36]

Terrace agriculture early appeared in Greece, probably to utilize the slopes of its fortress heights. This may be the significance of Homer's "terraced Ithome," a mountain stronghold of Thessaly. The steep hill whence Mycenæ ruled the Argive plain is scarred by concentric lines of old retaining walls, which suggest to the modern observer terraced vineyards and gardens to supply the table of Agamemnon. Slopes were thus cultivated in Greece more extensively in ancient times

than now, for age-long destruction of the forests has impaired
the conservation of the water supply and reduced the arable
land to 12.5 per cent of the total area.[37] Terracing was doubtless as common in the Ægean Isles as today, when the traveler
marvels at the tiers of cultivation rising from seashore to
mountain crest on Tenos, Cos, Thera and other islands. Their
bold relief and small area combine to restrict level land to a
minimum. Only Naxos among the Cyclades possesses a lowland. Thera (Santorin), which is the breached rim of an old
volcanic crater and measures only three miles in width, cul-
minates in a height of 1,860 feet. Melos, another half-submerged volcano, has an area of 57 square miles and a summit
elevation of 2,505 feet. Similar ratios of altitude and area
hold in nearly all the Cyclades and Sporades, which are handicapped also by a meager rainfall of 20 inches (500 mm.) or
less (Thera 14 inches, 362 mm.). Terracing alone could extend the crop land and conserve the water supply. Their
population, dense in very early times, implied a local food
supply; for their mineral wealth was small apart from their
marble. Homer speaks of "well-peopled Cos" and "well-peopled Lemnos." [38] Extensive colonization movements from many
Ægean Isles as early as the seventh century B.C. point to congested population; and the fame of their wines points to terraced vineyards like those covering the slopes of Cos and
Thera today.

Roman Italy, with its ampler endowment of plains, might
have postponed the hour of terracing; but the fertile soils of
volcanic peaks like Ætna and Vesuvius, and the wide distribution of rich volcanic ash and tufa in the Apennines made these
mountains early seats of sedentary population, which enjoyed
there also better climate and surer water supply than the plains
could offer. Hence ancient Italian tillage was associated with
terracing and irrigation wherever hill slopes were accessible to
distributing canals, or where populous hill towns like those of
Etruria, Latium, and Umbria, built in a warring age, exploited
all the tillage land within the protecting reach of their citadels.

IRRIGATION AND RECLAMATION OF FLOOD PLAINS—More important from an economic and social standpoint was the irrigation which attended the reclamation of river flood plains,

coastal marsh lands and swampy lake basins; because their abundant humus and composite soils repaid year-round cultivation. Upstream reservoirs and dyked channels made it possible to restrain the swollen winter torrents within their banks, and thus transform flooded wastes into ploughland; but they also provided for the summer irrigation of the low-lying fields. This dual process has been inaugurated from grey antiquity to the present. A recent contract (1928) let to an American construction company by the Grecian government provides for the reclamation and irrigation of the lower Vardar (Axius) valley in Macedonia. Its methods will duplicate in their basic features similar enterprises of nameless ancient engineers, whose accumulated works running through undated centuries were attributed to certain great national heroes.

The network of canals in the Nile floodplain drained or irrigated according to the way the water was controlled. The system of basin irrigation developed by the Pharaohs from the time of Menes (5000 B.C.) was the most efficacious one possible for the Egyptian climate and Nilotic conditions. Only the left bank of the Nile was first reclaimed. A longitudinal dyke was run parallel to the stream on the left bank, and tied by numerous cross dykes to the Libyan hill range on the west. Into these basins the "red water" of the Nile flood was conducted by natural or artificial channels and allowed to deposit its mud, while it thoroughly saturated the soil. Meantime, the whole right bank and trough of the river furnished passage for the floods to the sea. Reclamation of the right bank did not begin till the Twelfth Dynasty (1380 B.C.); it was a far more difficult project, involving the problem of disposal of excess water by escape-drains through the Delta, so that the water should not be held in the basins longer than forty-five days. Retention of the water for this period secured an adequate top-dressing of red mud and also saturated the subsoil, where this possessed the proper consistency; thus it provided plentiful ground-water which was used in winter and spring for irrigating later crops. It is a significant fact that all the ancient capitals of Egypt occupied sites with extensive subsoil water reserves, which permitted all-year irrigation. Abydos, where the philosopher king Akhnaton laid out his pleasure gardens, has the best subsoil water in the Nile valley; Thebes and Memphis have an excellent supply.[39]

The so-called "plagues of Egypt" were natural incidents of Nile control as practised in the lower Delta or "field of Zoan." In the old days of basin irrigation, and that too from earliest times, according to Sir William Willcocks, it was the Egyptian custom to build temporary earthen dams across the inferior Nile distributaries about twenty miles above their "tails," in order to hold back the flood water and let it overflow the maximum area of land. This was done at the peak of the flood about August first, when the fertilizing "red water" arrived; it was a method invariably adopted in years of "low Nile" to husband the water and extend the irrigated area to the utmost. The exclusion of the fresh water from the tails and the rapid evaporation in August combined to admit the salt water from the Mediterranean, with the result that the river fish died and the frogs beat a hasty retreat to the land. The Israelite settlers living in Goshen near the tails of the east Delta channels saw every year at the time of "red water" myriads of fish floating dead and attributed the phenomenon to "the water turned into blood."

The Pelusiac arm of the Nile, thus dammed below Bubastis during a low Nile to check the out-flow, flooded the Wadi Tumilat, irrigated the grain fields and pastures of Goshen, renewed its sweet subsoil water, and brought plenty to the immigrant Hebrew tribes thereabouts. But it condemned the district of Zoan or Tanis on the lower Pelusiac Nile to plagues of dead fish, frogs, sand-fleas, flies, polluted wells, with the consequent infection and death of cattle and babies. No miracles these: only the operation of natural laws set in motion by a certain human enterprise under certain geographic conditions. The first and second plagues were ordinary occurrences, produced "also by the Egyptian necromancers," according to biblical statement. The other six came only in a very low Nile, which might occur once in a century or two. "Darkness" was probably due to a protracted northwest wind, bringing clouds of dust to obscure the sun; and the swarms of locusts doubtless came from the deserts of Arabia as they do today. Hail, which is not unknown in the Nile Delta, probably came in late January, since it destroyed the barley crop, then nearly ripe, but did not injure the still immature wheat. The low Nile played no part in these last three plagues, which were fortuitous.[40]

The embanking of rivers for flood control was a common practice among the Homeric Greeks.[41] They knew "the winter torrent at the full that in swift course scatters the dykes; neither can the long line of mounds hold it in, nor the walls of the fruitful orchards stay its sudden coming, when the rain of heaven driveth it." [42] Yet earlier, in the legendary period, various heroes instituted combined drainage and irrigation works, so far back into the past did these undertakings reach. The characteristic labors of Heracles show him grappling with some problem of water control, whether in Thrace, Argolis, Elis or in Acarnania, where he reclaimed for tillage the flood plain at the mouth of the silt-bearing Achelous. This river, described in legend as a roaring bull when in flood and as a writhing serpent when shrunken to a meandering brook in the summer drought,[43] he embanked and diverted its surplus water by an artificial channel to irrigate the bordering tract of alluvium. The reclaimed tillage land and the crescent course of the new channel which irrigated it, the hero presented to the neighboring king "as the horn of plenty" which all summer produced abundant fruit like apples, grapes, and pomegranates.[44]

In like manner the Thessalians of Larisa, who occupied the richest portion of the lacustrine basin drained by the Peneus River, embanked this stream to protect their fields from the floods which often washed away the soil into the overflow basin of Lake Nesonis.[45] But the moderate annual rainfall of this district (20 inches, 502.4 mm.),[46] and the low summer minimum, which makes the Larisian plain in June as dry and dusty as Egypt,[47] offered inducements for irrigation, while the dyked stream, fed by the lingering snows on high Olympos and the Pindus Mountains, furnished a ready irrigation system. The abundant and varied food which weighed down the tables of the voracious Thessalians was partly supplied from irrigated gardens and orchards surrounding the capital city. Apparently, too, the low flooded basin of Nesonis, alternately swamp and lake,[48] was frequently reclaimed. Homer fails to mention Lake Nesonis, because, as Strabo surmises, the district was uninhabited owing to inundations; but Simonides of Ceos (556-469 B.C.) speaks of its Pelasgi population.[49] In the fourth century, possibly during the efficient administration of the tyrant Jason (369 B.C.), the swamp of Nesonis was drained so completely, that "after the water was drawn off and the land was dry, the air became colder and frosts more frequent," to the destruction of the fine old olive groves and the occasional injury of the vineyards.[50]

Reclamation produced similar results in the old Lake of Philippi, which occupied a valley basin in the Pangæus Mountains of southwest Thrace. When the native Thracians occupied the district, so tradition ran, the whole plain was a big forested swamp, a gathering place of the waters from the surrounding mountains,—"*multas aquarum collectiones et stationes habit*." "But after the basin was drained and for the most part dried out and the whole country brought under cultivation," the district became more subject to frosts.[51] This reclamation was probably instituted by Philip of Macedon after his conquest of the territory in 356 B.C., to furnish local supplies for his new town of Philippi, which was designed as market center for the rich gold mines in Mount Pangæus. Hence the enterprise was recent history to Theophrastus writing about it in 313 B.C. It was almost inevitably associated with irrigation, for this coastal belt suffered from scarcity of summer rains and failing streams.[52] Cvijic states that the practice was very ancient and widespread, tracing back to an oriental or Byzantine origin; that irrigation canals, constructed on the ancient plan, were mentioned in the charters of the Serbian kings of the thirteenth century. They are numerous today in the basin of the Meglen River, which formed the heart of Philip's Macedonia, and which now yields two crops annually under irrigation.[53]

Farther south, in the narrow peninsular area of Hellas and Peloponnesos, where the valley plains contract, the arable land shrinks, rainfall declines, and summer drought lengthens, reclamation and irrigation became increasingly urgent. The Eurotas River of Laconia was ascribed to a large canal constructed by Eurotas, a mythical king of Sparta, to drain the Spartan plain.[54]   The legend probably epitomized centuries of piece-meal reclamation; for this middle section of the Eurotas valley, blocked on the south by the Bardunochoria hill belt which cuts it off from the sea, was formerly a Pliocene inland lake, which was slowly drained as the Eurotas eroded its gorge through the limestone barrier to the Mediterranean.[55]   The process was incomplete even in historical times.   The ancient city park Plantanistas or Planetree Grove occupied an artificial island surrounded by channels of the braided stream [56]—evidence of water control,—while Limnæ, an urban district of Sparta in a depression by the Eurotas, had its name from the former marshes there.   Its temple of Dionysos occupied a wet site, which in the course of time was drained.[57]

IRRIGATION IN THE KARST COUNTRY—The karst country of Greece utilized for irrigation its great "fountain-heads" or kephalari, surface vents of underground rivers; these were often so copious and had so many "heads" or mouths that they formed considerable streams and necessitated reclamation enterprises to control and distribute the water.   The River Erasinos, which issues near Argos from its twenty-mile subterranean course from Lake Stymphalus, has force today to drive a dozen mills, and in ancient times served to water the adjacent Argive plain.[58]   In a cavern above the spring sacrifices were offered to Dionysos and Pan, both gods of husbandry; and now in mid-August a Panegyris is annually celebrated here, for the summer drought is just as severe and the human need is just as great.   Six miles south of Argos, on a narrow coastal strip at the base of Mount Pontinos is the gushing spring of Amymone, which forms the Lerna River and swamp. Here Heracles, "man's great benefactor," fought the monster Hydra or water snake with its nine heads; and as soon as he severed one head two others sprang out in its place.[59]   The spring gave evidence of strong hydraulic pressure.   In ancient times it watered a sacred grove of plane-trees, where solemn rites were celebrated in honor of Demeter and Dionysos, gods of tillage.

Bœotia was the scene of various reclamation projects from the legendary period to recent times.   Cadmus of Tyre, a typical Phœnician engineer and colonist, "was directed by the gods to fix his abode in the rich wheat lands where gushing Dirce's fair streams pour their water over green and fruitful fields." But a dragon had its lair in a limestone cave beneath the high Cadmean citadel; it ravaged the Theban plain and "watched with roving eye the watered vales and quickening rivulets." [60] This monster typified the mighty spring of Ares, which the hero snared in a network of canals and thus held captive. He converted its devastating streams into beneficent water conduits, and made the Theban district the most productive in Greece. An unknown writer about 250 B.C. thus describes the area: "All its parts are level, its form is circular, and its hue black like the earth. Everywhere well watered, verdant, undulating, it includes more gardens than any other city in Greece. For two rivers flow through its precincts, watering all the level land adjoining their banks, and hidden springs descend from the Cadmeia in artificial channels, said to have been constructed by Cadmus in very ancient times." [61] Today several large tanks of ancient masonry with inscribed tablets impound the water of the famous Dircean springs and distribute it to the surrounding gardens. They stand there, still performing their age-long service, mute intimations of the immortality of geographic forces in history.

Bœotia contained also several lake basins with underground outlets typical of the karst regions of Greece. They furnished admirable soil but were subject to inundation when the natural vents in the underlying limestone became choked up or proved inadequate to carry off the winter floods. [62] Lake Copais, the largest of these basins, shrank to a reedy swamp in late summer, but when it attained its highest level in late winter, covered an area of ninety square miles. [63] Theophrastus, on the basis of old traditions, estimated that this occurred about once every nine years; though its duration was variable. At the time of the battle of Chæronea (338 B.C.) and for several years before, Lake Copais was deep; it filled again later at the time of a severe plague, but failed again in winter. [64] During sustained droughts, the lake dried up so completely that the aquatic vegetation became sere. [65]

The earliest inhabitants of this lacustrine plain, dating back to Minyan Orchomenos (2000 B.C.) or yet earlier to the Stone Age, kept Lake Copais at a low level and thus reclaimed for tillage a wide zone of fertile land by constructing canals and enlarging the openings or katavothra to the underground channels.[66] These ran eastward under Mount Ptoon and debouched as great springs near Larymna on the Eubœan Sound.[67] The traveler in Bœotia today sees the masonry of the ancient dykes, and caverns in the mountain shore which mark the tunnel course of the katavothra. Drainage works, executed by a British company about 1890, consist of a girdle canal, which intercepts the affluent streams on two sides of the Copais basin, and discharges its water by a series of tunnels and minor katavothra lakes into the Eubœan Sound.[68] Significantly enough, it is a belated copy of a girdle canal described by Plato as encircling the mountain-rimmed plain of the mythical Atlantis and connected with a network of conduits intersecting the plain.[69] Plato doubtless copied the reclamation system in several lake basins of Greece.

These reclamation works about Lake Copais recovered many thousand acres of irrigable tillage land and founded the agricultural wealth of Gla, Orchomenos, Copæ, Acræphium, Coroneia, Haliartos, and other places. All these cities occupied hill or mountain sites for safety from the recurrent inundations. Even so, the rising waters often trapped them. The legendary history of Bœotia abounds in tales of towns swallowed up by floods; it had its local variants of the deluge myth with quite distinctive features. The underground outlets of Lake Copais became obstructed with serious results in the time of Alexander the Great, when Crates of Chalcis, a mining engineer, undertook the work of clearing out the channels; but he left his task unfinished when an insurrection broke out. This was the period of high water alluded to by Theophrastus.

A different method of combined drainage and irrigation was devised by the inhabitants of ancient Thisbe, who occupied a small katavothra lake basin on the southern slope of Mount Helicon in western Bœotia.[70] They ran a dyke through the lake along the axis of its drainage; every second year they diverted the water to one side of the dyke, and tilled the land on the other, which was soaked with moisture and naturally fertilized by decayed vegetation.[71]

The rugged highlands of Arcadia abound in similar lake basins, which in ancient times furnished the best arable land but were subject to inundation. Efforts of ancient engineers to control the fluctuating water level and reclaim the land for tillage were epitomized in the symbolic labors of Heracles. The hero, for instance, rescued the plain of Lake Stymphalos from a plague of foul birds, symbolizing the torrents which rushed down from the surrounding mountains and devastated the land.[72] Lake Pheneos, whose surface has for ages oscillated with the seasonal rains and the open or obstructed conditions of the underground discharges, was in antiquity a fertile plain.[73] The stream feeding the lake was conducted across the plain to a katavothra by an embanked canal, five furlongs long and thirty feet deep, ascribed to Heracles. When everything was in order above and below ground, it reclaimed nine square miles of fertile land, and made Pheneos a prosperous cantonal state in this ancient Switzerland of Greece. But the district was never safe from floods. Lying 2,470 feet above sea level, surrounded by mountains from 2,000 to 4,400 feet higher, and subject to sudden storms, the little state found it wise to locate its capital city six miles from the katavothra and well up on the rim of the basin; but even so it once suffered from inundation.[74]

Farther south, a series of four small katavothra basins, occupying the graben of eastern Arcadia and lying about 2,000 feet above the sea, were reclaimed for the sake of the rich brown loam which covered their floors. Gradual deposition of silt from the surrounding slopes tended to raise the level, clog the drainage canals and choke the underground outlets; but the work of reclamation went on. The lake plain which fed the lofty city of Orchomenos (3,070 feet) in the days of its greatness had an area of only four square miles. In the time of Pausanias it had reverted to a mere. The adjacent plain of Caphyæ had its stream canalled and conducted to a katavothra.[75] The larger basin of Mantinea was carefully drained by canals and katavothræ,[76] and formerly supported a considerable population on its fluctuating eight square miles of

fertile land.   But a hill range on the south separated the
Mantinean district from the larger basin of Tegea, which lay
100 feet higher and after heavy winter rains overflowed through
a narrow defile into the Mantinean mere.[77]   The regulation of
the water in this course occasioned continual strife between
the two towns.   Prior to the seventh century B.C. and even in
the pre-Dorian age, Tegea was a powerful state.   It evidently
inaugurated reclamation works at a very early date, to exploit
the fertile lacustrine soil which formed the heart of its territory.[78]   The main katavothra, a low cave in the rock wall at
the southwest corner of the marshy lake, can still be seen from
the highroad crossing the mountains to Sparta; and still it
serves to drain the vineyards and wheatfields which support
the modern town of Tripolis, successor of hoary Tegea as
metropolis of the basin.

RECLAMATION ENTERPRISES IN ITALY—Reclamation enterprises in Italy go back into grey antiquity and generally appear under Etruscan initiative.   Several lakes or swamps
(*paludes*) in and about Rome figured in the early chronicles
but disappeared later.   Such were the Goat's Marsh, where
Romulus was struck by lightning, the Curtian Lake mentioned
as existing in 745 B.C., Lake Regillus near Tusculum where the
Romans defeated the Latins in 496 B.C.[79]   The marshy valley
between the Palatine and Capitoline Hills of Rome was doubtless reclaimed and cultivated at an early period.   The Cloaca
Maxima, ascribed by tradition to the Tarquin kings, originally
served this purpose and may be classed with drains found in
other Etruscan towns like Graviscæ, port of Tarquinii, located
on a marshy coast.   Clusium, overlooking the swampy lake-
strewn valley of the Clanis River, rests upon a labyrinth of
underground passages which probably belonged to an elaborate
drainage system similar to that at Præneste.[80]   The district
below Velitræ, which lies in the southern slope of the Alban
Mountains, is honeycombed with a system of tunnels or *cuniculi*
running down towards the Pontine marshes.   They probably
served, as has been suggested, to carry off excess water from
the swollen torrents and reduce erosion in the bordering fields.
Ancient dams of polygonal masonry are found in the Scara-
bellata gorge, which scars the steep seaward slope of Monte

Gennaro (4,160 feet), the highest peak of the Sabine Mountains; [81] and they seem designed to check the run-off and conserve the water for irrigation. In all these districts, Etruscan influence once prevailed.

Another Etruscan method of reclaiming land consisted in drawing off water from volcanic lakes by cutting tunnels through the crater walls. All the crater lakes in the Alban Mountains were tapped in this way. The tunnel emissarium of Lake Albanus was 1,300 yards long. It was constructed, according to tradition, in 397 B.C. during the siege of Veii, when the lake filled up and threatened to overflow; but it was possibly much older. Livy's garbled account ascribed the plan to Etruscan soothsayers, who urged the Romans to use the water for irrigation and "scatter it harmless over the fields." [82] A longer emissarium tapped Lake Nemi at some unknown date, reclaimed for gardens and vineyards the shallow north end of the basin, and opened below through the old crater wall of Lake Aricia, which lay eighty-five feet lower. Thence its water was conducted in a canal which drained the shallow basin of Aricia, and issued by a tunnel through the low crater rampart on the southwest into a river. The old town of Aricia, whose citadel lay on a hill, belonged to the early Latin League; and its fertile basin, where irrigation is still maintained, became famous for its leeks and cabbages.[83] This lake region was the heart of the old Latin territory. Pressure of population doubtless forced it to these reclamation projects under Etruscan direction. The amount of arable land recovered was small, but its quality was excellent and facilities for irrigation lay at hand.

The tunnel and *cuniculi* drainage of Latium and southern Etruria, like the dyking of the lower Arno by Etruscans or Greek Pisans, belongs to prehistoric times; but similar reclamation enterprises were carried on with no appreciable break by the Latins and later Romans. The old lacustrine basin of the Velinus River in the Sabine country was subject to progressive inundation caused by deposits of travertine which dammed the outflow. It invited reclamation because its meadows and wet pastures were famous and were located only about fifty miles from Rome. Hence a succession of drainage canals were made, the first in 271 B.C. by Manius Curius Dentatus; but the rising of the river bed necessitated fresh cuttings in the old channels or the construction of new ones.[84] Efforts to drain Lake Fucinus, which occupies a shallow, mountain-locked basin in the central Apennines, were stimulated by the rich soil around its shelving shores. The width of this arable zone varied widely with the rising and falling of the water level, which was very irregular; for the lake was "vast as a sea and of great service to the Marsi and all the surrounding nations." [85] The drainage enterprise was a big one, therefore. It was attempted with partial success by the Emperor Claudius in 52 A.D.; renewed by Hadrian, but accomplished only in 1875 by Prince Torlonia, who constructed a double tunnel emissarium four miles through a range of the Apennines to the River Liris.

Attempts to reclaim the Pontine marshes of Latium and the Maremna of Etruria were also big undertakings and urgent ones, because they lay in the heart of the old Roman territory and fringed a much used coast. The Etruscan towns like Volci, Vetulonia, Rusellæ, Cossa, Tarquinii, and Cære were situated on spurs of the upland a few miles from the sea, and only their ports lay on the marshy shore. Populonia which occupied a lofty promontory (938 feet), an old "tied" island, with a little harbor at its base, was the only ancient Etruscan town located on the sea.[86] The Pontine marshes, reputed to have been once dotted with flourishing villages,[87] reverted to a permanent swamp during the Republic, probably due to slow subsidence of the basin or buckling of the coast. Efforts to drain the marshes were made by Appius Claudius in 312 B.C. according to tradition, by Cornelius Cethegus in 182 B.C., by Julius Cæsar, Augustus, Nerva, Trajan, and finally by Theodoric the Goth. All achieved only temporary results, because the problem was apparently a progressive one, which is still engaging the attention of the Italian government.[88] In the time of Strabo, the great drainage canal along the Via Appia from Terracina was used for canal boat transportation between Rome and the coast.[89] Reclamation was evidently stimulated after the Hannibalic War (204 B.C.) which was probably responsible for the introduction of malaria into Italy from Africa.

The canalization of the Po, which was subject to heavy spring floods, was begun by the Etruscans who diverted the sluggish waters of the river into the coastal swamps, in order to facilitate communication between the seaport Adria and the Adriatic.[90] Æmilius Scaurus in 109 b.c. drained the plains south of the Po between Placentia and Parma by means of navigable canals, in connection with the construction of the Æmilian Way.[91] This road traced the north base of the Apennines and ran through a succession of new colonies whose fertile territory, developed by drainage and irrigation, could profit by land and water communication to stabilize Roman power in this frontier province.

These government enterprises accomplished on a big scale what the Etruscan and Roman peasants had been doing on their farms every year on a small scale. With the advent of the autumn rains, Cato directs all farm hands to work with pick and shovel, clearing out the drainage ditches or making new ones to carry off the excess water.[92] Vergil, recalling his boyhood impressions of his father's farm by the Mincio River in the Po lowland, describes the whole country-side as "afloat with brimming ditches during the winter rains." In such districts a gridiron of trenches was necessary. From the furrows of the ploughland the water ran into transverse channels and thence into open ditches.[93] A heavy rain involved emergency work to prevent the canals from getting choked with mud and debris. Hence this was a permissible task for feast days, when other agricultural labor was forbidden.[94]

The Roman law reflected the necessity of water control. It required neighbors to maintain the dykes and clean the trenches forming part of a common drainage system, in order to expedite run-off and prevent overflows.[95] Down-hill estates were made subject to higher lands for drainage, a servitude imposed by nature but compensated in part by the rich soil washed down from the upper fields. However, the law (actio aquæ pluviæ arcendæ) provided redress if a farmer dammed a swamp or lake to exclude the flood water from his own land, and thereby forced it to seek new outlets to the detriment of a neighbor's land below; or if he diverted the rain water from its natural course on his own farm, and overloaded the channel running down into his neighbor's farm.[96] But the owner of the upper estate was free to impound water flowing on to his own land, for purposes of irrigation or other use, and could thereby intercept it from the farm below.[97]   The law authorized any man to embank a river flowing through his land, and also to construct dykes and ditches on a neighbor's estate, where these were essential to his plan for flood control.[98]   Moreover such works were protected by law.   If wantonly destroyed, they had to be restored by the offender; but if swept away by the violence of the river in spate, there was no redress.[99]

IRRIGATION IN DRY LAND REGIONS—Aside from irrigation associated with reclamation enterprises, the Mediterranean region presented many irrigation schemes by which the farmer merely endeavored to get available water onto the land.   His object was to vary and amplify the yield of his farm by raising summer crops; or to supplement the scant winter rains of dry years or of dry localities, where recurrent droughts brought recurrent failure to the winter crops and jeopardized the fodder supply of the farm animals.   The marked variability in the amount and duration of the winter rains in the Mediterranean climatic region, the growing density of population, the increasing wealth and culture in the big urban centers which made a demand for increasing table luxuries, all combined to stimulate irrigation.   Hence this particular form of intensive agriculture became widely distributed in the Mediterranean lands.   Some of its finest phases, like elaborate floriculture, trace back to extremely early times.   A detailed survey of its distribution will make this clear.

Control of the Nile floods was a preliminary to the regulation and distribution of its waters; for the problems attending these national tasks underlay all Egyptian government and science, animated much of its religion.   The peasant turned from the harvests of his flooded fields in March to the irrigation of his spring crops by well and shaduf.

Where the level expanse of the African coast domes up in Barca Plateau, this highland attains sufficient altitude (3,300 ft. or 1,000 m. in the west) to collect an annual rainfall of 11 inches (276 mm.) with wide fluctuation between 5.5 and 24 inches,[100]—enough for grain in average years by the help of the dews and dry-farming methods, as is the case today.[101] The products were typical of a good soil in a semi-arid karst

region. But one notes the presence of terrace springs and
short streams wherever gardens, orchards, and vineyards
flourished, as about Cyrene, Hesperides, Barca, and Darnæ.[102]
Diodorus Siculus lauds the fertile soil, the vines, olive groves,
trees, and herbs about Cyrene, and then adds, "It excels also
in the convenience of its streams. The land to the south where
the nitre comes out permits no tillage, being bereft of flowing
water, and it presents the appearance of the sea." [103]   The
coast town of Darnæ owed its existence to a little stream, fed
by two springs, which today serves to irrigate gardens in the
delta. Ruins of aqueducts and reservoirs show that the Romans conserved the water resources of Cyrenaica to the utmost, despite the difficulty of making storage tanks in the
porous limestone.[104]   The prosperity of ancient Cyrene was
based on silphium, a wild native plant of the steppes; and when
that was exhausted, the state declined.

Yet farther west, where a high escarpment of the African
plateau approaches close to the Mediterranean and suffices to
condense the winter rains (16 inches or 391 mm.) a few wadis
find their way to the shelving coast and maintain high ground
water in the littoral. Here in the Cinyps valley, where "the soil
is black and well watered with springs," grain fields flourished
under the combined effect of rain and dew; and irrigation
helped in years when the precipitation declined to nine inches
or less.[105]   At the head of the Syrtis Minor, in the rain-shadow
of the Atlas Mountains precipitation became negligible and
tillage frankly depended on irrigation. There lay the port of
Tacape (rainfall 7 in., 183 mm.) occupying a small district of
nine square miles but great fertility, located in the midst of the
sands. Through it flowed an unfailing spring, abundant to
be sure, but only at certain hours were its waters distributed
among the inhabitants; for its irrigation ditches fructified
orchards of olive, figs, and pomegranates, with fields of wheat,
pulses, and garden herbs growing beneath their grateful shade
among the murmuring rivulets. No wonder the ground was
costly.[106]

IRRIGATION IN THE ATLAS REGION—In North Africa, only
the high mass of the Atlas system, accessible to the rain-bearing winds from the west, ensured water for irrigation. The

Tell valleys, near the coast, get enough rain for winter tillage; but all the inland valleys were in ancient times, as today, dependent upon irrigation. When Agathocles of Sicily invaded Carthage in 310 B.C., he found the land beautified with gardens and fruit trees; sluices and canals conveyed the water by which the whole tract was abundantly irrigated. There were orchards of pomegranates, figs, olives, pears, and cherries, besides extensive vineyards, nearly all of which presupposed irrigation in this trade-wind district. The fact that Carthage was importing grain in the third century B.C., according to Diodorus Siculus, points to the larger profit of horticulture by irrigation.

Eight centuries later Procopius gave a similar description of Vandal Africa. Landing at Caputvada or Shoal Head with the army of Belisarius in 535 A.D., he marched northward along the coast of Byzacium 120 miles to Carthage. It was summer, but the orchards were full of fresh fruits. The soldiers, digging the trench about their camp on Shoal Head, struck a gushing stream of water a few feet below the surface in the midst of an arid steppe, evidence of high ground water; and the next morning they raided the fruit orchards of the nearby farms. Thence all the way north the country people sold abundant supplies to the army, which often pitched its tents amid trees laden with fruit, beside spring-fed rivulets.[107] Irrigation and high ground water explain the summer productivity of this coast land of Byzacium, where winter wheat throve from early times with a mean annual rainfall of scant sixteen inches (Hadrumetum or Sousse, 406 mm.).

Farther north about Utica and Carthage, where the Atlas ranges approach the sea, the summer crops had ample flowing water. The busy port of Hippo Diarrhytus (Bizerta, rainfall 642 mm.) got its name from the canals irrigating its little plain.[108] It is no wonder that Carthaginian fruits and vegetables, such as asparagus and artichokes, Numidian pears, and cherries, enjoyed a great reputation. But sixty miles west of Carthage, in the valley of the Bagradas River, was Vaga, the busiest market of northern Numidia, located in the rain shadow of the northern Atlas. When the Roman army camped there in the summer of 109 B.C., they found the country about "a

desert owing to the dearth of water, except the places along
the river; these were planted in orchards and were resorted to
by flocks and the cultivators," [109] who clearly brought their
stock to the irrigated meadows in the summer drought.

Nor was intensive tillage by irrigation restricted to the Ro-
manized population of the coastland. The native Massylii of
inland Numidia diverted the River Abigas (Wadi Bu Duda)
which flowed down from the high Aures Mountains (7,585 feet,
2,310 m.) past the town of Bagais (Baghai), into the Shott-el-
Tarf, and distributed it by canals over the arid piedmont plain.
They stopped the channels with earth to check the flow, and
opened them at will. Similar plains in this highland region,
where streams and springs sufficed, were made to produce excellent grain and fruits. [110] The districts of Tamugadi (Timgad), Lambæsis, and Lamasba, located at the northern base
of the Aures Mountains at an altitude of about 3,350 feet
(1,050 m., rainfall, 12.5 to 15.5 inches) had extensive storage
works for water, on which tillage depended. [111] The ruins of
Lamasba, which lay near the modern site of Batna on the
Trans-Atlas railroad, comprise an ancient inscription, dating
from 220 A.D. It records the water rights of forty-three or
more farms in the commune, and specifies the hours and exact
dates when each estate might receive water. Plots were classi-
fied as *declives* or below the reservoir level, and *acclives,* or
above, to which water had to be pumped. The "descendent"
water was left flowing for fewer hours than "ascendent" water,
because the latter was more slowly delivered. The amount of
water was determined also by the size of the estate or the size
of its harvests, it is not clear which. A small farm received
"descendent" water for an hour in late September, and one
four times as large received it for four and a half hours. Of
two farms, about equal in size or products, one received ascending water for sixteen and a half hours, and the other received
descending water for ten and a half hours. These regulations,
which aimed to secure impartial distribution in a region of
inadequate rainfall and intense evaporation, were issued by
the local senate and people. [112]

IRRIGATION IN SYRIA AND PALESTINE—In the lands bordering the eastern end of the Mediterranean, similar conditions

of long summer droughts and uncertain rainfall obtained, with the consequent need of artificial watering. The early Aramaic-Semitic peóples of Syria and Palestine brought this secret of desert tillage from the stream oases of highland Arabia, and the invading Israelites adopted it along with other practices of sedentary life.

In Palestine irrigation relied upon springs, underground water, cisterns, and a few perennial rivulets—"a fountain of gardens, a well of living waters, and streams from Lebanon." [113] It was constantly associated with horticulture in the Bible, where the well watered garden was the symbol of generous blessing. But irrigation was applied also to field and meadow,[114] to vineyards, orchards, and groves. "I made me gardens and orchards, and I planted in them all kinds of fruit; I made me pools of water to water therewith the wood that bringeth forth trees." [115]

The narrow margin between food and famine, resulting from variable rainfall and porous limestone soil, made irrigation in Palestine a desirable resource. In those year-long periods of drought from which the country frequently suffered, every drop of water was conserved. Hence the surface of the country is pitted with ancient cisterns and reservoirs, whose restoration would renew the productivity of the land. The three great "Pools of Solomon" near Jerusalem are artificial tanks, measuring from 127 to 194 yards in length, from 49 to 76 yards in width, and from 25 to 48 feet in depth, fed by conduits from neighboring springs.[116] The average rainfall in Jerusalem, at an altitude of 2,600 feet, is 26 inches (649 mm.); but it drops to 20 inches (520 mm.) at Joppa on the coast and to 16 inches (420 mm.) at Gaza farther south. Both districts require irrigation for complete exploitation in good seasons, and for a partial crop in years of diminished rainfall. Abundant springs issue from the western base of the Judean Plateau, fed by the seepage waters of the long western slope. They are in reality the surface mouths of underground streams, and are therefore copious enough to supply distributing canals. Others like them water the base of Mount Carmel and Gilboa.[117] All these doubtless served to irrigate the scattered gardens of Palestine during the five months of summer drought. At the seaward edge of the Maritime Plain, wells sunk to the ground water which everywhere underlay the fertile soil, kept alive the flourishing gardens and orchards of Ashdod, Askalon, and Gaza.

In the wilderness or desert of Judea, that arid eastern slope which sinks abruptly to the Dead Sea, no cultivation was possible, except where an occasional spring, like that of Engeddi, bursting forth from the porous limestone escarpment, created an oasis as far as its waters reached. In the time of King Saul, as in that of Josephus (75 A.D.), the oasis of Engeddi spread in a succession of vineyards and gardens,[118] fed by brimming canals, 600 feet down to the Dead Sea. A nearly rainless climate, due to descending winds and intense heat, prevailed along the whole eastern base of the Judean Plateau, where this joined the sunken Jordan plain. Fertile soil on the natural terraces of an old lake basin offered attractive conditions for tillage, while fountains and spring-fed wadis afforded water for irrigation. Hence these old Jordan lake strands became from remote times the sites of flourishing agricultural towns, like Jericho, Phaselis, and Bethshan.

The situation of Jericho was typical. Located on a broad lake terrace 470 feet above the Dead Sea and about eight miles from the Jordan, it enjoyed excellent irrigation and drainage for the palm and balsam groves which made it famous in antiquity.[119] These plantations, extending northward for a hundred stadia or twelve miles and merging into those of Phaselis at the mouth of the Wadi Ifjion, included also various other cultivated trees which produced excellent fruits.[120] A reputation for fertility, "the fattest of Judea," belonged to Jericho equally in the time of Joshua and of the Latin kings of Jerusalem.[121] The modern traveller visiting the site today sees above the town the ancient tanks, one of them six acres in extent, whose conduits once made this district a miniature paradise.

Yet farther north, in the canyon mouth of the Vale of Jezreel, lay the fortress city of Bethshan, surrounded by gardens and orchards on the last broad terrace of the Jordan graben. Its irrigation streams were so abundant that during a Saracen attack in 634 A.D., they were poured out to convert the surrounding flats into a marsh and thus held the enemy at bay.[122] When it is remembered that this western terrace of the Jordan lay from 430 to 830 feet below sea level in the superheated rift, and from 2,000 to 3,400 feet below the summit of the plateau, whence the drying winds descended, and that this district was famous in antiquity for its grain, dates, flax, balsam, and other products, as for its sugar-cane under thrifty Saracen tillage, the conclusion is unavoidable that this was a banner district for irrigation, a conclusion that is corroborated by the scattered ruins of tanks and aqueducts.

Phœnicia, owing to its more northern location and its mountain relief facing the rain-bearing winds from the west, had ample precipitation for winter tillage. But the steep slopes exposed the fields to over-rapid drainage and surface erosion, that would scour off the forest-made humus. Hence, physical conditions necessitated terracing at an early date, while the populous cities which exploited the patches of coastal plain made insistent demand for the additional food supply yielded by summer tillage. Consequently, both agriculture and irrigation were highly developed here in remote antiquity. Olive groves, orchards, vineyards and gardens, all requiring intensive cultivation, covered the littoral and dotted the slopes to an altitude of two thousand feet or more; [123] for at this elevation remains of ancient temples and other buildings have been found. Even today, the traveller coming from Damascus to the coast issues from the high tunnels of the Lebanon Mountains, as if he had thrust his head out of a window, and sees below him vineyards mantling the slopes up to a height of 2,500 feet, and terraces of irrigated cultivation climbing far up the wadi walls. The Phœnicians were masters in the art of embanking and irrigating and were regarded as such by the Greeks,[124] whose engineer heroes, like Cadmus and Heracles, came from Syria.

Behind the wind-shield of the Lebanon Mountains, the need for irrigation increases with every added mile away from the coast and with every drop in altitude. The long line of cities and towns, which from most ancient times traced the great north road through the Lebanon Trough from the sources of the Jordan to Antioch and Aleppo, owed their agricultural

wealth to the rich soil and abundant flowing water.[125]   The
great productivity of Cœle-Syria under imperial Rome was due
to effective equipment and administration of the water supply,
which was furnished by the Orontes River, its western tributaries, and the full springs on the Lebanon flank.[126]   Damascus,
located about seventy miles from the Mediterranean on the edge
of the Syrian Desert, behind the double screen of the Lebanon
and Anti-Lebanon, in the rain-shadow of their towering ranges,
has relied through the ages upon their snow-fed brooks to
water her wide expanse of gardens, fields, and orchards.   The
rushing Barada issues from its canyon and flings abroad tas-
sels of silver streams across the outstretched plain; the Phar-
phar brings its tribute from the copious springs of Mount
Hermon (9,050 feet).   Only this delta of fertility, murmurous
with the running water of countless canals, creates the Garden
of Damascus between the Syrian Desert in front and the sterile
plateau of Es-Sahara behind.   In spring a cloud of pink and
white blossoms broods over the oasis, when the almond and
plum trees are in bloom; in summer a vast stretch of green
foliage shades off into the grey rolling steppe and the gleaming
salt lake on the desert rim.

IRRIGATION OF THE DRY LANDS OF GREECE—The ancient
Greeks practiced irrigation from remote times, certainly before the tenth century B.C.   The fine passage in the *Iliad*, which
describes the peasant turning the stream into the ditch to water
his fields and garden,[127] is echoed in the *Odyssey*, where a
spring-fed canal waters the garden of Alcinous, and the waste
from a roadside fountain waters a group of thirsty plane-
trees.[128]   Sophocles, who belongs to the golden age of Athens,
describes the flowery fields of the Cephisos valley kept green
by irrigation.[129]

> And there, beneath the gentle dew of heaven,
> The fair narcissus with its clustered bells
>   Blows every day by day,
> Of old the wreath of mightiest goddesses,
>   And crocus golden-eyed;
>   And still unslumbering flow
>   Cephisos' wandering streams.

Today the parcelled waters of the Cephisos are still distributed to the fields and gardens of the peasants by small canals which are called, in modern Greek, by almost the identical word used by Sophocles.

The chief centers of population in ancient Greece were located on the eastern side of the peninsula within the Ægean sphere of influence, and therefore lay in the rain-shadow of the western mountains. Hence low and uncertain rainfall (16 to 20 inches) and long summer drought made irrigation imperative for summer tillage. Cadmus and Danaus, immigrants from the East, were the mythical founders of artificial irrigation. Danaus, the hero-king of "thirsty Argos," whose imputed works probably represented the collective achievements of generations of the agricultural Danæ tribe, introduced tillage and opened springs and wells, whereby he converted a barren waste into a fertile and well watered plain.[130]

In Plato's model republic, the citizens constructed aqueducts across valleys in order to irrigate outlying gardens;[131] they conserved the water supply and prevented floods by damming mountain torrents, that the water thus impounded "might produce streams and fountains for the fields below them and for all places, and thus cause the driest spots to possess water plentiful and good."[132] So familiar were the ancients with the principle of impounding water that certain early writers mistook Lake Gygæa or Coloe, located four miles from Sardis in the Pactolus valley, for an artificial reservoir.[133]

The long-established organization of irrigation is reflected in the system of water-rights which Plato formulated for his ideal Republic, doubtless in imitation of the Attic laws.[134] These were explicit and elaborate, as one would expect in a state which had no perennial streams and which had to depend upon springs or wells sunk to ground water,[135] or upon artificial ponds or tanks. The office of water commissioner in Athens was once held by no less a man than Themistocles, who made a bronze figurine called the Water-carrier from the fines imposed on those who had taken water illegally.[136]

IRRIGATION OF DRY LANDS IN ITALY AND SPAIN—Italy, though located farther north and west than Greece, and therefore blessed with more abundant precipitation, yet suffered

enough from summer drought to make irrigation necessary for
the Roman farmer, as it is for the modern Italian peasant.
Ancient Latin writers on agriculture recommended irrigation
for various crops. Horace praised "the orchards watered by
the flowing rills," but his fastidious palate condemned excessive
irrigation and found "nothing poorer than a washed-out garden" with its insipid vegetables.[137] But "the endive rejoices in
the rivulet that it sips," says Vergil.[138] Cicero enumerates
aqueducts, the damming of streams, the tapping of rivers, and
the irrigation of the soil as among the great works of man.[139]
Frontinus, water commissioner for the city of Rome in 97 A.D.,
reveals in his famous Report an old illicit trade in drawing off
water from the public aqueducts for irrigation, between the city
and the distant intakes in the mountains. But aqueduct water
from impure or muddy sources, like the River Anio, was regularly reserved for the irrigation of gardens in and about
Rome.[140]

Even in the Alpine piedmont of Italy, where summer showers
occur, irrigation was practiced in ancient times. In the second
century B.C. the people of the lower Doria Baltea valley utilized
that river to irrigate their fields; but the Alpine tribe of the
Salassi, who lived up-stream and worked extensive gold mines,
drew off practically all the water of the river to wash the gold.
The situation occasioned numerous conflicts between the upstream and down-stream peoples, until the Romans conquered
the country in 143 B.C.[141] Vergil, who doubtless in his boyhood
often saw the waters of the Mincio River diverted to his father's
farm near Mantua, beautifully describes the summer irrigation
of tillage lands. The good farmer "guides over the crops the
chasing runlets from the river; and when the blade is dying in
the scorched and feverish field, look! on the brow of the slope
he lures the water from her channels, and the rushing stream
wakens a hoarse clatter among the smooth pebbles, and gushes
cooling o'er the parched fields." [142]

Irrigation in Spain is rarely mentioned by the ancient authorities, but it may be inferred from the evidences of advanced agriculture under the climatic conditions of the Iberian
Peninsula. The productiveness of tillage in Lusitania (Portugal), indicated by the low price of food in the second century

B.C.,[143] doubtless resulted from the alluvial soil and ample rain-fall (25 to 40 inches) of the western littoral. The Mediter-ranean coastal strip, characterized by low rainfall (15 to 20 inches) and very dry summers,[144] was the most populous and productive section in Carthaginian and Roman times. Olives, figs, vines, and all kinds of fruit trees abounded where today flourish the famous *huertas* or irrigated gardens of Spain,[145] using water channels dating back to Roman times. Murcia was arid in ancient times as it is today (380 mm. or 15 inches). Its parched coastal plain near New Carthage was irrigated from the Tader River (Segura) to raise the spartum reed, which supplied the ancient port with cordage and later supported a big local industry.[146] Wheat fields and vineyards today in Murcia often need irrigation, just as they did in ancient times, according to Justinus.[147] In Spain it was not uncommon for the vintager to gather grapes in flooded vineyards, Pliny tells us.[148]

This expert irrigation agriculture in Spain was confined to the coasts which had long been under the stimulating influences of Phœnician and Greek colonies; it presented a marked con-trast to the backward tillage in the interior of the peninsula, where the absence of olive and vine only a few miles back from the sea, and the use of butter instead of oil, point to isolation from stimulating contacts.[149] Where such contacts had been old and active, progress was great.

Roman authorities agree as to the careful tillage, skilful mining, and advanced civilization of the native Tartessians or Turdetani of the Guadalquivir valley and the southern littoral. The language and burial customs of these ancient Spaniards point to immigration of far-ranging Mycenæan Greeks,[150] while the century-long presence of Phœnicians in their midst would amply explain their progress in mining and tillage. The mas-ter miners of the Lebanon Mountains, eager to trade in the copper, gold and silver of Spain, probably instructed the an-cient Tartessian miners in principles of hydraulics, which were applicable also to irrigation. These Spanish natives conducted water to their placer gold deposits in trenches, which they often carried by tunnel through the mountains. When they needed increased hydraulic pressure to wash out the copper and silver ores, they built reservoirs high up the valleys. Springs encountered in the mines were drained by the screw of Archimedes, the method used in ancient Egypt for raising water from the Nile to adjacent fields.[151] These same Turdetani cultivated the banks and islets of the Guadalquivir, and there maintained gardens and groves which delighted the eye.[152] They produced the finest olives, for which irrigation was necessary.[153] This high state of tillage and a rainfall between 10 and 20 inches are irreconcilable facts except upon the theory of irrigation. It is a suggestive parallel that irrigation in central California utilized mining ditches, and spread in the wake of the prospectors; for fruits and vegetables were needed in the mining camps remote from settlements. After the pay dirt was exhausted and the camps were abandoned, the old ditches continued to serve for irrigation along the foothills of the Sierras.[154]

ANCIENT IRRIGATION LAWS—The wide distribution of irrigation in the Mediterranean region was reflected in an elaborate system of water rights which gradually developed out of custom and statute. The problem of such rights arose wherever a city like Athens or a village like Lamasbe undertook by communal effort to utilize and control the common water supply. The resulting laws showed local variations, but deviated little from certain big underlying principles. Finally in 550 A.D. they were codified in the legal Digests of Justinian, which embodied the water rights recognized throughout the Roman Empire; and in this form they reveal the importance of irrigation in ancient economic organization.

The law recognized that irrigation systems were very old. Hence specific water rights which went back beyond the memory of man were considered well founded without legal record, and could not be contested. Moreover, the phrase "ante-dating the memory of man" was broadly interpreted.[155]

The importance of water rights in this Mediterranean region is attested by the legal safeguards thrown around them. The law forbade artificial works altering the normal flow of a public or perennial river, or its diversion into a different channel from that which it occupied the previous summer, lest the riparian rights of the abutting estates be invaded. Rectification even for the purpose of strengthening the river banks was open to question, if it impaired riparian rights, though the law recognized the public utility of security from river floods.[156]   But if a river shifted its course and thereby receded from its former position, water rights pertaining to the lands along its old channel were lost or at least interrupted till the river by deposition of alluvium gradually returned to its old course.   Meanwhile the opposite bank approached by the fickle stream profited by the new contact and secured unexpected favors; for the whole stretch of the river was subject to water rights.[157]

More people could draw water from a public river than from an ordinary irrigation ditch; but all were compelled by law to respect the rights of their riparian neighbors or, if the stream were a narrow one, the rights of the estates on the opposite bank.   The law provided in general that water taken from a public river should be apportioned to the size of the respective riparian estates, except where one owner could prove a special right to a larger share.[158]

Rights to the use of an irrigation channel, a reservoir or spring comprised the right of access to the same, in order to clean and repair it and to connect the private pipe or conduit; for only thus could an efficient irrigation system be maintained.[159]   As such water courses necessarily crossed private estates, the land along them or about them, in the case of reservoir or intake basin, was reserved from building, roadmaking or consecration for religious purposes, or any use that might interfere with the regular service of the water.[160]

Such an irrigation channel was called a *rivus*, and all persons participating in its water rights were *rivales* or rivals,[161] a term which came to be applied to rivals in love by the old Roman comedies,—with peculiar appropriateness, for competition in water rights was keen, equity in them was jealously guarded, illicit draughts were common, and quarrels were frequent.   The minuteness of the water laws and the analytical decisions of the prætors point to centuries of litigation in the effort to secure a fair distribution of the life-giving stream.   Where several farms or farmers shared the use of a certain water supply, all had to be consulted before additional rights might be granted.[162] *Rivales* and servient estates were treated impartially.   No one could do anything to the water course which might infringe on the rights of his associates. If a man was unjustly prevented by a "rival" or by the owner of the servient estate from drawing water, so that his meadow land or orchard or tree plantation was injured by the resulting drought, he could sue for damages.[163] Where part of an estate was sold, the water in the irrigation channel serving that estate was apportioned to the amount of land sold and retained without regard to the fertility of the land,conveyed away or its need of water.[164]

The law *de rivis* applied when the water came from springs, even thermal springs.[165] Though cold water was preferable for irrigation, yet in certain localities where hot springs furnished the only water available, this law became operative, as in the Hierapolis basin of Greater Phrygia.[166] This was an old volcanic district in the upper Meander valley of Asia Minor,[167] where the rainfall was less than 20 inches (500 mm.) but where countless hot springs supplied the irrigation trenches and also the bath houses of Hierapolis, a famous Roman Spa perched on a high travertine terrace above the fertile Lycus River plain. Today these waters still perform their beneficent task on peasant farm and orchard; but the ancient resort lies dead, wrapped in a winding sheet of travertine.[168]

Water rights varied greatly in time allotment for tapping aqueduct or reservoir. They might entitle a man to draw water all year round, or only in summer, or in certain months or certain days or certain hours. They were apparently regulated by the abundance of the supply, the seasonal need of irrigation, the size of the estate, and the purchasing power of the owner, though the latter point is only a matter of inference since no data are available. The law made a fundamental distinction between annual or daily water rights and summer water rights (*aqua cottidiana et æstiva*), a distinction based legally upon use but actually upon the reliability of the water supply. Only unfailing springs and streams which persisted through the summer drought could be subject to these two classes of rights. Daily water conferred annual use, available for both summer and winter, though its value in the cold rainy season was negligible except for watering cattle. Summer water, also derived from perennial sources, was drawn off only in summer and chiefly for irrigation. Such summer rights were determined by the purpose of the farmer and the nature of the district, which for climatic reasons required water only in the season between the vernal and autumnal equinox.[169] But the delivery of the water on March 25th enabled the farmer to turn it on his meadows and legume crops as soon as it was needed. However, restrictions of water in winter to estates entitled to *aqua cottidiana* certainly contributed to economy both as to use and leakage from the private conduits.

Summer rights were further restricted by allotment periods; and these differed greatly. From actual or suppositional cases cited by the prætors to elucidate the law, it appears that a grant might authorize a man to draw off water only in the daytime or only by night; or every day, or every other day (*tertio die*) or every fourth day (*quinto die*); or for one hour daily or on alternate hours daily, or for two or three hours on specified dates; or in alternate months or for one specified month during the summer. Moreover the water right was confined to the use of a certain aqueduct or reservoir or spring, and it was void for any other source. Withdrawal of water from any other source or at any other time than that specified involved forfeiture of the right. Forfeiture was also the penalty for non-use during a period fixed by statute.[170] Nothing was left to the discretion of the user; everything was fixed by the terms of the contract.

The object of this rigid control was clearly to maintain a steady flow of the water for all entitled to its use, and hence to guard against a heavy over-draft that might decrease or stop the flow. For instance, the choice time for irrigation was night, when the plants were cool and loss of water by evaporation was low. But if all the sluices into the private conduits were flung wide open at ten P.M., the aqueduct might be empty for those drawing water at four A.M. To avoid such an injustice, where several persons had servitude rights in a channel from a spring on an adjoining estate, each man on his particular day opened his private conduit or pipe from the common canal, the parties following each other in order of distance from the source. If one man drew no water during the prescribed period, he forfeited his water right by non-use. Nor could he let one of his associates draw water in his place, for each man was limited to a separate right for his separate farm. However, if all the men were joint owners in a syndicate estate, the law was differently applied.[171] In that case, it assumed a wise distribution of the water for the benefit of the group, without question of conflicting rights.

Safeguards for individual rights were judiciously applied. If the water supply in a channel were abundant, several persons might receive water grants on said channel for the same days or the same hours, though the usual grant specified different days or different hours.[172] If two persons who had been accustomed to draw water separately from the same irrigation channel at certain hours, agreed to exchange their hours of use for their mutual convenience, they did not forfeit their water rights, despite the fact that neither had adhered to the hours specified in his grant.[173]

Irrigation works could be installed, as a rule, only by concerted effort. A peasant might use a spring or well on his farm for this purpose; but more often it was a city or rural district which resorted to this corporate enterprise for the common good. All citizens, by labor or taxes, contributed to the construction and maintenance of the irrigation works, all were entitled to a share of the benefit, and all learned a lesson in the sovereignty of law.

16

AUTHORITIES—CHAPTER XVI

1. Theophrastus, *De Historia Plantarum*, VIII, 1, 4. Pliny, *Historia Naturalis*, XVIII, 30.
2. Columella, *De Agricultura*, II, 18.
3. Columella, II, 11. Pliny, XVIII, 43.
4. Xenophon, *Anabasis*, I, 2, 3.
5. Theophrastus, *Hist. Plant.*, VIII, 7, 3.
6. Vergil, Eclogue III, 111.
7. Theophrastus, *Hist. Plant.*, II, 7, 1. Pliny, XVII, 40.
8. *Odyssey*, VII, 129; XVII, 205-209.
9. Theophrastus, *Hist. Plant.*, VII, 1, 3. Pliny, XVII, 39.
10. Theognis, *Maxims*, 875-880.
11. *Ezekiel*, XVII, 8; XIX, 10.
12. Pliny, XVII, 41.
13. Ovid, Elegia, X, 3-4.
14. Theophrastus, *De Causis Plantarum*, I, 20, 3-5. Pliny, XV, 2-3.
15. Theophrastus, *Hist. Plant.*, II, 7, 1-3.
16. Sophocles, *Œdipus in Colonos*, 685-690.
17. Theophrastus, *Hist. Plant.*, IV, 3, 1. Plutarch, *Solon*, 23-24. Vergil, Georgic II, 519.
18. Theophrastus, *Hist. Plant.*, II, 5, 7; II, 7, 1.
19. *Iliad*, IX, 542. *Odyssey*, VII, 115, 120; XXIV, 34.
20. Athenæus, III, 20, 23. Theophrastus, *Hist. Plant.*, IV, 5, 3.
21. *Deuteronomy*, XI, 10. Theophrastus, *Hist. Plant.*, VII, 4, 6; VII, 5, 1-2. Columella, I, 6.
22. Pliny, XIX, 26-55.
23. Pliny, XIII, 47.
24. Wiskemann, *Die antike Landwirthschaft*, pp. 7-8. Leipzig, 1859.
25. Ivan Mueller, *Handbuch des klassischen Altertums*, Vol. IV, Part II, p. 2.
26. Columella, X, 443-480.
27. Pliny, XIX, 45.
28. Theophrastus, *Hist. Plant.*, VIII, 2, 8-11.
29. Herodotus, V, 57-61.
30. Philippson, *Das Mittelmeergebiet*, p. 117. Leipzig, 1907.
31. G. Adam Smith, *Historical Geography of the Holy Land*, pp. 181-182. 1897.
32. Theophrastus, *Hist. Plant.*, VII, 5, 2.
33. Philippson, *Das Mittelmeergebiet*, p. 173. Leipzig, 1907.
34. Article on Agriculture, *Jewish Encyc.* 1907.
35. E. Huntington, *Palestine and Its Transformation*, p. 124. Boston, 1911.
36. *Joshua*, XV, 19.
37. International Year Book of Agricultural Statistics, Table 15. Rome, 1928.
38. *Iliad*, XIV, 255-256; XXI, 39.
39. Willcocks and Craig, *Egyptian Irrigation*, Vol. I, pp. 299-301. London, 1913.
40. Sir William Willcocks, *From the Garden of Eden to the Crossing of Jordan*, pp. 51-62. Cairo, 1918.
41. A. G. Keller, *Homeric Society*, p. 78. New York, 1902.

42. *Iliad,* V, 87-89.
43. Sophocles, *Trachinæ,* 9.
44. Diodorus Siculus, Bk. IV, Chap. II. Strabo, X, Chap. II, 19.
45. Strabo, IX, Chap. 2, 19. Pliny, XVII, 3.
46. Mariolopoulos, *Climat de la Grèce,* Table I, p. 16. Paris, 1925.
47. W. M. Leake, *Travels in Northern Greece,* Vol. I, p. 436. Oxford, 1835.
48. *Ibid.,* Vol. IV, pp. 402-403.
49. Simonides quoted in Strabo, IX, Chap. V, 20.
50. Theophrastus, *Causis Plant.,* V, 14, 2.
51. *Ibid.,* V, 14, 5-6.
52. Herodotus, VII, 108-109.
53. Cvijic, *La Péninsule Balkanique,* p. 69. Paris, 1918.
54. Pausanias, III, 1, 2.
55. Philippson, *Der Peloponnes,* pp. 238-239. Berlin, 1892.
56. Pausanias, III, 11, 2; 14, 8.
57. Strabo, VIII, Chap. V, 1.
58. Herodotus, VI, 76. Strabo, VIII, Chap. VI, 8.
59. Strabo, VIII, Chap. VI, 2, 8.
60. Euripides, *The Phœnicians,* 657-670.
61. Pseudo-Dicæarchus, quoted in J. G. Frazer, *Pausanias,* Vol. I, XLV. 1898.
62. Strabo, IX, Chap. II, 16-20.
63. Neumann and Partsch, *Physikalische Geographie von Griechenland,* p. 144. 1885.
64. Theophrastus, *Hist. Plant.,* IV, 11, 2-3.
65. *Ibid.,* IV, 10, 7. Xenophon, *Hellenes,* VII, Chap. II, 8, 11.
66. Strabo, IX, Chap. II, 40.
67. Bursian, *Geographie von Griechenland,* Vol. I, pp. 195-199.
68. Baedeker, *Greece,* pp. 183-191. 1909.
69. Plato, *Critias,* Chap. XIII, p. 426. Translated by H. Davis. London, 1897.
70. Strabo, IX, Chap. II, 18.
71. Pausanias, IX, 32, 2, 3.
72. Bursian, *op. cit.,* Vol. II, p. 196. Strabo, VIII, Chap. VI, 8.
73. Strabo, VIII, Chap. VIII, 4.
74. Philippson, *Der Peloponnes,* pp. 144-146. Pausanias, VIII, 14, 1-3.
75. Pausanias, VIII, 23, 2.
76. Polybius, *Histories,* XI, Chap. XI, 15-16.
77. Philippson, *Der Peloponnes,* pp. 105-107. Berlin, 1892.
78. E. Curtius, *History of Greece,* Vol. I, p. 244. New York, 1867.
79. Livy, I, Chaps. XIII, XVI; II, Chap. XIX.
80. Strabo, V, Chap. III, 11.
81. Tenney Frank, *Economic History of Rome,* pp. 5-9. 1920.
82. Livy, V, Chaps. XV-XVI.
83. Pliny, XIX, 34, 41. Strabo, V, Chap. III, 12.
84. W. Deecke, *Italy,* p. 102. London, 1904.
85. Strabo, V, Chap. III, 13.
86. Strabo, V, Chap. II, 6.
87. Pliny, III, 9.
88. W. Deecke, *Italy,* p. 94. London, 1904.
89. Strabo, V, Chap. III, 6.

90. Pliny, III, 20.
91. Strabo, V, Chap. I, 11.
92. Cato, *De Re Rustica*, 155. Varro, *Rerum Rusticarum*, I, 35, 36.
93. Varro, I, 14. Columella, II, 29. Palladius, VI, 3.
94. Cato, 24. Vergil, Georgic I, 269.
95. *Digesta sive Pandectæ Justiniani, Lib.*, XXXIX, Tit. III, 2.
96. *Ibid., Tit.*, III, 1, 1-5.
97. *Ibid., Tit.*, III, 1, 8-12.
98. *Ibid., Tit.*, III, 1, 23.
99. *Ibid., Tit.*, III, 11.
100. Hildebrand, *Cyrenaika*, pp. 210-215. Bonn, 1904.
101. Pindar, Isthmian Ode, II, 91. G. Dainelli, "The Italian Colonies," *Geog. Rev.*, Vol. XIX, p. 411. 1929.
102. Scylax, *Periplus*, 108. Herodotus, IV, 159, 199. Strabo, II, Chap. V, 33.
103. Diodorus Siculus, II, 49, 2; 50, 1.
104. J. W. Gregory, "Cyrenaica," *Geog. Jour.*, Vol. 47, pp. 326-336. London, 1916.
105. G. Hildebrand, *op. cit.*, p. 112. Herodotus, IV, 198.
106. Pliny, XVIII, 51.
107. Procopius, Vandal War, I, Chap. XV, 34-35; Chap. XVII, 6-8; II, Chap. VI, 6.
108. Pliny, V, 3.
109. Sallust, *Bello Jugurt*, XVII-XIX.
110. Procopius, *op. cit.*, II, Chap. XIII, 20, 23-24; Chap. XIX, 7, 10-13, 20.
111. H. Dessau, *Inscript. Latinæ Selectæ*, Nos. 5752, 5778, 5786, 5787.
112. *Ibid.*, No. 5793. Discussed in Heitland, *Agricola*, p. 293. Cambridge, 1921.
113. *Canticles*, IV, 15.
114. *Isaiah*, XXXII, 20; *Proverbs*, XXI, 1.
115. *Ecclesiastes*, II, 5-6.
116. Baedeker, *Palestine*, pp. 108-109. 1906.
117. G. Adam Smith, *op. cit.*, pp. 77-79. London, 1896.
118. *Canticles*, I, 14.
119. Theophrastus, *Hist. Plant.*, IX, 6, 2-4.
120. Strabo, XVI, Chap. II, 41. Pliny, XII, 54; XIII, 6. Josephus, *Jewish Wars*, IV, Chap. VIII, 3.
121. G. Adam Smith, *op. cit.*, pp. 266-267.
122. *Ibid.*, pp. 354, 357-361.
123. Strabo, XVI, Chap. II, 9.
124. Maspero, *Struggle of the Nations*, p. 188. New York, 1897.
125. Strabo, XVI, Chap. II, 6-10.
126. Mommsen, *Provinces of the Roman Empire*, Vol. II, pp. 148-149. 1887.
127. *Iliad*, XXI, 257-262; 346-347.
128. *Odyssey*, VII, 111-132.
129. Sophocles, *Œdipus in Colonos*, 681-687.
130. Strabo, VIII, Chap. VI, 7, 8.
131. Plato, *Critias*, Chap. XIII, pp. 424-425. Translated by H. Davis. London, 1897.
132. Plato, *Laws*, VI, Chap. VIII. Translated by G. Burgess. London, 1872.

133. Strabo, XIII, Chap. IV, 7.
134. Plato, *Laws*, VIII, Chaps. IX, XI.
135. Plutarch, *Solon*, 89.
136. Plutarch, *Themistocles*, 31.
137. Horace, Satires, II, 4, 16.
138. Vergil, Georgic IV, 120.
139. Cicero, *De Officiis*, II, 4; *De Senectute*, XV, 53.
140. Frontinus, *De Aquis Romæ*, I, 11; II, 66, 75, 76, 92. Compare Livy, XXXIX, 44.
141. Strabo, IV, Chap. VI, 7.
142. Vergil, Georgic I, 106-110.
143. Polybius, XXXIV, 8, 9.
144. A. Woeikoff, *Die Klimate der Erde*, p. 106. Jena, 1887. T. Fischer, in Kirchhoff, *Länderkunde von Europa*, Part II, p. 655. 1893.
145. Strabo, III, Chap. IV, 13, 16.
146. Varro, I, 23. Strabo, III, Chap. IV, 9. Pliny, XIX, 7-8. Hann, Klimatologie. Stuttgart, 1911.
147. Justinus, *Historiæ*, Lib., XLIV, Chap. I.
148. Pliny, XVII, 40.
149. Diodorus Siculus, V, 34. Strabo, III, Chap. III, 7.
150. E. S. Bouchier, *Spain Under the Roman Empire*, pp. 4-8, 13. Oxford, 1914.
151. Diodorus Siculus, V, 35-37.
152. Strabo, III, Chap. II, 3, 6. Columella, X, 72-80, 215-226.
153. Pliny, XV, 3.
154. U. S. Geo. Survey Report for 1891-2. Part III, "Irrigation," p. 137. 1892.
155. *Digesta Justiniani, Lib.* VIII, *Tit.* V., 10; *Lib.* XXXXIII, *Tit.* XX, 3.
156. *Ibid., Lib.* XXXXIII, *Tit.* XIII-XIV.
157. *Ibid., Lib.* XXXXIII, *Tit.* XX, 3.
158. *Ibid., Lib.* VIII, *Tit.* III, 1.
159. *Ibid., Lib.* XXXXIII, *Tit.* XXI, 1 (1-9); 3; *Tit.* XXI, 1.
160. *Ibid., Lib.* VIII, *Tit.* III, 20; *Tit.* IV, 11.
161. *Ibid., Lib.* XXXXIII, *Tit.* XX, 26.
162. *Ibid., Lib.* XXXIX, *Tit.* III, 8.
163. *Ibid., Lib.* VIII, *Tit.* V, 18.
164. *Ibid., Lib.* VIII, *Tit.* III, 25.
165. *Ibid., Lib.* XXXXIII, *Tit.* XXII, 1 (1-8).
166. *Ibid., Lib.* XXXXIII, *Tit.* XX, 1 (13-14).
167. Strabo, XIII, Chap. IV, 14.
168. A. Philippson, *Reisung und Forschung in Westlichen Kleinasien*, pp. 68-69. *Peterm. Mitt. Ergänz. Heft.* No. 180. Banse, *Die Turkei*, pp. 122-123. Brunswick, 1919.
169. *Digesta Justiniani, Lib.* VIII, *Tit.* III, 1, 15. *Lib.* XXXXIII, *Tit.* XX, 1 (2-6, 28-32); *Tit.* XX, 2.
170. *Ibid., Lib.* VIII, *Tit.* VI, 7, 10, 18. *Lib.* XXXXIII, *Tit.* XX, 1 (22); 3.
171. *Ibid., Lib.* VIII, *Tit.* VI, 16.
172. *Ibid., Lib.* VIII, *Tit.* III, 2.
173. *Ibid., Lib.* XXXXIII, *Tit.* XX, 5.

CHAPTER XVII

ANCIENT MEDITERRANEAN PLEASURE GARDENS

Noonday in early May on the Isthmus of Corinth. Beneath a ledge of grey limestone a ribbon of mauve shadow stretches across the narrow beach to a sapphire sea. A stiff breeze blowing down from the Hellespont tips the Ægean waves with curling crests, sucks up the moisture from the lucid air, and sends the limestone dust swirling down the white road in the midday glare. The sun burns face and hands as if its rays came through a lens, while the alkaline dust makes the eyes and skin smart. Seeking a refuge from heat and glare, I creep into the purple shade beneath the narrow ledge, blessing this "shadow of a great rock in a thirsty land," to eat my Homeric lunch of bread and wine, goat's cheese and figs.

Climatic conditions go far towards explaining those lovely pleasure gardens which were so widely distributed in the ancient Mediterranean lands. They still persist in many of the old localities, retaining their traditional features of confining wall or hedge, their seclusion and shade, flower beds and ornamental fruit trees, their fountains and murmurous waters, their central pool, sunken paths, marble seats and colonnades, the gleam of statuary mid the green twilight of the shrubbery, and the vine-grown pergola for the outdoor repast.

The ancient Mediterranean garden was a place of retreat from the searching Mediterranean sun during the long summer drought, when the thirsty Etesian winds blew down from the north to drink up the moisture from air and vegetation; or when the Sirocco swept down from the parched plateau of Africa, wilted the trees in plantations and orchards, and sent the limestone dust flying in clouds along the highways or through the narrow streets. Only the garden kept moist and green and fresh. A high enclosing wall, screened by cypresses and box trees, and the marble portico opening from the dim re-

474

cesses of the house served to shut out from this shady retreat
the dust and glare and sere vegetation of the Mediterranean
summer outside. The spray of fountains cooled and moistened
the air within, while the slender runlets from the irrigation
channel distributed reviving waters to the garden beds.

The Mediterranean climate encouraged the maintenance of
pleasure parks and gardens because the mild temperatures kept
a succession of trees and plants in blossom all year round,
brought winter blooms to the rose and almond tree, even in
northern Italy, and renewed the freshness of the evergreen
foliage during the winter rains; hence it rewarded the labor of
the cultivator and preserved the beauty of the garden in the
cold season. But gardens were the boon of summer. The long,
hot, cloudless months made the shelter of vine-grown arbor and
cypress avenue a welcome refuge. Eyes tired by a relentless
sun and its reflection from the limestone roads rested grate-
fully upon the dark foliage of laurel or oleander. When the
stifling afternoon passed and the people issued from their dark-
ened houses, the garden paths invited to leisurely strolls between fragrant flower beds along murmurous irrigation conduits. In the Paradise legend, Adam and Eve heard "the voice
of Jehovah God walking in the garden in the cool of the evening," [1] after the custom of Palestine and other Mediterranean
lands. Likewise Ammon Ra "walked abroad" in his temple garden at Thebes, where Queen Hatshepsut had planted myrrh
trees imported from distant Punt.[2]

Other factors, social and economic, contributed to the development of these ancient gardens: the early concentration of
population in urban centers, the expansion of trade and accumulation of wealth, the stimulation of civilization by maritime
intercourse between the various Mediterranean shores, the
growth in every city of a cultured leisure class with its concern
for the amenities and luxuries of life. A more potent factor
still was the rapid advance of agriculture, till it attained the
esthetic stage of development, crowning evidence of its intensive character.

The cultivation of land for the mere embellishment of life is
a frequent concomitant of intensive tillage, even when scant
arable area makes such use of the soil seem extravagant. It is

conspicuous in warm countries where climatic conditions encourage an open-air life, but appears also in less exuberant
form in colder countries with a long growing season like England. As a native growth it meets us in modern Japan, the
Hawaiian Islands, in ancient Persia and Babylonia as in Kash-
mir and northern India under the Mogul rulers. All these
countries developed intensive agriculture and all had to rely
wholly or in part upon irrigation to secure an adequate food
supply.

ELEMENTS OF THE GARDEN—Ornamental gardening became
a feature of ancient Mediterranean civilization. It began at
the eastern end of the basin at an early period, and advanced
westward in the wake of trade and colonization. Everywhere it
took root, and became the fine efflorescence of that patient, tire-
less tillage which characterized Mediterranean lands. It grew
out of the widespread fruit, flower, and herb culture, which in
greater or less degree depended upon summer irrigation. The
pleasure gardens originated in walled orchards and vineyards,
in plantations of flowering pomegranates, quinces, plums, and
apricots, in groves of stately date-palms, all with their irrigation pools and canals. The spaces between the rows of trees,
for the more economic use of the precious soil, were often
planted with flowers at once useful and beautiful, like the
saffron-yielding crocus or the edible poppy,[3] or "the henna flowers in the vineyards of Engeddi," [4] or the violets, iris, and roses
raised in Bœotia,[5] Cyrenaica and other lands for the manufacture of perfumes and unguents.[6]

The bloom and fragrance of the blossoming grape, the flowers of the pomegranate and nut tree were prized by the ancient
Jews as were the fruits. "I went down into the garden of nuts
to see the green plants of the valley, to see whether the vine
budded and the pomegranates were in flower." [7] Fig trees with
their fresh spring foliage and grape vines trained up on trellis
or pergola offered shade through the hot summer days.
Orchards and vineyards, therefore, provided certain essential
elements of the pleasure garden—blossoms, fragrance and especially shade. Hence the ancient Mediterranean gardens, in
their long development, continued to employ vine-grown trellises, fruit trees, alleys of shade trees, and masses of dark-leaved

shrubbery, and relied for their artistic effect only in part upon
flower beds.   Even then they preferred flowering shrubs, like
myrtle, laurel, and oleander, which presented masses of green
picked out with pink or white blooms.   The esthetic value of the
ripe fruit was never discounted.

In point of size the ancient gardens varied from the ample
palace grounds and parks of kings,—which however reached
only moderate proportions as a rule,—to the private home
garden, whose size depended upon its location in town or country and upon the means of the owner.   One seems to detect
everywhere a certain restricting influence probably due to the
high cost of irrigable land and heavy irrigation charges.
Water theft from the public aqueducts was a common offence
among Athenian citizens [8] and the landed gentry of the Roman
suburbs.[9]   The typical private garden was small, even diminu-
tive.   It lay near or behind the house to form an outdoor extension of the residence itself; and here much of the family life
was led.   The master could step from his drawing-room or din-
ing-room to its flower-bordered terrace or shaded avenues.
Resting on a marble bench or walking beneath a colonnade, he
commanded a view of the whole.   Its small size encouraged perfect cultivation and ample use of water, and did not necessarily
lessen its beauty.   A little garden dedicated to Eros is made to
speak for itself in an anonymous Greek poem: "I am not great
among gardens, but I am full of charm." [10]

This small scale was yet further reduced in the exquisite
miniature gardens planted in the peristyles of Greek and Roman houses in the last century before Christ, or perhaps earlier.
The peristyle garden still survives in the patio of the modern
Spanish dwelling, with its arcade, its central fountain, and its
myrtles, pomegranates, jasmines, and palms growing in earthen
jars.   On the desert rim of the Mediterranean Orient, it survives also in the spacious court of the typical Damascus residence, whose tessellated floor is broken in the center by water
basin and fountain, surrounded by flowering plants.   Orange,
lemon, and pomegranate trees furnish masses of dark green
to rest the eyes.   The fragrance of the jasmine fills the air and
penetrates to the recessed colonnade or *liwan* whose cushioned
couches look out upon this charming enclosure.

In contrast to the small private gardens, the sacred groves and temple grounds reveal a larger scale. These also, like the peasant's orchard, felt the transforming touch of the ancient Mediterranean gardener, and became beautiful parks for religious or secular use. The Temple of Jerusalem was an exception to the rule, because the Jews feared that trees in the courtyard might savor of the hill-top gardens or groves of Baal-worship.

The summer drought dictated the introduction of water as an unfailing feature of the garden. The air was cooled by the shower of a fountain; flower beds and shade trees had to be irrigated. Hence water was handled as an artistic *motif* in countless ways. It was conducted about the garden in stone, cement or tiled runlets; it emerged from some decorative opening in a terrace wall or issued in jets from a statue; it was collected in fish pond or lotus pool; it flowed from artificial grotto or leaped from a rocky ledge into a marble basin. Moreover, the irrigation canals with their secondary furrows necessitated a regular system, which tended to throw the garden plan into geometric forms. The modern oriental garden always seems dominated by the irrigation scheme on which its life depends. In the exquisite Indian gardens which one sees about Jaipur and Amritsar, the water conduits dictate the basic lines of flower beds, tree plots and pools, just as they do in the garden plans depicted on ancient Egyptian tombs.

The same thing is true of the Persian rose gardens which in Shiraz today reproduce the ancient garden pattern. An old description of a sixth century Persian rug shows the design of a pleasure garden, planted in fruit trees and flowers, crossed by straight paths and irrigation conduits, while the border represents long flower beds. Persian garden rugs of 1600 and later show the traditional design—a central water basin with fish and ducks, canals leading thence in formal arrangement, narrow paths following the canals, cypress alleys or slender flower beds in the border, trees and shrubs growing in jars, while the weave in the streams resembles "watered ribbon." [11] The whole arrangement is rectilinear, reproducing the Persian garden plan as necessitated by irrigated horticulture in a semi-arid land.[12]

Like their Persian prototypes, the Mediterranean gardens were for the most part formal and architectural in style. They were not an idealized landscape like the English park, or a miniature landscape like the Japanese garden. They had no place for winding paths or pools with the sinuous outlines of natural shores. Back of the ancient Mediterranean garden we see the engineer with his problems of hydraulic pressure, his traditions of durable and economical construction, even when pursuing aims of beauty, and his architectural skill in utilizing the small garden space at his command.

So much for the general conclusions. A survey of the ancient Mediterranean gardens according to countries will demonstrate the truth of these conclusions, and show the types that developed in various districts, owing to local differences of geographic, economic, and social conditions.

ORIENTAL GARDENS—Paradise, that garden which "the Lord God planted eastward in Eden," was modeled upon the oriental gardens found in all the irrigated lands from Persia to Palestine; and it became in turn a prototype of those flowery retreats which attended Mediterranean civilization from Damascus, Jerusalem, and Antioch in the East to Roman Spain and Moorish Granada in the West. The river which watered Paradise was divided into several channels, after the manner of "the shorn and parcelled Oxus," the Nile and other irrigation streams. The garden contained "every tree that is pleasant to the sight and good for food." [13] The tree of knowledge and the tree of life were rare exotics introduced by the early dramatist who staged here the first great tragedy of man.

The desert Arabs who skirted the high rim of the Mediterranean Basin from Moab to Mount Hermon, and looked down upon the irrigated gardens of Damascus and Ramoth-Gilead, pictured their Paradise as a pleasure garden, abounding in fountains of pure water and traversed by rivulets. There in the noonday heat the saints reclined on silken couches spread in deep shade, and enjoyed the fruits always ripe on the trees.[14] It was the Garden of Resort in the Koran, the Garden of Eden, the Garden of the Most High. It contained everything to satisfy the taste and delight the eye of the blessed. "Close down upon them shall be its shadows and lowered over them its fruits to cull." [15] Though this Arab Paradise waited for the pen of Mohammed, it belonged of old to the Semites of desert and grassland; it doubtless lived in Arab poetry sung in moonlit tents, ages before the seer of Mecca.

The oriental models found apt imitators in Palestine, Philistia, Phœnicia, and northern Syria, where geographic conditions encouraged their introduction and further development, and where the rich and powerful maintained large estates; but the Judean peasant enjoyed his leisure beneath his own vine and fig tree, or raised a few flowers in his herb garden.[16] King Solomon had his pleasure park near Jerusalem, whither he was wont to go in the morning, Josephus tells us. It was laid out in fine gardens and abounded in rivulets of water.[17] The author of *Canticles* described an ideal garden to which he compared his beloved. A high wall ensured its privacy, and a never failing spring or mountain stream watered its thirsty plants. Almond trees raised their crowns of pale pink blossoms. The scarlet fruit of the pomegranate trees punctured the dark foliage with points of light. There were beds of lilies or narcissi, of saffron-yielding crocuses, of sweet-scented henna, and all the aromatic plants which could be made to grow, while the blossoming grape vines gave forth their perfume. "Awake, O North wind, and come thou, South; blow upon my garden that the spices thereof may flow out." [18]

The Bible in figurative language indicates the beauty of these gardens, specifies their trees and flowers, and suggests their wide prevalence. The Garden of Eden or the Garden of the Lord is the synonym for earthly beauty and productivity.[19] Jehovah, placated after one of the habitual backslidings of His people, promises to convert the desert into a tree garden: "I will plant in the wilderness the cedar, the shittah tree (acacia) and the myrtle and the oil tree; I will set in the desert the fir tree and the pine and the box tree together." [20] Balaam likens the encampment of the Israelites, with its orderly rows of tents, to a well-watered garden with its alleys of cedars bordering the irrigation channels and its plots of aloe trees.[21]

In the apocryphal book of *Ecclesiasticus,* Wisdom compares her glory to the beauties of a garden—to the cedar of Lebanon, to the cypress of Mount Hermon, to the palm tree, the olive and the plane, to the wide-spreading terebinth or pistachio tree, to the blossoming grape vine, and the roses of Jericho. From her issue pleasant odors like the fragrance of spices and sweet-scented shrubs. She invites all to come and eat of her fruits. Then the figure of speech shifts to another feature of the garden: "I came out as a stream from a river, and as a conduit into a garden. I said, I will water my garden, and will water abundantly my garden bed; and, lo, my stream became a river, and my river became a sea." [22] So full flow the well-springs of wisdom.

Gardens were doubtless familiar objects in the landscape of Palestine, especially after the Babylonian captivity, when the returning exiles brought back new standards of horticultural beauty. The Bible contains frequent allusions to their pools of water, luxuriant vegetation, fragrant shrubs and flowers, their grateful shade and seclusion. The world-weary author of *Ecclesiastes*, searching for diversion, made for himself "gardens of flowers and fruit trees, with pools of water therein." [23] To these green retreats water lent its beauty, either rushing along in stone-lined channels or collected into a basin which might serve for a bath, as the stories of Bathsheba and Susanna lead us to infer.[24]

Within the city of Jerusalem, only the royal rose garden was allowed,[25] because no dung might be brought within the walls; outside, practical considerations probably dominated, though the introduction from Greece of laurel, iris, ivy, mint, narcissus, box, and rue into Judean gardens indicates an esthetic motive.[26] Through the periods of Greek and Roman rule, when peace brought wealth and plenty, the environs of Jerusalem blossomed with gardens, orchards and olive groves. Those north of the Wall of Agrippa were destroyed by Titus in 71 A.D. during the siege of the city. On this side opened the Gate of Gennat or Garden Gate. East of Jerusalem, on the Mount of Olives lay the Garden of Gethsemane, much frequented by the people of the capital. When the April sun ripened the fields of barley and the first blast of the Sirocco heralded the Feast of the Passover, thither the men of Jerusalem in pairs or groups, escaping from the heat of the city streets, would walk out after supper to spend the evening or night. One such group of

friends, one such night, made this little pleasure park a synonym of agony.   Another such garden near the hill of Golgotha
received the body of the dead Christ.[27]   The ancient Jews used
these green enclosures as family burying grounds, in which a
natural or artificial cave served for the sepulcher.

Semitic garden technique was perfected in Syria, because this
land, more than Palestine, was constantly subjected to Persian
influences, both through trade and conquest.   There the imperial rulers established royal parks, where the cedars of Lebanon grew larger and finer than on their native mountains; [28]
and the common people expended their art on the sacred groves
or tree-gardens of Baal.   The palace of the Persian governor
of northern Syria, located at the springs of the little Dardes
River between Aleppo and the Euphrates, had a "beautiful garden containing all that the seasons produce," but it was destroyed by Cyrus the Younger in 401 B.C.[29]   Sidon contained
a pleasure garden which belonged to the Persian kings, and
which was demolished when the city revolted against Artaxerxes
Ochus in the fourth century B.C.[30]

Throughout Syria and Palestine the sacred groves on hill-
tops and "high places," consecrated by the native Semitic population to the worship of Baal and the generative forces of
nature, seem to have been improved by cultivation.   These
groves originated sometimes about high-laid springs, which
moistened the soil and later were distributed into water conduits; or they were set out as acts of merit near a spring or
well.   The sacred trees were oaks, tamarisks, poplar, palm,
and terebinth, all which were improved or maintained by irrigation.   As the groves were gradually provided with altars,
wood and stone symbols of the deity, and finally temples, the
efforts to beautify them converted them into gardens.

The native Canaanites and Phœnicians instituted these sacred gardens with obscene rites, but the Israelites also frequented them, and thereby provoked the denunciations of the
prophets.[31]   Such probably was the sacred grove and temple of
Astarte, located at the springs of the Adonis River (Nahr
Ibrahim) below the crest of the Lebanon Mountains.   Here the
people of Byblus and neighboring Phœnician cities celebrated
every spring the death and resurrection of the nature god

Adonis, youthful lover of Astarte (Aphrodite). Here the rose
and scarlet anemone, dyed in the blood of the slain god, bloomed
amid the cedars and walnut trees of Lebanon, and here the
mourning worshippers sacrificed the miniature "gardens of
Adonis" (*horti Adonis*), which figured in the Adonis rites practiced in Western Asia, Alexandria, and the Greek lands.[32]
They were small baskets or earthen pots planted with wheat,
barley, fennel, lettuce, and various flowers; epitomes of field
and garden, sprouting and withering in eight days,[33] they typified the ephemeral life of spring vegetation. The Adonis worship prevailed also in contaminated Jerusalem, where Ezekiel
saw the women wailing for the god in the temple gate.[34] Isaiah
describes the short-lived gardens which were placed before the
images of Adonis,[35] exactly as one sees them today in the Catholic churches of Italy on Good Friday, the vernal memorial of
the dead Christ.

The Phœnicians were commercial nurserymen in Homeric
times. Their ship cargoes included plants and trees, like the
rose, palm, fig, pomegranate, cassia, myrrh, plum, and almond,
which were disseminated over the whole Mediterranean from
their native habitats in the East, and early became commodities of international trade.[36] This process stimulated horticulture, spread information as to methods of cultivation, or led
to big-scale experiments in acclimatization. It is possible to
follow the introduction of the peach from Persia into Egypt,
thence into Rhodes where the tree long sulked and refused to
bear, and thence finally into Greece and Rome.[37]

EGYPTIAN GARDENS—Phœnicia and Palestine, through centuries of commercial and political affiliation with Egypt, drew
suggestions for their horticulture also from the Nile valley.
There all conditions encouraged the early development of pleasure gardens—the careful agriculture, the need of escape from
the relentless sun, the great length and heat of the summer,
the demand for flowers in the worship of nature gods like Isis
and Osiris, and finally the presence of a rich and refined leisure
class appreciative of this luxury. The Egyptian pleasure garden never lost the marks of its origin in orchard and vineyard,
and of its conformity to the requirements of irrigation. The
drawings in the tombs at Thebes and Tel-el-Amarna reveal

formal gardens laid out with geometrical precision. Their marble pools pink with lotus blossoms, their walks spanned by vine-grown trellises, their avenues of fruit trees, their flower beds and summer houses show how readily Egyptian horticulture developed into a fine art.[38]

Formal gardens existed in Egypt in the Fourth Dynasty (2800 B.C.).[39] In the Eighteenth Dynasty garden technique was fully developed, and served to beautify the country estates of the wealthy or their city homes. Local plant resources no longer sufficed; incense trees and other exotics were imported. A garden of this period, depicted at Thebes, shows a walled enclosure laid out in eight sections. The middle section is occupied by a long grape arbor shading a path which leads to the dwelling. Nearby are two water basins with pavilions on their margins, lotus flowers floating on their surface, and ducks swimming about. Two other rectangular tanks, bordered by avenues of alternate palms and fig trees, occupy the front part of the garden. An artistic balance marks the composition of the whole.[40]

A picture in a high priest's tomb at Tel-el-Amarna shows a complex of buildings comprising his residence and the storehouses of the temple, all surrounded by a garden. Trees set in depressions to hold water fill the spaces between the buildings. A palm garden has a square tank or pool in the center, around which other trees are planted in formal lines. Steps lead down to the water, while a summer house or kiosk overlooks the pool. This is a recurrent feature in the Egyptian gardens. A villa garden depicted on another Theban tomb has the usual combination of canal, water basin, shady avenues, and flower beds, but in addition shows an awning stretched over the entrance of the dwelling and projecting into the garden to form an outdoor room, where the mistress of the house is receiving guests.[41]

Reading of these ancient Egyptian gardens, one gets a vision of homes screened by plantations of fig and pomegranate trees from the outside world; one hears the ripple of water in the irrigation canal, the splash of ducks in the stone-lined pool. One catches vistas down shady walks beneath palm trees and acacias, where the fierce Egyptian sun can hardly penetrate; one smells the fragrance of flower beds when the slave moves about with his watering pot in the fading twilight. The Pharaohs themselves loved their trees and flowers. In his new capital in the Delta, Rameses III made "great vineyards; walks shaded by all kinds of sweet fruit trees with fruit; a sacred way splendid with flowers from all countries, with lotus and papyrus countless as the sands." [42]

Flowers were used profusely in the social and religious life of the ancient Egyptians. At banquets they decked both table and guests. The latter wore lotus-buds in their hair, and held out the open blossom to each other to smell. Garlands festooned the wine jars. Bouquets were offered to the gods; wreaths encircled the necks of sacrificial geese and bulls, and covered the mummy cases on their way to the tomb.[43] Finally, according to a love song of the Turin papyrus, a blooming garden is the trysting place of two lovers; and there beneath a wild fig tree they meet "on the festival of the garden." One is reminded inevitably of Japan, with its national flower festivals and its passion for gardens.

GREEK GARDENS—In contrast to the explicit testimony on esthetic gardens left by Egyptian tombs and papyri, the evidence of Greek development in this respect is fragmentary and meager, so far as private gardens are concerned, till Hellenic culture has passed its zenith; then the references become abundant. The pseudo-Platonic dialogue "Minos" alludes to authoritative books on gardening which have vanished,[44] and whose loss we deplore, since they might have yielded testimony. On the other hand, there is abundant evidence of a highly developed garden technique, which beautified the temple groves with flower beds and fountains, and converted prosaic orchards into recreation parks.

The Greeks, like the Hebrews, reveal a love of gardens in their mythology. As companion piece to the Garden of Eden, they give us the Garden of Hesperides, located in some fabled isle of far western seas. Pindar describes its beauty.[45]

There round the Islands of the Blest,
The Ocean breezes blow,
And golden flowers are glowing,
Some on trees of splendor growing

And some the water feedeth,
Fair wreaths they yield, wherewith
The happy ones do twine their hands.

A love of flowers and gardens is apparent in Homeric times.
They are frequently described in the *Iliad* and *Odyssey*, and
always with esthetic appreciation. The *Iliad* alludes to a garden "where heavy-headed poppies grow." [46]   Pallas Athene,
bestowing divine beauty on Ulysses, "made the curling locks to
cluster around his head like the blossoms of the hyacinth
flower." [47]   The young charioteer of Hector, struck by the
fatal arrow, "Even as in a garden a poppy droopeth its head
aside, being heavy with fruit and the showers of spring, so
bowed he aside his head, laden with his helmet." [48]   The entrance to Calypso's cave, supposedly a scene of natural beauty,
is depicted with the artistic touch of the landscape gardener.
All the elements of the pleasure garden are there—shade-trees,
vines, fragrance, springs, and interlacing water conduits; a
suggestion of formal arrangement is not wanting. "Around the
grotto trees grew luxuriantly, alder and poplar and sweet-
scented cypress, where long-winged birds had nests. . . . Here,
too, was trained over the hollow grotto a thrifty vine, luxuriant
with clusters; and four springs in a row were running with
clear water, making their way from one another here and
there." [49]

The garden of Alcinous also reveals the sense of horticultural
beauty, though planted for practical purposes. "Without the
courtyard hard by the door is a large garden covering four
acres; around it runs a hedge on either side. Here grow tall
thrifty trees—pears, pomegranates, apples with shining fruit,
sweet figs and thrifty olives. On them fruit never fails; it is
not gone in winter or in summer but lasts throughout the year.
. . . And here trim garden-beds, along the outer line, spring
up in every kind, and all the year are gay. Nearby two fountains rise, one scattering its streams throughout the garden,
one bounding by another course beneath the courtyard gate
toward the high house." [50]

From such farm gardens developed the Greek pleasure garden. Flowers were raised on all country estates to provide

"decorations for altars and statues and wreaths of beauty and fragrance for the person." [51] They were the chief crop in industrial gardens which supplied the perfumer and unguent manufacturers. Those in Cyrenaica were famous because the semi-arid climate made the roses, violets, and crocuses more fragrant than elsewhere. [52] Such commercial nurseries doubtless stimulated esthetic horticulture, which was also aided by Alexander's conquest of western Asia; for the victors returned with new fruits like the citron, new plants, and countless Semitic slaves trained in fine garden technique; finally they were filled with enthusiasm for the numerous Persian paradises which they had seen.

But Greek gardens had appeared in Athens before this. Aristophanes mentions "fragrant gardens" injured by insects, vine-grown gardens where the birds picked the berries of the myrtle, poppy, and sesame; [53] and he alludes to sweet violets growing by a fountain in a garden. [54] Demosthenes, who had a nephew living in a house and garden in Athens, records a rose garden with shrubbery beds and a fruit orchard, outside the city, which were all destroyed by a spiteful neighbor. [55] Aristotle had a home and garden in Chalcis in Euboea, where he spent his last years (322 B.C.). [56] The painter Protogenes lived and worked in his garden outside the city of Rhodes (304 B.C.). [57] Theocritus mentions "beds of roses blooming along the garden wall," maybe in Cos or Syracuse. [58] Such allusions are short and casual, but they indicate quiet green retreats like that Lesbian Garden of the Nymphs described by Sappho (600 B.C.): [59]

> Through orchard plots with fragrance crowned
> The clear cool fountain murmuring flows,
> And forest trees with rustling sound
> Invite to soft repose.

We hear more of private gardens which were thrown open to the public, and therefore figured in the common life. Cimon of Athens, general during the Persian War, pulled down the walls of his garden and grounds that his fellow citizens might share the fruit. [60] Plato, Epicurus and Theophrastus bought land and planted gardens, only to convert them into schools of philosophy, which came to rank among the glories of Athens.[61]

The architecture of the Grecian dwelling, with its open peristyle court suggested the interior garden as a natural accessory; yet in Homeric times, and long afterward, this court served as an outdoor work shop. Where or when it first came to be planted and beautified is unknown; for this evanescent art of flower and shrub would leave few traces. Yet the remains at Herculanæum and Pompeii reveal the perfect development of the peristyle garden in the Greco-Roman houses of the first and second centuries B.C. The Roman architect Vitruvius describes the Greek drawing-room in the Cyzicene style of house as facing north upon gardens in the rear and having windows like folding doors so that the garden view might be unobstructed.[62] To this and later periods belonged the perfected house garden of the widespread Greek cities. These were small, exquisite, planned with rigid symmetry, ornamented with statuary and marble colonnades. Shade trees and fountains cooled the air; flower beds were planted each with a separate kind, with lilies or roses, violets or crocuses, lest the large should rob the small of its nourishment.[63] Gardens by the sea had lagoons and navigable channels, in which grew marine plants, encircled by native trees and shrubbery.[64]

It was in their public parks, however, that the democratic Greeks developed their national talent for landscape gardening. These grew out of the sacred groves, which were transformed by every means of enhancing natural beauty known to the Greeks, and devoted to popular recreation and exercise.[65] The Academy of Athens, outgrowth of Athene's sacred olive grove in the Cephisus valley, was repeatedly beautified by tyrants and statesmen of the city. Hipparchus, son of Pisistratus, surrounded it with walls in the late sixth century B.C., and Cimon embellished it with walks, trees, and fountains. Here were alleys of elm and plane trees,[66] "sunless at noon," nightingales singing in the deep coverts, groves of sacred laurel and olive, narcissus and crocus blooming abundantly beside the irrigation rivulets.[67] Thus Sophocles knew it, as later did Plato and his followers. Gymnasia and *palestræ* were places not only of training but also of recreation; their plantations

of trees, shaded walks and fountains attracted old and young.
The ground plan of old gymnasia excavated at Delphi, Priene,
Epidaurus, and Pergamon indicate that landscape gardens
occupied the peristyle enclosures.[68]   Even prosaic Sparta located its wrestling ground in the lovely Plantanistas or Plane-
tree Grove on an island in the Eurotas River.[69]

The sacred groves of forest trees, which antedated temples,
were gradually improved by cultivation, diversified by ornamental trees, shrubs, and flowers, and beautified by marble
altars and columned fountains; for springs were invariably
present, whose nymphs were honored.   Fruit trees contributed
the beauty of their blossom and yielded revenue for the temple.
Strabo states that "flowery groves" surrounded the temples to
Artemis, Aphrodite, and the Nymphs in the Alpheus valley
about Olympia.[70]   Here Xenophon built a temple to Artemis in
an orchard of fruit trees.[71]   Pindar speaks of the "pleasant
garden" surrounding Aphrodite's temple in Cyrene,[72] where
the Greek colonists maintained consecrated groves.   The costly
marble sanctuary of Apollo at Grynium, near Cyme on the
Asia Minor coast, had a typical plantation, consisting "both
of cultivated fruit trees and of all trees which, without bearing
fruit, are pleasant to smell or see." [73]   Finest of all was the
Garden of Daphnæ, sacred to Apollo, near the city of Antioch.
It was famous for its laurel and cypress trees, its fountains
and streams, and its shining temple of Apollo, whose sumptuous
festival was held every August.[74]

A motive for the introduction of flower gardens into the
sacred groves lay in the demand for a particular flower in the
cult of each deity.   Aphrodite was the "violet crowned" pro-
tector of blooming gardens.   Sacred to her also were the rose
and bridal myrtle with its fragrant white blossoms.   The
laurel tree with its clustered bloom, essential in the worship of
Apollo, was always planted near his temples.   Laurel and
myrtle were not native to the chill Crimean shores of the
Euxine; the Greek colonists there tried by every known art
to propagate them for religious purposes, but in vain.   They
succeeded in raising figs and pomegranates whose foliage and
fruit graced many a Mediterranean garden, but had to cover
the trees in winter.[75]

Greek settlers on distant Mediterranean shores were constantly reclaiming some new spot to beauty. Colonists on the Asia Minor and Syrian coast were doubtless stimulated thereto by contact with the Persians and their garden art. Tissaphernes, Persian satrap of Lydia during the Peloponnesian War, had a lovely park, "a place charmingly wooded and watered, with delightful walks and summer houses." [76] Antioch was laid out by Seleucus Nicator on a magnificent scale with boulevards planted in flower gardens, which were bordered by colonnades, and ornamented with marble pavilions, baths, and fountains. From the west gate of the city an avenue led through a suburb of garden-set villas, vineyards, rose gardens, and groves to the Park of the Daphne. The Ptolemies laid out a succession of fine public gardens in Alexandria about the Museum and Gymnasium; the latter had porticoes six hundred feet long enclosing a shady garden. [77]

The social conditions of Hellenic Syria and Egypt, which assured a wealthy ruling class, recurred among the colonial Greeks of Sicily, and there too resulted in a display of gardens. Gelon, tyrant of Syracuse (476 B.C.), had a superb royal park. It was well irrigated and contained a wonderful "Horn of Amaltheia," a plot of blossoming fruit trees and flower beds, accounted a masterpiece of the gardener's art. [78] Dionysius the Great of Syracuse, a century later, had a garden near Rhegium; there he tried with much zeal but indifferent success to cultivate plane trees, which were aliens in Italy, but desirable for gardens on account of their shade. [79] Hiero II of Syracuse achieved the fantastic in horticultural art. On the upper deck of a monster pleasure ship he laid out a roof garden, which was provided with walks, pergolas and arbors covered with ivy and grape vines; shrubs and flowers were planted in casks of earth to complete the effect. [80]

The use of flowers runs through all Greek life. Every home seems to be in touch with some blooming garden. In all their celebrations, religious or secular, public or private, and in their common daily life, the Greeks made an extraordinary demand for flowers, which expert florists supplied all year round. There was a regular succession of blooms, from the white violet lifting up its pale face on mild days in winter and the early blossoming plum trees, to the autumn flowers which were made to protract their season far into the winter, when planted in sunny protected nurseries.[81]

On festal occasions the Greeks wore wreaths on their heads, garlands around their necks, and carried bouquets in their hands. A young dandy of Athens would stroll through the market place with a single rosebud or narcissus stuck behind his ear. The populace scattered roses as a sign of public joy, and placed cypress wreaths on the tombs of their heroes. Flowers were an essential part of every religious ceremony. Sappho bids the votary to approach the altar with wreathed hair, if he expect favor from the gods.[82] Wreaths decked the horns or necks of animals led to sacrifice. Garlands of fruits and leaves festooned the altars of the gods, and in this form were embodied as a *motif* of decoration in Greek art. Boys with crowns of narcissus or purple hyacinths on their heads walked in the sacred processions.[83] The Paralus, dispatch boat of the Athenian navy, entered the Piræus with its prow hung with wreaths when returning to announce a victory.[84]

"Violet-wreathed Athens" had daily flower markets where many varieties of roses and violets were sold, besides phlox, hyacinths, narcissi, irises, lychnis, myrtles, lilies, anemones, crocuses, and numerous sweet-smelling shrubs. Flower girls went from house to house, offering their tender wares for sale or filling a regular order,[85] as if they were delivering milk and eggs. These were the women garland-sellers satirized by the poet Eubulus.[86] Flowers were cultivated in market gardens in the outskirts of the city. Roses received special attention. The bushes were transplanted frequently and cut back to prevent deterioration of the bloom in size, color, and abundance; or they were burnt back,[87] a treatment applied to perennials by some modern European florists.

The Greeks constantly varied the native supply of garland flowers by foreign importations and domestication of wild species. They knew which Mediterranean lands produced the finest and most fragrant varieties,[88] but they had difficulty growing these in an alien climate and soil. Domestication presented similar problems. A species of wild thyme was transplanted from the mountains and cultivated at Athens and

Sicyon; but as wood plants were often sterile under domestication, considerable art was required to propagate them.[89]   A remarkable hundred-leaved rose was grown at Philippi in eastern Macedonia.   It had been domesticated by the townspeople from a many-leaved variety which grew wild on the slopes of Mount Pangæus nearby.[90]   As this coast had been colonized by Phœnicians from the neighboring island of Thasos, one surmises that this queenly rose of the Macedonian hills was perhaps an exile from some far Sidonian garden.   Or it may have traced back to that Macedonian garden attributed to Phrygian Midas by Herodotus, "in which wild roses grow, each one having sixty petals, and surpassing all others in fragrance." [91]   Some long and noble ancestry it had.

ROMAN GARDENS—The practical Romans, for centuries a race of farmers, reveal the slow evolution of esthetic horticulture from the merely economic; eventually they gave it the final touch of beauty and magnificence.   In ancient Latium, as in Greece, the garden was part of every *villa* or farm.   Primarily for fruits and vegetables, it included also flower beds for the garlands used in public and private ceremonies.   An ancient scene reported by Roman tradition is that of Tarquinius Superbus (534 B.C.) in his garden, showing a perturbed official how to handle a threatened revolt, by silently striking off the heads of the tallest poppies as he sauntered down a path.[92]   Cato (d. 149 B.C.) states that every farm garden should raise ceremonial flowers, like the nuptial myrtle, the Delphic and Cyprian laurel, and that it should be laid out near the house.[93]

Two centuries later, Columella, in his *Carmen Hortorum*, describes the garden of a large estate, emphasizing the flowers, which he calls "those earthly stars." [94]   He depicts them with fine poetic touch.   In the spring "the violet beds unfold their winking eyes . . . the rose abashed with modest blush unveils her virgin cheek." [95]   He enumerates daffodils, wild pomegranate flowers, sweet marjoram, lilies, hyacinths blue and white, flame-colored marigolds, fragrant balms, "the horned poppies with their wholesome fruit and poppies which fast bind eluding sleep."   He includes also fragrant plants from foreign lands, and sums them all up as "plants of a thousand colors."   This is a farm garden.   Its flowers, along with vegetables and fruits, are packed into osier baskets and sold in the nearest market town. The flower trade pays, for "the vendor, with staggering pace and soaked with wine, joyfully from town returns, weighed down with cash." [96]

Columella's garden had irrigation channels, sunken paths, raised borders to hold the water in the beds, a formal plan, and the enclosing wall or hedge to keep out marauders. Ornamental shade and fruit trees afforded shelter from the sun, and the abundant flowers required by Roman ceremonials gave the garden its masses of color. Here were all the elements of a pleasure garden.

The demand for flowers increased with increasing luxury in the late Republic and the Empire. In early times public benefactors were honored by simple chaplets of leaves; later crowns of blossoms became customary. From Rome's early days garlands decorated the temples of the gods, the domestic Lares and the sepulchers; but their uses later multiplied in private life.[97] At banquets wine and roses went together. Roses were scattered on the tables and crowned the guests. "Let not roses fail the feast, nor lasting parsley, nor the lily soon to die." [98] This lavish use of flowers was associated with appreciation of their beauty, as revealed in the poetry of Horace, Ovid, and Martial, and the sober prose of the Elder and Younger Pliny.

Horace states that in his time flower gardens had become a great national indulgence, displacing field crops.[99] The territorial expansion of imperial Rome caused an economic reaction upon production in Italy, a reaction that was strong and immediate, owing to easy maritime communication between Rome and remote parts of her empire. The importation of provincial grain discouraged field agriculture, and interrupted the normal evolution of tillage. But a partial readjustment followed when Roman farmers concentrated on intensive garden and fruit culture, and thus specialized in agricultural products proof against foreign competition. This change stimulated the finer aspects of horticulture, while increasing population and wealth multiplied the demand for the rarer products, whether flower, fruit, or vegetable. Thus improved floriculture constantly enlarged the element of beauty in the Roman kitchen garden.

Moreover, increasing contact with Greeks and Asiatics who

already had a highly developed horticulture, and the growing wealth of the patrician and equestrian orders at Rome combined to make the pleasure garden the fashion in Italy. Riches and slaves poured into the country from the Eastern provinces, till Italy swarmed with Syrian, Jewish, Phœnician, and Greek slaves, skilled in landscape gardening.[100]

A force of expert workmen was thus at hand just when a cultured capitalistic class at Rome was looking for new and refined enjoyments, and when the wear and tear of crowded city life and the recurring excitement of political campaigns drove the wealthy to provide rural retreats for themselves. They began to convert the old farm or *villa rustica* into a beautiful country estate with shady groves, formal garden and summer dining room in marble pavilion. Or they built smaller suburban villas, each with its pleasure garden, like Diomedes' villa near Pompeii and the Younger Pliny's villa at Laurentum. The millionaires laid out their gardens in the city and there, within enclosing walls, made their green retreats. The building and planning of villas became a passion among the Romans. Cicero, in addition to his ancestral estate at Arpinum, bought seventeen others which he improved and occupied from time to time. Lucretius, writing in 61 B.C., pictures the restless high class society of his day vibrating between town and country house.[101]

Private pleasure gardens therefore abounded within and without the capital. A map of imperial Rome shows them extending over the hills for two miles or more on both sides of the Tiber, almost encircling the city with a wreath of green.[102] The significant fact of their distribution is their paucity within the old city of the Seven Hills enclosed by the Servian walls, and their great number and expanse immediately outside these early fortifications. This inner city, even in imperial times, contained only the garden of Lollia and part of the garden of Mæcenas.

The outer girdle of green comprised the Pincian Hill, the ancient *collis hortorum*, where lay the gardens of the Acilian family and Pompey, the sumptuous gardens of Lucullus [103] and the beautiful grounds of the historian Sallust, which in the Italian Renaissance became the site of the famous Villa Ludovisi. The green belt curved east and south through a long series of gardens, most famous of which were the *Horti Mæce-natis*. This was laid out above an old potter's field and dumping ground of the Esquiline Hill, which Mæcenas covered with twenty feet of earth and converted from a plague spot into a place of beauty.[104] Here the great prime minister of Augustus entertained the literati of Rome. The low plain west of the Tiber and the slopes of the Janiculum and Vatican Hills were covered with imperial gardens. Lanciani estimates that the capital under the Cæsars had one-eighth of its area laid out in gardens, and therefore was provided with lungs as are few modern cities.

We have scant data as to the size of these gardens. Those of the emperors and nobles were undoubtedly large, like that of Mæcenas, which measured approximately 1,000 by 300 feet or about seven acres. However, this area comprised the palace, offices, pavilion, conservatory, and various other buildings which constituted a rich Roman establishment; so that the planted spaces were probably small.[105] The ruins of the imperial palace on the Palatine Hill contain traces of a formal garden two acres in extent, measuring 525 by 156 feet. Colonnades enclosed the two long sides and served as a protected walk. A marble canal surrounded the central space and supplied the garden with water, while a semi-circular fountain basin ornamented each end of the enclosure.[106] These gardens were large, considering their location within the city; but one represented wealth and the other imperial power.

The famous Porticoes and gardens of the Campus Martius presented a total length of over three miles of covered walk, and sheltered an area of about six acres; but they enclosed garden spaces amounting to sixteen acres. These were beautifully planted and ornamented with fountains and miniature lakes.[107] The *Porticus Liviæ*, which Augustus laid out as a public garden on the Esquiline Hill, has left remains sufficient to indicate its size and character. It was a sunken parterre two acres in extent (377 by 246 feet), approached by a flight of steps from above, and surrounded by a double colonnade which overlooked the central garden space. This contained a pool with trees and flower beds. Vine-grown pergolas shaded the paths, while the marble arcade offered sunshine or shadow according to the exposure. This isolated *Porticus* was probably typical of those in the Campus Martius, and suggests a taste for small and finished garden plots even as public parks.

Outside the city the gardens were large wherever wealth abounded. Magnificent villas with beautiful grounds were distributed along the main highroads within easy chariot ride of the capital. They occupied the choice sites in the Alban Mountains, an old volcanic region of fertile soil, deep woods, lakes and springs, fifteen miles southeast of Rome. High up on the northern slope, above modern Frascati, Cicero had his Tusculum villa with lovely gardens laid out in terraces and shady groves, one of which he called the Academy and another the Lyceum.[108] Nearby Lucullus had one of his sumptuous estates, with formal walks, open pavilions and outlook towers.

The Sabine Mountains on the western flank of the Apennines had many villas about Tibur (Tivoli), notably those of Mæcenas, Augustus and Hadrian. The seashore also had its country estates, not only Ostia and Laurentum, which were within easy reach of Rome, but also remoter points like Antium and the lovely region about the Bay of Naples. When the Italian Renaissance revived the ancient type of gardens, many estates like the Villa d'Este at Tivoli, the Villa Aldobrandini at Frascati, and the Villa Barberini at Rome occupied sites where once were the famous gardens of Hadrian, Lucullus and Nero. Moreover, they utilized ancient statues and vases which came to light when the soil was dug up for the new plantations.[109]

The detailed description left by the Younger Pliny of his suburban villa at Laurentum and his country estate in Tuscany reveal the leading features of ancient Roman pleasure gardens.[110] Like the Egyptian and Greek gardens, these were geometrical and formal in design and connected with the residence, so that life indoors and out was not divorced. The typical villa had a long portico opening upon a terrace or raised parterre. This was the *xystus* of the garden and served as an open-air drawing-room. Its level surface was covered with turf, broken here and there by beds of violets, crocuses, lilies or other low flowers, each kind to itself in a separate plot. Its outer edge was bordered by box or other shrubs, trimmed

often in fantastic shapes, as in Pliny's Tuscan garden; or by
a low marble balustrade recessed at intervals to hold a tall
marble vase or fountain basin, as depicted in the wall paintings
in the Palace of Livia at Prima Porta and the garden frescoes
of Pompeii.[111]

The *xystus* overlooked a lower garden or *ambulatio*, with
which it was connected by broad steps or a grassy ramp. Seen
from above, the *ambulatio* presented the appearance of a varied
mass of foliage grateful to the eye.[112] But the shining green
of the pomegranate trees was pricked by the nasturtium red
of its fruit.[113] The pure yellow of the citron and the pale buff
of the quince stood out against the dense green behind; for
these fruits served the same decorative purpose as the lemon
and orange later in the Renaissance gardens of Italy and the
Moorish gardens of Spain. Their points of color contrasted
with the solid masses furnished by the flowering laurel and the
pink or white oleander bushes, and their rounded tops of green
with the slender spires of the cypresses.

This *ambulatio* or second part of the typical Roman garden
was planned for leisurely strolls, when the host and his guests
after a morning or evening meal joined mild exercise to conver-
sation. It consisted, therefore, of shaded walks and alleys for
use when the sun was hot, and of open paths for twilight hours.
The spaces between the walks were planted with fruit or shade
trees; but where a vista opened to view of sea or mountains, the
eye ranged across low beds of hyacinths, asters, jasmine and
roses.[114]

The third section of the Roman garden was the *gestatio* or
shaded avenue where the master took his airing on horseback
or in a litter carried by slaves. It encircled the *ambulatio*, or
was laid out quite apart, usually in an oval form. In either
case it was bordered by a fancifully cut box hedge or by dwarf
plane trees; for the Romans had discovered the art of dwarfing
trees by methods of planting and topping them. The topiary
art of clipping trees and shrubs was introduced into Rome from
Syria about the Christian Era.[115]

The Roman garden was surrounded by a wall screened by
cypress trees and box, sometimes cut into a succession of miniature terraces; and it contained always summer houses, where

meals were served. These commanded views of mountain or sea, or an outlook over the garden itself. The stillness of the retreat was broken by the song of birds and the sound of water, falling in a cascade down a rocky slope, springing up into a fountain, chasing along a narrow runlet to a pool for gold fish, or trickling over a stone ledge into a marble basin. In Pliny's Tuscan estate, one such basin beneath a vine-grown arbor had a broad rim to hold the plates for an outdoor banquet, while the dishes floated on the water in miniature boats shaped like birds.[116] One can see the white-togaed guests reclining on the dining couches against the green background, wreaths of roses on their heads, silver wine cups in their hands, while they discuss a recent epigram of Martial or the latest scandal in the capital. Shouts of Olympian laughter go up, drowning the splash of the nearby fountain, while barefoot slaves move noiselessly about, serving the guests.

Gardens were not the monopoly of the rich and noble in ancient Italy. The remains of Pompeii show them attached to the average town residence, scaled down to the size of a town lot. The old Italic *atrium* house of Pompeii had a small garden in the rear, enclosed by extended side walls of the dwelling and a cross wall at the back. It was therefore the width of the house but usually quite shallow. The House of Sallust, built in this old style in the second century before Christ, had such a garden, 60 feet long and only 20 feet wide. Though small, it had all the elements of the traditional garden. In the back was a fountain and water basin, in the corner an open-air *triclinium* or dining pavilion, probably once covered by a grape arbor. A flower-bordered path ran down the length of the cramped enclosure, whose rear wall was frescoed to simulate a garden and thus extend the apparent space.[117]

Pompeii lay in a region of ancient Greek colonies and had a considerable Greek element in its population, as indicated by numerous family names. Hence the Greco-Roman peristyle residence was established here in the second century B.C. and prevailed in the handsomer homes. The peristyle court was adorned with flower beds, vases of growing plants, fountains, water basins, and statues. All were arranged with studied symmetry, as the traveler sees them today in the big peristyle

(33 by 65 feet) of the House of the Vetii, which has been restored and replanted according to the original ground plan.

Behind the peristyle and its apartments usually lay the garden or *viridarium.* The portico façade thrust out wings at either end, and enclosed the garden on three sides by colonnades. A Pompeian wall painting depicts this type of semi-enclosed garden, evidently borrowed from Greece, because it resembles the Cyzicene house garden described by Vitruvius. The House of Pansa had a portico the width of the building, opening upon a garden 124 feet wide by 100 feet deep. This was laid out in regular flower beds with paths between. It contained a fountain and a semi-circular pavilion, which doubtless served as a *triclinium.*[118]

As population increased in Rome and the private homes of the old city were superseded by tall tenement or apartment houses (*insulæ*), the little gardens were crowded out; but in their stead the flower-loving Romans introduced window-boxes and growing plants "to pasture the eyes on," Pliny says.[119] Roof gardens crowned the big city buildings with shrubs, grape arbors, fruit and shade trees, all planted in boxes of earth,[120] while high above the noisy street their marble-rimmed fish pools reflected the blue Mediterranean sky or the silent stars.

The Roman type of garden may have been transplanted to Carthage on the conquest of Africa in 146 B.C.; or the conquerors may have occupied unaltered the fine villas, which surrounded the Punic capital with their orchards and gardens. Yet earlier, in 310 B.C. when Agathocles of Sicily marched on Carthage, he passed through a cultivated and irrigated region, occupied by the landed estates of the Carthaginian nobles, "which they improved for their delight and pleasure," Diodorus tells us.[121] Esthetic gardening was a natural development for a people who inherited the principles of Phœnician horticulture, who produced an authority on tillage like Mago, and who, like the Romans, had a rich and privileged class.

Ancient Spain has left no record of pleasure gardens, though under the conditions of climate and relief they may have readily developed from the intensive tillage of the native Tartessians and the colonial Phœnicians, Greeks, and Romans who settled on Spanish shores. Strabo (b. 66 B.C.), sailing up the Guadalquivir River, described with enthusiasm the beauty of the "orchards and gardens which in this region are met with in highest perfection," [122] but he failed to specify pleasure gardens. Here at Gades (Cadiz) was born Columella of Roman blood, who more than any other writer on ancient horticulture sang the praises of flowers, as he had seen them grow in his father's gardens beside the Guadalquivir.

With the Saracen conquest in 711 A.D. Spain begins to glow with the beauty of its gardens. The Arab conquerors, conservators of ancient Mediterranean civilization in an age of barbarian invasions, had already mastered the art of gardening in their eastern homes; they embodied the ideal of their craft in the Moslem dream of Paradise. But the environment of Spain produced the perfect efflorescence of this art, because it gave to the craftsman incentive, opportunity, abundant material and abundant reward. The gardens of Spain became a revelation of the Saracen spirit, finer even than the dream of Paradise. Here race and environment seem to have combined to produce perfection; but it must not be forgot that the previous habitat of this conquering race lay among the flowering orchards of apricot and almond, among vineyards and balsam groves, by the high-laid pools and rushing rivulets of mountain Yemen and Mecca. Who tilled those narrow terraces, who watered those slender garden plots, earned beauty as well as life.

The Saracens in Spain made their cities places of gardens and waters. They multiplied shady enclosures where the green twilight beneath the trees was broken only by the gleam of marble columns or the sparkle of fountains, and where the still pool mirrored the peering faces of its bordering flowers. They gave poetical names to these retreats: "The Garden of the Waterwheel," "The Meadow of Murmuring Waters." For water was always present, handled with infinite artistic skill.[123]

Many of the old gardens of Granada have survived Christian depredations. The fact that impresses one here is the succession of small gardens incorporated in the architectural mass of the Alhambra and the Generalife—each in a setting of stone walls or stucco arcade, each exquisite and distinct in itself. Such is the little Patio of Lindaraja in the Alhambra, with its alabaster fountain, its thicket of roses and myrtles, citron and orange trees, tempering the noonday glare to a mysterious gloom. Such is the *Jardin los Adarves* on the Alhambra hill, with its vine-covered trellises and its blossoming trees looking toward the snowy Sierra Nevada.[124] The Generalife too reveals the charm of small perfect gardens. Here they glow with sun-lit flowers; there they are subdued to deep shade in a sunken water-garden, whose still green pool is overhung by rows of aged cypresses. This composite grouping recalls those complex gardens of Egyptian Thebes, Rome, Tibur, Tusculum, and the Naples district; and it makes one realize that the Egyptian Pharaohs, the Roman Cæsars, and the Moorish Sultans all planned their gardens after one common Mediterranean model.

The arcade about the Generalife "Garden of the Pond" bears the inscription: "Charming place! thy garden is adorned with flowers which rest on their stalks and exhale sweetest perfumes; fresh breezes stir the orange tree and spread abroad the fragrance of its blossoms. I hear voluptuous music mingled with the rustling of leaves in thy grove. Everything about is harmonious, green, flowering." [125]

"Awake, O North wind, and come, thou South; blow upon my garden that the spices thereof may flow out." East meets West, the garden of Palestine and the garden of Granada.

AUTHORITIES—CHAPTER XVII

1. *Genesis*, III, 8.
2. Breasted, *Records of Ancient Egypt*, Vol. II, par. 294-295.
3. Pliny, *Historia Naturalis*, XVIII, 51.
4. *Canticles*, VI, 11.
5. Pausanias, Bk. IX, 41, 7.
6. Theophrastus, *De Odoribus*, 23-31. Pliny, XXI, 10, 17-19.
7. *Canticles*, VII, 12, 13.
8. Plutarch, *Themistocles*.
9. Frontinus, *De Aquis Romœ*, II, 72-76.
10. W. R. Paton, *Greek Anthology*, Vol. III, p. 371. London, 1917.
11. M. L. Gothein, *Geschichte der Gartenkunst*, Vol. I, pp. 148-150. Jena, 1914.
12. *Oriental Carpets*, Vol. I, Part IV, Plate XXXI, *et passim*. Vienna, 1892.
13. *Genesis*, II, 8-17.
14. *Koran*, XXXII, 19; XXV, 25; XXXVI, 55; XXXVII, 40; XLIII, 70; XLVII, 10-15.
15. *Koran*, LXXVI, 10-20; LXXVII, 40.
16. I *Kings*, IV, 25.
17. Josephus, *Antiquities of the Jews*, Bk. VIII, Chap. XIV, 3.
18. *Canticles*, IV, 12-16; VI, 2, 11.
19. *Genesis*, XIII, 10; *Isaiah*, LI, 3; *Joel*, II, 3.
20. *Isaiah*, XLI, 19. Compare *Amos*, IX, 14.
21. *Numbers*, XXIV, 6.
22. *Ecclesiasticus*, XXIV, 13-32.
23. *Ecclesiastes*, II, 5-6.
24. II *Samuel*, XI, 2-3.
25. *Nehemiah*, III, 16.
26. Article, Horticulture, *Jewish Encyc.* London and New York, 1904.
27. *John*, XIX, 41; XX, 15.
28. Theophrastus, *Historia Plantarum*, Bk. V, 8, 1.
29. Arrian, *Anabasis of Alexander*, Bk. I, Chap. IV, 10.
30. Diodorus Siculus, Bk. XVI, Chap. VIII.
31. *Isaiah*, I, 29; LVII, 5-9; LXV, 3; LXVI, 17; *Hosea*, IV, 12-14.
32. J. G. Fraser, *Adonis Attis Osiris*, pp. 23-6; 183-5. London, 1907.
33. *Ibid.*, pp. 195-6. Theophrastus, *Hist. Plant.*, Bk. VI, 7, 3.
34. *Ezekiel*, VIII, 14.
35. *Isaiah*, XVII, 10-11. Bible translated by James Moffatt. New York, 1922.
36. A. G. Keller, *Homeric Society*, p. 20. New York, 1904.
37. Theophrastus, *De Causis Plantarum*, Bk. II, Chap. III, 7; *Hist. Plant.*, Bk. IV, Chap. II, 5.
38. Sir T. G. Wilkinson, *Manners and Customs of the Ancient Egyptians*, Vol. I, pp. 365-8; 375-9. New York, 1878.
39. A. Erman, *Life in Ancient Egypt*, pp. 196-7. London, 1894.
40. Sir T. G. Wilkinson, *op. cit.*, Vol. I, pp. 377-8. New York, 1878.
41. A. Erman, *op. cit.*, pp. 285-8. London, 1894.
42. *Ibid.*, pp. 194-7.
43. *Ibid.*, pp. 175, 179, 193-4.

44. Work of Plato, Vol. IV, p. 455. Translated by G. Burges. London, 1870.
45. Pindar, *Olympic Odes*, II, 68-72.
46. *Iliad*, VIII, 306.
47. *Odyssey*, VI, 227-232.
48. *Iliad*, VIII, 306-8.
49. *Odyssey*, V, 63-72.
50. *Odyssey*, VII, 112-132.
51. Xenophon, *Œconomicus*, V, 2, 3.
52. Theophrastus, *Hist. Plant.*, Bk. VI, 6, 5. Athenæus, XV, 29. Pliny, *Hist. Nat.*, XXI, 10.
53. Aristophanes, *Aves*, 1067, 1100.
54. Aristophanes, *Pax*, 577.
55. Demosthenes, Adv. Nicostratus, 1251.
56. Diogenes Laertes, V, 14.
57. Pliny, *Hist. Nat.*, XXXV, 36.
58. Theocritus, Idyl, V.
59. Nathan H. Dole, *The Greek Poets*, p. 137. New York, 1904.
60. Plutarch, *Cimon*, 13.
61. Strabo, Bk. IX, Chap. I, 17.
62. Vitruvius, *De Architectura*, Bk. VI, Chap. III, 10.
63. H. Inigo Triggs, *Garden Craft in Europe*, pp. 1-3. London, 1913.
64. W. R. Paton, *Greek Anthology*, Vol. III, pp. 369-371. London, 1917.
65. Plato, *Critias*, XII; *Laws*, VI, 8.
66. Aristophanes, *Clouds*, 1005-1011.
67. Sophocles, *Œdipus at Colonos*, 681-687.
68. M. L. Gothein, *op. cit.*, Vol. I, pp. 70-3. Jena, 1914.
69. Pausanias, Bk. III, 14, 8.
70. Strabo, Bk. VIII, Chap. III, 12.
71. Xenophon, *Anabasis*, Bk. V, Chap. III, 11-12.
72. Pindar, Pythian Ode, V, 22, 84.
73. Pausanias, Bk. I, Chap. XXI, 7.
74. Polybius, Histories, Bk. XXI, Chap. 3-4. Mommsen, *Provinces of the Roman Empire*, Vol. II, p. 140. New York, 1887.
75. Theophrastus, *Hist. Plant.*, Bk. IV, Chap. V, 3.
76. Plutarch, *Alcibiades*, XXIV.
77. Strabo, Bk. XVII, Chap. I, 8, 10.
78. Diodorus Siculus, Bk. III, Chap. IV.
79. Theophrastus, *Hist. Plant.*, Bk. IV, Chap. V, 6.
80. Athenæus, Bk. V, 41.
81. Theophrastus, *Hist. Plant.*, Bk. VI, Chap. VIII, 4.
82. Nathan H. Dole, *op. cit.*, p. 139.
83. Pausanias, Bk. II, 35, 5.
84. Xenophon, *Hellenica*, Bk. I, 6, 36.
85. H. Wiskemann, *Die Antike Landwirthschaft und das Thunenische Gesetz*, pp. 5-6. Leipzig, 1859. W. S. Davis, *A Day in Old Athens*, p. 20. New York, 1914.
86. Athenæus, Bk. V, 24.
87. Theophrastus, *Causis Plant.*, Bk. III, Chap. XIX, 1. *Hist. Plant.*, Bk. VI, Chap. VI, 6; Chap. VII, 5.
88. Theophrastus, *Causis Plant.*, Bk. VI, Chap. VIII, 1-3.
89. Theophrastus, *Hist. Plant.*, Bk. VI, Chap. VII, 2-3.

90. *Ibid.*, Bk. VI, Chap. VI, 4.
91. Herodotus, VIII, 138.
92. Pliny, *Hist. Nat.*, Bk. XIX, Chaps. 19, 53.
93. Cato, VIII.
94. Columella, *Carmen Hortorum*, line 147.
95. *Ibid.*, 400-402.
96. *Ibid.*, ·181-3; 255-267; 398-402; 443-480.
97. Whole subject of chaplets and garlands treated in Pliny, *Hist. Nat.*, Bk. XXI, Chaps. II-IV; Bk. XVI, Chaps. IV, V.
98. Horace, *Odes*, Bk. I, 36.
99. Horace, *Odes*, Bk. II, 15.
100. Karl Woksch, *Der Römische Lustgarten*, p. 6. Leitmeritz, Böhmen, 1881.
101. Lucretius, *De Natura Rerum*.
102. Lanciani, *Ruins and Excavations of Ancient Rome*, map, p. 394. Boston, 1897.
103. Tacitus, *Annales*, Bk. XI, Chap. I, 37.
104. R. Lanciani, *op. cit.*, pp. 394-427.
105. *Ibid.*, 409-10.
106. Baedeker, *Central Italy*, p. 319. 1909.
107. Lanciani, *op. cit.*, pp. 445-6, 459.
108. Plutarch, *Lucullus*, 34.
109. Lanciani, *op. cit.*, pp. 407-412.
110. Pliny the Younger, *Letters*, Bk. V, 6; Bk. II, 17.
111. *Antike Denkmäler, Band* I, *Heft*, I. Berlin.
112. A. Mau, *Pompeii: Its Life and Art*, pp. 279, 388. New York, 1899.
113. R. Lanciani, *Ancient Rome*, p. 273. Boston, 1888.
114. Pliny the Younger, *Letters*, Bk. II, 17.
115. Pliny, *Hist. Nat.*, Bk. XII, 6.
116. Pliny the Younger, *Letters*, Bk. V, 6.
117. A. Mau, *op. cit.*, pp. 240, 277-279. New York, 1899.
118. *Ibid.*, pp. 254-8, 296-7. Baedeker, *Southern Italy*, pp. 146-149. 1912.
119. Pliny, *Hist. Nat.*, XIX, 19.
120. Seneca, *Epistolæ*, 122.
121. Diodorus Siculus, Bk. XX, Chap. I.
122. Strabo, Bk. III, Chap. II, 3.
123. H. Inigo Triggs, *Gardencraft in Europe*, pp. 264-280. London, 1913.
124. Washington Irving, *Alhambra*, Chap. IV.
125. C. G. Hawley, *Things Seen in Spain*, pp. 33-5. London, 1911.

CHAPTER XVIII

CLIMATIC INFLUENCES IN ANCIENT MEDITERRANEAN RELIGION: GODS OF RAINFALL AND TILLAGE

Primitive religions embody the first halting efforts of untutored man to explain the world about him. They slowly build up a mythology reflecting the aspects of nature in the homeland, and they create gods who represent the forces of nature operating to the benefit or detriment of man. It is geography, therefore, which furnishes the clay out of which the gods are modeled, and geography supplies the vision by which the untrained sculptor works. If religions be studied in their native habitats, before they have been transplanted to new environments, and studied moreover in their native forms, before they have been seriously modified by imported ideas born of other environments, these religions are found to mirror that combination of earth and sea and sky which gave them birth. And if a group of such religions arise in a well defined natural region, which comprises common characteristics of climate and relief in its various component parts, these religions reveal in their fundamental aspects a family likeness traceable to their common geographical parentage; they may be differentiated, one from the other, by local variations of place and race in each individual homeland and by their respective stage of evolution, but they still remain true to the larger regional type.

The Mediterranean Region presents a natural environment in which such a kindred group of religions arose. It is an extensive region of prevailing highland relief, of sub-tropical warmth, of typical Mediterranean climate with its winter rains and summer droughts, of short wet-weather torrents, of rivers which swell to flood proportions in winter and shrink in summer to slender brooks trickling down from some nearby mountain source. It is a region where springs run dry in summer, where unfailing wells and perennial fountains are accounted blessings; a region where in the dry days "the hart panteth for the water-brook" which has become transformed into a river of sand, where Christ promised "I will be unto you a well of living water," where Pindar sang "Water is best of all," and where the modern Greek says to his departing guest, "May you have a safe journey and find good water."

MEDITERRANEAN CLIMATE—The circle of the Mediterranean lands forms approximately a climatic unit. The amount of the annual rainfall and the length of the rainy season decrease from west to east and from north to south; while the duration and intensity of the summer drought increase in the same directions, and thus curtail the length of the growing season for winter crops. Deviations from this law occur only where high mountains take toll of moisture from the reluctant clouds, prolong the rainy days on their slopes, and break the summer drought by an occasional local thunderstorm. From midday on their chilly summits are often enveloped in clouds, which seem to give delusive promises of rain to the sun-baked plains below.

Moreover, from north to south and from west to east the showers which open and close the wet season, "the former and the latter rains" of the Bible, become more variable and unreliable. They appear late or fail altogether, thus lopping off either end of the growing season and reducing the total rainfall. Especially is this the case in the southeast, in Syria and Palestine, where the supply of water, scant at best, assumes crucial importance; where any diminution in the amount or duration of the rains seriously jeopardizes the crops. Modern records show that the rainfall at Jerusalem fluctuates between 12.5 and 42 inches (318 mm. and 1,091 mm.); that during the sixty years from 1850 to 1910 it dropped twelve times below the critical 20 inches (500 mm.) and twelve times exceeded 32 inches (800 mm.). Thus every five years, on an average, the rainfall on the Judean Plateau drops below the annual mean of 26 inches (662 mm.) and causes alarming reduction of the harvests. Moreover, a succession of these dry years tends to occur, diminishing the reserves of moisture in the soil and lowering the ground-water table. During the half-decade from 1869 to 1873 inclusive, the rainfall averaged little over 17

inches (441 mm.).[1]   In Cyprus precipitation varies from 10 to
27 inches (265 to 696 mm.) on the coasts,[2] in Cyrenaica from
8.27 to 24.25 inches (210 to 616 mm.),[3] in Athens from 4.5 to
33.3 inches (116 to 847 mm.),[4] in Palermo from 22.8 to 39
inches, and Rome from 25 to 45 inches.[5]

ANCIENT DROUGHTS AND FAMINES—Ancient traditions and
history agree with the modern meteorological records; the two
together indicate stable climatic conditions from the earliest
times to the present in the Mediterranean Region.[6]   Severe
droughts, reported in history always as famines, were frequent
in the arid eastern end of the region.   Bible records, fragmentary as they are, show that the crops of ancient Palestine constantly suffered from insufficient rain.   The famines in the
time of Abraham, Isaac and Jacob were clearly due to drought,
because they were protracted, widespread, and attended by failure of the wild pastures as well as of the crops.[7]   A series of
dry years evidently caused the famine which lasted for the
Biblical seven years in the time of Jacob; it necessitated importations of grain from Egypt, and resulted in emigration
from Palestine to the Goshen district of the Nile delta.   The
famine in the time of the Judges mentioned in the Book of
Ruth lasted several years, and was probably due to drought,
though the cause is not stated.   Possibly to this period belonged the famine in northern Syria when Meneptah of
Egypt, about 1322 B.C. sent grain by sea to the Hittites there.[8]
The three years' famine in King David's reign [9] is ascribed by
Josephus to a long drought sent by Jehovah in punishment for
sin.   The sin being expiated, "God began to send rain at once,
and to make the earth again bring forth fruit as usual, and to
free it from the previous drought, so that the country of the
Hebrews flourished again." [10]   A three years' drought "without
rain or dew," attended by failure of springs and wells, pastures
and crops, occurred in King Ahab's reign in the ninth century
B.C., and ended with the dramatic competition of prayers for
rain on the summit of Mount Carmel.[11]   Menander mentions
this drought in his history of Ethbaal, King of Tyre and Sidon,
and states that no rain fell in Phœnicia for twelve months.[12]

Another destructive drought visited Judea in the seventh
century B.C. in the time of Josiah and Jeremiah, when fissures

formed in the sun-baked earth and the wild animals perished for lack of water and grass, when "the showers have been withholden and there hath been no latter rain." [13] This may have been the severe drought described by Joel, who lived then, when a plague of locusts increased the ravages of the drought till the blessed rains came.[14] Again about 520 B.C. the Jews, returned from exile in Babylonia, found "the heaven is stayed from dew and the earth is stayed from her fruit," when the drought destroyed the mountain pastures, grain fields, vineyards and olive harvests.[15] A like visitation is recorded as lasting two years during the reign of Herod the Great, in 24 and 23 B.C.; wheat was imported from Egypt and distributed to the people of Palestine to the amount of 400,000 Attic medimni or 600,000 bushels, while 100,000 medimni or 150,000 bushels were sent to relieve northern Syria; for all the countries about suffered from the same drought.[16] Palestine shared in the "great dearth throughout the world in the time of Claudius Cæsar," the wide extent of which indicates a meteorological cause. The price of wheat soared, and the distress in Jerusalem was relieved by the purchase of grain in Alexandria and dried figs in Cyprus.[17]

Greece, though located farther north and west than Palestine, nevertheless suffered from numerous droughts in ancient times; all its large and important city-states were situated on the ill-watered eastern side of the peninsula, in the rain-shadow of the western mountains, where the rainfall was scant and variable, as it is today. The mean rainfall of Athens is variously given as 16 inches, 15.2, and 13.2 inches (408 mm., 386 mm., 330 mm.). In 1882 only 8.4 inches (214.5 mm.) fell, and that year put Athens in a meteorological class with Alexandria. Hence severe droughts run through all Greek legendary history. One occurred during the time of the mythical Erectheus, and necessitated the importation of grain from Egypt;[18] another visited all Hellas and the Peloponnesos in the time of King Æacus of Ægina,[19] and yet another caused a devastating famine in fertile Bœotia during the reign of the legendary king Athamas. The myth runs that the women had been induced by evil council to parch the seed-corn, unknown to their husbands, so that it failed to sprout.[20] The islands of the Ægean suffered in the same way from thirst and famine, —Crete [21] and Ceos [22] and especially Thera, where seven rainless years in succession drove the people to colonize the Cyrene region of Africa, which lay beneath "a hole in the sky." [23]

In historical times the effect of the droughts became less disastrous, because Grecian maritime trade supplied imported food. However, frequent records of famine in Greece point to the recurrent cause in a scant rainfall. A period of scarcity prevailed in Athens in 445 B.C., when no war was going on to interrupt the work of tillage; the city was relieved by a gift of 40,000 medimni (60,000 bushels) of wheat from the King of Egypt.[24] Drought undoubtedly caused the great famine of the 105th Olympiad (about 360 B.C.) mentioned by Demosthenes, when Athens imported an unprecedented amount of grain from the Crimea.[25] A great famine occurred in 325-324 B.C., when not only Greece but also "other regions suffered severely and Egypt to a lesser degree." [26] In this case, a widespread drought happened to coincide with a "low Nile." Athens, unable to secure food from the Nile valley except at exorbitant rates, considered sending out a colony to Hadria at the Po mouth to establish a grain port there.[27]

The opposite coast of the Ægean Sea in Asia Minor normally received more rain (20 to 30 inches) than the Greek side;[28] but this region too had its record of famines. A dearth prevailed over all Lydia for several successive years in the mythical age of King Atys, and finally compelled the emigration of half the population, an exodus which peopled ancient Etruria with Greco-Asiatics.[29] The duration and extent of this famine are explicable only on the theory of a prolonged drought, like that which visited Lydia in the reign of Artaxerxes I (465 to 425 B.C.), and dried up every river, lake and well of the country, as reported by the historian Xanthus.[30]

Italy, owing to its more northern and more western location, was less subject than Greece to serious diminution of its rainfall, yet did not wholly escape the evil. A famine in 490 B.C. was attributed by Livy to neglect of tillage caused by the secession of the plebs, which was only a momentary episode. Far more significant is the fact that the grain agents, sent out by the Roman Government to purchase food from the neighbor-

ing tribes, were roughly handled and chased away by the
Volscians and the people of the Pontine plain; that immediately afterwards a pestilence broke out among the Volscians,
who were also apparently suffering from inadequate food and
a low water supply; and that the grain purchased by the
Roman agents farther south in the Neapolitan district was held
up there by the local tyrant and its export forbidden. These
facts point to a widespread famine due in all probability to
drought. Grain was finally procured only from the north, from
Etruria,[31] where the rainfall was more reliable. Again in 440
B.C. a famine in Rome, "due either to a bad season for the crops
or to neglect of tillage," Livy writes, necessitated the importation of grain, which again could be procured only in Etruria.[32] Failure to get it from other sources may have been due
either to widespread drought or to the political rivalry and
enmity of the neighboring tribes; but the latter reason would
not have applied to the distant Neapolitan district at this
period of history.

The year 425 B.C. in Latium was marked by a protracted
drought. Rivers and springs dried up, crops failed, cattle lay
dead from thirst along the exhausted streams, disease and
famine followed.[33] Such a drought with its manifold effects is
described by Vergil in his Eclogues and Æneid. One such visited Italy in 182 B.C., when for six months no rain fell.[34] A
widespread famine occurred in 5 A.D. and lasted for a year; it
set in again in 7 A.D. and extended over Dalmatia and Pannonia, and in both instances taxed the ingenuity of Augustus
to reduce the suffering in Rome.[35] Again about 44 A.D. in the
reign of Claudius, Italy suffered from crop failure and consequent famine, which put a special pressure upon the grain
trade from Egypt· and elsewhere.[36] Today the farmer of
southern Italy is familiar enough with the scourge of scant
rains and perishing crops.[37]

WEATHER GODS—The frequent threat of drought, the pow-
erlessness of the people to deduce any meteorological law, and
their helplessness before the forces of nature, all conspired to
unite rain and religion in the ancient Mediterranean mind. The
chief gods, reflecting these climatic conditions, became weather
gods, powerful to bestow or deny the life-giving water from

the sky. Their meteorological functions were primitive, fundamental, and persistent. Untrammeled by natural law, they sent
the drought or the blasting east wind in punishment for sin
or infringement of some man-made custom or some wholly un-
conscious offense. They were irascible deities, especially
Jehovah. The divine tempers varied with the variability of
the rainfall, and tended to increase in serenity from the eastern
towards the western end of the Mediterranean Region. When
angered or offended, they were appeased by prayers, offerings
and even by human sacrifice until they ceased to inhibit the
rain. Jupiter alone never exacted the maximum price for his
renewed favor.

Egypt, a fluvial oasis stretched across the desert of northern Africa, constituted a province by itself. Relying on the
irrigating waters of the Nile, quite independent of rainfall, it
bred a tribe of gods unrelated to the climatic conditions of the
Mediterranean Region. Palestine on the other hand gives us
Jehovah, armed with all the powers of a weather-god. He
commands the clouds, rain, hail, snow, dew, waterspout, thunder, lightning, wind, whirlwind, storm, flood, and rainbow; he
controls the underground waters in springs which feed the
irrigation ditches, and in wells which water the flocks and
herds.[38] "The Lord rideth on a swift cloud."[39] "He giveth
rain upon the earth and sendeth waters upon the fields."[40] He
makes or breaks the drought. "The grass withereth, the flower
fadeth because the Spirit of the Lord bloweth upon it."[41] In a
punitive mood, he withholds the spring showers and lets the
crops perish before they mature.[42] In a beneficent mood, he
sends the former and the latter rains in good season, when "the
threshing floors shall be full of wheat and the vats shall overflow with wine and oil."[43] "I will give waters in the wilderness
and rivers in the desert, to give drink to my people, my
chosen."[44]

The prophets of Jehovah are frequently weather-doctors,
like Moses, Samuel, Elijah and Elisha; they are endowed with
power to summon the rain, invoke the lightning, and control the
underground waters by producing springs in the desert.[45]
When the armies of Judea and Israel marched through the dry
plateau of Edom to invade Moab, men and cattle suffered from

thirst, till Elisha dug trenches in a wadi bed and caused them
to be filled with water, though no rain fell.[46] Josephus explains
the miracle: "The next day the torrent ran full of water, for
God had caused a great rain up in Edom a three days' journey
away." [47] Jehovah sometimes acts in conformity with obvious
meteorological laws. He calls the west wind, which "bears the
water of the sea," to moisten the fields; he employs the desiccating north wind and the east blast from the Syrian Desert to
parch the earth.[48] During persistent drought he remains ob-
durate to prayers, but may be finally conciliated by human
sacrifices. After the three dry years in the reign of David,
Jehovah's supposed wrath was appeased by the execution of
the seven sons of Saul, at the suggestions of the priests of
Gibeon, whose sanctuary had been desecrated by Saul.[49] Incidentally David eliminated seven possible pretenders to the
throne which he had usurped, a result which suggests some
underground connection between the palace at Jerusalem and
the sanctuary of Gibeon.

When the Jews settled in Palestine and exchanged the pastoral life of the grasslands for sedentary agriculture, Jehovah
like his people became adjusted to a changed environment.
He became primarily controller of the weather upon which
tillage depended. As the invading Israelites appropriated the
fields and adopted the agricultural methods of the Canaanites,
so the immigrant Jehovah assumed the meteorological functions of the local baalim of Palestine, Phœnicia and Moab,
though his distinctive origin was never forgotten by the Jews.[50]
The baalim, like Jehovah, are givers of rain and speak with
the voice of the thunder. The priests of Baal pray for rain
during the long drought in Ahab's reign; and Ethbaal, King
of Tyre and Sidon, making like supplications, is answered by
"great thunders," according to Menander.[51] The baalim are
the ultimate source of the gifts of the earth—wheat and barley,
wool and flax, oil and drink, vines and fig trees,[52] whose harvests
they insure by means of the fertilizing rain and dew, by irrigating waters from spring or well or stream. They are lords
of the underground waters so abundant in the porous limestones of Palestine and Syria, as well as of the showers from
the clouds. Their invisible presence, evidenced by the life-

giving water, rendered springs sacred throughout the land of the Semites.[53] As gods of fertility and reproduction in the widest sense, they were worshipped with obscene rites and orgies quite alien to the religion of Jehovah. But the rival deities possessed identical powers to determine the yield of the soil, as Hosea himself insisted, when defending Jehovah's claim to the veneration and gratitude of his people.[54]

As Baal, on the southern borders of Syria, blended with Jehovah, so on the northern frontier, from his outposts in Baal Tarsus in Cilicia and Baal Casius near the Orontes River mouth, he linked up with the ancient Hittite Tesub, a storm-god represented in sculpture with an emblem of forked lightning in one hand and an axe-hammer in the other. Thus he was pictured in bas-relief at Singerli on Mount Amanus 70 miles northeast of Antioch, and in the rock sanctuary above the old Hittite capital near Pteria in central Asia Minor.[55] On the Ægean coast of Caria this Hittite thunder-god appears trans-muted into the Zeus of Labranda, who has stolen the thunder emblem, the axe-hammer of Tesub.[56] This transmutation of the chief weather gods was common in the Mediterranean Region, owing to their community of function imposed by common climatic conditions. In many cases the change was merely one of name or outward symbol, while the essence of the deity remained the same. A whole series of these may be detected: Jehovah-Baal, Baal-Zeus, Baal-Tesub, Tesub-Zeus, Zeus-Jupiter, and Cronus-Baal, the last in Carthage. Old zones of blended or transmuted weather gods crop out in natural transition areas, and they multiply in periods of change or amalgamation stimulated by immigration and conquest.

ZEUS—All the Hellenic lands about the Ægean had reason to fear protracted droughts and rains too scant for maturing crops. They therefore attached great importance to the vernal thunder-storms which fortified wheat and barley fields against the approaching drought of summer. The Dorians even prayed for rain during the hay harvest; for any damage to the hay was compensated by the benefit to the wheat.[57] Therefore in the whole Ægean world primitive religion was bound up in the needs of tillage; the supreme god was he who sent the beneficent rains upon the thirsting fields.

"Hurler of thunderbolts unfaltering, the most high Zeus" [58] is the rain-giver of the Greek world. Like Jehovah the Most High, he is equipped with all the powers of a weather god. His epithets describe his activities. He is "showery Zeus," "cloud-compelling Zeus," "rain-bringing Zeus," "Zeus the thunderer," "the gatherer of lightning," "Zeus the moistener," "Zeus the pourer forth," "god of the storm cloud." [59] "From Olympos a cloud fares into heaven from the sacred air when Zeus spreadeth forth the tempest." [60] He commands the winds and sets the rainbow in the sky.[61] Clouds and rain, thunder and lightning, and the rain-loving oak grove are manifestations of his presence.[62] The marriage of Zeus and Hera on the cloud-wrapped summit of Mount Ida in Phrygia was the union of earth and the fertilizing rain. "Beneath them the divine earth sent forth new tender grass, and dewy lotus and crocus and hyacinth, thick and soft, that lifted them aloft from the ground. Therein they lay and were clad with a white cloud, whence fell drops of glittering dew." [63]

Throughout the Hellenic world from Ionia to Sicily, and especially on the dry eastern side of Greece, supplications ascended to Zeus for the life-giving rain. On the Acropolis of Athens was an image of Earth (*Ge*) imploring Zeus with up-lifted hands.[64] The Attic prayer in time of drought has come down to us: "Rain, rain, dear Zeus, upon the grainlands of the Athenians and upon their pastures." [65] Zeus controlled every sign of coming showers, such as the autumn lightning that heralded the end of the dry season. Athens had an altar to Zeus, Dispenser of Lightning, where for three months priests kept watch, looking northward towards Mount Parnes for the first flash denoting the presence of the god. When it lightened on the mountain near Harma and Phyle, they sent a sacrifice to Delphi to Apollo, god of agriculture.[66] Pelasgian Zeus the Thunderer had his sacred seat in the oak grove of Dodona in Epiros, on the rainy western side of the Pindus Mountains. There was the earliest shrine of the weather god, where now almost daily thunder-storms occur during June and July, where the annual precipitation is 51 inches (1,299 mm.) and the great Rain-giver abundantly manifests his presence.[67] Thence came the west wind, signalled by the lightning on Mount Parnes, which brought the rare summer thunderstorms to arid Attica.[68]

Aristophanes, rationalist and critic, reduces this meteorological mythology to its lowest terms: "The Clouds are our
only goddesses: all the rest are bunk." [69] Nevertheless prayers
and sacrifices, offerings of animals and of children, like those
immolated to Moloch, altars and temples to Zeus interceded
with the Father of the gods for rain in times of drought and
during the dog days, when Sirius hung his glowing lantern in
the evening sky.[70] More merciful than the Semites, the Greeks
early substituted a ram or kid for the human sacrifice; weaker
as to moral sentiment, they rarely interpreted the droughts as
punishment for sin; more rationalistic, they regarded their
priests as passive agents of Zeus, not endowed with rain-making powers as were the Hebrew prophets.   The sole exception
to this rule were the legendary Telchines, early emigrants from
Crete to Rhodes, who attended the infant Zeus at his birth on
Mount Dicte, and were accredited with power to produce rain
and snow.[71]

JUPITER—Like the Hellenic Zeus, Jupiter of the Latins and
Etruscans was in the historical period a weather-god, though
less conspicuously so in actual practice than his Greek counterpart, owing perhaps to the more reliable and abundant rains
of Italy. As head of the Roman state, he exercised important
functions which tended to overshadow his meteorological offices,
though violent thunder-storms and devastating strokes of
lightning were regularly interpreted as national omens.[72] The
Jupiter of the pre-Roman Latins and Sabines is only scantily
revealed to us; yet his oldest sanctuary presents an interesting
parallel to Baal of the springs and streams. Lavinium,
metropolis of Latium before the founding of Rome, had an
aboriginal sanctuary of Jupiter Numicius on the River
Numicius,[73] where the Lavinians identified the creative power
of Jove with the waters of this little stream as it irrigated the
tillage land of the city. Jupiter Latiaris, chief god of the
Latin League, revealed the symbol of the weather god in the
lapis manalis or thunder-bolt.

As Etruscan influence spread over Latium, Jupiter became
identified with the Etruscan weather god Tina or Tinia, who
embodied old Hellenic conceptions of the chief deity brought

from the Asia Minor coast, and was therefore modelled after
the Greek Zeus, hurler of the thunderbolt.[74]   Attached to his
worship in Etruria was a college of priests, the *Fulgatores*,
whose office was to observe the lightning, its character, location, direction, and the season of the year when it occurred.[75]
They were in effect a weather bureau, forecasting the thunder-
storms which were vitally important for ancient Etruscan
tillage.   Zeus, transplanted from western Asia Minor to
Etruria, needed little adjustment to the climatic conditions of
the new environment, which were only a little better than his
old ones.

The epithets of the Roman god parallel those of Zeus.   He
is Jupiter *Pluvius* or rainy, *Uvidus* or wet, *Imbricitor* or
shower-sender, and *Serenator* or giver of clear weather.   He
is Jupiter *Fulgur* or *Fulminator* in his power over the lightning, and Jupiter *Tonitrualis* or *Tonans* as hurler of the
thunderbolt.[76]   In Greek literature rain was the water of
Zeus;[77] so in Roman literature it is frequently the *Aqua Jovis*
or merely Jove, as when Vergil says, "Now Jove (rain) must
be feared for the ripe grapes."[78]   The oak tree, which in its
several varieties served as a rain gage throughout the Mediterranean region, was sacred to Jove all over Italy;[79] oak groves
originally surrounded his shrines and temples.   Jove it was
who sent the fructifying showers upon the thirsty fields and
gardens; hence prayers to Jove were a condition of successful
tillage.[80]   In times of drought, noble Roman matrons walked
barefoot in procession up the long slope of the Capitoline Hill
to the temple of Jove the Thunderer, to pray for rain.   So
effective were their prayers that "the rain came down in bucket-
fuls, and all the women smiled though wet as rats.   But now
the gods do not come to our help, because we are no longer
religious; so the fields lie barren," says Petronius.[81]

As the Latin Jupiter merged with the Greek Zeus in consequence of similar functions imposed by similar climatic conditions, so among the widely scattered Phœnician settlements of
the Western Basin, the old Semitic Baalim, who had migrated
from the slope of the Lebanon, retained their individuality so
long as Carthage maintained its political power, but when
Carthage fell, they gradually merged into the equivalent Greek

or Roman deity who acted as rain-giver or bringer of fertility
to the fields. It suggests perhaps a very early contact between
Carthage and the Italian folk that Baal of Carthage was
regularly identified with Saturn, forerunner of Jove in the
succession of Italian gods. Saturn was god, not of rain, but
of the rain-given productivity of the fields; he embodied the
effect rather than the natural cause. Baal like Saturn was
appeased by human sacrifices, preferably of children, who in
Carthage as in Tyre were immolated to him under his title of
Moloch or King in times of drought or pestilence or unsuccessful war. [82] He was worshipped throughout the immediate
Carthaginian territory, and in Numidia, Mauretania, Sardinia
and Spain; and as Baal Hammon he was identified both with
Zeus and Jupiter.[83]

MOUNTAIN GODS—The original seats of these divine rain-
givers—their first rude earthen altars, their shrines and
temples were located on hill-tops, mountain summits, lofty
peaks, "the high places of the earth." These were the "sacred
mounts," like Sinai, Zion, Hermon, Mount Ida of Phrygia and
of Crete, Mount Olympos with its cloud-walled city of the
gods, that unplaced "Mount of the Transfiguration," the countless altar-crowned peaks and templed hills of Greece and the
Ægean Isles, Sicilian Ætna, the Alban Mount with its sanctuary of the Latin tribes, the Capitoline Hill of Rome, and
hundreds more wherever they lifted their heads above the wave-
lapped shores of the Mediterranean. It was perhaps some
deathless memory of this ancient mode of thought, lingering in
the folk mind, that made tradition place the sanctuary of the
Holy Grail on Mont Serrat, rising from the Spanish shore of
the Mediterranean and looking eastward towards that sunrise
of the Christian faith on Mount Calvary.

What was the cogent reasoning that made men of all the
Mediterranean world see in these lofty seats the dwelling-places
of the Most High—that made Jew, Trojan, Greek, Lydian,
Roman and Carthaginian erect thereon the first rude shrines
or altars of the rain-gods, and mount these long slopes with
prayers and offerings in times of drought?

Below in the treeless plains a glare of light from cloudless
skies, a merciless sun beating down on shrivelled crops and

vineyards, meadows parched and sere, the soil baked and cracked with the heat, water courses dried up made a whole world athirst. Above on the heights clouds rested, and gathered at times for local storms, creating islands of moisture in a vast sea of aridity. There under a gray canopy, refreshed by showery afternoons and dewy nights, grew forests of oak and tamarisk, of chestnut and ash and cedar—sacred groves of all "high places," handiwork of the Rain-giver, evidence of his presence in this place of his abode. From these tree-grown slopes perennial springs sent their gift of water down to the irrigation ditches in the plains below. Even in summer those misty summits held out promise of rain, elusive though it might be; towards the end of the dry season their gathering clouds and the increasing play of lightning were harbingers of the autumn showers. Therefore when the Mediterranean peasant saw his meadow parched by the pitiless sun, his crops dying for lack of water, his irrigation stream shrinking to a trickle and his well or cistern giving out, in despair he looked towards the mountains for signs of rain: "I will lift mine eyes unto the hills whence cometh my help."

There the rain-god manifested himself by clouds, thunder, lightning, and storms. The groves which crowned the dewy summits became his sanctuary, and hence they were marked by rude altars, rarely by temples, because the sites were too remote from the haunts of men. The sanctuaries were often associated with nearby springs and wells, reminiscent of the older worship of the gods of the underground waters; and these waters figured in the cult of the rain-god as another sign of his presence. Such was the spring at the high place of Tarnaach on the north slope of Carmel near Megiddo, and the bell-shaped cistern beneath the high place of Gezer on a western spur of the Judean plateau; [84] and such were the springs and cavern streams that figured in many mountain sanctuaries of Zeus and Baal and Jove.

A survey of the distribution of these rain-giving mountain gods shows them widely distributed over the Mediterranean Region. They crop out also in Persia, where a semi-arid or arid climate is combined with rugged relief, and where, according to Herodotus, the people in their religious observances ascended to the summits of mountains and offered sacrifices to their chief god.[85] The sanctity of mountains among the western Semites was universal. Canaanites and Jews worshipped "upon the high mountains and upon the hills and under every green tree." [86] When colonists from Tyre founded Carthage in North Africa, they enthroned their god on a two-pronged mountain near the city and called him Bal-caranensis or "Baal of the Two Horns"; and on the higher summit they built a simple altar with a *temenos* but no temple—evidence of the antiquity of the sanctuary.[87] On a sacred knoll of the Judean Plateau, identified as Mount Zion or Mount Moriah, was staged the arrested tragedy of Abraham's sacrifice of his son Isaac to Jehovah. So universal was the cult of the high places in the early Semitic days, that the Aramæans of the trans-Jordan country characterized the Hebrew deities as "gods of the mountains." [88]

The holy mountains of Canaan, many of them sacred from the legendary time of Abraham, were Zion, Mount Moriah, Mount Bethel [89] which was a very ancient sanctuary of Canaanites and Jews, the Mount of Olives,[90] Ramah, Hebron, Ebal,[91] Gerizim, Gilboa, Tabor,[92] Mount Carmel, Mount Perazim with its Baal-Perazim,[93] and countless more. The Hebrew sanctuary of Ramah was merely a hill rising above the plateau town, and was evidently identical with an earlier Canaanite shrine.[94] Similar was the "great high place of Gibeon," seven miles from Jerusalem, where Solomon sacrificed to Jehovah before he built the temple. Mount Carmel, jutting out into the Mediterranean as a bold promontory, rising directly in the path of the rain-bearing winds from the western sea, clothed in forests that withered only in severe droughts, had an altar and spring sacred to Jehovah before the time of Elijah, and was a sanctuary through all ancient times.[95] Hence on this mountain was appropriately staged that dramatic contest between Elijah and the priests of Baal, to bring down upon their rival altars the lightning of fire from heaven which should herald the storm and end the disastrous drought.[96] Baal-Carmel became Zeus Carmel or Jove Carmel of Tacitus, of whom the historian writes: "Mount Carmel, such is the name given to the mountain and the god; nor is there any representation of the deity or temple, but according to ancient usage there is only an altar and worship." Here Vespasian sacrificed a lamb to the god of the mountain, while the local priest interpreted the entrails.[97] Today the spot is marked by a Carmelite monastery and chapel to Saint Elias. The sanctuary abides; only the divine incumbent shifts.

The trans-Jordan country, which in ancient as in modern times suffered from severe droughts, had its numerous high-places where the local god could be implored for rain. Such was Mount Peor [98] with its Baal-Peor, Mount Nebo and other hill sanctuaries of Moab; [99] Mizpeh of Gilead sacred both to Baal and Jehovah; [100] while far to the south, Petra of Edom, located on a high terrace (3,000 feet) of the Mount Hor range, had its sacred place on a rocky peak 700 feet above the ancient Nabatæan capital.[101] Far to the north, at the sources of the Jordan, lofty Mount Hermon (9,050 feet or 2,653 m.), wearing a coronal of snow till late summer, abounding in perennial springs and in oak forest, was a sacred mountain to all the dwellers about. The Hebrews valued it as a collector of clouds and dew,[102] and like the Canaanites they called it Mount Baal-Hermon, in recognition of the resident god.[103] Ruins of ancient shrines and altars, especially on its southern peak, testify to the ancient worship. Farther north the Lebanon range, mother of streams and forests, had its Baal-Lebanon; so had its companion range, the Anti-Lebanon. Mount Casius (5,800 feet) overlooking the mouth of the Orontes River, had its Baal Casius and later its Zeus Casius, after the Greek conquest of Syria.

These mountain tops were the natural stage for the revelation of a supreme god like Jehovah. On Horeb, a peak of Sinai, Jehovah first spoke to Moses, when the latter was pasturing the flocks of his Midian father-in-law on its northern slopes. Moses knew the weather conditions of Sinai and utilized them for the impressive drama of the promulgation of the ten commandments. He had doubtless seen the occasional thunderstorms that break forth on the summit and send torrential floods down the wadi beds to the desert of Paran below; [104] and he knew that to the thirsty caravans, travelling the old route between the Nile delta and Edom, the water sweeping down the rocky canyons came with a suddenness that suggested an answer to prayer. A tempest on the mountain, with all the spectacular effects of massing clouds, the roar of wind and rain, the flash of lightning and the reverberation of thunder which seemed to shake the rocky slopes, could be only the voice of Jehovah God speaking from his holy mountain.[105] Whether this mount of God was the Sinai of tradition, whose topmost peak rises to the height of 8,535 feet (2,602 m.) far to the south of the caravan route; or whether it was the minor northern spur (3,250 feet or 1,000 m.) above Kadesh Barnea which intercepts the winter storm clouds from the Mediterranean; or whether it was Mount Seir or Horeb (3,700 feet or 1,128 m.) northeast of the Gulf of Akabah,[106] matters little. All were mountain sanctuaries visited by rare storms in a region of prevailing aridity, and each in turn may have been appropriated by the wandering Israelites for their God.

In Judea, "Ziòn is the mount which God hath desired for his abode." [107] There the ark of the covenant was located on its arrival in Jerusalem, on what was probably an ancient high-place of the Jebusite stronghold.[108] The Israelites, on gaining Palestine, abandoned their pastoral nomadic life, gradually adopted the higher economic culture of the native Canaanites, and appropriated their mountain cult along with their fields. Even the prophets failed to preserve entire the original faith of Jehovah of the grasslands; but were compelled to magnify his rain-giving powers, in accordance with the needs of an agricultural people in a semi-arid land.

In the wide circle of Hellenic lands, Zeus was habitually worshipped on the heights, where the clouds first gathered and the storms first broke.[109] Like his Canaanite prototype, Baal-Hermon or Baal Carmel, he was identified with the lofty place of his abode; he was the Olympian Zeus or the Idæan or the Ætnæan Zeus. Apostrophizing the latter, Pindar sings: "Hurler of thunderbolts unfaltering, most high Zeus . . . to whom Ætna belongeth, the wind-beaten burden that crusheth fierce Typhon's hundred heads." [110] Zeus is represented as enthroned on a mountain in ancient Hellenic art, on coins, sculptured reliefs and pottery.[111] A hundred instances of this mountain cult of Zeus are found in classical literature, and yet

other cases may be surmised from the survival of ancient hill
ceremonies for rain into medieval and modern times. The worship of the mountain Zeus abounds in rites for invoking rain.
These are so archaic and persistent that they show this meteorological aspect of the god to have been fundamental.[112]   His
other rôles, such as the King of the Gods and Averter of Ills,
are secondary, derivative. To his sacred mountains processions repair in the recurrent season of the Dog Days or in times
of prolonged drought; and at the altars on the summit they
perform ceremonials which are dramatized prayers for rain.

The assignment of Zeus to the mountain-tops was a rational
process for the ancient Greeks. A race of farmers and seamen,
concerned for all atmospheric conditions, wind as well as rain,
they observed that the mountains gave the surest weather indications.   Certain peaks which acquired local fame as
"weather-breeders" became identified with Zeus. Theophrastus
states that, aside from particular constellations which were
the celestial timekeepers of the winter rains, weather signs
were found chiefly on high mountains, especially those rising
from the sea and exposed to rain-bearing winds.[113]   A latter-
day echo of the ancient meteorological principle persists
among the Spanish farmers of Granada, who take Mount
Parapanda as their weather prophet and say: "When Parapanda puts on his cap, it rains, though God himself may not
wish it." [114]   Similarly, to the ancient Greeks, a turban of cloud
on Mount Oros on the island of Ægina was a sign of rain.[115]
Hence this peak (1,745 feet or 532 m.), the most conspicuous
height in or about the Saronic Gulf, was the site of the ancient
altar of Panhellenic Zeus, possibly a remnant of the legendary
temple built there to Zeus, to secure the cessation of the long
drought in the time of Æacus.[116]   High up on the shoulder
of Mount Oros walls of Cyclopean masonry may be seen which
in the late sixth century B.C. supported a temple of Zeus Pan-
hellenius. Similarly, Mounts Hymettos (3,370 feet or 1,027
m.), Lycabettus and Parnes, overlooking the plain of Athens,
gave promise of rain, when clouds obscured top or slopes; so
they were crowned by altars to Showery Zeus.[117]

Mount Athos, "the Thracian watch-tower of Athoan Zeus,"
located on the eastern prong of the Chalcidice trident and lift-

ing its bold white marble summit 6,347 feet (1,935 m.), furnished a weather forecast for the north Ægean islands and
coasts, as it does today. A mantle of clouds about Athos
presaged a storm; a girdle of clouds half way up its slope
indicated a southerly wind and eventual rain.[118]   Therefore
Athos was sacred to Zeus, and has retained its sacred character
to the present. Vergil groups it with other great rain mountains of the Balkan Peninsula. "The god himself, either on
Athos or Rhodope or the high Caraunian range strikes with
the flaming bolt." [119]   Athos had one or more altars on its
summit and a bronze statue of Zeus, a local legend of which
still lingers on the promontory.[120]

The weather signs displayed by Mount Athos characterized
other conspicuous peaks rising immediately from the sea, and
hence entitled such mountains to become the abodes of Zeus.
Thessalian Olympos, loftiest mountain of all Greece (9,794
feet or 2,986 m.), lifting its majestic mass above the level
Thessalian plain, was the sacred mountain of Homer's Achæans.
Zeus haunted "the topmost peak of many-ridged Olympos," [121]
where his presence was commemorated by an altar. The elon-
gated massif of Olympos, mantled with snow most of the year
and harboring snow in its gorges till late summer, swept by
storms of rain and sleet frequently in August,[122] deeply impressed the northern Greeks by its beauty and its beneficence
as a source of the life-giving waters. Hence they took the
memory of the Olympian Zeus with them as they migrated east
into Mysia and Bithynia, south into the Peloponnesos, or
across the seas to Lesbos or Cyprus. Wherever they settled,
they installed him on the nearest mountain or high hill, which
they called Olympos, thus conferring his name and sanctity on
twenty or more heights.[123]   The name often survived long
after the altar of the god had been obliterated.

On the Asiatic coast of the Ægean, a like preëminence belonged to Phrygian Ida, the sacred mountain where the native
Trojans established their thundergod and where the Achæan
Zeus also held sway. Rising to a height of 5,480 feet, it
stretches its long ridge east and west across the path of the
Black Sea winds sweeping in from the north, and presents a
broad flank to the rain-bearing winds from the southwest.[124]

It brewed its local thunder-storms in early summer, one of which was violent enough to destroy a detachment of Xerxes' army encamped at the mountain's base.[125]   It abounded in springs and forests and highland pastures,—all evidences of plentiful rain.   Therefore Iris, searching for the father of the gods, "came to many-fountained Ida . . . and found far-seeing Zeus seated on its topmost peak Gargaros, and around him a fragrant cloud was circled like a crown."   There was his "domain and fragrant altar," and there he hid his horse and chariot in a mist.[126]   Throughout the Hellenic and Roman world this peak was "Sacred Ida."   The Dorian Greeks, invading Crete about 1300 B.C., installed their Zeus on the highest mountain of the island, and called it Mount Ida [127] (modern Psilorite Mountain, altitude 8,195 feet or 2,500 meters) ; and far up its slope, at an altitude of 5,055 feet, they made a vast rock-hewn altar to the god at the entrance to a cave.   Altar and grotto, sacred to the Idæan Zeus, remained a sanctuary from the end of the Mycenæan period to Roman times.[128]

Cretan Ida came to be known as a birthplace of Zeus, a distinction attributed to several other peaks ; for mountains, as storm-breeders, became the birthplace and nursery of the rain-god.   The most ancient shrine for the Zeus cult in Crete was a cave on lofty Mount Dikte (altitude 7,170 feet or 2,185 meters), celebrated as the birthplace of the god, and worshipped during all the Minoan periods till the Dorian invasion.[129]   There every ninth year Minos of Cnossus ascended to the sacred grotto to commune with the Diktæan Zeus, while his people waited below ; and there like Moses he received the laws to govern his people, laws which became famous throughout the Ægean world.[130]

An older and more famous sanctuary, reputed to be a birthplace of Zeus by some authorities, and by others the home of his infancy, was Mount Lycæus in southwest Arcadia.[131]   It was called also Olympos and the Sacred Peak (altitude 4,658 feet or 1,420 meters).   On its summit a primitive earthen altar and a never-failing spring, sacred to Zeus, formed a miracle-working shrine for the generation of rain.   Its operation has been described by Pausanias.   "If there is a long drought, and the seeds in the earth and the trees are withering, the priest

of Lycæan Zeus looks to the water and prays; and having
prayed and offered the sacrifice enjoined by custom, he lets
down an oak branch to the surface of the spring, but not deep
into it; and the water being stirred, there rises a mist-like
vapor, and in a little while the vapor becomes a cloud, and
gathering other clouds to itself, it causes rain to fall on the
land of Arcadia." [132] Very ancient traditions point to child
sacrifice in the ritual of the Lycæan Zeus; a passage in Plato's
Republic indicates that the practice had become obsolete in
historical times,[133] though according to Theophrastus in periods of drought the god was appeased by the sacrifice of a
boy as late as the fourth century B.C.[134] Traces of the ancient
altar survive today on the summit of Mount Lycæus in a cone
of ashes and calcined bones of animals.[135]

Zeus as the fertilizing rain is sometimes associated with Hera,
the productive Earth, on these mountain sanctuaries. After
the manner of Baal and the Syrian goddess Ashtaroth, their
marriage is celebrated on these heights, as Homer depicted
their union on Mount Ida; or they have two altars, or preside
over twin heights side by side, as do Jove and Juno in Italy.
This association is very old. On the sacred top of Mount
Helicon, the Muses "with delicate feet dance about the violet-
hued spring and altars of the mighty son of Cronus," where
they celebrate "Ægis-bearing Zeus and majestic Hera." [136]
The marriage was commemorated by Bœotian peasants in the
night festival of the Great Dædala, celebrated every sixty
years on the summit of Mount Cithæron with bon-fires and
sacrifices on the altar of Zeus.[137] The citizens of ill-watered
Argolis, in time of drought, had recourse to the altars of Zeus
and Hera on the summit of Mount Arachnea (3,933 feet, 1,200
meters), where they offered prayers and sacrifices for rain.[138]

The mountain sanctuaries of Zeus the Rain-giver were distributed over the whole Hellenic world from African Cyrene
to the Euxine shores, and from the Cilician Taurus in the east
to Mount Ætna and Agrigentum in the west. The severe
summer droughts which prevailed on the south coast of Asia
Minor gave an impulse to the mountain cult of Zeus. Hence
the Cilician capital of Olba had a temple of Olbian Zeus 6,000
feet up the slope of the Cilician Taurus, where the intrusive

Greek god seems to have usurped the sacred seat of an earlier, native weather god; [139] for even Greek tradition assigned the foundation of the temple to the legendary period. Farther west, Zeus Solymus was enshrined on Mount Solymos, an outlier of the Taurus in Lycia, whence the god looked down on the Greek maritime colonies of Olympos and Phaselis at his feet.[140] The city of Mylasa in Caria had a temple precinct with fountain and plane-tree grove sacred to Zeus Labrandeus, located up on a spur of Mount Latmus, seven miles from the city, with which it was connected by a Sacred Way for the passage of processions and votaries.[141] Here, too, as we have seen, Zeus occupied the throne of an earlier Hittite thunder-god and appropriated his *bi-pennis* sceptre.

Zeus had his high-places also in Lydia and Mysia, where the parallel rift valleys with their broad silted floors were devoted to tillage and hence needed the favors of the rain-god for their vineyards, olive and fig orchards during the three months' drought. Ephesos and the Cayster River plain had their sacred Mount Coressus with its altar and throne of Zeus; [142] Sardis and the Hermus River valley had a Birthplace of Zeus, probably located on the culminating peak of the Tmolus range, which rose as a bold gneiss pyramid to the height of 6,888 feet (2,100 m.) immediately south of the ancient Lydian capital; [143] the fertile Caicus valley had its vast altar of Zeus on the lofty acropolis of Pergamum, 1,000 feet above the sea and under the open sky; while the Trojans looked to the altar of Zeus on "the topmost peak" of Mount Ida, where Hector of Troy used to sacrifice.

In the Greek peninsula, the mountain cult of Zeus assumes great importance on the arid Ægean side, which lies in the rain-shadow of the western mountains, and was also the region of dense populations and big cities. The mountain shrines of the rain-god found on the western side of the peninsula, apart from the old Pelasgic sanctuary at Dodona, were located chiefly south of the Gulf of Ambracia (Arta), which marks the northern limit of very dry summers.[144] The island of Cephallenia, lying well within this drought belt, had a shrine to Zeus Ænesius on the summit of Mount Ænus (5,310 feet or 1,620 meters), the highest peak of the Ionian Isles.[145]

Today the spot is marked by a stone pyramid, surrounded by calcined bones of ancient sacrifices. Farther south, the rich agricultural land of Messenia looked for its gifts of rain to the altar of Zeus Ithomatus on the top of Mount Ithome, whither the migrating Dorians had brought him from an earlier seat on Thessalian Ithome. On the lofty summit of the Taygetos range (altitude 7,905 feet), intercepting the western winds on their passage across the Peloponnesos, dwelt the ancient Zeus of the Pelasgi, demanding human sacrifices like him of Mount Lycæus and Ithome.[146] The altar found there by Pausanias was sacred to Helios, but the rain-making ceremonies conducted on this mountain from ancient times to the present clearly point to Zeus.[147] Even the Olympian Games in honor of Zeus, though celebrated in the level plain of Elis, seem to have been localized there by an earlier hill-top worship of Cronus on Mount Cronius (405 feet), on the summit of which sacrifices were regularly offered at the vernal equinox.[148]

On the eastern front of the Greek peninsula the Zeus sanctuaries multiply. Argolis, lying within the rain-shadow of the Peloponnesian highlands and receiving only about 15 inches of rain annually, provided itself with mountain shrines in every part of its territory.[149] Argos itself, "thirsty Argos," had an altar of Rainy Zeus in the lower town; and on the Larisa, an acropolis rising 950 feet above the city proper, they built the temple of the Larisian Zeus, and below it on the slope a sanctuary of Hera of the Height.[150] Twelve miles north of Argos, on the highest point of the route from Mycenæ to Corinth, was the valley of Nemea (1,200 feet) with its temple of Nemean Zeus,[151] its sacred cypress grove and fountain, which constituted the national sanctuary of all the Peloponnesian Greeks, and the biennial scene of the Nemean Games in honor of Zeus. An ancient high-place of tradition seems to have localized the famous sanctuary[152] in the "well-watered" Nemean valley, as Theocritus describes it, where rivulets flowing down from the surrounding mountains may have been interpreted as favors of the Watery Zeus.[153]

Attica's meager rainfall of 16 inches (408 mm.) accounts for the numerous shrines of Zeus which capped the rocky peaks rising from the Cephisos plain,[154] while Mount Olympos

(1,600 feet) near the southern end of the Attic peninsula suggests another hill-top altar of the god. Bœotia, which comprised the best arable land in all Hellas, looked to the Rain-giving Zeus to help its tillage. Besides the altars of the god on Mount Helicon and Cithæron, it had a temple and statue of the Supreme Zeus on the top of Mount Hypatos (2,434 feet high) above the town of Glisas; an image of the Chæronean Zeus on the summit of the crag Petrachus above Chæronea; [155] and most famous of all, an altar with a sacred grotto and wonder-working spring located on Mount Laphystion (2,940 feet or 896 meters) near Lebadea or Coronea.[156] This cult, which was probably as ancient as Orchomenus, involved human sacrifices when the deadly sequence of drought, crop failure, and famine visited the land of Bœotia. In one such period of disaster, Athamas, a legendary king of Bœotia, was ordered by the Delphic oracle to sacrifice his children to Zeus. He had placed the boy Phryxos on the altar, when their mother Nephele ("Cloud") seized both children and set them on a golden ram, which flew away with them.[157] Here a ram was substituted for the human victim, as in the Semitic myth of Isaac.

Thessaly, though located farther north than Hellas, nevertheless was surrounded by mountains which tended to exclude the rains from its fertile lake plains. Therefore it had many sacred peaks capped with shrines.[158] A famous altar of Zeus crowned Mount Pelion, whose clouds were a weather-gage for all Thessaly.[159] This lofty massif (5,350 feet, 1,631 meters), rising from the Ægean coast, at times bred violent thunder storms and torrential rains, as it did in the midsummer of 480 B.C. when a tempest shattered the Persian fleet stationed off its base.[160] Therefore at the climax of the summer heat and drought, when the Dog Star rose (July 25), a procession of noble youths, clad as to their shoulders with fleecy sheep-skins, used to ascend through the leafy forests of Pelion to the altar of Zeus on its summit, and there offer sacrifices for rain.[161] Here we have another of those dramatized prayers. The white fleeces on the boys' shoulders represented the clouds which they hoped might gather on the mountain and bring the wished-for showers. Their purpose was scarcely protection against the

cold, as Leake suggests,[162] because the midsummer temperature
on Pelion would necessitate no such covering.

The islands of the Ægean Sea lie for the most part south of
the 40th parallel, in the region of almost rainless summers.
They therefore cherished the cult of the mountain Zeus, especially since their small area limited their water supply to the
rain which their mountains collected from the passing clouds.
A hill-top cult of Zeus is suggested for Lesbos by the presence
of a Mount Olympos there. The long mountain backbone of
Eubœa, which offered weather signs to Hellas,[163] had two
peaks consecrated to the rain-god. A possible doubt exists
in the case of Mount Ocha at the southern end of the island,[164]
which rises boldly from the sea to a height of 5,265 feet (1,604
meters); but the lofty Cenæum promontory at the northwest
extremity of the island had its altar and sacred grove of Zeus
Cenæus, which were consecrated by Heracles.[165] The Zeus cult
on Cos reveals the rain-bringing character of the god. The
islands of Minos were suffering from prolonged heat and
drought, when Aristæus, herd or tillage god, went to Cos and
there built an altar to Zeus Ikmaius (the Moistener) on a hill
and sacrificed to Sirius to avert the evil. "The priests of Cos
today sacrifice to Zeus just before Sirius rises," recalling the
cult on Mount Pelion.[166] Delos, though consecrated to Apollo,
had a temple of Zeus on Mount Cynthos (350 feet), "the
Cynthian rock with lofty horn," [167] highest point of the island.
Crete had not only its Idæan and Dictean Zeus, but also a temple of the latter on the citadel of the city of Præsus,[168] located
on the eastern end of Mount Dicte at 2,466 feet elevation.

MOUNTAIN CULT OF SAINT ELIAS—Many mountains once
sacred to Zeus now bear the name of Hagios Elias, or are
dedicated to that saint, whose chapel is generally perched on
the summit near the site of the old Zeus altar or shrine. The
connection is plain. Elias of Ilias, the prophet of Mount
Carmel, is the rain-giving saint of the Greek Catholic Church;
he has assumed the functions of Zeus and appropriated his
cloudy hill stations, for the office of rain-maker in this arid
region was so important that it had to be perpetuated in the
Christian hagiology. The saint's day of Elias is July 20th,
which nearly coincides with July 25th, when Sirius ushered

in the Dog days for the ancient Hellenes, and timed the processions ascending Mount Lycæus and Mount Pelion to implore Zeus to mitigate the summer drought. Numerous heights, which have lost all record or tradition of a Zeus cult, retain folk customs and Elias festivals which indicate the persistent power of the rain god.

The Hagios Elias peak (9,758 feet) of Mount Olympos in Thessaly is marked by a rude stone chapel, to which the monks of the monastery of Saint Dionysius, located in a ravine below, ascend in a procession by torch-light on the night of July 20th, and there say a mass.[169] In Messenia the monks of Saint Basil lead a procession of worshippers with offerings of cattle, sheep and goats up to the summit of Mount Ithome on August 12th to celebrate the Assumption of the Virgin. The date of the feast, August 15th, and its reported origin connect it with prayers to avert hail storms from vineyards and orchards just before the fruit harvest;[170] and suggest that it may be a survival of old appeals to the Ithomæan Zeus, like those which ascended to Jupiter at the *Vinalia rustica* on August 19th for good weather for the swelling grapes.[171] On the loftiest peak of East Helicon (5,010 feet), near the famous spring of Hippocrene, is a half-ruined chapel of Hagios Elias, apparently built of polygonal blocks from the enclosing walls of the ancient Zeus sanctuary.[172]

Saint Elias has succeeded Helios on Mt. Taletus, the highest summit of the Taygetos range (Mount Hagios Elias, 7,905 feet); but the modern procession of peasants up this peak at dusk, the huge bonfire on the summit visible from afar, and the incense cast into the flames as offerings to the saint[173] vividly recall the leading features of the Great Dædala, celebrated on the top of Cithæron to commemorate the marriage of Zeus and Hera. Pausanias, describing this festival with the vast wooden altar piled with burning brushwood, comments,— "I know of no blaze that rises so high and is seen so far."[174] Especially the date of the modern festival, July 20th, points to the survival of an old Zeus cult. Helios, who was a very ancient local god in the Peloponnesos, had like Zeus power over thunder-storms and tempests;[175] hence he may have been worshipped with similar rites. The identification of Saint Elias

with the sun-god, based on the resemblance of their names,
Helias and Helios, and the common feature of the fire-chariot
in the two myths,[176] is not convincing, because of the antagonis-
tic functions of the two divinities. The Saint is a useful
agent and therefore popular with the people during droughts,
so his little white chapel caps nearly every hill or mountain
top; whereas Helios had scant vogue as a deity in Greece,
where the sunshine was all too fervid and abundant. Moreover, only on Taletus and the acropolis of Acro-Corinth did
his altar occupy a conspicuous summit.[177] In contrast, the
Elias peaks are innumerable; in many instances they are clearly
identified with old Zeus sanctuaries, in others less obviously so.

These mountains of Elias multiply on the rugged islands of
the Ægean, where small area, rapid run-off and southern location combine to limit the water supply. Usually the highest
peak is dedicated to the saint, as on the volcanic islands of
Melos (2,526 feet), Santorin or Thera (1,887 feet), all three
of which must occasionally import water because the rainfall
is scant and the cisterns are inadequate.[178] Here if anywhere
prayers to Elias or Zeus would be in order. Sometimes the
Elias summit is the second highest of the island, as on Samothrace and Rhodes, where Mount Atabyrios retains its ancient name. Lesbos has two mounts of St. Elias, one identified
with the old Mount Olympos in the south, and a second in the
north. Others are found today in Thasos, Imbros, Chios,
Psara, Samos, and Patmos. In the Cyclades they are numerous. These link up with one Mount Hagios Elias on Ægina,
identical with the sacred high-place of Zeus, another in Salamis,
and another in southern Eubœa, identical with the ancient
Mons Ocha (5,265 feet) where the Saint's chapel lies near ancient ruins surmised to be a sanctuary of Zeus. In the islands
of the Ionian Sea, Saint Elias is established only on a secondary peak of the island of Levkas, which Döepfeld has identified
with the Ithaka of Ulysses. This hill-top worship of Elias
is explained by naïve Greek folk tales, which account for the
saint's own predilection for these lofty sites.

MOUNTAIN CULT OF JUPITER—The cult sites of Jupiter,
whether groves, altars or temples, point to the primitive worship of the god for the most part on the high places in Rome

as in all Italy, in pre-Roman and in Roman times.[179]   Jupiter
and Juno were described by the terms *Acræus* and *Acrea*,
"dwellers on the heights," Livy says, because their temples
stood on hills and mountains.[180]   Furthermore, the aboriginal
Italian god Saturn, possibly a forerunner of Jove, was associated with the period of the autumn rains as patron of the
sowing; and he too left his name on many hills and high places
of Italy which once bore his shrines.[181]

The earliest Latin sanctuary was that of Jupiter Latiaris,
located in a grove on the summit of *Mons Albanus* (3,115 feet
or 950 meters), the culminating peak of the Alban massif,
which overlooks the plains of Latium.[182]   There the common
festival of the Latin League, the *Feriæ Latinæ*, was annually
celebrated about the end of April, when the winter rains were
diminishing and the dry season approaching with its danger to
pastures and crops.   It was a rustic festival, with offerings
of cheese, sacrifice of a white heifer and libations of milk,
evidence of an early origin among a pastoral people; [183] and it
may have been a preliminary ceremony to the departure of the
flocks and herds to the highland pastures for the summer.
With the establishment of Roman leadership among the Latin
towns, the old cult was revived; a temple of Jupiter Latiaris
was built by a Tarquin king in place of the old shrine, and
became the terminus of the triumphal procession of Roman
victors and the place of sacrifice for every newly elected
consul.[184]

The glimpses which we get of the native gods of the Italian
tribes, before the levelling influence of Roman dominion and
of imported Hellenic deities had obliterated local religious
differentiations, are scant and fragmentary.   Yet they reveal
a mountain cult of Jupiter in the various tribal territories
which in time composed the mosaic state of Rome.   The Sabel-
lian tribe of the Marrucini on the Adriatic celebrated a festival of Jupiter and Juno of Mount Tarincris, possibly a spur
of the Abruzzi.   The Sabines had a mountain god in Jupiter
Cacunus, literally "Jupiter of the peak."   Umbria had its
native Jupiter cult, with official observation of weather conditions, as attested by the famous Tables of Iguvium.[185]   In
Etruria Jupiter, as the successor of the old Etruscan storm-

god Tina, was enthroned in a temple on the high fortress hill of every Etruscan town, where his cult showed close kinship with that of Zeus.[186]

Each Latin town probably had its hill-top shrine of Jupiter, beside the common sanctuary on Mount Albanus. Nearly all the seven hills of Rome were crowned with sanctuaries of Jupiter. Oldest and greatest was that of Jupiter Capitolinus, chief god of the Roman state. It occupied the southern peak of the Capitoline Hill, where Romulus first consecrated the spoils of war on a sacred oak tree and deposited the holy *lapis manalis* or *silex* or thunder-bolt in the little shrine, and where later Augustus built his great temple of Jupiter Capitolinus.[187] On the northern peak was the station of the augurs or *auguraculum*, for the interpretation of the heavenly phenomena by which Jove gave signs of his will. The Capitoline held also a shrine of Jupiter Summanus, god of lightning by night.[188]

Rich soil needed rain for its exploitation. Hence Jupiter Tifatinus, whose temple capped the singular horn-shaped height of Mount Tifata (1,975 feet or 602 meters) near ancient Capua, and Jupiter Vesuvius were doubtless early Campanian deities,[189] though they cannot escape the suspicion of a Greek origin in the Hellenic colonies on the Neapolitan coast. Ætnean Zeus, whose glory Pindar sang, was transmuted into the Ætnean Jove, in whose honor the Roman Senate caused altars to be erected.[190] Likewise the temple of Zeus Atabyrius, built by Rhodian colonists on the high citadel of Acragas in Sicily,[191] became the sanctuary of Jove of Agrigentum, when Sicily was incorporated in the Roman dominion. The Hellenization of Roman religion after the conquest of Greek Sicily possibly intensified the native bent of the Romans to enthrone their chief god on the heights, in imitation of the Zeus cult; for Roman frontiersmen of the Empire established a Jupiter Culminalis on some peak in the Danube country of Pannonia, and a *Jupiter Deus Pœninus* on the Great St. Bernard Pass in the Pennine Alps.[192] Even the little hill overlooking ancient Barcelona (Barcino) was sanctified as *Mons Jovis*, sacred to Jupiter.[193]

Thus the most high god, high both in a physical and a religious sense, recurs in all the Mediterranean lands which belong to the climatic region of winter rains and summer droughts, and to the physiographic region of young folded or block mountains rising from the blue waters of the *Mare Internum.*

AUTHORITIES—CHAPTER XVIII

1. E. Huntington, *Palestine and Its Transformation,* Table of rainfall, p. 425. Boston, 1911.
2. Hann, *Klimatologie,* Vol. III, p. 174. Stuttgart, 1911.
3. G. Hildebrand, *Cyrenaika,* pp. 210-212. Bonn, 1904.
4. Hann, *op. cit.,* Vol. III, p. 161.
5. W. Deecke, *Italy,* p. 82. 1904.
6. Hann, *op. cit.,* Vol. III, pp. 95-96, 166.
7. *Genesis,* XII, 10; XVI, 1; XLI, 54-57; LVII, 4, 13.
8. A. H. Sayce, *The Hittites,* p. 38. London, 1890.
9. II *Samuel,* XXI, 1-14.
10. Josephus, *Antiquities of the Jews,* Bk. VII, Chap. 12, 1.
11. I *Kings,* XVII, 1-10; XVIII, 1-5, 19-45.
12. Josephus, *op. cit.,* Bk. VIII, Chap. 13, 2.
13. *Jeremiah,* III, 3; XIV, 1-6.
14. *Joel,* I, 4-20; II, 19-25.
15. *Haggai,* I, 10-11.
16. Josephus, *op. cit.,* Bk. XV, Chap. IX, 1-2.
17. *Acts of the Apostles,* XI, 28. Josephus, *op. cit.,* Bk. IV, Chap. XV, 3; Bk. XX, Chap. II, 5.
18. Diodorus Siculus, I, 2.
19. *Ibid.,* IV, 60-61. Pausanias, Bk. I, Chap. XLIV, 13; Bk. II, Chap. XXIX, 6.
20. Keightley, *Mythology of Ancient Greece and Rome,* p. 294. London, 1896.
21. Vergil, *Æneid,* III, 141-142.
22. Apollonius Rhodius, II, 515. Translated by Arthur Way. London, 1901.
23. Herodotus, IV, 151.
24. Plutarch, *Pericles,* 37.
25. Strabo, VII, Chap. IV, 6.
26. Aristotle, *Economics,* II, 34.
27. Pauly-Wissowa, *Real-Ency.* Article *Frumentum.*
28. A. Philippson, *Das Mittelmeergebiet,* p. 104. Leipzig, 1907.
29. Herodotus, I, 94.
30. Quoted by Strabo, Bk. I, Chap. III, 4.
31. Livy, II, 34.
32. Livy, IV, 12.
33. Livy, IV, 30.
34. Livy, L, 29.
35. Dio Cassius, *Historia Romæ,* LV, 22, 26, 27, 31, 33.

36. Tacitus, *Annales*, XII, 43. Suetonius, Claudius, 18.
37. B. King and T. Okey, *Italy Today*, p. 178. London, 1901.
38. *Genesis*, IX, 13-14. *Exodus*, IX, 23-24. *Job*, XXVIII, 25-26. .*Isaiah*, XXX, 30; XLI, 17-20. *Psalms*, XXIX, 3-10; XVIII, 8-15; XLII, 7; LXV, 7-13. *Zech.*, X, 1.
39. *Isaiah*, XIX, 1.
40. *Job*, V, 10.
41. *Isaiah*, XL, 7.
42. *Amos*, IV, 7.
43. *Joel*, II, 23-24.
44. *Isaiah*, LIII, 20.
45. I *Samuel*, XII, 17-18. *Exodus*, XVII, 6. *Numbers*, XX, 8-11. I *Kings*, XVII, 1-14; XVIII, 1-5, 19-45. II *Kings*, I, 10-14; II, 14, 19-22.
46. II *Kings*, III, 6-20.
47. Josephus, *op. cit.*, Bk. IX, Chap. III, 1-2.
48. *Isaiah*, XXVII, 8; L, 7. *Hosea*, XII, 1; XIII, 15. *Habakkuk*, I, 9.
49. Josephus, *op. cit.*, Bk. VII, Chap. XII, 1; II *Samuel*, XXI, 1-14.
50. Cheyne and Black, *Biblical Ency.*, Article, "Jahveh."
51. I *Kings*, XVIII, 19-24. Josephus, *op. cit.*, Bk. VIII, Chap. XIII, 2.
52. *Hosea*, II, 5-17; *Ezekiel*, XVI, 19.
53. G. Adam Smith, *Historical Geography of the Holy Land*, p. 474. London, 1910. Hastings, *Ency. of Religion and Ethics*, article, "Baal of Springs." Edinburgh, 1909.
54. *Hosea*, IX, 9, 10; *Numbers*, XXV, 2-18.
55. Garstang, *The Land of the Hittites*, pp. 237, 291-292. New York, 1910. E. Meyer, *Geschichte des Alterthums*, p. 636. Stuttgart, 1909.
56. W. H. Roscher, *Lexikon der Griechischen und Römischen Mythologie*, article, "Labrandeus."
57. Plutarch, *Quæstiones Physicales*, II, IV, XIV. Theophrastus, *De Historia Plantarum*, VIII, Chap. VI, 6.
58. Pindar, Olympic Ode, IV, 1.
59. *Odyssey*, I, 63. *Iliad*, II, 411; XII, 24; XVI, 296. Hesiod, *Theogony*, 71.
60. *Iliad*, XVI, 362-364.
61. *Iliad*, XI, 25; *Odyssey*, XV, 295. Apollonius Rhodius, II, 515-527.
62. Aristophanes, *The Clouds*, 365-398.
63. *Iliad*, XIV, 347-351.
64. Pausanias, I, Chap. XXIV, 3.
65. Marcus Aurelius, V, 7.
66. Strabo, IX, Chap. II, 11.
67. A. Philippson, *Thessalien und Epirus*, pp. 201-205. Berlin, 1897. Leake, *Travels in Northern Greece*, Vol. I, 268; Vol. IV, 198. London, 1835.
68. Theophrastus, *De Signis Tempestatis*, 21.
69. Aristophanes, *The Clouds*, 365.
70. Herodotus, VII, 197. Pausanias, II, Chap. XXV, 10; Chap. XXIX, 7; Bk. VIII, Chap. II, 2-3. Apollonius Rhodius, II, 515-527. Translated by Arthur Way. London, 1901.
71. Diodorus Siculus, V, 55. Strabo, X, Chap. III, 7, 19; XIX, Chap. II, 7.

72. Livius, *Historiæ, passim.*
73. W. H. Roscher, *Lexikon der Griechischen und Römischen Mythologie,* Vol. II, Part I, pp. 645-646. Leipzig, 1897. Vergil, *Æneid,* V, 150.
74. Livy, V, 31.
75. Roscher, *op. cit.,* Vol. II, Part I, pp. 628, 634.
76. Georg Wissowa, *Religion und Kultus der Römer,* pp. 120-122. Munich, 1912. *The Golden Bough,* Part I, Vol. II, p. 183. London, 1913.
77. Plato, *Laws,* Bk. VI, 8.
78. Vergil, Georgics, II, 419.
79. Vergil, Georgics, III, 332.
80. Columella, *Carmen Hortorum,* 52; Varro, *Rerum Rusticarum,* Introduction.
81. Petronius, 44.
82. Diodorus Sic., XX, 14. *Deuteronomy,* XII, 31; XVIII, 9-12.
83. Diodorus Sic., II, 8. Vergil, *Æneid,* IV, 198-210. Herodotus, I, 181. Pauly-Wissowa, *op. cit.,* article, "Baal Hammon."
84. C. F. Kent, *Biblical Geography and History,* pp. 88-95. New York, 1911.
85. Herodotus, I, 131.
86. *Deuteronomy,* XII, 2. I *Kings,* III, 2-5; XII, 28-33; XIII, 32; XIV, 23; XV, 13-14.
87. Pauly-Wissowa, *Real-Ency.,* article, "Balcaranensis."
88. I *Kings,* XX, 23, 28.
89. *Genesis,* XXVIII, 16-19; XXXV, 7, 14. II *Kings,* XXIII, 15. *Amos,* VII, 13.
90. II *Kings,* XXIII, 13.
91. *Joshua,* VIII, 30.
92. *Psalms,* LXXXIX, 12.
93. II *Samuel,* V, 20; *Isaiah,* XXVIII, 21.
94. I *Samuel,* IX, 12-14.
95. G. Adam Smith, *Historical Geography of the Holy Land,* pp. 338-340. London, 1906. *Amos,* I, 2.
96. I *Kings,* XVII, 1-14; XVIII, 1-5, 19-45.
97. Tacitus, *Annales,* II, 78.
98. *Numbers,* XXV, 3-5, 18.
99. *Isaiah,* XV, 1; *Numbers,* XXI, 28.
100. *Judges,* XI, 11, 29; XX, 1.
101. Libbey and Hoskins, *The Jordan Valley and Beyond,* Vol. II, pp. 171-180.
102. *Psalms,* XCVIII, 12; CXXXIII, 3.
103. *Judges,* III, 3; I *Chronicles,* V, 23; *Deuteronomy,* XXXIII, 2.
104. W. Sievers, *Asien,* pp. 69-70. Leipzig, 1893.
105. *Exodus,* Chaps. XIX, XX, XXIV.
106. Sir Wm. Willcocks, *From the Garden of Eden to the Crossing of Jordan.* Cairo, 1918.
107. *Psalms,* LXVIII, 16; CXXXIII, 13.
108. I *Kings,* VIII, 1; *Amos,* IV, 13; *Isaiah,* XXX, 25; *Isaiah,* XIV, 14.
109. F. B. Farnell, *Cults of the Greek States,* Vol. I, pp. 50-51. Oxford, 1896.
110. Pindar, Olympic Odes, IV, 1.
111. A. B. Cook, *Zeus,* Vol. I, pp. 124-148. Cambridge, 1914.

112. M. M. P. Nilsson, *Griechische Feste von religioser Bedeutung*, pp. 1-3. Leipzig, 1906.
113. Theophrastus, *De Signis Tempestatis*, I, 3.
114. E. Reclus, *Europe*, Vol. I, p. 398.
115. Theophrastus, *De Sig.*, I, 24.
116. Pausanias, II, Chap. XXIX, 7.
117. Theophrastus, *De Sig.*, I, 20, 24; III, 43, 47. Pausanias, I, Chap. XXXII, 2. Aristophanes, *The Clouds*, 824.
118. Sophocles, *Fragment*, 229. Tozer, *Islands of the Ægean*, p. 240. Oxford, 1890. Theophrastus, *De Sig.*, II, 34, 35; III, 43, 51.
119. Vergil, Georgic I, 331-332.
120. Solinus, *Collectonea Rerum Memorabilium*, XI, 33. Tozer, *The Highlands of Turkey*, Vol. I, p. 102. London, 1869. A. B. Cook, *Zeus*, Vol. I, p. 121. Cambridge, 1914.
121. *Iliad*, V, 749-752; *Iliad*, I, 498-499; X, 76.
122. Tozer, *The Highlands of Turkey*, Vol. II, pp. 11, 18, 26. London, 1869.
123. Gilbert Murray, *Four Stages of Greek Religion*, pp. 63-64. London, 1912.
124. E. Banse, *Die Turkei*, pp. 65, 68. Berlin, 1919.
125. Herodotus, VII, 42.
126. *Iliad*, XV, 151-153; XIV, 158; VIII, 46-50.
127. Polybius, XXVII, 16; XXVIII, 14.
128. Vergil, *Æneid*, XII, 412. Ovid, *Metamorphoses*, IV, 293. A. B. Cook, *Zeus*, Vol. I, pp. 148-154. Cambridge, 1914.
129. R. M. Burrows, *Discoveries in Crete*, pp. 24-25, 116. New York, 1907.
130. Strabo, X, Chap. IV, 8, 19; XVI, Chap. II, 38. *Odyssey*, XIX, 178.
131. Strabo, VIII, Chap. III, 22; Chap. VIII, 2.
132. Pausanias, VIII, Chap. XXXVIII, 3-4, 7.
133. Pausanias, VIII, Chap. II, 2-3. Plato, *Republic*, VIII, 16.
134. Quoted in Pliny, *Historia Naturalis*, VIII, 81-82.
135. Baedeker, *Greece*, p. 391. 1909.
136. Hesiod, *Theogony*, 1-12.
137. Pausanias, IX, Chap. III, 2-8.
138. Pausanias, II, Chap. XXV, 10. Plutarch, *Aristides*, 11.
139. Strabo, XIV, Chap. V, 10. Frazer, *op. cit.*, Vol. V, pp. 148, 151-155.
140. Strabo, XIV, Chap. III, 9.
141. Herodotus, V, 119. Strabo, XIV, Chap. II, 23.
142. A. B. Cook, *Zeus*, Vol. I, pp. 134, 140-141. Cambridge, 1914.
143. E. Banse, *Die Turkei*, p. 140. Berlin, 1916.
144. Philippson, *Das Mittelmeergebiet*, Map IV, Table 12. Leipzig, 1907.
145. Strabo, X, Chap. II, 15. Baedeker, *Greece*, p. 272. 1909.
146. Ernst Curtius, *History of Greece*, Vol. I, p. 229. Translated from German. New York, 1867.
147. Pausanias, III, Chap. XX, 5.
148. Pausanias, V, Chap. VII, 4; VI, Chap. XX, 1. Frazer, *op. cit.*, Vol. IX, p. 354.
149. Pausanias, II, Chap. XXXVI, 1; Chap. XXV, 8.
150. Pausanias, II, Chap. XXIV, 1-4.
151. Strabo, VIII, Chap. VI, 19.
152. Pausanias, II, Chap. XV, 3.

153. Theocritus, XXV, 182.
154. Pausanias, I, Chap. XXXII, 1-2.
155. Pausanias, IX, Chap. XIX, 3; Chap. XLI, 3.
156. Herodotus, VII, 197. Plinius, XXXI, Chap. II. Pausanias, IX, Chap. XXXIV, 4.
157. Keightley, *Mythology of Ancient Greece and Rome*, p. 294. London, 1896.
158. Bursian, *Geographie von Griechenland*, Vol. I, p. 40. Leipzig, 1862.
159. Theophrastus, *De Sig.*, I, 22.
160. Herodotus, VIII, 12.
161. Dicæarchus, quoted in Frazer, Pausanias, Introduction, Vol. I, p. XLVII.
162. Leake, *Travels in Northern Greece*, Vol. IV, pp. 384-385. London, 1835.
163. Theophrastus, *De Sig.*, I, 22.
164. Neumann and Partsch, *Physikalische Geographie von Griechenland*, pp. 78-79. Breslau, 1885.
165. Homeric Hymn to Apollo, 219. Sophocles, *Trachiniæ*, 238, 752-754, 760-762, 993.
166. Apollonius Rhodius, Bk. II, 515-527. Translated by Arthur Way. London, 1901.
167. Aristophanes, *The Clouds*, 596.
168. Strabo, X, Chap. IV, 6, 12.
169. Tozer, *The Highlands of Turkey*, Vol. II, pp. 23-26. London, 1869.
170. Mary Hamilton, *Greek Saints and Their Festivals*, pp. 170-173. London, 1910.
171. Georg Wissowa, *op. cit.*, p. 101. Munich, 1902.
172. Baedeker, *Greece*, pp. 163-164. Leipzig, 1909.
173. A. B. Cook, *Zeus*, Vol. I, pp. 179-180. Cambridge, 1914.
174. Pausanias, IX, Chap. III, 2-4.
175. Pauly-Wissowa, *op. cit.*, article Helios.
176. Mary Hamilton, *op. cit.*, pp. 20-24. Tozer, *Islands of the Ægean*, pp. 126-127. Oxford, 1890.
177. Pauly-Wissowa, *op. cit.*, article Helios.
178. Tozer, *Islands of the Ægean*, pp. 96-98. Oxford, 1890.
179. Georg Wissowa, *op. cit.*, p. 116. 1912.
180. Livy, XXXII, 23; XXXVIII, 2.
181. Frazer, *op. cit.*, Vol. IX, p. 307.
182. Livy, I, 31; V, 31; XXI, 29.
183. W. W. Fowler, *Roman Festivals of the Republic*, pp. 95-97. London, 1908.
184. Livy, XXII, 1.
185. W. H. Roscher, *Lexikon der Griechischen und Römischen Mythologie*, Vol. II, Part I, p. 637-8. Leipzig, 1897.
186. W. H. Roscher, *op. cit.*, Vol. II, Part I, p. 628-630.
187. Georg Wissowa, *op. cit.*, p. 117. 1912.
188. Georg Wissowa, *op. cit.*, pp. 124-125. Munich, 1912.
189. *Ibid.*, p. 116, note 5.
190. Diodorus Siculus, XXXIV, 10.
191. Polybius, IX, 27.
192. Georg Wissowa, *op. cit.*, p. 116, note 5. Munich, 1912.
193. Pomponius Mela, II, 89-90.

CHAPTER XIX

CLIMATIC FACTORS IN SETTLEMENT AND WATER SUPPLY

The long summer drought made the presence of water a compelling factor in the distribution of the ancient rural population and in the size of the agricultural villages. As to the facts, history gives us scant information. The location of farms or the problems of peasant hamlets afforded no worthy theme for monument or inscription. From the influence of geographic conditions upon the present distribution of rural population, however, and from some scant negative evidence of antiquity, it is possible in a tentative way to reconstruct the ancient agrarian settlements.

WATER SUPPLY AND DISTRIBUTION OF SETTLEMENT—Climatic conditions, expressed in the rarity of a reliable supply of drinking water, forbade in general the isolated farm, just as they do today, except on the northern mountain rim of the Mediterranean Basin. This climatic inhibition was undoubtedly reinforced by the danger incident to life in remote spots, owing to rudimentary police systems and the imminence of attack in a military age. The local water supply was the dominant consideration, however; it determined both the size and location of the agricultural community, because irrigation was a factor in local production. Since unfailing streams were scarce, perennial springs or wells were essential. Where these were numerous, the villages could be numerous and small; population could be broken up into small groups, with their farm lands conveniently near. But where the springs were more sparsely scattered, population had to concentrate about them in fewer but larger groups, no matter how far might be the way from the home village to the outlying fields. Therefore the dry, porous limestone was likely to show a few large settlements; while the shales, sandstones, clays, and volcanic soils would show many small hamlets. The longer the summer

drought and the dryer the land, as found in the semi-arid east
and south of the basin, the sparser the villages in general.
But on alluvial plains with plenty of ground water accessible
through wells, or piedmont slopes blessed with rare perennial
streams, the abundance of fertile moist soil and of the life-giving water made the conditions for the numerous small villages.[1]
Such villages were strewn over the Nile flood plain, the Bœotian
Lake plain, in the Po valley, Etruria and Campania.

Ancient settlements had a linear arrangement along the eastern and western base of the Judean Plateau, where the springs
from this limestone highland burst forth. On the dissected plateau itself, where springs or wells were frequent, the map shows
the villages of northern Judea only five to ten miles apart, in
some cases less. But in Samaria and Galilee, of lower elevation and diminished rainfall, the distance from village to village
increased as it did also in the trans-Jordan district on the high
rim of the Syrian desert. There the canyon streams of the
deeply dissected escarpment offered few village sites accessible
to the water. Therefore settlements were distributed near the
spring heads of the streams, like Rabboth Ammon, Gerasa and
Edrei; or on small tributary wadis less deeply eroded, which
could be dammed for reservoirs. Where both springs and wells
were few or meager, cisterns supplemented the local water
supply.

VALUE OF ELEVATED TOWN SITES—The limited amount of
fertile arable land in the Mediterranean region necessitated, as
has been shown, the careful exploitation of the small alluvial
plains. These had rich, moist soil, and easy conditions for irrigation,—considerations which inevitably attracted population.
The settlements, however, systematically avoided the valley floor
and distributed themselves along the slopes of the enclosing hills
or mountains. These slightly elevated sites escaped the inundations of the valley stream during the winter rains, also in some
degree the mosquitoes and malaria in summer which the ancients
attributed to the mists from the marshes. For this reason Cato
recommended a high, well-drained location for a farm, and
Vitruvius advocated a similar site, "high, away from unhealthy
swamps," as the best for a city.[2] Natural drainage, accessibility to the swift course of stream or aqueduct where the water

was still uncontaminated, and the economy of the level land for tillage were other advantages. To these may be added the possession of an acropolis for defense in time of war. Even the seaports, as we have seen, avoided the river mouths; then veered off to one side where the rock structure of the land met the sea and offered a solid foundation for a settlement and safe anchorage or beach for boats drawn up on shore.

A study of any map of ancient Greece shows this to have been the characteristic distribution of settlement in the katavothra lake basins of Bœotia and Arcadia, in the plain of Macaria in Messenia, the Inachus valley in Argolis, the Marathon and Mesogæa plains of Attica, the Sperchius valley in Æniania and Malis, the Peneus in Thessaly, and the Axius in Macedonia. Wherever a city lay immediately on the lowland course of a river, it occupied some outlying spur of the mountain rim, as in the case of Anticyra on the lower Sperchius or Elis on the Elian Peneus, Athens in the Cephisos plain and Larisa on the Thessalian Peneus. It is interesting to compare a modern contour map of western Thessaly with a map of the ancient settlements and see how the towns, from the Homeric age onward, invariably clung to the slopes of the hills encircling the old lacustrine basin, and had their citadels on the rocky peaks above, whence they overlooked their deep-soiled wheat fields and irrigation ditches below.[3] This was conspicuously the location of Metropolis, Gomphi, Tricca, and Pelinnæum, the famous quadrilateral of strongholds with rocky Ithome "near their center."[4] Ithome occupied a spur of Mount Pindus which jutted out like a promontory into the sea-like level of the old lake plain. Even Piresiæ and Limnæum, located at the gathering of the waters, had their core in detached knobs of the Mount Titanus massif (modern Dobroudcha Dagh) only five miles away, and thus were lifted above the saturated lake plain. Similar was the site of ancient Ambrakia at the eastern end of a limestone ridge, which flanked the big deltaic plain of the Aracthus River. The position is held today by the city of Arta which, from its rocky eminence, surveys its gardens and orchards irrigated by the arms of the river.[5] The ancient roads also skirted the edge of these winter swamp lands, picking their way from town to town along the solid hem of the mountains,

18 *

while the flat plains remained untenanted and untraced except for the footpaths of the peasants going to and from their fields.[6]

Italy possesses geological, geographic and climatic conditions that have encouraged a wider distribution of agricultural towns and villages than was found in ancient Greece. Its extensive deposits of volcanic ash and tufa found in Etruria, Latium and Campania; its relatively large alluvial plains, notably that of the Po valley and Venetian coastland; its ampler rainfall and longer rainy season which insured a longer seasonal life to its rivers and springs, all combined to encourage numerous small agricultural villages or isolated farms in favored districts. From the evidence these seem to have existed in ancient times in the vicinity of large cities, after Roman dominion had brought order and security to the land. Originally clan villages, owning and tilling clan lands, united to form a tribe, and had their communal meeting place in a stronghold on the top of a hill (*capitolium*) where they took refuge with their families and cattle in time of war. The *arx* or stronghold was the nucleus of a town and often developed into a city, but the peasants continued to dwell in their open hamlets, looking to their town as market, voting place, and asylum.[7] Such were the ancient Latin, Sabine and Etruscan towns with their outlying rural hamlets.[8] Nemausus (Nîmes) near the Rhone delta ruled 24 such villages which dotted the fertile land round about.

Most of the towns and villages of modern Italy date back to Roman or pre-Roman times. They indicate that population was not distributed over the whole land, as in England or France, but was confined to choice districts where the people lived in well defined and well defended communes. Rome had to conquer these fortified rural communes and cities before she could extend her dominion over Italy;[9] and she found that this politico-social organization made her task harder. The limestone mountains of the Alps and Apennines, the scattered volcanic masses like the Alban Mountains, and especially the bold river peninsulas flanked by deep gullies cut in the soft volcanic tufa, all furnished rocky citadels for these strongholds. Such was the site of ancient Tibur, on an entrenched meander, or interfluvial Veii.[10] The rural villages persisted, even after the

Roman conquest, owing to the precarious water supply of summer, and gathered their peasant population around the perennial springs and streams. The fact that many rivers even of the northern Apennines run dry in July and August or shrink to a mere trickle indicates how necessary was this precaution.[11]

The rivers which bestowed the benefaction of water in summer for domestic use and irrigation, in spring and autumn threatened the settlements near their banks with inundation. Floods were sudden and violent in these mountain valleys. The swift run-off from the steep slopes, the heavy autumn rains which inaugurated the wet season, the sudden thaw of the snows on the ranges accompanied by the violent storms of February and March, all converted the trickling brook of summer into a raging torrent, tearing away its banks and sweeping with devastating force over the fertile land at the base of the highlands. In the mountains, where the channels were deeply eroded and therefore could carry off a greatly increased volume of water before the flood stage was reached, ancient Italian settlements could approach the river banks. But where these same rivers issued from the mountains and escaped the high banks which there confined them, their swollen current spread out over the coastal plains, and warned the settlements to seek protected sites on hill or eminence withdrawn from the shifting margin of the torrent. Such was the location of Canusium (Canosa) in Apulia. It lay on the slope of a hill at an altitude of 505 feet a mile or more back from the Aufidus River, whose devastating floods, fed by the snows on Monte Vultur (4,365 feet), have through the ages overwhelmed the lowland of Apulia.[12]

The limestone districts and the volcanic tufa have been dissected by the drainage streams, which have cut deep gorges and thus carved out protected town sites, such as were found in southern Etruria and the Sabine country. Ancient Tibur (Tivoli), which long resisted Roman conquest, was located on a limestone hill (760 feet) within a deeply entrenched serpentine or meander of the Anio River, where it was safe from flood and attack. Many ancient Etruscan towns sought protected sites in the salient angles at the confluence of two streams. Ancient Veii, Careiæ, and Falerii occupied such positions on tufa platforms between perpendicular valley walls, which rendered them nearly impregnable.

The Apennines enclose between their folded ranges many broad longitudinal valleys of gentle grade whose outlets were evidently blocked by the crustal movements of the late Pliocene. The drainage streams collected in these lake basins; their waters, being charged with lime from the surrounding strata, deposited travertine in large amounts. This with the detritus from the slopes leveled the valley floor, till the basin was gradually drained by erosion,[13] but the streams have not had sufficient fall to encise themselves deeply into the valley floor. For purposes of settlement, therefore, these valleys resemble alluvial plains and are subject to inundation. Such are the Clanis trough, the modern Valle di Chiana, of eastern Etruria, the Trerus-Liris or Sacco which forms an axis of depression through the length of Latium, and the Umbrian course of the Tiber. In them all the ancient towns and villages, like the modern settlements, scented danger in the low-lying valley floor and sought safety on the lower terraces of the mountains.

PIEDMONT TOWNS AND ROADS—These longitudinal valleys, moreover, were the natural thoroughfares of land communication up and down the Italian peninsula, as is the case in all mountain regions. They were therefore the routes taken by invading armies. Towns situated along them were exposed to attack, and for this reason also were impelled to seek high impregnable situations, which might be the asylum of the agricultural population during time of war. Here two geographic factors operated together to determine the location of the settlement. The motive of military security tended to run the towns higher up the mountains, like a centrifugal force, while the fertility of the lowlands tended to draw them to the lowest site above the plain consistent with safety. Such was the location of Tibur on a rocky peninsula lifted a few hundred feet above the productive plain of the lower course of the Anio. Towns on the great valley thoroughfares tended to scramble up the mountains to safety.[14] Others in secluded and fertile lateral valleys, settled at the foot of the mountain where these shelved off into the plain. Such was the site of the ancient Umbrian Iguvium (Gubbio) in a high lacustrine basin of the upper

Clasius (modern Chiaggio), at the foot of Monte Calvo, with the fruitful fields flush with the lower edge of the town.[15]   In general the original Nolscian, Æquian and Hernician towns had lofty sites and limited development.

Even after Rome had spread her dominion and the Roman peace over the peninsula, the towns and villages adhered to their old sites and later settlements chose similar locations, because inundation still continued and even grew worse owing to the denudation of the forests and the constant deposition of debris at the mouths of the lateral valleys, which dammed up the streams and prepared for wide inundation.   Then entered a new factor.   During the Second Punic War (218 to 204 B.C.) the mosquitoes which infested the marshes of these oft inundated valleys became inoculated with the malaria germ and supplied a fresh motive for population to stick to the well-drained slopes and live above the water-soaked lowlands.

A detailed examination of the distribution of ancient towns in these longitudinal valleys yields the data on which the generalization above is based.   The broad furrow of the Clanis valley, the modern Valle di Chiana, had a slight fall towards the Tiber from the low watershed separating it from the upper Arno, with which it was once connected.   The Clanis River had too weak a current to cut through the alluvial fans thrust out from the lateral tributaries, and therefore must have been converted into swamps for a considerable period of each year. This was its chronic condition from about 1200 to 1700 A.D.[16] The valley formed an important line of communication between the Arno and the Tiber.   Its rich moist soil produced the finest wheat of Italy, according to Pliny.   Such a district inevitably attracted settlement, and in fact it contained three cities of the twelve forming the ancient Etruscan League.   They were Cortona, Clusium and Volsinii (modern Orvieto) all located on the surrounding slopes from 500 to 1,300 feet above the valley floor.   This was the characteristic situation of the Clanis valley towns during the medieval and modern periods,[17] when the swamps had expanded and the whole district was fever-haunted. The ancient highways, like the modern railroads, skirted the valley on either side, keeping to the base of the mountains; the problem of cheap construction and operation, however, force the railroads to maintain a lower level than the ancient highroads. Consequently, the stations lie from one to six miles from the Tuscan hill-towns which the traveller wishes to visit.

Similar conditions held in Umbria in the Tineas-Clitumnus valley (modern Topino and Teverone) which forms the continuation of the longitudinal trough of the upper Tiber. Evidence of its being a lacustrine basin is found in the long survival of Lake Umber near the confluence of the Tineas and the Tiber, and in the well watered meadows of the Clitumnus which pastured famous cattle in ancient times. The towns which exploited the agricultural wealth of the fertile valley,—Asisium (Assisi), Hispellum, Mevania, Fulginium, Trebiæ and Spoletium, all looked down upon it from steep hillsides several hundred feet above the valley floor. The last three towns were connected by the *Via Flaminia*, which skirted the hilly edge of the Clitumnus valley; another road in a similar way traced the high eastern margin of the Tineas plain.[18]

In the longitudinal valley of the Trerus-Liris again the ancient towns warily draw their skirts away from the river as if to keep from getting wet; and again the ancient highway connecting them undulates up and down across the roots of the mountains enclosing the valley on the north. The road is the *Via Latina*, running southeast from Rome to Capua. It follows the northern base of the Alban Mountains and reaching the Trerus valley, it passes through or just below the high piedmont towns of Anagnia (1,510 feet elevation), Ferentinum (1,290 feet), Frusino (955 feet), Fregellæ, Aquinum and Casinum, all three located on low spurs of the Apennines jutting out into the old lake basin of the Liris.[19] Thence it continued south over the watershed and took a similar course through the piedmont cities of the fertile Campanian plain—Teanum Sidicinum, Cales and Casilinum to Capua.

The alluvial coastal plains and deltaic lowlands of Italy showed the same tendency to group their settlements on the piedmont rims, while a few unhealthy ports found a footing on the sand hills that rose above the marshes of the coast. The piedmont road of Campania ran from Capua southeast to Salernum, running through Calatia, Suessula, Nola, Ad Teglanum and Nuceria. All these towns were situated where the mountains joined the plain, and where the drainage streams from the highlands still had enough current to erode steep-sided channels in the volcanic tufa.   The volcanic district encircling the Campanian plain on the south furnished city and villa sites lifted well above the water-soaked plain of the interior, while the rich soil of the Phlegræan Fields attracted settlement to exploit the inexhaustible volcanic soil.   Mount Massicus forming the western border of the Campanian plain was the site of the famous vineyards producing the Massic wine.   From its base to the Save River was the famous Falernian district and to the north about Cales the Calemian, whence the Romans procured their finest wines.[20]   Vineyards point to intensive cultivation and a dense rural population, which probably had their hamlets and farm houses on the neighboring slopes.   The center of the Campanian plain showed only two ancient towns, Acerræ and Atella, both located on a low land-swell which formed the southern rim of the swampy Clanius valley, which here takes a westerly course.

The coastal plain of Latium shows the same distribution of population—towns, villages, and landed estates in a close linear arrangement where lowland and mountain meet, with scattered settlements in the higher land above.   The isolated volcanic mass of the Alban Mountains had its base encircled with a border of towns,[21]—Labicium, Tusculum, Castrimœnium, Bovillæ, Aricia, Corioli, and Velitræ.   But from these mountains to the sea, a distance of ten miles, no settlements broke the solitude except Ostia, Laurentum, Lavinium and Ardea on or near the coast, which Strabo tells us were surrounded by marshes.   The same vacancy marked the *Ager Romanus*, the Roman Campagna, on both sides of the lower Tiber.   Strabo states that Rome was the only city of Latium located directly on the Tiber.[22]   The hilly site of the imperial city lifted it above the river floods, except low-lying parts like the Circus Maximus, which occupied the valley between the Aventine and Palatine Hills.   This was inundated in 363 B.C. and again in 204 B.C. The river got far out of its banks twice in 218 B.C., flooding the neighboring fields, demolishing houses, and sweeping away cattle from the meadows.[23]   For 15 miles above Rome the Tiber valley has been eroded almost to base level.   The river meanders

through a flood plain two or three miles wide but narrowing to
one mile just before it issues upon the Roman depression.   The
hills rise steeply above this flood plain and held on their summits the ancient towns of Antemnæ, now the site of the Fortress
Antenne, Fidenæ (265 feet) which as the ally of Veii long resisted Roman conquest, and the village of Eretum.²⁴   All three
were located on the very ancient *Via Salaria,* which skirted the
river plain, traversed the roots of the hills above the reach of
the floods, and crossed the torrents draining the uplands at the
points where these could be most safely and easily bridged, i.e.,
just before they reached the plain and deposited their burden
of gravel.   Along the western edge of the flood plain, skirting
the western hills, ran the *Via Tiberina* from Rome all the way
to Feronia.   The fertile alluvial plain of the Tiber attracted
agriculture, despite the rush of floods; but the villages were
carefully placed within reach of the fields, above the swollen
waters in a commanding position safe also from hostile attack.

Between the Alban Mountains and the sea the plain of Latium
held no settlements except Ostia, Port of Augustus, Laurentum,
Lavinium, all on or near the coast, all surrounded by marshes
and therefore notoriously unhealthy in ancient as in modern
times.²⁵   Farther south the coast had the important ports of
Antium and Circei, where limestone cliffs emerged from the surrounding alluvium but gave no security from fever.   The level
ill-drained interior held few settlements and none of importance
except the piedmont towns which cling to the slopes of the
Volscian Mountains.   The Appian Way which traversed this
plain "bounds the maritime portion of Latium," Strabo says.
An older or original Appian Way followed the base of the
Volscian Mountains, following approximately the course of the
modern railroad; but the later highway struck out across the
Latium plain from Aricia on the slope of the Alban Mount.²⁶   It
passed through only *Tres Tibernæ,* which is supposed to be the
modern Cisterna, situated on the last hummock of solid ground
above the Pontine Marshes, and *Forum Appii* probably a
local market and stopping place for the boats which passed up
the canal along the Appian Way, from Tarracina.²⁷   The
Pontine Marshes, due to continued subsidence of the shallow
trough at the western foot of the Volscian Mountains, were

temporarily drained by the Censor Appius Claudius in 312 b.c. Reclamation was attempted again in 182 b.c., and yet later by Julius Cæsar and other Emperors. Pliny states that this marshland was once a cultivated plain, occupied by twenty-four villages; but towards the close of the Republic it fell into its present condition owing to the decline of agriculture.[28] The drainage canal of Appius Claudius points to swampy conditions at an earlier date than Pliny assigns, as does also the location of the ancient Volscian towns well up the hillsides. The rain which falls on the limestone surface of the Volscian Mountains issues from their base in countless springs, which owing to inadequate drainage caused swamps in ancient times immediately below the towns of Tarracina, Setia and Cora. Similar conditions east of the mountains compelled the Appian Way, like the modern highroad, to bend inland around the coastal swamps of the famous Cæcubum vine-growing district to Fundi,[29] and thence traversed the lower slopes of the mountains out to the sea at Formiæ.

The plain of the Arnus (Arno) and Anser (Serchio) presented similar conditions. Broken up into a succession of old lake basins in which abundant debris and beds of travertine have been deposited,[30] flooded spring and fall by springs and streams from the northern Apennines, this valley had only its rim dotted with ancient towns, Lucca, Pistoria, Fæsulæ and Florentia, the last situated where the river issues from the mountains upon the plain at an elevation of 180 feet. Pisa located near the ancient mouth of the Arnus was thrust out seaward as far as possible on a spur of solid ground jutting out from the base of Monte Pisani, which rises to the height of 3,010 feet only four miles to the east. The site was recognized as one exposed to possible inundation, but this disadvantage was counterbalanced by the productive hinterland and the maritime activities carried on from the river mouth as a seaport.[31]

The great plain of the Po Basin is so fertile and extensive that ancient settlements could not be restricted to its margin; there, however, they are ranged closely side by side. Moreover, the Po valley, flat as it appears, presents slight variations of relief in its several parts and hydrographic peculiarities which radically influenced the distribution of the ancient population.

The ancient province of Liguria, the modern Piedmont, even in its lowest portions is crossed by offshoots of the Apennines and southern Alps [32] which run out to the banks of the Po and provide good town sites between the drainage streams. In Cispadana Gaul from Placentia eastward, a considerable belt of lowland intervenes between the base of the Apennines and the Po. This is subject to inundation during the heavy autumn rains and again in March, when the streams are swollen by the melting of the snows in the Apennines and by the continuous spring rains. The same is true of the northern slope of the basin, but with this difference, that the water from the Alpine snows is partly taken up by the lakes through which the rivers run. The Apennine streams lack this regulation of their flow; hence they burst out of their mountain valleys in devastating floods, depositing their burden of gravel and silt at the outlets on the level plains, building up alluvial fans, down which they drain in divided channels till they again gather the strands of their braided streams into one channel.

Hence the ancient settlements, whether Umbrian, Etruscan, Gallic or Roman, or all four in succession, were located on the last offshoots of the Apennines,[33] 150 to 200 feet above sea level, usually between these braided streams near the point where their multiple currents reunited to erode a single channel. Along the roots of the mountains they stretched in a long series from Placentia to the Adriatic—Placentia, Fidentia, Palma, Regium, Mutina, Forum Gallorum, Bononia, Claterna, Forum Cornelii, Faventia, Forum Livii, Forum Popilii, Cæsena and Ariminum, where the Apennines reach the sea.

The site of Bologna (Bononia) was typical. It lay on a low spur of the Apennines between the Remus and Idex Rivers, here only six miles apart. The city was 165 feet (55 meters) above sea level; but a half mile from the town wall on the south the hills rise to 500 feet or more, and doubtless in ancient as in modern times were the sites of rich suburban villas.[34] Placentia alone was situated near the Po, because it was established as a military colony in 219 B.C. to command an important passage of the river. The Apennines here bend northward almost to the Po; but five miles west of Placentia the Trebia River, known for its disastrous floods, debouched into the Po and jeopardized

Placentia. Hence drainage canals furrowed the outlet of the river valleys from Placentia to Parma,[35] because the drainage streams here are fed by the heavy precipitation of the Ligurian Apennines. The rivers east of Bononia debouch upon the deltaic plain of the Po and therefore through the ages have caused destructive floods. Hence the line of the ancient Æmilian towns held the narrow middle ground between the flood of the lowlands and the famine of the sterile mountain hinterland. The reclaimed flood plains, though often endangered, yielded rich crops in good years. Irrigated fields during the summer months yielded meadows and pastures.

The *Via Æmilia* built in 187 B.C. was a typical piedmont road, running along the northern base of the Apennines and connecting these towns from Ariminum to Placentia. Thence the Postumian Way in like manner skirted the last low terrace of the Alpine piedmont, running through Cremona and Verona to Vicetia (Vicenza), whence the road bent south into the low Venetian plain, in order to avoid the broad braided streams of the Alpine rivers, here unregulated by any glacial lakes. The road was therefore compelled to take a middle course between the marshes of the coast and the wide multiple flood streams of the alluvial fans in the upper lowland. At Tarvisium (Treviso) it crossed the Plavis (Piave), which has since been deflected farther east and thence ran east near the old coastline to the outpost of Roman rule at Aquileia near the head of the Adriatic. Strabo described this road as running "by the roots of the Alps and encircling the marshes." [36]

The great extent of this north Italian lowland and its ample fertility, praised by Polybius and others, gave rise to widely scattered agricultural villages which are mentioned in connection with most of the large towns of antiquity. Such was Andes, Vergil's birthplace near Mantua, and Vercellæ [37] near which Marius in 101 B.C. defeated the invading Teutons. Water was found everywhere, either in the perennial streams from the Alps, or in the springs issuing below the moraine deposits at the outlets of the Alpine valleys,[38] or in the abundant ground water. Reclamation of flood plains by canals and dykes began at an early date, "after the manner of Lower Egypt," while rivers and ditches provided irrigation for summer crops and water transportation for marketing the harvests. Along the coast sand beaches and dunes afforded sites for fishing and trading towns like Ravenna, Spina, Adria, Altinum and Aquileia, connected by canals with the sea. Ravenna, originally located on a sand beach enclosing the great Laguna south of the Po mouth, was built entirely on piles and traversed by numerous canals which were crossed by bridges or ferry boats. It had the reputation of being a salubrious place because the tides at the head of the Adriatic washed away the sewage.[39]

Along the Mediterranean base of the Ligurian Apennines and Maritime Alps, the drainage streams were so small and swift, that their deeply eroded channels could carry off the flood waters. But even an inconsiderable river like the Varus (Var), which drew the boundary between Italy and Trans-Alpine Gaul, and which though a mere ribbon of water in summer, in winter swelled to the width of seven stadia or four-fifths of a mile,[40] was sufficiently threatening to push the ancient Massiliot Greek colony about 4 miles east of its mouth. On the other hand, the port of Forum Julii (modern Frejus) could take up its position at the mouth of the Argenteus (Argens River), because the stream, draining the low Provence hill country, escaped the floods due to the heavy rains and melting snows of mountain sources. The bold promontories and numerous bays of this coast multiplied sites for seaport towns.

When we come to the delta of the Rhone, we find that the two important seaports of the Sinus Gallicus (Gulf of Lyons), Massilia and Narbo, gave the swampy outlets of this river a wide berth, and took up their positions, one to the east and one to the west. Massilia, Aquæ Sextiæ and Tarascon were all safely ensconced on spurs of the Provence hill ranges protruding into the flood plain of the Rhone. Arelate (Arles) lay at the head of the delta, on the solid ground of a detached Provence hill. The road from Forum Julii and Italy traversed a longitudinal valley through the hills to Aquæ Sextiæ and Arelate, which became a considerable commercial town.[41] It was doubtless the river port for vessels coming up the Canal of Marius from the sea and the point where the native down-stream traffic was transhipped for land transportation to Italy. It is an interesting fact that the road to Spain did not cross the Rhone at

Arelate, but turned north ten miles to Tarusco (Tarascon), where a low ridge of the Provence hills, 16 feet high, runs out west to the river. Here the Rhone, being confined to a narrow channel,[42] offered a shorter passage to Ugernum (Beaucaire) for the ferry-boats, which Strabo tells us were used on these streams. Strabo makes it clear that Tarusco and not Arelate, marked the passage of the Rhone and the junction of the two roads from Italy, the one along the Mediterranean coast and the other across the Cottian Alps by the *Mons Matrona* (Mount Genevre) pass.[43] North of the Tarascon ridge, *les Alpines*, the Durance River brought a vast amount of detritus from the Maritime Alps and therewith built up an alluvial plain constantly subject to devastating floods. Hence the ancient city of Avennio (Avignon) was located about six miles north of the Durance mouth. Arausio, on the other hand, about 20 miles further up stream, was located on a river peninsula where the Alpine platform runs out quite to the Rhone.

West of the Rhone the alluvial plain is broader, unbroken by folded hill ranges; and hence the towns retired further from the river. Namausus (Nîmes) lay 15 miles from the river where a low shelf from the rainy Cevennes highlands runs out eastward into the Rhone alluvium, and affords a city site 154 feet (47 meters) above sea level. The solid margin of this plain was defined on the southwest by Ambrussum, Forum Domitii, the fortified town of Bæterræ (Béziers), located where the little river Orobis (Orob) issues from the Cevennes foothills upon the coastal plain. Mount Setium (Cette) and Agathe (the Cape of Agde), old volcanic islands tied to the mainland by silt, were utilized by Greek colonists from Massilia for dry seaport sites. The road passed through these towns to Narbo, the busiest seaport or emporium of the Roman Province, located at the foot of the Mount Corbières, a northeastern offshoot of the Pyrenees, where this ran out to meet the mouth of the Aude River. The southeast slope of this range held the ancient town of Ruscino near the modern Perpignan on the Tet River, while the northern foothills of the Pyrenees offered a solid foundation to Illiberis (modern Elne) on the River Tech.[44] The ancient road continued south from Narbo, ran along the inner edge of the narrow coastal plain and passed through these towns, but from Illiberis, it led over the Col de Perthus, a deep gap (950 feet elevation) in the Pyrenees, down to Gerunda (modern Gerona) in Spain. The road existed as a rough track, well travelled however, even in 218 B.C., when Hannibal marched over it.[45]

The location of settlement along the Mediterranean front of Spain was determined by a combination of geographic conditions and of motives growing out of the long retarded cultural and economic status of the interior. The protracted survival of intertribal wars among the native stocks and their stubborn resistance to Roman conquest emphasized the need of stronghold sites for their towns. But the generally meager rainfall, both on the Mediterranean coast belt and the highland interior, held the settlements to the water-courses where irrigation might be practised for grain field or vineyard. The prevailing mountain relief of the country offered little arable land accessible to irrigation streams. The best of this was to be found in small alluvial pockets about the mouths of the drainage streams along the Mediterranean coast and in old lacustrine basins between the outer mountain ranges exposed to the rain-bearing winds. But where the stream deposited its silt it also threatened to flood the fields. Therefore, an elevated site for a settlement was imperative; so the towns sought hills or spurs abutting upon the plain for safety.

This was to be found only on the western or inner edge of the coastal plain of Hither Spain, and therefore generally drew the towns a few miles back from the coast—a fortunate circumstance because this coast was for centuries harried by the pirates of the Balearic Islands nearby. As a matter of fact, only the colonies of the Phœnicians, Carthaginians and Greeks, all experts in naval warfare, were located immediately on the coast. For protection against both sea and land attack, these comprised an acropolis, as did Malaca (Malaga) and Hemeroscopium; or they lay at the head of a deep defensible inlet like Carthago Nova, Carteia and Rhoda; or they occupied a fortified island or peninsula like Gades (Cadiz), Calpe (Gibraltar) or Mellaria (Tarifa). Emporiæ was located at first on an island, but after the Greek colonists had established friendly relations with the native population, they moved to the mainland. The fertile alluvial plain of Ampurdan forming its immediate hinterland contributed to the prosperity, especially to its flax culture and linen industry.[46] The ancient Chersonesus [47] (modern Peniscola), 35 miles south of the Ebro mouth had a name and location typically Greek. It was situated on a rocky islet, lifted 220 feet above the waves, and tied to the mainland by a narrow sandy isthmus, a location which in the middle ages gained for this marine stronghold the name of the "Gibraltar of Valencia."

Considerations of defense and tillage determined the location of the ancient Iberian towns and most of the Roman colonies. These lay for the most part on the piedmont where this met the coastal plain, and preferably where it retired several miles from the sea. Where the rocky frame of the peninsula pushed out close to the Mediterranean, as it did between Tarraco (Tarragona) and the boundary of Gaul, the cities arose on their citadel several hundred yards from their port, and only at a later period grew downward to the shore. Such was Tarraco, which began on a steep hill 530 feet high, and nearly a mile from the sea, surrounded by the Cyclopean walls of the native Iberian builders. It was extended when it became the Roman capital of Hither Spain, but always adhered to its lofty site whence it overlooked the fertile plain of Tarraco, with its flax fields, vineyards and orchards irrigated by the waters of the little Tulcis (modern Francoli). The cities of the eastern coastal plain lay on the great north-and-south thoroughfare of Spain, which was traversed by invading barbarians and by the armies of Carthage and Rome. Hence they had an additional motive for protected sites.

North of the Ebro mouth where the mountains border the sea, the drainage streams are short torrents flowing in deep beds, meagerly supplied with water, and hence restricted in their capacity for floods, which were therefore readily controlled by reservoirs and drainage ditches. The *avenidas*, as the spates are called in modern times, were violent but brief. Therefore towns were located with relative impunity near their mouths. But the Sambroca and Rubricatus Rivers (Llobrega), which rise in the rainy Pyrenees and flow through the border ranges to the sea, and hence carry much water in spring and autumn, tolerated no settlements on their lower courses. Emporiæ shied off a few miles from the mouth of the Sambroca (Ter) as did Barcina (Barcelona) from the little delta of the Rubricatus, but each city relied in part for its prosperity upon the productivity of the neighboring river plain. Each river had a flourishing upstream town, Gerunda (615 ft.) and Munorisa (672 ft.) (Manresa) respectively, the latter being the capital of the ancient Iberian Jacetani. The Ebro, draining the southern Pyrenees and Cantabrians, has thrust an extensive delta, dotted with lagoons and netted with sluggish streams, out beyond the regular shoreline. The Roman colony of Dertosa (Tortosa) lay on high ground at the passage of the Ebro,[48] where the river emerged from the mountains. Thence it overlooked the fertile *campus*, whose tillage by irrigation was easy and remunerative.

South of the Ebro, the rainfall along the littoral declines to 19 inches in Valencia and 14 inches in Murcia and is combined with a low humidity (60 to 65 per cent) which causes rapid evaporation. The coast torrents are small; the longer rivers which flow from the arid plateau interior draw thence a meager tribute of water. Irrigation was imperative. The short-lived floods of the coast torrents were doubtless controlled by drawing off their surplus water into the irrigation ditches and reservoirs. The towns, with few exceptions, adhered to hill sites well above the streams and back from the coast. Such was the location of Saguntum on the Pallantias, and Ilice (Elche) on the Vinatapo, both six miles from the sea. The Roman colony of Valentia lay directly on the Turia or Quadalaviar, two miles from its mouth. The Jucar River (ancient Sucro) which gathers in its waters from the central highlands of Cuenca and is therefore subject to more copious floods, seems to have had no ancient town on its course across the coastal plain except the port of Sucro at its mouth; but this place was located on a bold promontory (Cape Cullera) formed by a detached range of hills, which deflects the river southward near its mouth. The prosperous town of Sætabis (Jativa) was located ten miles from the Jucar, in a broad lateral valley, whose well watered alluvium merged into that of the lower Jucar. On this rich soil grew the flax for the fine linen of Sætabis praised by Pliny

and Martial. The town itself occupied a commanding site at
the northern base of Monte Bernisa; it had the inevitable
acropolis, because it lay on the main road between Valentia
and Carthago Nova, and its city fountains were doubtless
fed then as now by the abundant springs of Belus two miles
to the south.

Along the southern littoral of Spain the ancient Phœnician
colonists found choice sites for their maritime settlements, similar to those of their homeland. The spurs of the Sierra Nevada
Mountains and other coast ranges ran out to sea in rocky promontories which enclosed small bays offering safe anchorage for
ships. Wherever a pocket of alluvium was deposited at the head
of such an inlet, a commercial town was established on the nearest citadel site overlooking the irrigable plain. The rainfall
along this coast though variable averages about 22 inches (550
mm.) falling on 52 days in the year. On the mountain heights
which wall in the coast on the north it increases to 40 inches or
more (1,000 to 1,500 mm.), and thus feeds the irrigation
streams which apparently throughout historical times have
watered the small deltaic plains of the littoral. The situation
of ancient Malaca (Malaga) was typical. It occupied the
lower slope of a rocky citadel, 560 feet high, rising from a
small harbor to the south, and overlooked the fertile alluvial
plain of the Guadalahorca River, which extended westward for
9 miles along the coast and penetrated 18 miles up the valley
into the interior.[49] The river, draining the Sierra de Tolox
(6,555 feet or 1,959 meters) to the west and the Sierra de
Abdalajis (4,517 feet or 1,377 meters) to the north, maintained
a supply of water in the irrigation ditches during the hot rainless summers, and nourished the garden, orchards and vineyards
of the ancient seaport. A geographical companionpiece to
Malaca was formed by the famous *Portus Magnus* or Urci of
the Romans, now Almeria. This city occupied the site of an
earlier Iberian town at the base of the Sierra de Enix, whence
it overlooked the small but fruitful deltaic plain of the Almeria
River and the admirable harbor doing a thriving trade with
Italy and the eastern Mediterranean ports.

The seaboard towns of Spain in general relied for their
economic prosperity upon the rich mines of their immediate hin-

terland, upon the coastal fisheries, and in a minor degree upon
the garden plots of alluvial soil, which doubtless supplied their
local needs only in part. Gades and the group of seaports
about it had an additional advantage in the large and fruitful
hinterland of the Guadalquivir basin, which furnished all manner of foodstuffs for export and provided an avenue of communication in the long navigable course of the Guadalquivir
River. The alluvial plain along the lower course of this river
was subject to inundations both from floods and the high tides
of the Atlantic which submerged all the channels and inlets of
this coast. The silt deposited by the river, however, served to
cement together numerous limestone spurs and reefs which run
out westward into the alluvium from the Andalusian Mountains.
These furnished in antiquity, as they do today, solid foundations for seaports and inland towns skirting the soft alluvium
and therefore accessible to its productive vineyards, fields and
pastures.[50]

The Phœnician Gadiz, Roman Gades, was situated on a low
limestone island twenty miles south of the Bætis or Guadalquivir mouth at the entrance of a commodious harbor. On the
mainland opposite at the mouth of the Guadalete, which was
formerly joined by a distributary with the lower Guadalquivir,
lay the *Portus Menesthei* of the ancients, on the site of the
modern Puerto de Santa Maria. At the innermost recess of the
Bay of Cadiz, on the lowest terrace of the hill ranges, lay the
ancient Portus Gaditanus of the Romans, now Puerto Real,
while about twelve miles to the south a rocky eminence rising
out of the flat outer coast once held the famous Temple of the
Tyrian Hercules,[51] venerated throughout antiquity and rich in
treasures. Even the colony of Asta Regia survives today in
La Mesa de Asta, a limestone height south of the modern
Jerez.[52] Another of these rocks, rising from the delta of the
Bætis, held the famous Tower of Cæpio, a beacon for ships to
warn them of the reefs and guide them to the mouth of the
Guadalquivir.

On the arid plateau of Spain, with a rainfall ranging from
8 to 20 inches (200 to 500 mm.), the ancient native tribes
sought the mountain slopes, where they could find natural
strongholds, like the site of Numantia in the high Sierra

Moncaya (7,596 feet, 2,316 meters), and unfailing springs and streams like those which lent fame to Roman Bibilis (Calatayud) on the southeast slope of this range.[53]   Even more in the valleys of the Ebro and the Guadalquivir, a low rainfall and wide stretches of steppeland combined to drive Roman settlements up the enclosing mountains to place their fields on irrigable slopes, while they reserved the drier plains below for olive-groves and pastures. The Guadalquivir received its largest tributaries from the southern highland, which therefore attracted the ancient population to its springs and streams. The old lake basin of the upper Genil, famous in medieval history as the fertile Vega of Granada, was in Roman times rimmed by ancient Iberian towns; while towns of Iberian names were thickly clustered about the head of the Guadalquivir valley. The working of the silver and lead mines near New Carthage required water [54] no less than the summer fields.   In the Ebro valley, the tendency of settlements to seek the surrounding heights was yet more pronounced. The course of the river through the plains below the Roman provincial capital of Cæsar Augusta (Saragossa) was marked by only one town, Celsa (Gelsa), a Roman colony guarding the stone bridge which carried the Roman road from Cæsar Augusta northeast to Ilerda (Lerida).   Ilerda seems to have been the most important town in Roman times, judging from Strabo's description of its location. It lay on the lowest terrace of the Pyrenees, at the foot of a natural citadel overlooking the Sicoris River (Segre) and a level plain accessible to irrigation streams. Strabo indicates that the main route from Tarraco to the Bay of Biscay was a piedmont road, running through Ilerda, Osca (Huesca), Pampælo (Pampeluna), to Œassa [55] near Fonterabia.

The Phœnician settlements in Africa, animated by the purposes of maritime commerce, combined seaport and coastal citadel, both side-stepping the river or torrent mouth, with a well watered alluvial plain for field and garden culture. All these requirements were met by Saldæ (Bougie) in eastern Mauretania, Ruscidæ (Philippeville) on the scant stretch of Numidian coast, Hippo Regius (Bone) and Hippo Diarrhytus (Bizerta) on the northern littoral of Carthaginian Africa, and especially by Utica and Carthage flanking the mouth of the Bagradas River. This stream opened a longitudinal valley highway into the interior, and debouched on the strategic Sicilian Strait with its control of the great east-and-west sea route running the length of the Mediterranean. Carthage particularly, with its site on an anvil-shaped promontory, its island citadel, the Byrsa, tied to the mainland by a narrow belt of silted plain, its twin harbors and its protected Bay of Carthage to constitute its home waters, had the further advantage of a pure and ample domestic water supply, brought by aqueduct from the Zaghouan Mountain (4,245 feet), 38 miles to the southwest, across the low neck of land to the Byrsa.

CLIMATE AND WATERWORKS—All ancient literatures reflect the concern of the Mediterranean people to secure a pure domestic water supply ample enough to carry them through the summer drought. Cities and individuals were haunted by the fear that their water might fail or be cut off or become polluted. Consequently they took every precaution against these evils by the gradual development of elaborate waterworks which were consigned to the care of their ablest citizens—men like Themistocles, Cato the Censor and Frontinus. Aristotle emphasizes the necessity of locating a city where it can command an ample water supply. "There should be a natural abundance of springs and fountains in the town, or lacking these, large reservoirs may be established for the collection of rain water, such as will not fail when the inhabitants are cut off from the country by war." He considered pure water a big factor in the health of a town. Hence, "if the water supply is not all equally good, the drinking water ought to be separated from that used for other purposes." [56]

Everywhere precautions were taken to protect the water against pollution and theft. For these crimes heavy punishments and fines were imposed in Greece [57] and Italy. Furthermore, the Roman plutocrats had their drinking water first boiled and then chilled by mountain snows; if the snow was not clean, it was strained through fine linen cloths.[58] In this they imitated the practice of Cyrus the Persian (d. 529 B.C.) who took his drinking water with him from Susa on his campaigns.

It was boiled and then carried in silver vessels by pack animals or wagons.[59]

SPRINGS, WELLS AND CISTERNS—As to the sources of drinking water, all authorities laud the superiority of spring water and rain water conducted to a reservoir in earthenware pipes, as opposed to that from muddy streams or stagnant pools and marshes, because the latter were not aerated.[60] Columella gave a second place to mountain streams tumbling over rocks.[61] He agrees with Hippocrates the great physician (d. about 377 B.C.), who preferred water "flowing from high ground and hills, sweet and clear" and water derived from deep wells. Hippocrates considers rain water excellent because distilled by the sun, but adds that it soon spoils and gets a bad odor, so that it needs to be boiled and strained.[62]

"The fountain of living water" was the great desideratum from Palestine to Spain. The spring was the nucleus of town and village life, the starting point around which the community grew up. It became identified with his home town in the mind of the native. Theognis of Megara (d. about 540 B.C.), disgusted when a political upheaval dislodged the oligarchs and placed the common people in power, decided to become a voluntary exile and emigrate. He expressed his purpose in terms of his native spring and not of his native town.[63]

> The years I dropped my pitcher
> In the cool, dark village spring,
> How sweet and good the water's taste did seem.
> But now the rains have flooded it,
> The mountain streams have muddied it—
> I'll seek another spring, a larger stream.[64]

About the village spring or its reservoir the women gathered in the twilight, water jars on their shoulders, as one sees them today in Nazareth or some hamlet in the Apennines, to linger and gossip. Here the men resorted at all hours to discuss local affairs and advertise matters of local concern. The importance of the town spring or pool is reflected in the care which Pausanias takes to mention its name, its site, its mountain or piedmont source; and if its water has been brought from a distance, he tells who installed the conduit. He does this for all the ancient Hellenic world from Antioch and the Asia Minor coast west to Syracuse with its Fountain of Arethusa. He includes even a village like Pyrrhichus near Cape Malea, whose sole water supply was provided by a conduit built by the demigod Silenus from a distant spring to the market place.[65] Many of these springs have a mythological or miraculous origin, like the Dirce Spring of Thebes; or the conduit from mountain spring to city tank is attributed to the legendary founder of the colony, like the aqueduct to the Theban Cadmeia from the Cithæron Mountains. In any event it is identified with the beginning of the city. The Fountain of Priene, the famous spring of Corinth, shows five building periods in its well-house, which goes back to the sixth century B.C.

Climatic and geographic conditions in Palestine and Syria favored an individual rather than community water supply. "Drink waters out of thy own cistern, and running waters out of thine own well," says the Hebrew proverb.[66] Better still was a spring or "fountain of living water," for cisterns hewn from the limestone rock often leaked through natural clefts.[67] Often the spring was underground, reached by a well-shaft; for the geology of Palestine made for underground drainage. Where the flow was very abundant, such a spring or well was sure to have a whole village or town grow up about it. Such is the Virgin's Spring of Nazareth, sole water supply of the town today as in the boyhood of Christ. The numerous place-names in Palestine beginning with *En* or *Ain*, meaning spring, point to the water supply as the determining factor in locating a town or village, like En-Gannin, on the slope of Mount Carmel.

Springs are copious and numerous along the western escarpment of the Judean Plateau, but shrink rapidly in size and number in the rain shadow to the east. The pastoral region of the Negeb to the south has always been a transition belt physically and climatically between the Judean Plateau with its moderate winter rains and the Desert of Paran. The few springs and wells of the Negeb were imperative for field or herd. Even Debir, located near the northern margin of Hebron, was scarcely habitable without the possession of springs.[68] Isaac, who occupied the southern district, always kept close to the well of Lahai-roi. Wells sunk in the dry wadi beds were private possessions which were fought over by the rival herdsmen of Abraham and the neighboring king of Gerar. This Philistine sheik filled up the wells. This was an ancient method of maintaining a waste boundary to exclude encroachments of neighboring nomads. It was adopted also by the kings of Judah and Israel, when they invaded the Moabite country east of the Dead Sea, as a punitive measure,[69] because the aridity of that region made wells imperative. Rock-hewn cisterns and wells were assets of Canaan when conquered by the Jews.[70]

CITY POOLS OR RESERVOIRS —The cities of Palestine, with their concentrated populations, felt the need of exploiting all local resources to assure their water supply. As walled towns, subjected to siege in a warlike age, they were peculiarly dependent upon the water supply of summer, because campaigns were generally made in this season. While each house had a cistern to store the rain water from its own roof, the city provided public pools or reservoirs, formed by damming a valley stream; in many cases these were supplemented by aqueducts bringing water from distant springs. Pools acted as settling tanks and were often connected with public baths. In this event, they were surrounded by porticoes where the bathers rested or lounged, protected from the sun. The Pool of Siloam at Jerusalem had four such porticoes, whose remains have been excavated, and the Pool of Bethesda had five, one of them running across the middle of the basin and dividing it into two parts. We will have occasion to note the beautification of springs, fountains and water basins throughout the Mediterranean region by architectural features. This gave rise to an elaborate and varied fountain architecture which later set the standard for other parts of the world. It must be interpreted both as an effort to express the importance of water in a semi-arid region, and to render beautiful and comfortable the spot to which all had to resort for water, and which therefore became the city club or gathering place.

Jerusalem was provided with an elaborate water system from the time of the prophets. It had its Upper Pool, its Lower Pool, the King's Pool, Old Pool, Hezekiah's Pool, besides

Siloam and Bethesda.[71] Josephus mentions also four others existing in the city at the time of the Roman conquest.[72] The Pools of Solomon, three large reservoirs ranging from over one to two acres in area, may be seen today beyond Bethlehem eight miles from the ancient capital. They are possibly the "pools of water" made by Solomon to irrigate the gardens and orchards of his summer palace; but their water was conveyed to Jerusalem by a very ancient conduit, over 13 miles long, which tunnels the hill of Bethlehem on its way to the city. The Pool of Siloam was fed in part by a tunnel conduit which brought water from the Fountain of the Virgin, and which from an inscription on it in Phœnician characters must be assigned to the eighth century B.C. or an even earlier date.[73] King Hezekiah dammed the upper watercourse of Gihon and relied on hydraulic pressure to bring the water by tunnel conduit to his Pool in the west side of the city of David.[74] These channels were often hewn in the rock and were always covered with stone slabs to keep the water pure, probably also to reduce loss by evaporation. The latter was no small consideration in view of the intense dryness of the summer atmosphere.

Other towns also had their pools, like Gibeon,[75] located ten miles northwest of Jerusalem and famous for its High Place where Solomon worshipped; Hebron [76] near the summit of the Judean Plateau where two ancient reservoirs survive, one 132 feet square; and the ancient city of Samaria.[77] The Bible mentions these pools as places where men gathered. On the arid eastern escarpment of the Judean Plateau, tanks and aqueducts fed by limestone springs supplied water to ancient cities like Jericho and Bethshan. Herod built reservoirs on a large scale to impound the local spring water in the citadel of Macherus, a natural fortress situated on a high headland overlooking the Dead Sea; and he also opened rock-hewn cisterns in the ancient stronghold of Masada, when he began to fortify the frontiers of his kingdom.[78]

Across Jordan, on the westward facing escarpment of the plateau of Arabia, poverty of water necessitated its early conservation wherever towns grew up along the ancient highway of traffic leading from the Red Sea north to Damascus and the great bend of the Euphrates. The Ammonite capital of

Heshbon, an important place when Moses travelled this way towards Canaan, had a pool which was famous for its beauty,[79] fed by springs or streams from Mount Pisgah. The ruins of a tank at Heshbon show it to have been 191 feet long, 139 feet broad and 10 feet deep. Mesha, King of the Moabites in the time of Jehoshaphat according to the famous "Moabite Stone," built reservoirs for Baalmeon and other cities of this high plateau. Medeba, which existed in Mesha's time, now shows the ruins of a pool which measures nearly three acres in area.[80]

On this western edge of the Syrian Desert, towns developed only where the water of a wadi could be impounded, or where a distant spring could be tapped and its water led by conduit to a reservoir in the city. Owing to the desolating incursions of desert tribes, extensive water works had to wait for the protective rule of the Romans, and were therefore chiefly of Roman construction; but in some instances the Roman and earlier native works lay side by side. Petra is an example. Known to the ancient Hebrews as Sela or the Rock, it was the capital of Edom when that country was conquered by King Amaziah of Judea;[81] but it began to attain importance as a desert market under the Nabateans about 100 B.C., and reached preëminence only after the Roman conquest. Located on a high arid plateau (elevation 3,000 feet), south of the Dead Sea, it depended on ancient aqueducts which brought water from springs two miles up the Wadi Musa valley above the towns. The earliest conduits were cut in the soft sandstone of the wadi walls, far above the variable stream, but the later Roman aqueducts of clay pipe were let into the opposite face of the cliff and secured by cement. The High Places also about the city were provided with small rock-hewn pools, which doubtless figured in the primitive ceremonies to rain-giving Baal. An extensive system of channels and small tanks for gathering the precious rain water equipped the long canyon approach to one of these High Places for the benefit of thirsty pilgrims,[82] in the dry season. These undoubtedly belonged to the earliest period of the city's life. Strabo tells us that in his time Petra derived from its springs enough water for domestic purposes and for irrigating the city gardens, but that the country about was for the most part desert.[83] These conditions point to careful exploitation of the local water supply.

A long list of ancient cities in Moab, Gilead and the Hauran, some of them powerful places like Edrei, Ramoth Gilead and Rabboth Ammon in early Semite times, and other thriving Greek commercial towns, all show elaborate systems of reservoirs and conduits.

Despite these provisions for a regular water-supply, there were times when successive years of diminished rainfall encroached upon the narrow margin of moisture; when men scoured the country for the last surviving trickle from some hidden spring, and "the hart panteth for the water-brook," which had become a bed of gravel. Then the prophet's promise to the righteous man, "Bread shall be given him; his waters shall be sure," [84] guaranteed something more than the commonplace. The Hebrew proverb "Stolen waters are sweet" [85] testifies to the fierce thirst that prompted the petty theft, rather than to a fictitious zest lent by an unlawful act. The Scriptures abound in instances of water miraculously supplied, generally in "the wilderness" or desert borders of Palestine to the east and south, but occasionally also on the Judean Plateau, and even on the wooded slopes of Mount Carmel.

East of the long rift valley of the Jordan and the Dead Sea, where the inner highlands were the last to intercept the rain-bearing winds from the Mediterranean, the constant threat of water famines necessitated careful provision for the dry season. Especially was this true in the southern district east of the Dead Sea, the ancient lands of Edom and Moab. There from the earliest times water was a precious commodity, and had to be purchased with money or taken by force by wandering tribes traversing the country.[86] All this region on the fringe of the Syrian Desert, from Palmyra in the north to Petra in the south, offered sites for settlement only where oasis conditions existed; where rare perennial streams like the Jabbok, Yarmuk and "the rivers of Damascus" offered an unfailing though variable water supply; or where water from distant wadi or springs could be brought by aqueduct or underground conduit to reservoirs in the town.

Owing to the constant incursions of desert nomads and their

desolating activities, most of the water systems, where constructed on a big scale, waited for the peace-bringing Roman rule, which held the desert tribesmen in check.   The copious streams which flowed down from the Anti-Lebanon range and Mount Hermon to the oasis of Damascus guaranteed that city's water supply because nature had made a system which needed little improvement from the hand of man, elsewhere the human task was vastly greater, and the accomplished work more easily jeopardized.   The remains of all the highland cities of eastern Syria show the ruins of Roman aqueducts, baths, reservoirs, and occasionally a *naumachia* or naval pool, like that at Gerasa.[87]   Gadara, which lay on the cross country route from the plain of Esdraelon across Jordan to Canatha and the wide wheat fields of the Hauran, occupied an admirable fortress site on an important highway, but had to depend on cisterns and a meager spring, till the Romans brought water by an aqueduct over thirty miles long.[88]   Their engineers also exploited the streams of the Hauran Mountains, whose great massif, 6,032 feet high, condensed abundant winter rains, and supplied water to Canatha, Bostra, Philippopolis and the 300 villages skirting the slopes.[89]

Other towns of Gilead and Bashan, whose history extends back through the Greek period of the Decapolis and the early Hebrew conquest to the legendary days of the Aramaic Semitic rulers, relied on cisterns, rock-hewn reservoirs, and wells, whose remains can be seen today amid the later remains of Roman baths and aqueducts.   Such were the pools in Madeba of the Moabites and Heshbon of the Ammonites.[90]   The ancient Ammonite capital, Rabbath Ammon, which was rebuilt by Ptolemy Philadelphus of Egypt, and later improved by the Romans, depended during the siege of the city by Antiochus (218 B.C.) upon an underground passage, by which the citizens descended to a deep subterranean reservoir,[91] such as abounded in that limestone country and were utilized by the natives from time immemorial in periods of danger.

Yet farther north Damascus drew its water from the perennial streams flowing down from mighty Hermon and Anti-Lebanon.   Its domestic supply was derived from the brimming irrigation canals which ran through and past the city out to the blooming gardens and orchards reclaimed from the Syrian Desert. Palmyra had a more difficult problem. It was described by Pliny as located "in a region that all around in a vast circle is a sand desert and separated by nature from other lands," yet famous for its fertile soil and pleasant waters.[92] These were brought by covered aqueducts from the distant hills to the west and stored in great reservoirs to supply the homes and gardens of the city. Palmyra, which was first historically mentioned in 41 B.C. and began to flourish in the imperial period of Rome,[93] owed the security of its water works to the partial protection extended over it by the Romans, whose trade the city forwarded to the Euphrates.

The long coastal plain of Palestine and Syria was supplied by the "fountain heads" or springs which burst forth near the base of the Judean and Lebanon highlands; and also by the wells which were sunk to the ground-water. In the Philistine plain this rose near the surface and supplied the ample wells of Gaza and Ashdod; but on the steep coast of Lebanon where the ground-water has a rapid run-off, the ancient Phœnicians probably placed their chief reliance upon mountain streams and springs. The authorities give meager material on this point, though the Phœnicians were famous throughout the Mediterranean Region as hydraulic engineers. Only Strabo reports the ingenuity of the island city of Aradus in achieving a water supply. Rain water from the roofs was stored in cisterns, and in addition a submarine spring, which welled up in the sea only a few hundred yards from the port, was tapped by sinking over it a great inverted funnel with a hose attached.[94]

MUNICIPAL WATER SUPPLY IN GREECE—The Hellenic cities show equal concern for their water supply and a high regard for springs, to which they often attributed great sanctity or a miraculous origin, probably as a method of social control to protect the water supply against pollution. Many of them sacred to Apollo and Demeter, divinities of agriculture, suggest the utilization of their waters for irrigation. Others poured out their limpid streams in the heart of sacred groves,[95] which probably owed their sanctity as well as their trees to the god-given waters. Others issuing from caves made the grottos holy places, devoted to the worship of certain gods, or the abode of beneficent nymphs. In the height of the summer droughts, when the rivers of Greece were drying up and the foliage was sere and brown, the undiscouraged flow of some rocky fountain, overhung by tender green, seemed to the thirsty wayfarer a perennial miracle. One sees him stoop and drink, notes the long-drawn sigh of gratification and hears him exclaim in Pindar's words: "Water is best of all." [96] In modern Greece, the good-bye words to the departing guest are: "I wish you a safe journey and fresh water."

Springs were of paramount importance to the ancient Greek cities, and therefore one factor in determining their sites. They provided the first local water supply. When this was outgrown, it was supplemented from more distant sources by more or less elaborate systems of aqueducts. These city springs meet us in Homer, in the fountain of Hyperia in Pegasæ [97] on the Gulf of Volo, in the roadside in the city of Alcinous,[98] and the Fountain of Arethusa in the capital of Ithaca.[99] The last became famous; its name reappeared in the city spring of Eubœan Calchis, and Sicilian Syracuse.

The Greek Tyrants justified their beneficent despotisms by improving the water supply of their respective capitals. Pisistratus of Athens (560 to 527 B.C.) adorned the city's chief spring with a hall of columns where the water issued from nine jets, giving it the name of Enneacronnus or fount of nine mouths.[100] To supplement its flow, water was brought by two conduits from the upper course of the River Ilissus, one of them passing underground out to the Piræus. Other aqueducts, one from Mount Hymettus and two from Lycabettus, contributed to the water supply of Athens, while a system of canals from the Cephisos irrigated the olive groves and gardens in the vicinity. The Greek conduits were generally subterranean channels, cut in the living rock. In order to supervise and cleanse them, shafts were sunk at intervals through the rock from the surface, and thus admitted light and air to the dark canals beneath. At the entrance to the city of Athens, the aqueducts discharged their water into rocky basins which acted as settling tanks. From these the water was distributed through the city.[101] When necessary, conduits pierced the hills by means of tunnels, as in Palestine.

Megara too had its water works in the form of a long canal, built by the tyrant Theagenes in 620 B.C., which brought water from the mountains to a beautiful basin in the market place. This basin was famous for its size, its decorations and the number of its columns.[102]   Polycrates of Samos, about 530 B.C., employed the leading hydraulic engineer of his time, a native of Megara, to supply Samos city with water.   The need was crucial for a big town on a small island, which however had a high mountain core.   The task was accomplished by piercing the mountain by a tunnel nearly a mile long to reach the springs of Mount Ampelus.   Thence water was distributed to the wells, pipes, and baths of the city, while the surplus went to cleanse the sewers.[103]   Corinth had the most famous city fountain of all Greece.   The upper spring, located in the high rock citadel of Acro-Corinth, was said to be the gift of the river-god Asophus.   So precious a boon on that bare rock could be explained only by a divine origin.   The lower Priene spring has a well-house indicating former architectural beauty.[104]   The colonnade over the basin and the bronze lion heads from which the water flowed are still to be seen.

More elaborate even than anything that democratic Greece could show were the water works and drainage system in the royal palaces of Crete, a thousand years before the time of the Greek tyrants.   The palace of Cnossus had lavatories and sinks equipped with terra cotta pipes and drains of stone or cement. That of Phæstos had bathrooms well constructed and amply equipped.[105]   The water was probably brought in artificial channels from the high mountain range which forms the backbone of the island.   These works ante-dated the Hellenic invasion of Greece, and may have furnished the models for the water systems which developed in Greece.   The widespread development of hydraulic engineers, however, must be attributed to the early institution of summer tillage by irrigation as well as the necessity of a reliable domestic water supply.   The dissemination of the art went hand in hand with trade and colonization.   The finest Grecian aqueducts were the underground conduits of Syracuse which brought drinking water to the city. These were destroyed by the besieging Athenian forces in 423 B.C.   But Syracuse was not the only city so supplied.   The vic-

tor of the Olympic Games in 452 B.C. returning to his native
Camarina in Sicily, praises "The River Oanis and the lake of
his native land, and the sacred channels where through doth
Hipparis give waters to the people." [106]   This lake was prob-
ably a tank or reservoir formed by damming the course of the
Oanis or Hipparis River.

THE WATER WORKS—The Greek colonies located about the
Bay of Naples may have given the first impulse to the utilization of the hot springs there for public baths and the consequent installation of the water-works which supplied these
baths and the fountains and piscina or pools in the private gardens of Herculaneum, Pompeii and Cumæ. But it was the city
of Rome, desirous of providing water for its large population,
that shows the most extensive water works. The report of
Sextus Julius Frontinus, water commissioner of Rome in 97
A.D., gives a complete survey of the water system of the city.
The nine Roman aqueducts ran for the greatest length underground and with a gentle gradient, because the water was carried by gravity from source to city. Hence the flumes crossed
valleys on high arches. The Appian aqueduct was brought
to the city in 313 B.C. It was over ten miles long and had its
intake at a spring on the estate of Lucullus. The Marcian
was 60 miles long and had its source in the Sabine Mountains
"where countless springs gush forth from caves in the rocks,
motionless as a pool, of deep green color." Such springs were
sought out, opened up to get an ampler flow of water, and then
walled in with concrete to keep the source intact. The old
Anio aqueduct, built in 273 B.C., came from the Anio River
above Tibur, 40 miles distant. Its water was often muddy during the winter rains. So was that of the New Anio conduit,
till a settling tank was built between the river and the intake.
This improved the water except in periods of very heavy rains.

Rigid distinction was made between pure and impure water
by the Roman water commissioner. The supply from the Alsie-
tina duct was drawn from a lake, none too clean; hence it was
not distributed to the public but was reserved for the *Naumachia* or naval lake of the Cæsars or for irrigating gardens.
The spring-fed aqueducts were considered the best, and these
were reserved for drinking water. The water system of Rome

supplied private houses, the 39 ornamental fountains of the city and 75 public structures, chiefly baths, like the Baths of Nero and the Baths of Caracalla. Gardens in and about the city also were supplied with water for their fountains, pools and irrigation canals.[107]

Fraudulent tapping of the public aqueducts and reservoirs was rife from early times. Illicit pipes were laid by the thieves, and the robbery was connived at by the watermen who had the reservoirs in charge. Landed proprietors having estates along the course of the aqueducts tapped them to water their gardens. Frontinus when appointed commissioner made a survey of the city's water supply and rounded up the delinquents.[108]

Owing to the recurring scarcity of water in the Mediterranean region, it was natural that springs should assume a sacred character, and thus be safeguarded against malicious pollution. The gods of rain, as we have seen, were also deities of the underground waters, whose ultimate source was in the sky; and therefore lent their sanctity to the springs. Curative power attributed to various pools and fountains and even rivers runs through all ancient Mediterranean life. The Pool of Bethesda at Jerusalem daily saw its porches filled with the blind, halt and withered, waiting for the angel to move the waters.[109] The healing power of hot. and medicinal springs was recognized and exaggerated in Italy, especially in the volcanic regions, where the baths of Baiæ and Naples became famous.[110]

Commensurate with the importance of springs under Mediterranean climatic conditions, and their large number wherever the limestones predominated, an elaborate fountain architecture developed which set the standard for later times. This was especially varied and beautiful in the fountains of gardens and peristyles, as we have seen, where the sculptured designs were the product of a fine art. It was stimulated also by the custom of erecting a *nymphæum* or temple above the spring where it issued from its mountain source, like that built by Carthage at the intake of the aqueduct which brought water 38 miles to the citadel. The object was to proclaim the sanctity of the spring; contamination of its water became an offense against a deity as well as a crime against a community.

Finally, Rome instituted the Fontinalia or religious festival of the fountains, when garlands were thrown into all the city fountains of Italy; and a god *Fons* appeared with the goddess Flora [111] to secure abundant water.

AUTHORITIES—CHAPTER XIX

1. Compare A. Philippson, *Das Mittelmeergebiet,* pp. 212-214. Leipzig, 1907.
2. Vitruvius, *De Architectura,* Bk. I, Chap. IV, 1.
3. A. Philippson, *Thessalien und Epirus,* pp. 118, 119, 132, 133. Berlin, 1897.
4. Strabo, IX, Chap. V, 17; *Iliad,* II, 729.
5. A. Philippson, *Thessalien und Epirus,* pp. 253-4. Berlin, 1897.
6. W. R. Shepherd, *Historical Atlas,* Map pp. 10-11. New York, 1911.
7. Mommsen, *History of Rome,* I, 45-47. New York, 1905. Strabo, V, Chap. III, 10.
8. Livy, I, 11, 13, 14; II, 23, 26, 39, 50; III, 6; IV, 21.
9. W. Deecke, *Italy,* p. 140. London, 1904.
10. *Ibid.,* p. 87.
11. *Ibid.,* p. 76.
12. Horace, *Carmina,* III, 4, 14.
13. W. Deecke, *op. cit.,* p. 51.
14. Strabo, V, Chap. III, 9-11.
15. See plan, Baedeker, *Central Italy,* p. 56-7. 1904.
16. W. Deecke, *op. cit.,* pp. 96-97. London, 1904.
17. See Baedeker, *Central Italy,* for detailed map of this district.
18. For altitude of towns see Baedeker, *Central Italy,* on Clitumnus Valley.
19. W. Deecke, *op. cit.,* pp. 51, 420. London, 1904. Strabo, V, Chap. III, 9-11.
20. Strabo, V, Chap. IV, 3-5, 8.
21. Strabo, V, Chap. III, 9-12. Shepherd's *Historical Atlas,* p. 35 inset map.
22. Strabo, V, Chap. III, 7.
23. Livy, VII, 3; XXIV, 9; XXX, 38.
24. Strabo, V, Chap. III, 1.
25. *Ibid.,* V, Chap. III, 5, 12.
26. Shepherd's *Historical Atlas,* p. 35, inset map.
27. Strabo, V, Chap. III, 6.
28. Pliny, *Historia Naturalis,* III, 5.
29. Strabo, V, Chap, III, 5, 6.
30. W. Deecke, *op. cit.,* p. 51, 95.
31. Strabo, V, Chap, II, 5.
32. W. Deecke, *op. cit.,* p. 52.
33. Strabo, V, Chap. I, 10, 11.
34. Baedeker, *Northern Italy,* Map p. 385. 1903.
35. Strabo, V, Chap. I, 11.
36. *Ibid.,* V, Chap. I, 11.

37. *Ibid.*, V, Chap. I, 2, 6, 11.
38. W. Deecke, *op. cit.*, p. 50.
39. Strabo, V, Chap. I, 5, 7-8.
40. *Ibid.*, IV, Chap. I, 3.
41. *Ibid.*, IV, Chap. I, 6, 8.
42. Élisée Reclus, *Europe,* Vol. II, 129-130. New York, 1882.
43. Strabo, IV, Chap. I, 3.
44. *Ibid.*, IV, Chap. I, 6-7
45. Polybius, *Histories,* III, Chap. 35; Chap. 40.
46. Strabo, III, Chap. IV, 8-9.
47. *Ibid.*, III, Chap. IV, 6.
48. *Ibid.*, III, Chap. IV, 9.
49. For site, see Baedeker, *Spain and Portugal,* p. 873. 1898. Murray,
    Handbook to Spain and Portugal, Vol. II, p. 383.
50. Strabo, III, Chap. I, 9; Chap. II, 4-6; Chap. V, 9.
51. *Ibid.*, III, Chap. I, 9; Chap. V, 3, 5, 7.
52. Baedeker, *Spain and Portugal,* p. 466. Strabo, III, Chap. II, 2.
53. Martial, X, 103.
54. Polybius, *Histories,* XXXIV, 9.
55. Strabo, III, Chap. IV, 10.
56. Aristotle, *Politics,* VII.
57. Hesiod, *Works and Days,* 758. Jouett's Plato, *Laws,* VIII, Chap. 11,
    844, 845.
58. Juvenal, *Satire,* V, 50. Suetonius, Nero, 48. Martial, Epigram, XIV,
    104, 116.
59. Herodotus, I, 188.
60. Pliny, *Hist. Nat.,* XXXI, 31; Plutarch, *Quæstiones Physikales,* 33.
61. Columella, *Rerum Rusticarum,* I, Chap. V.
62. Hippocrates, *Air, Water and Places,* Chaps. VII-VIII.
63. Theognis of Megara, *Maxims,* verse 953-956.
64. Alfred Zimmern, *The Greek Commonwealth,* p. 116. Oxford, 1911.
65. Pausanias, III, Chap. XXV.
66. *Proverbs,* V, 15; II *Kings,* XVIII, 31.
67. *Jeremiah,* II, 13.
68. *Joshua,* XV, 15-19. *Genesis,* XVI, 14; XXIV, 62; XXV, 11.
69. *Genesis,* XXVI, 15-33; II *Kings,* III, 19, 25.
70. *Deuteronomy,* VI, 11; *Nehemiah,* IX, 25.
71. II *Kings,* XVIII, 17; XX, 20. *Nehemiah,* II, 14; III, 15. *Isaiah,*
    XXII, 9, 11. *John,* V, 2, 4, 7; IX, 7.
72. Josephus, *Jewish Wars,* V, Chap. III, 2; Chap. IV, 2; Chap. XI, 4.
73. Hastings and Selbie, *Dict. of the Bible,* article, "Conduits." New
    York, 1903.
74. II *Chronicles,* XXXII, 30.
75. II *Samuel,* II, 13.
76. II *Samuel,* IV, 12.
77. I *Kings,* XXII, 38.
78. Josephus, *Jewish Wars,* VII, Chap. VI, 2, 3; Chap. VIII, 3.
79. *Canticles,* VII, 4. Libbey and Hoskins, *The Jordan Valley and Petra,*
    Vol. I, pp. 244-246. New York, 1905.
80. *Ibid.*, Vol. I, pp. 258-259, 278.
81. II *Kings,* XIV, 7.
82. Libbey and Hoskins, *op. cit.,* Vol. II, pp. 81-87, 168, 211.

CLIMATIC FACTORS IN SETTLEMENT   575

83. Strabo, XVI, Chap. IV, 21.
84. *Isaiah*, XXXIII, 7.
85. *Proverbs*, IX, 17.
86. *Deuteronomy*, II, 6, 24-28.   *Numbers*, XX, 14-20; XXI, 5, 16-18, 22-24.
87. Libbey and Hoskins, *op. cit.*, Vol. I, p. 203; Vol. II, pp. 81-82, 168.
88. George Adam Smith, *Historical Geography of the Holy Land*, pp. 601-603. 1897.
89. Mommsen, *Provinces of the Roman Empire*, Vol. II, pp. 169-171. 1887.
90. Libbey and Hoskins, *op. cit.*, Vol. I, pp. 173, 174, 245-246, 259, 278.
91. Polybius, V, 71.
92. Pliny, *Historia Naturalis*, V, Chap. 25.
93. Mommsen, *Provinces of the Roman Empire*, Vol. II, pp. 100-107. 1887.
94. Strabo, XVI, Chap. II, 13.
95. Pausanias, III, Chap. XXII, 8; IV, Chap. XXXI, 1. *Odyssey*, VI, 293.
96. Pindar, Olympian Odes, I, 1; III, 43.
97. *Iliad*, II, 734.
98. *Odyssey*, VI, 293.
99. *Odyssey*, XIII, 408-409. Strabo, X, Chap. I, 13.
100. Pausanias, I, Chap. XIV, 1.
101. Harper's *Dict. of Classical Literature and Antiquities*, article, "Aquæductus."
102. Pausanias, I, Chap. XL, 1.
103. Herodotus, III, 60. Strabo, XIV, Chap. I, 15. E. Curtius, *History of Greece*, Vol. II, Bk. II, Chap. V, p. 166. Translated by A. W. Ward. New York, 1871.
104. Strabo, VIII, Chap. VI, 21.
105. R. M. Burrows, *Discoveries in Crete*, pp. 8-9, 59, 81, 104-106. New York, 1907.
106. Pindar, Olympic Ode, V, 10-12.
107. Frontinus, *De Aquis Urbis Romæ*, I, 5-15, 78, 89-92.
108. *Ibid.*, II, 65-76, 112-115, 128-130.
109. *John*, V, 2-4, 9; IX, 7, 11.
110. Strabo, V, Chap. IV, 5, 7, 9.
111. W. Warde Fowler, *Roman Festivals of the Period of the Republic*, pp. 240-241. London, 1908.

PART IV

MARITIME ACTIVITIES

CHAPTER XX

GEOGRAPHIC CONDITIONS OF NAVIGATION : THEIR EFFECTS

The Mediterranean Sea presented a combination of geographic conditions highly conducive to the early development of navigation. Fertile coastal lowlands and valley plains opening seaward between sheltering promontories drew population to settle on the littoral. Amply articulated coasts with abundant harbors and broad home waters furnished ports and practise grounds for fishermen and maritime traders. Mountain forests rising directly from the littoral provided lumber for shipbuilding, while barring the way to the hinterland and emphasizing the feasibility of maritime communication. The long summer of cloudless days and starry nights, of steady winds and fogless atmosphere provided a favorable season for sailing, when the strong diurnal breezes favored the out-going and home-coming ships, and the countless promontories and mountainous islands, visible in the lucid air, furnished points to steer by before the invention of the compass.

WINDS AND NAVIGATION—The strongest single factor in stimulating early navigation was probably climate, though it crowded nautical activities into the warmer part of the year, when for most of the season the winds were steady. During the cyclonic storms of winter, Hesiod advised the sailor to "avoid the winter sea when the winds war aloud." [1] Horace thought that man had a heart of oak and bronze who feared not for his fragile bark "the squally southwest wind battling with the north." [2] For him and his kind "the sailing season begins in spring when the swallows build their mud nests under the eaves, when the meadows bloom, and the soft zephyrs blow over the unruffled sea." [3] This was the signal to make "the rollers draw to sea the long-dried hulls." [4]

The entire sailing season, when the northeast trade winds prevailed, lasted from March 10th to November 10th. During this period merchant ships might venture out for the sake of profit; but war vessels with their precious cargo of human lives were restricted to the sailing season par excellence between May 26th and September 14th, when the Etesian or north winds blew steadily. This period was prefaced and followed by about a month or more of variable winds when navigation was attended by some danger.[5] Hesiod, who was a farmer and lived before seamanship was well developed in Hellas, knew the sailing season as lasting for fifty days after the summer solstice in July and August. "Then relying on the steady winds, drag down your ships to the water, store in your cargo, but hurry home again before the new wine is made," he advised the seaman, "when autumnal storms stir up the deep." There was a sailing time in spring also, but it was perilous and ventured by the brave.[6]

Winter voyages were made rarely and only under stress of circumstances. During a serious grain shortage at Rome in winter, the Emperor Claudius tried to induce provision merchants to bring supplies to Rome by assuming any losses they might incur during the winter storms, and by insuring at his own cost ships built for this winter grain trade.[7] Winter voyages were resorted to in the period from 74 to 67 B.C., when piracy closed the summer seas. Merchants and even Roman troops destined for garrisons in the eastern provinces or to join the forces waging war against Mithradates feared the winter storms less than the pirate ships.[8] Lucullus made a winter voyage to Egypt to get ships, at a time when Mithradates (89-88 B.C.) had got command of the summer seas.[9] During the Peloponnesian War, in the winter of 427 B.C., the Athenian fleet in Sicily made a descent upon the Dorian colonies in the Lipari Islands, because this volcanic group could not be attacked at any other time, owing to the lack of water.[10]

The Etesian winds spring up about 9 A.M., increase to gale force in the early afternoon, and die down at night. In August they attain such violence that sailing vessels for weeks at a time cannot beat against them but have to tie up behind islands;[11] and in very ancient times this often endured till the sailors were threatened with starvation because their supplies were small.[12] They are too strong today at times even for

small steamers.   The local variety of the Etesian winds known
as the Hellespontine wind retarded ships bound from the
Ægean to the Pontus.   Demosthenes in his First Philippic describes with what concern Philip of Macedon watched this wind
at the height of summer, hoping it might detain the Athenian
fleet sailing for the relief of the Greek forces in eastern Thrace.
These long halts at the southern entrance to the Hellespont
were not rare; [13] and they help to explain the prosperity of
Troy, which became a local market and supply point.

The northeast trades prevailed in the West Basin of the
Mediterranean only to 40 degrees north; farther south the
winds swung to northwest or southwest, or were variable.   In
any event, the prevalence of the north winds in the sailing season made it desirable that seaports should have their harbors
sheltered on the north and open on the south, where ships would
most often enter.   It was better still if they had an anvil-shaped
harbor with entrances facing both north and south, like Tyre,
Cnidos, Cyzicus, Syracuse, Carthage and Athens with its
Piræus and Phaleros, the latter being the cargo port.   During
the entire period of navigation, from March 10th to November
10th, when the winds were variable, both entrances were
available.

In general the port with the south side entrance was imperative where the Etesian winds were strong as in Mytilene, or
where the north winds were augmented by some other powerful
air current, like the falling winds, to make them irresistible.
These develop at the southern base of all high coast ranges
facing southward to the Mediterranean.   A high cold hinterland and a warm sea foreland make the necessary conditions.
Then blows the fierce *mistral* or ancient Circius down from the
Cevenne Plateau of France, sweeping the Mediterranean littoral
with irresistible force as far as the Gulf of Luna (Spezia),
lending incalculable value to the port of Massilia and Antipolis
(Antibes) with their northern barrier.   In the Adriatic, which
is generally an area of low pressure, the northeast wind (Bora)
of the east coast quickly changes to a squally falling wind.[14]
In this sea the ancient pirates developed their expert seamanship and were embodied in the Roman navy as the "Liburnian

Squadron," for they were known to be trained in a severe school.[15]

These falling winds had an evil reputation among all navigators not familiar with their mountainous coast. "The violent blast of Strymonian Boreas" described the squalls that poured down the valley of the Strymon River and out to the Thracian Sea on the southern slope of the Rhodope Mountains.[16] The Cilician and Lycian coast of the Taurus Mountains had an ill repute owing to their winds, and often produced catastrophes for those unfamiliar with them. When Mithradates was attacking the island of Rhodes in 87 B.C., he sent his land forces in merchant vessels and triremes from the mainland. But a storm, blowing down from the hinterland towards the harbor of Rhodes, drove them into the arms of the enemy who rammed or burned them.[17]

Subordinate factors growing out of climatic conditions were the strong diurnal breezes which developed in these various seas and which the ancients utilized to approach their harbors in the evenings and leave them in early mornings, as the seamen do now; the starry skies which they used to steer by when night sailing became imperative; and the absence of fogs to confuse them when out on the sea.

CURRENTS AND TIDES—Other factors grew out of the conditions prevailing in the Mediterranean as an enclosed sea. Owing to this fact it had few marine currents strong enough to disconcert the ancient sailor, except the swift-flowing Bosporus and Hellespont which discharged the surplus waters collected from the large catchment basin of the Euxine.[18] This current zig-zagged from shore to shore in a way to determine natural landing places. Its velocity increased at the narrows and sharp bends, and during the early summer when thaws in the north brought on flood stage in the Euxine rivers and when the Hellespontine wind swept down the channel across the Ægean to Cape Malea. A less conspicuous current flowing from the higher *niveau* of the Atlantic into the *Mare internum* [19] was known to the ancients and was utilized by the Romans during the Second Punic War to put the Carthaginian fleet at a serious disadvantage in a naval engagement which ended in a debacle.[20]

Tides, which are faint and irregular in the Mediterranean as in all enclosed seas, were familiar to the ancients at the shallow heads of long inlets like the Malic Gulf,[21] the Adriatic, and the two Syrtes on the African coast;[22] but they played dangerous pranks with their craft only in funnel-shaped straits like the Messina channel and the tortuous Euripos. The tidal races in the Strait of Messina were scrutinized by naval commanders in the Second Punic War, lest their ships should be carried astray.[23] A Carthaginian fleet, about to ravage the coast of Sicily and Italy, was dispersed by a storm and three of its ships were driven by the tide into the Strait, where they were captured by Hiero of Syracuse.[24] Polybius stated that seamen had avoided the navigation of this passage ever since the time of Odysseus,[25] when the myth of Scylla and Charybdis expressed its reputation. The Euripos during spring tides was impassable to ships except during the pause at the turning of the current,[26] but this handicap did not prevent traffic in this strategic channel.

The ancients found the navigation of the Syrtes perilous because the ebb of the tides betrayed their ships to the quicksands lining those shallow bays;[27] but in the Gulf of Gades, the Atlantic tides flooded the shallow inlets and the river estuaries, rendering the whole land navigable, as Strabo expresses it, and this facilitated the import and export of merchandise.[28]

SUBSIDENCE COASTS—Nearly all parts of the Mediterranean coast had experienced an excess of subsidence over elevation. It therefore showed the typical subsidence littoral of high relief, broken up into a succession of rugged headlands and inshore islands by the drowned valleys of the old drainage streams dating from a period of more active erosion. This type of coast was widely distributed, corresponding to the prevailing mountain relief and the common history of subsidence. It reappeared with kindred features in nearly all parts sought by the ancient colonist and therefore reproduced his familiar home conditions in which he knew how to earn his livelihood. The Phocæans from the indented hill coast of western Asia Minor found a familiar site for their colony of Massilia where the hill ranges of Provence open out seaward with a safe port between. Where elevation succeeded subsidence, as on the maritime plain of Palestine, the irregularities of the coast disappeared, and the shore lifted only a featureless face.

PROMONTORIES—While abundant inlets and bays indenting Mediterranean coasts furnished a close succession of harbors of refuge for the early sailor, hardly less important to him were the intervening tongues of land—promontories or islands which stood out as sea marks to guide him in his creeping coastwise navigation. The bold relief of the Mediterranean shores made these sea marks conspicuous, and the clear, dry summer atmosphere rendered them visible from afar. Their importance is made evident in the early Greek voyages up the west coast of Italy, when the legend of Odysseus was transferred to the shore of the Tyrrhenian Sea. All the isles and headlands figure in the hero's wanderings. The Lacinian Cape on the southern coast of Italy became the Isle of Calypso. The Misenian Promontory at the entrance to the Bay of Naples became the Isle of the Sirens, and Cape Circei that of Circe. The steep promontory of Terracina seemed an appropriate site to mark with the burial mound of Elpenor.[29] Only the salient geographical features of the shore were embodied in the legends and thus were identified and located in their proper succession on the mental sailing chart of this new coast, for the benefit of later mariners.

This same emphasis on conspicuous sea marks along the coast appears again in Vergil's description of the wanderings of Æneas and in the geographical works of Strabo, Pliny, and Diodorus Siculus. Strabo traces the coast of each country by its promontories much as the ancient seaman steered from headland to headland; and it is from these outstretched arms of the land that he measures the distance from one country to another, as if quoting some early Greek sailor whose mind saw only the points where he abandoned and then regained the protecting line of the shore. He locates Crete by stating the distance of its various promontories from Cyrenaica, Egypt, Capes Malea and Sunium.[30] The Sacred Promontory (Cape St. Vincent) was the ancient boundary not only of Europe but of the habitable world.[31] The headlands of Calpe (Gibraltar) and Mount Abila (Ceuta) were the Pillars of Hercules marking the entrance to the Mediterranean.[32] The Hermæan Promontory (Cape Bon) was fixed as the eastern limit of Roman trading privileges in North Africa by an early treaty (circa 509 b.c.) with Carthage.[33]   A similar treaty with Tarentum excluded all Roman vessels from the Ionian Sea east of the Lacinian Promontory,[34] which was regarded as the boundary stone between the Sicilian and Ionian Seas.[35]   Strabo considered headlands and small coastal islands as obvious boundary marks comparable to columns and pillars.[36]

Numerous promontories which serrated the coasts of the Mediterranean were fortified and utilized as primitive coast defences or provided a protected base for the sinister operations of pirates.   The natural harbor formed by the jutting rock afforded safe anchorage for ships, and the elevated summit furnished an outlook point in time of war.   The Scyllæan headland overlooking the Strait of Messina was fortified by an early tyrant of Rhegium against the Etruscan pirates, to prevent the marauders from passing through the straits.[37] Rome's earliest coast defenses consisted in establishing Roman colonies in the newly conquered promontory towns of Antium, Terracina, Circei, and on the Island of Pontia in the fourth century before Christ.[38]   In the First Punic War, the turtle-shaped cape of Drepanum was fortified as naval base by the Carthaginians [39] to overlook the passage from Sicily to Carthage, just as Athens in the Peloponnesian War fortified Cape Sunium at the southern extremity of Attica, to protect the approaches for her ships from the Ægean.[40]   Sertorius, leading the revolt of Spain against Roman rule, seized the Artemisian promontory on the east coast of the peninsula "as an arsenal, convenient to the sea, both because it was fortified and fitted for piratical uses, and because it was visible from a great distance to vessels approaching." [41]   The southern coast of Asia Minor had a succession of these rocky fortresses where the buttresses of the Taurus ranges protruded into the sea.   Lycia had Cragos and Anti-Cragos, Pamphylia had Olympos and Phaselis, Cilicia had the notorious Coracesium, all of them pirate nests [42] which in the last half century of the Roman Republic levied toll upon Mediterranean commerce.

The long-continued importance of promontories and inshore islets to ancient seamen becomes apparent when we realize that coastwise navigation prevailed in the Mediterranean till a late date. When Athens was at the zenith of her maritime development, her naval expedition against Syracuse in 413 B.C. hugged the coast all the way, stopping at various cities along the course.[43] A fleet of transport vessels, carrying Peloponnesian forces from Laconia for the relief of Syracuse, was driven by a storm southward to Libya, touched at Cyrene to get pilots, coasted thence along the north shore of Africa to the Hermæan promontory (Cape Bon), whence was the shortest passage to Selinus in Sicily.[44] Two years later, when the Peloponnesians had developed their naval force to the utmost, and moreover were reinforced by powerful maritime allies who had revolted from Athens, they sent their fleet from Miletos to the Hellespont. Its voyage was typical. From Miletos the fleet was driven by a storm westward to Icaros island, where it was detained five or six days by bad weather; it sailed thence northward about fifty miles to Chios, where it remained two days provisioning. Leaving this island, it sought the mainland coast to avoid the Athenian fleet stationed on the west side of Lesbos, and touched at the inshore islet of Carteria near Phocæa to take the noonday meal. It sailed thence northward along the Æolian shore of Asia Minor, supped at the little port of Arginussæ, and there spent the night. The ships started again before dawn and reached Harmatus on the southern coast of the Troad in time for the noon meal. Thence they rounded the Lectum promontory, and reached the town of Rhœteum in the Hellespont before midnight.[45]

VISIBILITY DUE TO BOLD RELIEF AND CLIMATE—For creeping navigation such as this, the close-hugging shores of the sub-basins of the Mediterranean, the numerous islands and mountainous coasts lent the necessary encouragement. The outbound voyager was generally able to keep in view some beacon which beckoned him on. Even before he had left the home port, distant land faintly outlined on the far horizon stirred his spirit of enterprise. The Phœnician, pruning his vinestock on the terraced slope of Lebanon, could see distant Cyprus and its lofty peak of Olympos (6,403 feet or 1,952 meters) outlined against the sunset sky. From the mountains of Cyprus the view commands the Taurus range of Cilicia.[46] The island of Rhodes is within signalling distance of the Asia Minor coast; and from the high peak of Mount Atabyris (4,067 feet or 1,240 meters), where the ancient Rhodian sacrificed to Zeus, he could discern the far-away summit of Mount Ida in Crete.[47]   He made his voyage to Crete along an island-strewn course; and from Crete he sailed north past Ægilia and Cythera to the Laconian peninsula of the Peloponnesos, without losing sight of land.

The surface of the Ægean was so broken up by peninsulas and islands that a ship could not get farther than forty miles from some shore.   Moreover, owing to the prevailing high relief of the land, it was always in sight of peak or range in the clear summer weather.   Mount Athos (6,347 feet or 1,935 meters) was a guide to seamen in the North Ægean for a radius of a hundred miles.   At the summer solstice its shadow fell on the market place of Myrina in the island of Lemnos forty miles away.[48]   It is visible from Mount Olympos and Pelion in eastern Thessaly, from the summit of Mount Dirphys (Mount Delph, 5,725 feet or 1,745 meters) in eastern Euboea,[49] from the mouth of the Hellespont and from the west coast of Lesbos. The high peak of Samothrace, 5,250 feet (1,600 meters) in altitude, was visible for a radius of ninety-five miles.   Homer says that from its summit "was seen all Ida, the city of Priam and the ships of the Greeks." [50]   Æschylus, in his *Agamemnon*, describes how the news of Troy's fall was flashed by signal fires from peak to promontory and from island to mainland across the Ægean to the palace of Mycenæ in the Peloponnesos.[51]   The points which he enumerates had long been familiar sea marks to the ancient sailors.

For the middle Ægean this part of the mountain beacon was played by Dirphys in central Euboea and the Ocha Massif (4,607 feet or 1,404 meters) near the southern end of the island.   The former peak was visible from the bays of Macedonia and Chalcidice; the latter could be discerned from Halonnesos to the north, Naxos to the south, and Chios to the east.   Chios itself had a peak, Mount Pelinnaios (3,950 feet or 1,204 meters), which was visible for a radius of 75 miles or the distance across the Ægean to the eastern promontory of Euboea.   The south Ægean had similar beacons in Mount Atabyris of Rhodes (4,067 feet or 1,240 meters); in Mount

Ida of central Crete (8,195 feet or 2,498 meters) visible for 118 miles; and in other peaks of eastern and western Crete, ranging from seven to eight thousand feet in altitude, visible from the Cyclades to the north and half-way to Africa on the south.[52]

In other parts of the Mediterranean, shadowy shores on far horizons lured enterprising mariners to boldest ventures. The lofty Acroceraunian Mountains (highest peak, 6,620 feet or 2,018 meters), rising like a rampart on the northwest coast of Epiros, are visible across the Strait of Otranto, from the opposite Italian shore.[53] Africa is occasionally visible in winter from the peak of Eryx in Sicily,[54] across 85 miles of sea. The lofty range of northern Corsica (Mount Cinto 8,890 feet or 2,710 meters) looms up today like a gigantic piece of sculpture against the western sky of Tuscany, fifty miles away; and was discerned by the ancients from the Carrara Mountains overlooking Luna Bay (Gulf of Spezia), 70 miles away.[55] Two sea trails lead to Corsica, each staked out by a succession of mountainous islands, which the timid sailor kept in sight. The indented shoreline of Etruria, its ports sheltered by headlands, the numerous islands of the Tuscan Archipelago, outlying Corsica and Sardinia, all combined to make the school of navigation which turned out the wide-ranging Etruscan pirates and sea traders.

Corsica is only 85 miles from the sea-washed foot of the Maritime Alps; Sardinia lies only 112 miles from the Tunisian Peninsula, and even this short stretch is broken by a small group of islands twenty-five miles from the African shore. Hence it was possible for the ancient navigators to cross the western Mediterranean Basin from north to south at its widest part without losing sight of land. The broad expanse of water between Spain and Sardinia is half-way bridged by the Pityuses and Balearic Isles. These served to guide the ancient sailor across one belt of sea after another from shore to shore. The promontory of Artemisium on the Spanish coast commands a view of the nearer islands over fifty miles away in clear weather; but from the summit of Mount Mongo (2,495 feet or 7,600 meters), which occupies the northern side of this headland, the whole Balearic Archipelago can be seen. In the long marine corridor of the Iberian Sea, lying between Spain and Africa, the opposite coasts are rarely more than ninety miles apart. The snowy peaks of the Sierra Nevada, over 11,000 feet high, rise like watch-towers from the mountain rampart encircling the southern coast of Spain, and command a view of the Moroccan ranges opposite.[56] They doubtless beckoned the first Phœnician trireme which felt its way westward along the African littoral, and account in part for the constant intercourse between these neighboring coasts from the earliest times.

It cannot be sufficiently emphasized that in the Mediterranean we have to do with prevailing high reliefs, which are visible at great distances in the lucid air. This is true not only of the mainland but of the islands. Homer speaks of "the clear-seen islands" and "clear-seen Ithaca."[57] These are the crests of submerged mountain ranges, like the Sporades, Cyclades, Cyprus and Balearic Isles; or the summits of depressed plateaus, like Corsica, Sardinia and Malta; or the tops of submarine volcanic cones, which tower above the surrounding waves. The little island of Cossyra or Pantellaria, lying between Sicily and Tunisia only forty-three miles east of Cape Bon, contains a volcanic cone (2,743 feet high, 848 meters) visible from the isolated peak of San Salogero (1,272 feet) on the southern coast of Sicily near the ancient Selinunt.[58] Pantellaria was therefore an ancient seamark for vessels sailing between Carthage and the near Sicilian ports, and it was a way-station and supply point to ancient Phœnician navigators bound for Carthage and Spain.[59] The nearby islets of Lampione and Lampedusa, on the other hand, low mesa-like limestone rocks, rising only four hundred feet above the sea, derived their names from the custom of lighting fires to warn ships against shipwreck. It is a suggestive fact that all these islands are resting places for birds of passage on their air voyages between Europe and Africa.[60] The volcanic cones of the Æolian Isles (Lipari) were sea marks in the south Tyrrhenian Sea. They were visible in clear weather from the northern heights of Sicily; and the pulsating eruptions of Strongyle (Stromboli), smoke by day and flame by night, emitted every eight minutes, were a beacon to seamen. The appearance of the eruptions on Thermessa (Volcano), variable under different atmospheric conditions, enabled the seamen to foretell changes in the weather.[61]

The stimulus to ancient navigation of high reliefs on Mediterranean islands and coastlands lay not only in the fact that they provided seamarks and goals for voyages, but also in the fact that these mountains revealed to the inhabitants a wide prospect over the neighboring sea, and therefore extended the horizon of possible maritime enterprise. The summit of Mount Dirphys in Eubœa commands a view of distant Athos, but ancient Cyme on the shore at its feet could detect on the far horizon only a stationary mass of cloud, the white turban which Athos always wears.[62] The summit of Ætna (10,758 feet or 3,279 meters) commands a view 130 miles in radius, but fails to include either Malta or the African coast.[63] The range of vision from Mount Ida in Crete is almost as great, and includes those Cyclades islands which the Minoan kings of Crete colonized back in the youth of the world.[64]

Owing to geographic and climatic conditions, the ancient people of the Mediterranean basin lived on their heights to an unusual degree. These outlook towers therefore had always their watchmen. Tertiary terraces and a mild climate, as we have seen, combined to draw the husbandman to the mountain slopes, tillable up to an elevation of four or five thousand feet.[65] Shepherds with their flocks and herds occupied the highland pastures during the long summers. The forests on the mountains called the lumberman to his task before the autumn rains should make the sap begin to run. The summits of the peaks held the sanctuaries of the rain-giving gods, visited by priest and suppliant when the summer drought became intolerable. The grotto of Zeus on Mount Ida in Crete which was a place of pilgrimage, lies at an elevation of over five thousand feet; the earlier cave, sacred during the Minoan period as the mythological birthplace of Zeus, lay far up on the slope of Mount Dicte. Its votive offerings testify to the number of feet which climbed the sacred mount. The summit crater of Ætna was familiar to the Greeks of Sicily as early as 430 B.C., when it became renowned as the supposed grave of the philosopher Empedocles. Frequent ascents to the summit were made in the early days of the Roman Empire.[66] Drawn by these various economic and religious activities to the heights, men in ancient times grew curious about those distant lands within range of vision, and made them the goal of early maritime exploration.

FEAR OF LOW COASTS—Low coasts were in ill favor with the ancient seamen. They lacked the sea-marks necessary to the early Mediterranean navigator. Low featureless coasts of wide extent were found in the river deltas, like those of the Nile, Rhone, Po and the flat embayed coast of the Euxine between the Danube and the Dnieper. In other parts of the Mediterranean low shores are to be found, but they are backed a mile or two inland by hills or mountains visible from the sea.

The criticisms which Diodorus Siculus makes of the Mediterranean coast of Egypt are echoed by other ancient writers about this and other low littorals. Diodorus states that for 500 miles the Egyptian coasts had no harbors except the sheltered cove behind the island of Pharos, forming the port of Alexandria; that the Delta coast abounded in hidden rocks and sand reefs on which the ancient mariner was shipwrecked when attempting to land; and that the solid land lay so low that it could not be distinguished from the marshes, in which the boats would strand.[67] Hence the navigators of the *Odyssey* found "the way to Egypt is long and vexatious," [68] and had the perils of this coast impressed upon them by narrow escape from shipwreck. As the shore on either side of the Pharos harbor had nothing to distinguish it from the low marshy coast, Strabo tells us, a conspicuous mark was required to direct mariners to the entrance of the port. Therefore Ptolemy I and II erected on the eastern point of Pharos Island a high white marble tower, the first lighthouse of the world.[69] A few miles to the east between Alexandria and the Canobic mouth of the Nile, a long sand spit called Cape Zephyrium was distinguished from the flat featureless shore by a small temple of Venus Arsinoë,[70] erected as a sea-mark by Ptolemy II, doubtless in honor of his wife. But nearly four centuries before this at the Bolbitine (Rosetta) mouth of the Nile stood the Tower of Perseus, mentioned by Herodotus [71] but erroneously located by him at the western angle of the Delta. Near it, a short way up the Bolbitine channel, lay the so-called "Fortress of the Milesians," [72] built by a naval detachment of the Asia Minor Greeks who as mercenaries had helped Psammeticus I to expel the Assyrians and gain the Egyptian throne.[73] The tower at the mouth of the channel was the signpost on this unmarked coast to guide Greek reinforcements and merchant ships to the Bolbotine arm and the new Egyptian capital of Sais which lay about forty-five miles up this stream.

The same causes and effects are to be noted elsewhere on low coasts of the Mediterranean. The mouths of the Rhone were hard to navigate according to Strabo, owing to sandbars and the general flatness of the country, which rendered it impossible in foul weather to discern the land, even when near. Hence the Massiliots, who wished to make the Rhone accessible to foreign commerce, set up towers as beacons, and erected a temple to Diana of Ephesos on a deltaic island at the mouth of the river.[74] Among the various outlets of the Po, the navigable channels were hard to distinguish and difficult to enter; [75] they were indicated by no tower or temple, though from the time of the early Etruscans to that of Augustus, the various canal-builders endeavored to improve navigation through the coastal lagoons of the Po delta.[76] On the low coast of Scythia, however, incoming ships from Athens bound for Olbia to take on cargoes of grain were directed to their port by the temple of Ceres, located on the river peninsula between the mouth of the Dnieper and Bug where the two unite in a coastal lagoon.[77] The mouth of the Dniester was marked by the Tower of Neoptolemus,[78] while within its estuary lay the ancient Greek colony of Tyra.

Maritime activities of some kind have characterized nearly all the Mediterranean coasts. Their intensity of development has differed greatly; so have their date of origin and their duration. Some districts with excellent geographic conditions have been centers of nautical enterprise from the earliest days to the present. The Gulf of Volo today holds the busy Greek port of Volo on the site of ancient Iolkos, whence Jason with his fellow Argonauts sailed to explore the Euxine, and the son of Alcestis led his fleet to the Trojan War.[79] This protected inlet has had a succession of ports near the site of the ancient Iolkos, and has always centered in itself the maritime history of productive Thessaly. Seafaring activity has for ages characterized the Gulf of Corinth, with its series of great ports from ancient Corinth to modern Patras; also the Saronic Gulf with its group of busy harbors headed by the Piræus of Athens; and Greece as a whole, which still handles nearly all the local carrying trade of the eastern Mediterranean, though Greece is a small, poor state.

Maritime development of some kind, piratical, commercial and naval, merging one into the other, has stamped the history of the upper Adriatic, the Gulfs of Lyons, Genoa, Naples, Palermo, Tunis, Gibraltar and Cadiz, with few or no periods of quiescence during 2,500 years. Other littorals, with adverse local conditions of coastline, location and hinterland connections have failed to develop maritime enterprise under native initiative; but when colonized or conquered by a nautically efficient race, they have been brought to participate in the seafaring activities of their masters, because the geographic conditions of the Mediterranean as a whole insured profits to maritime trade.

FISHING INDUSTRIES—Fishing, which provides the first training for larger seafaring ventures, was almost universal in the ancient Mediterranean. This was due to the marked distribution of population along the small coastal lowlands in constant contact with the sea, discussed in a previous chapter, to the poor and limited pasturage which made fish an obvious substitute for meat, and to the abundant fisheries of the Mediterranean Sea. These comprised not only the various kinds of sea food, but also sponges and the purple-yielding murex. Hence the fisherman had a variety of wares to bring to market, and from his long voyages he normally brought back also articles of foreign production for sale.

The smaller the yield of the land, resulting either from barren soil or scant arable area, the more important were the fisheries and their associated commerce. This is the principle which we recognize in the economic history of Norway, Scotland, Japan and colonial New England,[80] and which meets us early in the Mediterranean. The Phœnicians and after them the Greeks followed the tunny into the Euxine in the legendary period. Homer emphasizes the striking feature of "the fishy

Bosporus." Outlook towers for tunny from early antiquity crowned bold headlands along the course of the moving shoals to brackish spawning grounds at the mouth of big rivers. The Phœnicians searched for the purple murex and located its haunts on the coast of Caria, the deep bays of Laconia and Argolis, the shores of Cythera, and the long Eubœan [81] Sound. This valuable mollusk gave rise to wide-sweeping voyages and extended the geographical horizon of Mediterranean navigators. It was a purple fisher of Itanus, a Phœnician settlement in eastern Crete, who guided colonists from Thera to the Barca peninsula in the sixth century before Christ and founded Cyrene.[82]

The geographic conditions which produced a typical fishing community are set forth by Dicæarchus in his description of the little Bœotian town Anthedon on the Eubœan Sound. It lay on a harbor, and behind it rose a belt of rough hills separating it from the Copaic Lake basin. Grain was scarce, for the soil was poor; but wine from the hillside vineyards and sea food were abundant. Nearly all the population got their living from the sea. They were fishermen or ship-builders or ferrymen who carried passengers across the sound. From its sheltered channel they drew the harvest of the deep—fish, sponges, and the purple murex, and their finger nails were corroded by constantly working in the salt water.[83]

The Phocæan exiles from Asia Minor who after the Persian conquest of the Ionian coast settled on the Italian shore at Hyela or Velia in Lucania, found their new home small and barren; so they resorted to maritime trade, salting of fish and such occupations to gain a livelihood.[84] Another group of these emigrants located at Massilia, where they found poor soil for grain crops, but good vineyard land on the hill slopes. Therefore, they also turned perforce to the resources of the sea and exploited their location for commerce at the terminus of the Rhone highway.[85] The colony from Cnidos and Rhodes which in 580 B.C. settled on Lipara Island north of Sicily, found geographic conditions similar to those in their previous homes and therefore maintained their wonted maritime activities. The land was fertile, but small in area.[86] A meager water supply also restricted tillage. On the other hand, their harbors were good, markets were near, fisheries were abundant, and the mineral products of the islands, like alum and sulphur, were valuable items of export trade. Hence they were strong enough to repel persistent attacks of the Etruscan pirates and rich enough to make generous offerings at the temple of Delphi.[87]

WHERE MARITIME ACTIVITY FAILED—This was the type of geographic environment which enforced intercourse with the sea on the eternal food quest. In the Mediterranean lands which failed to develop active maritime life, the pull of the geographic forces was landward, away from the coast. Their history was influenced not by sea power but by "bread power." Such countries were Egypt, lowland Cilicia, and Scythia; on a smaller scale also Bœotia and Latium. These showed little concentration of population on the coasts. In Bœotia and Latium the bulk of the people lived in the interior, where fertile valleys and wide meadows supported well-fed farming communities. Bœotia had an indented coastline along sheltered gulfs, but its enclosing mountains concentrated attention upon its golden crops and flowering gardens. Latium had no port except Formiæ [88] which lay far from the centers of population in the Tiber and Anio valley. Egypt too was a land of flesh pots. The harborless coast with its broad belt of marshes and mudflats, shifting river channels, barren sand-dunes and pestilential swamps on the seaward side of the Nile delta was doubtless always sparsely populated as today.[89] Only a limestone spur of solid Africa thrust out into the spongy alluvium gave a dry site and a harbor to Alexandria. Thus the Egyptian people were held at arm's length from the sea; and were slow to advance from river to marine navigation. Moreover, in this timberless land lumber was so expensive that only the prosperous few could own boats or ships. The frail reed skiffs wrought from papyrus and bulrushes sufficed to navigate the slow-flowing Nile, but not to withstand the break of the waves beyond the lagoons. The river provided fish; the swamps teemed with aquatic birds; the wet meadows pastured cattle, and the irrigated fields yielded food in abundance. That faroff sea could offer little more.

The advantages of a location on two seas, the Mediterranean

and the Red, were appreciated by a few progressive Egyptian rulers. Queen Hatasu sent out to the incense country on the Red Sea a royal fleet of vessels which resembled the large river boats of the period;[90] others transported troops to the Syrian coast in their Nile boats, when a northern campaign was on hand.[91] But the evidence seems to show that enterprising sovereigns employed chiefly Phœnicians and Greeks for this maritime intercourse, and failed to leave lasting results in a national maritime development. They moved their capitals to the Delta, however, to Tanis, Pelusium, Bubastis, and Sais, and made Lower Egypt in some degree receptive to oversea influences.

The Libyan dynasty, inaugurated about 650 B.C. by Psammeticus, followed the example of its ancestors, who had employed maritime raiders and pirates from the northern islands as allies in the conquest of Delta lands, and relied upon a Greek fleet to secure its hold upon the Egyptian throne. It opened the Canobic Nile to Greek trade, located Greek colonists at Naucratis, and founded a series of Ionian and Carian settlements on the Pelusiac Nile, below Bubastis.[92] Thus the two principal outlets of the Nile were occupied by Greek merchants. These increased in number, and by marriage with the natives gave rise to the important class of interpreters, who facilitated intercourse between Egypt and Greece. The enormous profits of the maritime trade,[93] the example of successful voyagers at their doors, the increased importation of suitable lumber for ships, its lower selling price, the presence of ship models on the lower Nile channels and the improved port facilities in the form of docks, all combined to convert Egyptians or Greco-Egyptian half-breeds into seamen. For by 480 B.C., when Xerxes collected his forces for the invasion of Greece, his fleet included two hundred Egyptian triremes; nor did the equipment of the sailors indicate them to be other than Egyptian.[94] Yet it is significant that Herodotus, who visited Egypt about 450 B.C., found that country had equivalents of all the Greek gods except Poseidon and the Dioscuri;[95] but these deities the priests of Egypt did not know. Moreover, the naval activity displayed in the Persian War was only momentary. Greek fleets sailed to Egypt again in 459 B.C. when the Delta endeavored to throw off the Persian yoke. And in the time of Herodotus, the Egyptians were again sea-shy, and left their foreign trade to Phœnicians and Greeks.

The Nile became the seat of sustained maritime activity only when Alexander the Great built a Greek city on the harbor of Pharos, and his successors made it the great commercial port of the Mediterranean world. They concentrated there all the trade from the Orient, diverting it from the Piedmont route through northern Mesopotamia and the Phœnician ports to the Red Sea and Nile route to Alexandria. After the decline of Athenian sea power, Egypt under the Ptolemies was for over a century the first commercial and maritime state of the Eastern Mediterranean.[95] She controlled for a time nearly all the coasts of the Levantine Sea, held Cyprus, the Cyclades, points on the west Asia Minor front and a seaboard strip in southern Thrace.[96] This oversea dominion she ruled from the capital of Alexandria, seat of a Greek court on the Mediterranean rim of Egypt. Greek maritime and commercial efficiency, transplanted thither, made Egypt a busy way-station in the world's sea trade, but failed to draw the native life into this imposed activity.

The northern littoral of the Euxine showed the same retarded maritime development under discouraging geographic conditions. Pasture lands and grain fields were extensive and productive, despite a low and uncertain rainfall, and hence furnished abundant food. The embayed river mouths provided numerous harbors and port sites, along which the tunny fish came to spawn at their door. The vast steppe hinterland bred a pastoral nomadic population, who in their seasonal wanderings came down to the coast only in winter,[97] when weather conditions for navigation were at their worst and the bays were often frozen over. Moreover, nomadism excluded that concentration of population in immediate contact with the sea which is a necessary condition of local maritime development. Therefore, the oversea commerce of the Euxine was started at an early period by the intruding Greeks. These utilized the geographic advantages of harbor and coastline which lay beyond the experience of the dwellers of the steppes. The agricultural Tauri of the Tauric Chersonesus (Crimea) who tilled the plains of the peninsula, imitated the example of the Greeks and sailed the sea. They seem to have pushed out first into the shallow Putrid Lake, a western arm of Lake Mæotis. This they navigated in their "sewn boats" or skiffs made of a wicker framework covered with sewn hides,[98] the materials for which abounded in the reeds of brackish lagoons and the herds of the pastureland. This boat was evidently a native product, and a type that develops in all semi-arid lands.[99] The abundant fisheries of Lake Mæotis probably drew the barbarians out upon its waters both in early times, and especially later when the Greek merchants created a heavy demand for the cured fish for export.[100] The Royal Scythians, who occupied the coast north of Lake Mæotis and the Crimean peninsula, sacrificed to a god of the sea corresponding to Poseidon.[101] The Scythians dwelling around this recess eventually developed into seamen after the Greek model, because we find them practising piracy against the Greek merchant ships,[102] and in 67 B.C. waging a naval battle against the fleet of Mithradates in the Crimean Bosporus (Kertch).[103]

In contrast with these regions of rudimentary or retarded maritime development, the Ægean Sea offered rare geographic conditions for early nautical enterprise. No other sub-basin of the Midland Sea could compare with it. It had every qualification for challenging the reluctant sea ventures of untutored and timid coast-dwellers, and gradually promoting intercourse along its easy sea paths. Its nautical and industrial efficiency produced a succession of Carian, early Ægean, Cretan and Greek sea-powers, based on a carrying trade to employ their numerous cargo boats, and on their own maritime enterprises. Thus geographic conditions on the land drove the people of these states out upon the sea, while the sea in front lured them by its ready accessibility from its inlets and harbors, by its outlying islands and neighboring coasts, and its profitable trade. Hence an important factor in the development of these maritime states was their location on routes of commerce.

MARITIME TRADE ROUTES—The chief trade routes of the Mediterranean Sea were main travelled roads. One system ran from the old industrial and civilized lands of the Levantine Sea to the pioneer West Basin, which was rich in raw materials and offered markets for the manufactured wares and fine wines of

the East. Another system, comprising many routes, crossed
the Mediterranean from north to south, connecting regions of
contrasted climates and generally contrasted degrees of culture. Hence they sought their termini in the big river ports
of southern Europe which gave access to the temperate regions
of the north.

The east-west trunk route of the Mediterranean was first explored by the Phœnicians. Likewise a Samian vessel, bound
for Egypt about 620 B.C., was carried west by a protracted
east wind past the Pillars of Hercules to Tartessus, then un-
frequented by the Greeks, and sold its cargo at huge profit.[104]
A little later some Phocæan Greeks from Ionia duplicated this
experience and were welcomed by the native king [105] who rejoiced to see the trade monopoly of the Phœnicians broken; for
the "silver-bedded River Tartessus" mentioned by the Sicilian
Greek, Stesichorus (570 B.C.), seems to have indicated the
island enclosed between the two outlets of the Bætis or Guadalquivir, where the port of Tartessus probably was situated and
where all the trade of the rich valley was concentrated.[106] But
the Phœnicians would not tolerate interlopers. They routed
out the Phocæans from their attempted colony at Mænaca
east of Malaca [107] and left them free to found Massilia. They
adopted the usual truculent method of middlemen. Eratosthenes said that the Carthaginians drowned any strangers who
sailed past their strait on their voyage to Sardinia or to the
Pillars of Hercules.[108]

This trunk route was long the monopoly of the Phœnicians.
It ran from Egypt, Tyre or Sidon north of Cyprus westward
in the lee of the Taurus Mountains past Side, Phaselis, Patara
and Myra in Lycia, where Saint Paul took ship for Rome; [109]
then on the southern or leeward side of Rhodes, Carpathos,
Crete, north past Cythera, Zachynthos and Corcyra, across
the Strait of Otranto to Hydruntum, along the coast of Magna
Græcia to Sicily, and thence by Cossyra island (Pantellaria) to
Utica or Carthage, and along the north coast of Africa to
Gades or Tartessus. An alternative route crossed the Ægean
Sea in the wind-shelter of the Cyclades Islands to Corinth from
Rhodes or Halicarnassos, passed the Isthmus on the roller
tramway, and joined the former route in the Sound between

Leucas and the mainland, where a gravel spit had been cut to form a channel. This last was short and the regular route for passenger travel, while cargo boats used it less often because of the heavy tolls on the Isthmian tramway.

The ancient coastwise route from Egypt and the Ægean to Sicily and Carthaginian Africa seems to have held at least till 1804. At that date, when sailing vessels were still in vogue, Leake found in the harbor of Avlona in western Epiros a grain ship, bound from Constantinople to Palermo; and outside the Gulf of Avlona he "met a vessel from Alexandria bound direct (sic) to Tunis" with pilgrims from Mecca.[110]

The ancient route from Phœnicia to Rhodes along the south coast of Asia Minor is followed by steamers today. Rhodes, which had a dominant interest in the Egyptian grain trade, had colonies or factories in the ports of call along this route, at Phaselis [111] and Gagæ in Lycia, Side and Soli farther east. Vessels travelling this route touched at Lindos in eastern Rhodes even in legendary times. Danaus and his fifty daughters stopped at Lindos on their way from Egypt to Argos; so did Cadmus on his journey from Phœnicia to Greece.[112] This route was travelled also by Pompey when fleeing from Philippi to Egypt,[113] and later by Saint Paul on his way from Greece to Jerusalem. Return voyages from Rhodes or eastern Crete to Egypt were made occasionally by sailing southeast before the Etesian wind to the Libyan coast at Apis near the Parartonian promontory, and thence east 200 miles to Alexandria. This route was taken by the young Ptolemy in 162 B.C.,[114] but owing to the barren nature of this littoral it had no attraction for merchant ships.

Rhodes enjoyed the immense advantage of a location at the busiest crossroads of the Eastern Mediterranean. Here the main sea route to the north and the Euxine branched off from the great trunk line between the Suez Isthmus and the Atlantic. There were three Ægean routes focusing on the Hellespont. This eastern one ran from Rhodes north along the coast of Asia Minor, threading its way between the islands and the mainland on a lee shore to the northeast Etesian winds, whose violence was therefore somewhat moderated. Vessels could conduct a drop-in trade on both sides of their course, for the insular capitals lay almost without exception on the continental side of the islands, facing the mainland ports and the river valley highways leading back into the interior. This was a populous coast, with ample resources considering the small arable area; but its citizens pushed their merchant ships into all the big markets of the Mediterranean, and carried on an active middleman business between the Euxine and the southern basins.

Another north-south route traced the western side of the Ægean. It ran from the group of cities clustered about the Saronic Gulf,—Corinth, Ægina, Megara, Athens—ran north through the Eubœan Sound behind the hundred-mile breakwater of Eubœa Island, issued from the Malic Gulf, and turned northeastward in the partial shelter of the Sporades islands and Lemnos to Tenedos near the mouth of the Hellespont.

A third route for vessels southward bound, ready to run before the Hellespontine wind, ran diagonally across the Ægean for 110 miles from Tenedos to the passage between southern Eubœa and Andros, and thence to the Saronic Gulf. In Homeric days this course was considered a test of a seaman's daring. The Greek leaders returning from Troy deliberated a long time whether they should venture on this open course, or follow the safer route south along the Asia Minor coast, thence west along the leeward side of Crete, and north to Nauplia and Argos, a voyage twice as long.

The Adriatic Sea, as a low pressure area, was a storm-breeder which could offer no advantage to ancient navigation. Its unproductive coasts had little attraction for traders or colonists. Only the fertile Po valley at its head could send out food stuffs to other lands; it therefore developed a succession of ports at the head of this embayment—Spina, an old Etruscan port, Adria, mentioned in 520 B.C., Ravenna, when the other ports became silted up, and finally Aquileia and Tergeste when Roman merchants began to develop trade across the Carso Plateau with the upper Save and Danube, after piracy had been suppressed on the Adriatic in the early days of the Empire.

The West Basin of the Mediterranean had its coast encircled by trade routes. The northward ones traced the west coast of Italy and the east coast of Spain, picking up a drop-in trade at the towns distributed along these shores. After leaving the stormy Sicilian Strait, vessels found safe winds until they came within range of the cyclonic storms that swept the northern part of the basin in late spring and early summer, or the mistral that sends down its squalls from the Cevenne Plateau against ships approaching Massilia and the other ports of the Gallic Gulf. Massilia's chief rival as northern terminus was Genoa, which had a poor harbor but was linked by a low pass (1,800 feet) across the Ligurian Apennines with the cities of the upper Po valley.

Certain maritime states lay at the crossroads of a land and sea route, like Corinth and Megara on the Isthmian highway north and south through Greece, and the busy marine track which ran from the Ægean to the western seas. This led west through the Saronic Gulf, over the Isthmus of Corinth by the roller tramway for the transfer of ships, thence by the Corinthian Gulf to the Ionian Sea and the Adriatic. Corinth and Megara stood astride the Isthmus, with a port on either sea. But Ægina, Athens, Epidaurus, Trœzene, and the Eubœan cities of Chalcis and Eretria were near enough to the Isthmus to profit by this western sea path. Chalcis and Eretria blazed the western trail. They planted way-stations in the vestibule of the Corinthian Gulf at a new Chalcis and on the island of Corcyra. Their termini they fixed at Cumæ in Italy, and Ortygia Island and Naxos in Sicily, prior to the coming of the Corinthians who in 735 B.C. followed in their tracks.[115]

The Eubœan cities, moreover, occupied a location closely analogous to that of Corinth, because at the port of Chalcis the Strait of the Euripos shrinks to so narrow a channel that in 411 B.C. it was bridged. Here passed the land road from the island into the heart of Bœotia at Thebes where it tapped the axial highway of the Greek peninsula, and ran thence westward to the port of Creusis on the Corinthian Gulf. Bœotia was rendered indifferent to maritime matters by her fertile soil and by the mountain rim of her old lake basin, which kept her chief centers of population secluded from the coast; hence Bœotia fed the trade of Chalcis, but offered no competition. A ferry kept Eretria in touch with the port of Oropus, which lay four miles away across the Strait on the Attic coast. Thus these Eubœan cities were in reach of a land road from the most fertile state of Greece, and they commanded the busy sea lane, the Eubœan Sound, which carried the bulk of north and south traffic along the Ægean coast of the peninsula. Chalcis, in other words, was situated on an isthmus that was pierced by a natural strait. A similar location on the Hellespont and Bosporus, where the straits between two continents are almost bridged, explain the nine successive cities on the site of ancient Troy, and the persistent commercial dominion of Byzantium and Constantinople.

A location at or near the crossroads of a north-south and east-west sea route contributed to the wide-reaching maritime enterprises of the seaports of the Saronic Gulf; for the latter also lay within easy reach of the Eubœan Sound. Therefore, the whole group of cities, Corinth and Athens as well as Chalcis and Eretria, sent out their trading and colonial expeditions north to the coast of Macedonia and Thrace, west to the coast of Sicily and southern Italy. Like location at the crossways of two important sea routes explains the ancient sea power of Rhodes, Crete, Naxos, Corcyra, Syracuse and Carthage. All were situated on the Oriental trade track, which followed the axis of the Mediterranean; and all commanded the outlets °of the northern sub-basins. Corcyra's position, though apparently sidetracked, lay right in the path of the old coastwise route to the west. Naxos occupied a pivotal position in the south Ægean, as indicated by its ancient slave market, and its early connections with Athens, Miletos and Samos.[116]

MARITIME LEAGUES—All these maritime states carried on extensive oversea trade, maintained navies to protect their commerce, and sent out colonies, both as outlets for their redundant population and as trading-stations on foreign coasts. Several states established for a time a thalassocracy or sea sovereignty, like· that of Crete in the Minoan period.[117] But more common was the maritime league, either with or without a chief city. Primarily an amphictyonic union grouped about a common sanctuary, it generally revealed also a selfish motive to secure itself against aggressive inland powers, or gain access to certain strategic trade routes, like the Eubœan Sound, the

Corinthian Gulf, the Hellespont and Bosporus, whence its ships might easily be excluded. These naval leagues were eminently characteristic of the Mediterranean Sea. They reflected the physical dismemberment of its coastlands; its small peninsulas, headlands, islands, and mountain-locked bays with their detached maritime communities; the dominant attraction of the sea, and the "short lap" of early coastwise voyages. They formed often a state within a state, after the manner of the medieval German Hansa, as in the case of the Magnesian League, which in the third century B.C. united certain Macedonian ports of the Pagasæ Gulf under the leadership of Demetrias. Sometimes they were international and linked the maritime subjects of different states, as in the case of Calaurian League of the seventh century B.C., which comprised seaports of Laconia, Argolis, Attica and Bœotia.

These maritime leagues prevailed in very ancient times. In the *Iliad* we get hints of them in the groups of vessels under their several leaders which figure in the Catalogue of the Ships.[118] The cities listed as subject to Argos included Tiryns, (whose port was Nauplia), Asine, Eiones, Mases, Hermione, Ægina and Epidauros,[119] all located in the broad coastal zone of ancient piratical days. After the Dorian invasion of Argolis and the consequent decay incident to war, the surviving coast towns of this list reappeared in the Ionic League of Calauria, which belonged to the seventh century B.C. Though outwardly an amphictyonic to maintain the worship of Poseidon on the little island of Calauria, it appears rather as a union of the earlier Ionian maritime population to preserve their rights against the Dorian conquerors.[120] This Calaurian League comprised eight members—Prasiæ, Nauplia, Hermione, Trœzene, Epidauros, Ægina, Athens and Bœotian Orchomenos,[121] which was a maritime state by reason of its seaports Anthedon and Larymna on the Eubœan Sound.[122] It is significant that Orchomenos was at this time resisting absorption into the racially alien Bœotian League, formed by the new conquerors from the north. Her adherence to the Calaurian League conferred a great advantage upon the trading cities of the Argolic and Saronic Gulfs; it gave them staple places for their trade and refuge ports at the door of the Euripos, probably at the time (seventh century B.C.) when the mercantile power of Chalcis and Eretria had been exhausted by the War of the Lelantian Plain,[123] and therefore, at an opportune moment for tapping the profitable Euripos commerce. Only a geographic factor like this adequately explains the presence of Orchomenos in the Calaurian League.

The confederation of the twelve Ionian cities on the west coast of Asia Minor was modelled after the old league of the Corinthian Gulf,[124] which probably had secured to its constituent cities a fair share or even predominance in the prehistoric trade with Italy. The mixed population of the Ionian colonies in Asia Minor speaking four different dialects, drawn from nearly every tribal stock in Greece and mingled with local Carians, gave a religious sanction to their union by setting up a federal shrine to Heliconian Poseidon on the Mycale Promontory.[125] Real enough was their need of mutual protection. Coming from the sea, they secured a mere *pied de terre* here and there on the fringed coasts of Lydia and Caria. Their neighbors were desirous of expanding seaward, and able to menace Ionian independence, as the campaigns of Gyges of Lydia in the seventh century B.C. indicated, and Lydian conquests of the coast in the sixth century abundantly proved.[126] And beyond lay the threat of barbarian aggressions from the heart of Asia. During the Persian conquest of Ionia and the Ionian revolt, the assemblies of the Panionium deliberated upon measures of common defense,[127] but the league was too loose for effective action.

The southern coast of Asia Minor, by reason of its geographic conditions, was destined for nautical activity, though its close hugging mountain barrier and its undeveloped hinterland prevented extensive trade. Therefore, Lycia, Pamphylia and Cilicia had their maritime leagues, the last chiefly of a piratical character, and developed fleets which were impressed into the Persian naval forces for the conquest of the Ægean Greeks.[128] The Phœnicians were the leading maritime power of the Levantine Basin, both in their navy and merchant marine. Their contingent in the fleet of Xerxes in 480 B.C. was 300 triremes; that of Cyprus was 150, and that of Egypt was 200. To both these countries Phœnicia gave standards of seamanship, through centuries of colonization in the case of the former and of long commercial intercourse in the case of the latter.   The line of detached Phœnician cities which occupied the sea base of the Lebanon Mountains, wherever a promontory or an inshore island or a line of reefs offered a harbor, never established a maritime empire as did their colony at Carthage in the West Mediterranean.   They had the small spacial ideals and the commercial purposes born of their environment.   They wanted only factories or trading stations on foreign soil, too small to arouse jealousy and easy to defend.   At home political isolation reflected their physical dismemberment.   At best there was only a political hegemony under the leadership of Sidon prior to the eleventh century, and after that under Tyre. Common interests gave rise to voluntary unions for the purpose of discussing and adopting joint politics.   During the seventh century, Tyre, Sidon and Aradus established a kind of federal capital at Tripolis where they held their joint meetings to consider important measures.   Whether the small towns took part in this federal congress is not known.[129]   As a rule, the Phœnician cities bowed their heads before the storms of conquest issuing from the Tigris and Nile valleys; by the payment of tribute they purchased immunity from interference, and profited by the enlarged hinterland markets for their commerce.

Phœnicians set a standard of seamanship and of sea craft for the whole Mediterranean, constantly improving the model of their vessels, constantly extending the reach of their voyages. They alone undertook extensive coastwise journeys up and down the Atlantic shores, from the coast of Cornwall to the Gulf of Guinea.   The early Minoan kings of Crete also had seals representing ships with sails and oars, and two crescent moons above to indicate a two-months' voyage.   One seal depicts a horse transport before 2200 B.C.[130]   But it remains a question who were the great inventors and distributors, Phœnicians or Cretans or both, but the teachers were Phœnicians.

NAUTICAL HERITAGE FROM THE MEDITERRANEAN SEA—A history of skilful navigation, in process of development from 3000 B.C. to the 14th century A.D., made the Mediterranean coasts a depositary of various nautical achievements.   These were finally concentrated in Italy, where the medieval trade of

Venice and Genoa kept alive the traditions of seafaring activities and the finished technique of great navigators. Wealth also sustained these activities, so long as Venice exploited the Oriental trade coming out from the port of Alexandria and shipped its commodities through the Strait of Gibraltar north to the ports of England and Flanders. There the tropical products of the Indies, the sub-tropical fruits and wines of the Mediterranean shores, and the finished industrial commodities of Italy, Sicily, Saracenic Africa and Spain were most in demand.

Italian vessels were the chief distributors to the north. *En route* to their distant markets, Italian navigators became familiar figures in the ports of Spain, Portugal, and France. Portugal was the first to escape Moorish rule in 1147 and soon afterwards opened Lisbon to Italian ships. King John II determined to build a Portuguese fleet, and in 1317 for this purpose called the Genoese Emmanuel Passagno to Lisbon, made him admiral and employed also twenty experienced seamen as captains and pilots. Other Genoese, especially members of the Passagno family, appeared as admirals and sea captains in the Portuguese service in the 14th and 15th centuries, and led the Portuguese fleet against the Sultans of Fez and Granada in naval engagements in the Strait of Gibraltar, and they achieved the conquest of Ceuta in 1415, which laid the foundation of Portugal's sea power.[131]

Genoese captains, accompanied by entire ships' crews of Italians took part in the discovery of the sea route to India around the Cape of Good Hope. Among these was Bartolemo Perestrelo, father-in-law of Columbus, and Columbus himself.[132]

As in Portugal, so in France and England, Italians tutored the captains of new fleets which were taking the Atlantic Ocean as their field of enterprise; for the decline of Genoese and Venetian sea powers within the Mediterranean Sea was synchronous with the rise of the new Atlantic navies and merchant marines, searching for new routes to the Indies and Cathay. Whole Genoese crews entered the service of King Louis the Good and Philip the Fair of France. Numerous Italians became French admirals like Verrazano, who explored the coast of Chesapeake Bay and the seaboard to the north. Leonardo Passagno's brother Emmanuel manned and armed five galleys in Genoa in 1317, and then commanded them for Edward II of England.[133]   Columbus visited the ports of Spain, Portugal, the Madeira, Canary and the Cape Verde Islands, where he became familiar with the northeast trade winds; then he went to England and Iceland, where he could study the prevailing westerlies.   Thus he widened his knowledge of the Atlantic wind systems.   He started from Bristol on his voyage to Iceland, and he possibly learned there of the Norse voyages to Greenland and Vinland.[134]

Giovanni Cabotto, described by a contemporary English historian as *Magister navis scientificus marinarius totius Angliæ* (Expert admiral of the fleet of all England), from the year 1491 made western voyages of discovery in high latitudes, where Cipango or Japan was supposed to lie.   His son Sebastiano, who also went on these voyages, was a short time in the service of Henry VII in 1517, when he searched for the northwest passage to China.   He resumed this service again in 1548, became Grand Pilot and undertook the usual duties of a trained technical navigator.   These included drawing geographical and hydrographic maps.   He also instructed the young prince Edward VI in nautical affairs and the use of the compass.[135] Sebastian Cabot's name was anglicized by this time, and only recent historians have debunked the "John and Sebastian Cabot" of English history text books.   Sebastian Cabot in 1556 became governor of the Muscovy Company, organized to stimulate English voyages to discover the northeast passage to China and to trade on the White Sea coast of Russia.

Prior to this period only North Germans and the Scandinavian family of nations—Norwegians, Swedes and Danes— revealed the maritime enterprise of natural seamen, independent of Italian guidance and instruction.   Saxons and Norse spread a coastal belt of settlement along the northern littoral of the continent from the Elbe River to the apex of Brittany; along the continental sides of Great Britain from the Southampton Water east and north to the Firth of Forth; along the shores of Celtic Scotland and Ireland, and the untenanted shore of southern Iceland.[136]   England's development of big sea enterprises, therefore, depended upon Italian stimulation until the time of Queen Elizabeth. That able ruler, with the help of her great sea captains of Cornwall and Devonshire, put through a program of legislative encouragement to navigation. She converted a coastal population of fearless fishermen, comprising the mackerel fleet of Cornwall and the herring fleet of the northern shores, into a force of incomparable seamen, ready to man the British navy and merchant marine.[137]

Thus from the time Phœnician triremes sought the Cornwall coast for tin to the days when Sebastiano Cabotto guided the English fleet, Mediterranean maritime influences linked together the great Midland Sea with the North Sea of British waters and English merchant ventures on the White Sea coast of Russia.

AUTHORITIES—CHAPTER XX

1. Hesiod, *Works and Days*, lines 619-625.
2. Horace, *Odes*, Bk. I, Ode III.
3. Antipater of Sidon, W. R. Paton, *Greek Anthology*, Vol. IV, p. 4. New York and London, 1917.
4. Horace, *Odes*, Bk. I, Ode IV.
5. Vegetius, *De Re Militari*, IV, 39; V, 9.
6. Hesiod, *Works and Days*, lines 662-677, 680-686.
7. Suetonius, *Claudius*, 18.
8. Mommsen, *History of Rome*, Vol. III, p. 308. New York, 1905.
9. Plutarch, *Lucullus*, II.
10. Thucydides, III, 18.
11. Philippson, *Das Mittelmeergebiet*, p. 94. Leipzig, 1907.
12. A. G. Keller, *Homeric Society*, p. 87. New York, 1902.
13. Herodotus, IX, Chap. 114.
14. Julius Hann, *Klimatologie*, Vol. I, pp. 311-313. Stuttgart, 1908.
15. Horace, *Odes*, I, 3, 19, 33, 37; II, 14.
16. Callimachus, *Hymn to Delos*, 26.
17. Appian, *Mithradatic Wars*, 26.
18. Philippson, *Das Mittelmeergebiet*, p. 52-53.
19. Aristotle, *De Mundo*, III.
20. Livy, Bk. 28, Chap. 30.
21. Herodotus, VII, 198.
22. Pliny, *Historia Naturalis*, V, Chap. 4.
23. Livy, Bk. XXIII, 41; XXIX, 7.
24. Livy, Bk. XXI, 49.
25. Polybius, XXXIV, 2, 4.
26. Philippson, *Das Mittelmeergebiet*, p. 55.
27. Pliny, *Historia Naturalis*, Bk. V, Chap. 4.
28. Strabo, III, Chap. 2, 4.
29. Mommsen, *History of Rome*, Vol. I, p. 177. New York, 1905.

30. Strabo, X, Chap. 4, 2, 5.
31. Strabo, III, Chap. 1, 4-5.
32. Pliny, III, Introduction.
33. Polybius, Bk. III, Chap. 22-25.
34. Mommsen, *op. cit.*, Vol. II, pp. 12, 42.
35. Pliny, III, Chap. 15.
36. Strabo, III, Chap. V, 5, 6.
37. Strabo, VI, Chap. I, 5.
38. Mommsen, *op. cit.*, Vol. I, p. 446; Vol. II, p. 42.
39. *Ibid.*, Vol. II, p. 178.
40. J. B. Bury, *History of Greece*, p. 486. London and New York, 1909.
41. Strabo, III, Chap. IV, 6.
42. *Ibid.*, XIV, Chap. III, 5; Chap. V, 2, 6, 7.
43. Thucydides, VII, 26, 31, 33, 35.
44. *Ibid.*, VII, 50.
45. *Ibid.*, VIII, 99, 101.
46. Franz von Löher, *Cyprus*, p. 61, 71, 94, 97.
47. *Ibid.*, p. 81.
48. Pliny, Bk. IV, 23.
49. Baedeker, *Greece*, p. 231. Leipzig, 1909.
50. *Iliad*, XIII, 13.
51. Æschylus, *Agamemnon*, lines 281-310.
52. Henkel, *Die Sichtbarkeit im Mittelmeergebiet*, Map plate 21. *Peterm. Geog. Mitt.* 1901. For figures of visibility see Neumann and Partsch, *Physikalische Geographie von Griechenland*. Breslau, 1885.
53. August J. Hare, *Cities of Southern Italy*, p. 325. New York, no date.
54. Baedeker, *Southern Italy*, p. 302. Leipzig, 1903.
55. Strabo, V, Chap. II, 5, 6, 8.
56. Baedeker, *Spain*, p. 321. Leipzig, 1901. Élisée Reclus, *Europe*, Vol. I, pp. 397-8. New York, 1881.
57. *Odyssey*, IV, 340-344.
58. Baedeker, *Southern Italy*, p. 304.
59. W. Deecke, *Italy*, pp. 449-50. London, 1904.
60. W. Deecke, *op. cit.*, p. 449. Compare Capri, in Axel Munthe, *San Michele*. New York, 1930.
61. Polybius, XXXIV, 11; Strabo, Bk. VI, Chap. II, 10, 11.
62. Neumann and Partsch, *op. cit.*, p. 147.
63. Baedeker, *Southern Italy*, p. 366.
64. Thucydides, I, 4.
65. Baedeker, *Greece*, p. 426.
66. Strabo, VI, Chap. 2, 8; Rycroft, "The Mediterranean Coast of Egypt," *Geog. Jour.*, Vol. 20, p. 502.
67. Diodorus Siculus, Bk. I., Chap. III.
68. *Odyssey*, IV, 485.
69. Strabo, XVII, Chap. I, 6.
70. *Ibid.*, Bk. XVII, Chap. I, 16.
71. Herodotus, II, 15.
72. Strabo, Bk. XVII, Chap. I, 18.
73. J. B. Bury, *op. cit.*, 114-115. London, 1909.
74. Strabo, IV, Chap. I, 8.
75. *Ibid.*, V, Chap. I, 5.
76. Pliny, III, 20.

77. Herodotus, IV, 53.
78. Strabo, VII, Chap. III, 16.
79. *Iliad,* II, 711-715.
80. Ellen C. Semple, *Influences of Geographic Environment,* pp. 261, 269-271, 330-333. New York, 1911.
81. Ernst·Curtius, *History of Greece,* Vol. I, p. 49. New York, 1871.
82. Herodotus, IV, 151.
83. Dicæarchus of Messina. Quoted in F. G. Frazer, *Introduction to Pausanias,* Vol. I, p. 46. London, 1898.
84. Strabo, VI, Chap. I, 1.
85. *Ibid.,* IV, Chap. I, 5.
86. Thucydides, III, 88.
87. Strabo, VI, Chap. II, 10; Pausanias, X, Chaps. 2, 16.
88. Strabo, V, Chap. III, 5, 6.
89. D. G. Hogarth, *The Nearer East,* pp. 84, 166. London, 1902.
90. J. H. Breasted, *History of Egypt,* pp. 276-277, 486. 1911. *Ancient Records of Egypt,* Vol. II, paragraphs 247-248, 263, 265, 272. Chicago, 1906.
91. G. C. Maspero, *Dawn of Civilization,* p. 391-2. New York, 1901. J. H. Breasted, *History of Egypt,* pp. 95, 127, 142, 153-4, 182, 274-8. New York, 1911.
92. Herodotus, II, 154.
93. Ernst Curtius, *op. cit.,* Vol. I, p. 451-452.
94. Herodotus, VII, 89-96.
95. *Ibid.,* II, 43, 50.
96. Mommsen, *op. cit.,* Vol. II, pp. 399-401.
97. Strabo, VII, Chap. III, 17.
98. *Ibid.,* VII, Chap. IV, 1, 6.
99. Ellen C. Semple, *op. cit.,* p. 296.
100. E. Curtius, *op. cit.,* Vol. I, p. 440-441.
101. Herodotus, IV, 20, 55-7, 59.
102. Strabo, VII, Chap. IV, 6.
103. *Ibid.,* VII, Chap. III, 18.
104. Herodotus, IV, 152.
105. *Ibid.,* I, 163.
106. Herodotus, IV, 8; Strabo, III, Chap. II, 11.
107. Strabo, III, Chap. IV, 2.
108. *Ibid.,* Bk. XVII, Chap. I, 19.
109. *Acts of the Apostles,* Chap. XX; Chap. XXVIII, 3-6.
110. Leake, *Travels in Northern Greece,* pp. 4-5. London, 1835.
111. Polybius, XXX, 9; XXXI, 26.
112. Diodorus Siculus, V, Chap. 58.
113. Cæsar, *Bello Civili,* III, Chaps. 102-105.
114. Polybius, XXXI, 26.
115. E. Curtius, *op. cit.,* Vol. I, p. 288; 292-3.
116. Herodotus, I, 64; V, 28-34; VII, 95-96.
117. Thucydides, I, 4-8.
118. *Iliad,* II, 494-877.
119. *Iliad,* II, 559-568.
120. E. Curtius, *op. cit.,* Vol. I, p. 112.
121. J. B. Bury, *op. cit.,* p. 68. London, 1909.

122. Strabo, VII, Chap. VI, 14; IX, Chap. II, 13.   Bury, *op. cit.*, p. 117-118.
123. J. B. Bury, *op. cit.*, pp. 151, 161.
124. Herodotus, I, 145.
125. *Ibid.*, I, 142-3; 146-8.
126. J. B. Bury, *op. cit.*, pp. 110-112, 222-225.
127. Herodotus, I, 170, 178; VI, 7.
128. *Ibid.*, VI, 17; VII, 91-2.
129. Hugo Winckler, "Phœnicia," in Helmolt, *History of the World*, Vol. III, p. 158-9, 163.   New York, 1903.   J. Kenrick, *Phœnicia*, pp. 272-3. London, 1855.
130. Harriet B. Hawes, *Crete, the Forerunner of Greece*, p. 45.   New York, 1911.
131. Th. Fischer, *Mittelmeerbilder*, pp. 8-9.   Leipzig, 1908.
132. John Fiske, *Discovery of America*, Vol. I, pp. 351-353.   Boston, 1892.
133. Th. Fischer, *op. cit.*, pp. 10-11.
134. Fiske, *op. cit.*, Vol. I, pp. 321-322, 382-386.
135. Fischer, *op. cit.*, pp. 10-11.
136. J. Richard Green, *The Making of England*, Vol. I, Chap. I.   London, 1904.   H. J. Mackinder, *Britain and the British Seas*, p. 189. London, 1904.   W. Z. Ripley, *Races of Europe*, pp. 312-315, map. New York, 1899.
137. H. D. Traill, *Social England*, Vol. III, pp. 493-494, 631-633, 638-642. London, 1920.

CHAPTER XXI

THE TEMPLED PROMONTORIES OF THE ANCIENT MEDITERRANEAN

The traveler who crosses the Ægean Sea from Smyrna to Athens is greeted at the threshold of Greece with a vision of ancient Hellenic beauty. As he rounds the bold promontory of Sunium, which marks the tip of the Attic peninsula, he beholds far up above him the temple of Poseidon crowning the headland, outlined against a sky blue as the cloak of the Madonna. Below it the cliffs of white crystalline limestone drop sheer for two hundred feet down to a cobalt sea, whose waves are fretted into lace as they break upon the rocks. Above, the white marble temple gleams in the early morning sunshine, poised between blue and blue. It is an arresting vision. No signs of life are near, except where a half-deserted cove, exposed to the fury of the southwest winds, receives an occasional boat or fisherman's smack. Why was the temple placed there? A location so striking seemed to indicate a compelling reason. One surmised that it might be the welcome home for the returning fleet or merchantman of ancient days, or a pious expression of thanks for a safe voyage which stirred in the hearts of the Attic sailors. But this reason seemed inadequate. Therefore one was moved to question whether there were other temples crowning other promontories on the busy sea lanes of the ancient Mediterranean. Moreover, out of the days of one's early Latinity, there loomed faint memories of temples along the southern promontories of Italy mentioned in the Æneid, shrines to Athene and Hera and Castor and Pollux, patron saints of ancient seamen. Investigation yielded one hundred and seventy-five of these promontory shrines, besides about twenty consecrated headlands, known to the ancients as sacred, but lacking any surviving record of altar or temple. Numerous other cases, not here included, rested upon suggestive but incomplete evidence.

These sanctuaries were found to be distributed from the tip
of the Sinai peninsula in the Red Sea,[1] a notorious spot for
conflicting winds and currents dreaded by Greek and Roman
seamen, all the way west to the angle of Portugal at Cape
St. Vincent, where a rude cairn of stones marked the consecrated worship of an ancient Melkart or Heracles.[2] They
reached also from the Crimean Bosporus, where they clustered
thick along the sea ways leading to the Scythian grain fields,
south to Egypt and west to the headland of the Pyrenees,[3]
where these mountains stretch out the rocky skeleton of an
arm before they dive beneath the waves of the Mediterranean.

From the accumulated data it became possible to formulate
certain generalizations as to the distribution of these headland
sanctuaries, and even to predict their former sites while the
facts were still unknown. Given certain winds and currents
at certain promontories, a summit shrine or altar was almost
inevitable, and it was eventually located nine times out of ten.
For instance, the port of Ancona on the northeast coast of
Italy, sheltered from the Bora by a rocky cape of elbow form,
is mentioned by Livy and Procopius as chief Adriatic naval
base of the Romans. Search for details about Ancona led
through the poems of Catullus and the satires of Juvenal,[4] and
established the fact of a temple to the marine Aphrodite, built
by the original Syracusan colonists to their tutelary deity.
Local tradition in Ancona places the site of this temple on the
tip of Monte Guasco promontory, whence the cathedral of
Saint Ciriaco now overlooks the town; but Peruzzi states that
the ruins of the ancient temple, together with the extremity
of Monte Guasco itself, fell into the Adriatic during an earthquake in 558 A.D.[5]

FORM AND AGE OF THE SANCTUARIES—The form of these
headland sanctuaries was varied. One type was the imposing
Doric temple to Poseidon on the Sunium promontory, or the
rich fane of Venus of Eryx on the northwest angle which
Sicily thrusts forward into the Tyrrhenian Sea.[6] A simpler
form was the sacred grove with its shrine or marble canopy
over the statue of the god, like the sacred precinct of Artemis
on the northeast promontory of Euboea.[7] Most primitive was
the wave-wrought cave which nature provided as a local shelter

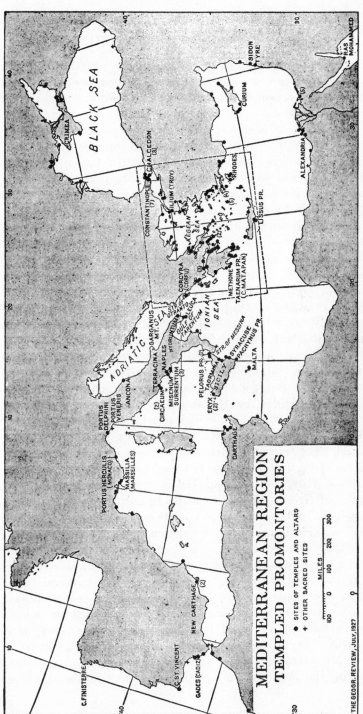

MAP 12—Location of Templed Promontories of the Mediterranean Region.

MEDITERRANEAN REGION
TEMPLED PROMONTORIES

● SITES OF TEMPLES AND ALTARS
+ OTHER SACRED SITES

MILES
100   0   100   200   300

THE GEOGR. REVIEW, JULY, 1927

BLACK SEA

CRIMEA

CHALCEDON (3)
CONSTANTINOPLE (7)
ILIUM (TROY)
RHODES
CURIUM
SIDON
TYRE
RAS MOHAMMED
ALEXANDRIA (5)
LISSUS PR.

AEGEAN SEA

METHONE
TAENARUM PR. (C. MATAPAN)

CORCYRA (CORFU)
STR. OF OTRANTO
HYDRUNTUM
GULF OF TARENTUM

ADRIATIC

MT. SARGANUS
TERRACINA
ANCONA
PORTUS DELPHINI
PORTUS VENERIS
CIRCAEUM (2)
MISENUM
NAPLES
SURRENTUM (3)

IONIAN SEA

PELORUS PR. (2)
TAORMINA
SICILY
SYRACUSE
PACHYNUS PR.
ERYX (2)
MALTA

STR. OF MESSINA

PORTUS HERCULIS (MONACO)
MASSILIA (MARSEILLES)

CARTHAGE

C. FINISTERRE
C. ST. VINCENT
GADES (CADIZ)
NEW CARTHAGE (2)

for altar or wooden image of the deity.[8]   On the limestone
walls of such grottoes grateful prayers have been found, inscribed by ancient seamen saved from shipwreck near the
stormy headlands.

Most of these headland sanctuaries date back to the gray
dawn of history.   They were ascribed by the ancients to
legendary builders of various races, like Orion, Dædalus,
Heracles, Jason and the Argonauts, Cadmus, Danaus and his
daughters, Neleus, Ulysses, Agamemnon and Æneas.   The
Tyrian Heracles or Melkart, sea Baal of Phœnicia, had a large
number to his credit.   Many of the famous temples of historical
times, like that of Sunium, Eryx and the Lacinian Cape (Capo
Colonne) of southern Italy, were erected on the foundations of
far earlier sanctuaries.[9]   The original temple of Apollo Bran-
chidæ or Didymus, crowning the Milesian promontory of the
Ionian coast, antedated the Ionian immigration and the founding of Miletos.[10]   The temple of Artemis on the Lindian promontory of Rhodes was also pre-Hellenic.[11]

In some cases a succession of deities were enthroned on these
promontories.   Maritime traders, colonists or oversea invaders
brought their new gods and grafted them upon local divinities
already established on the sacred headlands.   The primitive
sea goddesses Dictynna and Britomartis of Minoan Crete left
their names and legends attached to certain rocky capes of the
island,[12] but they themselves merged more or less into Artemis
of the Doric invaders; later in the composite form of Dictynna
Artemis they were transplanted in turn to various promontories of Greece and the Cyclades Islands.[13]   In all cases the
new incumbents succeeded to the site and its appropriate office,
for all performed the divine function of protecting seamen.

WINDS AND CURRENTS—The importance of these promontories to ancient seamen is apparent in all classical literature.
For the coastwise navigation of ancient and medieval times,
when no compass directed the timid sailor, these headlands were
sea marks for the groping prows of Greece and the adventurous sails of Tyre, for the beaked boat of the pirate as it
nosed its way along the trail of the prey.   The high relief of
the Mediterranean coasts made the headlands conspicuous
during the four summer months which formed the season of

navigation, for then no fog or mist blurred the outline of their
protruding form. But their high relief also converted the
straits and bays which they flanked into sea canyons, through
which the winds swept with restless violence in July and August
when the northern air currents, the Etesians of the Greeks,
reached their maximum strength. In June and September,
when the prevailing winds shifted from north to south or from
south to north, these headlands were points of conflicting
gales and raging surf. They were known to the ancient seamen
as places of severe storms, especially the wind storms of the
Mediterranean summer. The poet, Archilochus, who wrote in
700 B.C., gives us the picture:

> Behold, my Glaucus, how the deep
> Heaves, while sweeping billows howl,
> And round .the promontory steep
> The big black clouds portentous scowl.

Many of these promontories were notorious, like Cape Malea,
whence Jason, Ulysses, Menelaus, and countless other mariners
were swept by the violent north wind south past Cythera and
Crete to the African coast, hundreds of miles from their projected course.[14] The reputation of Malea was embodied in an
ancient adage of Greek sailors, "If you pass beyond Malea, for-
get your home." Equally notorious was Mount Athos, which
capped the long eastern prong of the Chalcidice peninsula with
a marble mass 6,347 feet high. It was a sea mark for all navigators in the North Ægean, visible for long distances. At the
summer solstice at sunset it cast a shadow fifty miles across the
Ægean to the Isle of Lemnos and made early twilight in the
market place of Myrina.[15] Thus it was a guide to seamen, but
also a terror. On its rocky base the Persian fleet in 492 B.C.
was dashed to pieces by the northeast wind;[16] therefore Xerxes
twelve years later cut a canal across the base of the peninsula,
that his fleet might pass in safety.[17] The headlands of Sicily
and Italy which abut upon the Strait of Messina converted the
local tidal currents into a whirlpool, whose perils were embodied by the ancients in the monster myths of Scylla and
Charybdis. Its evil reputation was not confined to legendary
times when Ulysses and Æneas shuddered at its terrors; for

its tidal eddies embarrassed the Roman and Carthaginian fleets during the Second Punic War.

These promontories often caused vexatious delays. Ancient sailboats, like modern steamers, had to wait for days till the contrary winds subsided enough for the vessels to round the headlands. The Lectum promontory, forming the southwest end of the Troad peninsula, was a critical point on the sailing route along the eastern shore of the Ægean; for the Etesian winds of midsummer swept down from the Black Sea and swirled around this headland with a force which daunted the bravest seaman. Here in the summer of 479 B.C. the Hellenic fleet, bound for the Hellespont from the victory over the Persians at Mycale on the Asia Minor coast, had to moor their ships on the leeward side of Lectum for several days, "being stopped from their voyage by the winds," Herodotus tells us.[18] This was a common experience, evidenced by an altar to the Twelve Great Gods which crowned the summit of Lectum and was said to have been dedicated by Agamemnon himself.[19] The fleet of Corcyra, summoned to aid the Greek forces at the battle of Salamis, arrived after the fighting was over, claiming that they had been unable to round Cape Malea against the Etesian winds, a plausible excuse.[20]

But these promontories were also the first points of the homeland to greet the returning seaman after his eventful voyage, or they marked his arrival in familiar waters. Hence at one of the harbors which usually flanked the ends of the headlands, he beached his ship if the sea was calm and climbed to the summit sanctuary to offer his thanks for a safe journey. Classical literature gives us many instances of this. Jason and the Argonauts, returning from the shadowy land of Colchis and the rocky coast of the Caucasus, rejoiced on reaching the headland that marked the northern entrance of the familiar Bosporus, and there built an altar to the Twelve Great Gods.[21] Ever afterwards this spot was sacred and became the site of a temple to Zeus. The Greeks returning from the siege of Troy under Nestor landed at the promontory of Geræstus, which formed the lofty southern tip of Eubœa, and there at the temple of Poseidon they sacrificed cattle as a thank offering for their safe return.[22] Another group of these victorious warriors had been shipwrecked on the notorious Cape Caphereus twenty miles to the north, and their fate served to emphasize the good fortune of Nestor and his companions.[23]

Hence these rock-bound capes became the sites of temples, mute prayers in stone for divine protection from the perils of the deep, till the Greek mind came to regard the wooded *temenos*, or sacred precinct, as the normal appurtenance of a promontory. Ajax, dying in the distant Troad, thus describes his native island of Ægina:

> Paths of the dashing surge,
> Caves by the ocean's edge,
> Grove on the promontory brow.[24]

This belief that promontories were the nature-made thrones, whence the sea gods watched over the maritime ventures of men, probably explains the ancient custom of commemorating naval victories by erecting trophies on these headlands, sometimes in an existing temple precinct. The Greeks set up a circle of white stone pillars around the temple on the Artemisian promontory of northeast Eubœa as a thank offering for the destruction of the Persian fleet off this headland in 480 B.C.[25] The Athenians, after their victory over the Spartans at the battle of Naupactus in 428 B.C., erected a trophy and dedicated a captured ship in the temple of Poseidon which from the promontory of Rhium looked down on the scene of the engagement.[26] Augustus Cæsar registered his gratitude for the naval victory of Actium by enlarging and beautifying the very ancient temple of Apollo which crowned this headland [27] and reviving its festivals.[28] Occasionally a promontory received its first dedication by such trophies; as when Corcyra won its great victory over the Corinthian fleet in 435 B.C. and, to commemorate the event, raised a monument on Cape Leucimne, a southern headland of the island [29] hitherto unmarked by any sanctuary, though one is prone to surmise there some native Corcyrean shrine whose god protected his own.

The sanctity attached to headlands probably explains the ancient custom of placing on them the tombs of heroes, consecrated with altars and monuments. In time these tombs developed into temples and the heroes into gods. The rocky capes that flanked the southern portal of the Hellespont were crowned with sepulchers, raised to the heroic dead of the Trojan War. The high tip of the Chersonesus near Elæus held the Protesilæum, tomb and temple of Protesilaus, the first Greek chief killed in the Trojan campaign.[30] The fane grew in sanctity and wealth for centuries; in 480 B.C. it was pillaged and defiled by the Persian viceroy, who, according to Herodotus,[31] paid dearly for the desecration. On a minor headland near by was the sepulcher of Hecuba, queenly victim of the war;[32] and four miles across the swift-flowing Hellespont was the Sigeum promontory, the Westminster Abbey of the early Hellenic race. There under blue Ægean skies rose the temple and tomb of Achilles, which held also the ashes of Patroclus[33] and on which the great Alexander placed a wreath of tribute; there also was the tomb of Antilochus. Three miles beyond, overlooking the mouth of the Scamander, was the Rhœteum promontory with its sepulchral temple of Ajax. Menelaus, homeward bound from Troy, came to sacred Sunium, and there he buried his pilot, who had died.[34]

This method of consecrating promontories was not confined to the heroic age. The tomb of Themistocles has recently been identified on the blunt headland overlooking the outer harbor of the Piræus from the north; and, with rare appropriateness, straight across the harbor channel on the Acte promontory rises the sepulchral monument of the Greek Miaulis, naval hero of the War of Liberation (died 1855). On the west coast of Italy, Cape Palinuri, Cape Miseno, and the promontory of Gæta all owe their names to the tombs of heroic seamen who explored this coast with Æneas.

Achilles, the son of Thetis, developed into a genuine promontory god. The Euxine and the Propontis became his special domain, and there he was worshipped as the "lord of the Pontus."[35] His altars tipped many a sand and boulder spit along those coasts, and he had a famous sanctuary on Leuce, "the shining island,"[36] near the mouth of the Danube whose warders were sea birds; but he also received divine honors on the Ægean island of Astypalea.[37]

PROMONTORY GODS—There was a large variety of these promontory gods. Some were primarily marine deities, like

Poseidon, Castor and Pollux, the deified Achilles [38] and his goddess mother Thetis, who presided over the rocky headland of Sepias. Here the northeast wind from the Black Sea dashed to pieces the Persian fleet of Xerxes as it was preparing to enter the rocky channel of the Euboean sound.[39] The universal maritime activity of the Mediterranean coast peoples, however, diverted other gods from their original tasks to assist the struggling sailor. Zeus became Zeus Soter, savior of seamen, and was assisted in this task by Hera or Juno. Apollo, Athene and Hermes, gods of travelers, were also enlisted in a like service.

Yet remoter deities from inland countries were set to work at the alien duty of helping the ancient navigators. Interesting in this connection is the evolution of Astarte, crescent-crowned moon goddess of Assyria, giver of fertility. She became known to the Phœnicians, who traded along the piedmont route of northern Mesopotamia, as a deity of great power; so they adopted her and took her to their crowded ports on the coast of the Lebanon Mountains. Having little use for her fertilizing powers, they made her patron goddess of their busy merchantmen. The Tyrians placed her figure at the prow of their boats where she breasted the Mediterranean waves; and they took her on all their wide voyages, to set her up on capes and headlands beside their distant factories and colonies. Tyrian traders introduced her among the Hellenic colonies of Asia Minor, where Astarte became identified with Artemis and achieved fame as the Diana of Ephesos. This hybrid goddess of the crescent was adopted by many Ægean Greek cities as the patron of seamen. She became identified with sea-born Aphrodite, goddess of love and fertility, and as such her worship spread from the Tyrian colony on the little island of Cythera among the peninsular Greeks; but she still retained her Phœnician rôle of patron goddess of seamen.[40] Among the Romans she merged into Venus. Under these various names, but maintaining an identical character, she can be traced all the way from Sidon and Ascalon to Massilia and the Spanish coast, along the sea tracks of Phœnician and Greek settlers.

The Tyrians gave a like distribution to the sanctuaries of their local sea Baal Melkart, who became identified with the

Greek Heracles, and in this character had his temples and altars on widely scattered headlands from Tyre to the Sacred Promontory of Iberia. Under his Roman name he presided over the Pillars of Hercules, where he looked down upon the full current and strong winds of the famous strait. Malign deities represented the terrors of dangerous headlands and were embodied in the Scylla monster who destroyed ships in the whirlpool of the Strait of Messina: [41] she also occupied the Scyllæan promontory of southeastern Argolis,[42] where the Etesian winds at midsummer swept around the end of this peninsula. Similar was the Italian Circe who lured seamen to their destruction on the surf-beaten rocks of the Circean promontory.[43] Similar too were the Sirens, localized by legend on the rocky islets off the Sorrento peninsula.

All of these deities, both beneficent and malignant, had their seats upon the wind-beaten headlands of the Mediterranean shores. A fragment of Sophocles thus apostrophizes the god of the sea:

Thou Poseidon, who art lord over the cliffs and glassy
Waves of the wind-swept Ægean, behold thy dwelling place
On the lofty crags of all the harbors.

Poseidon was "enthroned on Geræstos and Sunium bold," according to Aristophanes.[44] He had his famous sanctuary on the long promontory of Cape Matapan, the ancient Tænarum, where a grove and cave sheltered the image of the god.[45] The little harbor to the northeast of the sacred precinct was a refuge for storm-driven seamen; it was also the starting point for the voyage south to Crete and Africa, and thence to Egypt. The Venetians later called it the Bay of the Quails, because these birds of passage assembled there to fly to the winter grain fields of Egypt.[46]

In like manner Apollo was ensconced upon the windy promontories. "Many are thy fanes and groves, and dear to thee are all the headlands," sings the Homeric hymn to Apollo.[47] He frequently shared these sites with Artemis, who "was goddess of the stormy headlands." Aphrodite was called "the giver of fair voyages," "she who keeps a lookout from the headlands," "Aphrodite of the Heights." On a little promontory which sheltered the port of the city of Ægina from the north winds was a temple dedicated to "Aphrodite of the Harbor," now marked by a single surviving column.[48] Her character is described by Anyte of Arcadia, who wrote in 700 B.C. a poem to Aphrodite of the Sea:

> Cythera from the craggy steep
> Looks downward on the glassy deep,
> And hither calls the breathing gale
> Propitious to the venturous sail,
> While Ocean flows beneath serene,
> Awed by the smile of Beauty's Queen.

The ancient Greek city of Cnidos, which occupied the rocky tip of the Triopian promontory on the southwest coast of Asia Minor, dedicated its oldest sanctuary to the Bountiful Aphrodite, a later one to Aphrodite of the Height, and a third to the Aphrodite of the Fair Voyage.[49] This Cnidian Aphrodite was clearly a Greek form of the Phœnician Astarte, who appears on the island of Samos as Hera,[50] and as Artemis in Hellenic Eubœa and on the native shores of the ancient Argonauts. Orpheus, bard of these daring explorers, according to Apollonius Rhodius "sang of the Savior of Ships, Artemis, her that holds the headlands of these seas in her keeping." [51]

Athene also was drawn into the service of the Mediterranean seamen. She had her temple on "sacred Sunium," [52] near the famous shrine of Poseidon, and shared with him the task of assisting seamen to round this windy promontory. As "Guardian of the Anchorage" she had her sacred seat on a rocky cape sheltering the port of Hermione on the southern coast of Argolis, while a temple of Poseidon kept its lookout on a neighboring headland.[53] Athene was "mistress of the winds" in her sanctuary on the southwest promontory of Messenia, where she protected the sailors seeking their home port of Mothone; [54] for this point was exposed to the storms that swoop down from the Adriatic, and to the violent south winds of spring that bring rain from the coast of Africa.

These gods have passed, but their function still remains; their headlands are not deserted. In the Ægean Sea nearly all these high temple sites are occupied today by little chapels

of St. Nicholas, the patron saint of sailors trained in the
ritual and faith of the Greek Catholic Church. St. Nicholas
is dear to the heart of modern Ægean seamen. His icon is
fastened to the mast of every fishing boat, and below it hangs
an ever-burning lamp. Prayers ascend to him in every storm,
and sacrifices of salt and bread are cast into the sea by the
pious sailors when they round his promontories.[55] Many of
these little churches are located on the very site of the ancient
pagan sanctuaries, and one may see sculptured stones from
an Aphrodite or Poseidon temple built into the chapel walls.
In the Western Mediterranean, in the realm of the Roman
Catholic Church, the Virgin Mary is the *Stella Maris,* Star of
the Sea, to the modern sailor; humble successor of Artemis and
Venus, she has her chapel or church on the site of ancient
temples and is besought in prayer by the modern Sicilian or
Italian sailor for a safe voyage.

HARBOR SHRINES—These promontory sanctuaries reveal two
geographic principles in their distribution. They appear
singly or in groups about the harbor entrances of active seaboard towns, where headlands run out like piers and protect
the port from prevailing winds. The ancient sailing boats
evidently experienced difficulty in getting into harbor, though
they used the diurnal winds for this purpose, as the Mediter-
raneañ sailor does today. But these sea breezes were comparatively weak and often were overpowered by the stronger
currents of air. Moreover, along the steep coasts of the Mediterranean falling winds or squalls from the highland interiors
added to the complexity of the wind systems and increased the
difficulty of reaching port, especially on southward-facing
slopes.[56] They explain the successive headland temples along
the whole south coast of Asia Minor and of the Troad along
the base of Trojan Ida; of mountainous Crete and Rhodes,
southern Italy, and the seaboard of the Alps and northern
Apennines. Along the Italian Riviera, *Portus Herculis* of ancient Monaco,[57] *Portus Delphini* [58] near modern Rapallo, and
Portus Veneris near Spezia had their names from promontory
shrines.

These port sanctuaries were numerous. The ancient Hellenic colony of Massilia (Marseilles), by reason of its location

near the mouth of the Rhone, lay in the path of the mistral, the desolating wind that pours down the Rhone valley from northern France and the Cevennes. The ancients knew it in winter to overturn loaded wagons crossing the Rhone delta, and in the summer sailing season to buffet vessels entering or leaving the port of Massilia. The harbor was a natural basin between two limestone ridges of the Provence hills, which afforded protection against the mistral and determined the selection of the site by the ancient Phocæan colonists. These Asia Minor Greeks, coming from a region long impressed with Phœnician cults, brought with them the worship of Artemis of Ephesos, and they erected a temple to her on the northern headland protecting the port, where today rises the old cathedral of Marseilles. On other bold points abutting on their harbor they built sanctuaries to Apollo and Poseidon and thus fortified themselves against the stormy mistral. Nor was this all. They planted their colonies and temples along the whole Mediterranean shore of Gaul and the neighboring coast of Iberia.[59] The remoter Massiliot colonies on the Spanish coast often found it impossible for weeks at a time to send their ships northward to the mother city against the mistral. They found it especially perilous to round the bold Pyrenean promontory, which was therefore crowned with a temple to Aphrodite.[60]

The southwest coast of Asia Minor suffered from the falling winds from the highlands of Lycia and the plateau interior; so the Greek cities along this coast studded the promontory approaches to their harbors with sanctuaries of the helpful gods. The city of Cnidos was located on the tip of the Triopian peninsula and an islet which was linked with the mainland by a causeway and thus formed an anvil-shaped headland sheltering two harbors. On the bold island extremity Cnidos placed a famous temple of Apollo, sacred to seamen along all that coast,[61] and one to Poseidon, while in her three sanctuaries within the city Aphrodite was cherished above all its other gods.[62] Cnidos, by reason of its restricted territory, its barren rocky soil, its meager home resources, and its crossroad location on the great north-south and east-west trade routes of the Eastern Mediterranean, was early drawn into commercial and fishing ventures on the sea. Therefore its chief need was reflected in its worship of these sea deities. The nearby city of Halicarnassos, with a similar location and a similar career, had a harbor well protected both by nature and the gods. A northern headland, in the form of a precipitous rock, contained its citadel and a temple of Aphrodite, while another sanctuary crowned the corresponding promontory on the south.[63] The neighboring city of Miletos, famous in ancient commerce and colonization, was located on a club-shaped peninsula fronting the mouth of the Meander River. The southern tip of this peninsula held an altar to Poseidon, said to have been founded in gray antiquity by Neleus, who established the Ionian colony of Miletos; while two miles inland on the promontory summit was the famous temple of Apollo of Didymus.[64] This was a rich sanctuary visible from afar, sought as a place of prophecy by all the dwellers of the Ionian coast. The temple itself was of Ionian origin, but it occupied the site of a far earlier sanctuary, which had probably been established by the early Carians of this coast.[65]

On the peninsula of Greece the same story meets us. On Acte promontory, which sheltered the two ports of Athens, a temple of Artemis protected the home-coming sailor.[66] Corinth, located on the Isthmus of Corinth, had no available promontory, but she constructed a long mole to shelter Cenchreæ, her Ægean port, and on the tip she placed a bronze statue of Poseidon.[67] The high promontory (3,467 feet) on the western side of the Isthmus, which guarded the approach to her harbor on the Corinthian Gulf, was crowned with a temple of Hera Acræa.[68] This headland is now called Cape St. Nicholas, and bears on its summit an humble chapel to that helpful saint.[69] Even the land-loving Spartans had their two ports of Gytheum and Las, on the mountainous coast of the Laconic Gulf, protected by a promontory temple, one to Aphrodite and the other to Artemis Dictynna.[70] In like manner headland sanctuaries clustered thick about the ancient ports of Alexandria, Byzantium, Syracuse, Naples, Carthage, New Carthage, and Gades.

ALONG THE TRACK OF THE GRAIN SHIPS—The second principle of distribution is revealed along the main trade routes of the Mediterranean Sea. The temples are found on all these "wet ways" following the coast, where conflicting winds and currents meet and where the surf beats high. The long path of the Hellespontine wind, which blew from the Scythian coast of the Black Sea down through the Bosporus and Hellespont and swept southwestward across the Ægean, marked the great northern grain route of the ancient Mediterranean; hence it was marked by these templed promontories as if by road signs. The high water level in the Black Sea in early summer, due to the great volume of the northern rivers, caused a strong current out through the Crimean Bosporus, and again through the Thracian Bosporus and Hellespont into the Ægean. Ships northward bound to the Scythian grainfields had to sail up against the Hellespontine wind and also breast this current, which through the tortuous channels of the Straits rebounded from shore to shore and greatly complicated the problem of navigation. Hence the jutting banks of the Crimean Bosporus had their sanctuaries to Artemis, Heracles and Achilles.[71] Temples marked both headlands flanking the Euxine mouth of the Thracian Bosporus; and half way down the Strait other sanctuaries capped the promontories of Hermes and Heracles, which received the violent impact of the current rebounding from the Asian side.[72] At the southern end, where northbound vessels met the full force of current and Etesian wind, several temples marked the elbow of the Asian coast at Calchedon;[73] and the opposite headland of Byzantium was crowned by sanctuaries to Poseidon, Athene, Artemis, Aphrodite and Heracles, all within three hundred yards of its hilly extremity, while altars of Achilles and the twin Dioscuri lay near the city of Byzantium.[74] This diverse group of deities represented the patron gods of the various seamen who frequented the busy port of the Golden Horn.

The Hellespontine wind made perilous sailing at the entrance to the Malic gulf and the Eubœan sound, where the rocky headlands showed their teeth to approaching vessels. All these headlands, therefore, were capped with temples or altars to Artemis, Thetis, Athene and Zeus the Savior.[75] The Eubœan Sound itself is protected from the Hellespontine blast by the long mountainous island of Eubœa, which forms a breakwater

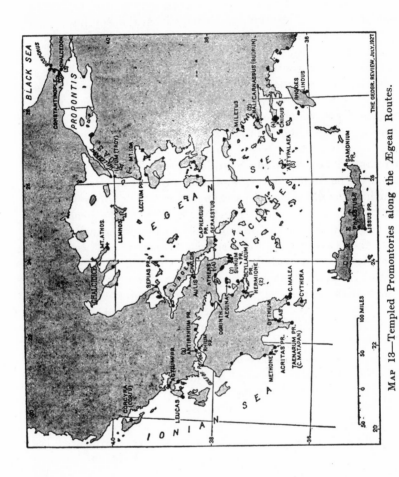

Map 13—Templed Promontories along the Ægean Routes.

and windshield. But the Euripos or stricture of the sound,
which contracts to two hundred feet, between Aulis and Chalcis,
was dreaded by ancient seamen because of the tidal rips which
formed here and shifted four times in the twenty-four hours;
and also because of the squalls dropping from the high massif
of Mount Dirphys (5,725 feet) in Eubœa.[76] With adverse
winds and tide it was impossible to pass these narrows. Here
under the lee of "Aulis rising high above the waves," was a
little harbor where vessels were wont to await a change of
wind and current.[77]   In this port of refuge Agamemnon and
the Greek fleet, assembled for the campaign against Troy, were
detained for weeks by head winds; and here finally at the
sanctuary of Artemis, Agamemnon sacrificed his daughter
Iphigenia, that the goddess might facilitate their departure.[78]
The temple of Artemis that crowned this little promontory
became a place of sacrifice for later military ventures setting
forth across the Ægean from the shores of Greece.[79]   The
pagan sanctuary has disappeared; the perils to navigators
have persisted; a little chapel to St. Nicholas watches here
today over the fate of the seamen.

AROUND MALEA—The Hellespontine wind carried the current from the Hellespont southwestward across the Ægean.
Side by side they swept around the southern end of Eubœa
and of Attica, where Poseidon from both rocky heights overlooked the stormy passage, and with undiminished force maintained their way southwestward to merciless Malea.   This
headland forms the eastern prong of the mountain trident of
southern Peloponnesos, the other two being Tænarum and
Acritas.   All three flanked the course of vessels seeking Italy
and the Western Mediterranean, and all were buffeted by conflicting winds.   Acritas on the west was swept by gales moving
southward out of the Adriatic.   All three at times were exposed to the southwest wind from Africa, and all knew the
squalls sweeping down from the highland of Arcadia.   They
felt "the south wind warring with the north" described by
Horace, the surf breaking on their hidden reefs, and the spume
of the sea on their rocky fronts.   Hence, besides the promontory sanctuaries there were altars to Apollo Acritas, to the
Malean Apollo, and to Tænarian Poseidon in the city of Sparta,

where prayers preceded every Laconian venture on the deep.[80]

But Malea was worst of all. "The blasts of whistling winds and swollen waves as huge as mountains," which drove the returning Menelaus south to Crete,[81] have continued to give the cape a bad name for storms and heavy seas through all time. The Spartan fleet that set out for Syracuse in the Peloponnesian War was caught by the Hellespontine wind off the cape and swept south to Africa. The fleet of Belisarius in 533 A.D., bound from Constantinople to Carthage, rejoiced to round Malea in calm weather.[82] Therefore the ancient seamen safeguarded themselves by establishing here four sanctuaries. A temple to Apollo Epidelius flanked the promontory on the east,[83] sanctuaries to Apollo,[84] Zeus and Athene [85] capped the bold spurs of the cape itself, while from the summit of Cythera a temple to Aphrodite or Astarte, of Phœnician origin, looked down on the boisterous channel between island and headland.[86] The Parnon range, which tapers off southward to form Malea, is a ridge of bare, black limestone, 2,600 feet high, dropping steeply to the surf at its base. A sheer cliff, 200 feet high, supports the last narrow ledge, on which are now two chapels and a hermit's cave.[87] Malea still retains its terrors. It overlooks a busy sea-lane, dotted by the sails of sponge fishermen in quiet weather, as by the boats of the Phœnician purple gatherers in ancient times. Ocean liners plough past, oil tankers and grain ships from the Black Sea hold their course westward; but in stormy weather, steamers and fishing smacks alike are delayed for days.

The ancient east-west sailing route may be traced by these promontory temples, set up like milestones at every port of call, all the way from Cyprus past Crete and Malta to the Pillars of Hercules. When vessels left the shelter of the Asia Minor coast on their sunset voyage, they sailed along the leeward side of Rhodes past Lindos to escape the north wind; but they encountered it again till they succeeded in passing the templed promontory of Samonium at the eastern extremity of Crete, a perennial point of danger.[88] Here the Apostle Paul met rough sailing on his voyage to Rome in the autumn of 40 A.D. His vessel found easy going along the sheltered southern coast of Crete, and was lucky in having a gentle south breeze for rounding the templed promontory of Lissus,[89] because it was mid-October and far too late even for a grain ship from Egypt to be abroad in the Mediterranean. So the inevitable happened: the wind circled around to the northeast and the tempestuous Euroclydon, counterpart of the Italian Bora, swept over the Mount Ida range (8,200 feet) of Crete and down the Bay of Phæstus (modern Bay of Messara). It pounded Paul's vessel and drove it with the Greek crew for nine days westward to Malta.[90] It was generally an involuntary voyage, captained by the arbitrary god of the winds, that carried an ancient vessel across the open sea from Crete to Malta. These were dangerous waters. The promontory protecting the bay of Malta was crowned in Cicero's time by a temple of Juno, very ancient, very rich and held in peculiar veneration; [91] and another headland was dedicated to Melkart from the early Phœnician appropriation of the island.[92]

ISTHMIAN ROUTE—To avoid Malea and shorten the voyage between the Saronic and Corinthian gulfs, ancient passenger vessels and small freighters with valuable cargoes took the isthmian route across Greece, making the four-mile transit of the Isthmus by the *diolchos* or roller tramway maintained by Corinth. The importance of this passage, despite the isthmian tolls, is attested by the promontory temples flanking the route. Westbound vessels issued from the narrow Corinthian Strait between two temples of Poseidon, crowning the Rhium and Antirrhium promontories,[93] and turned thence northward along the coast past the dreaded Leucadian headland to Corcyra, whence they crossed the Strait of Otranto to Italy.[94] They struck land near Hydruntum (Otranto) where a temple of Mercury welcomed them from afar; or, sailing twenty miles further south, they reached the port of Leuca on the Iapygian promontory of Italy. Its summit was crowned by the temple of Athene Leucadia, which Æneas saw on approaching the Italian shore.[95] This spot today is occupied by the church of Santa Maria di Leuca, or the Madonna in *Finibus Terræ*. Only the platform of the old temple remains, but in the white limestone cliff is a grotto containing ancient petitions of passing sailors to Jupiter Optimus,[96] the Italian successor of Zeus the Savior.

From this point the vessels steered across the broad opening of the Gulf of Tarentum to the Lacinian promontory, site of a temple to Hera, who was apparently successor to an earlier goddess, native to the place. This was once the most hallowed temple of Magna Græcia, and held annually a great panegyric.[97] Today a solitary column, twenty-six feet high, rises from the massive substructure and gives the headland the name of Capo delle Colonne,[98] while near by is the church of the Madonna del Capo, to which young girls go barefoot in procession every Saturday. Fifteen miles to the south is a second promontory, once sacred to Castor and Pollux.[99] The destination of most Greek ships coming from the Gulf of Corinth was Sicily, whose grain fields and pastures helped to supplement the meager food supplies of the old Greek cities. The eastern coast of Sicily was studded with templed promontories marking the entrances to the colonial ports,[100] while sanctuaries of Poseidon and Artemis on the Pelorus headland safeguarded the perilous Strait of Messina.[101]

All three corners of triangular Sicily endangered navigation, and all were sites of famous temples. The Pachynian promontory at the south, *imbriferos Pachynos*, with its Apollo sanctuary was swept by north winds streaming down the Strait of Messina, and also by southwest gales from the Atlas Mountains.[102] It was therefore the scene of frequent shipwrecks. The most famous templed promontory of perhaps the whole Mediterranean capped the northwestern angle of Sicily, where the massive headland of Eryx rose to the height of 2,463 feet and made a second Malea.[103] On its level summit the early Phœnician colonists established their goddess Astarte, and filled the grove about her temple with doves which figured in her worship. To the Greek colonists of Sicily she was Aphrodite of Eryx; she became Venus of Eryx when the Romans conquered the Island and embellished her shrine.[104] Today her sanctuary site is occupied by the cathedral of Our Lady of Eryx, patron saint of the Sicilian sailors, *Stella Maris* of the Sicilian sea. Hither pilgrims come from all parts of Sicily to make their offering for safe voyages, and they admire the doves which still wing their way from tree to tree in the surrounding grove. The sacred site has never changed, nor the human need; only the divine incumbent has assumed a different name and different guise.

SACRIFICES TO THE PROMONTORY GODS—The promontory gods, who were expected to rescue men from dire peril, were appeased by offerings of cattle and even of human lives. Artemis in her more primitive forms was propitiated by human sacrifices, like that of Iphigenia at the temple of Aulis. This barbarous phase of her cult tended to appear as a heritage from Astarte, wherever the Tyrians established their factories or fishing stations. It characterized the sanctuary of Artemis on the Parthenian promontory of southwestern Crimea among the Taurii, who cast shipwrecked seamen from the cliff of the headland as offerings to "Artemis of the deep"; [105] for the Taurii were fishermen and pirates, preying upon Greek vessels trading with the Crimean coast. The cult was either indigenous, belonging to a native Parthenia or Virgin goddess, on whom the Artemis worship was grafted; or it was borrowed from the Tyrians who maintained their purple-fishers' camp on the coast.[106] Certainly it was not borrowed from the Greeks. In the drama of Euripides the translated Iphigenia, who officiated as priestess in the gloomy Parthenian temple, voiced all the repugnance of the Hellenic mind to the barbarous features of the cult.[107]

Yet similar features characterized the cult of Apollo on the Curias promontory in southwestern Cyprus, long under Phœnician influence. There anyone who touched the altar of the god was cast into the sea to propitiate the deity.[108] But the most dramatic scene was yearly enacted at the temple to Apollo on the Leucadian promontory of southwestern Leukas. The forces of air and sea multiplied the dangers of rounding this headland, which thrust out a rocky spur six miles in length and 2,000 feet in height, rising in sheer cliffs of white limestone right across the path of the Adriatic winds. This was "the far projecting rock of woe," known and dreaded by ancient Greek and Roman sailors.[109] In order to avoid it, the sand and boulder reef which connected Leukas with the mainland was pierced as early as 500 B.C. by an artificial canal. But the waves and currents repeatedly barricaded the opening; again and again the boulder reef had to be cut, lest it should force vessels to round the Leucadian promontory. Here again the exigencies of the case demanded human sacrifices, which evidently figured in the cult of the Leucadian Apollo from the gray dawn of history. Strabo gives us the story. Once a year on the feast day of the god a criminal who had forfeited his life was cast from the top of the cliff into the sea. But the moral refinement of a more cultured age raised a protest against the barbarity. Hence, before the victim was thrown over the cliff, he was provided with crude Dædalian wings and numerous doves were attached by strings to his person, in order that the fluttering of their pinions might break the force of his fall. Below on the water a group of expectant fishermen waited in their boats, ready to pick up the victim, if he should survive the fall, and carry him as an exile out of the country. One can imagine the scene—the bold, gleaming cliffs, the temple of Apollo on the summit, down below the white-winged fishing boats, with their sturdy sailors looking upward for the appearance of the victim, awe and fear and hope depicted on their countenances. But the Leucadian promontory was merciless in a storm; the god up there held no sinecure; the divine laborer was worthy of his hire.

Though one hundred and seventy-five of these templed promontories have been identified, a few stormy headlands which by every law of geographical probability should have been sanctuary sites have not proved true to type. The Mount Garganus promontory (3,460 feet), the spur of Italy, though exposed to the dread Bora sweeping down the Adriatic, held minor local shrines, but none to a sea god. Notorious as Malea was Cape Caphereus "the Devourer," a rocky prong jutting out from the southeast coast of Eubœa into the teeth of the Hellespontine winds. It was the graveyard of the ancient Ægean; its funeral chants sound through all classical literature.[110] But it had no saving shrine. Its evil genius was represented by Nauplius, whose misleading fires lured to destruction the Greek heroes returning from the siege of Troy.[111] The few who were washed ashore on Caphereus found only a cave, containing an altar and image of Dionysus, but they welcomed the warming gift of the god of wine.[112]

THE TEMPLED PROMONTORIES 635

AUTHORITIES—CHAPTER XXI

1. Strabo, XVI, Chap. IV, 18.
2. *Ibid.*, III, Chap. I, 4.
3. *Ibid.*, IV, Chap. I, 3.
4. Catullus, 36, 13. Juvenal, IV, 40.
5. F. Hamilton Jackson, *The Shores of the Adriatic*, p. 225. London, 1906.
6. Polybius, I, 55. Diodorus Siculus, IV, 83.
7. Herodotus, VII, 176. Plutarch, *Themistocles*, VIII.
8. Pausanias, III, 25, 4.
9. M. P. Nilsson, *Griechische Feste von religiöser Bedeutung*, p. 63. Leipzig, 1906. E. A. Freeman, *History of Sicily*, Vol. I, pp. 199-209. Oxford, 1891.
10. Paus., VII, 2, 3.
11. Diodorus Siculus, V, 58. Herodotus, II, 182.
12. Herodotus, III, 59. Strabo, X, Chap. IV, 12-14.
13. Pauly-Wissowa, *Real Encyclopädie der classischen Altertumswissenschaft*, article, "Diktynna."
14. *Odyssey*, III, 387; IV, 514; IX, 79-83. Herodotus, IV, 179.
15. Apollonius Rhodius, I, 601-606.
16. Herodotus, VI, 44, 95.
17. *Ibid.*, VII, 22, 23.
18. *Ibid.*, IX, 114.
19. Strabo, XIII, Chap. I, 48.
20. Herod., VII, 168.
21. Pomponius Mela, I, 101. Polybius, IV, 39.
22. *Odyssey*, III, 176.
23. Ovid, *Metamorphoses*, IV, 472; XIV, 482.
24. Sophocles, *Ajax*, 412.
25. Plutarch, *Themistocles*, VIII. Herodotus, VIII, 8.
26. Thucydides, II, 84.
27. Suetonius, Augustus, 18; Dion. Cass., 51, 1.
28. Thucydides, I, 29.
29. Thucydides, I, 30.
30. *Ibid.*, VIII, 102. Strabo, XIII, 1, 31.
31. Herodotus, IX, 115.
32. Strabo, XIII, Chap. I, 28.
33. *Odyssey*, XXIV, 75. Arrian, *Anabasis of Alexander*, I, Chap. XI.
34. *Odyssey*, III, 277-279.
35. J. B. Bury, *History of Greece*, p. 92. London, 1909. Pauly-Wissowa, *op. cit.*, article, "Achilles."
36. Strabo, VII, Chap. 3, 16.
37. Cicero, *De Natura Deorum*, III, 45.
38. Bury, *op. cit.*, p. 92.
39. Herodotus, VII, 191.
40. Pauly-Wissowa, *op. cit.*, article, "Astarte."
41. H. F. Tozer, *Geography of Ancient Greece*, p. 77. London, 1873.
42. Pausanias, II, 34, 7-8.
43. Cicero, *op. cit.*, III, 19. Vergil, *Æneid*, VII, 10-24. Apollonius Rhodius, III, 312. Strabo, V, Chap. 3, 6.
44. Aristophanes, *The Knights*, 559-560.

45. Strabo, VIII, Chap. V, 1; X, Chap. 8. Pausanias, III, 25, 4.
46. Bursian, *Geographie von Griechenland*, Vol. II, p. 150. Leipzig, 1868.
47. Homeric Hymn to Apollo, lines 146-147.
48. Pausanias, II, Chap. 29, 6.
49. *Ibid.*, I, Chap. 1, 30.
50. *Ibid.*, VII, Chap. 4, 4-5; *Encyc. Brit.*, article, "Hera."
51. Apollonius Rhodius, I, 568.
52. *Odyssey*, III, 278.
53. Pausanias, II, Chap. 34, 8-10.
54. *Ibid.*, IV, Chap. 35, 1, 5, 6.
55. Mary Hamilton, *Greek Saints and Their Festivals*, pp. 28-31. London, 1918.
56. Neumann and Partsch, *Physikalische Geographie von Griechenland*, pp. 104-107. Breslau, 1885. Philippson, *Das Mittelmeergebiet*, pp. 98-99. Leipzig, 1907.
57. Strabo, IV, Chap. VI, 3. Lucan, I, 405.
58. Pliny, *Historia Naturalis*, III, 47.
59. Strabo, IV, Chap. I, 3-4.
60. *Ibid.*, IV, Chap. I, 6. Compare Poseidon temple on Nisyros. Strabo, X, Chap. V, 6.
61. Thucydides, VIII, 35.
62. Pausanias, I, Chap. 1, 3. Strabo, X, Chap. V, 6.
63. Diod. Sic., XVIII, 23, 4. Vitruvius, II, 8.
64. Strabo, XIV, Chap. I, 3, 5. Herod., V, 36; VI, 19. Pausanias, II, Chap. 10, 5.
65. Pausanias, VII, Chap. 2, 3. Compare port temple in Sheria, *Odyssey*, VI, 260-273.
66. Xenophon, *Hellenes*, II, Chap. IV, 11.
67. Pausanias, II, Chap, 2, 3.
68. Livy, XXXII, 23. Xenophon, *op. cit.*, IV, 5.
69. Philippson, *Der Peloponnes*, pp. 19-25. Berlin, 1892.
70. Pausanias, III, Chap. 22, 1. Bursian, *op. cit.*, Vol. II, p. 147.
71. Pliny, IV, 85. Strabo, XI, Chap. II, 6-8. E. H. Mimms, *Scythians and Greeks*, pp. 20-21. Cambridge, 1913.
72. Polybius, IV, 39, 40, 44. Strabo, VII, Chap. VI, 1.
73. Xenophon, *op. cit.*, I, Chap. III, 4, 7.
74. Pauly-Wissowa, *op. cit.*, article "Byzantium."
75. Sophocles, *Trachiniæ*, 238, 752-754, 993. Diod. Sic., XI, Chap. XII, 3. Strabo, IX, Chap. V, 22. Apol. Rhod., I, 568.
76. Livy, XXVIII, 6.
77. Euripides, *Iphigenia in Aulis*, 122, 157.
78. *Ibid.*, 90, 178, 350, 1450, 1740-1780.
79. Xenophon, *op. cit.*, III, Chap. IV, 3-4.
80. Pausanias, III, Chap. XII, 5, 8.
81. *Odyssey*, III, 287-290.
82. Procopius, *De Bello Vandalico*, III, Chap. XIII, 5-7.
83. Strabo, VIII, Chap. VI, 1.
84. Thucydides, VII, 26.
85. Pausanias, III, Chap. 22, 10; Chap. 23, 1.
86. Herod., I, 105.
87. Philippson, *Der Peloponnes*, p. 175.
88. Apol. Rhod., IV, 169.

89. Philostratus, *Life of Apollonius of Tyana*, IV, 34.
90. *Acts of the Apostles*, XXVII, 7-14. Revised version.
91. Cicero, *In Verrem*, IV, 46.
92. Ptolemy, *Geographia*, IV, 3, 37.
93. Thucydides, II, 86. Pliny, *Hist. Nat.*, IV, 6.
94. Vergil, *Æneid*, III, 275, 506-8. Thucydides, VI, 42-44.
95. *Ibid.*, III, 530.
96. A. J. Hare, *Cities of Southern Italy and Sicily*, p. 326. London, 1883.
97. Livy, XXIV, 3. Diod. Sic., IV, Chap. 24, 7. Aristotle, *De Mirabilibus*, 96.
98. A. J. Hare, *op. cit.*, pp. 349-350.
99. Pliny, *Hist. Nat.*, III, 95.
100. Appian, *De Bello Civili*, V, Chap. XII, 109. Thucydides, VI, 3.
101. Hesiod quoted in Diod. Sic., IV, Chap. V, 85. Strabo, VI, Chap. I, 5.
102. Ovid, *Met.*, XIII, 725. Macrobius, I, Chap. 17, 24; Polybius, I, Chap. 37, 54.
103. Polybius, I, 55. Vergil, *Æneid*, V, 759-773.
104. E. A. Freeman, *op. cit.*, Vol. I, pp. 277-280; 548-551.
105. Herod., IV, 103. Strabo, VII, Chap. IV, 2. Pomponius Mela, II, 3. Pliny, *Hist. Nat.*, IV, 26.
106. Euripides, *Iphigenia in Tauris*, 262-4.
107. *Ibid.*, 34-40, 380-404.
108. Strabo, XIV, Chap. VI, 3. Thucydides, III, Chap. 94, 2.
109. Strabo, X, Chap. II, 8-9.
110. Euripides, *The Trojan Women*, 102-104.
111. Euripides, *Helen*, 1129. Herod., VIII, 7. Ovid, *Tristia*, I, Chap. 1, 83; V, Chap. 7, 36. Propertius, III, 5, 55.
112. Pausanias, II, Chap. 23, 1; IV, Chap. 36, 6.

CHAPTER XXII

PIRATE COASTS OF THE MEDITERRANEAN SEA

The Mediterranean Sea has been the oldest and in some respects the greatest European training school of maritime activities. These it has coddled and guided and stimulated by a rare combination of geographic conditions. From time immemorial its coasts have sent out fishing fleets into all parts of the basin. From the days of the Cretan Minos it has produced a long succession of sea powers whose navies have sailed its waters far and wide and whose merchantmen have traded in its remotest ports.

A sinister form of maritime activity is found in the piracy which for ages was a recurrent phenomenon on many shores of the Mediterranean. It constituted a lawless combination of naval aggression and maritime commerce, seizure and sale without the formality of purchase. The blend of piracy and trade among early Phœnicians, Greeks and Etruscans belonged to a primitive, undeveloped period when warfare was chronic, when stranger meant enemy, and when buccaneers executed a crude form of navigation act designed to crush competition in the markets of the home sea. Such undoubtedly was the attitude of the ancient Etruscan pirates toward Greek and Carthaginian ships which ventured to sail the Tyrrhenian Sea. They asserted the priority of their claim to those waters by attacking the coast and island settlements of the Greeks in the vicinity, with the purpose of discouraging encroachments upon their maritime preserves.[1] Piratical attacks were especially common in the Ægean when many of the Cyclades islands were occupied by Carians and perhaps by Phœnicians, and when national antagonisms emphasized commercial rivalry on the sea. Finally the Cretan Minos employed his naval power to conquer these islands, suppress piracy, and protect the revenues from his maritime empire, so that commerce by sea became more general.[2]

The decay of Cretan sea power after the Dorian invasion made possible the revival of piracy in Homeric times,[3] and converted the former police of the Ægean into wide-ranging corsairs. A passage in the Odyssey indicates that it was not an uncommon event for Cretan freebooters to carry off plunder from the Egyptian coast.[4] Homer represents the Phœnicians as kidnapping men and women to sell as slaves. Taphian pirates, Greek natives of a small island group off the west coast of Acarnania, stole a Sidonian woman and sold her to a Syrian prince. Both Taphians and Cretans, in Homeric times, were more corsairs than traders, and both were skilful mariners.[5] When seamen landed on a strange coast, they were asked, quite naturally: "Outlanders, whence come ye? Are ye robbers that rove the sea?" The general custom of slaying shipwrecked mariners,[6] on the assumption of their being pirates, points to the prevalence of the evil in the Mediterranean in legendary and early historical times.

The conspicuous fact in Mediterranean piracy is its repeated recrudescence whenever maritime political control is relaxed, and especially its constant recurrence, from the dawn of history down to the nineteenth century, in certain coast districts which are natural breeding places of sea-robbers. The stable factors tending constantly to produce this phenomenon are to be found in the geographic conditions obtaining in the Mediterranean. Owing to the configuration of the basin, traffic was compressed into certain narrow trade routes. These threaded their way between island and peninsula, entered sub-basins by the only possible gateway of the strait, and, when bent upon tapping the hinterland trade, concentrated on ports like Massilia and Alexandria, commanding the few breaches in the barrier boundaries of the Mediterranean. Thus traffic was restricted to fixed lines in a way impossible on the open ocean.

The sea hunter, therefore, knew various points where he was sure to bag his game. The pirate was the robber of the sea highways; and the highways of the Mediterranean were well defined and well traveled. The Oriental commerce in slaves and luxuries yielded rich plunder to the freebooters, as it passed through Cretan waters between the Peloponnesos and Cyrene so that the pirates called this "the golden sea."[7] Just such

geographically determined routes attracted the buccaneers of
the American Mediterranean in the seventeenth century, as
they swarmed out of their hiding places in the Antilles, to seize
the gold and silver freight of the homebound Spanish caravels
or the useful cargoes of the outbound ships. Here Jamaica,
owing to its location, played the part of Crete as an advantageous piratical base; for it commanded several marine passages into the Caribbean Sea and was within striking distance
of the Spanish treasure ships as they left the Isthmus of
Panama and the Mexican ports.[8]

PIRACY AND CITY SITES—The Mediterranean afforded a
profitable field for the pirate, furthermore, because the wealth
of the bordering lands lay within reach of his pillaging expeditions ashore. Owing to the prevailing rugged relief, the consequent paucity of land roads, the importance of "the wet
ways" for communication and transportation, the scarcity of
level land for cultivation, and the general discouragement of
the barrier boundaries to inland expansion, population was concentrated on the coastal hems and small deltaic plains near the
sea. Piratical raids upon these littoral communities forced
the very early inhabitants of Greece, Thucydides tells us, to
locate their cities from two to ten miles back from the shore.[9]
Farther than this the pirates dared not penetrate, lest their
escape should be cut off. The location on the inner edge of the
coastal zone characterized not only the most ancient Greek
cities, like Athens, Argos, Tiryns, Mycenæ, Megara, and
Corinth, but also the earliest Cretan towns and palaces of the
Minoan period, such as Cnossos, Phæstos, Gortyna, Lyttos, and
Præsos. These lay several miles back from the shore where
each maintained a port or naval arsenal.[10]

The same cause and effect are manifest also in the western
Mediterranean. The Etruscans, owing to their nautical efficiency, might have risked coastal settlements; yet as a matter
of fact they placed their earliest towns several miles from the
shore. Such was the location of Pisa, twenty stadia up the
course of the Arno, which even in historical times was exposed
to robber raids from Sardinia.[11] Such was that of Vetulonium,
Volci, Cære, and Tarquinii on the Tyrrhenian littoral, as well
as Spina and Atria, their Adriatic ports.[12] Strabo makes the

generalization that the founders of the early Etruscan cities, as opposed to later ones, either avoided the coast or merely built fortifications there as defenses against pirates. The only exception to this rule was Populonia (Piombino), located on the walled summit of a lofty promontory, with its little port on the inlet at the base.[13] But this possibly was no exception after all, for Populonia may have been originally one of the earliest Greek factories which temporarily occupied several capes and islands of the Etruscan coast, until their occupants were dispossessed by the native inhabitants.[14]

The necessity of occupying these salient points as coast defenses against the maritime Greeks, and their own growing sea power, drew the Etruscans coastward. They occupied also the promontories of Antium, Circei, and Surrentum on the coast of Latium and Campania and utilized them as pirate strongholds from which to conduct their depredations.[15] Fearing these attacks, the agricultural Latins located their most ancient villages at a respectful distance from the sea, even those like Lavinium, Laurentum, and the Rutulian Ardea, which belonged to the coastal zone.[16]

With the general development of maritime activity in the Mediterranean, the consequent decrease of piracy and increase of oversea colonization, sites on the outer edge of the littoral were selected for their ready access to commerce. Such of the older towns as were not too far from the seaboard established there each its own port. Thus there developed twin cities, port and capital, such as Rome and Ostia, Trœzene and Pogon,[17] Athens and the Piræus, Gortyna and Leben in Crete,[18] Cythera and Scandia in the island of Cythera,[19] and countless other primitive towns of inland location. Many of these felt the necessity of securing their connection with the sea against interruption in time of war and therefore built "long walls" like those which enclosed the thoroughfare between Athens and the Piræus. Similar "long walls" connected Megara with its port of Nisæa [20] on the Saronic Gulf, Corinth with its port of Lechæum on the Corinthian Gulf,[21] and were projected by Argos to ensure its communication with the sea at Nauplia in the Peloponnesian War, but when half finished were destroyed by the Spartans.[22]

The decline of Roman sea power in the last decades of the Republic led to a widespread recrudescence of piracy. The freebooters were emboldened to seize many coast towns and to carry their pillaging expeditions farther inland than ever before. Therefore the Manilian Law, enacted in 67 B.C. for the suppression of piracy, conferred upon Pompey the dictatorship over the sea and over a coastal zone fifty miles wide, in order to include all the seaboard holdings and the inland refuges of the pirates.

The coastal population which was drawn shoreward when the seas were safe from marauders retreated anew to the interior on the revival of the buccaneer's trade. Thus the southern littoral of Italy, which was the site of flourishing seaboard settlements during the period of Greek colonial expansion, became well-nigh depopulated during the Middle Ages, owing to the century-long attacks of the Vandal, Saracen, and Algerine pirates,[23] who swooped down from the African coast, and the depredations of the Dalmatian corsairs, who issued from their haunts in the nearby Adriatic. Any one who has traveled along the seaboard railroad of southern Italy is familiar with the lonely little stations and the accompanying *marina*, or landing place, on the shore, while the unseen towns lie three to ten miles inland on acropolis sites in the mountains.[24] The same shifting of population has occurred on other seas where pirates have flourished. The German city of Lübeck was originally located nearer the sea than at present; but after it had been frequently demolished by the pirates who scoured the Baltic coast in the Middle Ages, it was rebuilt farther inland up the Trave River. Gradually, with the return of security, it built up its port of Travemünde at the mouth of the estuary.[25]

Thus geographic conditions made the Mediterranean basin a good hunting ground for the pirate. But they did more than this. They condemned certain districts of its coasts to be natural breeding places for corsairs and sent their inhabitants out upon the sea to earn an infamous livelihood. The fundamental geographic condition on these coasts is the same that makes for systematic robbery also in mountains and deserts, during their protracted centuries of backward economic development. The land yields only a scanty food supply, which

must be eked out therefore by raids upon neighboring territories.   The predatory expeditions of the mountaineers are
directed against the agricultural plains at the foot of the
highlands, as those of the ancient Alpine tribes against the
lowland settlements of northern Italy.   The son of the desert
turns his raid against the river-valley farm lands, like those of
the Libyan tribesmen against the neighboring Nile delta.[26]
Where the unproductive area abuts upon the sea, like the
Dalmatian or Caucasus coast, its people prey upon the nearest
thoroughfares of maritime commerce, like the brigand on the
mountain pass road, or pillage the nearest productive seaboard.

It is to be noted, moreover, that where mountain or desert
tribes or steppe nomads make their way out to such coasts, they
bring with them the mind of robbers and only alter their raiding method.   They adapt themselves to the seaboard environment, blend with the local inhabitants, from whom they learn
the art of navigation, and pursue their ancestral trade, ex-
changing the desert camel and steppe pony for the swift-moving ship.   The mental habit of the previous habitat harmonizes
with the economic conditions of the new one.   This was true of
the Illyrian pirates, whose highland brethren for centuries
raided the frontiers of ancient Macedonia; it was true of the
desert-bred Saracens wherever they touched the Mediterranean
coasts, though their inland settlements were models of careful tillage and thriving industries; it was true of the ancient
nomad Scythians [27] and later of the nomad Tatars when they
settled on the Black Sea shore, and the Zaporagian Cossacks
of the Russian steppes, who in the seventeenth century put out
from the Dnieper estuary in their frail skiffs to ravage the
Turkish coasts.[28]

RECURRENT PIRACY—Like a natural product of the soil,
pirates were a constant or recurrent phenomenon on the whole
southern coast of Asia Minor, comprising ancient Lycia,
Pamphylia, and Cilicia; [29] on the rugged littoral of Clazomenæ
peninsula of Asia Minor, where Mount Corycus rises abruptly
from the sea; [30] in many Ægean islands and especially Crete;
on the forbidding Caucasus coast of the Euxine where all geographical conditions were hostile to civilization; [31] on the

Illyrian or Dalmatian coast of the Adriatic; on the Atlas-walled front of the African shore, the so-called Barbary coast; and in the Balearic Archipelago and Corsica.

All these districts, whether on islands, peninsulas, or continental shores, have in common certain geographic conditions which combined to force or lure the inhabitants into a piratical mode of life. So soon as war interrupted their few regular industries, or a corrupt government failed to hold them under restraint, or the maritime powers which policed the Mediterranean became weak or disorganized, these regions flashed into piracy. They were all mountainous coasts, broken up into isolated coves and valleys in which a strong centralized government was next to impossible, and endowed with little alluvial land. Natural conditions reduced tillage to a minimum and prevented the concentration of population necessary for local industries as a basis for commerce. The islands suffered always from the handicap of limited land, and therefore were more addicted to piracy, Thucydides tells us, than the continents. Samos, only 182 square miles in area, laid the financial and naval foundations of its great power under Polycrates (532-522 B.C.) by a long career of piracy. Its penteconters cruised the Ægean, plundering Greek and barbarian alike, levying blackmail for safe conduct. After the tyrant had made his fleet supreme on the sea, he organized the coasts and islands into a maritime confederation of wide extent; but the restless Samians easily reverted to their freebooting activities when opportunity arose.[32] Crete, though it was a large island and had a fertile maritime plain of some extent at the northern base of its long mountain range, gave evidence of a constant food problem. Like mountainous Arcadia and Ætolia, in order to reduce the pressure of population upon the limits of subsistence, it became a standing source for mercenary troops in the ancient Mediterranean,[33] when a strong hand kept order on the sea. When the hand was removed, Crete became a chronic source of pirates. On these, as on other islands, human life has resorted to crime in order to equalize population and food supply.[34]

On the rugged continental coasts of the Mediterranean, the mountains provided timber for ships, but impeded communication with the hinterland. Moreover, that hinterland was un-developed on account of the mountain barrier, as in the case of the Illyrian interior; or unproductive on account of an arid climate, as in the case of the Cilician, Caucasus, and Atlas back-country. Hence it furnished no incentive for the commercial development of the littoral. This was the condition which for centuries made the Malabar coast of India and the Norwegian fiords nests of pirates. The Lebanon country had all the geographic conditions necessary for a pirate coast, with one exception. Trade here was more profitable than piracy, owing to the rich commerce from the Euphrates fords and the desert market of Damascus which forced its way through the mountain passes to the sea. But in Pompey's time, after two centuries of nerveless Seleucid rule in Syria, after the disorganization of the hinterland trade by the successive Armenian and Parthian conquest of northern Mesopotamia, and the diversion of the through Oriental commerce to the Red Sea and Nile route, robber chiefs held many coast cities of Phœnicia and made them pirate bases.[35] Joppa became a notorious haunt, and for this reason was destroyed by Vespasian in 68 A.D.[36]

The normal relation of coast to hinterland is a close interdependence. But in ancient times when the hinterland was impoverished and barred from the sea, and when the littoral itself afforded a slender basis of subsistence, the inhabitants of the seaboard were forced to live by a carrying trade under peaceful conditions, or by piracy, if the unorganized or disorganized state of society so permitted. The balance was easily disturbed and tipped from trade to freebooting at any jar to the social base.

Another common geographic condition was a multiplicity of small harbors and hidden recesses as lurking places for the robber fleets, with numerous headlands as outlook points and strongholds. In this respect the Ægean archipelagoes, the Balearic Isles, and the Illyrian coast were best equipped, because the maze of straits and inlets facilitated escape from pursuit. In this respect they resembled the Bahama Islands off the Florida coast,[37] which were long the hiding place of pirates operating about the Florida Straits and the Windward

Passage. They offered the same geographic conditions as the network of sounds and creeks, deposit islands and barrier beaches, forming the embayed coast of North Carolina; there for over a century American pirates lay in wait for merchantmen trading along the coast between the West Indies and New England and did their best to nullify the effects of the obnoxious Navigation Acts.[38]   Crete, like Cuba and Jamaica, had an admirable coastline for piratical purposes and nearby island-strewn seas in which its corsairs could safely operate. Lycia, Pamphylia, and Rugged Cilicia (Cilicia Trachea) had an abundance of small hidden ports and rock fortresses [39] but lacked the sheltering islands.

The Caucasus coast of the Euxine had nothing to recommend it for piratical purposes, except its poverty of resources and its ship-building timber. Its harbors were few and badly exposed to the prevailing winds. It had no islands and for long stretches not even a beach. The Caucasus buccaneers, when they returned in autumn from their marauding expeditions, lifted their slender *camaræ*, or boats, on their shoulders and hid them in the mountain forest until spring again opened their business season.[40]

TRADE ROUTE LOCATION OF PIRATE COASTS—All these pirate coasts lay on established trade routes. The robber fleets of the Caucasus swooped down upon the well-laden Greek ships making their usual coastwise voyage to the ports of the Crimean Bosporus, there to exchange wines and cloth for grain and cattle. In the third Mithradatic War, the Pontic corsairs who joined the fleet of the Asiatic king were doubtless recruited in part from this mountainous coast; for thither retreated the last remnants of the pirate bands who, for two years, withstood a Roman siege in Amisus, Sinope, and Heraclea on the seaboard of Asia Minor.[41]   During the time of Emperor Tiberius, we find the pirates from this east coast of the Euxine preying upon commerce and pillaging towns and villages of the surrounding lands. They were later reinforced by Scythian corsairs from the Dniester estuary, and in the third century these "*Scythicarum gentium catervæ*" ravaged the shores of the Propontis and Ægean.[42]   The Romans had two lonely stations, Dioscurias and Pityus, on the best harbors this Caucasus littoral could offer; and their remote outpost situation strongly suggests that they were designed to police this lawless coast.

In the Middle Ages the Caucasus pirates were still plying their ancestral trade, though their stock had probably received an infusion of fresh Tatar blood. This time they were looting the richly freighted caravels bound for the Genoese colonies in the Crimea. And again, in the eighteenth and early nineteenth centuries, they issued forth in their poor barks and seized any Turkish or Russian vessels which approached their shores.[43] Hence, Genoa, at some remote date, established a fort at Anapa on this coast for the protection of her commerce. Centuries later, on the ruins of this Genoese stronghold, the Turks built a fort in 1783, and transferred it to the Russians in 1828.[44]

The Ægean pirates, when anarchy reigned on the seas, waylaid ships at the various crossroads of that much-traveled basin in ancient and medieval times. The pirate-haunted coast of southern Asia Minor flanked the great Oriental trade track which skirted along this shore and ran thence westward past Rhodes, Crete, and Cythera. These islands afforded choice bases for depredations upon the eastern commerce and also upon the traffic passing in and out of the Ægean. Rhodes, however, seems always to have had both a firm, enlightened government and a strong fleet. Hence, she repeatedly fought the pirates on her own account and supported Rome in its efforts to suppress the evil. Cythera was long a depot of Phœnician pirates. Crete, though its Minoan kings enjoyed the distinction of being the first to put down piracy in the Ægean, became a nest of freebooters so soon as the decline of Greek naval power brought disorder upon the sea.[45] Finally, the extent and flagrancy of their depredations, in co-operation with the Cilician pirates, forced Rome, in 67 B.C., to conquer and annex the island as a police measure. Crete in Saracen hands, from 823 to 960 A.D., again became a formidable nest of corsairs and a great slave market.[46] But the location which made it a desirable pirate base also made it for over four centuries, from 1206 to 1669, the most important commercial base of Venice in eastern waters.

Pompey's famous campaign of 67 B.C. was directed against

the pirates who, for about thirty-five years (102 to 67 B.C.), had terrorized the Mediterranean, organizing themselves into an international sea power for robbery which embraced the whole basin.   They so effectually stopped traffic that dreadful scarcity of provisions prevailed in Italy and especially in Rome, which had come to rely on her oversea grain supply.   The buccaneers had their ports of refuge on all the chronic pirate coasts of the Mediterranean from Mauretania to Cilicia, but the latter was their acropolis.[47]   Nature had equipped it with every physical facility for the trade—timber, harbors, signal stations, coast fortresses, impregnable mountain retreats.[48] Moreover, its location, remote and inaccessible from the weak Seleucid capital, had placed it beyond reach of the arm of authority and left its people free to follow their marauding bent.   Hence the Cilician sea chiefs were the last to hold out against Pompey, and his strong repressive measures against piracy produced here only temporary results.   The corsairs of Cilicia resumed activities in the early years of Augustus. One of their tribes, the Clitæ, necessitated a Roman punitive expedition in 36 A.D. and again in 52 A.D.   In the third century the Cilician pirates emerged as the Isaurians, who from the Cilician mountains plundered on land and sea.[49]

PIRACY IN THE ADRIATIC—The Adriatic furnished a convenient thoroughfare for piratical operations.   Throughout ancient and medieval times the rich commerce which traversed this marine channel, to and from the ports about the Po mouth, had to run the gauntlet of Illyrian or Dalmatian pirates, whose haunts flanked the sea for four hundred miles.   These freebooters also pillaged vessels sailing across the basin from Italy and ravaged the western coasts of Greece from Epidamnos to Messenia.   When their sovereign, Queen Teuta of Scodra, or Scutari, provoked the Romans to punitive operations in 230 B.C., the Illyrian pirates could send out a fleet of a hundred vessels equipped with a force of five thousand men.   This first effort of the Romans to police the Adriatic resulted in the escape of Queen Teuta to Rhizon (Resine) in the marine labyrinth of the Gulf of Cattaro,[50] till 1919 the impregnable naval base of modern Austria in these waters; but the treaty of peace excluded Illyrian raids from the southern part of the

basin beyond Lissus (Alessio). Fifty years later the founding
of Aquileia at the northern end of the Adriatic helped to suppress piracy on those shores.[51]   The significant result of
Illyrian piracy in these waters was the first interference
of Rome in affairs of the Balkan Peninsula, the establishment
of Roman naval supremacy in the Adriatic, and the acquisition
of certain islands and ports on its eastern shore [52] which were
valuable bases for the later extension of Roman power in
Greece and Macedonia.

The Illyrian pirates still persisted in their depredations.
The robber confederacy which had its capital at Scodra, like
its brothers elsewhere in the Mediterranean, was open to engagements as a mercenary fleet.   In this capacity it took part
in the third Macedonian war against the Romans, and after
the battle of Pydna, in 168 B.C., saw its fleet captured and its
operations checked for a time.   Soon its neighbors, the Dalmatian tribe of pirates, who held the littoral from the Narenta
River northward beyond the Cetina, committed such widespread
depredations that the Romans sent punitive expeditions against
them in 156 B.C., again in 155 B.C. and again in 135 B.C.[53] This
last drove the pirate population inland and made them settle
in barren mountain valleys where they starved and pined away.
But their old haunts on the sea were soon reoccupied by remnants of the tribe, probably reinforced by refugees and outlaws, because the Romans had to punish the Dalmatians again
in 119 B.C.[54]   In seventy years they so recouped their fortunes
and extended their confederacy that, as allies of Pompey, they
offered long-continued resistance to the fleets of Cæsar sent
against them.[55]   After order was restored, Imperial Rome
established on this coast, at Pola and Salona, her most important Adriatic naval stations, because the opposite Italian coast
had no adequate harbors, and she drew from these former out-
law shores the marines to man the imperial navy.

The decline of Roman power during the *Völkerwanderung*
was followed by insecurity of traffic on all Mediterranean
routes.   In the Adriatic especially, the growing Venetian commerce of the eighth and ninth centuries and the richly freighted
vessels which traveled this long waterway furnished tempting
booty for piratical attacks.   Geographic conditions were un-

altered on the mountainous and island-strewn coast of Dalmatia, but the original Illyrian population had been largely diluted, and at many points even replaced, by the influx of Slavic Serbs and Croatians who poured down to this coast in the seventh century.[56] These interlopers, accustomed to the inland occupations of farming and cattle-herding, abandoned their ancestral callings and adapted themselves to their new environment. They learned from the surviving Illyrians the traditional trade of the coast, became the only expert navigators that the Slav race has ever turned out, and developed buccaneering aptitudes that would have elicited the admiration of old Queen Teuta. Therefore, when the Venetian galleys proved worthy prizes, this new race of freebooters issued from the old pirate haunts at the mouth of the Narenta and along the whole Dalmatian coast. The task of policing the Adriatic against the marauders began in 827 and continued without interruption till the end of the eighteenth century; because the richer grew Venetian trade, the greater was the temptation which it offered to the corsairs.[57]

At first the Venetian fleets were too weak to make effective resistarce. They seized pirate ships, to be sure, and carried the Slav captives in such numbers to Venice to be sold as slaves that the race name became the common term for human chattels in western Mediterranean lands; but only a large navy and systematic campaigns against the pirates could remedy the evil. The increased armament necessary for coping with the marauders undoubtedly contributed greatly to the development of Venetian sea power both within and without the Adriatic.[58] Moreover, the necessity of protecting Istria from depredations led finally to Venetian supremacy in that peninsula, while the yet stronger necessity of cleaning out the corsair nests on the whole Dalmatian coastland led to the conquest and annexation of the littoral in 998. This move was imperative, because the pirates had adopted the method of the ancient Illyrians and hired themselves out as a mercenary fleet to the enemies of Venice, who thus found a convenient base in the Adriatic.[59]

PIRATE COASTS IN THE WESTERN MEDITERRANEAN—The appearance of Genoese and Tuscan corsairs during the Middle

Ages in Adriatic waters looks like a recrudescence of the ancient piracy which emanated from the Etruscan and Ligurian coasts. Ancient Etruria lacked the essential geographic conditions for chronic piracy, owing to its fertile soil and varied relief; but its location conferred upon it control of the narrow channel of traffic between the islands of Elba and Corsica, and gave it ready access to the rich commerce passing through the Strait of Messina.[60] Undoubtedly this advantageous location, plus the desire to exclude Greek competition from the Tyrrhenian trade, contributed to the persistence of Etruscan piracy. In 482 B.C. we find Anaxilaus, tyrant of Rhegium and Zancle, fortifying the Scyllæum promontory to prevent the Etruscan sea-robbers from passing through the Strait of Messina; and thirty years later Hiero of Syracuse, who had established his naval power in the Tyrrhenian Sea, sending forth an expedition to ravage the coast of Corsica and Etruria, and to occupy the island of Elba, in order effectually to suppress piracy.[61] The evil recurred sporadically, however, for over a century after this.

Corsica, by reason of its rugged relief, poor soil, ample forests, and location on marine trade routes, had all the physical qualifications for chronic piracy. To these were added yet another. Its small geographical area, limited population, and political dismemberment, due to its physical dismemberment, all combined to weaken the island and make it a ready prey to every policy of expansion which emanated from the near mainland, whether from ancient Etruria, from Carthaginian, Vandal, or Saracen Africa, from Rome, Pisa, Genoa, or France. To all except the African states, the location of Corsica made it a constant menace if held by a hostile power. Hence, its football political experiences were the persistent result. The free spirit of the mountain islanders made them irreconcilable subjects under foreign rulers. Hence their constant rebellions through five centuries of Genoese rule, their chronic brigandage and feuds, all together yielded a crop of outlaws who found a ready outlet for their energy in piracy, while hatred for the mainland states gave them motive enough for depredations.[62]

The rugged coast of the Maritime Alps and Ligurian Apennines, with no harbors and few anchorages and only a slender strip of tillable soil here and there, occupied an advantageous position on the ancient line of coastwise traffic between Italy and the Rhone Valley. From the earliest times the Ligurians who held this mountainous littoral systematically pillaged by land and sea.[63] The little Stœchades Islands (Isles d'Hyères), which were cultivated by the Greek citizens of Massilia, were provided with garrisons to ward off piratical attacks, in the days before Imperial Rome brought order in these waters.[64] The Massiliot coast settlements to the west suffered as did the Pisans to the east. And only a century or more of constant conflict reduced the marauders to subjection.[65] By the second century B.C. their raids became intolerable, because they were in a position to threaten Rome's increasing coastwise trade with Massilia, the new *Provincia Romana,* and Spain, which was acquired in 201 B.C.

The Spanish commerce suffered also from buccaneers who had their base in the numerous lurking places of the Balearic Archipelago. These islands had been occupied by the Carthaginians at an early date [66] as outposts against the Massiliots, and long served as stations for piratical descents upon Massiliot merchantmen; [67] for this mode of warfare was more congenial than big conflicts to all representatives of the Phœnician race. After the Punic Wars, these islands continued to be haunts of sea-robbers, until in 123 B.C. the Romans were forced to seize them in order to secure Spanish trade from further molestation.[68]

These islands possessed for the most part a fertile soil and ample fisheries, which together yielded an adequate but by no means sumptuous food supply and inclined the inhabitants to peaceful pursuits.[69] But the frequent appearance of Balearic slingers among the Carthaginian mercenaries during the Punic Wars [70] points to a pressure of population upon the means of subsistence in the home islands which might readily tip the scales in favor of piracy. Furthermore, the abundant coves and hiding-places along their coasts suited to small craft and a location within striking distance of two important trade routes of the Western Mediterranean disposed the inhabitants to freebooting activities so soon as orderly control of the seas was

relaxed; and they likewise attracted both individuals and nations to whom lawless pursuits were congenial.   There is a
recognized law of such geographic polarity.[71]   Thus, the
Balearic Isles were seized by the Saracens in 798 and became
the haunt of pirates who were attracted thither from all the
surrounding coasts.   In 1009 they were erected into a separate
corsair kingdom, which for over two centuries preyed upon
the growing trade of Catalonia near by, especially the port of
Barcelona.   The Catalans and Pisans participated in a Cru-
sade against the islands; but not until James I, King of Aragon
and Count of Barcelona, conquered and annexed them in 1235,
were Catalan merchantmen safe on the sea.[72]   With the restoration of order, the archipelago became the center of a thriving
maritime commerce which justified the wisdom of the ancient
Rhodians [73] and Phœnicians [74] in placing trading colonies on
these islands.

The rugged mountainous front which Africa presents to the
Western Mediterranean possesses all the qualifications for a
typical pirate coast, except in the Tunisian peninsula, where
alluvial plains and broad intermontane valleys give access to a
fertile hinterland.   Here ancient Carthage found the land base
for her great territorial and maritime empire.   At several
points along the Atlas coast small alluvial plains, like that at
modern Oran, Mostaganem, Algiers, and Bona, break the continuity of the mountain rampart bordering the sea and afford
a local food supply, but they are barred from hinterland trade.
In front of them, on the other hand, from time immemorial
have passed fleets of merchantmen, laden with the products of
the East, to be exchanged in the markets of Spain; for along
this coast ran the great sea thoroughfare of ancient times,
leading to the Pillars of Hercules.   Hence this littoral in all
ages has sent out piratical raiders against the commerce of
the Western Basin and the opposite shores of Europe.[75]   Prior
to Pompey's great campaign it furnished retreats and markets
for the buccaneers who terrorized Italy and Sicily.   The Rif
coast, whose rugged mountains wall the African front of the
Iberian Sea for two hundred miles east of the Strait of Gibraltar, was an incorrigible pirate haunt.   Its native Mauri or
Berber sea-rovers found a profitable field of operations in the

nearby strait and the rich Spanish province of Bætica in the Guadalquivir valley, with its island port of Gades (Cadiz). In the second century of the Empire they repeatedly raided up the river as far as Italica (Seville), in spite of the Imperial troops stationed there to overawe the pirates. Tingis (Tangier) also had a garrison whose main duty.was to hold the Rif corsairs in check; but their inroads across the strait into the rich districts of southern Spain continued through the whole imperial period. In Nero's time they caused the Bætica shore to be described as *trucibus obnoxia Mauris*. They were troublesome in the reign of Marcus Aurelius, again under Septimus Severus, and again under Alexander.[76]

The geographical location of the Tunisian peninsula offered facilities for the conduct of wide-reaching maritime trade, when Carthaginians, Sicilian Greeks, and later the Romans maintained order on the sea; or for equally wide piratical depredations, when the decline of Imperial Rome gave free rein to the Vandal kingdom of North Africa. This ill-organized, barbarian community, bent upon spoils more than conquest or power, utilized the nautical aptitude of the local inhabitants and the commanding position of Carthage to pillage all the neighboring coasts from Spain to Venetia and western Greece.[77] Its maritime supremacy was maintained for thirty years during the life of King Genseric, but, gradually declining, was crushed in 533 with the downfall of the Vandal dominion.

The Mohammedan conquest of North Africa in the seventh century brought a new lease of life to piracy on this coast and intensified it by racial and religious wars which prolonged it through a thousand years. The disintegration of the Saracen dominion in Africa into several small states during the fourteenth century and the arrival here of the Moorish exiles from Spain in 1502 lent new motives, both of self-protection and vengeance, to the pirate communities of the African coast. Bougie, Algiers, and Saldae outside the Strait, became notorious haunts of the "sea-skimmers." Spain, in an effort to police the pirate coast, seized Tunis, Oran, and an island fort in the Bay of Algiers, but was soon forced to relinquish them, because new vigor was infused into this whole pirate coast by Turkish corsair captains from the Ægean. They seized Tunis,

Algiers, and Tripoli and formed them into military republics living by plunder under a nominal Turkish suzerainty. Here piracy reached its zenith in the seventeenth century but maintained itself till the French conquest of Algiers in 1830, though the Rif pirates continued their raids for several decades. The striking feature of Barbary piracy is its survival long after Mohammedan corsairs had elsewhere abandoned their trade.[78] This was made possible by the rivalry of England, France, and Turkey in the Mediterranean, the maritime weakness of Spain and Italy, the peculiar geographical fitness of the Barbary coast for piracy, and the elements of its population, constantly recruited from robber tribes of the desert and of the Atlas Mountains.

Piracy was a social-economic effect of geographic conditions in the Mediterranean basin, but it produced in turn certain political effects that played no small part in Mediterranean history. Instances have already been given where pirate fleets were employed as a mercenary navy. In all probability those were fleets maintained and trained by piracy which Xerxes drafted into his forces for the Grecian campaign from the shores of Cilicia, Pamphylia, and Lycia.[79] Organized Persian rule offered them a legitimate occupation for their energies. Several centuries later King Tryphon (146-139 B.C.), a usurper on the throne of Syria, encouraged the corsairs of Cilicia and used their help to maintain his position.[80] Spartacus in 72 B.C. relied on the aid of pirates in the Servile War.[81] The buccaneer allies of Sertorius in the Spanish uprising were a match for the Roman fleet, and from their stronghold at Diana on the Artemisian promontory they intercepted Roman supply ships on their way to the army in Spain.[82] Cilician pirates under the leadership of Sertorius attacked the Pityussæ Islands off the Spanish coast.[83] In the long-sustained Mithradatic Wars, all the pirate fleets of the Eastern Mediterranean were employed by the Asiatic king to reinforce his Pontic and Ægean navies. By their aid he established his supremacy on the sea, almost paralyzed the Roman offensive for several years in the first war and protracted the final conflict in the second.[84] The presence of large bodies of corsairs for hire introduced, therefore, an incalculable factor into many Mediterranean wars.

Constant piratical attacks had an important politico-economic effect upon the states assailed. These found it necessary to build up a standing navy to convoy their merchantmen, protect the home coasts, and destroy the marauding fleets. The increased maritime efficiency and daring which they thus attained reacted favorably upon their merchant marine. In all probability the sea power of Minoan Crete at the time it established its thalassocracy had been developed in part by wars against early Ægean corsairs. Negligent Rome in the last half century of the Republic was driven again and again to refit or supplement or rebuild its rotting fleet to cope with the Mediterranean pirates. Venice, as has been shown, was forced to adopt a big naval program by freebooting neighbors on the Dalmatian coast. Genoa, Pisa, Amalfi, and Barcelona, in their protracted naval wars with the Saracen pirates of the western Mediterranean, built up a sea power which inaugurated or greatly stimulated their successful careers as maritime states.[85]

Constant piratical attacks led not only to reprisals but also to conquest of the lawless coasts in order to police them. The captured ships and seamen went to swell the naval and merchant marine of the victorious nation, thus contributing to its sea power. The newly acquired coasts often proved so valuable as bases for extended maritime trade and military operations, that they whetted the national thirst for further territorial expansion. It was the revival of Barbary corsair activities after the Napoleonic Wars that in 1827 drew the unemployed energies of France to the occupation of Algiers and inaugurated her important North African policy. The French conquest of the strongest robber state dealt a serious blow to the Barbary pirates. Shortly before they had been chastised by American warships, which found themselves in good fighting shape but with nothing to do after the War of 1812. What whipped the Barbary corsairs was steam navigation. Their rugged coasts could not breed mechanics and engineers.

AUTHORITIES—CHAPTER XXII

1. Mommsen, *History of Rome*, Vol. I, pp. 181-182 and 186. New York, 1905.
2. Thucydides, I, 4-8.
3. Keller, *Homeric Society*, pp. 92-93. New York, 1902.
4. *Odyssey*, XIV, 245 *et seq.*
5. *Odyssey*, I, 181-185; XV, 426; XVI, 426. Strabo, Bk. X, Chap. II, 20. Herodotus, I, 2.
6. Herodotus, IV, 103. Strabo, Bk. XVII, Chap. I, 6, 19. *Odyssey*, III, 70-74.
7. Mommsen, *op. cit.*, Vol. IV, p. 309.
8. David Hanney, *The Sea Trader*, pp. 234-244. Boston, 1912.
9. Thucydides, I, 7.
10. Strabo, Bk. X, Chap. IV, 7, 11-14.
11. Strabo, Bk. V, Chap. II, 5, 7.
12. Mommsen, *op. cit.*, Vol. I, pp. 160-161, 179. Pliny, *Historia Naturalis*, III, 20.
13. Strabo, Bk. V, Chap. II, 6.
14. Mommsen, *op. cit.*, Vol. I, pp. 177-178.
15. *Ibid.*, Vol. I, p. 181.
16. Strabo, Bk. V, Chap. III, 2, 5.
17. Strabo, Bk. VIII, Chap. VI, 14.
18. Strabo, Bk. X, Chap. IV, 7, 11.
19. Pausanias, Bk. III, Chap. XXIII, 1.
20. Thucydides, I, 103.
21. Strabo, Bk. VIII, Chap. VI, 22.
22. Thucydides, V, 82-83.
23. Norman Douglas, *Old Calabria*, pp. 135-140. Boston, 1915.
24. Baedeker, *Southern Italy*, pp. 221-222, 225-228. Leipzig, 1903.
25. R. Reinhard, *Die wichtigsten deutschen Seehandelstädte*, p. 23. Stuttgart, 1901.
26. Friedrich Ratzel, *Anthropogeographie*, Vol. I, pp. 154 and 435. Stuttgart, 1899.
27. Strabo, Bk. VII, Chap. IV, 2, 6.
28. Gogol, *Taras Bulba*. Translation by Isabel Hapgood.
29. Strabo, Bk. IV, Chap. V, 1, 2, 3, 6.
30. Strabo, Bk. XIV, Chap. I, 35. Livy, *Historia*, XXXVII, 27.
31. Strabo, Bk. XI, Chap. II, 12, 15.
32. Herodotus, III, 39, 47, 57-59. Ernst Curtius, *History of Greece*, Vol. II, pp. 161-162, 170, 212. New York, 1871.
33. Thucydides, VI, 25, 43; VII, 67. Polybius, II, 66; III, 75; V, 13, 14, 65, 79; XIII, 6; XXXI, 26; XXXIII, 16.
34. E. C. Semple, *Influences of Geographic Environment*, pp. 67 and 461-465. New York, 1911.
35. Mommsen, *History of Rome*, Vol. IV, pp. 423-424, 430. 1905.
36. Strabo, Bk. XVI, Chap. II, 28. G. Adam Smith, *Geography of the Holy Land*, p. 138. New York, 1897.
37. David Hanney, *The Sea Trader*, p. 234. Boston, 1912.
38. S. C. Hughson, *Carolina Pirates and Colonial Commerce, 1670-1740*. Baltimore, 1894.
39. Strabo, Bk. IV, Chap. V, 1, 2, 3.

40. Strabo, Bk. XI, Chap. II, 12.
41. Mommsen, *op. cit.*, Vol. IV, pp. 333-335. 1905.
42. Mommsen, *Provinces of the Roman Empire*, Vol. I, pp. 262-263. New York, 1887.
43. Chevalier Marigny, *Three Voyages in the Black Sea to the Coast of Circassia*, pp. 9-10. London, 1837. Translated from the French.
44. *Blackwoods Magazine*, Vol. 42, 1837, p. 642.
45. Polybius, XIII, 8. Mommsen, *History of Rome*, Vol. III, pp. 291-292. New York, 1905.
46. Gibbon, *Decline and Fall of the Roman Empire*, Vol. VI, pp. 37-38, 46, 57. New York, 1907.
47. Mommsen, *History of Rome*, Vol. III, p. 292; Vol. IV, pp. 301-302, 307-312, 351-355, 396-405. 1905.
48. Strabo, Bk. IV, Chap. V, 1-6.
49. Mommsen, *Provinces of the Roman Empire*, Vol. I, pp. 363-365.
50. Polybius, II, 5, 6, 8-12.
51. Mommsen, *History of Rome*, Vol. II, p. 372. 1905.
52. *Ibid.*, Vol. II, pp. 218-219.
53. *Ibid.*, Vol. II, pp. 437, 505, 508-509; Vol. III, pp. 421-422, 426-427.
54. Strabo, Bk. VII, Chap. V, 4-6, 10.
55. Mommsen, *History of Rome*, Vol. V, pp. 103-104, 235-236, 284-285. 1905.
56. W. Z. Ripley, *Races of Europe*, pp. 404, 410-414. New York, 1889. E. W. Freeman, *Historical Geography of Europe*, p. 118. London, 1882.
57. W. C. Hazlitt, *The Venetian Republic*, Vol. I, p. 60. London, 1900.
58. W. R. Thayer, *Short History of Venice*, pp. 30-35. New York, 1905.
59. W. C. Hazlitt, *op. cit.*, Vol. I, pp. 78 and 106-109.
60. Strabo, Bk. VI, Chap. I, 5.
61. Mommsen, *History of Rome*, Vol. I, pp. 415-418.
62. David Hanney, *The Sea Trader*, p. 253.
63. Strabo, Bk. IV, Chap. VI, 2-4.
64. Strabo, Bk. IV, Chap. I, 10.
65. Mommsen, *History of Rome*, Vol. II, p. 375; Vol. III, p. 382, note. 1905.
66. Diodorus Siculus, Bk. V, Chap. 16.
67. Mommsen, *History of Rome*, Vol. II, p. 143. 1905.
68. *Ibid.*, Vol. III, pp. 233 and 291.
69. Diodorus Siculus, Bk. V, Chap. 17; Strabo, Bk. III, Chap. V, 1, 2.
70. Polybius, I, 67; III, 33, 72, 83, 113; XV, 11.
71. E. C. Semple, *Influences of Geographic Environment*, p. 160.
72. Ulick R. Burke, *History of Spain*, Vol. I, p. 258. London, 1900.
73. Strabo, Bk. XIV, Chap. II, 10.
74. John Kenrick, *Phœnicia*, pp. 116-118. London, 1855.
75. *Encyc. Brit.*, article, "Barbary Pirates," 11th edit., Vol. 3. 1910.
76. Mommsen, *Provinces of the Roman Empire*, Vol. I, pp. 73-74; Vol. II, p. 353.
77. Gibbon, *Decline and Fall of the Roman Empire*, Vol. IV, pp. 1 and 27. Edited by J. B. Bury. London, 1901.
78. *Encyc. Brit.*, article, "Barbary Pirates," 11th edit., Vol. 3. 1910. Hans Helmolt, *History of the World*, Vol. IV, pp. 251-254. New York, 1904.

79. Herodotus, VII, 91-92.
80. Mommsen, *History of Rome,* Vol. III, p. 292. 1905.
81. *Ibid.,* Vol. IV, p. 362.
82. *Ibid.,* Vol. IV, pp. 282 and 286.
83. Plutarch, *Sertorius,* Chap. VII.
84. Mommsen, *History of Rome,* Vol. IV, pp. 28, 33-43, 323-324, 333-334, 351-353, 400-402.
85. Bella Duffy, *The Tuscan Republics,* pp. 1, 2, 23-26, 34-35 and 115-117. New York, 1893. *Encyc. Brit.,* articles, "Genoa" and "Pisa," 11th edit., Vols. 11 and 21. 1910 and 1911.

CHAPTER XXIII

TRADE AND INDUSTRY

The Mediterranean Sea and its surrounding lands constituted a natural region highly conducive to those innumerable
movements and counter movements which, in Ratzel's estimation,
make up the very essence of history. He sums them up in the
general term Historical Movement.[1] In this he includes alike
every change of habitat whether of individuals, like exiles ban-
ished to lonely isles for a political offence, or of small groups of
traders, setting up their fort or stockade on some alien shore, or
of great mass migrations, attracted by a choice natural environment, promising to mitigate the struggle for existence. These
movements of almost unlimited variety have set up new contacts. They have produced amalgamation of races and the
blending of civilizations, with the ultimate result of lifting the
general niveau of culture, until the *Voelkerwanderung* overwhelmed early human achievements and inaugurated new ones.

Conditions of climate, soil, relief, coastline, and the small
naturally defined districts into which the Mediterranean lands
are subdivided, all combined to start men on that constant food
quest necessary to sustain the congested populations of the
seaboard. They gave rise also to trade and industries. Industries, produced by a congested labor force, yielded redundant
commodities for export to regions of raw materials, and paid
for these as well as food stuffs. Conditions of navigation stimulated overseas intercourse and multiplied the articles of trade
to be exchanged with the secluded hinterland, so far as valley
roads or navigable rivers rendered the hinterland accessible.
Contact with the sea encouraged coast fisheries for mullet, shellfish, the purple-yielding murex, and sponges, as well as for the
wide-ranging tunny. Sponges were an article of commerce in
Homer's time. Hephæstus sponges off his face and chest preparatory to making the shield of Achilles.[2] Restless movement
got into the mentality of these coast-dwellers as it did into the

western pioneers of the United States. Unknown shores had few terrors for trader or navigator. They drew the adventurous spirit of Ulysses and his son Telemachus, as that of the explorers Hanno and Pytheas, and the colonizers of Tartessus and Massilia. Through the gateways of the enclosing mountain walls and desert barriers, trade moved inland along commercial routes to the English Channel, North Sea, and Baltic coasts of Europe, to pick up tin and amber, east into Asia or south into the Africa of gold dust and ivory.

Trade was most active between the ancient industrial regions, like Phœnicia, Syria, Egypt and the Hellenic seaboard of Asia Minor on the one hand and the backward regions of raw production, like the Euxine shores, the Adriatic, and the Western Basin littoral on the other; between the tropical Orient and the sub-tropical Mediterranean lands, between the latter and the temperate regions of Middle Europe, where the production of raw materials long predominated.

The relative uniformity of climate over all the coastlands resulted in uniformity of the chief articles of food. Wheat, barley, olives, figs, raisins and wine were produced everywhere among the settled communities, and hence figured little in local exchange until big centers of congested population developed. The semi-arid climate and dry summers condemned portions of the bordering lands to arid pastures which supported large herds of sheep and goats. These provided ample hair and wool for the domestic looms on every farm and hence supplied the ordinary clothing for masters and slaves. They provided also sufficient meat to supplement the common salt-fish diet, so long as population remained relatively sparse. Only big textile centers like the Phœnician cities or the Ionian cities of Asia Minor —Smyrna, Miletos, Clazomenæ, Ephesos, Teos, and Phocæa— had to import raw materials to sustain their chief industries, because their territorial base was too small for adequate supplies of wool, hair or food. Excessive competition for the nearby wool of inland Asia Minor forced Miletos to establish trading stations or colonies around all the coasts of the Euxine in the 8th and 7th centuries before Christ, till she had made this basin a Milesian sea for a time.

A temporary check to commercial expansion was probably

22

found in the high mountain relief which permitted a variety of exchanges between coast and summit, beginning with fisheries and salt concretions along the seaboard, followed by grain in the coast plains, figs and olives on the piedmont slope up to 2,000 feet, vineyard products from 100 to 3,500 feet, wheat and barley up to 5,000 feet, and various trees for lumber and mast from 2,000 to 6,000 feet, according to latitude and exposure. Here each zone of altitude yielded products complementary to those above and below; hence neighborhood barter prevailed, warranted to satisfy the chief necessary wants. Only articles of luxury, like the choice wines, perfumes, fine textiles and skilled slaves imported in Homeric times, pointed to overseas trade. Hesiod enjoyed the Byblian wine from the Lebanon slope, brought by Phœnician traders, and Ulysses knew the potent draught from the Ismarus Mountain range of Thrace which could stand dilution with twenty parts of water.

ORGANIZATION OF TRADE—Population increased rapidly at strategic points which facilitated import of raw materials and export of finished wares. Commerce fed industries and industries widened the circle of commerce. Exchanges became more varied and complex as they increased in amount, and they became also more vital to the survival of the industrial state. Hence a closer organization of trade ensued, in order to protect it from fluctuations detrimental to the industrial state. This elaborate organization reveals the importance of ancient trade under Mediterranean conditions which emphasized the interdependence of the various contrasted sections of the basin. Organization reached its climax in Athens, but there is abundant evidence that it was carried far in other industrial states like Miletos, Teos, Corinth, Ægina, Heraclea, and Rhodes. Seaports were equipped with all facilities for maritime commerce. The Piræus, for instance, had its *Zea* or grain port and the *Kantharos* with its naval supplies, its *Long Stoa* or market for the sale of goods, and its *deigma* for the inspection of goods exposed for sale.[3] Rhodes also had its *deigma*.[4] An informal consular service provided for the care of commercial property when a merchant died in a foreign port, as the records show both for Rhodes and Heraclea as well as Athens. Customs duties were low, profits were often large, loans on ship and cargo frequently cost 30 per cent for the summer.[5]

Drastic laws for the protection of the creditor in commercial transactions existed in Athens: "for all commerce emanates from loans and is based on credit," says Demosthenes, "for without credit no vessel, no sea captain, no traveller can make a voyage; commerce does not emanate from the debtor or borrower." Hence imprisonment or death was the mead of the dishonest commercial creditor but not the private creditor. Commercial courts convened in winter, so that ships might not be detained after the sailing season had opened in late spring.[6]

Custom duties were imposed only to yield revenue, not to hamper trade or to favor industrial enterprises at the cost of the farmers. Embargoes were enforced on the export of raw materials which were essential to the well-being of the state, or became scarce when war checked the flow of raw materials from oversea sources to the home market. Compare the control of the grain trade, both as to imports and exports, in Athens, Teos, Selymbros, Egypt and Sicily, and of the lumber trade in Athens and Macedonia.[7] In the fifteenth year of the Peloponnesian War, Athens declared a blockade of Macedonia and undertook to control all Ægean commerce in naval supplies, which included flax for canvas sails, pitch, wax, rope, copper and iron, lest these should be diverted to enemy ports.[8] During this war Athens prohibited the passage of grain through the Bosporus or Hellespont except for certain favored city states, which had to declare their needs.

No citizen of Athens or of a confederate state was permitted to loan money on a vessel, unless it brought its return cargo to the Piræus; because the city fathers, in view of the small area (750 square miles), limited resources and dense population of Attica, had to ensure a steady supply of grain and other raw materials.[9] As a rule this involved little hardship, because Athens afforded a good market. It had more coined money, probably, than any other Ægean state after the destruction of Miletos, and therefore could pay higher prices. Incoming raw materials and outgoing manufactured wares guaranteed vessels full cargoes and protected them against leakage due to half-empty space. Small city states like Megara, Ægina, Mytilene and Rhodes offered a like advantage, but not so the ports of Egypt, lowland Cilicia, Magna Græcia and Sicily, which commanded both food supplies and industrial products. Roman Italy and Spain, on the other hand, till the Second Punic War reproduced the trading conditions of Homeric Greece. They imported luxury articles from the advanced states of the Orient and the Eastern Basin, and exported raw materials like lumber, wool and metals.[10]

Early Mediterranean commerce was also organized for protection against piracy and hostile attacks at sea during periods of war.[11] Enterprising states like ancient Cnossos, Samos, Rhodes, Ægina and Athens policed the Ægean and Levantine seas to suppress piracy, and provided naval convoys for their commercial fleets. The Héllenic cities of Sicily and nearby Italy performed the same service against the Etruscan pirates of the Western Basin and against Carthaginian attacks on Sicilian commerce. Roman Italy, which was the youngest child in the political family of the Western Basin, became of age and assumed mature responsibility when in 229 B.C. it began to control the Illyrian pirates of the Adriatic. From that time, the steady territorial expansion of Roman power and the increasing importance of Roman commerce forced upon the imperial government the task of policing the Mediterranean Sea against the recurrent outbreaks of piracy.

Fluctuations of trade were forestalled by commercial treaties, such as Athens made with the Kingdom of the Crimean Bosporus to stabilize the grain trade with that section. Athens negotiated a treaty also with the cities of Ceos to secure the monopoly of the cinnabar export from the island, which was the best in the Eastern Mediterranean.[12] That from Lemnos ranked second, and that from Cappadocia, which reached Mediterranean commerce through the port of Sinope, ranked third.[13] This mineral was used for medicinal purposes, and for making a red paint for vessels, which Athens needed. Perdiccas of Macedonia (423 B.C.) guaranteed to the Chalcidian League the export of pitch, building and ship timber, but only enough firwood for the use of the state.[14] In like manner Carthage imposed on the young Roman state (508-7 B.C.) a treaty agreement restricting its trade to coasts west of the Lacinian Promontory and Cape Hermæum, thus excluding it from the industrial cities of the Eastern Basin.[15]

Other aids to early commerce were the spread of astronomy from Egypt, which enabled Phœnician and Greek seamen to sail at night by the stars; improvement in the size and shape of vessels, which increased the speed and lowered the relative cost of the crew, while reducing the chance of shipwreck; the increase of colonization, which multiplied the seaboard trading stations and varied the products drawn into Mediterranean commerce; and finally the political unification of the Mediterranean coasts under the Roman Empire in 31 B.C., which introduced the *pax Romana* or universal peace on the seas.

SALT TRADE—The first commodity to become an article of trade between the Mediterranean coast and its hinterland was salt, in all probability. As an article of general use, it was in universal demand; and owing to natural conditions, it formed all along the seaboard and was rare in the interior. An almost continuous series of lagoons fringes the Mediterranean lowland shores, where the little rivers, failing in the summer drought, are powerless to keep their course open to the sea. The saline waters evaporate under the strong Etesian winds of summer and salt concretions form.[16] The silt of the river mouth is easy to shape into basins of any size and depth. Fresh water is at hand in autumn to wash out adulterations from the salt, which is piled up in gleaming white mounds on shore. These were a familiar sight near the docks of ancient Carthage, as they are today in the port of Smyrna. The salt hardens and bakes in the dry hot air, and suffers little diminution from evaporation.

Salt figures in the earliest trade with the interior. It gave the name of *Via Salaria* to the first road which led from Rome across Latium back into the Sabine country of the Apennines. The salt ships ascended the Tiber from the salt pans established at Ostia by Ancus Martius to the magazines at the Roman *Porta Trigemina*.[17] Corresponding to the *Salinæ Romanæ* were the *Salinæ Herculæ* near Herculanæum. This term, like *Halæ* on Hellenic shores, has given its name to many old seaboard settlements that grew up about salt works. The Halys River in Asia Minor had its name from a like source.[18] Where no river was at hand to wash out impurities, the natives depended on the moist south wind for this service. Treaties often secured this salt trade, like that between the Romans and the Sabines,[19] or that between the Pæonians of the upper Axius River and Salonica, which exchanged its salt for the lumber of the mountainous hinterland.

Malaca and Mellaria had their names from Phœnician salt pans and salting stations for fish on the southern coast of Spain, whence salted food was exported to the nomads of Mau retania.[20] This Malacan salt industry persisted for centuries. The New England marine carried rough lumber, barrel staves, and naval stores to Malaga and brought back Spanish wines and salt to preserve their cod fish for the West Indian trade. They once tried salt from the Tortugas of the Florida Straits, but the result was bad, and they returned to the Mediterranean supply. After the War of 1812, when the American Republic had a vigorous but idle navy, spoiling for a fight, it attacked the Rif pirates who were interfering with this salt and wood trade, and administered the first effective chastisement the outlaws had received.

The south shore of the Mediterranean abounded in salt pans, where fresh water for washing the salt was present. Those of Salamis in Cyprus gave a famous yield, also those near the Nile mouth and near Utica at the Bagradas mouth, where the hills of salt were so hard and dry that they had to be broken with iron implements.

The ancients were familiar with rock salt but preferred the marine variety. Salt mines were few. They were found in Sicily near Gela and Agrigentum, in central Asia Minor at Lake Tatta.[21] In the interior of Illyria the Ardiæi mountaineers exploited brine springs to evaporate salt for their cattle, because the coast was so inaccessible over the rugged mountains that transportation was practically impossible.[22] Aristotle assigned this manufacture of salt from brine to things marvelous. A factor was of course the abundance of forest growth on the coastal ranges of the Adriatic.

SLAVE TRADE—Such manufacture required little labor. The slave trade found its human commodities a drug on the market soon after any protracted war. Primitive wars involved small armies, and provided slaves for the most part from de-

feated combatants and captives of the immediate vicinity. Such
was the case in the Trojan War. In the Roman wars the
armed forces greatly increased; as the number of combatants
increased, the prices of slaves rapidly decreased, especially
where the prisoners were distant from the big markets for such
slaves in Italy, where estates were large and employed them by
the thousand.

The price of slaves varied according to supply, age, beauty,
health, strength, skill in handicrafts and mental endowments.[23]
Their industrial, intellectual, and artistic skill made them a
factor in disseminating art and culture through the Mediterranean world. Their sources were generally captives of war
and piracy and prisoners for debt. Agricultural slaves or
"serfs" were generally subjugated natives, like the Helots of
Sparta and Crete or the Penestæ of Thessaly. These were
rarely for sale. All citizens who were left free on the Scythian
plains were prized as "tame natives" and encouraged to cultivate the land for the export of wheat. Others, who were captured and taken to Athens, were employed as the city police
and served as cavalry in war. As nomads, they were natural
horsemen, and their previous training gave them some military
experience, which was maintained by their tent life in Athens
as municipal slaves and police.[24] When the street gamin of
Athens saw a policeman coming, he doubtless shouted, "Here
comes a Scyth!" Other city slaves were used in the mines of
Laurium or Mount Pangæus of Macedonia, or were rented out
at a small sum a day, as a source of revenue for the capital.

Islands or cities located on the chief trade routes and commanding small areas or limited resources were the chief slave
markets. Such were Corinth, Ægina, Crete, Rhodes, Chios,
Delos, and Naxos. In Delos 1,000 slaves were often sold in a
day; but Lucullus was known to sell 40,000 captives in a single
day after one battle in Greece, at a nominal price *per capita*.
The islands were located where they could readily pick up their
human commodities. Lesbos, Lemnos and Imbros bargained
for such wares after the Trojan War.[25] The turnover had to
be quick, for food-supply was scant; but the distance was
short from big cities like Mytilene, Samos, Miletos, Athens and
Corinth where industrial slaves found ready sale.

Skilled slaves came from the island of Lesbos and the eastern shores of the Levantine Sea. Men metallurgists came from the Phœnician coast cities and women weavers and embroiderers came from Babylonia, Egypt, and Syria. Phœnicia provided gardeners, foresters, besides dyers and weavers. The Hellenic coasts provided pedagogues for children, tutors, men skilled in music, art, philosophy, secretaries, accountants, business managers, foremen of mines and factories, philosophers and copyists in private libraries and all such cultural positions. And their rental fixed their sale price. They came from refined eastern cities of industry and wide trade connections.

INDUSTRY—Solon, about 594 B.C., owing to the mediocre and limited soil of Attica, turned the attention of the citizens to manufacture. He compelled every father to teach his son a trade, since tillage made no adequate return for the labor expended; and he insisted that every industry should be considered an honorable calling. Hence in time distinguished men like Pericles and Alcibiades owned and controlled factories, and saw therein no loss of social or political prestige. Solon allowed only olive oil to be sold out of Athens,[26] though in time he probably permitted figs also to be exported, as these crops were abundant.

The expansion of industry and trade necessitated the extension of port facilities and their protection; and this was adumbrated before the time of Solon, in about the seventh and eighth centuries B.C.[27] Athens began about this period to annex the islands of Salamis and Ægina, for both islands had excellent ports and they blanketed the Piræus and the Phaleros, the two important western harbors of Athens facing the Isthmus of Corinth. Hence Athens increased her port areas by the annexation of these two islands, and was able to differentiate her ports. Increase of industry called forth increased grain imports, and gave rise to the Zea or grain port as a special section of the Piræus. The soil of Attica, as we have seen, was better suited to barley than to wheat. Wheat imports increased, as the choice grain of a capitalistic population, and small peasants multiplied in number. Society became increasingly democratic, though the vote was still restricted to landholders, and was not extended to the metics or alien residents. However, the aliens were generously treated, so that they were attracted to Athens, felt an affection for the state even beyond that of the confederates of Delos later, and frequented the emporium of the Piræus.

The industrial and commercial city-states had three elements of population: (1) The free citizen landowners, engaged in any activity. (2) Foreign residents or metics without vote. (3) Slaves in great number who provided the labor force. If we take Attica or the city-state of Athens as a standard, we find its population in 431 B.C. comprised 100,000 free citizens with their families, 30,000 metics, and 100,000 slaves,[28] though Boeckh estimates the slaves as 400,000 at this date. The area of Attica from 431 to 412 B.C. was 750 square miles. The peninsula of Attica alone comprised 700 square miles; but this area was increased during the Bœotian War (c. 506 B.C.) by the annexation of the fertile Asopus border valley of Bœotia containing the town of Tanagra.[29]

Real industrial development began in congested coast districts where population of superior ability congregated, especially where these locations commanded active trade routes. Corinth in such a location had in 480 B.C. 40,000 to 50,000 free citizens and about 60,000 slaves on a total area of 340 square miles. Ægina, according to Aristotle, had 470,000 slaves, many of them for sale, in a total population of 500,000 on an island only 32 square miles in extent. The island of Chios in 431 B.C. had 30,000 freemen, about 100,000 slaves and a variable number of metics on an island of 300 to 325 square miles. Corcyra in 431 B.C. on 240 square miles had 30,000 free men and 40,000 slaves at the lowest estimate. Rhodes in 300 B.C.[30] had about 30,000 free citizens in its total population; but the area of this state's territory was sometimes limited to the island, and sometimes included mainland districts of variable extent and considerable fertility. This was the typical *Peræa* or continental holding that often characterized insular possessions.[31] It represented the effort of the island state to extend its political territory to the mainland, where the water supply might be more ample and the resources of the soil more abundant, and where both might be close at hand in times of war or piratical activity.

These commercial cities did everything in their power to attract traders, although the visiting merchants were controlled by stringent laws, as shown in Chapter XIII. A busy metropolis like Corinth had a famous temple of Aphrodite which employed more than a thousand priestesses to be at the service of the visiting merchants.[32] Temple and city were both enriched by shipmasters and seamen who often squandered all their wealth on the sacred courtesans and thus put money into circulation. The economic result was an increase of the coined money, rising prices, and an enhanced reputation of the city as a desirable market, where the shipmaster could rely on the best return on his cargo. It mattered little that he had to buy a license to trade in the Piræus, if his profits were ample, and if he could find in this market all the products of the Mediterranean coastlands from the Caucasus to the Pillars of Heracles, and all the languages.[33]

Moreover wares of Athenian manufacture enjoyed an enviable reputation throughout the Mediterranean world; they were greatly superior to those produced at Carthage, which catered to the backward markets of the Western Basin and therefore turned out cruder commodities. Athenian weapons, tools, utensils and other metal wares were considered excellent. Lamps were made of bronze or pottery, but in either case were varied in form and artistic in design. The Hellenic sense of the beautiful was irrepressible. The factories were numerous and employed a large number of slave workmen, but large-scale production did not impair the beauty of the output. Prices were apparently moderate, though workmen and in many cases foremen or managers were slaves. Rates of interest were high and the risks of long voyages in oversea commerce were considerable, so that the merchant calculated for big profits in order to cover possible losses in a bad season.[34]

Owing to the geographic conditions of coastline and relief—conditions typified in Attica, Lesbos and Crete—the picture that we get of the ancient Mediterranean world, especially in the Eastern Basin, is that of a marked or even excessive development of urban centers and urban population. Rome in the time of Augustus numbered fully one million. Carthage at the time of its fall in 146 B.C. had a population of 700,000.[35]

Rhodes, Corinth, Samos, Alexandria and other cities at their zenith represented agglomerations of people out of proportion to the little Mediterranean world. But these big human groups stimulated culture, because contacts were active and new ideas accompanied every outbound ship to other coasts.

Larger aspects of commerce have been considered in earlier chapters in connection with the production of grain, cattle, hides, wool, hair, lumber, honey, wax, and salt fish together with sponges and the purple murex along shallow littorals, where these products abound. These are the raw products of forests, fields, grazing lands, and pelagic pastures, where shoals of tunny used to crowd into the brackish-waters of river mouths and the shallow coastal lagoons abounding in littoral life. These were the fundamental commodities of very ancient trade; they involved little or no industry, because the raw material was subjected to practically no modification by the hand of man.

INDUSTRY AND RAW MATERIALS—Industry in the real sense began when raw materials were transformed by craftsmanship and greatly enhanced in value. It began as a rule with some home-grown product, which was put through various simple processes, such as grape juice for its conversion into wine. Wine-making differed greatly in various localities, according to local geographic conditions and degree of economic development. To this group belonged the manufacture of olive oil, by the primary process of expressing the oil in an oil press; the making of cheeses from the milk of cows, ewes and goats, and their modification by the method of preserving and flavoring them. Finally came the genuine industrial products like textiles, manufactured from the home supply of wool, ranging from thin fine woolen cloth for clothing to blankets and carpets; goats' hair cloth ranging from the fine mohair of the Angora goat of ancient Anatolia to the coarse cloak for shepherds or slaves woven notably in the Po valley; linens from flax, ranging from the coarse canvas for sails made in Homeric Greece to the sheer linen muslins of Egypt like that in Tutankhamen's tomb, or the fine linen robes of the Temple priests used in Hebraic Palestine. All these lines of industry involved home-grown raw materials, which were readily increased by imports; but each in turn reveals an increasing amount and skill

of handicraft, both in relation to its own simpler forms and
to the culminating complexity of the highly developed textile
industry.

WINE TRADE—The widespread cultivation of vineyards in
the Eastern Basin and the universal use of wine as a beverage
in the Mediterranean world stimulated the early manufacture
of wine. Varieties multiplied because the juice of the grape
changed its flavor with every change of soil, climate and exposure. New wines were made by mixture of various grapes, by
slight modification of treatment, by the kind of cask in which
the juice was preserved, and by the addition of pitch to the
amphora or cask lining. Consequently the varieties were endless and greatly stimulated trade. Lesbian wine, which was
choice, entered the Piræus free of duty by treaty, but its sales-
man was inhibited from selling even a pint of it in any other
port.[36]

Athenæus states that the best wines came from the islands,
like Lesbos, Lemnos, Thasos, Cos, Chios, Icaros, Naxos and
Sciathos; and each wine had a distinctive flavor appealing to a
different palate. He praises also the mountain wines of Italy,
especially the products of the vineyards of Mount Massicus in
western Campania and the hills of Cæcuba in southern Latium;
but the wine of the Surrentum and Tibur districts were rather
inferior. That of Tarentum was very sweet like the wines of
Naxos, Lesbos and Phœnician Byblos, but the latter was less
heady.[37]

This development of varieties inevitably stimulated the wine
trade. The invention of wine was ascribed to gods and heroes
by the ancients—to Osiris in Egypt, to Dionysus in Greece, to
Bacchus or Liber in Latium and to Noah in Palestine. The
early development of the trade cannot be distinguished from
that of olive oil; the tonnage of ships was estimated in amphora,
earthenware vessels holding nearly seven gallons; but the wine
measure among the Greeks was the *metretes*, holding about ten
gallons and one pint. The wine trade is mentioned in Hesiod,
Homer, Ezekiel of the sixth century B.C. and later writers.
Ezekiel mentions the choice wine of Chalybon, made in the
Damascan district, and sold by the Phœnician merchants, together with Greek wines, as far as southern Gaul and Spain.

Homer mentions the wine of Mount Ismarus in southern Thrace
which Pliny states could be diluted with twenty parts of water.
Hesiod regarded the wine of Phœnician Byblos as the choicest
of his time, and selected this for his refreshment in hours of
leisure.

As the product of every little Mediterranean farm, wine of
some sort was available to all; but the imported wines were
long restricted till the oversea wine trade had developed to surprising proportions.   For instance during the Mithradatic
War (61 B.C.) the Rhodians sold to Sinope 10,000 *metretes* of
wine, besides 1,000 suits of armor, 15,000 pounds of prepared
hair for weaving and other materials of war.[38]   Even excellent
wine was cheap.   The best product of Chios in Socrates' time
sold for $1.70 a gallon in Athens.   Wine production in Italy
did not increase till after the decline of field agriculture subsequent to the Second Punic War.   Then Roman law, in the
interest of Italian landowners and merchants, prohibited the
manufacture of wine and olive oil from about 150 B.C. in the
district dependent upon Massilia west of the Maritime Alps,
and thus enlarged the Roman market.[39]

OLIVE OIL AND UNGUENTS—These industrial products derived their fundamental constituent from the widespread olive
groves.   Olive presses from 1000 B.C. were found widely distributed in ancient Palestine, and presses dating back to 2000
B.C. were unearthed in ancient Thera, overlaid by volcanic ash.
"Rose-scented oil," used by the dandy Paris in the *Iliad* points
to the early manufacture or importation of unguents.[40]   The
Bible describes sacred ointments and perfumes used for anoint-
ing the Ark of the Tabernacle, made of about a gallon of oil
compounded with a wealth of various oriental drugs, spices and
perfumes.[41]   Olive oil was sometimes compounded with oil of
sesame or almond and added to alum, sulphur, salt or tar as a
curative element to make a healing salve.   The manufacture was
usually simple except when numerous flower extracts were added
to make something superfine.[42]   The elaborate and costly varieties described in Pliny's *Natural History* indicate the need for
these commodities, and also the extensive trade in these luxury
articles.[43]   The Royal Unguent had twenty-seven ingredients.
Industrial flower gardens, like the iris fields of Bœotia and rose

gardens of Philippi, were maintained to provide blossoms to lend fragrance to the unguents; and the total number of vegetable ingredients was large enough to constitute a considerable industry.[44]

These costly unguents were the luxury of the rich, but the use of equivalents by peasants or even barbarians prevailed, owing to climatic conditions. At the great festival of Apollo held at Daphnæ near Antioch in Syria in 165 B.C. by Antiochus Epiphanes, the athletic contestants in the games had their bodies anointed with oil scented with saffron on the first day, with nard and cinnamon on the second day, fenugreek on the third day, marjoram on the fourth, and lily on the fifth, and all these ointments were contained in golden boxes.[45] On the other hand, the barbarians of the Balearic islands, so backward that they were without iron, met the climatic needs by expressing oil from the lentiscus plant, because they had no olive trees;[46] and the Judean peasant anointed his head with plain olive oil to ease his parched skin.

Though the manufacture of unguents and perfumes had gone thus far, the bulk of the oil trade was in crude or clarified oil. The export of oil to Carthage from Agrigentum in southern Sicily (c. 350 B.C.) brought wealth to the Greek colony and was the basis of an active exchange trade. Ship size was estimated in "amphorage" or its wine or oil contents.[47] The industry originated in the Eastern Basin, and moved westward with the spread of Phœnician and Greek colonization. Though oil export from Sicily to Carthage throve in the fourth century B.C., the declining price of olive oil in Italy did not permit exports till about 75 B.C. The manufacture of unguents appeared in Italy first in Campania, about Capua and Naples where industrial rose gardens stimulated the industry[48] and a dense population provided the labor force. Moreover, the increasing power, refinement and wealth of Rome stimulated the purchase market, while the decline of field agriculture encouraged this new phase of tillage.

TEXTILES AND RAW MATERIALS—Trade and industries made a distinct forward step with the development of textile manufactures; because these were sufficiently complex in their processes to compare with really mature industries. They began their development undoubtedly at a very early date because of imperative demand for clothing, and the abundant raw material at hand in the nomadic stage of development, found in the wool of sheep, camels' wool and hair, and goats' hair. This presupposes an extraordinarily long evolution of the industry with steady improvement of method and increasing variety of product. In time the career of woolen textiles was paralleled by that of hempen and flaxen weaves, though never on so large a scale, owing to climatic conditions; and eventually after the sixth century A.D. by sericulture and the manufacture of silken goods. Subsidiary to the exploitation of the wools and hairs, the animals of the farm and mountain pastures provided leather for sandals and shoes, which became an advanced industry in the city state of Sicyon, especially for ladies. Sicyon had its wet meadows along the sea front on the Gulf of Corinth where herds of kine and horses pastured, and its hinterland mountains where sheep and goats grazed in large numbers and provided unlimited amounts of leather. Great luxury was displayed in shoes both by men and women, and striking variety of styles, which were known by their place of origin.[49]

It was the textiles that showed the greatest possibilities of development. The process involved cleansing the wool or hair by the fullers, who in some large cities formed guilds, carding, dyeing the yarn and finally spinning and weaving under the supervision of the house mistress, as represented by Penelope in the *Odyssey* and Helen in the *Iliad*. Even the demoralized daughters of the Emperor Augustus directed their slave women in the same way. This was the household aspect of the industry; in addition the factory system for textile production prevailed widely, where raw materials were abundant, and yielded a great variety of fabrics.

The question of colors or dyes was an important one. Many wools were utilized in their native shades which were very fine where the animals fed on natural saline pastures,—a fact realized by the oriental rug weavers today. The tans varied from a delicate cream through all the deeper hues to brown and black. The "yellow-yielding saffron" which throve in the industrial gardens of the African coastland figured largely in the dye trade. Blue was derived from indigo imported from India and was used in mummy linen from the early Egyptian dynasties. Other vegetable dyes were procured in large quantities from roots in interior Spain.[50]

The fertile source for reds and purples was the murex univalve, found widely distributed on the Mediterranean littoral, wherever streams were confined to small torrents which did not render the coastal waters brackish. There were many species of the murex, and heaps of their shells are found where the coast favored their exploitation. Those found off Sigeum and Lectum of the Troad were large, those in the Euripos and the Carian shore were small, though the latter made the basis of industry of Cos. The small ones had a reddish hue, and the large ones were dark even to blackness. The shellfish were caught in spring when constructing the roe, for after this process the color was poor.[51] Superior murex abounded on the Lebanon coast and led to the development of an active dye industry at Tyre. The product was used to color the fine wool from the high Anatolian pastures. These goods excelled all others of the coast and their export brought wealth to the busy merchants.[52] The Phœnicians on their trading expeditions scoured the Mediterranean littoral for the murex to conserve the superior supply on the Lebanon coast from Sidon south to Dora below Mount Carmel. They early discovered the murex beds in the Laconian Gulf near Gytheum, the port of Sparta, and by 720 B.C. they had revealed to the Laconians the ample beds in the Gulf of Tarentum. In 706 B.C. these attracted Laconian colonists, a disgruntled political group, and in time formed the basis of the thriving dye industry established at Tarentum in connection with a textile factory instituted by immigrants from Miletos, who wished to take advantage of the fine wool of the nearby mountain pastures and the big merchant fleet in the harbor of Tarentum.[53]

Carthage, Utica and the nearby Phœnician cities enjoyed similar raw materials. The arid, shallow coast of the Syrtis Minor afforded thriving murex fisheries, which supported dye factories. Saline pastures provided ample wool and goats' hair, and under the Roman Empire even camels' hair. All dyes had to be fixed with alum, which the Rhodian colonists of the Lipari Islands and Gela in southern Sicily carried in their cargo

boats to the textile centers of this coast. In the Eastern Basin
alum was procured from volcanic islands of the Ægean Sea
and from Egypt.

The quality or character of the textiles varied widely, both
according to the quality of the raw material,—wool, hair, flax
or hemp, the purpose which the textile was to serve, the evolution of the industrial technique as advanced or backward, and
the general character of the markets where the commodities
were to be sold, especially the purchasing power and its degree
of culture. The coarsest textile was undoubtedly the black felt
of long coarse camels' hair, which from time immemorial constituted the covers of the nomad tents, as the traveller sees them
on the heights of Moab and Gilead today. The finest was probably the delicate fabric made from the soft down growing close
to the camel's skin. It doubtless provided the textile for those
renowned "Babylonian garments," embroidered and fringed,
which constituted the vestments of the Mesopotamian emperors
as seen depicted in the rock sculptures of the Lebanon coast
near Berytus. The art spread thence to Cyprus.[54]

Fine toga wool was procured from choice breeds of sheep
raised for this purpose. The final textile was that exquisite
fabric falling into graceful folds which we are familiar with in
the Elgin marbles and the Venus of Melos. The finest wool came
from selected breeds and the sheep were pastured on dry grazing grounds. Fine wool of Italy was derived from superior
Milesian sheep, which grazed in Apulia about Luceria and
Canusium and in the Sybaris and Crathis valleys in the rain-
shadow of the Apennines near Tarentum.[55] There it was woven
into cloth. Equally fine wool was later raised about Pollentia,
Parma and Mutina in Cisalpine Gaul, on the leeward side of the
Apennines, but in early times when this was all a frontier district, it manufactured only rough cloth of coarse wool and
goats' hair for slaves' clothes.[56] Old industrial centers famous
for their textiles, like Miletos, Megara, Corinth, Athens, Tarentum, Corduba and the far earlier Phœnician cities were all located near dry pastures, and in every case the local sheep were
improved by artificial selection or the importation of choice
Greek or Syrian breeds. Megara, with small territory and
meager soil resources, carried on large textile manufactures by

means of slave labor. In the fifth and fourth centuries B.C. it
was still one of the richest states of Greece.[57] Most of the industrial city states of Greece were clustered about the Isthmus
of Corinth,—Megara, Corinth, Athens, Ægina and Sicyon. In
461 B.C. Athens made a brief alliance with Megaris, secured
thereby access to Pagæ, Megara's port on the Corinthian Gulf,
and gained an outlet for Attica's western markets in Italy and
Sicily.

The inferior wools were utilized for making blankets, carpets
and occasionally canopies or awnings for boats or house entrances. Fine carpets from Miletos sought the market place
of the Piræus.[58] Rich carpets from Carthage and Sardinia
were in wide demand, the latter industry doubtless having been
introduced into Sardinia by Carthaginian colonists.[59] Blankets
were made in Corinth and beautiful purple coverlets in Cyprus.[60]

FLAX AND LINEN TEXTILES—A different textile, sparsely
distributed as an industrial product over the Mediterranean
coastlands, was linen. Its raw material was derived from flax
fields, which required a light fertile soil and ample water for
irrigation. These conditions existed on a large scale only in
Egypt, which therefore early evolved a refined linen industry
cultivated through many ages. It produced every grade of the
textile from heavy sail cloth to sheer linen muslin. Linen
breast-plates from Egypt were sold by the Phœnicians in
Greece in Homer's time. The linen cuirass of King Amasis of
Egypt, preserved in Rhodian Lindus, was woven of threads
each of which consisted in turn of 365 threads.[61] Pharaoh arrayed his prime minister Joseph "in garments of fine linen."
The annual flax (*linum usitatissimum*) was cultivated for five
thousand years in Mesopotamia and Babylonia, and provided a
second source for the linens in the Tyrian and Sidonian cargoes
sold on the Mediterranean coasts. In Greece both climate and
soil were adverse to flax production; so also in Palestine. Here
the fine linen curtains in blue, purple and scarlet, which made
the inner hangings of the Tabernacle described in Exodus,[62]
were doubtless Egyptian or Phœnician textiles. But Pausanias
describes a fine flax raised in Elis, which led to the development

of a textile industry among the women of Patræ, who wove linen for dresses and nets for the hair.[63]

Italy had the necessary raw materials and the resulting linen industry in the Po valley, but this industry came late into Italy.[64] Linen was sparingly used for clothing even by the Emperors in the first century of the Empire, when it was a luxury article only for the rich.[65] The flax districts in Cisalpine Gaul lay between the Ticinus River and the Po, near Retovium in eastern Liguria, ten miles south of the Po, and about Taventia in eastern Gallia Cispadana not far from Ravenna. These districts produced linens of excellent quality. All Gaul produced coarse linen for sail cloth also, which met a constant demand.[66] Flax was extensively raised in fertile districts on the east coast of Spain between the Sucro River on the south and the Sambroca River on the north. At various points like Sætabis, Tarraco and Emporiæ at the base of the Pyrenees, it gave rise to a superior linen industry which produced a textile like linen cambric.[67] Coastal lagoons near Saguntum in eastern Spain yielded a species of rushes under irrigation, and these supported an active cordage industry whose product was exported to the neighboring coasts and especially to Italy. Flax was raised also in Carthaginian Africa,[68] and doubtless helped to support the textile industry of the capital, though Punic ships could bring Egyptian flax in their return cargoes from Egypt.

Silken fabrics were known to the Mediterranean world at an early date by imports from the Orient. The women of Cos learned the art of unwinding the cocoons of the silk worms and weaving the filaments into a transparent gauze in the time of Aristotle.[69] The fabric was used for veils or fine garments known as the *Coæ vestes*, much in demand among the rich.[70] A fine textile produced at Amorgos may also have been of silk.[71] Gisela Richter, of the Metropolitan Art Museum of New York, has surmised an early manufacture of silken textiles in the Ægean lands, certainly in the fifth century before Christ, on a larger scale than was formerly supposed, since the drapery of the Parthenon Fates, Balustrade Victory and certain other statues clings like silk and not like any woolen or linen fabric.[72] Sericulture was developed first in the reign of Justinian (c. 550 A.D.), when two monks secreted silk worms out of Chinese terri-

tory or the Oxus valley, where the secret of silk production was
jealously guarded.

The textile industry made a distinct contribution to ancient
Mediterranean civilization.   Its long evolution in Babylonia
and Egypt on the eastern flank of the Mediterranean Basin
from 4000 B.C. resulted in the production of exquisite fabrics.
These served as models for designs and technique in other Mediterranean coastlands, and afforded a basis for comparison and
selection, wherever textiles were woven with increasing variety
in new localities and with increasing demands of trade.   Comparison and selection stimulated development and gave a new
cultural value to the advanced textile industry, which produced
fabrics of real beauty with colored or embroidered borders, and
interwoven threads of gold.   These facts may be recognized
from ancient sculptures, whose draperies reveal the quality of
the textiles, and from Tanagra figurines which show the colors.   If it be true that "civilization began when things became
more beautiful than they need be," textiles were one index of
progress.

POTTERIES AND RAW MATERIAL—A like contribution to the
advance of civilization was made by the evolution of potteries,
which ran back into prehistoric times.   This long and leisurely
development produced vases that were indeed the "foster child
of silence and slow time," endowed with a perfection of beauty
that called forth Keats' *Ode on a Grecian Urn.*

The raw materials were at hand in the widespread deposits
of excellent clays found everywhere in the Mediterranean lands
from Egypt and Syria west to Spain.   They were the product
both of crystalline and volcanic rocks, and were found in various colors—white, cream, tan and the coral red resulting from
the oxide of iron accumulated in the limestone soils.   The technique was simple.   The implements were the potter's wheel, one
of the most ancient human inventions, a commonplace in early
Egyptian equipment and in Homeric Greece; [73] moulds for designs of flowers or figures to be attached to the jar or vase in
high or low relief; gravers or scalpels to finish or perfect the
decorations, and furnaces for baking the clay.   The articles
manufactured included the seven-gallon amphora for wine and
oil; the huge jars, *dolia*, containing about 200 gallons and often

four or five feet in height, used for storing reserve supplies of
grain, oil, wine, raisins, beans and fresh grapes, and found in
Cnossos in Crete in 1800 B.C. in enormous quantities; various
containers for household use and receptacles in shops,[74] as one
sees 'them today in Pompeii; water-jars, cinerary urns for the
poor, jugs with stoppers and handles, pots, pans, wash basins,
cups and innumerable clay lamps [75] that lighted every Grecian
or Italian hovel with its wick of Carpasian flax floating in
olive oil.

The earliest receptacles for water and wine were goatskins,
earthen and bronze jars, and their use probably developed in
this order. Goatskins for wine were long used in ancient Palestine, though "old bottles" could ill resist the pressure of fer-
menting new wine. Bronze jars were rare, owing to the scarcity
of tin, but earthenware amphora were countless. All pottery
products were decorated, even the simplest and coarsest. These
were graded up to the colored glazed urns and the exquisite
"tear bottles" of iridescent glass.[76] The art of making this
iridescent glass, which throve in ancient Egypt and Phœnicia,
has never been recovered.

The pottery industry spread from east to west down the
length of the Mediterranean Basin. Fine ceramic art developed
successively in Egypt, Phœnicia and Crete, where a climax of
beauty was attained by 1800 B.C., as if beauty were a natural
feature of mere growth. The famous "cuttle-fish vase" discovered by Harriet Hawes near Gournia in eastern Crete shows
a realistic cuttle-fish in high relief, with two tentacles forming
the handles. Dating back to 1800 B.C. it nevertheless reveals
a standard of form and beauty of decoration unsurpassed by
any modern product. Another early Cretan vase reproduced in
bas-relief an epitome of the animal and vegetable life of the
neighboring seas.[77] The nations developed the potter's art
along individualistic lines. The Egyptians excelled in their
color schemes of decorations; the Greeks in their exquisite plas-
tic forms and their reliefs representing sacred processions of
women, whose forms were perfectly apportioned to the size and
shape of the urn; the ancient Cretans in their naturalistic decorations, realistic as those of modern Japan.

Potteries both fine and coarse were made widely through the

Mediterranean coasts, as in Rhodes, Cyprus, Samos, Corinth and Sicyon. The Athenian product was very fine, and the chief industrial district of the city was called the *Keramaikos* where the potteries congregated. A deposit of superior clay on the Colian Promontory near the Phaleros Port may have contributed to this excellence, combined with the early industrial development of the city. Choice vases were often exhibited at the Panathenæan games and presented to the victors. As early as 462 B.C. Athens was exporting its black-on-red figured pottery to Italy; and when its industrial development and maritime trade were fairly launched under Pericles, its potteries, both fine and coarse, sought various Mediterranean shores. The distribution of Athenian potteries coincided approximately with the limits of the Athenian maritime empire, just as centuries before Cretan vases had spread to Philistia and Egypt, to the Troad, Greece and Sicily, with every outreach of Cretan commerce in the Middle Minoan Period (1800 B.C.) [78]

The pottery of ancient Etruria was a distinctive type of advanced art. It developed especially in ancient Arretium and Tarquinii, and produced life-sized statuary in red baked clay, like the famous "Apollo" which the tourist sees in the Etruscan Museum of Rome today. Another feature was the large sarcophagi of terra cotta ornamented with figures in bas-relief, and supporting on their lids recumbent figures in life size, presumably portraits of the deceased.

The Romans inherited the technique of the pottery industry, and spread it over their territory west to the Atlantic and north into Britain. A period of decline followed in the Mediterranean lands, till the Arab conquest brought a remarkable revival of the art in Spain in the 12th century. Then Moorish potters, after the Arab conquest of Persia, gradually became skilled in the art that had raised Persian potteries to surpassing excellence, and they contributed to the renaissance of the artistic pottery industry in Italy in the 15th and 16th centuries.[79]

METAL WORK AND TRADE—Metals were unevenly distributed over the Mediterranean lands, on the borders of the old crystalline areas. This fact forced the manufacturers to search for the rarer ones like tin and gold. The distribution and trade in tin, necessary for the manufacture of bronze implements and weapons, has been discussed. Copper, the other ingredient in bronze, was found widely distributed from the Lebanon Mountains to Spain. Hence, some of the older bronze pieces contained only eight per cent of tin, the rarer element before the discovery of the Spanish and Cornish deposits, though the best weapons with strong blades required fifteen per cent. Bronze continued in demand after the introduction of iron; for the *Odyssey* shows both metals in use side by side.

Gold was the rarest metal and the one most wanted. It was used for coins, often mixed with silver to form electrum; for ornaments of dress, like necklaces, *fibulæ* or clasps to fasten garments; and also for flagons like the famous Spartan "cup of Vaphio," of supposed Cretan Minoan origin with its repoussé decoration representing a bull-baiting scene. Gold was familiar to Homer.[80]

The Phœnicians were the great metallurgists of ancient times and therefore were always found on the trails to tin and gold deposits. They fixed their factories on the gold coast of Thasos Island, near the deposits on the slope of the Rhodope massif; and they were early drawn to Siphnos, one of the Cyclades Islands, where a crystalline outcrop brought gold with it. Their vessels trading along the Carian and Ionian coasts doubtless acquired gold which came from the Pactolus River of inland Lydia. The Egyptians, who were also skilful workers in metal, conquered the Sinai massif for the sake of the copper, lapis lazuli and malachite, which they used in decorations, and visited the old crystalline mountains bordering the Red Sea for gold. They also bought gold from the Phœnicians, who knew every source of supply. After the latter opened up Spain, they secured not only tin and gold, but also silver, lead, copper, iron, and cinnabar from which the highly prized vermilion was made, and shipped to Rome in sealed packages.[81]

The Hellenes had little of the precious metals at their command. They mined the Astyra district near Abydos for gold in Xenophon's time;[82] the Thessalian Greeks made the Argonautic Expedition to Colchis at the head of the Euxine in search of the golden fleece long before the Trojan War. Hence the eagerness of Athens to secure the gold mines of the Pangæus Mountains to assist her in the Peloponnesian War,[83] and later the effort of Philip of Macedon (342 b.c.) to secure control of this region to finance his conquest of Greece.[84] The Persian Wars unloaded vast Asiatic resources of gold into Greece through bribes, subsidies to allies, payment to sailors and soldiers in Persian employ, and thus assisted the commercial expansion of Athens after the war. Alexander's conquest of Asia had a similar effect on a larger scale.[85] The large imports of Asiatic gold advanced prices and stimulated trade.

The desire to create artistic ornaments resulted in demand for other rare minerals to combine with gold, like the lapis lazuli and malachite which the Egyptians sought at Sinai as early as 4000 b.c., and later the emeralds they found in the Red Sea coastal ranges near Berenice. The Phœnicians participated actively in this trade in decorative articles according to Homer; they sold beads of agate and blue fluorite, also of iridescent glass. Other articles were carved seals of sardonyx, onyx and amethyst; but the Cretans of the Middle and Late Minoan Ages also made these artistic seals with figures cut in intaglio. Everywhere in the Mediterranean Basin amber was in demand from the earliest time. Amber beads were found in the ruins of Troy and Cnossos. They doubtless came from the Baltic Samland, passing from tribe to tribe, to the eastern piedmont of the Carpathians at the San River, and thence down the Bug and Dniester and through the Bosporus and Hellespont to Troy, where they entered the Ægean trade. Herodotus frequently mentions the inland tribe of the Neuri on the upper Dniester [86] who were doubtless middlemen in the amber trade. The Cretan amber was of Baltic origin, as shown by its silicate element. The Samland amber emerged also at the head of the Adriatic, having come by the Moravian Gate and the Peartree Pass. Amber from the Frisian Islands of the North Sea found its way to the Mediterranean by the Rhine-Rhone route, and like that from the Samland was distributed by Etruscan traders who controlled the Po valley, the Brenner Pass and other routes through the Alps.

When the Hellenes introduced the use of iron, they found the ore widely distributed in the Pontic ranges of Asia Minor, Syria, Greece, Sardinia, Elba and Spain. The copper and iron mines of Elba (Æthalia) probably attracted Greek settlement at an early date, for it seems to have been one of the earliest Greek places in Italy.[87] The mines in the Pontic ranges, worked by the Calybes tribes, were the chief sources of iron in the Eastern Mediterranean.

MARBLES AND BUILDING STONES—The paucity of wood in the Mediterranean Region, the early exhaustion of the supply in the old settled regions, and the difficulty of reforestation combined to necessitate a greater reliance upon stones and marbles than was the case in Middle Europe. Marbles, resistant to weathering, beautiful, varied, and easily worked as compared to granite, were widely distributed. They were found mid crystalline rock outcrops in Lydia and southwest Asia Minor, eastern Thessaly, southern Euboea, the Cyclades and eastern Attica. Granites come to the surface in some of the Cyclades, but were sparingly used because hard to work. The marbles had generally a white or creamy surface, flecked or veined in delicate colors; and they took a fine polish. Hence they were used for sculpture and fine architecture in the Eastern Basin, while common limestones served for the homes of the poorer class.

The evidence showed that stones and marbles early supplanted wood in architecture, and modified the type of construction and the style of decoration. Long familiarity with a medium like marble led to growing perfection in technique. The archaic wooden images of the gods were early superseded by marble statues. The marble cinerary urns and carved sarcophagi, the countless inscriptions on marble *stelæ*, the statues of the gods, the altars of temples or theaters, the numerous portrait busts of Greece and Rome are so many imperishable records of ancient life and thought. Whether the sculptured forms of the bare Grecian mountains, with their unblurred outline, were a stimulus to ancient sculpture, as Henri Taine states, it is difficult to maintain.

Italy had quarries of fine white Carrara marble, overlooking the Bay of Spezia (Luna), which was considered equal to the best Greek marble for sculpture in imperial times. It provided material for fine buildings in Rome in Cæsar's time. The buildings of Luna and even the town walls were made of this material,[88] recalling the marble houses of Paros.

Italy had extensive deposits of calcareous tufa or travertine,

which was soft when first quarried but hardened on exposure to
the air. It was found along the western Apennines and made
good building stone, used in the Colosseum, Pantheon, and older
houses of Rome. Lava blocks, available in old volcanic districts, served for paving roads, like the old Appian Way, the
streets of Pompeii and Syracuse; but they became slippery and
deeply rutted when worn, as the traveller sees them today.
Italian quarries, like the Grecian mines, were worked by criminals, prisoners of war and convicted slaves. Craftsmen in the
industry were differentiated into stonemasons, who squared and
laid stones for houses, and the skilled *marmorarii* who veneered
walls with marble and carved ornamental work for buildings.[89]

Traders were the apostles of civilization in the Mediterranean
Basin. Every commercial center in greater or less degree disseminated elements of civilization or higher culture. Familiarity with life in Athens and the Piræus reveals these two cities as
teeming centers of thought and progress. The same was true
of Massilia. The Rhone valley people brought raw materials
to market there, but they took back with them various elements
of Hellenic culture. The great universities, poets, philosophers
and artists of the ancient world were found in commercial cities
like Athens, Corinth, Rhodes, Miletos, Tarsus, Alexandria and
Massilia, for here the currents of thought flowed full and fast.

AUTHORITIES—CHAPTER XXIII

1. F. Ratzel, *Anthropogeographie*, Vol. I, pp. 119-204. Stuttgart, 1899.
E. C. Semple, *Influences of Geographic Environment*, Chap. IV.
New York; 1911.
2. *Iliad*, XVIII, 500.
3. Xenophon, *Hellenes*, V, Chap. I, 21.
4. Polybius, V, Chap. 88, 8. Diodorus Siculus, Chap. 45, 4.
5. Boeckh, *Staatshaushaltung der Athener*, Vol. I, pp. 75-77. Berlin, 1886.
6. *Ibid.*, Vol. I, pp. 64-65.
7. See chapters on Forests and the Lumber Trade and the Grain Trade.
Boeckh, *op. cit.*, Vol. I, pp. 68-69. Thucydides, V, 83.
8. Xenophon, *The Athenian State*, II, 12. Aristophanes, *Frogs*, 362-367.
9. Principle in Aristotle, *Rhetoric*, I, 4. Plutarch, *Solon*.
10. Mommsen, *History of Rome*, Vol. II, pp. 252-257. New York, 1900.
11. See chapters on Grain Trade and Pirate Coasts.
12. Boeckh, *op. cit.*, Vol. II, p. 315. Berlin, 1886.
13. Strabo, XII, Chap. II, 11.
14. Boeckh, *op. cit.*, Vol. I, p. 68. Berlin, 1886.
15. Pauly-Wissowa, *Real-Ency.* Article, "Carthage."
16. Strabo, XIII, Chap. I, 48.
17. Livy, I, 33; V, 45; VII, 19. Pliny, *Hist. Nat.*, XXXI, 39.
18. Strabo, XII, Chap. III, 12.
19. Pliny, XXXI, 89.
20. Strabo, III, Chap. II, 6-8; IV, 2-6.
21. Strabo, XII, Chap. V, 4.
22. Aristotle, *De Mirabilibus*, No. 138.
23. Boeckh, *op. cit.*, Vol. I, pp. 86-87. 1886.
24. *Ibid.*, Vol. I, pp. 81-85. 1886.
25. *Iliad*, VI, 427. Leaf, *Troy*, pp. 248-251. London, 1912.
26. Plutarch, *Solon*, 22, 24.
27. Pauly-Wissowa, *Real-Ency.* Article, "Attika."
28. J. B. Bury, *History of Greece*, pp. 407-408. London, 1913.
29. *Ibid.*, p. 218.
30. Diodorus Siculus, Bk. 20, Chap. 84.
31. E. C. Semple, *op. cit.*, p. 454. New York, 1911.
32. Strabo, VIII, Chap. VI, 20.
33. Thucydides, II, 38. Boeckh, *op. cit.*, Vol. I, pp. 59-60. 1886.
34. Boeckh, *op. cit.*, Vol. I, pp. 58-59. 1886.
35. Mommsen, *op. cit.*, Vol. II, p. 157. 1900.
36. Boeckh, *op. cit.*, Vol. II, p. 316.
37. Athenæus, I, Chaps. 48-57.
38. Polybius, IV, 56. Boeckh, *Public Economy of the Athenians*, p. 136.
Boston, 1857.
39. Mommsen, *op. cit.*, Vol. III, p. 415. 1900.
40. *Iliad*, Bk. XXIV, 186.
41. *Exodus*, XXX, 23-38.
42. H. Blümner, *Gewerbe und Künste der Griechen und Römer*, Vol. I,
pp. 350-356. 1875.
43. Pliny, *Hist. Nat.*, XIII, Chaps. 1-5; XIV, 1-2.
44. *Ibid.*, *Hist. Nat.*, XIII, Chaps. 26-63.

45. Polybius, XXXI, 3-4.
46. Diodorus Siculus, V, Chap. 17.
47. Livy, XXI, 63. Cicero, *Literæ Fam.*, XII, 15, 2.
48. Pliny, *Hist. Nat.*, XIII, Chap. 6.
49. Boeckh, *Staatshaushaltung der Athener*, Vol. I, p. 146. 1886.
50. Strabo, III, Chap. IV, 16.
51. Aristotle, V, Chap. 15, 547 A.
52. Strabo, XVI, Chap. II, 23.
53. Strabo, XVI, Chap. III, 4.
54. Athenæus, II, Chap. 30.
55. Strabo, VI, Chap. III, 5.
56. Strabo, IV, Chap. IV, 3; V, Chap. I, 7. See also chapter on Pastures and Stock-raising.
57. G. B. Grundy, *Thucydides and the History of His Age*, p. 75. London, 1911.
58. Boeckh, *op. cit.*, Vol. I, p. 60. Berlin, 1886. Thucydides, II, 38.
59. Athenæus, I, 49, 50; II, 30.
60. *Ibid.*, II, 30.
61. Pliny, *Hist. Nat.*, XIX, 2.
62. *Exodus*, XXXVII, 8, 14, 35, 37.
63. Pausanias, V, Chap. V, 2; VII, Chap. XXI, 7.
64. Pliny, *Hist. Nat.*, XIX, 9.
65. H. Blümner, *Die Römischen Privataltertümer*, p. 241. Munich, 1911.
66. Pliny, *Hist. Nat.*, XIX, Chap. 2.
67. Strabo, III, Chap. IV, 9. Pliny, *op. cit.*, XIX.
68. Polybius, V, 26.
69. Aristotle, V, Chap. XVII, 6.
70. Propertius, *History of the Wars*, I, Chap. XX, 9-12.
71. Aristophanes, Lysistrate, line 150.
72. Gisela Richter, "Silk in Greece," *Amer. Jour. Archæology*, Vol. 33, pp. 27-33. 1929.
73. *Iliad*, XVIII, 600.
74. R. M. Burrows, *The Discoveries in Crete*, p. 3. New York, 1907.
75. H. Blümner, *op. cit.*, pp. 145-149. Munich, 1911.
76. A. Erman, *Life in Ancient Egypt*, pp. 456-459. London, 1894.
77. Harriet Boyd Hawes, *Excavations at Gournia.* Angelo Mosso, *The Palaces of Crete*, pp. 46, 54-55, 61-62, 81. London, 1907.
78. James Baikie, *The Sea Kings of Crete*, p. 276. London, 1920. Burrows, *op. cit.*, p. 244.
79. *Ency. Brit.*, Article, "Ceramics."
80. *Iliad*, XVIII, 576.
81. *Ezekiel*, XXVII, 12. Diodorus Siculus, V, Chap. II. E. S. Boúchier, *Spain Under the Roman Empire*, pp. 82-91. Oxford, 1914.
82. Xenophon, *Hellenes*, IV, Chap. 8, 37.
83. Strabo, *Fragment 36*.
84. Strabo, VII, Chap. VII, 5.
85. Boeckh, *op. cit.*, Vol. I, pp. 9-11. Berlin, 1886.
86. Herodotus, IV, 17, 51, 105.
87. Mommsen, *History of Rome*, Vol. I, p. 178. New York, 1900.
88. Pliny, *Hist. Nat.*, XXXVI, 5-6.
89. Blümner, *Die Römischen Privataltertümer*, p. 596. Munich, 1911.

CHAPTER XXIV

COLONIZATION AND CULTURE

Ancient Mediterranean coast peoples, like the Cretans, Phœnicians and Greeks, were encouraged to send out colonies not only by their need of distant trading-posts, but also by their nautical efficiency, their familiarity with remote shores acquired by fishing and trading expeditions, and also by involuntary voyages, like that of the Samian ship which was swept westward to the southern coast of Spain by a protracted east wind, as recounted by Herodotus.

Moreover, the Midland Sea, owing to its latitudinal direction and the mild equable climate prevailing on nearly all its coasts, presented few deterrents to colonization. Similar conditions of temperature, seasonal rainfall and winds met the outward-bound settler when he arrived on unknown but familiar shores. The general history of subsidence in the sub-basins and inlets and of mountain folding on the land insured to the colonist the necessary harbors on some sheltered bay and familiar conditions of relief, so that his home-grown methods of tillage brought from the Lebanon slope or the Meander River plain and his system of navigation required little or no modification. Nearly every change of condition meant a gain—more abundant land, better soil, "tame natives" to do the rough work and deliver raw materials for exchange, neighbors unsophisticated and friendly unless ruthlessly antagonized.

CAUSES OF COLONIZATION—The geographic conditions which stimulated ancient trade and industry also at an early date gave an impulse to colonization. These conditions were the small size of the ancient states, the limited amount of arable land even in a larger state like Palestine or Judea, the constant threat of drought and famine, the consequent reduction of an already deficient food supply, and the need of importing food even in a fertile state like Bœotia, as indicated in Hesiod.[1] The tradition of over-population in Greece survived to the time of

Thucydides, who records that the great naval states of early days subjugated the islands to relieve the pressure of over-population. The economic motive of colonization was indicated by its search for productive grain land, like the Scythian plains, the coastal belt of Thrace, the Magna Græcia shore and the Neapolitan basin of Italy, and the fertile soils of Sicily.[2] The Phœnicians planted their colonies on similar productive coasts of North Africa, Sardinia and Spain; and like the Ionians of western Asia Minor had their factories on the Pelusiac arm of the Nile to balance Greek Naucratis on the Canobic arm.

This colonization movement was very active during the eighth and seventh centuries, long before industrial development and trade had reached their zenith. It was a process of blood-letting to draw off the turbulent population who created political disturbance over the unequal distribution of the land. Land, being scant, accumulated in the hands of a few oligarchs, and left a landless peasantry. The out-going colony moved under the direction of the state,[3] but thereafter had only a filial relation to its motherland. The Temple of Delphi, which was the Mediterranean clearing-house for geographical information, owing to its numerous visitants, was ready to indicate good locations for the new homes to be established. Colonization tended to relieve congestion of population, and it also opened the way for importation of overseas foods, which the colonials sold to the old city-states.

Similar conditions prevailed in Phœnicia. The big profits reaped by merchants conducting the overland trade between Orient and Mediterranean Occident occasioned over-population in the small deltaic plains at the seaward base of the Lebanon Mountains, and stimulated political dissensions. The harsh rule of the upper classes and the turbulent nature of the proletariat led to uprisings and regicides, as in ancient Tyre, followed by the expulsion and flight of the guilty, or the escape of innocent victims to distant lands, where they set up colonies. Thus Dido established Carthage in the eighth century before Christ, taking with her the people dispossessed in the dynastic quarrels of Tyre.

Every city had its poorer class to form the raw material of colonists, whom the oligarchs were glad to see depart for new and distant coasts where they could satisfy their land-hunger. Local physical causes, as earthquakes, droughts, famines and locust pests furnished recurrent motives for an exodus. Finally the frequent invasions from the Asiatic hinterland, from Babylonia, Assyria, Persia and Parthia and their seizure of the rich coast cities admonished the timid to find safe homes farther west, while the ease of sea-transportation, the prospect of gain and generous land allotments aided the colonial movement.[4]

Phœnicia maintained hinterland colonies or trading stations at Laish (Dan) near the source of the Jordan, Hamath in the Lebanon trough, Edessa on the Euphrates bend, possibly at Thapsacus and also Nisibis. These secured its access to the Piedmont route. Strabo indicates that Phœnician settlements existed on the Persian Gulf [5] at the south end of the great trunk road between Orient and Occident. Punic colonies also clustered about the Bay of Issus, as indicated by local myths, cùlts, place-names, and coins. The cult of Baal of Tarsus which prevailed throughout Cilicia resembled the Baal worship of Tyre and Carthage.[6] The chief colonies in the Gulf of Issus district were Rhosus, Myriandus, Ægeæ, Mallus, and Heraclea on the site of the later Daphnæ. Founded or largely inhabited by Phœnicians, these coast towns were emporia of the Euphrates trade. They had fair harbors, fertile land, secured copper, iron and ship timber from the Taurus Mountains, and commanded the opposite coast of Cyprus. Hence both Cilicia and Cyprus belonged to Phœnicia during the zenith of Punic power, from the twelfth to the eighth century before Christ, till the Assyrians conquered both districts.[7]

Drought and famine stimulated colonization, especially in islands where the boundaries were fixed. A seven years' drought in the island of Thera (Santorin) led to the colonization of Cyrene, at the suggestion of the Delphi oracles; one person from each family joined the exodus,[8] which therefore comprised about twenty per cent of Thera's population. Paros Island, small in size and poor in soil, was originally inhabited by Cretans and Arcadians, later by Ionians. Over-population ensued and caused Parian colonies to be sent to Thasos, to Parium on the Propontis and Pharus on the Illyrian coast.[9] Andros, an island of meager resources, sent out colonies to Acanthus and

Stagira on the Chalcidice peninsula in 654 B.C.[10] Fugitives from Samos colonized the island of Samothrace, which received settlers also from Epidauros.[11] Rhodes, which had only a fringe of coastal plain around its mountain core of the island, and by its location was subject to frequent droughts, sent out colonists to Phaselis on the Lycian coast,[12] to Gela in southern Sicily and to the Lipari Islands. Homer speaks of "well-peopled Cos" and "well-peopled Lemnos," selecting an adjective that suggests over-population. The "hundred cities of Crete" mentioned by Homer and the six city-states of Lesbos forced these islands at an early date to send away the superfluous citizens.

Drought and famine on the mainland worked to the same end. The prolonged famine in Lydia in the time of King Attys gave rise to the exodus of half the population to Etruria, where they built cities and instituted early Etruscan trade [13] and industry. The ancient Italian peoples, when crops failed, used to send out from their territory every living creature born the next spring, when these reached maturity, as an offering to the gods. This was the "sacred spring" and was accountable for a system of internal colonization, which relieved the pressure of population on the native sources of subsistence. Various sub-tribes of the Sabines, like the Samnites, Piceni and Hirpini owed their origin to a sacred spring.[14]

Natural catastrophes like the earthquakes and tidal waves which swept the Corinthian Gulf, invasions of migrant peoples like the successive Hellenic tribes, who overwhelmed Greece, and wars of conquest from the continental hinterlands, like Persian attacks on Asia Minor and Greece, all led to colonization, because they destroyed productive fields and increased the pressure of population upon local means of subsistence. The Persian conquest (512 B.C.) of the Ionian coast started colonies moving out in search of safe homes and independence, like the exodus of Phocæans [15] to Corsica, Samians to Sicily, and of Teians to Abdera on the Thracian coast, while the Ionians of Miletos considered colonizing Sardinia.[16] The Hellenic invasions from the north in the thirteenth century B.C. started a trans-Ægean movement to the Asia Minor coast of Æolian, Ionian and Dorian Greeks, till the whole seaboard was Hel-

lenized.   The latest arrivals were the Dorians or Heraclidæ;
and when these crossed from the Peloponnesos to Crete, the
fugitive Cretans fled to North Africa and Philistia about 1230
B.C.   Assyrian and Egyptian attacks upon Phœnicia had a similar effect.

So severe was the pressure of population upon the limits of
subsistence in these Eastern Mediterranean lands, that the
equilibrium was easily disturbed.   The eternal food quest had
mobilized the minds of the inhabitants long before the need to
depart arose, and informed them as to the best sites for colonies.   Megaris, which comprised a rugged country of 143
square miles with poor soil predominating, was forced to send
out colonies during the eighth and seventh centuries before
Christ, in spite of the careful native tillage.   She founded
Megara in Sicily in 734 B.C.,[17] Astacus in Bithynia in 712 B.C.,
Cyzicus on the Propontis in 675 B.C., Calchedon at the mouth
of the Bosporus in 674 B.C., and Heraclea Pontica about the
same time.   Meanwhile in this same period, Miletos by the help
of her neighbors made the Euxine a Milesian lake, with her
colonies established at every feasible coastal point.   The rich
raw materials of this northern sea attracted them with its
woods, cattle, hides, grains, fisheries, wool, and metals.   Political squabbles at home between land-holding nobles and a landless peasantry provided the occasion for outward movements
from Megara.[18]   Commercial profits drew the citizens of Miletos, Teos, Clazomenæ, Phocæa, Samos and other Ionian cities
from their homes, while paucity of arable land and uncertain
rainfall spurred them on.   Thus three geographic factors operated in the same direction, according to a familiar geographical principle,[19] and sprinkled colonies along the Mediterranean
coasts.

LOCATION AND SITES OF COLONIES—The location of such colonies was determined by economic and commercial motives.
Hence they were distributed along the great north-south and
east-west trade routes, especially at the crossroads where
streams of commodities converged.   Such was the location of
Rhodes, Byzantium on the Bosporus, Syracuse, Carthage and
Utica.   Megara threw out her colonies north to the Euxine and
west to Megara Hyblæa in Sicily.   Corinth and Chalcis of

Eubœa did the same, establishing way-stations north to the
Chalcidice peninsula, and west along the Gulf of Corinth and
the Magna Græcia coast of Italy to the nearer coast of Sicily.
Phœnician factories were established at an early date in Cyprus, eastern Crete, the island of Cythera (Cerigo), Corinth,
Malta, Utica, Sicilian coast and various points along the south
Iberian shores to Gades (Cadiz). Traces of them were to be
found also along the northern route to the Euxine,—on the
Carian coast at Erythræ [20] and Lampsacus at the entrance to
the Propontis, while traditions of Phœnician fishermen lingered
on the Crimean coast, according to Euripides. Lingering evidences of Cretan factories could also be detected on all this
west coast of Asia Minor from Rhodes and Lycia northward to
Troy.[21]

Strategic points exist at the termini of these main-travelled
marine routes, especially where they meet inland roads opening
up the hinterland. Therefore colonies abounded at the sea end
of the breaches in the barriers enclosing the Mediterranean
Basin. As we have seen, Naucratis and Alexandria were Greek
commercial colonies which handled the Nile River trade. Ancient Phœnician colonies clustered about the Gulf of Issus and
the later Greek colonies of Alexandretta; Antioch and its port
of Seleucia commanded the entrance to the Piedmont route of
northern Mesopotamia. The series of Hellenic trading stations along the Hellespont, Propontis and Bosporus bore witness to the importance of this breach, while more remote termini
on the Euxine coasts were marked by Grecian factories or markets in Colchis at Phasis and Bathys Limen (Batum); on
the north shore at Panticapæum, Tanais, Olbia and Tyras.
Therma (Saloniki) and Pydna giving access to the Axius
(Vardar) valley, handled the sluggish trade of the Vardar-
Maritza breach. Aquileia and Tergeste (Trieste) marked the
Adriatic termini of the Carso Plateau route to the Danube. A
succession of ports comprising Atria, Spina, Ravenna and
finally Venice, of various Etruscan, Greek, Roman and Venetian
origins, dotted the distributaries of the Po, and provided commercial outlets for the Po valley. The Mediterranean approaches to the Rhone valley breach were marked by Massilia
and a long cordon of colonies stretching from Forum Julii west

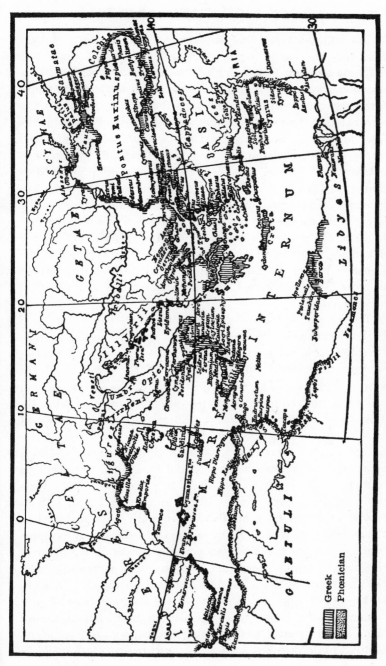

Map 14—Ancient Phoenician and Greek colonies.

to Narbo, which in turn was entrepôt for the Gap of Carcassonne.

Colonies of this type which occupied strategic positions possessed enormous importance for the mother country, and therefore were often kept under government control. Such were the
cleruchies or dependent colonies established by Pericles in the
Chersonesos, probably also in Lemnos and Imbros, the island
warders of the Hellespont.[22] One such, Oreos, at the northern
extremity of Eubœa, guarded the entrance to the Eubœan
Sound, and another on the island of Andros guarded the approach to Cape Sunium and the Saronic Gulf. These settlements were colonies of territorial expansion and were comparable to the military colonies which Rome established on her
advancing frontiers at danger points. Such was Aquileia, designed to control the Carso Plateau breach (184 B.C.), and the
colonies later established at Narbo, Carthage and countless
other points.

The prime requirement for the site of colonies was a good
harbor combined with local security against hostile natives.
Most desirable was a double harbor with access from two sides,
so that ships could enter regardless of the direction of the
wind. High ground on the seaward side of the port was essential to. protect shipping from prevailing storms and from the
Etesian winds of late summer. These requirements were met
by a situation on an anvil or club-shaped headland of bold relief, or on an inshore island, connected with the mainland by a
causeway, which could be pierced and bridged to unite the two
harbors. The headland or island site promised safety from
native attack. Such was the site of ancient Carthage, with its
citadel of Byrsa on a headland—originally an island tied to
the mainland by a neck of silt and gravel—flanked by two harbors; Cnidos on the Triopian peninsula, with its double port
sheltered by a hilly rocky islet from west and northwest winds;
the grain port of Perinthos on a headland jutting out from the
east coast of Thrace; [23] Cyzicos on the landward side of Arc-
tonnesos in the Propontis, originally an island but in ancient
times linked by sand reefs forming two causeways from island
to the Phrygian shore, with a lagoon between, which could be

entered by a channel from either side,[24] Sinope, Myndos, and many more.

A slightly different site was that of Syracuse on the east coast of Sicily and of Mytilene in Lesbos. Mytilene was situated on an islet, separated from Lesbos by a narrow channel which in time was spanned by stone bridges and which had a large port at either end. It could be entered by a north or south wind, and enabled ships to pass from one harbor to the other, as was done by the Athenian Conon and his fleet in the Peloponnesian War.[25] The north harbor was sheltered from the Etesian winds [26] by a mole, while the mountainous mass of Lesbos protected shipping from the west winds. The little island of Ortygia, the insular part of Syracuse, was connected with the Sicilian mainland at one time by a mole and later by a bridge.[27] These islet or headland sites with their double harbors abounded on the Mediterranean coasts, providing both safety and access to the sea. They afforded only a foothold on the land, but this sufficed for the ancient colonist, who found the small area easier to defend and less likely to antagonize the natives, because it indicated no purpose of territorial aggression. Moreover, it harmonized with the contracted land policy of the ancient Phœnician, Cretan and Grecian city-states.[28] Only Carthage and Rome adopted a policy of territorial expansion. Hence the small island site prevailed. Such was the site of Clazomenæ, an Ionian colony in the Gulf of Smyrna; [29] of Apollonia on the west coast of the Euxine, a remote settlement of Miletos mid the barbarous Thracians; [30] of Phanagoria on the Asian shore of the Crimean Bosporus, a busy market for the raw materials coming from the Don River valley and Lake Mæotis; [31] of Emporiæ at the eastern foot of the Pyrenees, which like most of these island colonies soon outgrew its narrow confines and spread over to the mainland; [32] and of Gades (Cadiz) on the island of Gadeira, little over a mile long and in some places only 200 yards wide.[33] These little islands afforded protection for shipping on their landward side, and safeguarded the colonists against hostilities from the mainland, but exposed them to piratical depredations and the attack of enemy fleets in time of war. However, the colonists were generally experts in naval warfare, and in case of defeat, they retreated to the main-

land,[34] where they usually owned a *peræa* or subsidiary territory.   Colonies on thalassic islands like Lesbos and Melos
lacked the mainland asylum, and were therefore more vulnerable.

Where such inshore islets were lacking, a narrow headland
or cape, whose base could be fortified by a rampart and moat,
answered the purpose, if it helped to inclose a small bay or inlet
which provided a single or double port.   Such was the site of
Potidæa at the base of the Pallene peninsula,[35] Acanthus and
Sane at the neck of the Mount Athos promontory on the edge
of the Persian canal,[36] Cardia on the four-mile isthmus of the
Chersonesos, founded by Milesians owing to its strategic location
and later re-colonized by the Athenians,[37] and finally the grain
port of Perinthos on the Thracian coast of the Propontis which
long withstood a siege by Philip of Macedon.   Various headlands on the coast of Sicily and Sardinia were occupied by
Punic colonies.   Carales (Cagliari) occupied a rocky spur
flanking the Gulf of Carales on the east; Nora on the west side
of the inlet had its port protected from the west winds by the
mountain mass of southern Sardinia.

Though a double port was desirable, it was not essential if
the colony had one deep capacious harbor like the Golden Horn
of Byzantium, sheltered from the Etesian gales by a wind-break
of hills; or like the roomy harbor of Massilia, or the narrow
inlet of Kallone Bay, which penetrated the island of Lesbos for
ten miles on the south and provided the city of Pyrrha with safe
harborage for a large fleet.   The city lay at the head of the
inlet on a table hill with sheer walls of rock on three sides, which
provided a perfect acropolis for a Grecian colony.[38]   Brundusium had one large harbor with a single entrance but compounded of several inlets, so that its outline resembled the ant-
lers of a stag.[39]   Hence it was easily defended, like the Euripos
passage into Kallone Bay.

LAND DETOURS—Even favorable harbor conditions might be
nullified, if the approach to the port was a devious passage,
studded with windy headlands, difficult to round or liable to
blockade by hostile fleets in time of war or by pirate ships.
Such a passage was the Bosporus-Hellespont, the Hermæus Gulf
(Gulf of Smyrna) which was dotted with busy ports—Phocæa,

Smyrna and Clazomenæ—but flanked by the stormy promontory of Mount Mimas (c. 3,000 feet); the marine channel, defined by the dangerous headlands of Caphereas, Geræstos, Sunium and Scyllæum, which afforded uncertain access to the Saronic and Argolic gulfs before the southwest winds of spring and early summer gave way in mid-July to the Etesian winds; the sea passage between Cape Malea and Cythera, between Ithaca and Leucas; the Strait of Otronto, of Messina and various others. (See Chapter XXI, "Templed Promontories.")

The imperative nature of trade in the ancient Mediterranean required that the flow of commodities should not be checked. Since these sea channels in many cases washed the shores of peninsulas, which characterized the highly articulated coasts of the Mediterranean Sea, the solution of the problem lay in breaking bulk and forwarding wares by short safe roads across the base of the peninsulas to a trans-isthmian port, where the voyage was resumed. The land route had the advantage not only of safety but also of brevity, because it avoided the long detour around the end of the peninsula.

The geographical principle was early recognized by the Phœnicians who placed their trading stations on many a narrow isthmus of the Ægean, where they survived as *astypalaia* or "old towns" to the arriving Greeks, and were found on the coast of Asia Minor, the little island of Astypalæa, and the west coast of Attica.[40] The low narrow isthmus of eastern Crete, eight miles across from north to south, between Minoa (or Gournia) and Hierapytna (Hierapetra) was evidently used as a land road or portage path by ancient sailors who wished to avoid the stormy headlands at the eastern end of the island, for a chain of settlements grew up along its course by 1500 B.C.[41]

The site of ancient Troy, in the opinion of Bérard, owed its successive cities to the fact that it dominated a land route which obviated the necessity for ancient sailing vessels to round the promontories of Lectum and Sigeum, when the Etesian winds made it impossible for them to approach the Hellespont. A larger peninsula, comprising all the Troad and Hellespontine Phrygia, and involving a long, difficult voyage, was evaded by a base road running from Cyzicos southward up the valley of the Æsepos River past Scepsis and around the eastern end of

Mount Ida to the Gulf of Adramyttium. Miletos, which settled most of the colonies along the Hellespont, Bosporus and Propontis, is accredited by Strabo with the founding of inland Scepsis, evidently as a half-way station between the two seas.[42] Walter Leaf, on the contrary, thinks the obvious land route ran from Assas on the leeside of Lectum, traversed a low gap near the western end of Mount Ida, and thence crossed the plain of the Scamander and Æsepos rivers to one of the numerous seaports on the Propontis.[43] The Æsepos valley was well tilled and had many towns on both sides of the river,—a fact that suggests a busy thoroughfare. Scepsis was evidently a very old town, as there was also a Palæscepsis.[44] Another longer isthmian route ran from Cyzicos or Cios southward up the Macestos valley to Mandræ, thence over a low divide to the head of the Caicos'River which the Macestos had decapitated, and past the inland capital Pergamum to the Ægean at the port of Atarneos.[45] Cyzicos therefore had an immense asset in the three isthmian routes, when perils beset the sea.

Bérard calls this location of ports "the law of the isthmus." It is strikingly illustrated by the situation of Teos and Lebedos, port of Colophon, on the Ionian coast in relation to Smyrna and Clazomenæ at the northern base of a three-pronged peninsula. The Gulf of Smyrna was guarded by the high Mimas promontory (1,000 meters), which made the entrance impassable with adverse winds. It was 70 kilometers (43 miles) long and 300 kilometers (186 miles) in a circuit, so ancient sail boats took three or four days to round it. Winds here were uncertain and often involved long delays. Hence it was frequently found advisable to deposit goods at Teos, with its hospitable double harbor, and send them overland twelve miles to Clazomenæ, or to unload the cargo at Lebedos and transport it via Colophon twenty-five miles direct to Smyrna. The latter road utilized two small river valleys,[46] which the modern traveller now traverses on his railroad journey from Smyrna to Ephesos. This isthmian road explains the location of Colophon and the flourishing trade of Teos as out-port of Smyrna in ancient times.[47]

Much depends upon the relief of the isthmus, which determines the feasibility of the land route. The neck of the Chalcidice peninsula on the Macedonian coast is a narrow furrow formed by a rift valley, which drops nearly to sea-level and extends from the Gulf of Saloniki eastward to the Strymonic Gulf. The valley is filled by two narrow shallow lakes except at its west end, where the smaller lake approaches within thirteen kilometers (eight miles) of Saloniki. There a low ridge (200 meters or 656 feet) of schistose rocks forms the threshold of the isthmian route and the back door of Saloniki.[48] This land road, only 36 miles long, linked the ancient Grecian colonies of Therma (Saloniki) on the west with Arethusa and Amphipolis on the east, and enabled ancient traffic to avoid the long detour by sea (160 miles) around the three stormy headlands of the Chalcidice peninsula when squalls swept down from the Strymon valley and the Hellespontine wind blew a gale. Hence this isthmian road helped to forward the ample resources of Chalcidice[49] to the terminal ports, and in time it formed a section of the *Via Egnatia* which the Romans constructed across the base of the Grecian peninsula from Apollonia or Durrachium on the Illyrian coast east to the Hellespont.[50]

Colonies or city-states in control of such isthmian routes enjoyed commercial opportunities, and increased their revenues by the imposition of transit tolls and port dues. The wealth and power of Agamemnon probably depended upon his control of the land route from Nauplia on the Gulf of Argolis north to Corinth and Sicyon, though the rough track had to climb to a considerable height as it traversed the fault valley of Nemea (c. 1,800 feet) and Cleonæ. Nevertheless it was one of the most important land routes of ancient Greece.[51] The high ridge of the Apennines running through Bruttium did not deter certain towns of Magna Græcia from founding colonies on the west coast; but these seaboard cities were agricultural, not commercial, with the single exception of Tarentum which had a good harbor. Croton, which had only a mediocre roadstead, set up its colonies of Laus and Posidonia on the Tyrrhenian Sea, but developed only incidental land traffic between. Milesians, Etruscans and Carthaginians managed the commerce for these well-fed Grecian colonists.[52] The Etruscans, on the other hand, who occupied northern Italy from sea to sea, developed the isthmian route from Pisa to Spina at the Po mouth on the Adriatic.

The long detour around the toe of Italy, the perilous navigation of the Adriatic Sea and the Strait of Messina were arguments for the land journey across the narrow base of the Italian peninsula, especially as the Etruscans dealt in the silver of
Populonia, iron from Elba, copper from Volterræ, and amber
from the Baltic,[53] all articles of considerable value in relation
to their bulk.

ETHNIC INTERMIXTURE IN ANCIENT COLONIES—The colonizing movements which characterized Mediterranean social-economic life from the Middle Minoan period onward resulted in
a stratification of races, more or less complex, along all the
coasts of the Midland Sea, with a final amalgamation both of
races and cultures. The seaboard of North Africa was occupied by a Libyo-Phœnician stock from the Syrtis Major west
to the Strait of Gibraltar and beyond. The coastal belt of
Cyrenaica was inhabited by Libyo-Hellenes. The west side of
the Nile delta was to some degree Hellenized by the Grecian
colonies of Naucratis and Alexandria, while the Pelusiac arm
received a steady infusion of Phœnician elements which resulted
in a hybrid race of interpreters, invaluable in commercial transactions. Greek colonies from 800 B.C. wove a border of Hellenic race and culture all around the Euxine littoral, except
along the inhospitable coast of the Caucasus, and left there a
Greco-Scythian people who were effective intermediaries in the
commerce of this coast.

The Ægean Sea, which invited mass movements of population, produced a far more complex combination on the western
front of Asia Minor, which invited colonization. Here Phrygians in the north, Leleges in the middle section and Carians in
the south furnished the underlying native stocks. These were
modified in time by a sprinkling of Cretan traders and colonists;[54] but after the arrival of the Hellenes on the Ægean
shores, they were overlaid by Pelasgi and Æolian, Ionian and
Dorian colonies, which appropriated the seaboard, crowded the
native inhabitants back into inland parts, or absorbed them
by intermarriage. Thus we find a Greco-Phrygian stock in the
north, and a Greco-Carian stock in the south.

The complexity of race intermixture was greater than even
these various elements implied. For instance Chios, an Ionian

colony, considered the Pelasgi from Thessaly their original settlers,[55] but Leleges from Asia Minor had previously occupied the island and various stocks arrived later. Ionia was colonized by Ionians, but received settlers also from the Abantes of Euboea, a wholly different stock, and from the Æolians of Boeotia, Dorians of Epidaurus, Arcadians who claimed to be Pelasgians, and Molossians from Epiros of primitive race. Certain colonists from Athens brought no wives with them but appropriated the Carian women, after killing their husbands. Thereafter the women never ate with their husbands or called them by name.[56] Aristotle warned against the reception of aliens into colonies at their foundation or later, because they created political unrest and often stirred up revolution, as exemplified by the history of Syracuse, Zancle or Messana, and many more.[57]

The amalgamation of the Greek colonists with the native inhabitants was the rule. Cedreæ on the Ceramic Gulf of Caria had a mixed population of Greeks and barbarians.[58] So had Argos Amphilochia on the Gulf of Ambracia (Arta); its natives adopted the Greek language,[59] a rather exceptional case. More often the colony became bi-lingual, as did the settlers on the peninsula of Mount Athos,[60] or they spoke a mixed dialect of Greek and native words, as was the case in a Greek settlement among the Budini of Scythia.[61] Strabo comments upon the various dialects spoken in the Ionian colonies on the coast of Asia Minor. The Roman military colonists intermarried on a large scale in the remote provinces of the Empire, and thereby fostered friendly relations with the conquered territory; but the Latin speech suffered in the mouth of barbarians, as Cicero reveals in his scorn of the uncouth language of a Spanish colonial poet. On the other hand, Greek persisted in its purity in Sicily, where the Hellenic colonies dislodged the native Siculi and drove them back from the coast. Hence Syracuse could produce a poet like Theocritus.

COLONIZATION AND CIVILIZATION—The first seats of commerce became also the seats of earliest culture and civilization. More than other city-states they were under the necessity of founding distant colonies as collecting and distributing depots, and through the agency of these they disseminated their cultural achievements to various coasts. Commerce and its attendant colonization exercised a marked influence not only on seamanship, tillage, politics, domestic life and the standard of living, but also on art, science, and religion. Phœnician merchantmen sold imported plants and fruits, like the cassia, peach, plum and citron, in the Mediterranean markets, and domiciled them in Punic colonies wherever they could be made to grow. Culture followed the paths of commerce in the ancient world, and throve in great terminal colonies like Alexandria, Byzantium, Mytilene, and Massilia. Ports like the Golden Horn, the Piræus, Corinthian Cenchreæ, Pharos or Puteoli became clearing houses of commodities, opinions, and ideas. Despite distinctions due to differences of race and character in the peoples of the Mediterranean Basin, a common type of cultural development finally prevailed among them, and differentiated them from the people of the interior who remained aloof from this commercial intercourse.[62]

Colonies were carriers of this civilization, and wove a band of Mediterranean culture around the coasts, while the hinterland remained backward, arrested like the interior of Spain, Illyria and Anatolia. The art of the Mediterranean peoples, architecture, painting and sculpture, drew upon the resources of Egypt, Crete, Assyria and Greece, while the Romans fell heir to their achievements. Increase of wealth and the growth of a leisure class created patrons of the arts, like the *chôregoi* of Athens who became financially and artistically responsible for the annual dramatic performances in honor of Dionysus. The ruins of magnificent theaters which the traveller sees in Cnidos, Ephesos, Epidauros, Syracuse and Taormina, not to mention the amphitheaters at Arelate (Arles) and Nemausus (Nîmes) indicate in these colonial cities a leisure class devoted to the drama, a companion group to the great poets and philosophers who sustained the culture of Lesbos and the Ionian coast of Asia Minor.

The colonists took with them memories of the drama and literature of their home land. Plutarch in his *Nicias* related the story [63] that Athenian prisoners made captive in Syracuse in 413 B.C. were given their freedom if they could recite in public passages from the drama of *Alcestis* by Euripides—an episode which Browning has used in his lovely paraphrase of Euripides, *Balaustion's Adventure*. The Syracusans greatly admired the poetry of Euripides, and the presentation of the *Alcestis* on the stage at Athens was a recent dramatic event, the fame of which had spread to Sicily, despite the Peloponnesian War. Books appeared occasionally in the colonial trade. Xenophon found a chest of books from a ship-wrecked boat at Salmydessos on the Thracian coast; and Plato's works were regularly exported to the cultivated cities of Sicily, though the book trade was not organized in Hellas as it later was in Rome.[64]

The intimate communication stimulated by commerce and colonization, between the different coasts of this enclosed sea, had the further effect of widely disseminating the various religions. The worship of Serapis spread along the grain track from Egypt to Rhodes, and thence to the grain port of Pozuoli (Puteoli) near Naples, where the traveller today sees the half submerged Serapheum on the sunken shore.

The worship of Astarte, under the name of Artemis, Diana, Aphrodite or Venus, spread around all the Mediterranean coasts, while that of Melkart, as Heracles or Hercules, appeared wherever Phœnician merchants set up a trading-station or colony. Hence their voyages can be traced by these Heracles shrines or temples. The Zeus worship spread from Greece to Asia Minor and there displaced the Mother of the Gods, while this archaic deity was introduced into Italy during the Second Punic War for the salvation of Rome. These frequent voyages of commerce and colonization finally obliterated the distinctions between the ancient faiths, except in Egypt and Judea which clung to their old beliefs. Hence a complete religious tolerance arose and cleared the way for Christianity by the collapse of the old religions. This tolerance must be regarded as only another aspect of ancient Mediterranean culture, since it represented emancipation of the intellect.

The high-water mark of Mediterranean civilization is to be found in the polished manners which characterized these ancient peoples. Their manners were a conscious acquisition. We have only to read the *Heracles* of Euripides to observe the perfect manners of the slaves of Queen Alcestis, who would not violate the laws of hospitality by letting the hero see that his visit was inopportune, since his hostess had just died. The same grace is to be observed in the slaves of Odysseus, who avoid any embarrassment to their ragged guest. When faultless manners descend from kings to slaves, the social polish is perfect and culture has attained its utmost. When the Rhodians, denied the export of lumber from Macedonia by the Romans, received their financial death blow, their ambassador, returning from the imperial capital, stood up in the breathless assembly and said: "This means our economic ruin; but we can still maintain our reputation of being the best mannered people of the Mediterranean world." [65] Thus they held their heads, "bloody but unbowed."

AUTHORITIES—CHAPTER XXIV

1. Hesiod, *Works and Days*, p. 236 *et seq.*
2. G. B. Grundy, *Thucydides and the History of His Age*, pp. 63-66. London, 1917.
3. A. Zimmern, *The Greek Commonwealth*, p. 252. Oxford, 1915.
4. F. C. Mövers, *Die Phoenizier*, Vol. II, pp. 5-9. Berlin, 1849-1850.
5. Strabo, XVI, Chap. III, 4. *Ezekiel*, XXVII, 15.
6. F. C. Mövers, *op. cit.*, Vol. II, pp. 170-174.
7. *Ibid.*, Vol. I, pp. 306-310; Vol. II, pp. 161-169. Berlin, 1849-1850.
8. Herodotus, IV, 151, 153, 156-158.
9. Thucydides, IV, 104, 107. Strabo, VII, Chap. V, 5.
10. Thucydides, IV, 84, 88.
11. Pausanias, VII, Chap. 4, 3.
12. Herodotus, II, 178. Thucydides, II, 69; VIII, 88-89.
13. Herodotus, I, 94.
14. Vergil, *Æneid*, VII, 796. Strabo, V, Chap. IV, 2, 12. Livy, XXXIV, 44.
15. Herodotus, I, 165.
16. Herodotus, I, 168, 170; V, 124; VI, 22-24.
17. Strabo, VI, Chap. II, 2.
18. Theognis of Megara, *Epigrams*.
19. Ratzel, *Anthropogeographie*, Vol. I, pp. 289-293. Stuttgart, 1899. E. C. Semple, *Influences of Geographic Environment*, pp. 14-15. New York, 1911.
20. Hugo Gaebler, Dissertation, *Erythra*, p. 4. Berlin, 1892.
21. Herodotus, I, 172, 173. Pausanias, VII, Chap. III, 7. Strabo, XIII, Chap. I, 4, 8; XIV, Chap. I, 6.
22. J. B. Bury, *History of Greece*, pp. 365-366. London, 1913.
23. Diodorus Siculus, XVI, 76.
24. Frontinus, III, Chap. 13. F. W. Hasluck, *Cyzicus*, pp. 2-5. Cambridge, 1910.
25. Diodorus Siculus, XIII, 77-79.
26. Strabo, XIII, Chap. II, 2.

27. Strabo, VI, Chap. II, 4.
28. Thucydides, VI, 2. E. C. Semple, *op. cit.*, pp. 195-196.
29. Thucydides, VIII, 14. Strabo, I, Chap. II, 17.
30. Strabo, VII, Chap. VI, 1.
31. *Ibid.*, XI, Chap. II, 9-10.
32. *Ibid.*, III, Chap. IV, 8.
33. *Ibid.*, III, Chap. V, 3.
34. Thucydides, VII, 14.
35. Strabo,·*Fragment 25; Fragment 27.*
36. Thucydides, IV, 88, 109. Herodotus, VII, 22. Strabo, *Fragment 31; Fragment 33.*
37. Strabo, *Fragment 52.*
38. Strabo, XIII, Chap. II, 2. Tozer, *Islands of the Ægean*, pp. 130-133. Oxford, 1890.
39. Strabo, VI, Chap. III, 6.
40. Victor Bérard, *Les Phéniciens et L'Odyssée*, Vol. I, pp. 30-42. Paris, 1902.
41. C. H. and H. B. Hawes, *Crete the Forerunner of Greece*, p. 94. New York, 1911.
42. Bérard, *op. cit.*, p. 74.
43. Walter Leaf, *Troy*, pp. 200, 260-261. London, 1912.
44. Strabo, XIII, Chap. I, 43-45.
45. F. W. Hasluck, *Cyzicus.*
46. A. Philippson, *Reisen und Forschungen in westlichem Kleinasien*, pp. 50-57. Peterm. Ergänz. No. 177, 1914. Bérard, *op. cit.*, p. 77. C. Schaeffler, Dissertation, *De Rebus Teorum.* Leipzig, 1882.
47. Strabo, XIV, Chap. I, 30-31. Livy, XXXVII, 27-28.
48. Th. Fischer, *Die Balkan Halbinseln* in Kirchoff's *Europa*, pp. 119-120. 1893.
49. Xenophon, *Hellenes*, V, Chap. II, 16.
50. Mommsen, *History of Rome*, Vol. III, p. 263; Vol. IV, p. 168.
51. Bérard, *op. cit.*, Vol. I, p. 78. Philippson, *Der Peloponnes*, pp. 63-64. 1892.
52. Mommsen, *op. cit.*, Vol. I, pp. 171-172. New York, 1905.
53. *Ibid.*, Vol. I, pp. 162, 182.
54. Pausanias, VII, Chapters II-V.
55. Strabo, XIII, Chap. III, 3.
56. Herodotus, I, 18, 142, 146.
57. Aristotle, *Politics*, Bk. V. Herodotus, VI, 22-25. Thucydides, VI, 4.
58. Xenophon, *Hellenes*, Bk. II, Chap. I, 15.
59. Thucydides, II, 68.
60. *Ibid.*, IV, 109.
61. Herodotus, IV, 108-109.
62. Ratzel, *Anthropogeographie*, Vol. I, p. 214. Leipzig, 1882.
63. Plutarch, *Nicias*, 29.
64. A. Boeckh, *Staatshaushaltung der Athener*, Vol. I, pp. 60-62. Berlin, 1886.
65. Polybius, XXV, 4.

GENERAL BIBLIOGRAPHY

ANCIENT AUTHORITIES

Æschylus, Tragedies.

Apollonius Rhodius, *Argonautæ.*

Appian, *Illyrian Wars.*

Aristophanes, *Clouds; Knights; Wasps.*

Aristotle, *Politics; Animalia; De Mirabilibus.*

Arrian, *Anabasis of Alexander; Indica.* Trans. by E. Chinnock. London, 1893.

Athenæus, *The Deipnosophists.* Trans. by C. D. Yonge. London, 1853.

The Bible.

Cæsar, *De Bello Gallico; De Bello Civili.*

Callimachus, *Hymns to Artemis and Zeus.*

Cato, *De Re Rustica.*

Cicero, *Orationes; Litteræ; De Natura Deorum.*

Columella, *De Agricultura; Carmen Hortorum.*

Demosthenes, *Contre Parmenis, Œuvres Complettes.* 4 vols. Trans. by Abbé Auger. Paris, 1777. Selected Orations. English translation by Charles Rann Kennedy.

Diodorus Siculus, Historical Library.

Euripides, Tragedies.

Frontinus, *De Aquis Urbis Romæ.*

Grundy, G. B., *Greek Anthology.*

Herodotus, *History.*

Hesiod, *Works and Days; Catalogue of Women* and *Eoiæ.* Loeb Lib. London, 1914.

Hippocrates, *Air, Water and Places.*

Homer, *Homeric Hymns; Iliad; Odyssey.*

Horace, *Carmina, Odes and Satires.*

Josephus, *Antiquities of the Jews; The Jewish Wars.*

Justinian, *Digesta.*

709

Livius, *Historia.*
Lucanus, *De Bello Civili.*
Lucretius, *De Natura Rerum.*

Martialis, *Epigrams.*

Ovid, *Metamorphoses; Tristia.*

Pater, Walter H., *Anthology of Greek Poetry.* 4 vols.
Pausanias.
Periplus of the Erythræan Sea. Trans. by Schoff. London and
　　New York, 1912.
Philostratus, *Vita Sancti Apolloni Tyanæ.*
Pindar, *Odes.*
Plato, *Laws; Phædo; Critias.*
Pliny, *Historia Naturalis.*
Pliny the Younger, *Epistulæ.*
Plutarch, *Lives of Solon, Sertorius, Cato the Younger, Nicias,*
　　Alexander.
Polybius, *Histories.*
Pomponius Mela, *Geographia.*
Procopius, *De Bello Vandalico.*
Propertius, *De Historia Bellorum.*
Ptolemy, *Geography.*

Scylax, *Periplus.*
Seneca, *Physical Science.*
Sophocles, Tragedies.
Strabo, *Geography.*

Tacitus, Histories; Annals.
Theocritus, *Idyls.*
Theognis of Megara, *Epigrams.*
Theophrastus, *De Historia Plantarum.* Eng. trans. Loeb Library.
　　De Causis Plantarum; Characters.
Thucydides, *History of the Peloponnesian Wars.*

Varro, *Tres Libri de Agricultura.*
Vergil, *Æneid; Georgics.*
Vitruvius, *De Architectura.*

Xenophon, *Anabasis; Cyropædia; Hellenes; Œconomicus.*

Modern Authorities

Baedeker, *Austria, Eastern Alps, Egypt, Greece, Italy, Northern Italy, Central Italy, Southern Italy, The Mediterranean, Palestine, Spain.*

Banse, E., *Die Turkei.* Braunschweig, 1919.

—— *Die Altasländer.* 1910.

Bérard, V., *Les Phéniciens et l'Odyssée.* 2 vols. Paris, 1902.

Berg, L., *Das Problem der Klimaänderung in geschichtlicher Zeit.* Leipzig, 1914.

Blümner, H., *Gewerbe und Kunste der Griechen und Römer.* 2 vols. 1875.

—— *Die Römischen Privataltertümer.* Munich, 1911.

Boeckh, A., *Public Economy of the Athenians.* English trans. London and Boston, 1857.

—— *Die Staatshaushaltung der Athener,* 1886.

Boúchier, E. S., *Spain Under the Roman Empire.* Oxford, 1914.

Breasted, J. H., *History of Egypt.* New York, 1909.

—— *Ancient Records of Egypt.* 2 vols. Chicago, 1906.

Brooks, C. E. P., *Evolution of Climate.* London, 1922.

Bunbury, *History of Ancient Geography.* 2 vols.

Burrows, R. W., *Discoveries in Crete.* New York, 1907.

Bursian, Conrad, *Geographie von Griechenland.* 3 vols. Leipzig, 1862.

Bury, J. B., *History of Greece.* London, 1913.

Casson, Stanley, *Macedonia, Thrace and Illyria.* Oxford, 1926.

Ceznola, *Cyprus.* 1872.

Curtius, Ernest, *History of Greece.* Trans. from the German. New York, 1907.

Cvijic, *La Péninsule Balkanique.* Paris, 1918.

Deecke, W., *Italy.* London, 1904.

Erman, A., *Life in Ancient Egypt.* London, 1894.

Fischer, Theobald, *Mittelmeerbilder.* Leipzig, 1905.

—— *Die sudoestlichen europaeischen Halbinseln,* in Kirchhoff's *Europa.*

—— *Studien über das Klima der Mittelmeerländer.* Pet. Mitt. Ergänz. No. 58, 1879.

Fitzner, *Niederschlag und Bewölkung in Kleinasien.* Pet. Mitt. Ergänz. No. 40, 1902.

Frank, Tenney, *Economic History of Rome.*

Freeman, E. A., *Historical Geography of Europe.* London, 1882.

—— *History of Sicily.* 4 vols.

Garstang, J., *Land of the Hittites.* New York, 1910.

Glinka, K., *Die Typen der Bodenbildung.* Berlin, 1914.

Glotz, G., *Ancient Greece at Work.* New York, 1926.

Götz, W., *Die Verkehrswege im Dienste des Welthandels.* Stuttgart, 1888.

Grundy, G. B., *Thucydides and His Age.* London, 1911.

Hann, J., *Handbuch der Klimatologie.* 3 vols. Stuttgart, 1908-1911.

Harrison, Fairfax, *Roman Farm Management.* New York.

Hawes, Charles H. and Harriet B., *Crete, the Forerunner of Greece.* New York, 1911.

Helmolt, H., *History of the World.* Vol. IV. New York, 1903.

Hildebrand, G., *Cyrenaika.* Bonn, 1904.

Hodgkin, T., *Italy and Her Invaders.* Oxford, 1911.

Hogarth, D. G., *The Nearer East.* London, 1902.

—— *Ionia and the East.* Oxford, 1909.

Huntington, E., *Palestine and Its Transformation.*

Huntington, E. and Visher, S., *Climatic Changes: Their Nature and Causes.* New Haven, 1922.

Keller, A. G., *Homeric Society.* New York, 1902.

Kenrick, *Phœnicia.* London, 1855.

King, Bolton and Okey, Thomas, *Italy Today.*

Launay, L. de, *Géologie de la France.* Paris, 1921.

Leaf, Walter, *Troy: A Study in Homeric Geography.* New York, 1912.

Leake, W. M., *Travels in Northern Greece.* 4 vols. London, 1835.

—— *Travels in the Morea.* 3 vols.

Leiter, H., *Die Frage der Klimaänderung während historischer Zeit in Nordafrika.* Vienna, 1909.

Le Strange, Guy, *Lands of the Eastern Caliphate.* Cambridge, 1905.

MacIver, David Randall, *The Etruscans.* London, 1927.

Mariolopoulos, E. G., *Etude sur le climat de la Gréce.* Paris, 1925.

Maspero, G. C., *The Dawn of Civilization.* New York, 1901.

—— *The Struggle of the Nations.* Ed. by A. H. Sayce. New York, 1897.

Meyer, Eduard, *Geschichte des Altertums.* Stuttgart, 1909.

Mimms, E. H., *The Scythians and the Greeks.* Cambridge, 1913.

Mommsen, T., *History of Rome.* New York, 1900.

—— *Provinces of the Roman Empire.* New York, 1887.

Mövers, C., *Die Phoenizier.* 4 vols. Berlin, 1840-1856.

Myres, J. L., *The Dawn of History.* New York, 1911.

Neumann and Partsch, *Physikalische Geographie von Griechenland.* Breslau, 1885.

Newbigin, M. I., *The Mediterranean Lands.* New York and London, 1924.

—— *Modern Geography.* New York and London, 1911.

Oberhummer, E., *Das Insel Cypern.* 4 vols. Munich, 1903.

Penck, A., *Die tecktonischen Grundzüge West Kleinasiens.* Stuttgart, 1918.

Perthes, J., *Atlas antiquus.* Gotha.

Philippson, A., *Das Mittelmeergebiet.* Leipzig, 1907.

—— *Der Peloponnes.* Berlin, 1892.

—— *Westlichen Kleinasien.* Petermanns Ergänzhefte, No. 177 and 180.

Playfair, Sir Lambert, *The Mediterranean, Physical and Historical.* Smithsonian Report, 1890. Pp. 259-276.

Ramsey, W. M., *The Historical Geography of Asia Minor.* London, 1890.

Ratzel, F., *Anthropogeographie.* Stuttgart, Vol. I, 1882, Vol. II, 1899.

Rawlinson, G., *The Five Great Monarchies of the Ancient Eastern World.* New York, 1870.

Reclus, E., *The Earth and Its Inhabitants.* Vol. II, Europe. New York, 1882.

Ripley, W. Z., *The Races of Europe.* New York, 1910.

Semple, E. C., *Influences of Geographic Environment.* New York, 1911.

Seymour, T. D., *Life in the Homeric Age.* New York, 1907.

Shaw, Sir Napier, *Manual of Meteorology.* 2 vols. Cambridge, 1926.

Shepherd, W. R., *Historical Atlas.* New York, 1911.

Smith, George Adam, *Historical Geography of the Holy Land.* London, 1895.

Speck, E., *Die Handelsgeschichte des Altertums.* 2 vols. Leipzig, 1900.

Suess, E., *The Face of the Earth.* Vol. I. Oxford, 1904.

Tozer, H. F., *Geography of Ancient Greece.* London, 1873.

Trzebitsky, F., *Studien über der Niederschlags verhältnisse auf den Sudösteuropäischen Halbinseln.* 1911.

Vidal de la Blache, *Géographie de la France.* Vol. I in Lavisse, *Histoire de France.* Paris, 1903.

Vogelstein, H., *Die Landwirthschaft in Palästina zur Zeit der Mishnah.* Berlin, 1894.

Willcocks, W. and Craig, J., *Egyptian Irrigation*. 2 vols. London, 1913.

Winckler, Hugo, *Geschichte Babyloniens und Assyriens*. Leipzig, 1892. Trans. and edit. by J. A. Craig. New York, 1907.

Zimmern, A. E., *The Greek Commonwealth*. Oxford, 1911.

INDEX

Abila, Mt., 36, 80-81, 283
Abraham, 190, 195
Abruzzi Plateau, 287
Absalom, 89
Abydos, 66
Abyssinian Highland, 158, 163
Academy of Athens, 435, 488
Acanthus, 698
Acarnania, 37, 122, 281, 322
Achaia, 9, 46, 280, 350, 366
Achaian League, 75
Achelous R., 281; floods and flood control, 108, 110, 444; navigation, 123, 127
Achilles, 620, 627
Acritas, 629
Acte promontory, 626
Actium, 619
Adana, 169
Aden, Gulf of, 164, 168
Adonis, 483
Adrasteia, 317
Adria, 126, 552, 601, 640
Adrianople, 218
Adriatic Sea, 21; bora in, 581; east and west coasts contrasted, 25, 217, 221, 228, 235; form, 17, 63; piracy on, 68, 648-650; ports of, 601; seamanship in, 581
Æacus of Ægina, 508, 522
Ædui, 248, 249
Ægean Isles, droughts in, 509; culture and racial stocks in, 69-70; earthquakes and tidal waves in, 39, 40, 42, 43, 44, 47, 53; origin of, 22, 65
Ægean Sea, 4, 65, 89; enclosure by folded mountains, 20; maritime activity, 11, 69-71; piracy in, 643, 645, 647, 664; race amalgamation, 69-70; seamanship in, 598; strait gateways, 74; sub-basins, 61; timber trade, 270, 277; trade routes, 600-601; visibility in, 586-588
Ægina, Isle of, annexed by Athens,

668; area and population, 669; drought in, 522; earthquake rift, 47; soil, 415; grain supply, 350-351; industry, 678; piracy, 664; promontory temple, 619; trade of, 70, 662, 663, 667
Ægium, 46
Ægyra, 24
Æmonia, 229, 230
Ænaria. See Ischia
Ænos, 116, 129
Æolian Isles. See Lipari Islands
Æschylus, 36
Æsepos R. route, 699-700
Æsop, 398
Ætna, Mt., 52, 53, 54; forests, 285; outlooks, 590; sacred to Zeus, 521, 525; terraces of rich soil, 441; wines, 401
Ætolia, 98, 322; league of, 75
Africa, contribution to Mediterranean civilization, 6; lumber trade of northern, 271, 282; of the ancients, 153; Phœnician settlements in, 559-560; plateau of, 16, 23, 146-148; races in northern, 8; relation to Mediterranean Sea, 4, 5, 6; saffron, 675; sea route of northern, 146-147; stock-raising in northern, 334; Vandal, 143, 144, 148, 456, 654
Agamemnon, 48, 163
Agatha, 124
Agathocles of Syracuse, 79
Agde. See Agatha
Agriculture, cultivation of grains, 342-344; decline of, 100, 370; dry-farming, 385-388; esthetic, 475-476; fallow system, 386-388; geographic conditions of, 376-381; irrigation, 434; land utilization, 381, 389; manures, 406-418; orchards and vineyards, 388-401; rotation of crops, 418-419; season and system of tillage, 427-428;

715

24